THE FABLE OF THE BEES • BERNARD MANDE

Publisher's Note

The book descriptions we ask booksellers to display prominently warn that the book may have numerous typos, missing text, images and indexes.

We scanned this book using character recognition software that includes an automated spell check. Our software is 99 percent accurate if the book is in good condition. However, we do understand that even one percent can be a very annoying number of typos! And sometimes all or part of a page is missing from our copy of a book. Or the paper may be so discolored from age that you can no longer read the type. Please accept our sincere apologies.

After we re-typeset and design a book, the page numbers change so the old index and table of contents no longer work. Therefore, we often remove them.

We would like to manually proof read and fix the typos and indexes, manually scan and add any illustrations, and track down another copy of the book to add any missing text. But our books sell so few copies, you would have to pay up to a thousand dollars for the book as a result.

Therefore, whenever possible, we let our customers download a free copy of the original typo-free scanned book. Simply enter the barcode number from the back cover of the paperback in the Free Book form at www.general-books. net. You may also qualify for a free trial membership in our book club to download up to four books for free. Simply enter the barcode number from the back cover onto the membership form on the same page. The book club entitles you to select from more than a million books at no additional charge. Simply enter the title or subject onto the search form to find the books.

If you have any questions, could you please be so kind as to consult our Frequently Asked Questions page at www. general-books.net/faqs.cfm? You are also welcome to contact us there.

General Books LLC®, Memphis, USA, 2012. ISBN: 9781150182167.

❧ ❧ ❧ ❧ ❧ ❧ ❧ ❧

PREFACE.

Jlaws and government are to the political bodies of civil societies, what the vital spirits and life itself are to the natural bodies of animated creatures; and as those that study the anatomy of dead carcases may fee, that the chief organs and nicest springs more immediately required to continue the motion of our machine, are not hard bones, strong muscles and nerves, nor the smooth white skin, that so beautifully covers them, but small trifling silms, and little pipes, that are either overlooked or else seem inconsiderable to vulgar eyes; so they that examine into the nature of man, abstract from art and education, may observe, that what renders him a sociable animal, consists not in his desire of company, good nature, pity, affability, and other graces of a fair outside; *but* that his vilest and most hateful qualities are the most necessary accomplishments to sit him for the largest, and, according to the world, the happiest and most flourishing societies.

The following Fable, in which what I have said is set forth at large, was printed above eight years ago , in a six penny pamphlet, called, The Grumbling Hive, or Knaves turn'cl Honest; and being soon after pirated, cried about the streets in a halfpenny sheet. Since the sirst publishing of it, I havs met with several that, either wilfully or ignorantly mistaking the design, would have it, that the scope of it was a satire upon virtue and morality, and the whole wrote for the encouragement of vice. This made me resplve, whenever it should be reprinted, some way or other to inform the reader of the real intent this little poem was wrote with. I do not dignify these few loose lines with the name of Poem, that *I* would have the reader expect any poetry in them, but barely because they are rhyme, and I am in reality puzzled what name to give

them, for they are pastoral, satire, burlesque, nor heroicomic; to be a tale they want probability, and the whole is rather too long for a fable. All t can fay of them is, that they are a story told in doggerel, which, without the least design of being witty, I have endeavoured to do in as easy and familiar a manner as I was able: the reader shall be welcome to call them what he pleases. It was said of Montagne, that he was pretty well versed in the' defects os mankind, but unacquainted with the excellencies of human nature: if I fare no worse, I shall think myself well used.

` This was wrote in 1714.

What country soever in the universe is to be understood by the Bee-Hive represented here, it *k* evident, from what is said of the laws and constitution of it, the glory, wealth,' power, and industry of its inhabitants, that it must be a large, rich and warlike nation, that is happily governed by a limited monarchy. The satire, therefore, to be met with in the following lines, upon the several professions and callings, and almost every degree and dation of people, was not made to injure and point to particular persons, but only to mow the viieness of the ingredients that altogether compose the wholesome mixture of a well-ordered society; in order to extol the wonderful power of political wisdom, by tire help of which so beautiful a machine is raised from the most contemptible branches. For the main design of the Fable (as it is briefly explained in the Moral), is to show the impossibility of enjoying all the most elegant comforts of life, that are to be met with in an industrious, wealthy and powerful nation, and at the fame time, be blelied with all the virtue and innocence that can be wished for in a golden age; from thence to expose the unreasonableness and foJly of those, that desirous of being an opulent and flourishing people, and wonderfully greedy after all the benessits they can receive as such, are yet always murmuring at and exclaiming against those vices and inconveniences, that from the beginning of the world to this present day, have been inseparable from all kingdoms and states, that ever were famed, for strength, riches, and politeness, at the fame time.

To do this, I sirst slightly touch upon some of the faults and corruptions the several prosessions and callings are generally charged with. After that I show that those very vices, of every particular person, by skilful management, were made subservient to the grandeur and worldly happiness of the whole. Lastly, By setting forth what of necessity must be the consequence of general honesty and virtue, and national temperance, innocence and content, I demonstrate that if mankind could be cured of the failings they are naturally guilty of, they would cease to be capable of being raised into such vast potent and polite societies, as they have been under the several great commonwealths and monarchies that have flourished since the creation.

If you ask me, why I have done all this, *cut bono?* and what good these notions will produce? truly, besides the reader's diversion, I believe none at all;,but if I was asked what naturally ought to be expected from them, I would answer, that, in the sirst place, the people who continually find fault with others, by reading them, would be taught to look at home, and examining their own consciences, be made ashamed of always railing "at what they are more or less guilty of themselves; and that, in the next,-those who are so fond of the ease and comforts, and reap all the benesits that are the consequence of a great and flourishing nation, would learn more patiently to submit to those inconveniences, which no government upon earth can remedy, when they should fee the impossibility of enjoying any great fliarc of the sirst, without partaking likewise of the latter.

This, I fay, ought naturally to be expected from the publishing of these notions, if people were to be made better by any thing that could be said to them; but mankind having for so many ages

remained slill the lame, notvwthilanding the many instructive and elaborate writings, by which their amendment has been endeavoured, I am not so vain as to hope for better success from so inconsiderable a triste.

Having allowed the small advantage this little whim is likely to produce, I think myself obliged to show that it cannot be prejudicial to any; for what is publisoed, if it does no good, ought at least to do no harm: in order to this, I have made some explanatory notes, to which the reader will sind himself referred in those passages that seem to be most liable to exceptions.

The censorious, that never saw the Grumbling Hive, will tell me, that whatever I may talk of the Fable, it not taking up a tenth prt of the book, was only contrived to introduce the Remarks; that instead of clearing up the doubtful or obscure places, I have only pitched upon such as I had a mind to expatiate upon; and that far from striving to extenuate the errors committed before, I have made bad worse, and shown myself a more barefaced champion for vice, in the rambling digressions, than I had done in the Fable itself.

I shall spend no time in answering these accusations: where men are prejudiced, the best apologies are lost; and I know that thole who dunk it criminal to suppose a necessity of rice in any case whatever, will never be reconciled to any part of the performance; but if this be thoroughly examined, all the offence it can give must result from the wrong inferences that may perhaps be drawn from it, and which I desire nobody to make. When I assert that vices are inseparable from great and potent societies, and that it is impossible their wealth and grandeur should subsist without, I do not say that the particular members of them who are guilty of any should not be continually reproved, or not be punished for them when they grow into crimes.

There are, I believe, few people in London, of those that are at any time forced to go a-foot, but what could wish the itreets of it much cleaner than generally they are; while they regard noth-

ing but their own clothes and private conveniency; but when once they come to consider, that what offends them, is the result of the plenty, great trassic, and opulency of that mighty city, if they have any concern in its welfare, they will hardly ever wish to see the streets of it less dirty. For if we mind the materials of all sorts that must supply such an insinite number of trades and handicrafts, as are always going forward; the vast quantity of victuals, drink, and fuel, that are daily consumed in it; the waste and superfluities that must be produced from them; the multitudes of horses, and other cattle, that are always dawbing the streets; the carts, coaches, and more heavy carriages that are perpetually wearing and breaking the pavement of them; and, above all, the numberless swarms of people that arc continually harassing and trampling through every part of them: If, I fay, we mind all these, we shall sind, that every moment must produce new silth ; and, considering how far distant the great streets are from the river side, what cost and care soever be bestowed to remove the nastiness almost as. fast as it is made, it is impossible London should be more cleanly before it is less flourishing. Now Would I asle, isa good citizen, in consideration of what has been said, might not aflert, that dirty streets are a necessary evil, inseparable from the felicity of London, without being the least hinderance to the cleaning of shoes, or sweeping of streets, and consequently without any prejudice either to the blackguard or the scavingers.

But if, without any regard to the interest or happiness of the city, the question was put, What place I thought most pleasunt to walk in? Nobody can doubt, but before thq stinking streets of London, I would esteem a fragrant garden, or a shady grove in the country. In the fame manner, if laying aside all worldly greatness.and vain glory, I should be asked where I. thought it was most probable that men might enjoy true happiness, I would prefer a small peaceable society, in which men, neither envied nor esteemed by neighbours, mould be contented to live upon the natural product of the spot they inhabit, to a vast multitude abounding in wealth and power, that should always be conquering others by their arms abroad, and debauching themselves by foreign luxury at home.

Thus much I had said to the reader in the sirst, edition; and have added nothing by way of preface in the second. But since that, a violent outcry has been made against the book, exactly answering the expectation I always had of the justice, the wisdom, the charity, and fair-dailing of those whose good will 1 despaired of. It has been presented by the Grand Jury, and condemned by thousands who never saw a Word of it. It has been preached against before my Lord Mayor; and an utter refutation of it is daily expected from a reverend divine, who has called me names in the advertisements, and threatened to answer me in two months time for above sive months together. What I have to fay for myself, the reader wdl see in my Vindication at the end of the book, where he will likewise sind the Grand Jury's Presentment, and a letter to the Right Honourable Lord C. which is very rhetorical beyond argument or connection. The author shows a sine talent for invectives, and great sagacity in discovering atheism, where others can sind none. He is zealous against wicked books, points at the Fable of the Bees, and is very angry with the author: He bestows four strong epithets on the enormity of his guilt, and by several eiegant inuendos to the multitude, as the danger there is in sullcung such authors to live, and the vengeance of Heaven upon a whole nation, very charitably recommends him to their care.

Considering the length of this epistle, and that it is not wholly levelled at me only, I thought at sirst to have made some extracts from it of what related to myself; but sinding, on a nearer inquiry, that what concerned me was so blended and interwoven with what did not, 1 was obliged to trouble the reader with it entire, not without hopes that, prolix as it is, the extravagancy of it will be entertaining to to those who have perused the treatise it condemns with so much horror.

THE GRUMBLING HIVE: OR, KNAVES TURN'D HONEST.

A Spacious hive well stock'd with bees,
That liv'd in luxury and ease;
And yet as fam'd for laws and arms,
As yielding large and early swarms;
   Was counted the great nursery 5
   Of sciences and industry.
No bees had better government,
More sickleness, or less content:
They were not Haves to tyranny,
   Nor rul'd by wild democracy; 10
   But kings, that could not wrong, because
Their power was circumscrib'd by laws.
These insects liv'd like men. and all
Our actions they perform'd in small:
   They did whatever's done in town, 15
   And what belongs to sword or gown:
Though th' artful works, by nimble slight
Of minute hmbs,'scap'd human light;
Yet we've no engines, labourers,
   Ships, castles, arms, artisicers, 20
   Craft, science, shop, or instrument,
But they had an equivalent:
Which, lince their language is unknown,
Must be call'd, as we do our own.
   As grant, that among other things, 25
   They wanted dice, yet they had kings;
And thole had guards; from whence we may / '
   Justlv conclude, they had some play;
   B
   Unless a regiment be shown
Of soldiers, that make use of none. 30
Vast numbers throng'd the fruitful hive;
Yet those vast numbers made 'em thrive;
Millions endeavouring to supply
Each other's lust and vanity;
   While other millions were employ'd, 35
   To fee their handy-works destroy'd ;
They furnish'd half the Universe;
Yet had more work than labourers.
Some with vast stocks, and little pains,
   Jump'd into business of great gains; 40
   And some were damn'd to scythes and spades,
.And all those hard laborious trades;
Where willing wretches daily sweat,

And wear out strength and limbs to eat:
While others follow'd mysteries, 45
   To which few folks binds 'prentices;
That want no stock, but that of brass,
And may set up without a cross;
As sharpers, parasites, pimps, players,
   Pickpockets, coiners, quacks, fouthsayers, 50
   And all those, that in enmity,
With downrright working, cunningly
Convert to their own use the labour
Of their good-natur'd heedless neighbour.
These were call'd Knaves, but bar the name, 55
   The grave industrious were the fame:
All trades and places knew some cheat,,
   No calling was without deceit.
The lawyers, of whole art the basis
Was raising feuds and splitting cases, 60
Oppos'd all registers, that cheats
Might make more work with dipt estates;
As were't unlawful, that one's own,
Without a law-suit, should be known.
   They kept ost' hearings wilfully, 65
   To singer the refreshing fee;
And to defend a wicked cause,
Examin'd and survey'd the laws,
As burglar's shops and houses do,
To sind out where they'd best break through. 70
   Physicians valu'd fame and wealth hove the drooping patient's health, r their own skill: the greatest part tudy'd, instead of rules of art, rave pensive looks and dull behaviour, o gain th' apothecary's favour; he praise of midwives, priests, and all hat serv'd at birth or funeral, b bear with th' ever-talking tribe, nd hear my lady's aunt prescribe; Tith formal smile, and kind how d'ye, 0 fawn on all the family; nd, which of all the greatest curse is, endure th' impertinence of nurses. Among the many priests of Jove, ir'd to draw bleffings from above, cine few were learn'd and eloquent, ut thoufands hot and ignorant: et all pals'd muster that could hide heir sloth, lust, avarice and pride; or which they were as fam'd as tailors or cabbage, or for brandy sailors, *jme,* meagre-look'd, and meanly clad, ('ould mystically pray for bread, leaning by

that an ample store, et lit"rally received no more; nd, while these holy drudges starv'd, he lazy ones, for which they serv'd, idulg'd their ease, with all the graces f health and plenty in their faces. The soldiers, that were forc'd to sight, they surviv'd, got honour by't; hough some, that shunn'd the bloody fray, ad limbs shot off, that ran away: me valiant gen'rals fought the foe; thers took bribes to let them go: jme ventur'd always where 'twas warm, ost now a leg, and then an arm; ill quite dislabled, and put by, hey liv'd on half their salary; thile others never came in play, nd staid at home for double pay.

II Their kings were serv'd, but knavisldy,
Cheated by their own ministry;
Many, that for their welfare slaved,
Robbing the very crown they saved:
Pensions were small, and they liv'd high,
Yet boasted of their honesty.
Calling, whene'er they strain'd their right,
The slipp'ry trick a perquisite; 12;
And when folks understood their cant,
They chang'd that for emolument;
Unwilling to be short or plain,
In any thing concerning gain;
   For there was not a bee but would j2
   Get more, 1 won't fay, than he should;
But than he dar'd to let them know,
That pay'd for't; as your gamesters do,
That, though at fair play, ne'er will own
Before the losers that they've won. j o,
But who can all their frauds repeat?
The very stuff which in the street
Tiiey fold for dirt t' enrich the ground,
Was often by the buyers found
   Sophisticated with a quarter 1,
   Of good for-nothing stones and mortar;
Though Flail had little cause to mutter,
Who sold the other salt for butter.
Justice herself, fam'd for fair dealing,
By blindness had not lost her feeling; y.
   Her left hand, which the scales should hold,
Had often dropt 'em, brib'd with gold;
And, though she seem'd impartial,
Where punishment was corporal,
   Pretended to a reg'lar course, j

In murder, and all crimes of force;
Though some sirst pillory'd for cheating,
Were hang'd in hemp of their own beating;
Yet, it was thought, the sword she bore
Check'd but the desp'rate and the poor; 1
   That, urg'd by mere necessity,
Were ty'd up to the wretched tree
For crimes, which not deferv'd that fate,
But to secure the rich and great.
   Thus every part was full of vice, Yet the whole mass a paradise; Flatter'd in peace, and fear'd in wars They were th' esteem of foreigners, knd lavish of their wealth and lives, The balance of all other hives, such were the blessings of that state; Their crimes conspir'd to make them great nd virtue, who from politics tfas learn'd a thousand cunning tricks, kVas, by their happy influence, rtade. friends with vice: And ever since, she worst of all the multitude Did something for the common good.
   This was the state's craft, that maintain'd The whole of which each part complain'd: This, as in music harmony tlade jarrings in the main agree, 'arties directly opposite, Vffist each other, as 'twere for spite; ind temp'rance with sobriety, erve drunkenness and gluttony.
   The root of evil, avarice, 'hat damn'd ill-natur'd baneful vice; i'as stave to prodigality, hat noble sin; whilst luxury 'mploy'd a million of the poor, nd odious pride a million more: nvy itself, and vanity, ere ministers of industry; heir darling folly, sickleness, i diet, furniture, and dress, hat strange ridic'lous vice, was made he very wheel that turn'd the trade, heir laws and clothes were equally bjects of mutability! ar, what was well done for a time, i half a year became a crime; et while they alter'd thus their laws, ill sinding and correcting flaws, hey mended by inconstancy aults, which no prudence could foresee;
   Thus vice nurs'd ingenuity, Which join'd the time and industry, Had carry'd life's conveniences,
   Its real pleasures, comforts, ease, 2C(
   To such a height, the very poor 1
   Liv'd better than the rich before.

And nothing could be added more.
How vain is mortal hapiness!
Had they but known the bounds of bliss; 20;
   And that perfection here below
Is more than gods can well bestow;
The grumbling brutes had been content
With ministers and government.-
   But they, at every ill success, 21
   Like creatures lost without redress,
Curs'd politicians, armies, fleets;
While every one cry'd, damn the cheats,
And would, though conscious of his own,
In others barb'rously bear none. 21
   One, that had got a princely store,
   By cheating master, king, and poor,
Dar'd cry aloud, the land must sink
For all its fraud; and whom d'ye think
The sermonizing rascal chid?
A glover that sold lamb for kid.
The least thing was not done amiss,
   Or cross'd the public business;
But all the rogues cry'd brazenly,
   Good gods, had we but honesty '. 2:
Merc'ry smil'd at th' impudence,
And others call'd it want of fense,
Always to rail at what they lov'd:
But Jove with indignation mov'd,
At last in anger swore, he'd rid 2
The bawling hive of fraud; and did.
The very moment it departs,
And honesty sills all their hearts;
There shows 'em, like th' instructive tree,
   Those crimes which they're asham'd to fee ;
   Which now in silence they confess,
   By blushing at their ugliness:
Like children, that would hide their faults. And by their colour own their thoughts: Imag'ning, when they're loook'd upon, That others fee what they have done.

   But, O ye gods! what consternation, How vast and sudden was th' alteration! In half an hour, the nation round, Meat fell a penny in the pound. The mask hypocrisy's sitting down, From the great statesman to the clown: And in some borrow'd looks well known, Appear'd like strangers in their own. The bar was silent from that day; For now the willing debtors pay, Ev'n what's by creditors forgot; Who quitted them that had it not. Those that were in the wrong, stood mute And dropt the patch'd vexatious suit: On which since nothing else can thrive, Than lawyers in an honest hive, All, except those that got enough, With inkhorns by their sides troop'd oss.

Justice hang'd some, set others free; And after gaol delivery, Her presence being no more requir'd, With all her train and pomp retir'd. First march'd some smiths with locks and Fetters, and doors with iron plates: Next gaolers, turnkeys and aflistants: Before the goddess, at some distance, Her chief and faithful minister, 'Squire Catch, the law's great sinisher, Bore not th' imaginary sword, But his own tools, an ax and cord: Then on a cloud the hood-wink'd fair, Justice herself was push'd by air: About her chariot, and behind, Were serjeants, bums of every kind, Tip-staffs, and all those osficers, That squeeze a living out of tears.

Though physic liv'd, while folks were None would prescribe, but bees of skill,

Which through the hive dispers'd so wide, 280

That none of them had need to ride;

Wav'd vain disputes, and strove to free

The patients of their misery;

Left drugs in cheating countries grown,

And us'd the product of their own; 285

Knowing the gods lent no disease,

To nations without remedies.

Their clergy rous'd from laziness, Laid not their charge on journey-bees; But serv'd themselves, exempt from vice, 290

The gods with pray'r and sacrisice; All those, that were unsit, or knew, Their service might be spar'd, withdrew:

Nor was their business for so many, (If th' honest stand in need of any,) 295

Few only with the high-priest staid, To whom the rest obedience paid: Himself employ'd in holv cares; Relign'd to others itate-affairs.

He chas'd no starv'ling from his door, 300

Nor pinch'd the wages of the poor: But at his house the hungry's fed, The hireling sinds unmeasur'd bread, The needy trav'ller board and bed.

Among the king's great minsters, 305

And all th' inferior ossicers,

The change was great; for frugally They now liv'd on their salary: That a poor bee should ten times come To ask his due, a trifling sum, 310

And by some well-hir'd clerk be made

To give a crown, or ne'er be paid, Would now be call'd a downright cheat, Though formerly a perquisite.

All places manag'd sirst by three, 315

Who watch'd each other's knavery And often for a fellow-feeling,. Promoted one another's stealing, Are happily supplv'd by one, By which some thousands more are gone. » 320

No honour now could be content, To live and owe for what was spent -

Liv'ries in brokers shops are hung, They part with coaches for a song;

Sell stately horses by whole, sets; 325

And country-houses, to pay debts.

Vain cost is shunn'd as much as fraud; They have no forces kept abroad; Laugh at th' esteem of foreigners, And empty glory got by wars; 330

They sight but for their country's fake,

When right or liberty's at stake. Now mind the glorious hive, and fee How honesty and trade agree.

The show is gone, it thins apace; 335

And looks with quite another face.

For 'twas not only that they went, By whom vast sums were yearly spent; But multitudes that liv'd on them,

Were daily forc'd to do the fame. 34O

In vain to other trades they'd fly; All were o'er-stock'd accordingly. The price of land and houses falls; Mirac'lous palaces, whose walls,

Like those of Thebes, were rais'd by play, 345

Are to be let; while the once gay, Well-seated household gods would be More pleas'd to expire in flames, than fee

The mean inscription on the door

Smile at the lofty ones they bore. 350

The building trade is quite destroy'd, Artisicers are not employ'd; No limner for his art is fam'd, Stone-cutters, carvers are not nam'd.

Those, that remain'd, grown temp'rate, strive, 355

Not how to spend, but how to live; And, when they paid their tavern score, Resolv'd to enter it no more: No vintner's jilt in all the hive

Could wear now cloth of gold, and thrive; 360

Nor Torcol such vast sums advance, For Burgundy and Ortelans; The courtier's gone that with his miss Supp'd at his house on Christmas peas;

Spending as much in two hours stay, 365

As keeps a troop of horse a day.

The haughty Chloe, to live great, Had made her husband rob the state: But now she sells her furniture,

Which th' Indies had been ransack'd for; 370

Contracts the expensive bill of fare, And wears her strong suit a whole year: The flight and sickle age is past; And clothes, as well as fashions, last.

Weavers, that join'd rich siIk with plate, 375

And all the trades subordinate, Are gone; still peace and plenty reign, And every thing is cheap, though plain: Kind nature, free from gard'ners force, Allows all fruits in her own course; 3So

But rarities cannot be had, Where pains to get them are not paid. As pride and luxury decrease, So by degrees they leave the seas.

Not merchants now, but companies 385

Remove whole manufactories. All arts and crafts neglected lie; Content, the bane of industry, Makes 'em admire their homely store, And neither leek nor covet more. 390 So few in the vast hive remain, The hundredth part they can't maintain Against th' insults of numerous foes; Whom yet they valiantly oppose;

'Till some well fene'd retreat is found, 395

And here they die or stand their ground.

No hireling in their army's known;
But bravely sighting for their own,'
Their courage and integrity
At last were crown'd with victory. 400
They triumph'd not without their cost,
For many thousand bees were lost.
Harden'd with toils and exercise,
They counted ease itself a vice;

Which so improv'd their temperance;
405

That, to avoid extravagance,
They flew into a hollow tree,
Blest with content and honesty.
THE MORAL.

Then leave complaints: fools only strive

To make a great dn honest hive. 4
T' enjoy the world's conveniences,
Be fam'd in war, yet live in ease,
Without great vices, is a vain
Eutopia seated in the brain.
Fraud, luxury, and pride must live, 4S
While we the benesits receive:
Hunger's a dreadful plague, no doubt,

Yet who digests or thrives without?
Do we not owe the growth of wine
To the dry shabby crooked vine? 420
Which, while its shoots neglected stood,

Chok'd other plants, and ran to wood;
But blest us with it$ noble fruit,
As soon as it was ty'd and cut:
So vice is benesicial found, 42 5
When it's by justice lopp'd and bound;

Nay, where the people would be great,

As necessary to the state,
As hunger is to make 'em eat.
Bare virtue can't make nations live 430

In splendor; they, that would revive
A golden age, must be as free,
For acorns as for honesty. 433 THE
INTRODUCTION.

One of the greatest reasons why so few people understand themselves, is, that most writers are always teaching men what they should be, and hardly ever trouble their heads with telling them what they really are. As for my part, without any compliment to the courteous reader, or myself, I believe man (besides skin, flesh, bones, &-c.

that are obvious to the eye) to be a compound of various passions; that all of them, as they are provoked and come uppermost, govern him by turns, whether he will or no. To show that these qualisications, which we all pretend to be ashamed of, are the great support of a flourishing society, has been the subject of the foregoing poem. But there being some passages in it seemingly paradoxical, I have in the preface promised some explanatory remarks on it; which, to render more useful, I have thought sit to inquire, how man, no better qualisied, might yet by his own imperfections be taught to distinguish between virtue and vice: and here I must desire the reader once for all to take notice, that when 1 say men, 1 mean neither Jews nor Christians; but mere man, in the state of nature and ignorance or the true Deity.

AN INQUIRY INTO THE ORIGIN OF MORAL VIRTUE.

All untaught animals are only solicitous of pleasing themselves, and naturally follow the bent of their own inclinations, without considering the good or harm that, from their being pleased, will accrue to others. This is the reason that, in the wild state of nature, those creatures are sittest to live peaceably together in great numbers, that discover the least of understanding, and have the fewest appetites to gratify; and consequently no species of animals is, without the curb of government, less capable of agreeing long together in multitudes, than that of man; yet such are his qualities, whether good or bad I shall not determine, that no creature besides himself can ever be made sociable: but being an extraordinary selsish and headstrong, as well as cunning animal, however he may be subdued by superior strength, it is impossible by force alone to make him tractable, and receive the improvements he his capable of.

The chief thing, therefore, which lawgivers, and other wife men that have laboured for the establishment of society, have endeavoured, has been to make the people they were to govern, believe, that it was more benesicial for every body to conquer than indulge his

appetites, and much better to mind the public than what seemed his private interest. As this has always been a very dissicult talk, lo no wit or eloquence has been left untried to compass it; and the moralists and philosophers of all ages employed their utmost skill to prove the truth of so useful an assertion. But whether mankind would have ever believed it or not, it is not likely that any body could have persuaded them to disapprove of their natural inclinations, or prefer the good of others to their own, if, at the fame time, he had not showed them an equivalent to be enjoyed as a reward for the violence, which, by so doing, they of necessity must commit upon themselves. Those that have undertaken to civilize mankind, were not ignorant of this; but being unable to give so many real rewards as would satisfy all persons for every individual action, they were forced to contrive an imaginary one, that, as a general equivalent for the trouble of self-denial, should serve on all occasions, and without costing any thing either to themselves or others, be yet a most acceptable recompence to the receivers.

They thoroughly examined all the strength and frailties ot our nature, and observing that none were either so savage as not to be charmed with praise, or so despicable as patiently to bear contempt, justly concluded, that flattery must be the most powerful argument that could be used to human creatures. Making use of this bewitching engine, they extolled the excellency of our nature above other animals, aud setting sorth with unbounded praises the wonders of our sagacity and vastness of understanding, bestowed a thousand encomiums on the rationality of our fouls, by the help of which we were capable of performing the most noble atchievemcnts. Having, by this artful way of flattery, insinuated themselves into the hearts of men, they began to instruct them in the notions of honour and shame; representing the one as the worst of all evils, and the other as the highest good to which mortals could aspire: which being done, they laid before them how unbecoming it was the dignity of such sublime creatures to be solicitous about gratifying those appetites, which they had in common with brutes, and at the fame time unmindful of those higher qualities that gave them the preeminence over all visible beings. They indeed confessed, that those impulses of nature were very pressing; that it was troublesome to resist, and very dislicult wholly to subdue them. But this they only used as an argument to demonstrate, how glorious the conquest of them was on the one hand, and how scandalous on the other not to attempt it.

To introduce, moreover, an emulation amongst men, they divided the whole species into two classes, vastly differing from one another: the one consisted of abject, low-minded people, that always hunting after immediate enjoyment, were wholly incapable of self-denial, and without regard to the good of others, had no higher aim than their private advantage; such as being enslaved by voluptuousness, yielded without resistance to every gross desire, and make no use of their rational faculties but to heighten their sensual pleasure. These wild grovelling wretches, they said, were the dross of their kind, and having enly the shape of men, differed from brutes in nothing but their owtward sigure. But the other class was made up of lofty high-spirited creatures, that, free from sordid selsishness, esteemed the improvements of the mind to be their fairest possessions; and, setting a true value upon themselves, took no delight but in embellishing that part in which their excellency consisted; such as despising whatever they had in common with irrational creatures, opposed by the help of reason their most violent inclinations; and making a continual war with themselves, to promote the peace of others, aimed at no less than the public welfare, and the conquest of their own passion.

Fortior est qui se quum qui fortistima
Vincit
Mœnia ——

These they called the true representatives of their sublime species, exceeding in worth the sirst class by more degrees, than that itself was superior to the beasts of the sield.

As in all animals that are not too imperfect to discover pride, we sind, that the sinest, and such as are the most beauiiful and valuable of their kind, have generally the greatest share of it; so in man, the most perfect of animals, it is so inseparable from his very essence (how cunningly soever some may learn to hide or disguise it), that without it the compound he is made of would want one of the chiesest ingredients: which, if we consider, it is hardly to be doubted but lesions and remonstrances, so skilfully adapted to the good opinion man has of himself, as those 1 have mentioned, must, if scattered amongst a multitude, not only gain the assent of most of them, as to the speculative part, but likewise induce several, especially the siercest, most resolute, and best among them, to endure a thousand inconveniences, and undergo as many hardships, that they may have the pleasure of counting themselves men of the second class, and consequently appropriating to themselves all the excellencies they have heard of it.

From what has been said, we ought to expect, in the sirst place, that the heroes who took such extraordinary pains to master some of their natural appetites, and preferred the good of others to any visible interest of their own, would not lecede an inch from the sine notions they had received concerning the dignity of rational creatures; and having ever the authority of the goverment on their side, with all imagmable vigour assert the esteem that was due to thole of the second class, as well as their superiority over the rest of their kind. In the second, that those who wanted a sussicient stock of either pride or resolution, to buoy them up in mortifying of what was dearest to them, followed the sensual dictates of nature, would yet be ashamed of confessing themselves to be those despicable wretches that belonged to the inferior class, and were generally reckoned to be so little removed from brutes; and that therefore, in their own defence, they would fay, as others did, and hiding their own imperfections as well as they could, cry up self-denial and public spiritedness as much as any: for it is highly probable, that some of them, convinced by the real proofs of fortitude and self-conquest they had seen, would admire in others what they found wanting in themselves; others be afraid of the resolution and prowess of those of the second class, and that all of them were kept in awe by the power of their rulers; wherefore is it reasonable to think, that none of them (whatever they thought in themselves) would dare openly contradict, what by every body else was thought criminal to doubt of.

This was (or at least might have been) the manner after which savage man was broke; from whence it is evident, that the sirst rudiments of morality, broached by skilful politicians, to render men useful to each other, as well as tractable, were chiefly contrived, that the ambitious might reap the more benessit from, and govern vast numbers of them with the greater ease and security. This foundation of politics being once laid, it is impossible that man should long remain uncivilized: for even those who only strove to gratify their appetites, being continually crossed by others of the fame stamp, could not but observe, that whenever they checked their inclinations or but followed them with more circumspection, they avoided a world of troubles, and often escaped many of the calamities that generally attended the too eager pursuit aster pleasure.

First, they received, as well as others, the benesit of those actions that were done for the good of the whole society, and consequently could not forbear wishing well to those of the superior class that performed them. Secondly, the more intent they were in seeking their own advantage, without regard to others, the more they were hourly convinced, that none stood so much in their way as thole that were most like themselves.

It being the interest then of the very worst of them, more than any, to preach up public-spiritednefs, that they might reap the fruits of the labour and self-denial ii" others, and at the fame time indulge their own appetites with less disturbance, they agreed with the rest, to call every tiling, which, without regard to the public, man should commit to gratify any of his appetites, Vice; if in that action there could be observed the least prospect, that it might either be injurious to any of the society, or ever render himself less serviceable to others: and to give the name of Virtue to every performance, by which man, contrary to the impulse of nature, should endeavour the benesit of others, or the conquest of his own passions, out of a rational ambition of being good.

It shall be objected, that no society was ever any ways civilized before the major part had agreed upon some worship or other of an over-ruling power, and consequently that the notions of good and evil, and the distinction between virtue and vice, were never the contrivance of politicians, but the pure effect of religion. Before I answer this objection, I must repeat what I have said already, that in this inquiry into the origin of moral virtue, I speak neither of Jews or Christians, but man in his state of nature and ignorance of the true Deity; and then I assirm, that the idolatrous superstitions of all other nations, and the pitiful notions they had of the Supreme Being, were incapable of exciting man to virtue, and good for nothing but to awe and amuse a rude and unthinking multitude. It is evident from history, that in all considerable societies, how stupid or ridiculous soever people's received notions have been, as to the deities they worshipped, human nature has ever exerted itself in all its branches, and that there is no eari hly wisdom or moral virtue, but at one time or other men have excelled in it in all monarchies and commonwealths, that for riches and power have been any ways remarkable.

The Egyptians, not satissied with having deisied all the ugly monsters they could' think on, were so silly as to adore the onions of their own sowing; yet at the same time their country was the most famous nursery of arts and sciences in the world, and themselves more eminently lkilled in the deepest mysteries of nature than any nation has been since.

No states or kingdoms under heaven have yielded more or greater patterns in all forts of moral virtues, than the Greek C and Roman empires, more especially the latter; and yet how loose, absurd and ridiculous were their sentiments as to sacred' matters? For without reflecting on the extravagant number of their deities, if we only consider the infamous stories they fathered upon them, it is not to be denied but that their religion, far from teaching men the conquest of their passions, and the way to virtue, seemed rather contrived to justify their appetites, and encourage their vices. But if we would know what made them excel in fortitude, courage, and magnanimity, we must cast our eyes on the pomp of their triumphs, the magnisicence of their monuments and arches; thi'ir trophies, statues, and inscriptions; the variety of their military crowns, their honours decreed to the dead, public encomiums on the living, and other imaginary rewards they bestowed on men of merit; and we shall sind, that what carried so many of them to the utmost pitch of self-denial, was nothing but their policy in making use of the most effectual means that human pride could be flattered with.

It is visible, then, that it was not any heathen religion, or other idolatrous superstition, that sirst put man upon crossing his apperites and subduing his dearest inclinations, but the skilful management of wary politicians; and the nearer we search into human nature, the more we (hall be convinced, that the moral virtues are the political osfspring which flattery begot upon pride.

There is no man, of what capacity or penetration soever, that is wholly proof against the witchcraft of flattery, if artfullv performed, and suited to his abilities. Children and fools will swallow personal praise, but those that are more cunning, must be managed with much greater circumspection; and the more general the flattery is, the less it is suspected by those it is levelled at. What you fay in commendation of a whole town is received with pleasure by all the inhabitants: speak in commendation of letters in general, and every man of learning will thir.K himself in particular obliged to you. You may lately praise the employment a man is of, or the country he was born in;' because you give him an opportunity of screening the joy he seels upon his own account, under the esteem which he pretends to have for others.

It is common among cunning men, that understand the power which flattery has upon pride, when they are afraid they shall be imposed upon, to enlarge, though much against their conscience, upon the honour, fair dealing, and integrity of the family, country, or sometimes the profession of him they suspect; because they know that men often will change their resolution, and act against their inclination, that they may have the pleasure of continuing to appear in the opinion of some, what they are conscious not to be in reality. Thus sagacious moralists draw men like angels, in hopes that the pride at least of some will put them upon copying after the beautiful originals which they are represented to be.

When the incomparable Sir Richard Steele, in the usual elegance of his easy style, dwells on the praises of his sublime species, and with all the embellishments of rhetoric, sets forth the excellancy of human nature, it is impossible not to be charmed with his happy turns of thought, and the politeness of his expressions. But though I have been often moved by the force of his eloquence, and ready to swallow the ingenious sophistry with pleasure, yet i could never be so serious, but,reflecting on his artful encomiums, I thought on the tricks made use of by the women that would teach children to be mannerly. When an awkward girl before she can either speak or go, begins after many entreaties to make the sirst rude essays of curtesying, the nurse falls in an ecstacy of praise; " There is a delicate curtely! O line Mils! there is a " pretty lady! Mamma! Miss can make a better curtsey than " her sister Molly!" The fame is echoed over by the maids, whilst Mamma almost hugs the child to pieces; only Miss Molly, who being four years older, knows how to make a very handsome curtesy, wonders at the perverienefs ot their judgment, and swelling with indignation, is ready to cry at the injustice that is done her, till, being whispered in the ear that it is only to please the baby, and that Hie is a woman, she grows proud at being let into the secret, and rejoicing at the superiority of her understanding, repeats what has been said with large additions, and insults over the weaknels of her siller, whom all this while sile fancies to be the only bubble among them. These extravagant praises would by any one, above the capacity of an infant, be called fulsome flatteries, and, if you will, abominable lies; yet experience teaches us, that bv the help of such gross encomiums, young misses will be brought to make pretty tutrtesies, and behave themselves womanly much sooner, and with less trouble, than they would without them. It is the fame with boys, whom they will strive to persuade, that all sine gentlemen do as they are bid, and that none but beggar boys aje rude, or dirty their their clothes; nay, as soon as the wild brat with his untaught sid begins to fumble for his hat, the mother, to make him pull it osf, tells him before he is two years old, that he is a man; and if he repeats that action when she delires him, he is presently a captain, a lord mayor, a king, or something higher if she can think of it, till edged on by the force of praise, the little urchin endeavours to imitate man as well as he can, and strains all his faculties to appear what his shallow noddle imagines he is believed to be.

The meanest wretch puts an inestimable value upon himself, and the highest wish of the ambitious man is to have all the world, as to that particular, of his opinion: ib that the most insatiable thirst aster same that ever heroe was inspired with, was never more than an ungovernable greediness to engross the esteem and admiration of others in future ages as well as his own; and (what mortisication soever this truth might be to the second thoughts of an Alexander or a Cæsar) the great recompence in view, for which the most exalted minds have with so much alacrity sacrisiced their quiet, health, sensual pleasures, and every inch of themselves, has never been any thing else but the breath of man, the aerial coin of praise. Who can forbear laughing when he thinks on all the great men that have been so serious on the subject of that Macedonian madman, his capacious soul, that mighty heart, in one corner of which, according to Lorenzo Gratian, the world was so commodiously lodged, that in the whole there was room for six more? Who can forbear laughing, I fay, when he compares the sine things that have been laid of Alexander, with the end he proposed to himself from his vast exploits, to be proved from his own mouth; when the vast pains he took to pass the Hydaipes forced him to cry out? Oh ye Athenians, could you believe what dangers I expose myself to, to be praised by you! To desine then, the reward of glory in the amplest manner, the most that can be said of it, is, that it coniists in a superlative felicity which a man, who is conscious of having performed a noble action, enjoys in self-love, whilst he is thinking on the applause he expects of others.

But here 1 shall be told, that belides the noisy toils of war and public bustle of the ambitious, there are noble and generous actions that are performed in silence; rh.n virtue being its own reward, thole who are really good have a iatissaction in their consciousness of being so, which is all the recompence they expect from the most worthy performances; that among the heathens there have been men, who, when they did good to others,'were so far from coveting thanks and applause, that they took all imaginable care to be for ever concealed from those on whom they bestowed their benesits, jfand consequently that pride has no hand in spurring man on to the highest pitch of self-denial.

In answer to this, I fay, that it is impossible to judge of a man's performance, unless we are thoroughly acquainted with the principle and motive from which lie acts. Pity, though it is the most gentle and the least mischievous of all our passions, is yet as much a frailty of our nature, as anger, pride, or fear. The weakest minds have generally the greatest share of it, for which reason none are more compassionate than women and children. It must be owned, that of all our weaknesses, it is the most amiable, and bears the greatest resemblance to virtue; nav, without a considerable mixture of it, the society could hardly subsist: but as it is an impulse of nature, that consults neither the public interest nor our own reason, it may produce evil as well as good. It has helped to destroy the honour of virgins, and corrupted the integrity of judges; and whoever acts from it as a principle, what good soever he may bring to the society, has nothing to boast of, but that he has indulged a passion that has happened to be benesicial to the public. There is no merit in saving an innocent babe ready to drop into the lire: the action is neither good nor bad, and what benesit soever the infant received, we only obliged ourselves; for to have seen it fall, and not strove to hinder it, would have caused a pain, which self preservation compelled us to prevent: Nor has a rich prodigal, that happens to be of a commiserating temper, and loves to gratify his passions, greater virtue,to boast of, when he relieves an object of compassion with what to himself is a trifle. But such men, as without complying with any weakness of their own, can part from what they value themselves, and, from no other motive but there love to goodness, persorm a worthy action in silence: such men, 1 confess, have acquired more resined notions of virtue than those 1 have hitherto spoke of, yet even in theie (with which the world has yet never swarmed) we may discover no small symptoms of pride, and the humblest man alive must confess, that the reward of a virtuous action, which is the satisfaction that ensues upon it, consuls in a certain pleasure he procures to himself by contemplating on his own worth: which pleasure, together with the occasion of it, are as certain signs of pride, as looking pale and trembling at any imminent danger, are the symptoms of fear.

If the two scrupulous reader should at sirst view condemn ihese notions concerning the origin of moral virtue, and think them perhaps offensive to Christianity. 1 hope he will forbear his censures, when lie mall consider, that nothing can render the unsearchable depth of the Divine Wisdom more conspicuous, than that man, whom Providence had designed for society, should not only by his own srailties and imperfections, be led into the road to temporal happiness, but likewise receive, from a seeming necessity of natural causes, a tincture of that knowledge, in which he was afterwards to be made perfect by the true religion, to his eternal welfare.

RliMARK S.

Line 45. Whilst others follow'd mysteries,

To which few folks bind 'prentices.

I

N the education of youth, in order to their getting of a livelihood when they shall be arrived at maturity, most people look out for some warrantable employment or other, of which there are.whole bodies or companies, in every large society of men. By this means, all arts and sciences, as well as trades and handicrafts, are perpetuated in the commonwealth, as long as they are found useful; the young ones that are daily brought up to them, continually supplying the losoftheold ones that die. But some of these employments being vastly more creditable than others, according to the great difference of the charges required to let up in each of them, all prudent parents, in the choice of them, chiefly consult their own abilities, and the circumstances they are in. A man that gives three or four hundred pounds with his son to a great merchant, and has not two or three thousand pounds to spare against he is out of his time to begin business with, is much to blame not to have brought his child up to something that might be followed with less money.

There are abundance of men of a genteel education, that have but very small revenues, and yet are forced, by their reputable callings, to make a greater sigure than ordinary people of twice their income. If these have any children, it often happens, that as their indigence renders them incapable of bringing them up to creditable occupations, so their pride makes them unwilling to put them out to any of the mean laborious trades, and then, in hopes either of an alteration in their fortune, or that some friends, or favourable opportunity shall offer, they from time so time put off the dilposing of them, until insensibly they come to be of age, and are at last brought up to nothing. Whether this neglect be more barbarous to the children, or prejudicial to the society, I shall not determine. At Athens all children were forced to assist their parents, if they came to want: But Solon made a law, that no son should be obliged to relieve his father, who had not bred him up to any calling. Some parents put out their ions to good trades very suitable to their then present abilities, but happen to die, or fail in the world, before their children have sinished their apprenticeships, or are made sit for the business they are to follow: A great many young men again, on the other hand, arc handsomely provided for and set up for themselves, that yet (some for want of industry, or else a susssicient knowledge in their callings, others by indulging their pleasures, and some few by misfortunes) are reduced to poverty, and altogether unable to maintain themselves by the businels they were brought up to. It is impossible but that the neglects, mismanagements, and misfortunes I named, must very frequently happen in populous places, and consequently great numbers of people be daily flung unprovided for into the wide world, how rich and potent a commonwealth may be, or what care soever a government may take to hinder it. How must these people be disposed of? The sea, 1 know, and armies, which the world is seldom without, will take osf some. Those that are honest drudges, and of a laborious temper, will become journeymen to the trades they are of, or enter into some other service: such of them as studied and were sent to the university, may become schoolmasters,

tutors, and some lew of them get into some ossice or other: But what must become of the lazy, that care for no manner of working, and the sickle, that hate to be consined to any thing?

Those that ever took delight in plays and romances, and have a spice of gentility, will, in all probability, throw their eyes upon the stage, and if they have a good elocution, with tolerable mien, turn actors. Some that love their bellies above any thing else, if they have a good palate, and a little knack at cookery, will strive to get in with gluttons and epicures, learn to ennge and bear all manner of usage, and so turn parasites, ever flattering the master, and making mischief among the rest of the family. Others, who by their own and companions lewdness, judge of people's incontinence, will naturally fall to intriguing, and endeavour to live by pimping for such as either want leisure or address to speak for themlelves. Thole of the most abandoned principles of all, if they are fly and dexterous, turn sharpers, pickpockets, or coiners, if their skill and ingenuity give them leave.. Others again, that have observed the credulity of simple wo. men, and other fooiiih people, if they have impudence and a little cunning, either let up for doctors, or elle pretend to tell fortunes; and every one turning the vices and frailties of others to his own advantage, endeavours to pick up a living the. easiest and shortest way his talents and abilities will let him.

These are certainly the bane of civil society; but they are fools, who, not conlidering what has been said, storm at the remisthefs of the laws tttat fuller them to live, while wife men content themselves with taking all imaginable care not to be circumvented by them without quarrelling at what no human prudence can prevent.

Line 55. These we call'd Knaves, but bar the name,

The grave industrious were the fame.

1 His, I confess, is but a very indifferent compliment to all the trading part of the people. But if the word Knave may be understood in its full latitude, and comprehend every body that is not sincerely honest, and does to others what he

would distike to have done to himself, J do not question but 1 shall make good the charge. To pass by the innumerable artisices, by which buyers and fellers outwit one another, that are daily allowed of and practised among the fairest of dealers, show me the tradesmen that has always discovered the defects of his goods to those that cheapened them; nay, where will you sind one that has not at one time or other industriously concealed them, to the detriment of the buyer? Where is the merchant that has never, against his conscience, extolled his wares beyond their worth, to make them go off the better.

Decio, a man of great sigure, that had large commissions. for sugar from scveral parts beyond sea, treats about a considerable parcel of that commodity with Alcander, an eminent West India merchant; both understood the market very well, but could not agree: Decio was a man of substance, and thought no body ought to buy cheaper than himself; Alcander was the fame, and not wanting money, stood for his price. While they were driving their bargain at a tavern near the exchange, Alcander's man brought his master a letter from the West Indies, that informed him of a much greater quantity of sugars coining for England than was expected. Alcander now wished for nothing more than to!cll at Decio's price, before the news was public; but being a cunning fox, that he might not seem too precipitant, nor yet lose his customer, he drops the discourse they were upon, and putting on a jovial humour, commends the agreeablenefs of the weather, from whence falling upon the delight he took in his gardens, invites Decio to go along with him to his country house, that was not above twelve miles from London. It was in the month of May, and, as it happened, upon a Saturday in the afternoon: Decio, who was a tingle man, and would have no business in town before Tuesday, accepts of the other's civility, and away they go in Alcander's coach. Decio was splendidly entertained that night and the day following; the Monday morning, to get himself an appetite, he goes to take the air upon a pad of Alcander's, and coming back meets with a gentleman of his acquaintance, who tells him news was come the night before that the Barbadocs fleet was destroyed by a storm, and adds, that before he came out-it had been consirmed at Lloyd's cosil-e house, where it was thought sugars would rife 25 per cent, by change-time. Decio returns to his friend, and immediately resumes the discourse they had broke off at the tavern: Alcander, who thinking himself sure of his chap, did not design to have moved it till after dinner, was very glad to fee himself so happily prevented; but how desirous soever he was to fell, the other was yet more eager to buy; yet both of them afraid of one another, for a considerable time counterfeited all the indifference imaginable; until at last, Decio sired with what he had heard, thought delays might prove dangerous, and throwing a guinea upon the table, struck the bargain at Alcander's price. The next day they went to London; the news proved true, and Decio got sive hundred pounds by his sugars, Alcander, whilst he had strove to over-reach the other, was paid in his own coin: yet all this is called fair dealing; but 1 am lure neither of them' would have desired to be done to by, as they did to each other.

Line Ioi. The soldiers that were fore'd to sight,
If they surviv'd got honour by't.
bo unaccountable is the desire to be thought well of in men, that though they are dragged into the war against their will, and some of them for their crimes, and are compelled to sight with threats, and often blows, yet they would be esteemed for what thev would have avoided, if it had been in their power: whereas, if reason in man was of equal weight with his pride, he could never be pleased with praises, which he is conscious he does not deserve.

By honour, in its proper and genuine signisication, we mean nothing else but the good opinion os others, which is counted more or less substantial, the more or less noise or bustle there is made about the demonstration of it; and when we fay the sovereign is the fountain of honour, it signisies that he has the power, by titles or ceremonies, or both together, to stamp a mark upon whom he pleases, that shall be as current as his coin, and procure the owner the good opinion of every body, whether he deserves it or not.

The reverse of honour is dishonour, or ignominy, which consists in the bad opinion and contempt of others; and as the sirst is counted a reward for good actions, so this is esteemed a punislnnent for bad ones; and the more or less public or heinous the manner is in which this contempt of others is shown, the more or less the person so suffering is degraded by it. This ignominy is likewise called soame, from the effect it produces; for though the good and evil of honour and dishonour are imaginary, yet there is a reality in lhame, as it signisies a passion, that has its proper symptoms, over-rules our reason, and requires as much labour and self-denial to be subdued, as any of the rest; and since the most important actions of life often are regulated according to the influence this passion has upon us, a thorough understanding of it must help to illustrate the notions the woild has of honour and ignominy. I shall therefore describe it at large.

First, to desine the passion of shame, I think it may be called a sorrowful reflection on our own unworthiness, proceeding from an apprehension that others cither do, or might, if they knew all, deservedly despise us. The only objection of weight that can be raised against this desinition is, that in-nocent virgins are often ashamed, and blush when they are guilty of no crime, and can give no manner of reason for this trailty: and that men are otten ashamed for others, for, or with whom, they have neither friendship or assinity, and consequently that there may be a thousand instances of lhame given,to which the words of the desinition are not apphcaole. To answer this, 1 would have it sirst considered, that the modesty of women is the result of custom and education, by which all unfashionable denudations and silthy expressions are rendered frightful and abominable to them, and that notwithstanding this, the most virtuous young woman alive will often, in spite of her teeth, have thoughts and confused ideas of things arise in her imagination, which she would not reveal to some people for a thousand worlds. Then, 1 fay, that when obscene words are spoken in the presence of an unexperienced virgin, she is afraid that some body will reckon her to understand what they mean, and consequently that she understands this, and that, and several things, which she desires to be thought ignorant of. The reflecting on this, and that thoughts are forming to her disadvantage, brings upon her that passion which we call shame; and whatever can sting her, though never so remote from lewdness, upon that let of thoughts 1 hinted, and which she tlunks criminal, will have the fame effect, especially before men, as long as her modesty lasts.

To try the truth of this, let them talk as much bawdy as they please in the room next to the same virtuous young woman, where she is sure that she is undiscovered, and she will hear, if not hearken to it, without blushing at all, because then sire looks upon herself as no party concerned; and if the disceurse should stain her cheeks with red, whatever her innocence may imagine, it is certain that what occasions her colour, is a passion not half so mortifying as that of shame; but if, in the same place, sire hears something said of herself that must tend to her disgrace, or any thing is named, of which she is secretly guilty, then it is ten to one but she will be ashamed andblush, though nobody sees her; because she has room to fear, that she is, or, if all was known, should be thought of contemptibly.

That we' are often ashamed, and blush for others, which was the second part of the objection, is nothing else but that sometimes we make the cafe of others too nearly our own; so people shriek out when they fee others in danger: Whilst we are reflecting with too much earnest on the effect which such a blameable action, if it was ours, would

produce in us, the spirits, and consequently the blood, are insensibly moved, after the same manner as if the action was our own, and so the fame symptoms must appear.

The shame that raw, ignorant, and ill-bred people, though seemingly without a cause, discover before their betters, is always acompanied with, and proceeds from a consciousness of their weakness and inabilities; and the most modest man, how virtuous, knowing, and accomplished soever he might be, was never yet ashamed without some guilt or dissidence. Such as out of rusticity, and want of education are unreasonably subject to, and at every turn overcome by this passion, we call bashful; and those who out of disrespect to others, and a false opinion of their own sussiciency, have learned not to be affected with it, when they ffiould be, are called impudent or shameless. What strange contradictions man is made of! The reverse of shame is pride, (fee Remark on 1. 182) yet no body can be touched with the sirst, that never felt any thing of the latter; for that we have such an extraordinary concern in what others think of us, can proceed from nothing but the vast esteem we have of ourselves.

That these two passions, in which the feeds of most virtues are contained, are realities in our frame, and not imaginary. qualities, is demonstrable, from the plain and different effects, that, in spite of our reason, are produced in us as soon as we are affected with cither.

When a man is overwhelmed with shame, he observe; a sinking of the spirits! the heart feels cold and condensed, and the blood flies from it to the circumference of the body; the sace glows, the neck and part of the breast partake of the sire: he is heavy as lead; the head is hung down, and the eyes through a mist of confusion are sixed on the ground: no injuries can move him; he is weary of his being, and heartily wishes he could make himself invisible: but when, gratifying his vanity, he exults in his pride, he discovers quite contrary symptoms; his spirits swell and fan the arterial blood; a more than ordinary warmth strengthens and dilates the heart; the ex-

tremities arc cool; he feels light to himlelf, and imagines he could tread on air; his head is held up, his eyes rolled about with iprightliness; he rejoices at his being, is prone to anger, and would be glad that aljthe world could take notice of him.

It is incredible how necessary an ingredient shame is to make us sociable; it is a frailty in our nature; all the world, whenever it affects them, submit to it with regret, and would prevent it if they could; yet the happiness of conversation depends upon it, and no society could be polished, if the generality of mankind were not subject to it. As, therefore, th-: ienle of shame is troublesome, and all creatures are ever labouring for their own defence, it is probable, that man striving to avoid this uneasiness, would, in a great measure conquer his shame by that he was grown up; but th» would be detrimental to the society, and therefore from his infancy, throughout his education, we endeavour to increase, instead of lessening or destroying this fense of shame; and the onlyremedy prescribed, is a strict observance of certain rules, to avoid those things that might bring this troublesome sense of shame upon him. But as to rid or cure him of it, the politician would sooner take away his life.

The rules I speak of, consist in a dextrous management of ourselves, a stifling of our appetites, and hiding the real sentiments of our hearts before others. Those who are not instructed in these rules long before they come to years of maturity, seldom make any progress in them afterwards. To acquire and bring to perfection the accomplishment 1 hint at, nothing is more assisting than pride and good fense. The greediness we have after the esteem of others, and the raptures we enjoy in the thoughts of being liked, and perhaps admired, are equivalents that over pay the conquest of the strongest passions, and consequently keep us at a great distance from all such words or actions that can bring shame upon us. The passions we chiesly ought to hide, for the happiness and embellishment of the society, are lust, pride, and selsishness; therefore the word modesty has three disferent acceptations, that vary with the passions it conceals.

As to the sirst, I mean the branch of modesty, that has a general pretension to chastity for its object, it consists in a sincere and painful endeavour, with all our faculties, to stifle and conceal before others, that inclination which nature has given us to propagate our species. The lessons of it, like those of grammar, are taught us long before we have occasion for, or understand the usefulness of them; for this reason children often are ashamed, and blush out of modesty, before the impulse of nature 1 hint at makes any impression upon them. A girl who is modestly educated, may, before she is two years old, begin to observe how careful the women she converses with, are of covering themselves before men; and the fame caution being inculcated to her by precept, as well as example, it is very probable that at six ihe will be ashamed of showing her leg, without knowing any reason why such an act is blameable, or what the tendency of it is.

To be modest, we ought, in the sirst place, to avoid all unfashionable denudations: a woman is not to be found fault with for going with her neck bare, if the custom of the country allows of it; and when the mode orders the stays o be cut very low, a blooming virgin may, without fear of rational censure, show all the world:

How firm her pouting breasts, that white as snow,
On th' ample chest at mighty distance grow.

But to suffer her ancle to be seen, where It is the fashion for women to hide their very feet, is a breach of modesty; and she is impudent, who shows half her face in a country where decency bids her to be veiled. In the second, our language must be chaste, and not only free, but remote from obscenities, that is, whatever belongs to the multiplication of our species is not to be spoke of, and the least word or expression, that, though at a great distance, has any relation to that performance, ought never to come from our lips. Thirdly, all postures

and motions that can any ways fully the imagination, that is, put us in mind of what 1 have called obscenities, are to be forbore with great caution.

A young woman, moreover, that would be thought wellbred, ought to be circumspect; before men in all her behaviour, and never known to receive from, much less to bestow savours upon them, unless the great age of the man, near consanguinity, or a vast superiority on either side, plead her excuse. A young lady of resined education keeps a strict: guard over her looks, as well as actions, and in her eyes we may read a consciousness that she has a treasure about her, not out of danger os being lost, and which yet she is resolved not to part with at any terms. Thousand satires have been made against prudes, and as many encomiums to extol the careless graces, and negligent air of virtuous beauty. But the wiser sort of mankind are well assured, that the free and open countenance of tie smiling fair, is more inviting, and yields greater hopes to the seducer, than the ever-watchful look of a forbidding eye.

This strict reservedness is to be complied with by all young women, especially virgins, if they value the esteem of the polite and knowing world; men may take greater liberty, because in them the appetite is more violent and ungovernable. Had equal harshness of discipline been imposed upon both, neither of them could have made the sirst advances, and propagation must have stood still among all the fashionable people: which being far from the politician's aim, it was advisable to ease and indulge the sex that suffered most by the severity, and make the rules abate of their rigour, where the passion was the strongest, and the burden of a strict restraint would have been the most intolerable.

For this reason, the man is allowed openly to profess the veneration and great esteem he has for women, and mow greater satisfaction, more mirth and gaiety in their company, than he is used to do out of it. He may not only be complaisant and serviceable to them on all occasions, but it is reckoned his du-

ty to protect and defend them. He may praise the good qualities they are possessed of, and extol their merit with as many exaggerations as his invention will let him, and are consistent with good fense. He may talk of love, he may sigh and complain of the rigours of the fair, and what his tongue must not utter he has the privilege to speak with his eyes, and in that language to fay what he pleases; so it be done with decency, and short abrupted glances: but too closely to pursue a woman, and fasten upon her with ones eyes, is counted very unmannerly; the reason is plain, it makes her uneasy, and, if me be not sussiciently fortisied by an and dissimulation, often throws her into visible disorders. As the eyes are the windows of the soul, lo this staring impudence flings a raw, unexperienced woman, into panic fears, that she may be seen through; and that the man will discover, or has already betrayed, what passes within her: ir keeps her on a perpetual rack, that commands her to reveal her secret wishes, and seems designed to extort from her the grand truth, which modesty bids her with all her faculties to deny.

The multitude will hardly believe the excessive force of education, and in the difference of modesty between men and women, ascribe that to nature which is altogether owing to early instruction: Miss is scarce three years old, but me is spoke to every day to hide her leg, and rebuked in good earnest if she shows it; while little Master at the lame age is bid to take up his coats, and piss like a man. It is shame and education that contains the feeds of all politenels,.and he that has neither, and offers to speak the truth of his heart, and what he feels within, is the most contemptible creature upon earth, though he committed no other fault. Isa man should tell a woman, that he could like no body so well to propagate his species upon, as herself, and that he found a violent desire that moment to go about it, and accordingly offered to lay hold of her for that purpose; the consequence would be, that he would be called a brute, the woman would run away, and himself be never admitted in any civil company. There is no body that has any fense of shame, but would conquer the strongest passion rather than be so served. But a man need not conquer his passions, it is sussicient that he conceals them. Virtue bids us subdue, but good breeding only requires we should hide our appetites. A fashionable gentleman may have as violent an inclination to a woman as the brutish fellow; but then he behaves himself quite otherwise; he sirst addresses the lady's father, and demonstrates his ability splendidly to maintain his daughter; upon this he is admitted into her company, where, by flattery, submission, presents, and assiduity, he endeavours to procure her liking to his person, which if he caii compass, the lady in a little while resigns herself to him before witnesses in a most solemn manner; at night they go to bed together, where the most reserved virgin very tamely susfers him to do what he pleases, and the upshot is, that he obtains what he wanted without ever having asked for it.

The next day they receive visits, and no body laughs at them, or speaks a word of what they have been doing. As to the young couple themselves, they take no more notice of one another,! speak of well-bred people, than they did the day before; they eat and drink, divert themselves as usually, and having done nothing to be ashamed of, are looked upon as what in reality they may be, the most modest people upon earth. What I mean by this, is to demonstrate, that by being well-bred, we susfer no abridgement in our sensual pleasures, but only labour for our mutual happiness, and assist each other in the luxurious enjoyment of all worldly comforts. The sine gentleman 1 spoke of need not practise any greater self-denial than the savage, and the latter acted more according to the laws of nature and lincerity than the sirst. The man that gratisies his appetites after the manner the custom of the country allows of, has no censure to fear. If he is hotter than goats or bulls, as soon as the ceremony is over, let him fate and fatigue himself with joy and ecstacies of pleasure, raise and indulge his appetites by turns, as extravagantly as his strength and manhood will give him leave, he may with safety laugh at the wise men that mould reprove him: all the women, and above nine in ten of the men are of his side; nay, he has the liberty of valuing himself upr,n the fury of his unbridled passion, and the more he wal

D lows in lust, and straius every faculty to be abandonedly voluptuous, the sooner he shall have the good-will and gain the direction of the women, not the young, vain, and lascivious only, but the pru lent, grave, and moll sober matrons.

Because impudence is a vice, it does not follow that modesty is a virtue; it is built upon shame, a pastion in our nature, and may be either good or bad according to the actions performed from that motive. Shame may hinder a prostitute from yielding to a man before company, and the fame shame may cause a bashful good-natured creature, that has been overcome by frailty, to make away with her infant. Passions may do good by chance, but there can be no merit but in the conquest of them.

Was there virtue in modesty, it would be of the fame force in the dark as it is in the light, which it is not. This the men of pleasure know very well, who never trouble their heads with a woman's virtue, so they can but conquer her modesty; seducers, therefore, do not make their attacks at noon-day, but cut their trenches at night.

Ilia verecundis luxest præbenda pufllis,
Qua timidu latebras fperat habere pudor.

People of substance may sin without being exposed for their stolen pleasure; but servants, and the poorer fort of women, have seldom the opportunity of concealing a big belly, or at least the consequences of it. It is impossible that an unfortunate girl of good parentage may be left destitute, and know no shift for a livelihood than to become a nursery, or a chambermaid: she may be deligent, faithful, and obliging, have abundance of modesty, and if you will.be religious: slie may resill temptations, and preserve her chastity for years together, and yet at last meet with an unhappy moment in which she gives up her honour to a powerful deceiver, who afterwards neglects her. If she proves with child, her sorrows-are unspeakable, and she cannot be reconciled with the wretchedness of. her condition; the fear of shame attacks her so lively, that every thought distracts her. All the family she lives in have a great opinion of her virtue, and her last mistress took her for a faint. How will her enemies, that envied her character,, rejoice! How will her relations detest her! The more modest she is now, and the more violently the dread of coming to shame hurries her away, the more wicked and more cruel her resolutions will be, either against herself or what stie bears.

It is commonly imagined, that she who can destroy her child, her own flesh and blood, must have a vast stock of barbarity, and be a savage monster, different from other women; but this is likewise a mistake, which we commit for the want of understanding nature and the force of passions. The fame woman that murders her bastard in the most execrable manner, if she is married afterwards, may take care of, cherish, and feel all the tenderness for her infant that the fondest mother can be capable of. All mothers naturally love their children: but as this is a passion, and all passions centre in self-love, so it may be subdued by any superior passion, to sooth that same self-love, which if nothing had intervened, would have bid her fondle her offspring. Common whores, whom all the world knows to be such, hardly ever destroy their children; nay, even those who assist in robberies and murders seldom are guilty of this crime; not because they are less cruel or more virtuous, but because they have loll their modesty to a greater degree, and the fear of shame makes hardly any impression upon them.

Our love to what never was within the reach if our fenses is but poor and inconsiderable, and therefore women have no natural love to what they bear; their affection begins after the birth: what they feel before is the result of reason, education, and the thoughts of duty. Even when children sirst are born, the mother's love is but weak, and increases w ith the sensibility of the child, and grows up to a prodigious height, when by signs it begins to express his lorrows and joys, makes his wants known, and dilcovers his love to notify and the multiplicity of his desires. What labours and hazards have not women undergone to maintain and i'ave their children, what force and fortitude beyond their sex have they not shown in their behalf! but the vilest women have exerted themselves on this head as violently as the best. All are prompted to it by a natural drift and inclination, without any consideration of the injury or benesit the society receives from it. There is no merit in pleasing ourselves, and the very offspring is often irreparably ruined by the excesive fondness of parents: for though infants, for two or three years, may be the better for this indulging care of mothers, yet afterwards, if not moderated, it may totally spoil them, and many it h:is brought to the gallows.

If the reader thinks 1 have been too tedious on that branch of modestv, by the help of v, hicb we endeavour to appear chaste, I shall make him amends in the brevity with which I design to treat of thegmaining part, by which we would make others believe, that the esteem we have for them exceeds the value we have for ourselves, and that we have no disregard so great to any interest as we have to our own. This laudable quality is commonly known by the name of Manners and Good-breeding, and consists in a fashionable habit, acquired by precept and example, of flattering the pride and selsishness of others, and concealing our own with judgment and dexterity. This must be only understood of our commerce with our equals and superiors, and whilst we are in peace and amity with them; for our complaisance must never interfere with the rules of honour, nor the homage that is due to us from servants and others that depend upon us.

With this caution, I believe, that the desinition will quadrate with every thing that can be alleged as a piece, or an example of either good-breeding or ill manners; and it will be rery disficult

throughout the various accidents of human life and conversation, to sind out an instance of modesty or impudence that is not comprehended in, and illustrated by it, in all countries and in all ages. A man that asks considerable favours of one who is a stranger to him, without consideration, is called impudent, because he mows openly his-selsishness, without having any regard to the selsishness of the other. We may fee in it, likewise, the reason why a man ought to speak of his wife and children, and every thing that is dear to him, as sparing as is possible, and hardly ever of himself, especially in commendation of them. A well-bied man may be desirous, and even greedy after praise and the esteem of others, but to be praised to his face offends his modesty: the reason is this; all human creatures, before they are yet polistied, receive an extraordinary pleasure in hearing themselves praised: this we are all conscious of, and therefore when we fee a man openly enjoy and feast on this delight, in which we have no share, it rouses our selsishness, and immediately we begin to envy and hate him. For this reason, the well-bred man conceals his joy, and utterly denies that he feels any, and by this means consulting and soothing our selsishness, he averts that envy and hatred, which otherwife he would have justly to fear. When from our childhood we observe how those are ridiculed who calmly can hear their own praises, it is possible that we may strenuously endeavour to avoid that pleasure, that in tract of time we grow uneasy at the approach of it: but this is not following the dictates of nature, but warping her by education and custom; for if the generality of mankind took no delight in being praised, there could be no modesty in refusing to hear it.

The man of manners picks not the best, but rather takes the worst out of the dish, and gets of every thing, unless it be forced upon him, always the most indii'erent share. By this civility the best remains for others, which being a compliment to all that are present, every body is pleased with it: the more they love themselves, the more they arc

forced to approve of his behaviour, and gratitude stepping in, they are obliged almost, whether they will or not, to think favourably of him. After this manner, it is the well-bred man insinuates himself in the esteem of all the companies he comes in, and if he gets nothing else by it, the pleasure he receives in reflecting on the applause which he knows is secretly given him, is to a proud man more than an equivalent for his former self-denial, and overpays to self love with interest, the loss it sustained in his complaisance to others.

If there are seven or eight apples or peaches among six people of ceremony, that are pretty near equal, he who is prevailed upon to choose sirst, will take that, which, if there be any considerable difference, a child would know to be the worst: this he does to insinuate, that he looks upon those he is with to be of superior merit, and that there is not one whom he wishes not better to than he does to himself. It is cullom and a general practice that makes this modish deceit familiar to us, without being shocked at the absurdity of it; for if people had been used to speak from the sincerity of their hearts, and act according to the natural sentiments they felt within, until they were three or four and twenty, it would be impossible for them to assist at this comedy of manners, without either loud laughter or indignation; and yet it is certain, that such behaviour makes us more tolerable to one another, than we could be otherwise.

It is very advantageous to the knowledge of ourselves, to be able well to distinguish between good qualities and virtues. The bond of society exacts from every member a certain regard for others, which the highest is not exempt from in the presence of the meanest even in an empire: but when we are by ourselves, and so far removed from company, as to be beyond the reach of their fenses, the words modesty and impudence lose their meaning; a person may be wicked, but he cannot be immodest while he is alone, and no thought can be impudent that never was communicated to another. A man of exalted pride may so hide it, that no body sliall be able to discover that he has any; and yet receive greater satisfaction from that passion than another, who indulges himselfin the declaration of it before all the world. Good manners having nothing to do with virtue or religion; instead of extinguishing, they rather inflame the passions. The man of fense and education never exults more in his pride than when he hides it with the greatest dexterity; and in feasting 0'1 the applause, which he is sure all good judges will pay to his behaviour, he enjoys a pleasure altogether unknown to the shortlighted surly alderman, that lhows his haughtiness glaringly in his face, pulls off his hat to nobody, and hardly deigns to speak to an inferior.

A man may carefully avoid every thing that in the eye of the world, is esteemed to be the.result of pride, without mortifying himself, or making the least conquest of his passion. It is possible that he only sacrisices the insipid outward part of his pride, which none but lilly ignorant people take delight in, to that part we all feel within, and which the men of the highest spirit and most exalted genius feed on with so much ecstacy in lilence. The pride of great and polite men is no where more conspicuous than in the debates about ceremony and precedency, where they have an opportunity of giving their vices the appearance of virtues, and can make the world believe that it is their care, their tenderness for the dignity of their ossice, or the honour of their masters, what is the result of their own personal pride and vanity. This is most manifest in all negotiations ot ambassadors and plenipotentiaries, and must be known by all that observe what is transacted at public treaties; and it will ever be true, that men of the best taste have no relish in their pride, as long as any mortal can sind out that they are proud.

Line I 25. For there was not a bee but would

Get more, 1 won't fay, than he should;
But than, &c.

The vast esteem we have of ourselves, and the small value ve have for others, make us all very unfair judges in our own cases. Few men can be persuaded that they get too much by those they sell to, how extraordinary soever their gains are, when, at the fame time, there is hardly a prosit so inconsiderable, but they will grudge it to those they buy from; for this reason the smallest of the seller's advantage being the greatest persuasive to the buyer; tradesmen are generally forced to tell lies in their own defence, and invent a thousand improbable stories, rather than discover what they really get by their commodities. Some old slanders, indeed, that pretend to more honesty (or what is more likely, have more pride), than their neighbours, are used to make but few words with their customers, and refuse to sell at a lower price than what they ask at sirst. But these are commonly cunning foxes that are above the world, and know that those who have money, get often more by being surly, than others by being obliging. The vulgar imagine they can sind more sincerity in the sour looks of a grave old fellow, than there appears in the submissive air and inviting complacency of a young beginner. But this isa grand mistake; and if they are mercers, drapers, or others, that have many forts of the lame commodity, you may soon be satissied; look upon their goods and you will sind each of them have their private marks, which is a certain sign that both are equally careful in concealing the prime cost of what they fell.

Line 12S. —As your gamesters do,
That, though at fair play ne'er will own
Before the losers what they've won.

This being a general practice, which no body.can be ignorant of, that has ever seen any play, there must be something in the make of man that is the occasion of it: but as the searching into this will seem very trifling to many, I desire the reader to skip this remark, unless he be in perfect good humour, and has nothing at all to do.

That gamesters generally endeavour to conceal their gains before the losers, seems to me to proceed from a mixture of gratitude, pity, and self-preservation. All men are naturally grateful while they receive a benesit, and what they say or do, while it affects and feels warm about them, is real, and comes from the heart; but when that is over, the returns we make generally proceed from virtue, good manners, reason, and the thoughts of duty, but not from gratitude, which is *a* motive of the inclination. If we consider, how tyrannically the immoderate love we bear to ourselves, obliges us to esteem every body that with or without design acts in our favour, and how often we extend our affection to things inanimate, when we imagine them to contribute to our present advantage: if, I say, we consider this, it will not be dissicult to sind out which way our being pleased with those whose money we win is owing to a principle of gratitude. The next motive is our pity, which proceeds from our consciousness of the vexation there is in losing; and as we love the esteem of every body, we are afraid of forfeiting theirs by being the cause of their loss. Lastly, we apprehend their envy, and so self-preservation makes that we strive to extenuate sirst the obligation, then the reason why we ought to pity, in hopes that we shall have less of their illwill and envy. When the passions show themselves in their full strength, they are known by every body: When a man in power gives a great-place to one that did him a small kindness in his youth, we call it gratitude: When a woman howls and wrings her hands at the loss of her child, the prevalent passion is grief; and the uneasiness we feel at the sight of great misfortunes, as a man's breaking his legs, or dashing his brains out, is every whs re called pity. But the gentle strokes, the slight touches of the passions, are generally overlooked or mistaken.. To prove my assertion, we have but to observe what generally passes between the winner and the loser. The sirst is always complaisant, and if the other will but keep his temper, more than ordinary obliging; he is ever ready to humour the loser, and willing to rectify his mistakes with precaution, and the height of good manners. The loser is uneasy, captious, morose, and perhaps swears and storms; yet as long as he fays or does nothing designedly asfronting, the winner takes all in good part, without offending, disturbing, or contradicting him. Losers, fays the proverb, must have leave to rail: All which shows that the loser is thought in the right to complain, and for that very reason pitied. That we are afraid of the loser's ill-will, is plain from our being conscious that we are displeased with those we lose to, and envy we always dread when we think ourselves happier than others: From whence it follows, that when the winner endeavours to conceal his gains, his design is to avert the mischiefs he apprehends, and this is self-preservation; the cares of which continue to asfect us as long as the motives that sirst produced them remain.

But a month, a week, or perhaps a much shorter time after, when the thoughts of the obligation, and consequently the winner's gratitude, are worn off, when the loser has recovered his temper, laughs at his loss, and the reason of the winner's pity ceases; when the winner's apprehension of drawing upon him the ill-will and envy of the loser is gone; that is to fay, as soon as all the passions afe over, and the cares of self-preservation employ the winner's thoughts no longer, he will not only make no scruple of owning what he has won, but will, if his vanity steps in, likewise, with pleasure, brag off, if not exaggerate his gains.

It is possible, that when people play together who are at enmity, and perhaps desirous of picking a quarrel, or where men playing for trifles contend for superiority of skill, and aim chiefly at the glory of conquest, nothing shall happen of what 1 have been talking of. Different passions oblige us to take different measures; what 1 have said I would have understood of ordinary play for money, at which men endeavour to get, and venture to lose what they value: And even here 1 know it will be objected by many, that though they have been guilty of concealing their gains, yet they never observed those passions which I allege as the causes of that frailty; which is no wonder, because few men will give themselves leisure, and fewer

yet take the right method of examining themselves as they should do. It is with the passions in men, as it is with colours in cloth: It is easy to know a red, a green, a blue, a yellow, a black, &c. in as many different places; but it must be an artist that can unravel all the various colours arid their proportions, that make up the compound of a well-mixed cloth. In the fame manner, may the passions be discovered by every body whilst they are distinct, and a single one employs the whole man; but it is very dissicult to trace every motive of those actions that are the result of a mixture of passions.

I

Line 163. And virtue, who from politics

Has learn'd a thousand cunning tricks,

Was, by their happy influence,

Made friends with vice

It may be said, that virtue is made friends with vice, when indullrious good people, who maintain their families, and bring up their children handsomely, pay taxes, and are several ways useful members of the society, get a livelihood by something that chiefly depends on, or is very much influenced by the vices of others, without being themselves guilty of, or accessary to them, any otherwise than by way of trade, as a druggist may be to poisoning, or a sword-cutler to bloodshed.

Thus the merchant, that fends corn or cloth into foreign parts to purchase wines and brandies, encourages the growth or manufactoiy of his own country; he is a benefactor to navigation, increases the customs, and is many ways benesicial to the public; yet it is not to be denied, but that his greatest dependence is lavislmefs and drunkenness: For, if none were to drink wine but such only as stand in need of it, nor any body more than his health required, that multitude of wine-merchants, vintners, coopers, &-c. that make such a considerable mow in this flourishing city, would be in a miserable condition. The same may be said not only of card and dice-makers, that are the immediate ministers to a legion of vices; but that of mercers, upholsterers, tailors, and many

others, that would be starved in half a year's time, if pride and luxury were at once to be banished the nation.

Llne 167. The worst of all the multitude

Did something for the common good. JL His, I know, will seem to be a strange paradox to many; and I shall be asked what benesit the public receives from thieves and house-breakers. They are, I own, very pernicious to human society, and everjj. government ought to take all imaginable care to root out and destioy them; yet if all people were strictly honest, and nobody would middle with, or pry into any thing but his own, halt the smiths ot the nation would want employment; and abundance of workmanship (which now serves for ornament as well as defence) is to be seen every where both in town and country, that would never have been thought of, but to secure us against the attempts of pilferers and robbers.

If what I have said be thought far fetched, and my assertion seems still a paradox, I desire the reader to look upon the consumption of things, and he will sind that the laziest and most unactive, the profligate and most mischievous, are all forced to do something for the common good, and whilst their mouths are not sowed up, and they continue to wear and otherwise destroy what the industrious are daily employed about to make, fetch and procure, in spite of their teeth obliged to help, maintain the poor and the public charges. The labour of millions would soon be at an end, if there were not other millions, as I fay, in the fable.

Employ'd,

To fee their handy-works destroy'd.

But men are not to be judged by the consequences that may succeed their actions, but the facts themselves, and the motives which it shall appear they acted from. If an ill-natured miser, who is almost a plumb, and spends but sifty pounds a-year, though he has no relation to inherit his wealth, should be robbed of sive hundred or a thousand guineas, it is certain, that as soon as this money should come to circulate, the nation would be the better for the robbery, and receive the fame, and as real a benesit from it, as if an archbishop had left the fame sum to the public; yet justice, and the peace of society, require that he or they who robbed the miser should be hanged, though there were half a dozen of them concerned.

Thieves and pick-pockets steal for a livelihood, and either what they can get honeflly is not sussicient to keep them, or else they have an aversion to constant working: they want to gratify their senses, have victuals, strong diink, lewd women, and to be idle when they please. The victualler, who entertains them, and takes their money, knowing which way they come at it, is very near as great a villain as his guests. But if he fleeces them well, minds his business, and is a prudent man, he may get money, and be punctual with them he deals with: The trusty out-clerk, whose chief aim is his master's prosit, fends him in what beer he wants, and takes care not to lose his custom; while the man's money is good, he thinks it no business of his to examine w horn he gets it by. In the mean time, the wealthy brewer, who leaves all the management to his servants, knows nothing of the matter, but keeps his coach, treats his friends, and enjoys his pleasure with ease and a good conscience; he gets an estate; builds houses, aud educates his children in plenty, without ever thinking on the labour which wretches perform, the shifts fools make, and the tricks knaves play to come at the commodity, by the vast sale of which he amasses 1ns great riches.

A highwayman having met with a considerable booty, *l* gives a poor common harlot, he fancies, ten pounds to newrig her from top to foe; is there a spruce mercer so conscientious that he will refuse to sell her a thread sattin. though he knew who she was? She must have shoes and dockings, gloves, the stay and mantua maker, the sempstress, the linendraper, all must get somerhing by her, and a hundred different tradesmen dependent on those she laid her money out with, may touch part of it before a month is at an end. The generous gentleman, in the mean time, his money being near spent, ventured again on the road, but the second day having committed a robbery near Highgate, he was taken with one of his accomplices, and the next sessions both were condemned, and suffered the law. The money due on their conviction fell to three country fellows, on whom it was admirably well bestowed. One was an honest farmer, a sober pains-taking man, but reduced by misfortunes: The summer before, by the mortality among the cattle, he had lost six cows out often, and now his landlord, to whom he owed thirty pounds, had seized on all his stock. The other was a day-labourer, who struggled hard with the world, had a sick wife at home, and several small children to provide for. The third was a gentleman's gardener, who maintained his father in prison, where, being bound for a neighbour, he had lain for twelve pounds almost a year and a half; this act of silial duty was the more meritorious, because he had for some time been engaged to a young woman, whose parents lived in good circumstances, but would not give their consent before our gardener had sifty guineas of his own to show. They received above fourscore pounds each, which extricated every one of them out of the dissiculties they laboured under, and made them, in their opinion, the happiest people in the world.

Nothing is more destructive, either in regard to the health or the vigilance and industry of the poor, than the infamous liquor, the name of which, derived from Juniper in Dutch, is now, by frequent use, and the laconic spirit of the nation, from a word of meddling length, shrunk into a monosyllable, intoxicating gin, that charms the unactive, the desperate and crazy of either sex, and makes the starving sot behold his rags and nakedness with stupid indolence, or banter both in senseless laughter, and more inlipid jests! It is a siery lake that sets the brain in flame, burns up the entrails, and scorches every part within; and, at the fame time, a Lethe of oblivion, in which the wretch immersed drowns his mest pinching cares, and with his reason, all anxious reflection on brats that cry for food, hard winters frosts, and horrid empty home.

In hot and adust tempers it makes men quarrelsome, renders them brutes and savages, sets them on to sight for nothing, and has often been the cause of murder. It has broke and destroyed the strongest constitutions, thrown them into consumptions, and been the fatal and immediate occasion of apoplexies, phrenzies, and sudden death. But, as these latter mischiefs happen but seldom, they might be overlooked and connived at: but this cannot be said of the many diseases that are familiar to the liquor, and which are daily and hourly produced by it; such as loss of appetite, fevers, black and yellow jaundice, convulsions, stone and gravel, dropsies, and leucophlegmacies.

Among the doting admirers of this liquid poison, many of the meanest rank, from a sincere affection to the commodity itself, become dealers in it, and take delight to help others to what they love themselves, as whores commence bawds to make the prosits of one trade subservient to the pleasures of the other. But as these starvelings commonly drink more than their gains, they seldom, by seising, mend the wretchedness of condition they laboured under while they were only buyers. In the fag-end and outskirts of the town, and all places of the vilest resort, it is fold in some part or other of almost every house, frequently in cellars, and sometimes in the garret. The petty traders in this Stygian comfort, are supplied by others in somewhat higher station, that keep professed brandy shops, and are as little to be envied as the former; and among the middling people, I know not a more miserable shift for a livelihood than their calling; whoever would thrive in it must, in the sirst place, be of a watchful and suspicious, as well as a bold and resolute temper, that he may not be imposed upon by cheats and sharpers, nor out-bullied by the oaths and imprecations of hackney coachmen and foot soldiers: in the second, he ought ro be a dabster at gross jokes and loud laugtiter, and have all the winnmg ways to allure customers and draw out their money, and be well versed in the low jests and raileries the mob make use of to banter prudence and frugality. He must be affable and obsequious to the most despicable; always ready and ossicious to help a porter down with his load, shake hands with a balket woman, pull off his hat to an oyster wench, and be familiar with a beggar; with patience and good humour he must be able to endure the silthy actions and viler language of nasty drabs, and the lewdest rakehells, and without a frown, or the least aversion, bear with all the stench and squalor, noise and impertinence, that trie utmost indigence, laziness, and ebriety, can produce in the most shameless and abandoned vulgar.

The vast number of the mops I speak of throughout the city and suburbs, are an astonishing evidence of the many seducers, that, in a lawful occupation, are accessary to the introduction and increase of all the sloth, sottishness, want, and misery, which the abuse of strong waters is the immediate cause of, to lift above mediocrity perhaps half a score men that deal in tiie same commodity by wholesale, while, among the retailers, though qualisied as 1 required, a much greater number are broke and ruined, for not abstaining from the Circean cup they hold out to others, and the more fortunate are their whole lifetime obliged to take the uncommon pains, endure the hardships, and swallow all the ungrateful and shocking things 1 named, for little or nothing beyond a bare muenance, and their daily bread.

The short-sighted vulgar in the chain of causes seldom can see further than one link; but those who can enlarge their view, and will give themselves the leisure of gazing on the prospect of concatenated events, may, in a hundred places, fee good spring up and pullulate from evil, as naturally as chickens do from eggs. The money that arises from the duties upon malt is a considerable part of the national revenue, and ihould no spirits be distilled from it, the public treasure would prodigiously suffer on that head. But if we would set in a true light the many advantages, and large catalogue of solid blessings that accrue from, and are owing to the evil I treat of, we are to consider the rents that are received, the ground that is tilled, the tools that are made, the cattle that are employed, and above all, the multitude of poor that are maintained, by the variety of labour, requited in husbandry, in maltmg, in carriage and distillation, before we can have the product of malt, which we call low wines, and is but the beginning from winch the various spirits are afterwards to be made.

Besides this, a sharp-sighted good-humoured man might pick up abundance of good from the rubbish, which 1 have all flung away for evil. He would tell me, that whatever sloth and sottistinel's mirht be occasioned bv the abuse of malt-spirits, the moderate use of it was of inestimable benesit to the poor, who could purchase no cordials of higher prices, that it was an universal comfort, not only in cold and weariness, but most of the afflictions that are peculiar to the necessitous, and had often to the most destitute supplied the places of meat, drink, clothes, and lodging. That the stupid indolence in the most wretched condition occasioned by those composing draughts, which I complained of, was a blessing to thousands, for that certainly those were the happiest, who felt the least pain. As to diseases, he would fay, that, as it caused some, so it cured others, and that if the excess in those liquors had been sudden death to some few, the habit of drinking them daily prolonged the lives of many, whom once it agreed with; that for the loss sustained from the insignisicant quarrels it created at home, we were overpaid in the advantage we received from it abroad, by upholding the courage of soldiers, and animating the sailors to the combat; and that in the two last wars no considerable victory had been obtained without.

To the dismal account I have given of the retailers, and what they are forced to submit to, he would answer, that not many acquired more than middling riches in any trade, and that what I had counted so osfensive and intolerable in the calling, was trifling to those who were used to it; that what seemed irksome and calamitous to some, was delightful and often ravishing to others; as men differed in circumstances and education. He would put me in mind, that the prosit of an employment ever made amends for the toil and labour that belonged to it, nor forget, *Dulc'u odor lucri e re qualibet;* or to tell me, that the smell of gain was fragrant even to night-workers.

If 1 should ever urge to him, that to have here and there one great and eminent distiller, was a poor equivalent for the vile means, the certain want, and lasting misery of so many thousand wretches, as were necessary to raise them, he would answer, that of this 1 could be no judge, because I do not know what vast benesit they might afterwards be of to the commonwealth. Perhaps, would he fay, the man thus railed will exert himself in the commission of the peace, or other station, with vigilance and zeal against the diflbiute and disaflected, and retaining his stirring temper, be as industrious in spreading loyalty, and the reformation of manners, throughout every cranny of the wide populous town, as once he was in silling it with spirits; till he becomes at last the scourge os whores, of vagabonds and beggars, the terror of rioters and discontented rabbles, and conllant plague to sabbath-breaking butchers. Here my good-humoured antagonist would exult and triumph over me, especially if he could instance to me such a bright example, what an uncommon blessing, would he cry out, is this man to his country! how shining and illustrious his virtue!

To justify his exclamation, he would demonstrate to me, that is was impossible to give a fuller evidence of self-denial in a grateful mind, than to see him at the expence of his quiet and hazard of his life and limbs, be always harassing, and even for trifles, persecuting that very class of men to whom he owes his tortune, from no other motive than his aversion to idleness, and great concern for religion and the public welfare.

Line 173. Parties directly opposite,
Assist each other, as 'twere for spite.

Nothing was more instrumental in forwarding the Reformation, than the sloth and stupidity of the Roman clergy; yet the fame reformation has roused them from the laziness and ignorance they then laboured under; and the followers of Luther, Calvin, and others, may be said to have reformed not only those whom they drew into their sentiment, but likewise those who remained their greatest opposers. The clergy of England, by being severe upon the Schismatics, and upbraiding them with want of learning, have raised themselves such formidable enemies as are not easily answered; and again, the Dissenters by prying into the lives, and diligently watching all the actions of their powerful antagonists, render those os the Established Church more cautious of giving offence, than in all probability they would, if they had no malicious over-lookers to fear. It is very much owing to the great number of Hugonots that have always been in France, since the late utter extirpation of them, that that kingdom has a less dissolute and more learued clergy to boast of than any other Roman Catholic country. The clergy of that church are no where more sovereign than in Italy, and therefore no wh-'re more debauched; nor any where more ignorant than they are in Spain, because their doctrine is nowhere less opposed.

Who would imagine, that virtuous women, unknowingly, should be instrumental in promoting the advantage of prostitutes? Or (what still seems the greater paradox; that incontinence should be made serviceable to the preservation of chastity? and yet nothing is more true. A vicious young fellow, after having been an hour or two at church, a ball, or any other assembly, where there is a great parcel of handsome women dressed to the best advantage, will have his imagination more sired, than if he had the fame time been poling at Guildhall, or walking in the country among a flock of sheep. The consequence of this is, that he will strive to satisfy the appetite that is raised in him; and when he sinds honest women obstinateand uncomatable, it is very natural to think, that he will hasten to others that are more compilable. Who

would so much as surmise, that this is the fault of the virtuous women? They have no thoughts of men in dressing themselves, poor fouls, and endeavour only to appear clean and decent, every one according to her quality,

I am far from encouraging vice, and think it would be an unspeakable felicity to a state, if the sin of uncleanness could he utterly banished from it; but 1 am afraid it is impossible: The passions of some people are too violent to be curbed by any law or precept; and it is wisdom in all governments to bear with lesser inconveniencies to prevent greater. If courtezans and strumpets were to be prosecuted with as much rigour as some silly people would have it, what locks or bars would be sussicient to preserve the honour of our wives and daughters? For it is not only that the women in general would meet with far greater temptations, and the attempts to ensnare the innocence of virgins would seem more excuseable, even to the sober part os mankind, than they do now: but some men would grow outrageous, and ravishing would become a common crime. Where six or seven thousand sailors arrive at once, as it often happens, at Amsterdam, that! have seen none but their own sex for many months together, how is it to be supposed that honest women should walk the streets unmolested, if there were no harlots to be had at reasonable prices? for which reason, the wife rulers of that wellordered city always tolerate an uncertain number of houses, in which women are hired as publicly as horses at a livery.stable; and there being in this toleration a great deal of prudence and economy to be seen, a short account of it will b« no tiresome digression.

E

In the sirst place, the houses I speak of are allowed to be *n,* where but in the most slovenly and unpolished part of the town, where seamen and strangers of no repute chiefly lodge and resort. The street in which most of them stand is counted scandalous,-and the infamy is extended to all the neighbourhood round it. In the second, they are only places to meet and bargain in, to make

appointments in order to promote interviews of greater secrecy, and no manner of lewdness is ever susfered to be transacted in them: which order is so strictly observed, that bar the ill manners and noise of the company that frequent them, you will meet with no more indecency, and generally less lascivioufness there, than with us are to be seen at a playhouse.

Thirdly, the female traders that come to these evening exchanges are always the scum of the people, and generally such as in the day time carry fruit and other eatables about in wheel-barrows. The habits, indeed, they appear in at night are very different from their ordinary ones; yet they are commonly ib ridiculously gay, that they look more like the Roman dresses of strolling actresses than gentlewomen's clothes: if to this you add the awkwardness, the hard hands, and course breeding of the damsels that wear them, there is no great reason to fear, that many of the better sort of people will be tempted by them.

The music in these temples of Venus is performed by organs, not out of respect to the deity that is worshipped in them, but the frugality of the owners, whose business it is to procure as much sound for as little money as they can, and the policy of the government, who endeavour, as little as is possible to encourage the breed of pipers and scrapers. All seafaring men, especially the Dutch, are like the element they belong to, much given to loudness and roaring, and the noise of half a-dozen of them, when they call themselves merry, is susssicient to drown, twice the number of flutes or violins; whereas, with one pair of organs, they can make the whole house ring, and are at no other charge than the keeping of one scurvy musician, which can cost them but little: yet notwithstanding the good rules and strict discipline that are observed in these markets of love, the fchout and his ossicers are always vexing, mulcting, and, upon the least complaint, removing the miserable keepers of them; which policy is of two great uses; sirst, it gives an opportunity to a large parcel of ossicers, the magistrates make use of fefl many occasions, and which they could not be without, to squeeze a living out of the immoderate gains accruing from the worst of employments, and, at the fame time, punish those necessary profligates, the bawds and panders, which, though they abominate, they desire yet not wholly to destroy. Secondly, as on several accounts it might be dangerous to let the multitude into the secret, that those houses and the trade that is drove in them are connived at, so by this means appearing unblameable, the wary magistrates preserve themselves in the good opinion of the weaker sort of people, who imagine that the government is always endeavouring, though unable, to suppress what it actually tolerates: whereas, if they had a mind to root thejn out, their power in the administration of justice is so sovereign and extensive, and they know so well how to have it executed, that one week, nay, one night might send them all a packing.

In Italy, the toleration of strumpets is yet more barefaced, as is evident from their public stews. At Venice and Naples, impurity is a kind of merchandise and trassic; the courtezans at Rome, and the cantoneras in Spain, compose a body in the stare, and are under a legal tax and impost. It is well known, that the reason why so many good politicians as these tolerate lewd houses, is not their irresigion, but to prevent a worse evil, an impurity of a more execrable kind, and to provide for the safety of women of honour. " About two hundred and sifty years ago," fays Monsier de St. Di" dier, Venice being in want of courtezans, the republic " was obliged to procure a great number from foreign parts." Doglioni, who has written the memorable affairs of Venice, highly extols the wisdom os the republic in this point, which secured the chastity of women of honour, daily exposed to public violences, the churches and consecrated places not being a sussicient asylum for their chastity.

Our universities in England are much belied, if in some colleges there was not a monthly allowance *ad expvrgan-*

dos renes: and time was when monks and priests in Germany were allowed concubines on paying a certain yearly duty to their prelate. " It is generally believed" says Monsieur Bayle, (to whom 1 owe the last paragraph) " that avarice was the cause of this shameful indulgence; but it is more probable their design was to prevent their tempting modest women, and to quiet the uneasiness of husbands, Whose resentments the ciergy do well to avoid. From what has been said, it is manifest that there is a necessity of sacrisicing one part of womankind to preserve the other, and prevent a lilthiness of a more heinous nature. From whence I think I may justly conclude (what was the seeming paradox I went about to prove) that chastity may be supported by incontinence, and the best of virtues want the assistance of the worst of vices.

Line 177. The root of evil, avarice,
That darhn'd ill-natur'd baneful vice,
Was stave to prodigality.

I Have joined so many odious epithets to the word avarice, in compliance to the vogue of mankind, who generally bestow more ill language upon this than upon any other vice, and indeed not undeservedly; for there is hardly a mischief to be named which it has not produced at one time or other: but the true reason why every body exclaims so much against it, is, that almost every body lusters by it; for the more the money is hoarded up by some, the scarcer it must grow among the rest, and therefore when men rail very much at misers, there is generally self-interest at bottom.

As there is no living without money, so those that are unprovided, and have nobody to give them any, are obliged to do some service or other to the society, before they can come at it; but every body esteeming his labour as he does himself, which is generally not under the value, most people that want money only to spend it again presently, imagine they do moie for it than it is worth. . Men cannot forbear looking upon the necessaries of life as their-due, whether they work or not; because they sind that nature, without consulting whether they have victuals or not, bids them eat

whenever they are hungry; for which reason, every body endeavours to get what he wants with as much ease as he can; and there sore when men sind that the trouble they are put to in getting money is either more or less, according as those they would have it from are more or less tenacious, it is-very natural for them to be angry at covetousness in general; for it obliges them either to go without what they have occasion fer, or else to take greater pains for it than they are willing`.

Avarice, notwithstanding it is the occasion ot so may evils, is yet very necessary to the society, to glean and gather what has been dropt and scattered by the contrary vice. Was it not for avarice, spendthrifts would soon want materials; and if none would lay up and get faster than they spend, rery few could spend taster than they get. That it is a stave to prodigality, as 1 have called it, is evident from so many misers as we daily fee toil and labour, pinch and starve themselves, to errrich a lavish heir. Though these two vices appear very opposite, yet they often assist each other. Florio is an extravagant young blade, of a very profuse temper; as he is the only son of a very rich father, he wants to live high, keep horses and dogs, and throw his money about, as he fees some of his companions do; but the old hunks will parr. with no money, and hardly allows him necesiaries. Florio would have borrowed money upon his own credit long ago; but as all would be lost, if he died before his father, no prudent man would lend him any. At last he has met with the greedy Cornaro, who lets him have money at thirty *per cent.* and now Florio thinks himself happy, and spends a thousand a-year. Where would Cornaro ever have got such a prodigious interest, if it was not for such a fool as Florio, who will give so great a price for money to fling it away? And how would Florio get it to spend, it he had not lit of such a greedy usurer as Cornaro, whole excessive covetousness makes him overlook the great risk he runs in venturing such great sums upon the life of a wild debauchee.

Avarice is no longer the reverse of

profuseness, than while it signisies thai sordid love of money, and narrowness of soul that hinders misers from parting with what they have, and makes them covet it only to hoard up. But there is a sort of avarice which consists in a greedy desire of riches, in order to spend them, and this often meets with prodigality in the fame persons, as is evident in most courtiers and great osficers, both civil and military. In their buildings and furniture, equipages and entertainments, their qnllantry is displayed with the greatest profusion; while the base actions they submit to for lucre, and the many frauds and impositions they are guilty of, discover the utmost avarice. This mixture as contrary vices, comes up exactly to the character of Catiline, of whom it is said, that he was *appeiens alieni 13sui prefusus,* greedy after the goods of others, and lavisli ofh's own.

Line 180. That noble sin *L* He prodigality, I call a noble sin, is not that which has avarice for its companion, and makes men unreasonably profuse to some of what they unjustly extort from others, but that agreeable good-natured vice that makes the chimney smoke, and all the tradesmen smile; I niean the unmixed prodigality of heedless and voluptuous men, that being educated in, plenty, abhor the vile thoughts of lucre, and lavish away only what others took pains to scrape together; such as indulge their inclinations at their own expence, that have the continual satisfaction of bartering old gold for new pleasures, and from the excessive largeness of a disfusive foul, are made guilty of despising too much what most people overvalue

When I speak thus honourably of this vice, and treat it with so much tenderness and good manners as I do, I have the fame thing at heart that made me give so many ill names to the reverse of it, viz. the interest of the public; for as the avaricious does no good to himself, and is injurious to all the world besides, except his heir, so'the prodigal is a blessing to the whole society, and injures no body but himself. It is true, that as most of the sirst are knaves, so

the latter are all fools; yet they are delicious morsels for the public to feast on, and may with as much justice, as the French call the monks the patridges of the women, be styled the woodcocks of the society. Was it not for prodigality, nothing could make us amends for the rapine and extortion of avarice in power. When a covetous statesman is gone, who spent his whole life in fattening himself with the spoils of the nation, and had by pinching and plundering heaped up an immense treasure it, ought to sill every good member of the society with joy, to behold the uncommon profuseness of his son. This is refunding to the public what was robbed from it. Resuming of grants is a barbarous way of stripping, and it is ignoble to ruin a man faster than he does it himself, when he sets about it in such good earnest. Docs he not feed an insinite number of dogs of all sorts and sizes, though he never hunts; keep more horses than any nobleman in the kingdom, though he never rides them; and give as large an allowance to an ill-favoured whore as would keep a dutchess, though he never lies with her? Is he not itill more extravagant in those things he makes use of? Therefore let him alone, or praise him, call him public spirited "ford, nobly bountiful and magnisicently generous, and in a few years he will suffer himself to be stript his own way. As long as rhe nation has its own back again, we ought not to quarrel with the manner m which the plunder is repaid.

Abundance of moderate men, I know, that are enemies to extremes, will tell me, that frugality might happily supply the place of the two vices 1 speak of, that if men had not so many profuse ways of spending wealth, they would not be tempted to so many evil practices to scrape it together, and consequently that the same number of men, by equally avoiding both extremes, might render themselves more happy, and be less vicious without, than they could with them. Whoever argues thus, shows himself a better man than he is a politician. Frugality is like honesty, a mean starving virtue, that is only sit for small so-

cieties of good peaceable men, who are contented to be poor, so they may be easy; but, in a large stirring nation, you may have soon enough os it. It is an idle dreaming virtue that employs no hands, and therefore very useless in a trading country, where there are vast numbers that one way or other must be all let to work. Prodigality has a thousand inventions to keep people from sitting still, that frugality would never think of; and as this must consume a prodigious wealth, so avarice again knows innumerable tricks to raise it together, which frugality would scorn to make use of.

Authors are alwaysallowed to compare small things to great ones, especially if they ask leave sirst. *Si licit exemplis, is 'c.* but to compare great things to mean trivial ones, is unsufferable, unless it be in burlesque; otherwise 1 would compare the body politic (I confess the simile is very low) to a bowl of punch. Avarice should be the souring, and prodigality the sweetening of it. The water 1 would call the ignorance, folly, and credulity of the floating insipid multitude; while wisdom, honour, fortitude, and the rest of the sublime qualities of men, which separated by art from the dregs of nature, the sire of glory has exalted and resined into a spiritual eflence, should be an equivalent to brandy. I do not doubt but a Westphalian, Laplander, or any other dull stranger that is unacquainted with the wholesome composition, if he was to sell the several ingredients apart, would think it impossible they should make any tolerable liquor. The lemons would be too four, the sugar too luicious, the brandy he will fay is too strong ever t© be drank in any quantity, and the water he will call a tasteless liquor, only sit for cows and horses; *yet* experience teaches us, that the ingredients I named, judiciously Txed, will make an excellent liquor, liked of, and admired by men of exquiflte palates.

As to our vices in particular, I-could compare avarice, that causes so much mischief, and is complained of by every body who is not a miser, to a griping acid that sets our teeth on edge, and is unpleasant to every palate that is not debauched c I could compare the gaudy trimming and splendid equipage of a profuse beau, to the glillening brightness of the sinest loaf sugar; for as the one, by correcting the sharpness, prevent the injuries which a gnawing four might do to the bowels, so the other is a pleasing balsam that heals and makes amends for the smart, which the multitude always suffers from the gripes of the avaricious; while the substances of both melt away alike, and they consume themselves by being benesicial to the several compositions they belong to. I could carry on the simile as to proportions, and the exact nicety to be observed in them, which would make it appear how little any of the ingredients could be spared in either of the mixtures j but 1 will not tire my reader by pursuing too far a ludicrous comparison, when I have other matters to entertain him with of greater importance; and to sum up what 1 have said in. this and the foregoing remark, shall only add, that I look upon avarice and prodigality in the society, as I do upon twa contrary poisons in physic, of which it is certain that the noxious qualities being by mutual mischief corrected in both, they may assist each other, and often make a good medicine between them.

Line J So. Whilst luxury

Employ'd a million of the poor, &c.

If every tiling is to be luxury (as in strictness it ought) that is not immediately necessary to make man subsist as he is a living creature, there is nothing else to be found in the world, no not even among the naked savages; of which it is not probable that there are any but what by this time have made some improvements upon their former manner of living; and either in the preparation of their eatables, the ordering of their huts, or otherwise, added something to what once sussiced them. This desinition every body will fay is too rj gorous: I am of the fame opinion; but if we are to abate one inch of this severity, 1 am afraid we (hall not know where to stop. When people tell us they only desire to keep themselves sweet and clean, there is no understanding what they would be at: if they made use of these words in their genuine proper literal fense, they might be soon satissied without much cost or trouble, if they did not want water: but these two little adjectives are so comprehensive, especially in the dialect of some ladies, that nobody can guess how far they may be stretched. The comforts of life are likewise so various and extensive, that nobody can tell what people mean by them, except he knows what fort of life they lead. The fame obscurity I observe in the words decency and conveniency, and I never understand them, unless I am acquainted with the quality of the persons that make use of them. People may go to church together, and be all of one mind as much as they please, I am apt to believe that when they pray for their daily bread, the bishop includes several things in that petition which the sexton does not think on.

By what I have said hitherto I would only show, that if once we depart from calling every thing luxury that is not absolutely necessary to keep a man alive, that then there is no luxury at all; for if the wants of men are innumerable, then what ought to supply them has no bounds; what is called superfluous, to some degree of people, will be thought requisite to those of higher quality; and neither the world, nor the skill of man can produce any thing so curious or extravagant, but some most gracious sovereign or other, if it either eases or diverts him, will reckon it among the necessaries of life; riot meaning every body's life, but that of his sacred person.

It is a received notion, that luxury is as destructive to the wealth of the whole body politic, as it is to that of every individual person who is guilty of it, and that a national frugality enriches a country in the fame manner, as that which is less general increases the estates of private families. 1 confess, that though I have found men of much better understanding than myself of this opinion, I cannot help dissenting from them in this point. They argue thus: We feud, fay they, for example, to Turkey of woollen manufactury, and other things of our own growth, a million's worth ever year; for this we bring back silk, mohair, drugs, &c. to the value of twelve hundred thousand pounds, that are all spent in our pwn country. By this, fay they, we get nothing; but if most of us would be content with our own growth, and so consume but half the quantity of those foreign commodities, then those in Turkey, who would still want the same quantity of our manufactures, would be forced to pay ready money for the rest, and so by the balance of that trade only, the nation should get six hundred thousand pounds *per annum.*

To examine the force of this argument, we will suppose (what they would have; that but half the silk, &c. shall be consumed in England of what there is now; we will suppose likewise, that those in Turkey, though we refuse to buy above half as much of their commodities as we used to do, either can or will not be without the same quantity of our manufactures they had before, and that they will pay the balance in money; that is to fay, that they shall give us as much gold or silver, as the value of what they buy from us, exceeds the value of what we buy from them. Though what we suppose might perhaps be done for one year, it is impossible it should last: Buying is bartering; and no nation can buy goods of others, that has none of her own to purchase them with. Spain and Portugal, that are yearly supplied with new gold and silver from their mines, may for ever buy for ready money, as long as their yearly increase of gold or silver continues; but then money is their growth, and the commodity of the country. VVe know that we could not continue long to purchase the goods of other nations, if they would not take our manufactures in payment for them; and why should we judge otherwise of other nations? If those in Turkey, then, had no more money fall from the skies than we, let us fee what would be the consequence of what we supposed. The six hundred thousand pounds in silk, mohair, &c. that are left upon their hands the sirst year, must make those commodities fall considerably: Of this the Dutch and French will reap the benesit as much as ourselves; and if we continue to refuse taking their commodities in payment for pur manufactures, they can trade no longer with us, but must content themselves with buying what they want of such nations as are willing to take what we refuse, though their goods are much worse than ours; and thus our commerce with Turkey must in few years be insallibly lost.

But they will fay, perhaps, that to prevent the ill consequence I have showed, we shall take the Turkish merchandises as formerly, and only be,io frugal as to consume but half the quantity of them ourselves, and fend the rest abroad to be sold to others. Let us fee what this will do, and whether it will enrich the nation by the balance of that trade with six hundred thousand pounds. In the sirst place, I will grant them that our people at home making use of so much more of our own manufactures, those who were employed in silk, mohair, &c. will get a living by the various preparations of woollen goods. But, in the second, I cannot allow that the goods can be fold as formerly; for suppose the half that is wore at home to be fold at the fame rate as before, certainly the other half that is sent abroad will want very much of it: For we must send those goods to markets already supplied; and besides that, there must be freight, insurance, provision, and all other charges deducted, and the merchants in general must lose much more by this half that is reshipped, than they got by the half that is consumed here. For, though the woollen manufactures are our own product, yet they stand the merchant that ships them osf to foreign countries, in as much as they do the shopkeeper here that retails them: so that if the returns for what he fends abroad repay him not what his goods cost him here, with all other charges, till he has the money and a good interest for it in cash, the merchant must run out, and theupshot would be, that the merchants in general, sinding they lost by the Turkish commodities they lent abroad, would ship no more of our manufactures, than what would pay for as much silk, mohair, &-c. as would be consumed here. Other nations' would soon sind ways to supply them

with as much as we should fend short, and some where or other to dispose of the goods we should refuse: So that all we should get by this frugality, would be, that those in Turkey would take but half tha quantity of our manufactures of what they do now, while we encourage and wear their meichandises, without which they are not able to purchase ours.

As 1 have had the mortisication, for several years, to meet with abundance of sensible people against this opinion, and who always thought me wrong in this calculation, so I had the pleasure at last to see the wisdom of the nation full into the same sentiments, as is so manifest from an act of parliament made in the year 1721, where the legislature disobliges a powerful and valuable company, and overlooks very weighty inconveniences at home, to promote the interest of the Turkey trade, and not only encourages the consumption of silk and mohair, but forces the subjects, on penalsies, to make use of them whether they will or not.

What is laid to the charge of luxury besides, is, that it increases avarice and rapine: And where they are reigning vices, offices of the greatest trust are bought and sold; the ministers that should serve the public, both great and small, corrupted, and the countries every moment in danger of being betrayed to the highest bidders: And, lastly, that it esfeminates and enervates the people, by which the nations become an easy prey to the sirst invaders. These are indeed terrible things; but what is put to the account of luxury belongs to male-administration, and is the fault of bad politics. Every government ought to be thoroughly acquainted with, and stedfastly to pursue the interest of the country. Good politicians, by dexterous management, laying heavy impositions on some goods, or totally prohibiting them, and lowering the duties on others, may always turn and divert the course of trade which way they please; and as they will ever prefer, if it be equally considerable, the commerce with such countries as can pay with money as'well as goods, to those that can make no re-

turns for what they buy, but in the commodities of their own growth and manufactures, so they will always carefully prevent the trassic with such nations as. refuse the goods of others, and will take nothing but money for their own. But, above all, they will keep a watchful eye over the balance of trade in general, and never suffer that all the foreign commodities together, that arc imported in one year, mall exceed in value what of their own growth or manufacture is in the fame imported to others. Note, That I speak now of the interest of those nations that have no gold or silver of their own growth, otherwise this maxim need not to be so much insisted on..

If what 1 urged last, be but diligently looked after, and the imports are never allowed to be superior to the exports, no nation can ever be impoverished by foreign luxury; and they may improve it as much as they please, if they-can but in proportion raise the fund of their own that is to purchase it.

Trade is the principal, but not the only requisite to aggrandize a nation: there are other things to be taken care of besides. The. *mjum* and *tuum* must be secured, crimes punistied, and nil other laws concerning the adminiliration-of justice, wdcly contrived, and strictly executed. 1 oreign affairs must lie likewise prudently managed, and the ministry of every nation ought to have a good intelligence abroad, and be well acquainted with the public transactions of all those countries, that either by their neighbourhood, strength, or interest, may be hurtful or benessicial to them, to take the necessary measures accordingly, of crossing some, and assisting others, as policy, and the balance of power direct. The multitude must be awed, no man's conscience forced, and the clergy allowed no greater share in state asfairs, than our Saviour has bequeathed in his testament. These are the arts that lead to wordly greatness: VJ hat sovereign power soever makes a good use of them, that has any considerable nation to govern, whether it be a monarchy, a commonwealth, or a mixture of both, can never fail of making it flourish in spite of all the other powers upon earth, and no luxury, or other vice, is ever able to shake their constitution But here I expect a full-mouthed cry against me; What! has God never punished and destroyed great nations for their sins? Yes, but not without means, by infatuating their governors, and suffering them to depart from dither all or some ot those general maxims I have mentioned; and of all the famous states and empires the world has had to boast of hitherto, none ever came to ruin, whose destruction was not principally owing to the bad politics, neglects, or mismanagements of the rulers.

There is no doubt, but more health and vigour is expected among the people, and their offspring, scorn temperance and sobriety, than there is from gluttony and drunkenness; yet I confess, that as to luxury's effeminating and enervating a nation, 1 have not such frightful notions now, as 1 have had formerly. W hen we hear or read of things which we are altogether strangers to, they commonly bring to our imagination such idess of what we have seen, as (according to our apprehension) must come the nearest to them: And I remember, that when I have read of the luxury of Persia, Egypt, and other countries where it has been a reigning vice, and that were esseminated and enervated by it, it has sometimes put me in mind of the cramming and swilling of ordinary tradesmen at a city feast, and the beastliness their overgoiging themselves is often attended with; at other times, it has made me think on the distraction of dissolute sailors, as I had seen them in company of halt a dozen lewd women, roaring along with iiddles before them; and was I to have been carried into any of their great cities, I would have expected to have found one third of the people sick abed with surfeits; another laid up with the gout, or crippled by a more ignominious distemper; and the rest, that could go without leading, walk along the streets in petticoats.

It is happy for us to have fear for a keeper, as long as our reason is not strong enough to govern our appetites: And I believe, that the great dread 1 had more particularly against the word, to enervate, and some consequent thoughts on the etymology of it, did me abundance of good when I was a school boy: But since I have seen something in the world, the consequences of luxury to a nation seem not so dreadful to me as they did. As long as men have the fame appetites, the fame vices will remain. In all large societies, some will love whoring, and others drinking. The lustful that can get no handsome clean women, will content themselves with dirty drabs: and thole that cannot purchase true Hermitage or Pontack, will be glad of more ordinary French claret. Those that cannot reach wine, take up with most liquors, and a foot soldier or a beggar may make himself as drunk with stale beer or malt spirits, as a lord with Burgundy,Champaign, or Tockay. The cheapest and most slovenly way of indulging our passions, does as much mischief to a man's constitution, as the most elegant and expensive.

The greatest excesses of luxury are shown in buildings, furniture, equipages, and clothes: Clean linen weakens a man no more than flannel; tapestry, sine painting, or good wainscot, are no more unwholesome than bare walls; and a rich couch, or a gilt chariot, are no more enervating than the cold floor, or a country cart. The resined pleasures of men offense arc seldom injurious to their constitution, and there are many great epicures that will refuse to eat or drink more than their heads or stomachs can bear. Sensual people may take as great care of themselves as any: and the errors of the most viebusly luxurious, do not so much consist in the frequent repetitions of their lewdnels, and their eating and drinking too much (which are the things which would most enervate them), as they do in the operosc contrivance?, the profuscness and nicety they are served with, and the vail expence they are at in their tables and amours.

But let us once suppose, that the ease and pleasures, the grandees, and the rich people of every nation live in, render them unsit to endure hardships, and undergo the toils of 3

Vrar. I will allow that most of the common council of the city would make but very indifferent foot soldiers; and I believe heartily, that if your horse was to be composed of aldermen, and such as most of them are, a small artillery of squibs would be sussicient to route them. But what have the aldermen, the common council, or indeed all people of any substance to do with the war, but to pay taxes? The hardships and fatigues of war that are personally suffered, fall upon them that bear the brunt of every thing, the meanest indigent part of the nation, the working staving people: For how excessive soever the plenty and luxury of a nation may be, some body must do the work, houses and ships must be built, merchandises must be removed, and the ground tilled. Such a variety of labours in every great nation, require a vast multitude, in which there are always loose, idle, extravagant fellows enough to spare for an army; and those that are robust enough to hedge and ditch, plow and thrash, or else not too much enervated to be smiths, carpenters, sawyers, clothworkers, porters or carmen, will always be strong and hardy enough in a campaign or two to make good soldiers, who, where good orders are kept, have seldom so much plenty and superfluity come to their share, as to do them any hurt.

The mischief, then, to be feared from luxury among the people of war, cannot extend itself beyond the ossicers. The greatest of them are either men of a very high birth and princely education, or else extraordinary parts, and no less experience; and whoever is made choice of by a wife government to command an army *en chef,* should have a consummate knowledge in martial affairs, intrepidity to keep him calm in the midst of danger, and many other qnaliflcations that must be the work of time and application, on men of a quick penetration, a distinguished genius, and a world of honour. Strong sinews and supple joints are trifling advantages, not regarded in persons of their reach and grandeur, that can destroy cities a-bed, and ruin whole countries while they are at dinner. As they are most commonly men of great age, it would be ridiculous to expect: a hale constitution and agility of limbs from them: So their heads be but active and well furnished, it is no great matter what the rest of their bodies are. If they cannot bear the fatigue of being on horseback, they may ride in coaches, or be carried in litters. Mens conduct and sagacity are never the less for thejr being cripples, and the best general the king of France has now, can hardly crawl along. Those that are immediately under the chief commanders must be very nigh of the fame abilities, and are generally men that have raised themselves to those posts by their merit. The other ossicers are all of them in their several stations obliged to lay out so large a share of their pay in sine clothes, accoutrements, and other things, by the luxury of the times called necessary, that they can spare but little money for debauches; for, as they are advanced, and their salaries raised, so they are likewise forced to increase their expences and their equipages, which, as well as every thing else, must still be proportionable to their quality: by which means, the greatest part of them are in a manner hindered from those excesses that might be destructive to health; while their luxury thus turned another way, serves, moreover, to heighten their pride and vanity, the greatest motives to make them behave themselves like what they would be thought to be (See Remark on 1. 321)

There is nothing resines mankind more than love and honour. Those two passions are equivalent to many virtues, and therefore the greatest schools of breeding and good manners, are courts and armies; the sirst to accomplish the women, the other to polish the men. What the generality of ossicers among civilized nations affect, is a perfect knowledge of the world and the rules of honour an air of frankness, and humanity peculiar to military men of experience, and such a mixture of modesty and undauntedness, as may bespeak them both courteous and valiant. Where good fense is fashionable, and a genteel behaviour is in esteem, gluttony and drunkenness can be no reigning vices.

What ossicers of distinction chiefly aim at, is not a beastly, but a splendid way of living, and the wishes of the most luxurious, in their several degrees of quality, are to appear handsomely, and excel each other in sinery of equipage, politeness of entertainments, and the reputation of a judicious fancy in every-thing about them.

But if there should be more dissolute reprobates among officers, than there are among men of other professions, which is not true, yet the most debauched of them may be very serviceable, if they have but a great share of honour. It is this that covers and makes up for a multitude of defects in them, and it is this that none (how abandoned soever they are to pleasure) dare pretend to be without. But as there is noargument so convincing as matter of fact, let us look back on what so lately happened in our two last wars with France. How many puny young striplings have we had in our armies, tenderly educated, nice in their dress, and curious in their diet, that underwent all manner of duties with gallantry and cheerfulness?

Those that have such dismal apprehensions of luxury's enervating and effeminating people, might, in Flanders and Spain have seen embroidered beaux with sine laced shirts and powdered wigs stand as much sire, and lead up to the mouth of a cannon, with as little concern as it was possible for the most stinking slovens to have done in their own hair, though it had not been combed in a month, and met with abundance of wild rakes, who had actually impaired their healths, and broke their constitutions with excesses of wine and women, that yet behaved themselves with conduct and bravery against their enemies. Robustness is the least thing required in an officer, and if sometimes strength is of use, a sirm resolution of mind, which the hopes of preferment, emulation, and the love of glory inspire them with, will at a push supply the place of bodily force.

Those that understand their business, and have a sussicient sense of honour, as soon as they are used to danger will always be capable ossicers: and their

luxury, as long as they spend nobody's money but their own, will never be prejudicial to a nation.

By all which, 1 think, I have proved what I designed in this remark on luxury. First, that in one sense every thing may be called so, and in another there is no such thing. Secondly, that with a wile administration all people may swim in as much foreign luxury as their product can purchase, without being impoverished by it. And, lastly, that where military affairs are taken care of as they ought, and the soldiers well paid and kept in good discipline, a wealthy nation may live in all the ease and plenty imaginable; and in many parts of it, show as much pomp and delicacy, as human wit can invent, and at the fame time be formidable to their neighbours, and come up to the character of the bees in the fable, of which I said, that

Flatter'd in peace, and fear'd in wars,
They wereth' esteem of foreigners;
And lavish of their wealth and lives,
The balance of all other hives.

F (See what is farther said concerning luxury in the Remarks online 182 and 3J7.)

Line 182. And odious pride a million more.

Pride is that natural faculty by which every mortal that ha any understanding over-values, and imagines better thmgs of himself than any impartial judge, thoroughly acquainted with all his qualities and circumstances, could allow him. We are possessed of no other quality so benesicial to society, and so necessary to render it wealthy and flourishing as this, yet it is that which is most generally detested. What is very peculiar to this faculty of ours, is, that those who are the fullest of it, are the least willing to connive at it in others; whereas the heinousness of other vices is the most extenuated by those who are guilty of them themselves. The chaste man hates fornication, and drunkenness is most abhorred by the temperate; but none are so much offended at their neighbour's pride, as the proudest of all; and if any one can pardon it, it is the most humble: from which, I think, we may justly infer, that it being odious to all the world, is a certain sign that all the world is troubled with it. This all men offense are ready to confess, and nobody denies but that he has pride in general. But, if you come to particulars, you will meet with tew that will own any action you can name ol theirs to have proceeded from that principle. 1 here are likewise many who will allow, that among the sinful nations of the times, pride and luxury are the great promoters of t ade but they refuse to own the necessity there is, that in a more'virtuous age (such a one as should be tree from pride), trade would in a great measure decay..

The Almightyf they say, has endowed us with the donunion over all things which the earth and sea produce or con"ah, there is nothing to be found in either, but what was rnade for the use of man; and his skill and industry above other animals were given him, that he might render both them and every thing else within rhe reach of his senses, noS serviceable to him. Upon this consideration they think "impious to imagine, that humility, temperance, and other virtues should debar people from the enjoyment of those comforts of life, which are not denied to the moss wicked 2 and so conclude, that without pride or luxury "he fame things might be eat, wore, and consumed the same number of handicrafts and artisicers employed, and a nation be every way as flourishing as where those vices are the most predominant.

As to wearing apparel in particular, they will tell you, that pride, which sticks much nearer to us than our clothes, is only lodged in the heart, and that rags often conceal a greater portion of it than the most pompous attire; and that as it cannot be denied but that there have always been virtuous princes, who, with humble hearts, have wore their splendid diadems, and swayed their envied sceptres, void of ambition, for the good of others; so it is very probable, that silver and gold brocades, and the richest embroideries may, without a thought of pride, be wore by many whole quality and fortune are suitable to them. May not (say they) a good man

of extraordinary revenues, make every year a greater variety of suits than it is possible he should wear out, and yet have no other ends than to set the poor at work, to encourage trade, and by employing many, to promote the welfare of his country? And considering food and raiment to be necessaries, and the two chief articles to which all our worldly cares are extended, why may not all mankind set aside a considerable part of their income for the one as well as the other, without the least tincture of pride? Nay, is not every member of the society in a manner obliged, according to his ability, to contribute toward the maintenance of that branch of trade on which the whole has so great a dependence? Besides that, to appear decently is a civility, and often a duty, which, without any regard to ourselves, we owe to those we converse with.

These are the objections generally made use of by haughty moralists, who cannot endure to hear the dignity or their species arraigned; but if we look narrowly into them, they may soon be answered.

If we had vices, I cannot fee why any man should ever make more suits than he has occasion for, though he was never so desirous of promoting the good of the nation: for, though in the wearing of a well-wrought silk, rather than a 'light stusf, and the preferring curious sine cloth to coarse, he had no other view but the setting of more people to work, and consequently the public welfare, yet he could consider clothes no otherwise than lovers of their country do taxes now; they may pay them with alacrity, but nobody gives more than his due; especially where all are justly rated ac

Fa cording to their abilities, as it could no otherwise be expected in a very virtuous age. Besides, that in such golden times nobody would dress above his condition, nobody pinch his family, cheat or over reach his neighbour to purchase sinery, and consequently there would not be half the consumption, nor a third part of the people employed as now there are. But, to make this more plain, and demonstrate, that for the support of trade there can be nothing equiv-

alent to pride, I shall examine the several views men have in outward apparel, and set forth what daily experience may teach every body as to dress.

Clothes were originally made for two ends, to hide our nakedness, and to fence our bodies against the weather, and other outward injuries: to these our boundless pride has added a third, which is ornament; for what else but an excess of stupid vanity, could have prevailed upon our reason to fancy that ornamental, which must continually put us in mind of our wants and misery, beyond all other animals that are ready clothed by nature herself? It is indeed to be admired how so sensible a creature as man, that pretends to so many sine qualities of his own, mould condescend to value himself upon what is robbed from so innocent and defenceless an animal as a sheep, or what he is beholden for to the most insignisicant thing upon earth, a dying worm; yet while he is proud of such trifling depredations, he has" the folly to laugh at the Hottentots on the furthest promontory of Afric, who adorn themselves with the guts of their dead enemies, without considering that they are the ensigns of their valour those barbarians are sine with, the true*spolia opima,* and that if their pride be more savage than ours, it is certainly less ridiculous, because they wear the spoils of the more noble animal.

But whatever reflections may be made on this head, the world has long since decided the matter; handsome apparel is a main point, sine feathers make sine birds, and people, where they are not known, are generally honoured according to their clothes and other accoutrements they have about them; from the richness of them we judge of their wealth, and by their ordering of them we guess at their understanding. It is this which encourages every body, who is. conscious of his little merit, if he is any ways able to wear clothes above his rank, especially in large and populous cities, where obscure men may hourly meet with sifty strangers to one acquaintance, and consequently have the pleasure of being esteemed by a vast majority, not as what they are, but what they appear to be: which is a greater temptation than most people want to be vain.

Whoever takes delight in viewing the various scenes of low life, may, on Easter, Whitsun, and other great holidays, meet with scores of people, especially women, of almost the lowest rank, that wear good and fashionable clothes: if coming to talk with them, you treat them more courteously and with greater respect than what they are conscious they deserve, they will commonly be ashamed of owning what they are; and often you may, if you are a little inquisitive, discover in them a most anxious care to conceal the business they follow, and the place they live in. The reason is plain; while they receive those civilities that are not usually paid them, and which they think only due to their betters, they have the satisfaction to imagine, that they appear what they would be, which, to weak minds, is a pleasure almost as substantial as they could reap from the very accomplishments of their wishes: this golden dream they are unwilling to be disturbed in, and being sure that the meanness of their condition, if it is known, must link them very low in your opinion, they hug themselves in their disguise, and take all imaginable precaution not to forfeit, by a useless discovery, the esteem which they flatter themselves that their good clothes have drawn from you.

Though every body allows, that as to apparel and manner of living, we ought to behave ourselves suitable to our conditions, and follow the examples of the most sensible, and prudent among our equals in rank and fortune: yet how few, that are not either miserably covetous, or else proud of singularity, have this discretion to boast of? We all look above ourselves, and, as fast as we can, strive to imitate those that some way or other are superior to us.

The poorest labourer's wife in the parish, who scorns to wear a strong wholesome frize, as she might, will half starve herself and her husband to purchase a second-hand gown and petticoat, that cannot do her half the service; because, forsooth, it is more genteel.

The weaver, the shoeaiaker, the tailor, the barber, and every mean working fellow, that can set up with little, has the impudence, with the sirst money he gets, to dress himself like a tradesman of substance: the ordinary retailer in the clothing of his wife, takes pattern from his neighbour, that deals in the fame commodity by wholesale, and the reason he gives for it is, fhat twelve years ago the other had not a bigger shop than himself. The druggist, mercer, draper, and other creditable shopkeepers, can sind no difference between themselves and merchants, and therefore dress and live like them. The merchant's lady, who cannot bear the assurance of those mechanics, flies for refuge to the other end of the town, and scorns to follow any fashion but what she takes from thence; this haughtiness alarms the court, the women of quality are frightened to fee merchants wives and daughters dressed like themselves: this impudence of the city, they cry, is intolerable; mantua-makers are sent for, and the contrivance of fashions becomes all their study, that they may have always new modes ready to take up, as soon as those saucy cits shall begin to imitate those in being. The same emulation is continued through the several degrees of quality, to an incredible expence, till at last the prince's great favourites and those of the sirst rank of all, having nothing left to outstrip some of their inferiors, are forced to lay out vast estates in ponipous equipages, magnisicent furniture, sumptuous gardens, and princely palaces.

To this emulation and continual striving to out-do one another it is owing, that after so many various shiftings and changes of modes, in trumping up new ones, and renewing of old ones, there is still a *plus ultra* left for the ingenious; it is this, or at least the consequence of it, that sets the poor to work, adds spurs to industry, and encourages the skilful artisicer to search after further improvements.

It may be objected, that many people of good fashion, who have been used to be well dressed, out of custom, wear rich clothes with all the indifference

imaginable, and that the benesit to trade accruing from them cannot be ascribed to emulation or pride. To this 1 answer, that it is impossible, that those who trouble their heads ib little with their dress, could ever have wore those rich clothes, if both the stuffs and fashions had not been sirst" invented to gratify the vanity of others, who took greater delight in sine apparel, than they; besides that every body is not without pride that appears to be so; all the symptoms of that vice are not easily discovered; they are manifold, and vary according to the age, humour, circumstances, and often constitution of the people.

The choleric city captain seems impatient to come to action, and expressing his warlike genius by the sirmness of his steps, makes his pike, for want of enemies, tremble at the valour of his arm: his martial sinery, as he marches along, inspires him with an unusual elevation of mind, by which, endeavouring to forget his shop as well as himself, he looks up at the balconies with the sierceness of a Saracen conqueror: while the phlegmatic alderman, now become venerable both for his age and his authority, contents himself with being thought a considerable man; and knowing no easier way to express his vanity, looks big in his coach, where being known by his paultry livery, he receives, in sullen state, the homage that is paid him by the meaner sort of people.

The beardless ensign counterfeits a gravity above his years, and with ridiculous assurance strives to imitate the stern countenance of his colonel, flattering himself, all the while, that by his daring mien you will judge of his prowess. The youthful fair, in a vast concern of being overlooked, by the continual changing of her posture, betrays a violent desire of being observed, and catching, as it were, at every body's eyes, courts with obliging looks the admiration of her beholders. The conceited coxcomb, on the contrary, displaying an air of susssiciency, is wholly taken up with the contemplation of his own perfections, aqd in public places discovers such a dis. regard to others, that the ignorant must imagine, he thinks himself to be alone.

These, and such like, are all manifest, though different tokens of pride, that are obvious to all the world; but man's vanity is not always so soon found out. When we perceive an air of humanity, and men seem not to be employed in admiring themselves, nor altogether unmindful of others, we are apt to pronounce them void of pride, when, perhaps, they are only fatigued with gratifying their vanity, and become languid from a satiety of enjoyments. That outward mow of peace within, and drowsy composure of careless negligence, with which a great man is often seen in his plain chariot to loll at ease, are not always so free from art, as they may seem to be. Nothing is more ravishing to the proud, than to be thought happy.

The well-bred gentleman places his greatest'pride in the skill he has of covering it with dexterity, and some are so expert in concealing this frailty, that when they are the most guilty of it, the vulgar think them the most exempt from it. Thus the dissembling courtier, when he appears in state, assumes an air of modesty and good humour; and while he is ready to burst with vanity, seems to be wholly ignorant of his greatness; well knowing, that those lovely qualities must heighten him in the esteem of others, and be an addition to that grandeur, which the coronets about his coach and harnesses, with the rest of his equipage, cannot fail to proclaim without his assistance.

And as in these, pride is overlooked, because industriously concealed, so in others again, it is denied that they have any, when they show (or at least seem to show) it in the most public manner. The wealthy parson being, as well as the rest of his profession, debarred from the gaity of laymen, makes it his business to look out for an admirable black, and the sinest cloth that money can purchase, and distinguishes himself by the fullness of his noble and spotless garment; his wigs are as fashionable as that form he is forced to comply with will admit of; but as he is only stinted in their shape, so he takes care that for good-

ness of hair, and colour, few noblemen shall be able to match him; his body is ever clean, as well as his clothes, his steek face is kept constantly shaved, and his handsome nails are diligently pared; his smooth white hand, and a brilliant of the sirst water, mutually becoming, honour each other with double graces; what linen he discovers is transparently cur ous, and he scorns ever to be seen abroad with a worse beaver than what a rich banker would be proud of on his wedding day; to all these niceties in dress he adds a majestic gait, and expresses a commanding loftiness in his carriage; yet common civility, notwithstanding, the evidence of so many concurring symptoms, will not allow us to suspect any of his actions to be the result of pride: considering the dignity of his ossice, it is only decency in him, what would be vanity in others; and in good manners to his calling we ought to believe, that the worthy gentleman, without any regard to his reverend person, puts himself to all this trouble and expence, merely out of a respect which is due to the divine order he belongs to, and a religious zeal to preserve his holy function from the contempt of scoffers. With all my heart; nothing of all this shall be called pride, let me only be allowed to fay, that to our human capacities it looks very like it.

But if at last I should grant, that there are men who enjoy all the sineries of equipage and furniture, as well as clothes, and yet have no pride in them; it is certain, that if all should be such, that emulation I spoke of before must 7 cease, and consequently trade, which has so great a dependence upon it, suffer in every branch. For to say, that if all men were truly virtuous, they might, without any regard to themselves, consume as much out of zeal to serve their neighbours and promote the public good, as they do now out of self-love and emulation, is a miserable shift, and an unreasonable supposition. As there have been good people in all ages, so, without doubt, we are not destitute of them in this; but let us inquire of the periwig-makers and tailors, in what gentlemen, even of the greatest wealth

and highest quality, they ever could discover such public-spirited views. Aflc the lacemen, the mercers, and the linen-drapers, whether the richest, and if you will, the most virtuous ladies, if they buy with ready money, or intend to pay in any reasonable time, will not drive from shop to shop, to try the market, make as many words, and stand as hard with them to save a groat or sixpence in a yard, as the most necessitous jilts in town. If it be urged, that if there are not, it is possible there might be such people; I answer that it is as possible that cats, instead of killing rats and mice, should feed them, and go about the house to suckle aad nurse their young ones; or that a kite ihould call the hens to their meat, as the cock does, and lit brooding over their chickens instead of devouring them; but if they should all do so, they would cease to be cats and kites; it is inconsistent with their natures, and the species of creatures which now we mean, when we name cats and kites, would be extinct as soon as that could come to pass.

Line 1S3. Envy itself, and vanity,
Were ministers of industry.

Jlnvy is that baseness in our nature, which makes us grieve and pine at what we conceive to be a happiness in others. I do not believe there is a human creature in his fenses arrived to maturity, that at one time or other has not been carried away by this passion in good earnest; and yet I never met with any one that dared own he was guilty of it, but in jest. That we are so generally ashamed of this vice, is owing to that strong habit of hypocrisy, by the help of which, we have learned from our cradle to hide even from ourselves the vast extent of self-love, and all its different branches. It is impossible man ihould wilh better for another than he does for himself, unless where he supposes an impossibility that himself should attain to those wishes; and from hence we may easily learn after what manner this passion is raised in us. In order to it, we are to consider sirst, that as well as we think of ourselves, so ill we think of our neighbour with equal injustice; and when we apprehend, that others do or will enjoy what we think they do not deserve, it afflicts and makes us angry with the cause of that disturbance. Secondly, That we are employed in wishing well for ourselves, every one according to his judgment and inclinations, and when we observe something we like, and yet are destitute of, in the possession of others; it occasions sirst sorrow in us for not having the thing we like. This sorrow is incurable, while we continue our esteem for the thing we want: but as selfdefence is restless, and never suffers us to leave any means untried how to remove evil from us, as far and as well as we are able; experience teaches us, that nothing in nature more alleviates this sorrow, than our anger against those who are possessed of what we esteem and want. This latter passion, therefore, we cherish and cultivate to save or relieve ourselves, at least in part, from the uneasiness we felt from the first.

Envy, then, is a compound of grief and anger; the degrees of this passion depend chiefly on the nearness or remoteness of the objects, as to circumstances. If one, who is forced to walk on foot envies a great man for keeping a coach and six, it will never be with that violence, or give him that disturbance which it may to a man, who keeps a coach himself, but can only afford to drive with four horses. The symptoms of envy are as various, and as hard to describe, as those of the plague; at some time it appears in one shape, at others in another quite different. Among the fair, the disease is very common, and the signs of it very conspicuous in their opinions and censures of one another. In beautiful young women, you may often discover this faculty to a high degree; they frequently will hate one another mortally at sirst sight, from no other principle than envy; and you may read this scorn, and unreasonable aversion, in their very countenances, if they have not a great deal of art, and well learned to dissemble.

In the rude and unpolished multitude, this passion is very bare-faced, especially when they envy others for the goods pf fortune: They rail at their bet-

ters, rip up their faults, and take pains to misconstrue their most commendable actions: They murmur at Providence, and loudly complain, that the good things of this world are chiefly enjoyed by those who do not deserve them. The grosser sort of them it often affects so violently, that if they were not withheld by the fear of the laws, they would go directly and beat those their envy is levelled at, from no other provocation than what that passion suggests to them.

The men of letters, labouring under this distemper, discoTer quite different symptoms. When they envy a person for his parts and erudition, their chief care is industriously to conceal their frailty, which generally is attempted by denying and depreciating the good qualities they envy: They carefully peruse his works, and are displeased with every sine passage they meet with; they look for nothing but his errors, and wish for no greater feast than a gross mistake: In their censures they are captious, as well as severe, make mountains of molehills, and will not pardon the least shadoAv of a fault, but exaggerate the most trifling omission into a capital blunder.

Envy is visible in brute-beasts; horses show it in their endeavours of outstripping one another; and the best spirited will run themselves to death, before they will suffer another before them. In dogs, this passion is likewise plainly to be seen, those who are used to be caressed will never tamely bear that felicity in others. I have seen a lap-dog that would choke himself with victuals, rather than leave any thing for a competitor of his own kind; and we may often observe the same behaviour in those creatures which we daily see in infants that are froward, and by being over-fondled made humoursome. If out of caprice they at any time refuse to eat what they have asked for, and we can but make them believe that some body else, nay, even the cat or the dog is going to take it from them, they will make an end of their oughts with pleasure, and feed even against their appetite.

If envy was not rivetted in human nature, it would not be so common in chil-

dren, and youtn would not be so generally spurred on by emulation. Thole who would derive every thing that is benesicial to the society from a good principle, ascnbe the elsects of emulation in school-boys to a virtue of the mind; as it requires labour and pains, so it is evident, that they commit a self-denial, who act trom that disposition; but if we look narrowly into it, we shall hnd, that this sacrisice of ease and pleasure is only made to envy, and the love of glory. If there was not something very like this passion, mixed with that pretended virtue, it would be impossible to raise and increase it by the same means that create envy. The boy, who receives a reward for the superiority of his performance, is conscious of the vexation it would have been to him, if he should have fallen short of it: This reflection makes him exert himself, not to be outdone by those whom he looks upon as his inferiors, and the greater his pride is, the more self-denial he will practise to maintain his conquest. The other, who in spite of the pains he took to do well, has missed of the prize, is sorry, and consequently angry with him whom he mull look upon as the cause of his grief: But to show this anger, would be ridiculous, and of no service to him, so that he must either be contented to be less esteemed than the other boy; or, by renewing his endeavours, become a greater prosicient: and it is ten to one, but the disinterested, good humoured, and peaceable lad, will choose the sirst, and so become indolent and inactive, while the covetous, peevish, and quarrelsome rascal, lhall take incredible pains, and make himself a conqueror in his turn.

Envy, as it is very common among painters, so it is of great use for their improvement: I do not mean, that little dawbers envy great masters, but most of them are tainted with this vice against those immediately above them. If the pupil os a famous artist is of a bright genius, and uncommon application, he sirst adores his master; but as his own skill increases, he begins insensibly to envy what he admired before. To leain the nature of this pallion, and that it consists in what 1 have named, we are but to observe, that, if a painter, by exerting himself, comes not only to equal, but to exceed the man he envied, his sorrow is gone, and all his anger disarmed; and if he hated him before, he is now glad to be friends with him, if the other will condescend to it.

Married women, who are guilty of this vice, which few are not, are always endeavouring to raise the same passion in their spouses; and where they have prevailed, envy and emulation have kept more men in bounds, and reformed more ill husbands from sloth, from drinking, and other evil courses, than all the sermons that have been preached since the time of the Apostles.

As every body would be happy, enjoy pleasure, and avoid pain, if he could, so self-love bids us look on every creature that seems satissied, as a rival in happiness; and the satisfaction we have in feeing that felicity disturbed, without any advantage to oiirselves, but what springs from the pleasure we have in beholding it, is called loving mischief foe mischief's fake; and the motive of which that fiailty is the result, malice, another osfspring derived from the fame original; tor if there was no envy, there could be no malice. When the passions lie dormant, we have no apprehension of them, and often people think they have not such a frailty in their nature, because that moment they are not affected with it.

A gentleman well dressed, who happens to be dirtied all over by a coach or a cart, is langhed at, and by his inferiors much more than his equals, because they envy him more: they know he is vexed at it, and, imagining him to be happier than themselves, they are glad to fee him meet with displeasures in his turn! But a young lady, if Hie be in a serious mood, instead of laughing at, pities him, because a clean man is a sight me takes delight in, and there is no room for envy. At disasters, we either laugh, or pity those that befal them, according to the stock we are possessed of either malice or compassion. If a man falls or hurts himself so (lightly, that it moves not the latter, we laugh, and here

our pity and malice shake us alternately: Indeed, Sir, I am very sorry for it, 1 beg your pardon for laughing, 1 am the lilheit creature in the world, then laugh again; and again, 1 am indeed very sorry, and 1b on Some are so malicious, they would laugh if a man broke his leg, and others are so compassionate, that they can heartily pity a man for the least spot in his clothes; but nobody is to savage that no compassion can touch him, nor any man so good-natured, as never to be affected with any malicious pleasure. How strangely our passions govern us! We envy a man for being rich, and then perfectly hate him: But if we Come to be his equals, we are calm, and the least condescension in him makes us friends; but if we become visibly superior to him, we can pity his misfortunes. The reason why men of true good fense envy less than others, is because they admire themselves with lels hesitation than fools and silly people; for, though they do not mow this to others, yet the lolidity of their thinking gives them an assurance of their real worth, which men of weak understanding can never feel within, though they often counterfeit it.

The ostracism of the Greeks was a sacrisice of valuable men made to epidemic envy, and often applied as an infallible remedy to cure and prevent the mischiefs of popular spleen and rancour. A victim of state often appeases the murmurs of a whole nation, and after-ages frequently wonder at barbarities of this nature, which, under the fame circumstances, they would have committed themselves. They are compliments to the people's malice, which is never better gratisied, than when they can fee a great man humbled. We believe that we love justice, and to fee merit rewarded; but if men continue long in the sirst posts of honour, half of us grow weary of them, look for their faults, and, if we can sind none, we suppose they hide them, and it is much if the greatest part of us do not wish them discarded. This foul play, the best of men ought ever to apprehend from all who are not their immediate friends or acquaintance, because nothing is more

tiresome to us, than the repetition of praises we have no manner of share in.

The more a passion is,a compound of many others, the more dissicult it is to desine it; and the more it is tormenting to those that labour under it, the greater cruelty it is capable of inspiring them with against others; Therefore nothing is more whimsical or mischievous than jealousy, which is made up of love, hope, fear, and a great deal of envy: The last has been sussiciently treated of already; and what I have to say of fear, the reader will sind under Remark on 1. 321. So that the better to explain and illustrate this odd mixture, the ingredients I shall further speak of in this place, are hope and love.

Hoping is wishing with some degree of considence, that the thing wished for will come to pass. The sirmness and imbecillity of our hope depend entirely on the greater or lesser degree of our considence, and all hope includes doubt; for when our considence is arrived to that height, as to exclude all doubts, it becomes a certainty, and we take for granted what we only hoped for before. A silver inkhorn may pass in speech, because every body knows what we mean by it, but a certain hope cannot: For a man who makes use of an epithet that destroys the essence of the substantive he joins it to, can have no meaning at all; and the more clearly we understand the force of the epithet, and the nature of the substantive, the more palpable is the.nonsense of the heterogeneous compound. The reason, therefore, why it is not so shocking to some to hear a man speak of certain hope, as if he should talk of hot ice, or liquid oak, is not because there is less nonsense contained in the sirst, than there is in either of the latter; but because the word hope, I mean the essence of it, is not so clearly understood by the generality of the people, as the words and essence of ice and oak are.

Love, in the sirst place, signisies affection, such as parents and nurses bear to children, and friends to one another; it consists in a liking and well-wishing to the person beloved. We give an easv construction to his words and actions, and feel a proneness to excuse and forgive his faults, if we fee any; his interest we make on all accounts our own, even to our prejudice, and receive an inward satisfaction for sympathising with him in his sorrows, as well as joys. What I said last is not impossible, whatever it may seem to be; for, when we are sincere in sharing with one another in his misfortunes, self-love makes us believe, that the sufferings we feel must alleviate and lessen those of our friend; and while this fond reflection is soothing our pain, a secret pleasure arises from our grieving for the person we love.

Secondly, by love we understand a strong inclination, iir its nature distinct from all other affections of friendship, gratitude, and consanguinity, that persons of different sexes, after liking, bear to one another: it is in this signisication, that love enters into the compound of jealousy, and is the effect as well as happy disguise of that passion that prompts us to labour for the preservation of our species. This latter appetite is innate both in men and women, who are not defective in their formation, as much as hunger or thirst, though they are seldom affected with it before the years of puberty. Could we undress nature, and pry into her deepest recesses, we should discover the seeds of this passion before it exerts itself, as plainly as we fee the teeth in an embryo, before the gums are formed. There are few healthy people of either sex, whom it has made no impreflion on before twenty: yet, as the peace and happiness of the civil society require that this should be kept a secret, never to be talked of in public; so, among well-bred people, it is counted highly criminal to mention, before company, any thing in plain words, that is, relating to this mystery of succession: by which means, the very name of the appetite, though the most necessary for the continance of mankind, is become odious, arid the proper epithets commonly joined to lust, are silthy and abominable.

This impulse of nature in people of strict morals, and rigid modesty, often disturbs the body for a considerable time before it is understood or known to be what it is, and it is remarkable, that the most polished, and best instructed, are generally the most ignorant as to this affair; and here I can but observe the difference between man in the wild state of nature, and the same creature in the civil society. In the sirst, men and women, if left rude and untaught in the sciences of modes and manners, would quickly sind out the cause of that disturbance, and be at a loss no more than other animals for a present remedy: besides, that it is not probable they would want either precept or example from the more experienced. But, in the second, where the rules of religion, law, and decency, are to be followed, and obeyed, before any dictates of nature, the youth of both sexes are to be armed and fortisied against this impulse, and from their infancy artfully frightened from the most remote approaches of it. The appetite itself, and all the symptoms of it, though they are plainly felt and understood, are to be stifled with care and severity, and, in-women, flatly disowned, and if there be occasion, with obstinacy denied, even when themselves are affected by them. If it throws them into distempers, they must be cured by physic, or else patiently bear them in silence; and it is the interest of the society to preserve decency and politeness; that women should linger, waste, and die, rather than relieve themselves in an unlawful manner; and among the fashionable part of mankind, the people of birth and fortune, it is expected that matrimony should never be entered upon without a curious regard to family, estate, and reputation, and, in the making of matches, the call of nature be the very last consideration.

Those, then, who would make love and lust synonymous, confound the effect with, the cause of it: yet such is the force of education, and a habit of thinking, as we are taught, that sometimes persons of either sex are actually in love without feeling any carnal desires, or penetrating into the intentions of nature, the end proposed by her, without which they could never have been affected with that sort of paflion. That there are such is certain, but many more whole pietences to those resined notions are only upheld by art and dissimulation. Those, who are really such Platonic lovers, are commonly the pale-faced weakly people, of cold and phlegmatic constitutions in either sex; the hale and robust, of bilious temperament, and a sanguine complexion, never entertain any love so spiritual as to exclude all thoughts and wishes that relate to the body; but if the mull seraphic lovers would know the original of their inclination, let them but suppose that another should have the corporal enjoyment of the person beloved, and by the tortures they will suffer from that reflection they will soon discover the nature of their passions: whereas, on the contrary, parents and friends receive a satisfaction in reflecting on the joys and comforts of a happy marriage, to be tasted by those they wish well to. The curious, that are skilled in anatomizing the invisible part of man, will observe that the more sublime and exempt this love is from all thoughts of sensuality, the more spurious it is, and the more it degenerates from its honest original and primitive simplicity. The power and sagacity as well as labour and care of the politician in civilizing the society, has been no where more conspicuous, than in the happy contrivance of playing our passions against one another. By flattering our pride, and still increasing the good opinion we have of ourselves on the one hand, and inspiring us on the other with a superlative dread and mortal aversion against shame, the artful moralists have taught us cheerfully to encounter ourselves, and if not subdue, at least, so to conceal and disguise our darling passion, lust, that we scarce know it when we meet with it in our breads: Oh! the mighty prize we have in view for all our fell-denial! can any man be so serious as to abstain from laughter, when he considers, that for so much deceit and insincerity practised upon ourselves as well as others, we have no other recompense than the vain satisfaction of making our species appear more exalted and remote from that of other animals, than it really is; and we, in our consciences, know it to be? yet this is fact, and in it we plainly perceive the reason why it was necessity to render odious every word or action by which we might discover the innate desire we feel to perpetuate our kind; and why tamely to submit to the violence of a furious appetite (which is painful to resist) and innocently to obey the most pressing demand of nature without guile or hypocrisy,

G like other creatures, should be branded with the ignominious name of brutality.

What we call love, then, is not a genuine, but an adulterated appetite, or rather a compound, a heap of several contradictory passions blended in one. As it is a product of nature warped by custom and education, so the true origin and sirst motive of it, as I have hinted already, is stifled in well-bred people, and concealed from themselves: all which is the reason, that, as those assected with it, vary in age, strength, resolution, temper, circumstances, and manners, the esfects of it are so different, whimsical, surprising, and unaccountable.

It is this passion that makes jealousy so troublesome, and the envy of it often so fatal: those who imagine that there may be jealousy without love, do not understand that passion. Men may not have the least affection for their wives, and yet be angry with them for their conduct, and suspicious of them either with or without a cause: but what in such cases affects them is their pride, the concern for their reputation. They feel a hatred against them without remorse; when they are outrageous, they can beat them and go to sleep contentedly: such husbands may watch their dames themselves, and have them, observed by others; but their vigilance is not so intense; they are not so inquisitive or industrious in their searches, neither do they feel that anxiety of heart at the fear of a discovery, as when love is mixed with the passions.

What consirms me in this opinion is, that we never observe this behaviour between a man and his mistress; for when his love is gone and he suspects her to be false, he leaves her, and troubles his head no more about her: whereas, it is the greatest dissiculty imaginable, even to a man of fense, to part with his mistress as long as he loves her, whatever faults she may be guilty of. If in his anger lie strikes her, he is uneasy after it; his love makes him reflect on the hurt he has done her, and he wants to be reconciled to her again. He may talk of hating her, and many times from his heart wish her hanged, but if he cannot get entirely rid of his frailty, he can never disentangle himself from her: though she is represented in the most monstrous guilt to his imagination, and he has resolved and swore a thousand times never to come near her again., there is no trusting him, even when he is fully convinced of her infidelity, if his love continues, his despair is never so lasting, but between the blackest sits of it he relents, and sinds lucid intervals of hope; he forms excuses for her, thinks of pardoning, and in order to it racks his invention for possibilities that may make her appear less criminal.

Line 200. Real pleasures, comforts, ease.

That the highest good consisted in pleasure, was the doctrine of Epicurus, who yet led a life exemplary for continnence, sobriety, and other virtues, which made people of the succeeding ages quarrel about the signisication of pleasure Those who argued from the temperance of the philosopher, said, That the delight Epicurus meant, was being virtuous; so Erasmus in his Colloquies tells us, that there are no greater Epicures than pious Christians. Others that reflected on the dissolute manners of the greatest part of his followers, would have it, that by pleasures he could have understood nothing but sensual ones, and the gratisication of our passions. I shall not decide their quarrel, but am of opinion, that whether men be good or bad, what they take delight in is their pleasure; and not to look out for any further etymology from the learned languages, I believe an Englishman may justly call every thing a pleasure that pleases him, and according to this desinition, we ought to dispute no more about men's pleasures than their tastes:

Trabit sua quemque voluptas.

The worldly-minded, voluptuous, and ambitious man, notwithstanding he is void of merit, covets precedence every where, and desires to be dignisied above his betters: he aims at spacious palaces, and delicious gardens; his chief delight is in excelling others in stately horses, magnisicent coaches, a numerous attendance, and dear-bought furniture. To gratify his lust, he wishes for genteel, young, beautiful women of different charms and complexions, that mall adore his greatness, and be really in love with his person: his cellars he would have stored with the flower of every country that produces excellent wines: his tables he desires may be served with many courses, and each of them contain a choice variety of dainties not easily purchased, and ample evidences of elaborate and judicious cookery; while harmonious music, and well-couched flattery, entertain his hearing by turns. He employs even in the meanest trisles, none but the ablest and most ingenious workmen, that his judgment and fancy may as evidently appear in the least things that belong to him as his wealth and quality are manifested in those of greater value. He desires to have several sets of witty, facetious, and polite people to converse with andamongthem he would have some sami'us for learning and universal knowledge: for his serious affairs, he wishes to sind men of parts and experience, that should be diligent and faithful. Those that are to wait on him he would have handy, mannerly, and discreet, of comely aspect, and a graceful mien: what he requires in them besides, is a respectful care of every thing that is his, nimbleness without hurry, dispatch without noise, and an unlimited obedience to his orders: nothing he thinks more troublesome than speaking to servants; wherefore he will only be attended by such, as by observing his looks have learned to interpret his will fiom the llightest motions. He loves to fee an elegant nicety in every thing that approaches him, and in what is to be employed about his person, he desires a superlative cleanliness to be religiously observed. The chief ofsicers of his household he would have to be men of birth, honour and distinction, as well as order, contrivance, r. nd economy; for though he loves to be honoured by every body, and receives the respects of the common people with joy, yet the homage that is paid him by persons of quality is ravishing to him in a more tranlcendant manner.

While thus wallowing in a sea of lust and vanitv, he is wholly employed in provoking and indulging his appetites, he desires the world should think him altogether free from pride and sensuality, and put a favourable construction upon his most glaring vices: nay, if his authority can purchase it, he covets to be thought wife, brave, generous, good-natured, and endued with the virtues he thinks worth having. He would have us believe that the pomp and luxury he is served with are as many tiresome plagues to him; and all the grandeur he appears in is an ungrateful burden, which, to his sorrow, is inseparable from the high sphere he moves in; that his noble mind, so much exalted above vulgar capacities, aims at higher ends, and cannot relish such worthless enjoyments; that the highest of his ambition is to promote the public welfare, and his greatest pleasure to see his country flourish, and every body in it made happy. These are called seal pleasures by the vicious and earthly-minded, and whoever is able, either by his skill or fortune, after this resined manner at once to enjoy the world, and the good opinion of it, is counted extremely happy by all the moil fashionable part of the people.

But, on the other side, most of the ancient philosophers and grave moralists, especially the Stoics, would not allow any thing to be a real good that was liable to be taken from them by others. They wisely considered the instability of fortune, and the favour of princes; the vanity of honour, and popular applause; the precariousness of riches, and all earthly possessions; and therefore placed true happiness in the calm serenity of a contented mind, free from guilt and ambition; a mind that, having subdued every sensual appetite, despises the smiles as well as frowns of fortune, and taking no delight but in contemplation, desires nothing but what every body is able to give to himself: a mind that, armed with fortitude and resolution, has learned to sustain the greatest losses without concern, to endure pain without affliction, and to bear injuries without resentment. Many have owned themselves arrived to this height of self-denial, and then, if we may believe them, they were raised above common mortals, and their strength extended vastly beyond the pitch of their sirst nature: they could behold the anger of threatening tyrants and the most imminent dangers without terror, and preserved their tranquillity in the midst of torments: death itself they could meet with intrepidity, and left the world with no greater reluctance than they had showed fondness at their entrance into it.

These among the ancients have always bore the greatest sway; yet others that were no fools neither, have exploded those precepts as impracticable, called their notions romantic, and endeavoured to prove, that what these Stoics asscrted of themselves, exceeded all human force and possibility; and that therefore the virtues they boasted of could be nothing but haughty pretence, full of arrogance and hypocrisy; yet notwithstanding these censures, the serious part of the world, and the generality of wife men that have lived ever since to this day, agree with the Stoics in the most material points; as that there can be no true felicity in what depends on things perishable; that peace within is the greatest blessing, and no conquest hke that of our passions; that knowledge, temperance, fortitude, humility, and other embellishments of the mind are the most valuable acquisitions; that no man can be happy but he that is good: and that the virtuous are only capable of enjoying real pleasures.

1 expect to be asked, why in the fable I have called those pleasures real, that are directly opposite to those which I own the wise men of all ages have extolled as the most valuable? My answer is, because 1 do not call things pleasures which men fay are best, but such as they seem to be most pleased with; how can I believe that a mans chief delight is in the embellishment of the mind, when l fee him ever employed about and daily pursue the pleasures that are contrary to them? John never cuts any pudding, but just enough that, you cannot fay he took none: this little bit, after much chomping and chewing, you fee goes down with him like chopped hay; after that he falls upon the beef with a voracious appetite, and crams himself up to his throat. Is it not Erevoking, to hear John cry every day that pudding is all is delight, and that he does not value the beef of a farthing. 1 could swagger about fortitude and the contempt of riches as much as Seneca himself, and would undertake to write twice as much in behalf of poverty as ever he did; for the tenth part of his estate, I could teach the way to his *summum bonum* as exactly as 1 know my way home: I could tell people to extricate themselves from all worldly engagements, and to purify the mind, they must divest themselves of their passions, as men take out the furniture when they would clean a room thoroughly; and I am clearly of the opinion, that the malice and most severe strokes of fortune, can do no more injury to a mind thus stripped of all fears, wishes, and inclinations, than a blind horse can do in an empty barn. In the theory of all this I am very perfect, but the practice is very dissicult; and if you went about picking my pocket, osiered to take the victuals from before me when 1 am hungry, or made but the least motion of spitting in my face, 1 dare not promise how philosophically 1 should behave myself. But that I am forced to submit to every caprice of my unruly nature, you will say, is no argument, that others are as little masters of theirs, and therefore, 1 am willing to pay adoration to virtue wherever I can meet with it, with a proviso that I shall not be obliged to admit any as such, where I can see no ielf-denial, or to judge of mens sentiments from their words, where I have their lives before me.

I have searched through every degree and station of men, and confess, that 1 have found no where more austerity of manners, or greater contempt of earthly pleasures, than in some religious houses, where people freelv resigning and retiring from the world to combat themselves, have no-other business but subdue their appetites. What can be a greater evidence of perfect chastity, and a superlative love, to immaculate purity in men and women, than that in the prime of their age, when lust is most raging, they should actually seclude themselves from each others company, and by a voluntary renunciation debar themselves for life, not onlv from ur. cleanness, but even the most lawful embraces? those that abstain from flesh, and often all manner of food, one would think in the right way, to conquer all carnal desires; and I could almost swear, that he does not consult his ease, who daily mauls his bare back and shoulders with unconscionable stripes, and constantly roused at night from his sleep, leaves his bed for his devotion. Who can despise riches more, or show himself less avaricious than he, who will not so much as touch gold or silver, no not with his feet? Or can any mortal show himself less luxurious or more humble than the man, that making poverty his choice, contents himself with scraps and fragments, and refuses to eat any bread but what is bestowed upon him by the charity of others.

Such fair instances of self-denial, would make me bow down to virtue, if I was not deterred and warned from it by so many persons of eminence and learning, who unanimously tell me that 1 am mistaken, and all 1 have seen is farce and hypocrisy; that what seraphic love they may pretend to, there is nothing but discord among them; and that how penitential the nuns and friars may appear in their several convents, they none of them sacrilice their darling lusts: that among the women, they are not all virgins that pass for such, and that if I was to be let into their secret?, and examine some of their subterraneous privacies, 1 mould soon be convinced by scenes of horror, that some of them must have been mothers. That among the men 1 should sind calumny, envy, and ill-na-

ture, in the highest degree, or else gluttony, drunkenness, and impurities of a more execrable kind than adultery itself: and as for the mendicant orders, that they fer in nothing but their habits from other sturdy beggars, who deceive people with a pitiful tone, and an outward stiow of misery, and as soon as they are out of light, lay by their cant, indulge their appetites, and enjoy one another.

If the strict rules, and so many outward signs of devotion. observed among those religious orders, deserve such harfli censures, we may well despair of meeting with virtue anywhere else; for if we look into the actions of the antagonists and greatest accusers of those votaries, we shall not sind so much as the appearance of self-denial. The reverend divines of all sects, even of the most reformed churches in all countries, take care with the *Cyclops Evangeliphorus* sirst; *ut ventri benefit,* and afterwards, *ne quid defit iis quæsub ventre sunt.* To these they will desire you to add convenient houses, handsome furniture, good sires in winter, pleasant gardens in summer, neat clothes, and money enough to bring up their children; precedency in all companies, rcipect from every body, and then as much religion as you please. The things 1 have named are the necessary comforts of life, which the most modest are not ashamed to claim, and which they are very uneasy without. They are, it is true, made of the fame mould, and have the fame corrupt nature with other men, born with the fame insirmities, subject to the same pastions, and liable to the fame temptations, and therefore if they are diligent in their calling, and can but abstain from murder, adultry, swearing, drunkenness, and other heinous vices, their lives are all called unblemished, and their reputations, unspotted; their function renders them holy, and the gratisication of lo many carnal appetites, and the enjoyment of so much luxurious ease notwithstanding, they may set upon themselves what value their pride and parts will allow them.

All this I have nothing against, but 1

fee no self-denial, without which there can be no virtue. Is it such a mortisication not to desire a greater share os worldly blessings, than what every reasonable man ought to be satissied with? Or, is there any mighty merit in not being flagitious, and forbearing indecencies that are repugnant to good manners, and which no prudent man would be guilty of, though he had no religion at all?

1 know I shail be told, that the reason why the clergy are so violent in their resentments, when at any time they are but in the least asfronted, and show themselves so void of all patience when their rights are invaded, is their great care to preserve their calling, their profession from contempt, not for their own fakes, but to be more serviceable to others. It is the fame reason that makes them solicitous about the comforts and conveniencics ot life; for mould they luster them-r selves to be insulted over, be content with a coarser diet, and wear more ordinary clothes than other people, the multitude, who judge from outward appearances, would be apt to think that the clergy was no more the immediate care of Providence than other folks, and so not only undervalue their persons, but despise likewise all the reproofs and instructions that came from them. This is an admirable plea, and as it is much made use of, I will try the worth of it. lam not of the learned Dr. Echard's opinion, that poverty is one of those things that bring the clergy into contempt, any further than as it may be an occasion of discovering their blind side: for when men are always struggling with their low condition, and are unable to bear the burden of it without reluctancy, it is then they show how uneasy their poverty sits upon them, how glad they-would be to have their circumstances meliorated, and what a real value they have for the good things of this world. He that harangues on the contempt of riches, and the vanity of earthly enjoyments, in a rusty threadbare gown, because he has no other, and would wear his old greasy hat no longer if any body would give him a better; that drinks small beer at home with a

heavy countenance, but leaps at a glass of wine if lie can catch it abroad; that with little appetite feeds upon his own coarse mess, but tails to greedily where he can please his palate, and expresses an uncommon joy at an invitation to a splendid dinner: it is he that is despised, not because he is poor, but because he knows not how to be so, with that content and resignation which he preaches to others, and so discovers his inclinations to be contrary to his doctrine. But, when a man from the greatness of his soul (or an obstinate vanity, which will do as well) resolving to subdue his appetites in good earnest, refuses all the offers of ease and luxury that can be made to him, and embracing a voluntary poverty with cheerfulness, rejects whatever may gratify the senses, and actually sacrisices all his passions to his pride, in acting this part, the vulgar, far from contemning, will be ready to deify and adore him. How famous have the Cynic philosophers made themselves, only by residing to dissimulate and make use os superfluities? Did not the most ambitious monarch the world ever bore, condescend to visit Diogenes in his tub, and return to a studied incivility, the highest compliment a man of his pride was able to make?

Mankind are very willing to take one anothers word, when they see some circumstances that corroborate what is told them; but when our actions directly contradict what we fay, it is counted, impudence to desire belief. If a jolly hale fellow, with glowing cheeks and warm hands, newly returned from some smart exercise, or else the cold bath, tells us in frosty weather, that he cares not for the sire, we are easily induced to believe him, especially if he actually turns from it, and we know by his circumstances, that he wants neither fuel nor clothes: but if we mould hear the fame from the mouth of a poor starved wretch, with swelled hands, and a livid countenance, in a thin ragged garment, we should not believe a word of what he said, especially if we saw him making and shivering, creep toward the sunny bank; and we would conclude, let him say what he could, that warm clothes, and a good

sire, would be very acceptable to him. The application is easy, and therefore if there be any clergy upon earth that would be thought not to care for the world, and to value the soul above the body, let them only forbear showing a greater concern for their sensual pleasures than they generally do for their spiritual ones, and they may rest satissied,' that no poverty, while they bear it with fortitude, will ever bring them into contempt, how mean soever their circumstances may be.

Let us suppose a pastor that has a little flock intrusted to him, of which he is very careful: lie preaches, visits, exhorts, reproves among his people with zeal and prudence, and does them all the kind osssices that lie in his power to make them happy. There is no doubt but those under his care must be very much obliged to him. Now, we shall suppose once more, that this good man, by the help of a little self-denial, is contented to live upon half his income, accepting only of twenty pounds a-year instead of forty, which he could claim; and moreover, that he loves his parishioners so well, that he will never leave them for any preferment whatever, no not a bishoprick, though it be otFered. 1 cannot fee but all this might be an easy task to a man who professes mortisication, and has no value for worldly pleasures; yet such a disinterested divine, I dare promise, notwithstanding the degeneracy of mankind, will be loved, esteemed, and have every body's good word; nay, I would swear, that though he should yet further exert himself, give above half of his small revenue to the poor, five upon nothing but oatmeal and water, lie upon straw, and wear the coarsest cloth that could be made, his mean way of living would never be reflected on, or be a disparagement either to himself or the order he belonged to; bm that on the contrary his poverty would never be mentioned but to his glory, as long as his memory should last.

But (fays a charitable young gentlewoman) though you have the heart to starve your parson, have you no bowels of compassion for his wife and children? pray what must remain of forty

pounds a year, after it has been twice so unmercifully split? or would you have the poor woman and the innocent babes likewise live upon oatmeal and water, and lie upon straw, you unconscionable wretch, with all your suppositions and self-denials; nay, is it possible, though they should all live at your own murdering rate, that less than ten pounds a-year could maintain a family? Do not be in a passion, good Mrs. Abigail, I have a greater regard for your sex than to prescribe such a lean diet to married men; but I confess 1 sorgot the wives and children: The main reason was, because 1 thought poor priests could have no occasion for them. Who could imagine, that the parson who is to teach others by example as well as precept, was not able to withstand those desires which the wicked world itself calls unreasonable? What is the reason when an apprentice marries before he is out of his time, that unless he meets with a good fortune, all his relations are angry with him, and every body blames him? Nothing else, but because at that time he has no money at his disposal, and being bound to his master's service, has no leisure, and perhaps little capacity to provide for a family. What must we fay to a parson that has twenty, or, if you will, forty pounds a-year, that being bound more strictly to all the services a parish and his duty require, has little time, and generally much less ability to get any more? Is it not very reasonable he mould marry? But why should a sober young man, who is guilty of no vice, be debarred from lawful enjoyments? Right; marriage is lawful, and so is a coach; but what is that to people that have not money enough to keep one? If he must have a wife, let him look out for money, or wait for a greater benesice, or something else to maintain her handsomely, and bear all incident charges. But nobody that has any thing herself will have him, and he cannot stay: He has a very good stomach, and all the symptoms of health; it is not every body that can live without a woman; ft is better to marry than burn What a world of self-denial is here? The sober young man is very willing to be virtuous, but you must hot cross his inclinations; lie promises never to be a deer-stealer, upon condition that he shall have venison of his own, and no body must doubt, but that if it come to the push, he is qualisied to susfer martyrdom, though he owns that he has not strength enough, patiently to bear a scratched singer.

When we see so many of the clergy, to indulge their lust, a brutish appetite, run themselves after this manner upon an inevitable poverty, which, unless they could bear it with greater fortitude, than they discover in all their actions, must of necessity make them contemptible to all the world, what credit must we give them, when they pretend that they conform themselves to the world, not because they take delight in the several decencies, conveniences, and ornaments of it, but only to preserve their function from contempt, in order to be more useful to others? Have we not reason to believe, that what they say is full of hypocrisy and falsehood, and that concupiscence is not the only appetite they want to gratify; that the haughty airs and quick fense of injuries, the curious elegance in dress, and niceness of palate, to be observed in most of them that are able to show them, are the results of pride and luxury in them, as they are in other people, and that the clergy arc not possessed of more intrinsic virtue than any other profeflion?

I am afraid, by this time I have given many of my readers a real displeasure, by dwelling so long upon the reality of pleasure; but I cannot help it, there is one thing comes into my head to corroborate what I have urged already, which I cannot forbear mentioning: It is this: Those who govern others throughout the world, are at least as wife as the people that are governed by them, generally speaking: If, for this reason, we would take pattern from our superiors, we have but to cast our eyes on all the courts and governments in the universe, and we shall soon perceive from the actions of the great ones, which opinion they side with, and what pleasures thole in the highest stations of all seem to be molt fond of": For, if it be allowable

at all to judge of people's inclinations, from their manner of living, none can be less injured by it, than those who are the most at liberty to do as they please.

If the great ones of the clergy, as well as the laity of anycountry whatever, had no value for earthly pleasures, and did not endeavour to gratify their appetites, why are envy and revenge so raging among them, and all the other passions improved and resined upon in courts of princes more than any where else, and why are their repasts, their recreations, and whole manner of living always such as are approved of, coveted, and imitated by the most sensual people of that same country? If despising all visible decorations they were only in love with the embellishments of the mind, why should they borrow so many of the implements, and make use of the most darling toys of the luxurious? Why mould a lord treasurer, or a bishop, or even the grand signior, or the pope of Rome, to be good and virtuous, and endeavour the conquest of his passions, have occasion for greater revenues, richer furniture, or a more numerous attention, as to personal service, than a private man? What virtue is it the exercise of which requires so much pomp and superfluity, as are to be seen by all men in power? A man has as much opportunity to practise temperance, that has but one dish at a meal, as he that is constantly served with three courses, and a dozen dishes in each: One may exercise as much patience, and be as full of self-denial on a few flocks, without curtains or tester, as in a velvet bed that is sixteen foot high. The virtuous possessions of the mind are neither charge nor burden: A man may bear misfortunes with fortitude in a garret, forgive injuries a-foot, and be chaste, though he has not a shirt to his back: and therefore I shall never believe, but that an indifferent sculler, if he was intrusted with it, might carry all the learning and religion that one man can contain, as well as a barge with six oars, especially if it was but to cross from Lambeth to.Westminster; or that humility is so ponderous a virtue, that it requires six horses to draw it.

To fay that men not being so easily

governed by their equals as by their superiors, it is necessary, that to keep the multitude in awe, thole who rule over us should excel others in outward appearance, and consequently, that all in high stations should have badges of honour, and ensigns of power to be distinguished from the vulgar, is a frivolous objection. This, in the sirst place, can only be of use to poor princes, and weak and precarious governments, that being actually unable to maintain the public peace, are obliged with a pageant show to make up what they want in real power: so the governor of Batavia, in the East Indies, is forced to keep up a grandeur, and live in a magnisicence above his quality, to strike a terror in the nativesofjava, who, if they had skill and conduct, are strong enough to destroy ten times the number of their masters; but great princes and states that keep large fleets at sea, and numerous armies in the sield, have no occasion for such stratagems; for what makes them formidable abroad, will never fail to be their security at home. Secondly, what must protect the lives and wealth of people from the attempts of wicked men in all societies, is the severity of the laws, and diligent administration of impartial justice. Theft, house-breaking, and murder, are not to be prevented by the scarlet gowns of the aldermen, the gold chains of the sherisss,the sine trappings of the irhorses.or any gaudy show whatever: Those pageant ornaments are benesicial another way; they are eloquent lectures to apprentices, and the use of them is to animate, not to deter: but men of abandoned principles must be awed by rugged ossicers, strong prisons, watchful jailors, the hangman, and the gallows. If London was to oe one week destiutte of constables and watchmen to guard the houses anights, half the bankers would be ruined in that time, and if my lord mayor had nothing to defend himself but his great two handed sword, the huge cap of maintenance, and his gilded mace, he would soon be stripped, in the very streets to the city, of all his sinery in his stately coach.

But let us grant that the eyes of the mobility are to be dazzled with a gaudy outside; if virtue was the chief delight of great men, why mould their extravagance be extended to things not understood by the mob, and wholly removtd from public view, I mean their private diversions, the pomp and luxury of the dining-room and the bed-chamber, and the curiosities of the closet? few of the vulgar know that there is wine of a guinea the bottle, that birds, no bigger than larks, are often sold for half-a guinea a piece, or that a single picture may be worth several thousand pounds: besides, is it to be imagined, that unless it was to please their own appetites, men should put themselves to such vast expences for a political show, and be so solicitous to gain the esteem of those whom they so much despise in every thing else? if we allow that the splendor and all the elegancy of a court insipid, and only tiresome to the prince himself, and are altogether made use of to preserve royal majesty from contempt, can we say the same of half a dozen illegitimate children, most of them the offspring of adultery, by the fame majesty, got, educated, and made princes at the expence of the nation! therefore, it is evident, that this awing of the multitude, by a distinguished manner of living, is only a cloak and pretence, under which, great men would shelter their vanity, and indulge every appetite about them without reproach.

A burgomaster of Amsterdam, in his plain black suit, followed perhaps by one footman, is fully as much respected, and better obeyed, than a lord mayor of London, with all his splendid equipage, and great train of attendance. Where there is a real power, it is ridiculous to think that any temperance or austerity of life should ever render the person, in whom that power is lodged, contemptible in his ossice, from an emperor to the beadle of a parish. Cato, in his government of Spain, in which he acquitted himself with so muchglory, had only three servants to attend him; do we hear that any of his orders were ever flighted for this,notwithstandingthat heloved his bottle? and, when thatgreatman marched on foot through the scorching sands of Libya, and parched

up with thirst, refused to touch the water that was brought him, before all his soldiers had drank, do we ever read that this heroic forbearance weakened his authority, or lessened him in the esteem of his army? but what need we go so far off? there has not, for these many ages, been a prince less inclined to pomp and luxury than the present king of Sweden, who, enamoured with the title of hero, has not only sacrisiced the lives of his subjects, and welfare of his dominions, but (what is more uncommon in sovereigns) his own ease, and all the comforts of life, to an implacable spirit of revenge; yet he is obeyed to the ruin of his people, in obstinately maintaining a war that has almost utterly destroyed his kingdom.

Thus 1 have proved, that the real pleasures of all men in nature are worldly and sensual, if we judge from their practice; I say all men in nature, because devout Christians, who alone are to be excepted here, being regenerated, and preternaturally assisted by the Divine grace, cannot be said to be in nature. How strange it is, that they mould all ib unanimously deny it! ask not only the divines and moralists of every nation, but likewise all that are rich and powerful, about real pleasure, and they will tell you, with the Stoics, hat there can be no true felicity in things mundane and corruptible: but then look upon their lives, and you will sind they take delight in no other.

This was wrote in 1714

What must we do in this dilemma? shall we be so uncharitable, as judging from mens actions, to say, that all the world prevaricates, and that this is not their opinion, let them talk what they will? or shall we be so silly, as relying on what they fay, to think them sincere in their sentiments, and so not believe our own eyes? or sluill we rather endeavour to believe ourselves and them too, and fay with Montagne, that they imagine, and are fully persuaded, that they believe what they do not believe? these are his words: " some im" pose on the world, and would be thought to belive what " they really do not: but much the greater number impose " upon them-

selves, not considering, nor thoroughly appre" hending what it is to believe. " But this is making all mankind either fools or impostors, which, to avoid, there is nothing left us, but to fay what Mr. Bayle has endeavoured to prove at large in his Reflections on Comets: " that man is " so unaccountable a creature as to act most commonly a" gainst his principle;" and this is so far from being injurious, that it is a compliment to human nature, for we must fee either this or worse.

This contradiction in the frame of man is the reason that the theory of virtue is so well understood, and the practice of it so rarely to be met with. If you aik me where to look for those beautiful shining qualities of prime ministers, and the great favourites of princes that are so sinely painted in dedications, addresses, epitaphs, funeral sermons, and inscriptions, I answer, there, and no where else. Where would you look for the excellency of a statue, but in that part which you see of it? It is the polished outside only that has the skill and labour os the sculptor to boast of; what is out of sight is untouched. Would you break the head, or cut open the breast to look for the brains or the heart, you would only show your ignorance, and destroy the workmanship. This has often made me compare the virtues *ot* great men to your large China jars: they make a sine show, and are ornamental even to a chimney; one would, by the bulk they appear in, and the value that is set upon *them,* think they might be very useful, but look into a thousand ot them, and youwill sind nothing in them but dust and cobwebs.

Line 201 The very poor
Liv'd better than the rich before.

Jf we trace the most nourishing nations in their origin, we shall sind, that in the remote beginnings of every society, the richest and most considerable men among them were a great while destitute of a great many comforts cf lite that are now enjoyed by the meanest and most humble wretches: so that many things which were once looked upon as the invention of luxury, are now allowed, even to those that are so miserably poor as to become the objects of public charity, nay, counted so necessary, that we think no human creature ought to want them.

In the sirst ages, man, without doubt, fed on the fruits of the er.rth, without any previous preparation, and reposed himself naked like other animals on the lap of their common parent: whatever has contributed since to make life more comfortable, as it must have been the result of thought, experience, and some labour, so it more or less deserves the name of luxury, the more or less trouble it required, and deviated from the primitive simplicity. Our admiration is extended no further than to what is new to us, and we all overlook the excellency of things we are used to, be they never io curious. A man would be laughed at, that should discover luxury in the plain dress of a poor creature, that walks along in a thick parish gown, and a coarse shirt underneath it; and yet what'a number of people, how many different trades, and what a variety.of skill and tools must be employed to have the most ordinary Yorkshire cloth? What depth of thought and ingenuity, what toil and labour, and what length of time must it have cost, before man could learn from a seed, to raise and prepare so useful a product as linen.

Must that society not be vainly curious, among whom this admirable commodity, after it is made, sha.ll not be thought sit to be used even by the poorest of all, before it is brought to a perfect whitenels, which is not to be procured but by the assistance of all the elements, joined to a world of industry and patience? 1 have not done yet: can We reflect not only on the cost laid out upon this luxurious invention, but likewise on the little time the whiteness of it continues, in which part of its beauty consists, that every six or seven days at farthest it wants cleaning, and while it lasts is a continual

H charge to the wearer; can we, I say, reflect on all this, and not think it an extravagant piece of nicety, that even thole who receive alms of the parish, should not only have whole garments made of this operose manufacture, but likewise that as soon as they are soiled, to restore them to their pristine purity, they should make use of one of the most judicious as well as difficult compositions that chemistry can boast of; with which, dissolved in water by the help of sire, the most detersive, and yet innocent lixivium is prepared that human industry has hitherto been able to invent?

It is certain, time was that the things I speak of would have bore those lofty expressions, and in which every body would have reasoned after the same manner; but the age we live in would call a man fool, who should talk of extravagance and nicety, if he saw a poor woman, after having wore her crown cloth smock a whole week, wash it with a bit of stinking soap of a groat a pound.

The arts of brewing, and making bread, have by slow degrees been brought to the perfection they now are in, but to have invented them at once, and a priori, would have required more knowledge and a deeper insight into the nature of fermentation, than the greatest philosopher has hitherto been endowed with; yet the fruits of both are now enjoyed by the meanest of our species, and a starving wretch knows not how to make a more humble, or a more modest petition, than by asking for a bit of bread, or a draught of small beer.

Man has learned by experience, that nothing was softer than the small plumes and down of birds, and found that heaped together, they would by their elasticity, gently resist any incumbent weight, and heave up again of themselves as soon as the pressure is over. To make use of them to steep upon was, no doubt, sirst invented to compliment the vanity as well as ease of the wealthy and potent; but they are long since become so common, that almost every body lies upon fearherbeds, and to substitute stocks in the room of them is counted a miserable so is t of the most necessitous. What a vast height must luxury have been arrived to, before it could be reckoned a hardship to repose upon the soft wool of animals!

From caves, huts, hovels, tents, and barracks, with which mankind took up at sirst, we are come to warm and well-wrought houses, and the meanest habitations to be seen in cities, are regular buildings, contrived by persons skilled in proportions and architecture. If the ancient Britons and Gauls should come out of their graves, with what amazement would they gaze on the mighty structures every where raised for the poor! Should they behold the magnisicence of a Chelsey-College, a Greenwich-Hospital, or what surpasses all them, a Des Invatides at Paris, and fee the care, the plenty, the superfluities and pomp, which people that have no possessions at all are treated with in those stately palaces, those who were once the greatest and richest of the land would have reason to envy the most reduced of our species now,

Another piecehf luxury the poor enjoy, that is not looked upon as such, and which there is no doubt but the wealthiest in a golden age would abstain from, is their making use of the flesh of animals to eat. In what concerns the fashions and manners of the ages men live in, they never examine into the real worth or merit of the cause, and generally judge of things not as their reason, but custom direct them. Time was when the funeral rites in the disposing of the dead, were performed by sire, and the cadavers of the greatest emperors were burnt to ashes. Then burying the corps in the ground was a funeral for slaves, or made a punishment for the worst of malefactors. Now nothing is decent or honourable but interring; and burning the body is reserved for crimes of the blackest dye. At some times we look upon trifles with horror, at other times we can behold enormities without concern. If we see a man walk with his hat on in a church, though out of service time, it mocks us; but if on a Sunday night we meet half a dozen fellows drunk in the street, the sight makes little or no impression upon us. Isa woman at a merry-making dresses in man's clothes, it is reckoned a frolic amongst friends, and he that sinds too much fault with it is counted censorious: upon the stage it is done without reproach, and the most virtuous ladies will dispense with it in an actress, though every body has a full view of her legs and thighs; but if the fame woman, as soon as fae has petticoats on again, should show her leg to a man as high as her knee, it wouid be a very immodest action, and every body will call her impudent for it.

I have often thought, if it was not for this tyranny which custom usurps over us, that men of any tolerable good-nature could never be reconciled *to* the killing of so many animals, for their daily food, as long as rhe bountiful earth so plentifully provides them with varieties of vegetable dainties. I know that reatb-nexcites our compassion but faintly, and therefore I would not wonder how men should so little commiserate such imperfect creatures as cray-sish, oysters, cockles, and indeed all sish in general: as they are mute, and their inward formation, as well as outward sigure, vastly different from ours, they express themselves unintelligibly to us, and therefore it is not strange that their grief should not affect our understanding which it cannot reach; for nothing stirs us to pity so effectually, as when the symptoms of misery strike immediately upon our fenses, and I have seen people moved at the noise a live lobster makes upon the spit, that could have killed half a dozen fowls with pleasure. But in such perfect animals as sbeep and oxen, in whom the heart, the brain and nerves differ so little from ours, and in whom the separation of the spirits from the blood, the organs of fense, and consequently feeling itself, are the same as they are in human creatures; I cannot imagine how a man not hardened in blood and mastacre, is able to fee a violent death, and the pangs of it, without concern.

In answer to this, most people will think it sussicient to say, that all things being allowed to be made for the service of man, there can be no cruelty in putting creaturas to the use they were designed for; but I have heard men make this reply, while their nature within them has reproached them, with the falsehood of the assertion. There is of all the multitude not one man in ten but what will own (if he was not brought up in a staughter-house), that of all trades he could never have been a butcher; and I question whether ever any body so much as killed a chicken without reluctancy the sirst time. Some people are not to be persuaded to taste of any creatures they have daily seen and been acquainted with, while they were alive; others extend their, scruple no further than to their own poultry, and refuse to eat what they fed and took care of themselves; yet all of them will feed heartily and without remorse on beef, mutton, and fowls, when they are bought in the market. In this behaviour, methinks, there appears something like a consciousness of guilt, it looks as if they endeavoured to save themselves from the imputation of a crime (which they know sticks some,,where) by removing the cause of it as far as they can from themselves; and I can discover in it some strong remains of primitive pity and innocence, which all the arbitrary power of custom, and the violence of luxury, have not yet been able to conquer.

What I build upon I shall be told is a folly that wife men are not guilty of: I own it; but while it proceeds from a real passion inherent in our nature, it is sussicient to demonstrate, that we are born with a repugnancy to the killing, and consequently the eating of animals; for it is impossible that a natural appetite should ever prompt us to act, or defire others to do, what we have an aversion to, be it as foolish as it will.

Every body knows, that surgeons, in the cure of dangerous wounds and fractures, the extirpations of limbs, and other dreadful operations, are often compelled to put their patients to extraordinary torments, and that the more desperate and calamitous cafes occur to them, the more the outcries and bodily suferings of others mutt become familiar to them; for this reason, our English law, out of a most asfectionate regard to the lives of the subject, allows them not to be of any jury upon life and death, as supposing that their practice itself is sussicient to harden and extinguish in them that tenderness, without which no man is capable of setting a true value upon the lives of his fellow-creatures.

Now, if we ought to have no concern for what we do to brute beasts, and there was not imagined to be any cruelty in killing them, why should of all callings butchers, and only they, jointly with surgeons, be excluded from being jury-men by the fame law?

I shall urge nothing of what Pythagoras and many other wife men have said concerning this barbarity of eating flesh; I have gone too much out of my way already, and shall therefore beg the reader, if he would have any more of this, to run over the following fable, or cjse, if he be tired, to let it alone, with an assurance that in doing of either he mall equally oblige me.

A Roman merchant, in one of the Cathaginian wars, was cast away upon the coast of Afric: himself and his flave with great difficulty got safe ashore; but going in quest of relief, were met by a lion of a mighty size. It happened to be one of the breed that ranged in Æsop's days, and one that could not only speak several languages, but seemed, moreover, very wellacquainted with human asfairs. The flave got upon a tree, but his master not thinking himself safe there, and having heard much of the generosity of lions, fell down prostrate be fore him, with all the signs of fear and submission. The lion who had lately silled his belly, bids him rife, and for a while lay by his fears, assuring him withal, that he should not be touched, if he could give him any tolerable reasons why he should not be devoured. The merchant obeyed; and having now received some glimmering hopes of safety, gave a dismal account of the shipwreck he had sufered, and endeavouring from thence to raise the lion's pity, pleaded his cause with abundance of good rhetoric; but observing by the countenance of the beast, that flattery and sine words made very little impression, he betook himself to arguments of greater solidity, and reasoning from the excellency of man's nature and abilities, remonstrated how improbable it was that the gods should not have designed him for a better use, than to be eat by savage beasts. Upon this the lion became more attentive, and vouchsafed now and then a reply, till at last the following dialogue ensued between them.

Oh vain and covetous animal (said the lion), whose pride and avarice can make him leave his native foil, where his natural wants might be plentifully supplied, and try rough seas and dangerous mountains to sind out superfluities, why should you esteem your species above ours? And if the gods have given you a superiority over all creatures, then why beg you of an inferior? Our superiority (answered the merchant) consists not in bodily force, but strength of understanding; the gods have endued us with a rational soul, which, though invisible, is much the better part of us. I delire to touch nothing of you but what is good to eat; but why do you value yourself so much upon that part which is invisible? Because it is immortal, and shall meet with rewards after death for the actions of this life, and the just shall enjoy eternal bliss and tranquillity with the heroes and demigods in the Elysian sields. What life have you led? 1 have honoured the gods, and studied to be benesicial to man. Then why do you fear death, if you think the gods as just as you have been? 1 have a wife and sive small children that must come to want if they lose me. I have two whelps that are not big enough to shift for themselves, that are in want now, and must actually be starved if I can provide nothing for them: Your children will be provided for one way or other; at least as well when 1 have eat you, as if you had been drowned.

As to the excellency of either species, the value of thing?
among you has ever increased with the scarcity of them, and to a million of men there is hardly one lion; besides that, in the great veneration man pretends to have for his kind, there is little sincerity farther than it concerns the share which every one's pride has in it for himself; it is a folly to boast of the tenderness shown, and attendance given to your youngones, or the excessive and lasting trouble bestowed in the education of them: Man being born the most necessitous and most helpless animal, this is only an instinct of nature, which, in all

creatures, has ever proportioned the care of the parents to the wants and imbecillities of the osfspring. But if a man had a real value for his kind, how is it possible that often ten thousand of them, and sorrtetimes ten times as many, mould be destroyed in few hours, for the caprice of two? All degrees of men despise those that are inferior to them, and if you could enter into the hearts of kings and princes, you would hardly sind any but what have less value for the greatest part of the multitudes they rule over, than those have for the cattle that belong to them. Why mould so many pretend to derive their race, though but spuriously, from the immortal gods; why mould all of them suffer others to kneel down before them, and more or less take delight in having divine honours paid them, but to insinuate that themselves are of a more exalted nature, and a species superior to that of their subjects?

Savage I am, but no creature can be called cruel, but what either by malice or insensibility extinguishes his natural pity: The hon was born without compassion; we follow the instinct of our nature; the gods have appointed us to live upon the waste and spoil of other animals, and as long as we can meet with dead ones, we never hunt after the living. It is only man, mischievous man, that can make death a sport. Nature taught your stomach to crave nothing but vegetables; but your violent fondness to change, and great eagerness after novelties, have prompted you to the destruction of animals without justice or necessity, perverted your nature, and warped your appetites which way soever your pride or luxury have called them. The lion has a ferment within him that consumes the toughest skin and hardest bonesas well as the flesh of all animals without exception: Your squeamish stomach, in which the digestive heat is weak and inconsiderable, will not so much as admit of the most tender parts of them, unless above half the concoction has been performed by artisic'ral sire before hand; and yet what animal have you spared to sa isfy the caprices of a languid appetite? Languid

I fay; for what is man's hunger, if compared to the lion's? Yours, when it is at the worst, makes you faint, mine makes me mad: Oft have I tried with roots and herbs to allay the violence of it, but in vain; nothing but large quantities of stesh can anywise appease it.

Yet the sierceness of our hunger notwithstanding, lions have often requited benesits received; but ungrateful and persidious man feeds on the sheep that clothes him, and spares not her innocent young ones, whom he has taken into his care and custody. If you tell me the gods made man mailer over all other creatures, what tyranny was it then to destroy them out of wantonness? No, sickle, timorous animal, the gods have made you for society, and designed that millions of you, when well joined together, should compose the strong Leviathan. A single lion bears some sway in the creation, but what is single man? A small and inconsiderable part, a trifling atom of one great bead.. What nature designs, slic executes; and it is not safe to judge of what she purposed, but from the effects she shows: If she had intended that man, as man from a superiority of species, should lord it overall other animals, the tiger, nay, the whale and eagle would have obeyed his voice.

But if your wit and understanding exceeds ours, ought not the lion, in deference to that superiority, to follow the maxims of men, with whom nothing is more sacred, than that the reason of the strongest is ever the most prevalent? Whole multitudes of you have conspired and compasscd the destruction of one, after they had owned the gods had made him their superior; and one has often ruined and cut off whole multitudes, whom, by the fame gods, he had sworn to defend and maintain. Man never acknowledged superiority without power, and why should 1? The excellence I boast of is visible, all animals tremble at the sight of the lion, not out of panic fear. The gods have given me swiftness to overtake, and strength to conquer whatever comes near me. Where is there a creature that has teeth and claws like mine, behold the thickness of these masty jaw-bones, consider the Width of them, and feel the sirmness of this brawny neck. The nimblest deer, the wildest boar, the stoutest horse, and strongest bull, are my prey wherever I meet them. Thus spoke the lion, and the merchant fainted away.

The lion, in my opinion, has stretched the point too far; yet,' when to soften the stem of male animals, we have by castration prevented the sirmness their tendons, and every sibre would have come to, without it, 1 confess, i think it ought to move a human creature, when he reflects upon the cruel care with which they are fattened for destruction. WliL-n a large and gentle bullock, after having resisted a ten times greater force of blows than would have killed his murderer, falls stunned at last, and his armed head is fastened to the ground with cords; as soon as the wide wound is made, and the jugulars are cut asunder, what mortal can, without compassion, hear the painful bellowings intercepted by his blood, the bitter sighs that speak the sharpness of his anguisti, and the deep sounding groans, with loud anxiety, setched from the bottom of his strong and palpitating heart; look on the trembling and violent convulsions of his limbs; lee, while his reeking gore streams from him, his eyes become dim and languid, and behold his strugglings, gasps, and last efforts for life, the certain signs of his approaching fate? When a creature has given such convincing and undeniable proofs of the terrors upon him, and the pains and agonies he feels, is there a follower of Descartes so inured to blood, as not to refute, by his commiseration, the philosophy of that vain reasoner?

Lin E 3 o 7. For frugal Iy
They now liv'd on their salary.

W Hen people have small comings in, and are honest withal, it is then that the generality of them begin to be frugal, and not before. Frugality in ethics is called that virtue, from the principle of which men abstain from superfluities, and, despising the operose contrivances of art to procure either cafe or pleasure, content themselves with the natural simplicity of things, and are carefully temperate in the enjoyment of them,

without any tincture of covetousness. Frugality thus limited, is perhaps scarcer than many may imagine; but what is generally understood by it, is a quality more often to be met with, and consists in a medium between profuseness and avarice, rather leaning to the latter. As this prudent economy, which some people call saving, is in private families the most certain method to increase an estate. So some imagine, that whether a country be barren or fruitful, the same method, if generally pursued (which they think practicable), will have the same effect upon a whole nation, and that, for example, the English might be much richer than they are, if they would be as frugal as some of their neighbours. This, I think, is an error, which to prove, I shall sirst refer the reader to what has been said upon this head in Remark on 1. 180. and then go on thus.

Experience teaches us.sirst, that as people differ in their views and perceptions of things, so they vary in their inclinations; one man is given to covetousness, another to prodigality, and a third is only saving. Secondly, that men are never, or at least very seldom, reclaimed from their darling passions, either by reason or precept, and that if any thing ever draws them from what they are naturally propense to, it must be a change in their circumstances or their fortunes. If we reflect upon these observations, we shall sind, that to render the generality of a nation lavish, the product of the country must be considerable, in proportion to the inhabitants, and what they are profuse of cheap; that, on the contrary, to make a nation generally frugal, the necessaries of life must be scarce, and consequently dear: and that, therefore, let the best politician do what he can, the profuseness or frugality of a people in general, must always depend upon, and will, in spite of his teeth, be ever proportioned to the fruitfulness and product of the country, the number of inhabitants, and the taxes they are to bear. If any body would refute what I have skid, let them only prove from history, that there ever was in any country a national frugality without a national

necessity.

Let us examine then what things are requisite to aggrandize and enrich a nation. The sirst desirable blessings for any society of men, are a fertile soil, and a happy climate, a mild government, and more land than people. These things will render man easy, loving, honest, and sincere. In this condition they may be as virtuous as they can, without the least injury to the public, and consequently as happy as they please themselves. But they shall have no arts or sciences, or be quiet longer then their neighbours will let them; they must be poor, ignorant, and almost wholly destitute ot what we call the comforts of life, and all the cardinal virtues together would not so much as procure a tolerable coat or a porridge-pot among them: for in this state of slothful ease and stupid innocence, as you need not fear great vices, so you must not expect any considerable virtues. Man never exerts himself but when he is roused by his desires: while they lie dormant, and there is nothing to raise them, his excellence and abilities will be for ever undiscovered, and the lumpish machine, without the influence or his passions, may be justly compared to a huge wind-mill without a breath of air.

Would you render a society of men strong and powerful, you must touch their passions. Divide the land, though there be never so much to spare, and their posscisions will make them covetous: rouse them, though but in jest, from their idleness with praises, and pride will set them to work in earnest: teach them trades and handicrafts, and you will bring envy and emulation among them: to increase their numbers, set up a variety of manufactures, and leave no ground uncultivated; let property be inviolably secured, and privileges equal to all men; sufser nobody to act but what is lawful, and every body to think what he pleases; for a country where every body may be maintained that will be employed, and the other maxims are observed, must always be thronged, and can never want people, as long as there is any in the world. Would you have them bold and warlike, turn to military discipline, make good use of their sear, and flatter their vanity with art and assiduity: but would you, moreover, render them an opulent, knowing, and polite nation, teach them commerce with foreign countries, and, if possible, get into the sea, which to compass spare no labour nor industry, and let no disficulty deter you from it; then promote navigation, cherish the merchant, and encourage trade in every branch of it; this will bring riches, and where they are, arts and sciences will soon solsow: and by the help of what 1 have named and good management, it is that politicians can make a people potent, renowned, and flourishing.

But would you have a frugal and honest society, the best policy is to preserve men in their native simplicity, strive not to increase their numbers; let them never be acquainted with strangers or superfluities, but remove, and keep from them every thing that might raise their desires, or improve their understanding.

Great wealth, and foreign treasure, will ever scorn to come among men, unless you will admit their inseparable companions, avarice and luxury: where trade is considerable, fraud will intrude. To be at once well-bred and sincere, is no less than a contradiction; and, therefore, while man advances in knowledge, and his manners are polished, we must expect to fee, at the fame time, his desires enlarged, his appetites resined, and his vices increased.

The Dutch may ascribe their present grandeur to the virtue and frugality of their ancestors as they please; but what made that contemptible spot of ground so considerable among the pi incipal powers of Europe, has been their political wisdom in postponing every thing to merchandise and navigation, the unlimitted liberty of conscience that is enjoyed among them, and the unwearied application with which they have always made use of the most effectual means to encourage and increase trade in geneial.

They never were noted for frugality before Philip II. of Spain began to rage over them with that unheard of tyranny. Their laws were trampled upon, their

rights and large immunities taken from them, and their constitution torn to pieces. Several of their chief nobles were condemned and executed without legal form of process. Complaints and remonstrances were punished as severely as resistance, and those that escaped being massacred, were plundered by ravenous soldiers. As this was intolerable to a people that had always been used to the mildest of governments, and enjoyed greater privileges than any of the neighbouring nations, so they chose rather to die in arms than perish by cruel executioners. If we consider the strength Spain had then, and the low circumstances those distresied states were in, there never was heard of a more unequal strife; yet, such was their fortitude and resolution, that only seve.n of those provinces, uniting themselves together, maintained against the greatest and best disciplined nation in Europe, the most tedious and bloody war, that is to be met with in ancient or modern history.

Rather than to become a victim to the Spanisti fury, they were contented to live upon a third part of their revenues, and lay out far the greatest part of their income in defending themselves against their merciless enemies. These hardships and calamities of a war within their bowels, sirst put them upon that extraordinary frugality; and the connuance under the fume dillicullics for above fourscore years, could not but render it customary and habitual to them. But all their arts of saving, and penurious way of living, could never have enabled them to make head against so potent an enemy, if their industry in promoting their sishery and navigation in general, had not helped to supply the natural wants and disadvantages they laboured under.

The country is so small and so populous, that there is not land enough (though hardly an inch of it is unimproved) to seed the tenth part of the inhabitants. Holland itself is full of large rivers, and lies lower than the sea, which would run over it every tide, and wash it away in one winter, if it was not kept out by vast banks and huge walls: the repairs of those, as well as

their sluices, quays, mills, and other necessaries they are forced to make use of to keep themselves from being drowned, are a greater expence to them, one year with another, than could be raised by a general land tax of four millings in the pound, if to be deducted from the neat produce of the landlord's revenue.

Is it a wonder, that people, under such circumstances, and loaden with greater taxes, besides, than any other nation, should be obliged to be saving? but why must they be a pattern to others, who, besides, that they are more happily situated, are much richer within themselves, and have, to the fame number of people, above ten times the extent of ground? The Dutch and we often buy and fell at the fame markets, and so far our views may,be said to be the lame: otherwise the interests and political reasons of the two nations, as to the private economy of either, are very different. It is their interest to be frugal, and spend little; because they must have every thing from abroad, except butter, cheese, and sish, and therefore of them, especially the latter, they consume three times the quantity, which the fame number of people do here. It is our interest to eat plenty of beef and mutton to maintain the farmer, and further improve our land, of which we have enough to feed ourselves, and as many more, if it was better cultivated. The Dutch perhaps have more shipping, and more ready money than we, but then thole are only to be considered as the tools they work with. So a carrier may have more horses than a man of ten times his worth, and a banker that has not above sifteen or sixteen hundred pounds in the world, may have generally more ready calh by him, than a gentleman of two thousand a-year. He that keeps three or four stage-coaches to get his bread, is to a gentleman that keeps a coach for his pleasure, what the Dutch are in comparison to us; having nothing of their own but sish, they are carriers and freighters to the reft of the world, while the basis of our trade chiefly depends upon our own product.

Another instance, that what makes

the bulk of the people saving, are heavy taxes, scarcity of land, and such things that occasion a dearth of provisions, may be given from what is observable among the Dutch themselves. In the province of Holland their is a vast trade, and an unconceivable treasure of money. The land is almost as rich as dung itself, and (as 1 have said once already) not an inch of it unimproved. In Gelderland, and Overyssel, there is hardly any trade, and very little money: the soil is very indiserent, and abundance of ground lies waste. Then, what is the reason that the same Dutch, in the two latter provinces, though poorer than rhe sirst, are yet less stingy and more hospitable? Nothing but that their taxes in most things are lets extravagant, and in proportion to the number of people, they have a great deal more ground. What they save in Holland, they save out of their bellies; it is eatables, drinkables, and fuel, that their heaviest taxes are upon, but they wear better clothes, and have richer furniture, than you will sind in the other provinces.

Those that are frugal by principle, are so in every thing; but in Holland the people are only sparing in such things as are daily wanted, and soon consumed; in what is lasting they are quite otherwise: in pictures and marble they are profuse; in their buildings and gardens they are extravagant to folly. In other countries, you may meet with stately courts and palaces of great extent, that belong to princes, which nobody can expect in a commonwealth, where so much equality is observed as there is in this; but in all Europe you shall sind no private buildings so sumptuously magnisicent, as a great many of the merchants and other gentlemen's houses are in Amsterdam, and some other great cities of that small province; and the generality of those that build there, lay out a greater proportion of their estates on houses they dwell in, than any people upon the earth.

The nation 1 speak of was never in greater straits, nor their affairs in a more dismal posture since they were a republic, than in the year 1671, and the beginning of 1672. What we know of their economy and constitution with any certainty, has been chiesly owing to Sir William Temple, whole observations upon their manners and government, it is evident from several passages in his memoirs, were made about that time. The Dutch, indeed, were then very frugal; but since those days, and that their calamities have not been so pressing (though the common people, on whom the principal burden of all excises and impositions lies, are perhaps much as they were), a great alteration has been made among the better fort of people in their equipages, entertainments, and whole manner of living.

Those who would have it, that the frugality of that nation flows not so much from necessity, as a general aversion to vice and luxury, will put us in mind of their public administration, and smallness of salaries, their prudence in bargaining for, and buying stores and other necessaries, the great care they take not to be imposed upon by those that serve them, and their severity against them that break their contracts. But what they would ascribe to the virtue and honesty of ministers, is wholly due to their strict regulations, concerning the management of the public treasure, from which their admirable form of government will not suffer them to depart; and indeed one good man may take another's word, if they so agree, but a whole nation ought never to trust to any honesty, but what is built upon necessity; for unhappy is the people, and their constitution will be erer precarious, whose welfare must depend upon the virtues and consciences of ministers and politicians.

The Dutch generally endeavour to promote as much frugality among their subjects as it is poflible, not because it is a virtue, but because it is, generally speaking, their interest, as 1 have shown before; for, as this latter changes, so they alter their maxims, as will be plain in the following instance.

As soon as their East India ships come home, the Company pays off the men, and many of them receive the greatest part of what they have been earning in seven or eight, or some sifteen or sixteen years time. These poor fellows are encouraged to spend their money with all profuseness imaginable; and considering that most of them, when they set out sirst, were reprobates, that under the tuition of a strict discipline, and a miserable diet, have been so long kept at hard labour without money, in the midst of danger, it cannot be dissicult to make them lavish, as soon as they have plenty.

They squander away in wine, women, and music, as much as people of their taste and education are well capable of, and are suffered (so they but abstain from doing of mischief), to revel and riot with greater licentiousness than is customary to be allowed to others. You may in some cities fee them accompanied with three or four lewd women, few of them sober, run roaring through the streets by broad day-light with a lidler before them: And if the money, to their thinking, goes not fast enough these ways, they will sind out others, and sometimes fling it among the mob by handfuls. This madness continues in most of them while they have any thing left, which never lasts long, and for this reason, by a nick-name, they are called, *Lords of fix Weeks,* that being generally the time by which the Company has other ships ready to depart; where these infatuated wretches (their money being gone) arc forced to enter themselves again, and may have leisure to repent their folly.

In this stratagem there is a double policy: First, if the sailors that have been inured to the hot climates and unwholesome air and diet, should be frugal, and stay in their own country, the Company would be continually obliged to employ fresh men, of which (besides that they are not so sit for their business), hardly one in two ever lives in some places of the East Indies, which often would prove great charge as well as disappointment to them. The second i?, that the large sums so often distributed among those sailors, are b this means made immediately to circulate throughout the country, from whence, by heavy excises, and other impositions, the greatest part of it is soon drawn back into the public treasure.

To convince the champions for national frugality by another argument, that what they urge is impracticable, we will suppose that I am mistaken in every thing which in Remark, L 180, 1 have said in behalf of luxury, and the necessity of it to maintain trade: after that let us examine what a geneial frugality, if it was by art and management to be forced upon people whether they have occalion for it or not, would produce in such a nation as ours. We will grant, then, that all the people in Great Britain ihall consume but four-sifths of what they do now, and ib lay by one-sifth part of their income; I shall not speak of what influence this would have upon almost every trade, as well as the farmer, the grazier, and the landlord, but favourably suppose (what is yet impossible), that the fame work shall be done, and consequent ly the same handicrafts be employed as there are now. The consequence would be, that unless money should all at once fall prodigiously in value, and every thing else, contrary to reason, grow very dear, at the sive years end all the working people, and the poorest of labourers (for I would not meddle with any of the rest), would be worth in ready cash as much as they now spend in a whole year; which, by the bye, would be more money than ever the nation had at once.

Let us now, overjoyed with this increase of wealth, take a view of the condition the working people would be in, and, reasoning from experience, and what we daily observe of them, judge what their behaviour would be in such a case. Every body knows that there is a vast number of journeymen weavers, tailors, clothworkers, and twenty other handicrafts, who, if by four days labour in a week they can maintain themselves, will hardly be persuaded to work the sifth; and that there are thousands of labouring men of all forts, who will, though they can hardly subsist, put themselves to sifty inconveniences, disoblige their masters, pinch their bellies, and run in debt to make holidays. When men show such an extraordinary proclivity to idleness and pleasure, what

reason have we to think that they would ever work, unless they were obliged to it by immediate necessity? When we see an artisicer that cannot be drove to his work before Tuesday, because the Monday morning he has two shillings left of his last week's pay; why should we imagine he would go to it at all, if he had sifteen or twenty pounds isi his pocket?

What would, at this rate, become of our manufactures? If the merchant would fend cloth abroad, he must make it himself, for the clothier cannot get one man out of twelve that used to work for him. If what I speak of was only to befal the journeymen shoemakers, and nobody else, in less than a twelvemonth, half of us would go barefoot. The chief and most; pressing use there is for money in a nation, is to pay the labour of the poor, and when there is a real scarcity of it, those who have a great many workmen to pay, will always feel it sirst; yet notwithstanding this great necellity of coin, it would be easier, where property was well secured, to live without money, than w-ithout poor; for who would do the work? For this reason the quantity of circulating coin in a country, ought always to be nroportioned to the number of hands that are employed; and the wages of labourers to the price of provisions. From whence it is demonstrable, that whatever procures plenty, makes labourers cheap, where the poor are well managed; who as they ought to be kept from starving, so they should receive nothing worth saving. If here and there one of the lowed class by uncommon industry, and pinching his belly, lifts himself above the condition he was brought up in, nobody ought to hinder him; nay, it is undeniably the wisest course for every person in the society, and for every private family to be frugal; but it is the interest of all rich nations, that the greatest part of the poor Ihould almost never be idle, and yet continually spend what they get.

All men, as Sir William Temple observes very well, arc more prone to ease and pleasure than they are to labour, when they are not prompted to it by pride and avarice, and those that get

their living by their dady labour, are seldom powerfully influenced by either: so that they have nothing to stir them up to be serviceable but their wants, which it is prudence to relieve, but folly to cure. The only thing, then, that can render the labouring man industrious, is a moderate quantity of money; for as too little will, according as his temper is, either dispirit or make him desperate, so too much will make him insolent and lazy.

A man would be laughed at by most people, who should maintain that too much money could undo a nation: yet this has been the fate of Spain; to this the learned Don Diego Savedra ascribes the ruin of his country. The fruits of the earth in former ages had made Spain so rich, that King Lewis xi. of France being come to the court of Toledo, was astonished at its splendour, and said, that he had never seen any thing to be compared to it, either in Europe or Alia; he that in his travels to the Holy Land had run through every province of them. In the kingdom of Castile alone (if we may believe some writers), there were for the holy war, from all parts of the world got together one hundred thousand foot, ten thousand horse, and sixty thousand carriages for baggage, which Alonso 111. maintained at his own charge, and paid every day, as well soldiers as ossicers and princes, every one according-to his rank and dignity: nay, down to the reign of Ferdinand and Isabella (who equipped Columbus), and some time after, Spain was a fertile Country, where trade and manufactures stounihed, and had a knowing industrious people so. boast of. But as soon as that mighty treasure, that was obtained with more hazard and cruelty than the world until then had known, and which to come at, by the Spaniard's own confesiion, had cost the lives of twenty millions of Indians; as soon, I fay, as that oceari of treasure came rolling in upon them, it took away their senses, and their industry forsook them. The farmer left his plough, the mechanic his tools, the merchant his comptmghouse, and every body scorning to work, took his pleasure and turned gentleman. They thought they had reason to value themselves above all their neighbours, and now nothing but the conquest of the world would serve them.

The consequence os this has been, that other nations have supplied what their own sloth and pride denied them; and when every body saw, that notwithstanding all the prohibitions the government could make against the exportation of bullion, the Spaniard would part with his money, and bring it you aboard himself at the hazard of his neck, all the world endeavoured to work for Spain. Gold and lilver being by this means yearly divided and shared among all the trading countries, have made all things dear, and most nations of Europe industrious, except their owners, who, ever since their mighty acquisitions, sit with their arms across, and wait every year with impatience and anxiety, the arrival of their revenues from abroad, to pay others for what they have spent already: and thus by too much money, the making of colonies and other mismanagements, of which it was the occasion, Spain is, from a fruitful and well-peopled country, with all its mighty titles: id poslessions, made a barren and empty thoroughfare, through which gold and silver pass from America to the rest of the world; and the nation, from a rich, acute, diligent, and laborious, become a slow, idle, proud, and beggarly people: So much for Spain. The next country where money is called the product, is Portugal, and the ngure which that kingdom with all its gold makes in Europe, 1 think is not much to be envied.

The great art then to make a nation happy, and what we call flourishing, consists i:i giving every body an opportunity of being employed; which to compass, let a government's sirst care be to promote as great a variety of manufactures, arts, and handicrafts, as human wit can invent; and the second, to encourage agriculture and sishery in all their branches, that the whole earth inav be sorced to exert itself as well as man; for as the one is an infallible maxim to draw vast multitudes of people into a nation, so the other is the only method to maintain them.

It is from this policy, and not the trifling regulations of lavishness and frugality (which will ever take their own course, according to the circumstances of the people), that the greatness and felicity of nations must be expected; for let the value of gold and silver either rile or fall, the enjoyment of all societies will ever depend upon the fruits of the earth, and the labour of the people; both which joined together are a more certain, a more inexhaustible, and a more real treasure, than the gold ofBraz.il, or the silver of Potosi.

Line 321 No honour now, &c.

XJ.ONOUR, in its sigurative fense, is a chimera without truth or being, an invention of moralists and politicians, and signisies a certain principle of virtue not related to religion, found in some men that keeps them close to their duty and engagements whatever they be; as for example, a man of honour enters into a conspiracy with others to murder a king; he is obliged to go thorough stitch with it; and if overcome by remorse or good nature, he startles at the enormity of his purpose, discovers the plot, and turns a witness against his accomplices, he then forfeits his honour, at least among the party he belonged to. The excellency of this principle is, that the vulgar are destitute of it, and it is only to be met with in people of the better fort, as some oranges have kernels, and others not, though the outsit be the fame. In great families, it is like, the gout, generally counted hereditary, and all the lords children are born with it. In some that never felt any thing of it, it is acquired by conversation and reading (especially of romances), in others by preferment; but there is nothing that encourages the growth of it more than a sword, and upon the sirst wearing of one, some people have felt considerable moots of it in four and twenty hours.,

The chief and most important care a man of honour ought to have, is the preservation of this principle, and rather than forfeit it, he must lose his employments and estate, nay, life, itself; for which reason, whatever humility he may show by way of good-breeding, he is allowed to put an inestimable value upon himself, as a pollcflor of this invisible ornament. The only method to preserve this principle, is to live up to the rules of honour, which are laws he is to walk by: himself is obliged always to be faithful to his trust, to prefer the public interest to his own, not to tell lies, nor defraud or wrong any body, and from others to susser no affront, whicli is a term of art for every action designedly done to undervalue him.

The men of ancient honour, of which I reckon Don Quixote to have been the last upon record, were very nice observers of all these laws, and a great many more than I have named; but the moderns seem to be more remiss: they have a profound veneration for the last of them, but they pay not an equal obedience to any of the other; and whoever will but strictly comply with that I hint at, shall have abundance of trespasses against all the rest connived at.

A man of honour is always counted impartial, and a man of fense of course; for nobody never heard of a man of honour that was a fool: for this reason, he has nothing to do with the law, and is always allowed to be a judge in his own cafe; and if the least injury be done either to himself or his friend, his relation, his servant, his dog, or any thing which he is pleased to take under his honourable protection, satisfaction must be forthwith demanded; and if it proves an affront, and he that gave it likewise a man of honour, a battle must ensue. From all this it is evident, that a man of honour must be possessed of courage, and that without it his other principle would be no more than a sword without a point. Let us, therefore, examine what courage consists in, and whether it be, as most people will have it, a real something that valiant men have in their nature distinct from all their other qualities or not.

There is nothing so universally sincere upon earth, as the love which all creatures, that are capable of any, bear to themselves; and as there is no love but what implies a care to preserve the thing beloved, so there is nothing more sincere in any creature than his will, wishes, and endeavours, to preserve himself. This is the law of nature, by which no creature is endued with any appetite or passion, but what either directly or indirectly tends to the preservation either of himself or his species.

The means by which nature obliges every creature continually to stir in this business of self-preservation, are grafted in him, and, in man, called desires, which either compel him him to crave what he thinks will sustain or please him, or command him to avoid what he imagines might displease, hurt, or destroy him. These desires or passions have all their different symptoms by which they manifest themselves to those they disturb, and from that variety of disturbances they make within us, their various denominations have been given them, as has been shown already in pride and shame.

The passion that is raised in us when we apprehend that /nischief is approaching us, is called fear,: the disturbance it makes withm us is always more or less violent in proportion, not of the danger, but our apprehension of the mischief dreaded, whether real or imaginary. Our scar then bein always proportioned to the apprehension we have of the danger, it follows, that while that apprehension lasts, a man can no more shake olF his fear than he can a leg or an arm. In a fright, it is true, the apprehension of danger is io sudden, and attacks us so lively (as sometimes to take away reason and senses), that when it is over we often do not remember we had any apprehension at all; but, from the event, it is plain we had it, for how could we have been frightened if we had not apprehended that some evil or other was coming upon us?

Most people are of opinion, that this apprehension is to be conquered by reason, but 1 confess I am not: Those that have been frightened will tell you, that as soon as they could recollect themselves, that is, make use of their reason, their apprehension was conquered. But this is no conquest at all, for in a fright the danger was either altogether imaginary, or else it is past by that tune they can make use os their reason; and therefore if they sind there Is no danger, it is no wonder that they should not appre-

hend any: but, when the danger js permanent, let them then make use of their reason, and they will sind that it may serve them to examine the greatness and reality of the danger, and that, if they sind it less than they imagined, the apprehension will be lessened accordingly'; but, is the danger proves real, and the fame in every circumstance as they took it to be at sirst, then their reason, instead of diminishing, will rather increase their apprehension. While this fear lasts, no creature can sight osfensively; and yet we fee brutes daily sight obstinately, and worry one another to death; so that some other pasiion must be able to overcome this fear, and the most contrary to it is anger: which, to trace to the bottom, I must beg leave to make another digression.

No creature can subsist without food, nor any species of them (I speak of the more perfect animals) continue long unless young ones are continually born as fast as the old ones die. Therefore the sirst and siercest appetite that nature has given them is hunger, the next is lust; the one prompting them to procreate, as the other bids them eat. Now, if we" observe that anger is that paflion which is raised in us when we are crossed or disturbed in our desires, and that, as it sums up all the strength in creatures, so it was given them, that by it they might exert themselves more vigorously in endeavouring to remove, overcome, or destroy whatever obstructs them in the pursuit of self preservation; we shall find that brutes, unless themselves or what they love, or the liberty of either are threatened or attacked, have nothing worth notice that can move them to anger, but hunger or lust. It is they that make them more sierce, for we must observe, that the appetites of creatures are as actually crossed, whde they want and cannot meet with what they desire (though perhaps with less violence) as when liindercd fiom enjoying what they have in view. What I have said will appear more plainly, if we but.mind what nobody can be ignorant of, which is this: all creatures upon earth live either upon the fruits and product of it, or else the siesh of other animals, their fellow-

creatures.. The latter, which we call beasts of prey, nature has armed accordingly, and given them weapons and strength to overcome and tear asunder those whom me has deligned for their fcod, and likewise a much keener appetite than to other animals that live upon herbs, &c. For, as to the sirst, if a cow loved mutton as well as she does grafs, being made as she is, and having no claws or talons, and but one row of teeth before, that are all of an equal length, she would be starved even among a flock of sheep. Secondly, as to their voraciousness, if experience did not teach us, our reason might: in the sirst place, it is highly probable, that the hunger which can make a creature fatigue, harass and expose himself to danger for every bit he eats, is more piercing than that which only bids him eat what stands before him, and which he may have for stooping down. In the second, it is, to be considered, that as beasts of prey have an instinct by which they learn to crave, trace, and discover those creatures, that are good food for them; so the others have likewise an instinct that teaches them to shun, conceal themselves, and run away from those that hunt aster them: from hence it must follow, that beasts of prey, though they could almost eat forever, go yet more often with empty bellies than other creatures, whose victuals neither fly from nor oppose them. This must perpetuate as well as increase their hunger, which hereby becomes a constant fuel to their anger.

If you ask me what stirs up this anger in bulls and cocks that will sight to death, and yet are neither animals of prey, nor very voracious, I answer, lust. Those creatures, whose rage proceeds from hunger, both male and female, attack every thing they can master, and sight obstinately against all: But the animals, whose fury is provoked by a venereal ferment, being generally males, exert themselves chiefly against other males of the fame species. They may do mischief by chance to other creatures; but the main objects of their hatred are their rivals, and it is against them only that their prowess and fortitude are shown. We fee likewise in all those creatures, of which the male is able to satisfy a great number of females, a more considerable superiority in the male, expressed by nature in his make and features, as well as sierceness, than is observed in other creatures, where the male is contented with one or two females. Dogs, though become domestic animals, are ravenous to a proverb, and those of them that will sight being carnivorous, would soon become beasts of prey, if not fed by us; what we may observe in them is an ample proof of what I have hitherto advanced. Those of a true sighting breed, being voracious creatures', both male and female, will fasten upon any thing, and suffer themselves to be killed before they give over. As the female is rather more salacious than the male; so there is no disference in their make at all, what distinguishes the sexes excepted, and the female is rather the siercest of the two. A bull is a terrible creature when he is kept up, but where he has twenty or more cows to range among, in a little time he will become as tame as any of them, and a dozen hens will spoil the best game cock in England. Harts and deers are counted chaste and timorous creatures, and so indeed they are almost all the year long, except in rutting time, and then on a sudden they become bold to admiration, and often make at the keepers themselves.

That the influence of those two principal appetites, hunger and lust, upon the temper of animals, is not so whimsical as some may imagine, may be partly demonstrated from what is observable in ourselves; for, though our hunger is insinitely less violent than that of wolves and other ravenous creatures, yet we fee that people who are in health, and have a tolerable stomach, are more fretful, and sooner put out of humour for trifles when they stay for their victuals beyond their usual hours, than at any other time. And again, though lust in man is not so raging as it is in bulls, and other salacious creatures, yet nothing provokes men and women botli sooner, and more violently to anger, than what crosses their amours, when

they are heartily in love; and the most fearful and tenderly educated of either sex, have slighted the" greatest dangers, and let aside all other considerations, to compass the destruction of a rival.

Hitherto 1 have endeavoured to demonstrate, that no creature can sight offensively as long as his feir lasts; that feat cannot be conquered but by another passion; that the most contrary to it, and most effectual to overcome it, is anger; that the two principal appetites which, disappointed, can stir up this last-named passion, are hunger and lust, and that, in all brute beasts, the proneness to anger and obstinacy in sighting, generally depend upon the violence of either or both thole appetites together: From whence it must follow, that what we call prowess, or natural courage in creatures, is nothing but the effect of anger, and that all sierce animals must be either very ravenous, or very lustful, if not both.

Let us now examine what by this rule we ought to judge of our own species. From the tenderness of man's skin, and the great care that is required for years together to rear him; from the make of his jaws, the evenness of his teeth, the breadth of his nails, and the slightness of both, it is not probable that nature should have designed him for rapine; for this reason his hunger is not voracious as it is in beasts of prey; neither is he so salacious as other animals that are called so, and being besides very industrious to supply his wants, he can have no reigning appetite to perpetuate his anger, and must consequently be a timorous animal.

What 1 have said last must only be understood of man in his savage state; for, if we examine him as a member of a society, and a taught animal, we mall sind him quite another creature: As loon as his pride has room to play, and envy, avarice, and ambition begin to catch hold of him, he is roused from his natural innocence and stupidity. As his knowledge increases, his delires are enlarged, and consequently his wants and appetites are multiplied: Hence it must follow, that he will often be crolled in the pursuit of them, and meet with abundance more disappointment to

stir up his anger in this than his former condition, and man would in a little time become the most hurtful and obnoxious creature in the world, islet alone, whenever he could overpower his adversary, ifhehadno mischief to fear but from the person that angered him.

The sirst care, therefore, of all governments is, by severe punishments to curb his anger when it does hurt, and so, by increasing his fears, prevent the mischief it might produce. When various laws to restrain him from using force are strictly executed, self-preservation must teach him to be peaceable; and, as it is every body's business to be as little disturbed as is possible, his fears will be continually augmented and enlarged as he advances in experience, understanding, and foresight. The consequence of this must be, that as the provocations he will receive to anger will be insinite in the civilized state, so his fears to damp it will be the fame, and thus, in a little time, he will be taught by his fears to destroy his anger, and by art to consult, in an opposite method, the same self-preservation for which nature before had furnished him with anger, as well as the rest of his pasiions.

The only useful pastion, then, that man is posfesled of toward the peace and quiet of a society, is his fear, and the more you work upon it the more orderly and governable he will be; for how useful soever anger may be to man, as he is a single creature by himself, yet the iociety has no manner of occasion for it: But nature being always the fame, in the formation of animals, produces all creatures as like to thole that beget and bear them, as the place she forms them in, and the various influences from without, will give her leave; and consequently all men, whether they are born in courts or forests, are susceptible of anger. When this passion overcomes (as among all degrees of people it sometimes does) the whole set of fears man has, he has true courage, and will right as boldly as a lion or a tiger, and at no other time; and I shall endeavour to prove, that whatever is called courage in man, when he is not angry, is spurious and artisicial.

It is possible, by good government, to keep a society always quiet in itself, but nobody can ensure peace from without for ever. The society may have occasion to extend their limits further, and enlarge their territories, or otners iy invade theirs, or something else will happen that man must be brought to sight; for how civilized soever men may he, they never forget that force goes beyond reason: The politician now must alter his measures, and take oti lom of man's fears; he must strive to persuade him, that all what was told him before of the barbarity of killing men ceases, as soon as these men are enemie9 to the public, and that their adversaries are neither so good nor so strong as themselves. These things well managed will seldom fail of drawing the hardiest, the most quarrelsome, and the most mischievous into combat; but unless they are better qualisied, I will not answer for their behaviour there: If once you can make them undervalue their enemies, you mny soon stir them up to anger, and while that lasts they wiil sight with greater obstinacy than any disciplined troops: But if any thing hap-, pens that was unforeseen, and a sudden great noise, a tempest, or any strange or uncommon accident that seems to threaten them, intervenes, fear seizes them, disarms their anger, and makes them run away to a man.

This natural courage, therefore, as soon as people begin to have more wit, must be soon exploded. In the sirst place, those that have felt the smart of the enemy's blows, will not always believe what is said to undervalue him, and are often not easily provoked to anger. Secondly, anger consisting in an ebullition of the spirits, is a passion of no long continuance (jra furor brevis qjl), and the enemies, if they withstand the sirst shock of these angry people, have commonly the better of it. Thirdly, as long as people are angry, all counsel and discipline are lost upon them, and they can never be brought to use art or conduct in their battles. Anger then, without which no creature has natural courage, being altogether useless in a war to be managed by stratagem, and

brought into a regular art, the government must sind out an equivalent for courage that will make men sight.

Whoever would civilize men, and establish them into a body politic, must be thoroughly acquainted with all tne passions and appetites, strength and weaknesies of their lrame, aud understand how to turn their greatest frailties to the advantage of the public. In the Inquiry into the Origin of Moral Virtue, I have stiown how easily men were iniuced to believe any thing that is said in their praise. If, therefore, a lawgiver or politician, whom they have a great veneration for, should tell them, that the generality of men had within them a principle of valour distinct from anger, or any other passion, that made them to despise danger, and face death itself with intrepidity, and that they who had the most of it were the most valuable of their kind, it is very likely, considering what has been said, that most of them, though they felt nothing of this principle, would swallow it for truth, and that the proudest, feeling themselves moved at this piece of flattery, and not well versed in distinguishing the passions, might imagine that they felt it heaving in their breasts, by mistaking pride for courage. If but one in ten can be persuaded openly to declare, that he is possessed of this principle, and maintain it against all gainfayers, there will soon be half a dozen that shall assert the fame. Whoever has once owned it is engaged, the politician has nothing to do but to take all imaginable care to flatter the pride of those that brag of, and are willing to stand by it a thousand different ways: The fame pride that drew him in sirst will ever after oblige him to defend the assertion, till at last the fear of discovering the reality of his heart, comes to be so great, that it outdoes the fear of death itself. Do but increase man's pride, and his fear of shame will ever be proportioned to it: for the greater value a man sets upon himself, the more pains he will take, and the greater hardships he will undergo, to avoid fliame.

The great art to make man courageous, is sirst to make him own this principle of valour within, and after-

wards to inspire him with as much horror against shame, as nature has given him against death; and that there are things to which man has, or may have, a stronger aversion than he has to death, is evident from suicide. He that makes death his choice, must look upon it as less terrible than what he shuns by it; for whether the evil dreaded be present or to come, real or imaginary, nobody would kill himself wilfully but to avoid something. Lucretia held out bravely against all the attacks of the ravisher, even when he threatened her life; which shows that she valued her virtue beyond it: but when he threatened her reputation with eternal infamy, she fairly surrendered, and then flew herself; a certain sign that she valued her virtue less than her glory, and her life less than either. The fear of death did not make her yield, for she 4 resolved to die before she did it, and her compliance must only be considered as a bribe, to make Tarquin forbear sullying her reputation; so that life had neither the sirst nor second place in the esteem of Lucretia. The courage, then, which is only useful to the body politic, and what is generally called true valour, is artisicial, and consists in a superlative horror against shame, by flattery infused into men of exalted pride.

As soon as the notions of honour and shame are received among a society, it is not dissicult to make men sight. First, take care they are persuaded of the justice of their cause; for no man sights heartily that thinks himself in the wrong; then show them that their altars, their possessions, wives, children, and every thing that is near and dear to them, is concerned in the present quarrel, or at least may be influenced by it hereafter; then put feathers in their caps, and distinguish them from others, talk of public-spiritedness, the love of their country, facing an enemy with intrepidity, despising death the bed of honour, and such like high-sounding words, and every proud man will take up arms and sight himself to death before we will turn tail, if it be by daylight. One man in an army is a check upon another, and a hundred of them, that single and without witness, would be all cowards, are, for fear of incurring une another's contempt, made valiant by being together. To continue and heighten this artisicial courage, all that run away ought to be punished with ignominy; those that fought well, whether they did beat or were beaten, must be flattered and solemnly commended; those that lost their limbs rewarded; and those that were killed, ought, above all to be taken notice of, artfully lamented, and to have extraordinary encomiums bestowed upon them; for to pay honours to the dead, will ever be a sure method to make bubbles of the living.

When I fay, that the courage made use of in the wars is artisicial, I do not imagine that by the fame art, all men may be made equally valiant: as men have not an equal share of pride, and differ from one another in shape and inward structure, it is impossible they should be all equally sit for the some uses, Some men will never be able to learn music, and yet make good mathematicians; others will play excellently well upon the violin, and yet be coxcombs as long as they live, let them converse with whom they please. But to show that there is no evasion, I (hall prove, that setting aside what I said of artisicial courage already, what the greatest heroe differs in from the rankest coward, is altogether corporeal, and depends upon the inward make of man. What I mean is called constitution; by which is understood the orderly or disorderly mixture of the fluids in our body: that constitution which favours courage, consists in the natural strength, elasticity, and due contexture of the siner spirits, and upon them wholly depends what we call stedfastness, resolution, and obstinacy. It is the only ingredient that is common to natural and artisicial bravery, and is to either what size is to white walls, which hinders them from coming osf, and makes them lasting. That some people are very much, others very little frightened at things that are strange and sudden to them, is likewise altogether owing to the sirmness or imbecillity in the tone of the spirits. Pride is of no use in a fright, because while it lasts we can-

not think, which, being counted a disgrace, is the reason people is always angry with any thing that frightens them, as soon as the surprise is over; and when at the turn of a battle the conquerors give no quarter, and are very cruel, it is a sign their enemies fought well, and had put them siist into great fears.

That resolution depends upon this tone of the spirits, appears likewise from the effects of strong liquors, the siery particles whereof crowding into the brain, strengthen the spirits; their operation imitates that of anger, which I said before was an ebullition of the spirits. It is for this reason, that most people when they are in drink, are sooner touched and more prone to anger, than at other times, and some raving mad without any provocation at all. It is likewise observed, that brandy makes men more quarrelsome at the fame pitch of drunkenness than wine; because the spirits,of distilled waters have abundance of fiery particles mixed with them, which the other has not. The contexture of spirits is so weak in some, that though they have pride enough, no art can ever make them fight, or overcome their fears; but this is a defect in the principle of the fluids, as other deformities are faults of the solids. These pusillanimous people, are never thoroughly provoked to anger, where there is any danger, and drinking makes them bolder, but seldom so resolute as to attack any, unless they be women or children, or such who they know dare not resill. This constitution is often influenced by health and sickness, and impaired by great lofles'ot blood; sometimes it is corrected by diet; and it is this which the Duke de la Rochefocault means, when he fays; vanity, iliame, and above all constitution, make up very often the courage of men, and virtue of women.

There is nothing that more improves the useful martial courage I treat of, and at the same time shows it to be artisicial, than practice; for when men are disciplined, come to be acquainted with all the tools of death, and engines of destruction, when the shouts, the outcries, the sire and smoke, the grones of

wounded, and ghostly looks of dying men, with ail the various scenes of mangled carcases and bloody limbs tore osf, begin to be familiar to them, their fear abate apace; not that they are now lel's afraid to die than before, but being used so often to see the same dangers, they apprehend the reality of them less than they did: as they are deservedly valued for every siege they are at, and every battle they are in, it is impossible but the several actions they share in, must continually become as many solid steps by which their pride mounts up; and thus their fear of shame, as I said before, will always be proportioned to their pride, increasing as the apprehension of the danger decreases, it is no wonder that most of them learn to discover little or no fear: and some great generals are able to preserve a presence of mind, and counterfeit acalm serenity within the midst of all the noise, horlor, and confusion, that attend a battle.

So lilly a creature is man, as that, intoxicated with the fumes of vanity, he can feast on the thoughts "of the praises that mall be paid his memory in future ages, with so much ecilacy, as to neglect his present life, nay, court and covet death, if he but imagines that it will add to the glory he had acquired before. There is no pitch of self-denial, that a man of pride and constitution cannot reach, nor any passion so violent but he will sacrisice it to another, which is superior to it; and here I cannot but admire ar the simplicity of some good men, who, when they hear of the joy and alacrity with which holy men in persecutions have suffered for their faith, imagine that such constancy must exceed all human force, unless it was supported by some miraculous aflistance horn Heaven. As most people are willing to acknowledge all the frailties of their species', so they arc unpequainted with the strength of our nature, and know not that some men of sirm constitution may work themselves up into enthusiasm, by no other help than the violence of their passions; yet, it is certain, that there have been men who only assisted with pride and constitution to maintain the worst of causes, have undergone death and torments, with as much cheerfulness as the best of men, animated with piety and devotion, ever did for the true religion.

To prove thk assertion, I could produce many instances; but one or two will be sussicient. Jordanus Bruno of Nola, who wrote that silly piece of blasphemy, called *Spaccio della Bejlia triumpbante,* and the infamous Vanini, were both executed for openly professing and teaching of atheism: the latter might have been pardoned the moment before the execution, if he would have retracted his doctrine; but rather than recant, he chose to be burnt to ashes. As he went to the stake, he was so far from showing any concern, that he held his hand out to a physician whom he happened to know, desiring him to judge of the calmness of his mind by the regularity of his pulse, and from thence taking an opportunity of making an impious comparison, uttered a sentence too execrable to be mentioned. To these we may join one Mahomet Effendi, who, as Sir Paul Ricaut tells us, was put *to* death at Constantinople, for having advanced some notions against the existence of a God. He likewise might have saved his life by confessing his error, and renouncing it for the future; but chose rather to persist in his blasphemies, faying, " Though he had no reward to expect, the love of truth " constrained him to suffer martyrdom in its defence.

1 have made this digression chiefly to show the strength of human nature, and what mere man may perform by pride and constitution alone. Man may certainly be as violently roused by his vanity, as a lion is by his anger; and not only this, avarice, revenge, ambition, and almost every passion, pity not excepted, when they are extraordinary, may, by overcoming fear, serve him instead of valour, and be mistaken for it even by himself; as daily experience must teach every body that will examine and look into the motives from which some men act. But that we may more clearly perceive what this pretended principle is really built upon, let us look into the management of military affairs, and we shall sind that pride is no where so

openly encouraged as there. As lor clothes, the very lowest of the commission ossicers have them richer, or at least more gay and splendid, than are generally woie by other people of four or sive times their income. Most of them, aud especially those that have families, and can hardly subsist, would be very glad, all Europe over, to be less expensive that way; but it is a force put upon them t6 uphold their pride, which they do not think on.

But the ways and means to rouse man's pride, and catch him by it, are nowhere more grossly conspicuous, than in the treatment which the common soldiers receive, whose vanity is to be worked upon (because there must be so many) at the cheapest rate imaginable. Things we are accustomed to we do not mind, or else what mortal that never had seen a soldier, could look without laughing upon a man accoutred with so much paltry gaudiness, and affected sinery? The coarsest manufacture that can be made of wool, dyed of a brickdust colour, goes down with him, because it is in imitation of scarlet or crimson cloth; and to make him think himself as like his ossicer as it is possible, with little or no cost, instead of silver or gold lace, his hat is trimmed with white or yellow worsted, which in others would deserve bedlam; yet these sine allurements, and the noise made upon a calf's skin, have drawn in, and been the destruction of more men in reality, than all the killing eyes and bewitching voices of women ever flew in jest. To-day the swine herd puts on his red coat, and believes every body in earnest that calls him gentleman; and two days after-Serjeant Kite gives him a swinging wrap with his cane, for holding his musket an inch higher than he should do. As to the real dignity of the employment, in the two last wars, ossicers, when recruits were wanted, were allowed to list fellows that were convicted of burglary and other capital crimes, which shows that to be made a soldier is deemed to be a preferment next to hanging. A trooper is yet worse than a foot soldier; for when he is most at ease, he has the mortisication of being groom to a horse, that

spends more money than himself. When a. man reflects on all this, the usage they generally receive from their ossicers, their pay, and the care that is taken of them, when they are not wanted, must he not wonder how wretches can be so silly as to be proud of being called gentlemen soldiers? Yet if there were not, no art, dicipline, or money, would be capable of making them so brave as thousands of them are.

If we will mind what effects man's braveiy, without any other qualisications to sweeten him, would have out of an army, we shall sind that it would be very pernicious to the civil society; for if man could conquer all his fears, you nould hear of nothing but rapes, murders, and violences of

K all sorts, and valiant men would be like giants in romances: politics, therefore, discovered in men a mixed-metal principle, which was a compound of justice, honesty, and all the moral virtues joined to courage, and all that were possessed of it turned knights-errant of course. They did abundance of good throughout the world, by taming monsters, delivering the distressed, and killing the oppressors: but the wings of all'the dragons being clipped, the giants destroyed, and the damsels every where set at liberty, except some few in Spain and Italy, who remained still captivated by their monsters, the order of chivalry, to whom the standard of ancient honour belonged, has been laid aside some time. It was like their armours very massy and heavy; the many virtues about it made it very troublesome, and as ages grew wiser and wiser, the principle of honour in the beginning of the last century was melted over again, and brought to a new standard; they put in the fame weight of courage, half the quantity of honesty, and a very little justice, but not a scrap of any other virtue, which has made it very easy and portable to what it was. However, such as it is, there would be no living without it in a large nation; it is the tie of society, and though we are beholden to our frailties for the chief ingredient of it, there is no virtue, at least that I am acquainted with, that has been half so instrumental to the civilizing of mankind, who in great societies would soon degenerate into cruel villians and treacherous staves, were honour to be removed fiom among them.

As to the duelling part which belongs to it, I pity the unfortunate whose lot it is; but to fay, that those who are guilty of it go by false rules, or mistake the notions of honour, is ridiculous; for either there is no honour at all, or it teaches men to resent injuries, and accept of challenges. You may as well deny that it is the fashion what you fee every body wear, as to fay that demanding and giving satisfaction is against the laws of true honour. Those that rail at duelling do not consider the benesit the society receives from that fashion: if every illbred fellow might use what language he pleased, without being called to an account tor it, all conversation w-ould be spoiled. Some grave people tell us, that the Greeks and Romans were such valiant men, and yet knew nothing of duelling but in their country s quarrel. This Is very true, but, for that reason, the kings and princes in Homer gave one another worse language than

But porters and hackney coachmen would be able to bear without resentment.

Would you hinder duelling, pardon nobody that offends that way, and make the laws as severe as you can, but do not take away the thing itself, the custom of it. This will not only prevent the frequency of it, but likewise, by rendering the most resolute and most powerful cautious and circumspect in their behaviour, polhh and brighten society in general. Nothing civilizes a man equally as his fear, and if not all (as my lord Rochester said), at least most men would be cowards if they durst. The dread of being called to an account keeps abundance in awe; and there are thousands of mannerly and well-accomplished gentlemen in Europe, who would have been insolent and insupportable coxcombs without it: besides, if it was out of fashion to ask satisfaction for injuries which the law cannot take hold of, there would be twenty times the mischief done there is now,

or else you must have twenty times the constables and other ossicers to keep the peace. I confess that though it happens but seldom, it is a calamity to the people, and generally the families it falls upon; but there can be no perfect happiness in this world, and all felicity has an allay. The act itself is uncharitable, but when above thirty in a nation destroy themselves in one year, and not half that number are killed by others, 1 do not think the people can be said to love their neighbours worse than themselves. It is strange that a nation stiould grudge to fee, perhaps, half-a-doz.en men sacrisiced in a twelvemonth to obtain so valuable a blessing, as the politeness of manners, the pleasure of conversation, and the happiness of company in general, that is often ib willing to expose, and sometimes loies as many thousands in a few hours, without knowing whether it will do any good or not.

1 would have nobody that reflects on the mean original of honour, complain of being gulled and made a property by cunning politicians, but desire every body to be satissied, that the governors of societies, and those in high llations, are greater bubbles to pride than any of the rest. If some great men had not a superlative pride, and every body understood the enjoyment of life, who would be a lord chancellor of England, a prime minister of state in France, or what gives Wore fatigue, and not a stxth part of the prosit of either, grand pensionary of Holland? The reciprocal services which all men pay to one another, are the foundation of the society. The great ones are not flattered with their high birth for nothing: it is to rouse their pride, and excite theni to glorious actions, that we extol their race, whether it deserves it or not; and some men have been complimented with the greatness of their family, and the merit of their ancestors, when in the whole generation you could-not sind two but what were uxorious fools, silly biggots, noted poltrons, or debauched whore-masters. The established pride that is inseparable from those that are possessed of titles already, makes them often strive as much not to seem unworthy of them,

as the working ambition of others that are yet without, renders them industrious and indefatigable to deserve them. When a gentleman is made'a baron or an earl, it is as great a check upon him in many respects, as a gown and cassock are to a young student that has been newly taken into orders.

The only thing of weight that can be said against modern honour is, that it is directly opposite to religion. The one bids you bear injuries with patience; the other tells you if you do not resent them,you are not sit to live. Religion commands you to leave all revenge to God; honour bids you trust your revenge to nobody but yourself, even where the law would do it for you: religion plainly forbids murder; honour openly justisies it: religion bids you not shed blood upon any account whatever; honour bids you sight for the least trifle: religion is built on humility, and honour upon pride: how to reconcile them must be left to wiser heads than mine.

The reason why there are so few men of real virtue, and so many of real honour, is, because all the recompence a man has of a virtuous action, is the pleasure of doing it, which most people reckon but poor pay; but the self denial a man os honour submits to in one appetite, is immediately rewarded by the satisfaction he receives from another, and what he abates of his avarice, or any other passion, is doubly repaid to his pride: besides, honour gives large grains of allowance, and virtue none. A man of honour must not cheat or tell a lie; he mustpunctually repay what he borrows at play, though the creditor has nothing to show for it; but he may drink, and swear, and owe money to all the tradesmen in town, without taking notice of their dunning. A man of honour must be true to his prince and country, while he is in their service; but if he thinks himself not well used, he may quit it, and do them all the mischief he can A man of honour must never change his religion for interest; but he may be as debauched as he pleases, and never practise any. He must make no attempts upon his friend's wife, daughter, sister, or any body that is trusted to his care; but he may lie with all the world besides.

Line 353. No limner for his art is fam'd,

Stone-cutters, carvers are not nam'd.

It is, without doubt, that among the consequences of a national honesty and frugality, it would be one not to build any new houses, or use new materials as long as there were old ones enough to serve. By this three parts in four, of masons, carpenters, bricklayers, &c. would want employment; and the building trade being once destroyed, what would become of limning, carving, and other arts that are ministering to luxury, and have been carefully forbid by those law-givers that preferred a good and honest, to a great and wealthy society, and endeavoured to render their subjects rather virtuous than rich. By a law of Lycurgus, it was enacted, that the cielings of the Spartan houses lhould only be wrought by the ax, and their gates and doors only smoothed by the saw; and this, fays Plutarch, was not without mystery: for if Epaminondas could fay with so good a grace, inviting some of his friends to his table; " Come, " gentlemen, be secure, treason would never come to such " a poor dinner as this:" Why might not this great lawgiver, in all probability, have thought that such ill-favoured houses would never be capable of receiving luxury and superfluity?

It is reported, as the fame author teJJs us, that Leotichidas, the sirst of that name, was so little used to the sight of carved work, that being entertained at Corinth in a stately room, he was much surprised to see the timber and ceiling so sinely wrought, and asked his host whether the trees grew so in his country.

The lame want of employment would reach innumerable callings; and, among the rest, that of the

Weavers that join'd rich silk, with plate,

And all the trades subordinate,

(as the fable has it) would be one of the sirst; that should have reason to complain; for the price of land and houses. being, by the removal of the vast numbers that had left the hive, funk very low on the one side, and every body ab-

horring all other ways of gain, but such as were strictly honest on the other, it is not probable that many without pride or prodigality should be able to wear cloth of gold and silver, or rich brocades. The consequence of which would be, that not only the weaver, but likewise the silver-spinner, the statter, the wire-drawer, the bar-man, and the resiner, would, in a little time be asfected with this frugality.

Line 367. To live great,

Had made her husband rob the state.

W Hat oiir common rogues,-when they are going to be hanged, chiefly complain of, as the cause of their untimely end, is, next to the neglect of the Sabbath, their having kept company with ill women, meaning whores; and I do not question, but that among the lesser villains, many venture their necks to indulge and satisfy their low amours. But the words that have given occasion to this remark, may serve to hint to us, that among the great ones, men are often put upon such dangerous projects, and forced into such pernicious measures by their wives, as the most subtle mistress never could have persuaded them to. I have shown already, that the worst of women, and most profligate *ot'* the sex, did contribute to the consumption of superfluities, as well as the necessaries of life, and consequently were benesicial to many peaceable drudges, that work hard to maintain their families, and have no worse design than an honest livelihood. Let them be banished, notwithstanding, says a good man: When evtry strumpet is gone, and the land wholly freed from lewdness, God imighty will pour such bleflings upon it, as will vastly exceed the prosits that are now got by harlots. This perhaps would be true; but I can make it evident, that, with or without prostitutes, nothing could make amends, for the detriment trade would sustain, if all those ot. that sex, who enjoy the happy state of matrimony, stiould act and behave themselves as a sober wise man could wish them.

The variety of work that is performed, and the number of hands employed to gratify the fickleness and lux-

ury of women, is prodigious, and if only the married ones should hearken to reason and just remonstrances, think themselves suf-. siciently answered w"ith the sirst refusal, and never ask a second time what had been once denied them: If, I say, married women would do this, and then lay out no money but what their husbands knew, and freely allowed of, the consumption of a thousand things, they now make use of, would be lesscned by at least a fourth part. Let us go from house to house, and observe the way of the world only among the middling people, creditable shop-keepers, that spend two or three hundred a-year, and we shall sind the women when they have half a score suits of clothes, two or three of them not the worse for wearing, will think it a sussicient plea for new ones, if they can fay that they have never a gown or petticoat, but what they have been often seen in, and are known by, especially at church; I do not speak now of profuse extravagant women, but such as are counted prudent and moderate in their desires.

If by this pattern we mould in proportion judge of the highest ranks, where the richest clothes are but a trifle to their other expences, and not forget the furniture of all forts, equipages, jewels, and buildings of persons of quality, we should sind the fourth part I speak of a vast article in trade, and that the loss of it would be a greater calamity to iuch a nation as ours, than it is possible td conceive any other, a raging pestilence not excepted: for the death of half a million of people could not cause a tenth part of the disturbance to the kingdom, than the same number of poor unemployed would certainly create, if at once they were to be added to those, that already, one way or other, are a burden to the society.

Some few men have a real passion for their wives, and are fond of them without reserve; others that do not care, and have little occasion for women, are yet seemingly uxorious, and love out of vanity; they take delight in a handsome wife, as a coxcomb does in a sine horse, not for the use he makes of it, but because it is his: The pleasure lies in the consciousness of an uncontrolable pcllellion, and what follows srom it, the reslection on the mighty thoughts he imagines others to have of bis happiness. The men of either fort may be very lavish to their wives, and often preventing their wishes, crowd new clothes, and other sinery upon them, suster than they can atk it, but the greatest part are wiser than to indulge the extravagances of their wires so far, as to give them immediately every thing they are pleased to fancy. It is incredible what vast quantity of trinkets, as weil as apparel, are purchased and used by women, which they could never have come at by any other means, than pinching their families, marketing, and other ways of cheating and pilfering from their husbands: Others, by ever teazing their spouses, tire them into compliance, and conquer even obstinate churls by perseverance, and their assiduity of asking: A third sort "are outrageous at a denial, and by downright noise and scolding, bully their tame fools out"of any thing they have a mind to; while thousands, by the force of wheedling, know how to overcome the best weighed reasons, and the most poiitive reiterated refusals; the young and beautiful, especially, laugh at all remonstrances and denials, and few of them scruple to employ the most tender minutes of wedlock to promote a sordid interest. Here, had I time, I could inveigh with warmth against those base, those wicked women, wh© calmly play their arts and false deluding charms against our strength and prudence, and act the harlots with their husbands! Nay, she is worse than whore, who impiously profanes and prostitutes the sacred rites of love to vile ignoble ends; that sirst excites to passion, and invites to joy with seeming ardour, then racks our fondness for no other purpose than to extort a gift, while full of guile in counterfeited transports, she watches for the moment whennien can least deny.

I beg pardon for this start out of my way, and desire the experienced reader duly to weigh what has been said as to the main purpose, and after that call to mind the temporal blessings, which men daily hear not only toasted and wished

for, when people are merry and doing of nothing; but likewise gravely and solemnly prayed for in churches, and other religious assemblies, by clergymen of all sorts and sizes: And as soon as he shall have laid these things together, and, from what he has observed in the common asfairs of life, reasoned upon them consequentially without prejudice, I dare slatter myself, that he will be obliged to own, that a considerable portion of what the prosperity of London and trade in general, and consequently the honour, strength, safety, and all the wordly interest of the nation consist in, depend entirely on the deceit and vile stratagems of women; and that humility, content, meekness, obedience to reasonable husbands, frugality, and all the virtues together, if they were possessed of them in the most eminent degree, could not possibly be a thousandth part so serviceable, to make an opulent, powerful, and what we call a flourishing kingdom, than their most hateful qualities.

I do not question, but many of my readers will be startled at this assertion, when they look on the consequences that may be drawn from it; and I shall be asked, whether people may not as well be virtuous in a populous, rich, wide, extended kingdom, as in a small, indigent state or principality, that is poorly inhabited? And if that be impossible, Whether it is not the duty of all sovereigns to reduce their subjects, as to wealth and numbers, as much as they can? If I allow they may, I own myself in the wrong; and if I asfirm the other, my tenets will justly be called impious, or at least dangerous to all large societies.. As it is not in this place of the book only, but a great many others, that such queries might be made even by a well-meaning reader, 1 shall here explain myself, and endeavour to solve those dissiculties, which several passages might have raised in him, in order to demonstrate the consistency of my opinion to reason, and the strictest morality.

I lay down as a sirst principle, that in all societies, great or small, it is the duty of every member of it to be good,

that virtue ought to be encouraged, vice discountenanced, the laws obeyed, and the transgressors punished. After this I asfirm, that if we consult history, both ancient and modern, and take a view of what has passed in the world, we shall sind that human nature, since the fall of Adam, has always been the fame, and that the strength and frailties of it have ever been conspicuous in one part of the globe or other, without any regard to ages, climates, or religion. I never said, nor imagined, that man could not be virtuous as well in a rich and mighty kingdom, as in the most pitiful commonwealth; but I own it is my fense, that no society can be raised into such a rich and mighty kingdom, or so raised, subsill in their wealth and power for any considerable time, without the vices of man.

This, I imagine, is sussiciently proved throughout the book j and as human nature still continues the fame, as it has always been for so many thousand years, we have no great reason to suspect a future change in it, while the world endures. Now, I cannot fee what immorality there is in showing a man the origin and power of those passions, which so often, even unknowingly to himself, hurry him away from his reason; or that there is any impiety in putting him upon his guard against himself, and the secret stratagems of selflove, and teaching him the difference between suqh actions as proceed from a victory over the passions, and those that are only the result of a conquest which one passion obtains over another; that is, between real and counterfeited virtue. It is an admirable saying of a worthy divine, That though many discoveries have been made in the world of self-love, there is yet abundance of *terra incognita* left behind. What hurt do I do to man, if I make him-more known to himself than he was before? But we are all so desperately in love with flattery, that we can never relish a truth that is mortifying, and I do not believe that the immortality of the soul, a truth broached long before Christianity, would have ever found such a general reception in human capacities as it has, had it not been a pleasing one, that extolled, and was a compliment to the whole species, the meanest and most miserable not excepted.

Every one loves to hear the thing well spoke of that he has a share in, even bailisfs, goal-keepers, and the hangman himself would have you think well of their functions; nay, thieves and house breakers have a greater regard to those of their fraternity, than they have for honest people; and 1 sincerely believe, that it is chiefly self-love that has gained this little treatise (as it was before the last impression), so many enemies; every one looks upon it as an asfront done to himself, because it detracts from the dignity, and lessens the sine notions he had conceived of mankind, the most worshipful company he belongs to. When I fay that societies cannot be raised to wealth and power, and the top of earthly glory, without vices, 1 do not think that, by so saying, 1 bid men be vicious, any more than I bid them.be quarrelsome or covetous, when I assirm that the profession of the law could not be maintained in such numbers and splendor, if there was not abundance of too selfish and litigious people.

But as nothing would more clearly demonstrate the falsity of my notions, than that the generality of the people should fall in with them, so 1 do not expect the aporobation of the multitude. 1 write not to many, nor leek for any wellwifhers, but among the few that can think abstractly, and have their minds elevated above the vulgar. If I have shown the way to worldly greatness, I have always, without hesitation, preferred the road that leads to virtue.

Would you banish fraud and luxury, prevent profaneness and irreligion, and make the generality of the people charitable, good, and virtuous; break down the printing-prestes-, melt the founds, and burn all the books in the illand, except those at the universities, where they remain unmolested, and susfer no volume in private hands but a Bible: knock down foreign trade, prohibit all commerce with strangers, and permit no ships to go to sea, that ever will return,

beyond sisher-boats. Restore to the clergy, the king and the barrens their ancient privileges, prerogatives, and professions: build new churches, and convert all the coin you can come at into sacred utensils: erect monasteries and alms-houses in abundance, and let no parish be without a charity-schook Enact sumptuary laws, and let your youth be inured to hardship: inspire them with all the nice and most resined notions of honour and shame, of friendship and of heroism, and introduce among them a great variety of imaginary rewards: then let the clergy preach abstinence and self-denial to others, and take what liberty they please for themselves; let them bear the greatest sway in the management of state-affairs, and no man be made lord-treasurer but a bishop.

But by such pious endeavours, and wholfome regulations, the scene would be soon altered; the greatest part of the covetous, the discontented, the restless and ambitious villains, would leave the land; vast swarms of cheating knaves would abandon the city, and be dispersed throughout the country: artisicers would leavn'to hold the plough, merchants turn farmers, and the sinsul overgrown Jerusalem, without famine, war, pestilence, or compulsion, be emptied in the most easy manner, and ever after cease to be dreadful to her sovereigns. The happy reformed kingdom would by thi means be crowded in no part of it, and every thing necessary for the sustenance of man, be cheap and abound: on the contrary, the root os so many thousand evils, money, would be very scarce, and as little wanted, where every man should enjoy the fruits of his own labour, and our own dear manufacture unmixed, be promiscuously wore by the lord and the peasant. It is impossible, that such a change of circumstances mould not influence the manners of a nation, and fender them temperate, honest, and sincere; and from the t generation we might reasonably expect a more healthy and robust osfspring than the present; an harmless, innocent, and well-meaning people, that would never dispute the doctrine of passive obedience, nor any other orthodox

principles, but be submissive to superiors, and unanimous in religious worship.

Here I fancy myself interrupted by an Epicure, who, not to want a restorative diet in case of necessity, is never without live ortelans; and I am told that goodness and probity are to be had at a cheaper rate than the ruin of a nation, and the destruction of all the comforts of life; that liberty and property may be maintained without wickedness or fraud, and men be good subjects without being staves, and religious though they refused to be priest-rid; that to be frugal and saving is a duty incumbent only on those, whose circumstances require it, but that a man of a good estate does his country a service by living up to the income of it; that as to himself, he is so much master of his appetites, that he can abstain from any thing upon occalion; that where true Hermitage was not to be had, he could content himself with plain Bourdeaux, if it had a good body; that many a morning, instead of St. Lawrence, he has made a shift with Fronteniac, and after dinner given Cyprus wine, and even Madeira, when he has had a large company, and thought it extravagant to treat with Tockay; but that all voluntary mortisications are superstitious, only belonging to blind zealots and enthusiasts. He will quote my Lord Shaftsbury against me, and tell me that people may be virtuous and sociable without self-denial; that it is an affront to virtue to make it inaccessible, that 1 make a bugbear of it to frighten men from it as a thing impracticable; but that for his part he can praise God, and at the same time enjoy his creatures with a good conscience; neither will he forget any thing to his purpose of what I have said, page *66*. He will ask me at last, whether the legislature, the wisdom of the nation itself, while they endeavour as much as possible, to discourage profaneness and immorality, and promote the glory of God, do not openly profess, at the fame time, to have nothing more at heart, than the ease and welfare of the subject, the wealth, strength, honour, and what else is called the true interest of the country?

and, moreover, whether the most devout and most learned of our prelates, in their greatest concern for our conversion, when they beseech the Deity *to* turn their own as well as our hearts, from the world and all carnal desires, do not in the fame prayer as loudly solicit him to pour all earthly blessings and temporal felicity, on the kingdom they belong to?

These are the apologies, the excuses, and common pleas, not only of those who are notoriously vicious, but the generality of mankind, when you touch the copy-hold of their inclinations; and trying the real value they have for spirituals, would actually strip them of what their minds are wholly bent upon. Ashamed of the many frailties they feel within, all men endeavour to hide themselves, their ugly nakedness, from each other, and wrapping up the true motives of their hearts, in the specious cloak of sociableness, and their concern for the public good, they are in hopes of concealing their silthy appetites, and the deformity of their desires; while they are conscious within of the fondness for their darling lulls, and their incapacity, bare-faced, to tread the arduous, rugged path of virtue.

As to the two last questions, 1 own they are very puzzling: to what the Epicure asks, I am obliged to answer in the afsirmitive; and unless I would (which God forbid!) arraign the sincerity of kings, bishops, and the whole legislative power, the objection stands good against me: all 1 can fay for myself is, that in the connection of the facts, there is a mystery past human understanding; and to convince the reader, that this is no evasion, I shall illustrate the incomprehensibility of it in the following parable.

In old heathen times, there was, they fay, a whimsical country, where the people talked much of religion, and the greatest part, as to outward appearance, seemed really devout: the chief moral evil among them was thirst, and to quench it a damnable sin; yet they unanimously agreed that every one was born thirsty, more or less: small beer in moderation was allowed to all, and he was counted an hypocrite, a cynic, or a mad-

man, who pretended that one could live altogether without it; yet those, who owned they loved it, and drank it to excess, were counted wicked. Ail this, while the beer itself was reckoned a blessing from Heaven, and there was no harm in the use of it; ail the enormity lay in the abuse, the motive of the heart, that made them drink it. He that took the least drop of it to quench his thirst, committed a heinous crime, while others drank large quantities without any guilt, so they did it indisferently, and for no other reason than to mend their complexion.

They brewed for other countries as well as their own, and for the small beer they sent abroad, they received, large returns of Westphalia-hams, neats tongues, hung-beef, and Bologna sausages, red-herrings, pickled sturgeon, cavear, anchovies, and every thing that was proper to make their liquor go clown with pleasure. Those who kept great stores of small beer by them without making use of it, were generally envied, and at the same time very odious to the public, and nobody was easy that had not enough of it come to his own soare. The greatest calamity they thought could befal them, was to keep their hops and barley upon their hands, and the more they yearly consumed of them, the more they reckoned the country to flourish.

The government had many very wise regulations concerning the returns that were made for their exports, encouraged very much the importation of salt and pepper, and laid heavy duties on every thing that was not well seasoned, and might any ways obstruct the sale of their own hops and barley. Those at helm, when they acted in public, mowed themselves on all accounts exempt and wholly divested from thirst, made several laws to prevent the growth of it, and punish the wicked who openly dared to quench it. If you examined them in their private persons, and pry ed-narrowly into their lives and converlations, they seemed to be more sond, or at least drank larger draughts of small beer than others, but always under pretence that the mending of complexions required

greater quantities of liquor in them, than it did in those they ruled over; and that, what they had chiefly at heart, without any regard to themselves, was to procure great plenty of small beer, among the subjects in general, and a great demand for their hops and barley.

As nobody was debarred from small beer, the clergy made use of it as well as the laity, and some of them very plentifully; yet all of them desired to be thought less thirsty by their function than others, and never would own that they drank any but to mend their complexions. In their religious assemblies they were more sincere; for as soon as they came there, they all openly confessed, the clergy as well as the laity, from the highest to the lowest, that they were thirsty, that mending their complexions was what they minded the least, and that all their hearts were set upon small beer and quenching their thirst, whatever they might pretend to the contrary, "What was remarkable, is, that to have laid hold of those, *truths* to any ones prejudice, and made use of those confessions afterwards out of their temples, would be counted very impertinent, and every body thought it an heinous asfront to be called thirsty, though you had seen him drink small beer by whole gallons. The chief topics of their preachers, was the great evil of thirst, and the folly there was in quenching it. They exhorted their hearers to resist the temptations of it, inveighed against small beer, and often told them it was poison, if they drank it with pleasure, or any other design than to mend their complexions.

In their acknowledgements to the gods, they thanked them for the plenty of comfortable snlall beer they had received from them, notwithstanding they had so little deserved it, and continually quenched their thirst "with it; whereas, they were so thoroughly satissied, that it was given them for a better use. Having begged pardon for those offences, they desired the gods to lesten their thirst, and give them strength to resist the importunities of it; yet, in the midst of their sorest repentance, and most humble supplications, they never forgot small beer, and prayed that they niight continue to have it in great plenty, with a solemn promise, that how neglectful soever they might hitherto have been in this point, they would for the future not drink a drop of it, with any other design than to mend their complexions.

These were standing petitions put together to last; and having continued to be made use of without any alterations, for several hundred years together; it was thought by some, that the gods, who understood futurity, and knew that the fame promise they heard in June, would be made to them the January following, did not rely much more on those vows, than we do on those waggish inscriptions by whicli men offer us their goods; to-day for money, and to-morrow" for nothing. They often began their prayers very mystically, and spoke many things in a spiritual sense; yet, they never were so abstract from the world in them, as to end one without beseeching the gods to bless and prosper the brewing trade in all its branches, and for the good of the whole, more and more to increase the consumption of hops and barley.

Line 388. Content, the bane of industry.

1 Have been told by many, that the bane of industry is laziness, and not content; therefore to prove my assertion, which seems a paradox to some, I shall treat of laziness and content separately, and afterwards speak of industry, that the reader may judge which it is of the two former, that is opposite to the latter.

Laziness is an aversion to business, generally attended with an unreasonable desire of remaining unuctiye; and every body is lazy, who, without being hindered by any other warrantable employment, refuses or puts otf any business which he ought to do for himself or others. We seldom call any body lazy, but such as we reckon inferior to us, and of whom we expect some service. Children do not think their parents lazy, nor servants their masters; and isa gentleman indulges his ease and sloth so abominabh, that he will not put on his own shoes, though he is young and slender, nobody mall call him lazy for it,

if he can keep but a footman, or some body else to do it for him.

Mr. Dryden has given us a very good idea of superlative flothfulness, in the person of a luxurious Icing of Egypt. His majesty having bellowed some considerable gifts on several of his favourites, is attended by some of his chief ministers with a parchment, which he was to sign to consirm those grants. First, he walks a few turns to and fro, with a heavy uneasiness in his looks, then sets himself down like a man that is tired, and, at last, with abundance of reluctancy to what he was going about, he takes up the pen, and falls a complaining very seriously of the length of the word Ptolemy, and expresses a great deal of concern, that he had not some short monosyllable for his name, which he thought would save him a world of trouble.

We often reproach others with laziness, because we are guilty of it ourselves. Some days ago, as two young women sot knotting together, fays one to the other, there comes a wicked cold through that door; you are the nearest to it, lister, pray shut it. The other, who was the youngest, vouchsafed, indeed, to cast an eye towards the door, but fat still. and said nothing; the eldest spoke again two or three times, and at last the other making her no answer, nor offering to stir, she got up in a pet, and shut the door herself; coming back to sit down again, she gave the younger a very hard look; and said, Lord, sister Betty, I would not be so lazy as you arc for all the world; which she spoke so earnestly, that it brought a colour in her face. The youngest should have risen, I own; but if the eldest had not overvalued her labour, she would have shut the door herself, as soon as the cold was osfensive to her, without making any words of it. She was not above a step farther from the door than her sister, and as to age, there was not eleven months disference between them, and they were both under twenty. I thought it a hard matter to determine which was the laziest of the two.

There are a thousand wretches that are always working the marrow out of

their bones for next to nothing, because they are unthinking and ignorant of what the pains they take are worth: while others who are cunning, and understand the true value of their work, refuse to be employed at under rates, not because they are of an unactive temper, but because they will not beat down the price of their labour. A country gentleman sees at the back side of the Exchange a porter walking to and fro with his hands in his pockets. Pray, fays he, friend, will you step for me with this letter as far as Bow-church, and I will give you a penny? I will go with all my heart, fays the other, but I must have twopence, master; which the gentleman refusing to give, the fellow turned his back, and told him, he A$puld rather play for nothing than work for nothing. The gentleman thought it an unaccountable piece of laziness in a porter, rather to saunter up and down for nothing, than to be earning a penny with as little trouble. Some hours after he happened to be with some friends at a tavern in Threadneedle-street, where one of them calling to mind that he had forgot to send for a bill of exchange that was to go away with the poll that night, was in great perplexity, and immediately wanted some body to go for him to Hackney with all the speed imaginable. It was after ten, in the middle of winter, a very rainy night, and all the porters thereabouts were gone to bed. The gentleman grew very uneasy, and said, whatever it cost him, that somebody he must send; at last one of the drawers seeing him sp very prefling, told him that he knew a porter, who would rise, if it'was a job worth his while, Worth his while, said the gentleman very eagerly, do not doubt of that, good lad, if you know of any body, let him make what haste he can, and I will give him a crown if by *h* be back by twelve o'clock. Upon this the drawer took the errand, left the room, and in less than a quarter of an hour, came back with the welcome news that the message wouid be dispatched with all expedition, The, company in the mean time, diverted themselves as they had done before; but when it began to be towards twelve, the watches were pulled out, and the porter's return was all the discourse. Some were of opinion he might yet come before the clock had struck; others thought it impossible, and now it wanted but three minutes of twelve, when in comes the nimble messenger smoking hot, with his clothes as wet as dung with the rain, and his head all over in a bath of sweat. He had nothing dry about him but the inside of his pocket-book, out of which he took the bill he had been for, and by the drawer's direction, presented it to the gentleman it belonged to; who, being very well pleased with the dispatch he had made, gave him the crown he had promised, while another silled him a bumper, and the whole company commended his diligence. As the fellow came nearer the light, to take up the wine, the country gentleman I mentioned at sirst, to his great admiration, knew him to be the fame porter that had refused to earn his penny, and whom he thought the laziest mortal alive.

The story teaches us, that we ought not to confound those who remain unemployed for want of an opportunity of exerting themselves to the best advantage, with such as for want of spirit, hug themselves in their sioth, and will rather starve than stir. Without this caution, we must pronounce all the world more or less lazy, according to their estimation of the reward they are to purchase with their labour, and then the most industrious may be called lazy.

Content, I call that calm serenity of the mind, which men enjoy while they think themselves happy, and rest satissied with the station they are in: It implies a favourable construction of our present circumstances, and a peaceful tranquillity, which men are strangers to as long as they are solicitous about mending their condition. This is a virtue of which the applause is very precarious and uncertain: for, according as mens circumstances vary, they will either be blamed or commended for being possessed of it.

A single man that works hard at a laborious trade, has a hundred a year left him by a relation: this change of fortune makes him soon weary of work-ing, and not having industry enough to put himself forward in the world, he resolves to do nothing at all, and live upon his income. As long as he lives within compass, pays for what he has, and offends nobody, he shall be called an honest quiet man. The victualler, his landlady, the tailor, and others, divide what he has between them, and the society is every year the better for his revenue; whereas, if he should follow his own or any other trade, he must hinder others, and some body would have the less for what he should get; and therefore, though he sliould be the idlest fellow in the world, lie a-bed fifteen hours in four and twenty, and do nothing but sauntering up and down all the rest of the time, nobody would discommend him, and his unactive spirit is honoured with the name of content.

But if the fame man marries, gets three or four children, and still contines of the fame easy temper, rests satissied with what he has, and without endeavouring to get a penny, indulges his former sloth: sirst, his relations, afterwards, all his acquaintance, will be alarmed at his negligence: they foresee that his income will not be sussicient to bring up so many children handsomely, and are afraid, some of them may, if not a burden, become a disgrace to them. When these fears have been, for some time, whispered about from one to another, his uncle Gripe takes him to task, and accosts him in the following cant: " What, nephew, no " business yet! sie upon it! 1 cannot imagine how you do " to spend your time; if you will not work at your own " trade, there are sifty ways that a man may pick up a pen" ny by: you have a hundred a-year, it is true, but your " charges increase every year, and what must yon do when " your children are grown up? 1 have a better estate than " you my self, and yet you do not see me leave offmy business; " nay, 1 declare it, might I have the world 1 could not " lead the life you do. It is no business of mine, I own, " but every body cries, it is a shame for a young man, as " you are, that has his limbs and his health, should not turn " his hands to something or other." If these admonitions do not reform him in a little time, and he continues half-a-year longer without employment, he will become a discourse to the whole neighbourhood, and for the same qualisications that once got him the name of a quiet contented man, he stiall be caUed the worst of" husoands, and the laziest fellow upon earth: from whence it is manifest, that when we pronounce actions good or evil, we-only regard the hurt or benesit the society receives from them, and not the person who commits them. (See page 17.)

Diligence and industry are often used promiscuously, to signify the fame thing, but there is a great difference between them. A poor wretch may want neither diligence nor ingenuity, be a saving pains-taking man, and yet without striving to mend his circumstances, remain contented with the station he lives in; but industry implies, besides the other qualities, a thirst after gain, and an indefatigable destre of meliorating our condition. When-men think either the customary prosits of their calling, or else the share of business they have too small, they have two ways to deserve the name of industrious; and they must be either ingenious enough to sind out uncommon, and yet warrantable methods to increase their business or their prosit, or else supply that defect by a multiplicity of occupations. If a tradesman takes care to provide his shop, and gives due attendance to those that come to it, he is a dilligent man in his business; but if, besides that, he takes particular pains to fell, to the fame advantage, a better commodity than the rest of his neighbours, or if, by his obsequiousness, or some other good quality, getting into a large acquaintance, he uses all possible endeavours of drawing customers to his house, he then may be called industrious. A cobler, though he is not employed half of his time, if he neglects no business, and makes dispatch when he has any, is a diligent man; but if he runs of errands when he has no work, or makes but shoe-pins, and serves as a watchman a-nights, he deserves the name of industrious.

If what has been said in this remark

be duly weighed, we shall sind either, that laziness and content are very near a-kin, or, if there be a great disference between them, that the latter is more contrary to industry than the former.

Line 410. To make a great an honest hive.

X His perhaps might be done where people are contented to be poor and hardy; but if they would likewise enjoy their ease and the comforts of the world, and be at once an opulent, potent, and flourishing, as well as a warlike nation, it is utterly impossible. 1 have heard people speak of the mighty sigure the Spartans made above all the common-wealths of Greece, notwithstanding their uncommon frugality and other exemplary virtues. But certainly there never was a nation whose greatness was more empty than theirs: The splendor they lived in was inferior to that of a theatre, and the only thing they could be proud of, was, that they enjoyed nothing. They were, indeed, both feared and esteemed abroad: they were so famed for valour and skill in martial asfairs, that their neighbours difl not only court their friendship and assistance in their wars, but were satissied, and thought themselves sure of the victory, if they could but get a Spartan general to command their armies. But then their discipline was so rigid, and their manner of living so austere and void of all comfort, that the most temperate man among us would refuse to submit to the harshness of such uncouth laws. There was a perfect equality among them: gold and silver coin were cried down; their current money was made of iron, to render it of a great bulk, and little worth: To lay up twenty or thirty pounds, required a pretty large chamber, and to remove it, nothing less than a yoke of oxen. Another remedy they had against luxury, was, that they were obliged to eat in common of the fame meat, and they so little allowed any body to dine, or sup by himself at home, that Agis, one of their kings, having vanquished the Athenians, and sending for his commons at his return home (because he desired privately to eat with his queen) was refused by the Polemarchi.

In training up their youth, their chief care, says Plutarch, was to make them good subjects, to sit'them to endure the fatigues of long and tedious marches, and never to return without victory from the sield. When they were twelve years old, they lodged in little bands, upon beds made of the rushes, which grew by the banks of the river Eurotas; and because their points were sharp, they were to break them off with their hands without a knife: If it were a hard winter, they mingled some thistle-down with their rushes to kept them warm (fee Plutarch in the life of Lycurgus.) From all these circumstances it is plain, that no nation on earth was less effeminate; but being debarred from all the comforts of life, they could have nothing for their pains, but the glory of being a warlike people, inured to toils and hardships, which was a happiness that few people would have cared for upon the fame terms: and, though they had been masters of the world, as long as they enjoyed no more of it, Englishmen would hardly have envied them their greatness. What men want now-a-days has sussiciently heen shewn in Remark on line 200, where I have treated of real pleasures.

Line 411. T" enjoy the world's conveniencies.

x Hat the words, decency and conveniency, were very ambiguous, and not to be understood, unless we were acquainted with the quality and circumstances of the persons that made use of them, has been hinted already in Remark online 177. The goldsmith, mercer, or any other of the moil creditable shopkeepers, that has three or four thousand pounds to set up with, must have two dimes of meat every day, and something extraordinary for Sundays. His wife must have a damask bed against her lying-in, and two or three rooms very well furnished: the following summer she must have a house, or at least very good lodgings in the country. A man that has a being out of town, must have a horse; his footman must have another. If he has a tolerable trade, he expects in eight or ten years time to keep his coach, which, notwithstanding, he hopes, that after he has slaved (as

he calls it) for two or three and twenty years, he lhall be worth at least a thousand a-year for his eldest son to inherit, and two or three thousand pounds for each of his other children to begin the world with; and when men of such circumstances pray for their daily bread, and mean nothing more extravagant by it, they are counted pretty modest people. Call this pride, luxury, superfluity, or what you please, it is nothing but what ought to be in the capital of a flourishmg nation: those of inferior condition must content themselves with less costly conveniencies, as others of higher rank will be sure to make theirs more expensive. Some people call it but decency to be served in plate, and reckon on a coach and six among the neceflary comforts of life; and if a peer has not above three or four thousand a-year, his lordship is counted poor. 6

Oince the sirst edition of this book, several have attacked me with demonstrations of the certain ruin, which excessive luxury must bring upon all nations, who yet were soon answered, when I showed them the limits within which I had consined it; and therefore, that no reader for the future may misconstrue me on this head, I shall point at the cautions I have given, and the privisos I have made in the former, as well as this present impression, and which, if not overlooked, must prevent all rational censure, and obviate several objections that otherwise might be made against me. I have laid down as maxims never to be departed from, that the poor should be kept strictly to work, and that it was prudence to relieve their wants, but folly to cure them; that agriculture f and sishery should be promoted in all their branches, in order to render provisions, and consequently labour cheap. I have named ignorance as a necessary ingredient in the mixture of society: from all which it is manifest that I could never have imagined, that luxury was to be made general through every part of a kingdom. I have likewise required § that property should be well secured, justice impartially administred, and'in everything the interest of the nation taken care of: but what I have insisted on the most, and repeated more than once, is the great regard that is to be had to the balance of trade, and the care the legislature ought to take, that the yearly j imports never exceed the exports; and "where this is observed, and the other things I spoke of are not neglected, I still continue to assert that no foreign luxury can undo a country: the height of it is never seen but in nations that are vastly populous, and there only in the upper part of it, and the greater, that is, the larger still in proportion must be the lowest, the basis that supports all, the multitude of working poor.

Those who would too nearly imitate others of superior fortune, must thank themselves if they are ruined. This is nothing against luxury; for whoever can subsist, and lives above his income is a fool. Some persons of quality may keep three or four coaches and six, and at the fame time lay up Kney for their children: while a young shopkeeper is un

P. 212, 213. First Edit. 175, 176. t P. 215. First Edit. 178. t P. 106. First Edit. 77. $ P. 116. First Fdit. 87.) P. 115, 116. First Edit. 86, 87.

done for keeping one sorry horse. It is impossible there should be a rich nation without prodigals, yet I never knew a city so full of spendthrifts, but there were covetous people enough to answer their number. As an old merchant breaks for having been extravagant or careless a great while, so a young beginner falling into the fame business, gets an estate by being saving or more industrious before he is forty years old: besides, that the frailties of men often work by contraries: some narrow souls can never thrive because they are too stingy, while longer heads amass great wealth by spending their money freely, and seeming to despise it. But the vicissitudes of fortune are necessary, and the most lamentable are no more detrimental to society, than the death of the individual members of it. Christenings are a proper balance to burials. Those who immediately lose by the misfortunes of others, are very sorry, complain, and make a noise; but the others who get by them, as there always are such, hold their tongues, because it is

odious to be thought the better for the losses and calamities of our neighbour. The various ups and downs compose a wheel, that always turning round, gives motion to the whole machine. Philosophers, that dare extend their thoughts beyond the narrow compass of what is immediately before them, look on the alternate changes in the civil society, no otherwise than they do on the risings and fallings of the lungs; the latter of which are much a part of respiration in the most perfect animals as the sirst; so that the sickle breath of never-stable fortune is to the body politic, the fame as floating air is to a living creature.

Avarice then, and prodigality, are equally necessary to the society. That in some countries, men are most generally lavish than in others, proceeds from the difference in circumstances that dispose to either vice, and arise from the condition of the social body, as well as the temperament of the natural. 1 beg pardon of the. attentive reader, if here, in behalf of short memories, I repeat some things, the substance of which they have already seen in Remark, line 307. More money than land, heavy taxes and scarcity of provisions, industry, laboriousness, an active and stirring spirit, ill-nature, and saturnine temper; old age, wisdom, trade, riches, acquired by our own labour, and liberty and property well secured, are all things that dispose to avarice. On the contrary, indolence, content, good-nature, a jovial temper, youth, folly, arbitrary power, money easily got, plenty of provisions and the uncertainty of possessions, are circumstances that render men prone to prodigality: where there is the most of the sirst, the prevailing vice will be avarice, and prodigality where the other turns the scale; but a national frugality there never was nor never will be without a national necessitySumptuary laws, may be of'use to an indigent country, aster great calamities of war, pestilence, or famine, when work has stood still, and the labour of the poor been interrupted; but to introduce them into an opulent kingdom, is the wrong way to consult the interest of it. I shall end my remarks on the Grumbling-Hive, with assuring

the champions of national frugality, that it would be impossible for the Perlians and other eastern people, to purchase the vast quantities of sine English cloth they consume, mould we load our women with less cargoes of Asiatic silks.

ESSAY ON CHARITY, AKQ CHARITY-SCHOOLS.

Vharity, is that virtue by which part of that sincere love we have for ourselves, is transferred pure and unmixed to others, not tied to us by the bonds of friendship or consanguinity, and even mere strangers, whom we have no obligation to, nor hope or expect any thing from. If we lessen any ways the rigour of this desinition, part of the virtue must be lost. What we do for our friends and kindred, we do partly for ourselves: when a man acts in behalf of nephews or neices, and fays they are my brother's children, I do it out of charity; he deceives you: for if he is capable, it is expected from him, and he does it partly for his own fake: if he values the esteem of the world, and is nice as to honour and reputation, he is obliged to have a greater regard to them than for strangers, or else he must suffer in his character.

The exercise of this virtue, relates either to opinion, or to action, and is manifested in what we think of others, or what we do for them. To be charitable, then, in the sirst place, we ought to put the best construction on all that others do or fay, that things are capable of. If a man builds a sine house, though he has not one symptom of humility, furnishes it richly, and lays out a good estate in plate and pictures, we ought not to think that he does it out of vanity, but to encourage artists, employ hands, and set the poor to work for the good of his country: and if a man steeps at church, so he does not snore, we ought to think he shuts his eyes to increase his attention. The reason is, because in our turn we desire that our utmost avarice mould pass for frugality; and that for religion, which we know to be hypocrisy. Secondly, that virtue is conspicuous in us, when we bestow our time and labour for nothing, or employ our credit with others, in behalf of those who stand in need of it, and yet could not expect such an assistance from our friendship or nearness of blood. The last branch of charity consists in giving away (while we are alive) what we value ourselves, to such as I have already named; being contented rather to have and enjoy less, than not relieve those who want, and shall be the objects of our choice.

This virtue is often counterfeited by a passion of ours, called Pity orCompassion, whichconsists in a fellow-feeling and condolence for the misfortunes and calamities of others: all mankind are more or less affected with it; but the weakest minds generally the most. It is raised in us, when the sufferings and misery of other creatures make so forcible an impression upon us, as to make us uneasy. It comes in either at the eye, or ear, or both; and the nearer and more violently the object of compassion strikes those senses, the greater disturbance it causes in us, often to such a degree, as to occasion great pain and anxiety.

Should any of us be locked up in a ground-room, where in a yard joining to it, there was a thriving good humoured child at play, of two or three years old, so near us that through the grates of the window we could almost touch it with our hand; and if while we took delight in the harmless diverlion, and imperfect prittle-prattle of the innocent babe, a nasty overgrown sow mould come in upon the child, set it a screaming, and frighten it out of its wits; it is natural to think, that this would make us uneasy, and that with crying out, and making all the menacing noise we could, we should endeavour to drive the sow away. But if this ssiould happen to be an half-starved creature, that, mad with hunger, went roaming about in quest of food, and we should behold the ravenous brute, in spite of our cries, and all the threatening gestures we could think of, actually lay hold of the helpless infant, destroy and devour it; to fee her widely open her destructive jaws, and the poor lamb beat down with greedy haste; to look on the defenceless posture of tender limbs sirst trampled on, then

tore asunder; to see the stithy snout digging in the yet living entrails, fuck up the smoking blood, and now and then to hear the crackling of the bones, and the cruel animal with savage pleasure grunt over the horrid banquet; to hear and see all this, what tortures would it give the soul beyond expression! let me fee the most shining virtue the moralists have to boast of, so manifest either to the person possessed of it, or those who behold his actions: let me fee courage, or the love of ones country so apparent without any mixture, cleared and distinct, the sirst from pride and anger, the other from the love of glory, and every sliadow of self-interest, as this pity would be cleared and distinct from all other passions. There would be no need of virtue or self-denial to be moved at such a scene; and not only a man of humanity, of good morals and commiseration, but likewise an highwayman, an housebreaker, or a murderer could feel anxieties on such an occasion; how calamitious soever a man's circumstances might be, he would forget his misfortunes for the time, and the most troublesome passion would give way to pity, and not one of the species has a heart so obdurate or engaged, that it would not ache at such a sight, as no language has an epithet to sit it.

Many will wonder at what I have laid of pity, that it comes in at the eye or ear, but the truth of this will be known when we consider that the nearer the object is, the more we suffer, and the more remote it is, the less we are troubled with it. To fee people executed for crimes, if it is a great way off, moves us but little, in comparison to what it does when we are near enough to fee the motion of the soul in their eyes, observe their fears and agonies, and are able to read the pangs in every feature of the face. When the object is quite removed from our fenses, the relation of the calamities or the reading of them, can never raise in us the passion called pity. We may be concerned at bad news, the loss and misfortunes of friends and those whose cause we espouse, but this is not pity, but grief or sorrow; the same as we feel for the death of those we love, or the de-

struction of what we value.

When we hear that three or four thousand men, all strangers to us, are killed with the sword, or forced into some river where they are drowned, we say, and perhaps believe, that we pity them. It is humanity bids us have compassion with the sufferings of others; and reason tells us, that whether a thing be far off or done in our sight, our sentiments concerning it ought to be the fame, and we should be ashamed to own, that we felt no commiseration in us when any thing requires it. He is a cruel man, he has no bowels of companion; all these things are the estects of reason and humanity, but nature makes no compliments; when the object does not strike, the body does not feel it; and when men talk of pitying people out ot sight, they are to be believed in the fame manner as when they fay, that they are our humble servants. In paying the usual civilities at sirst meeting, those who do not see one another every day, are often very glad and very sorry alternately, for sive or six times together, in less than two minutes, and yet at parting carry away not a jot more of grief or joy than they met with. The fame it is with pity, and it is a choice no more than fear or anger. Those who have a strong and lively imagination, and can make representations of things in their minds, as they would be if they were actually before them, may work themselves up into something that resembles compassion; but this is done.by art, and often the help of a little enthusiasm, and is only an imitation of pity; the heart feels little of it, and it is as faint as what we suffer at the acting of a tragedy; where our judgment leaves part of the mind uninformed, and to indulge a lazy wantonness, suffers it to be led into an error, which is necessary to have a passion raised, the slight strokes of which are not unpleasant to us, when the foul is in an idle unactive humour.

As pity is often by ourselves and in our own cafes mistaken for charity, so it assumes the shape, and borrows the very name of it; a beggar alks you to exert that virtue for Jesus Christ's fake, but all the while his great design is to raise your pity. He represents to your view the sirst side of his ailments and bodily insirmities; in chosen words he gives you an epitome of his calamities, real or sictitious; and while he seems to pray God that he will open your heart, he is actually at work upon your ears; the greatest profligate of them flies to religion for aid, and assists liis cant with a doleful tone, and a studied dismality of gestures: but he trusts not to one passion only, he flatters your pride with titles and names of honour and distinction; your avarice he sooths with often repeating to you the smallness of the gift he sues for, and conditional promises of future returns, with an interest extravagant beyond the statute of usury, though out of the reach of it. People not used to great cities, being thus attacked on all sides, are commonly forced to yield, and cannot help giving something though they can hardly spare it themselves. How oddly are we managed by self-love! It is ever watching in our defence, and yet, to sooth a predominant passion, obliges us to act against our interest: for when pity seizes us, if we can but imagine, that we contribute to the relief of him we have "compassion with, and are instrumental to the lessening of his sorrows, it eases us, and therefore pitiful people often give an alms, when they really seel that they would rather not.

When sores are very bare, or seem otherwise afflicting in au extraordinary manner, and the beggar can bear to have them exposed to the cold air, it is very (hocking to some people; it is a shame, they cry, such sights should be susfered; the main reason is, it touches their pity feelingly, and at the fame time they are resolved, either because they are covetous, or count it an idle expence, to give nothing, which makes them more uneasy. They turn their eyes, and where the cries are dismal, some would willingly stop their ears if they were not ashamed, What they can do is to mend their pace, and be very angry in their hearts that beggars should be about the streets. But it is with pity as it is with fear, the more we are conversant with objects that excite either passion, the

less we are disturbed by them, and those to whom all these scenes and tones are by custom made familiar, they make little impression upon. The only thing the industrious beggar has left to conquer those fortisied hearts, if he can walk either with or without crutches, is to follow close, and with uninterrupted noise teaze and importune them, to try if he can make them buy their peace. Thus thousands give money to beggars from the fame motive as they pay their corn-cutter, to walk easy. And many a halfpenny is given to impudent and designedly persecuting rascals, whom, if it could be done handsomely, a man would cane with much greater satisfaction. Yet all this, by the courtesy of the country, is called charity.

The reverse of pity is malice: I have spoke of it where I treat of envy. Those who know what it is to examine themselves, will soon own that it is very dissicult to trace the root andorigin of this passion. It is one of those we are most ashamed of, and therefore the hurtful part of it is easily subdued and corrected by a judicious education. When any body near us stumbles, it is natural even before reslection, to stretch out our hands to hinder, or at least break the fall, which shows that while we are calm we are rather bent to pity. But though malice by itself is little to be feared, yet assisted with pride it is often mischievous, and becomes most terrible when egged on and heightened by anger. There is nothing that more readily or more effectually extinguishes pity than this mixture, which is called cruelty: from whence we may learn, that to perform a meritorious action, it is not sussicient barely to conquer a passion, unless it likewise be done from a laudable principle, and consequently how necessary that clause was in the desinition of virtue, that our endeavours were to proceed from a rational ambition of being good.

Pity, as I have said somewhere else, is the most amiable of all our passions, and there are not many occasions, on which we ought to conquer or curb it. A surgeon may be as compassionate as he pleases, so it does not make him omit

or forbear to perform what he ought to do. Judges likewise, and juries, may be influenced with pity, if they take care that plain laws and justice itself are not infringed, and do not suffer by it. No pity does more mischief in the world, than what is excited by the tenderness of parents, and hinders them from managing their children, as their rational love to them would require, and themselves could wish it. The sway likewise which this passion bears in the asfections of women, is more considerable than is commonly imagined, and they daily commit faults that are altogether ascribed to lust, and yet are in a great measure owing to pity.

What 1 named last is not the only passion that mocks and resembles charity; pride and vanity have built more hospitals than all the virtues together. Men are so tenacious of their possessions, and selsishness is so riveted in our nature, that whoever can but any ways conquer it shall have the applaule of the public, and all the encouragement imaginable to conceal his frailty, and sooth any other appetite he shall have a mind to indulge. The man that supplies, with his private fortune, what the whole must otherwise have provided for, obliges every member of the society, and, therefore, all the world are ready to pay him their acknowledgement, and think themselves in duty bound to pronounce all such actions virtuous, without examining, or so much as looking into the motives from which they were performed. Nothing is more destructive to virtue or religion itself, than to make men believe, that giving money to the poor, though they laould not part with it till after death, will make a full atonement in the next world, for the sins they have committed in this. A villain, who has been guilty of a barbarous murder, may, by the help of false witnesses, escape the punishmcnt he deserved: he prospers, we will fay, heaps up great wealth, and, by the advice of his father confessor, leaves all his estate to a monastery, and his children beggars. What sine amends has this good Christian made for his crime, and what an honest man was the priest who directed his conscience? He who parts with all he has in his lise-time, whateyer principle he

"7 ' acts from, only gives away what was his own; but the rich miser who refuses to assist his nearest relations while he is alive, though they never designedly disobliged him, and disposes of his money, for what we call charitable uses, after his death, may imagine of his goodness what he pleases, but lie robs his posterity. I am now thinking of a late instance of charity, a prodigious gift, that has made a great noise in the world: I have a mind to set it in the light 1 think it deserves, and beg leave, for once, to please pedants, to treat it somewhat rhetorically.

That a man, with small skill in physic, and hardly any learning, should, by vile arts, get into practice, and lay up great wealth, is no mighty wonder; but, that he should so deeply work himself into the good opinion of the world as to gain the general esteem of a nation, and establish a reputation beyond all his contemporaries, with no other qualities but a perfect knowledge of mankind, and a capacity of making the most of it, is something extraordinary. If a man arrived to such a height of glory should be almost distracted with pride, sometime give his attendance on a servant or any mean person for nothing, and, at the same time, neglect a nobleman that gives exorbitant fees, at other times refuse to leave his bottle for his business, without any regard to the quality of the persons that sent for him, or the. danger they are in: if he should be surly and morose, affect to be an humourist, treat his patients like dogs, though people of distinction, and value no man but what would deify him, and never call in question the certainty of his oracles: if he should insult all the world, asfront the sirst nobility, and extend his insolence even to the royal family: if, to maintain as well as to increase the fame of his sussiciency, he lhould scorn to consult with his betters on what emergency soever, look down with contempt on the most deserving of his prosellion, and never confer with any other physician but what will pay homage to his

superior genius, creep to his humour, and never approach him but with all the slavish obsequiousness a court-slatterer can treat a prince with: Isa man, in his lifetime, should discover, on the one hand, such manifest symptoms of superlative pride, and an insatiable greediness after wealth at the fame time, and, on the other, no regard to religion or affection to his kindred, no compassion to the poor, and hardly any humanity to his fellow-creaturps, if he gave no proofs that he loved his

M country, had a public spirit, or was a lover of arts, of books, or of literature, what must we judge of his motive, the principle he acted from, when, after his death, we sind that he has left a trifle among his relations who stood in need of it, and an immense treasure to an university that did not want it. "i

Let a man be as charitable as it is possible for him to be without forfeiting his reason or good sense: can he think otherwise, but that this famous physician did, in the making of his will, as in every thing else, indulge his darling pallion, entertaining his vanity with the happiness of the contrivance? when he thought on the monuments and. inscriptions, with all the sacrisices of praise that would be made to him, and, above all, the yearly tribute of thanks, of reverence, and veneration that would be paid. to his memory, with so much pomp and solemnity; when he considered, how in all these performances, wit and invention would be racked, art and eloquence ransacked to sind out encomiums suitable to the public spirit, the munisicence and the dignity of the benefactor, and the artful gratitude of the receivers; when he thought on, 1 fay, and considered these things, it must have thrown his ambitious foul into vast ecstasies of pleasure, especially when he ruminated on the duration of his glory, and the perpetuity he would by this means procure to his name. Charitable opinions are often stupidly false; when men are dead and gone, we ought to judge of their actions, as we do of books, and neither wrong their understanding nor our own. The British Æsculapius was undeniably a man of fense, and if he had been in-

fluenced by chanty, a public spirit, or the love of learning, and had aimed at the good ol mankind in general, or that of his own profession in particular, and acted from any of these principles, he could neer have made such a will; because so much wealth might have been better managed, and a man of much less capacity would have found out several better ways of laying out the money. But if we consider, that he was as undeniably a man of vast pride, as he was a man offense, and give ourselves leave only to surmise, that this extraordinary gift might have proceeded from such a motive, we shall presently discover the excelller.cy of his parts, and his consummate knowledge of the world: for, if a man would render himself immortal, be ever praised and deisied after his death, and have all the acknowledgement, the honours, and compliments paid to his memory, that vain glory herself could wilh for, I do not think it in human skill to invent a more effectual method. Had he followed arms, behaved himself in sive-and-twenty sieges, and as many battles, with the bravery of an Alexander, and exposed his life and limbs to all the fatigues and dangers of war for sifty campaigns together; or devoting himself to the muses, sacrisiced his pleasure, his rest, and his health to literature, and spent all his days in a laborious study, and the toils of learning; or else, abandoning all worldly interest, excelled in probity, temperance, and austerity of life, and ever trod in the strictest path of virtue, he would not so effectully have provided for the eternity of his name, as after a voluptuous life, and the luxurious gratisication of his passions, he has now done without any trouble or self-denial, only by the choice in the disposal of his money, when he was forced to leave it.

A rich miser, who is thoroughly selsish, and would receive the interest of his money, even after his death, has nothing else to do than to defraud his relations, and leave his estate to some famous university; they are the best markets to buy immortality at with little merit: in them knowledge, wit, and penetration are the growth, I had almost said the manufacture of the place: there men are profoundly stalled in human nature, and know what it is their benefactors want; and their extraordinary bounties shall always meet with an extraordinary recompence, and the measure of the gift is ever the standard of their praises, whether the donor be a physician or a tinker, when once the living witnesses that might laugh at them are extinct. I can never think on the anniversary of the thanksgiving-day decreed to a great man, but it puts me in mind of the miraculous cures, and other surprising things that will be said of him a hundred years hence; and I dare prognosticate, that before the end of the present century, he will have stories forged in his favour (for rhetoricians are never upon oath) that mall be as fabulous, at least, as any legends of the saints.

Of all this our subtle benefactor was not itrnorant; he tinderstood universities, their genius, and their politics, and from thence foresaw and knew, that the incense to be offered to him would not cease with the present or few succeeding generations, and that it would not only for the trifling space of three or four hundred years, but that it would continue to be paid to him through all changes and revolutions of government and religion, as long as the nation subsists, and the island itself remains.

It is deplorable that the proud should have such temptations to wrong their lawful heirs: For when a man in ease and affluence, brim-full of vain glory, and humoured in his pride by the greatest of a polite nation, has such an infallible security in petto for an everlasting homage and adoration to his manes to be paid in such an extraordinary manner, he is like a hero in battle, who, in feasting of his own imagination, tastes all the felicity of enthusiasm. It buys him up in sickness, relieves him in pain, and either guards him against, or keeps from his view all the terrors of death, and the most dismal apprehensions of futurity.

Should it be said, that to be thus censorious, and look into matters, andmensconsciences with that nicety, will discourage people from laying out their

money this way; and that, let the money and the motive of the donor be what they wist, he that receives the benesit is the gainer, I would not disown the charge, but am of opinion, that this is no injury to the public, should one prevent men from crowding too much treasure into the dead stock of the kingdom. There ought to be a vast disproportion between the active and unactive part of the society to make it happy, and where this is not regarded, the multitude of gifts and endowments may soon be excessive and detrimental to a nation Charity, where it is too extensive, seldom fails of promoting sloth and idleness, and is good for little in-the commonwealth but to breed drones, and destroy industry. The more colleges "and aimhouses you build, the more you may. The sirst founders and benefactors may have just and good intentions, and would perhaps, for their own reputations, seem to labour for the most laudable purposes, but the executors of those wills, the governors that come after him, have quite other views, and we seldom see charities long applied as it was sirst intended they should be.-1 have no design that is cruel, nor the least aim that savours of inhumanity. To have sussicient hospitals for sick and wounded, I look upon as an indispensible duty both in peace and war: Young children without parents, old age without support, and all that are disabled from working, ought to be taken care of with tenderness and alacrity. But as, on the one hand, I would have none neglected that are helpless, and really necessitous without being wanting to themselves, so, on the other, I would not encourage beggary or laziness in the poor: All should be set to work that are anywise able, and scrutinies should be made even among the insirm: Employments might be found out for most of our lame, and many that are unsit for hard labour, as well as the blind, as long as their health and strength would allow of it. What I have now under consideration leads me naturally to that kind of distraction the nation has laboured under for some time, the enthusiastic passion for Charity-Schools.

The generality are so bewitched with the usefulness and excellency of them, that whoever dares openly oppose them is in danger of being stoned by the rabble. Children that are taught the principles of religion, and can read the word of God, have a greater opportunity to improve in virtue and good morality, and must certainly be more civilized than others, that are susfered to run at random, and have nobody to look after them. How perverse must be the judgment of those, who would not rather see children decently dressed, with clean linen at least once a-week, that, in an orderly manner, follow their master to church, than in every open place, meet with a company of blackguards without shirts or any thing whole about them, that, insensible of their misery, are continually increasing it with oaths and imprecations 1 Can any one doubt but these are the great nursery of thieves and pickpockets? What numbers of felons, and other criminals, have we tried and convicted every sessions 1 This will be prevented by charity-schools; and when the childern of the poor receive a better education, the society will, in a few years, reap the benesit of it, and the nation be cleared of so many miscreants, as now this great city, and all the country about it, are silled with.

This is the general cry, and he that speaks the least word against it, an uncharitable, hard-hearted and inhuman, if not a wicked, profane, and atheistical wretch. As to the comeliness of the light, nobody disputes it; but I would not have a nation pay too dear for so transient a pleasure; and if we might set aside the sinery of the siiow, every thing that is material in this popular oration might soon be answered.

As to religion, the most knowing and polite part of a nation have every where the least of it; craft has a greater hand in making rogues than stupidity, and vice, in general, is nowhere more predominant than where arts,and »ciences flourisli. Ignorance is, to a proverb, counted to be the mother of devotion; and it is certain, that we shall sind innocence and honesty nowhere more general than among the most illiterate, the poor silly country people. The next to be considered, are the manners and civility that by charityschools are to be grafted into the poor of the nation. I confess that, in my opinion, to be in any degree possessed of what I named, is a frivolous, if not a hurtful quality, at least nothing is less requisite in the laborious poor. It is not compliments we want of them, but their work and assiduity. But I give up this article with all my heart; good manners we will fay are necessary to all people, but which way will they be furnished with them in a charity-school? Boys there may be taught to pull off their caps promiscuously to all they meet, unless it be a beggar: But that they should acquire in it any civility beyond that I cannot conceive.

The master is not greatly qualisied, as may be guessed by his salary, and if he could teach them manners he has not time for it: while they are at school they are either learning or saying their lesson to him, or employed in writing or arithmetic; and as soon as school is done, they are as much at liberty as other poor people's children. It is precept, and the example of parents, and those they eat, drink and converse with, that have an influence upon the minds of children: reprobate parents that take ill courses, and are regardless to their children, will not have a mannerly civilized offspring though they went to a charity-school till they were married. The honest painstaking people, be they never so poor, if they have any notion of goodness and decency themselves, will keep their children in awe, and never suffer them to rake about the streets, and lie out a-nights. Those who will work themselves, and have any command over their children, will make them do something or other that turns to prosit as soon as they are able, be it never so little; and such are so ungovernable, that neither words nor blows can work upon them, no charity-school will mend; nay, experience teaches us, that among the charity-boys there are abundance of bad ones that swear and curse about, and, bar the clothes, are as much blackguard as ever Tower-hill or St. James's produced.

I. am now come to the enormous crimes, and vast multitude of malefactors, that are all laid upon the want of this notable education. That abundance of thefts and robberies are daily committed in and about the city, and great numbers yearly fuller death for those crimes is undeniable: but because this is ever hooked in, when the usefulness of charity-sdhools is called in question, as if there was no dispute, but they would in a great measure remedy, and in time prevent those disorders; 1 intend to examine into the real causes of those mischiefs so justly complained of, and doubt not but to make it appear that charity-schools, and every thing else that promotes idleness, and keeps the poor from working, are more accessary to the growth of villany, than the want of reading and writing, or even the grossest ignorance and stupidity.

Here I must interrupt myself to obviate the clamours of some impatient people, who, upon reading of what I said last, will cry out, that far from encouraging idleness, they bring up their charity-children to handicrafts, as well as trades, and all manner of honest labour. I promise them that I shall take notice of that hereafter, and answer it without stifling the least thing that can be said in their behalf.

In a populous city, it is not dissicult for a young rascal, that has pushed himself into a crowd, with a small hand and nimble singers, to whip avay a handkerchief or snuff-box, from a man who is thinking on business, and regardless of his pocket. Success in small crimes seldom fails of ushering in greater; and he that picks pockets with impunity at twelve, is likely to be a house-breaker at sixteen, and a thoroughpaced villain long before he is twenty. Those who are cautious as well as bold, and no drunkards, may do a world of mischief before they are discovered: and this is one of the greatest inconveniencies of such vast overgrown cities, as London or Paris; that they harbour rogues and villains as granaries do vermin; they asford a perpetual shelter to the worst of people, and'are places of safety to thousands of criminals, who daily commit

thefts and burglaries, and yet, by often changing their places of abode, may conceal themselves for many years, and will perhaps for ever escape the hnnds of justice, unless by chance they are apprehended in a fact. And when they are taken, the evidences perhaps wants clearness, or are otherwise insussicient; the depositions are not strong enough; juries and often judges are touched with compassion; prosecutors though vigorous at sirst, often relent before the time of trial comes" on: few men prefer the public safety to their own ease; a man of good-nature is not easily reconciled with taking away of another man's life, though he has deserved the gallows. To be the cause of anv ones death, though justice requires it, is what most people is startled at, especially men of conscience and probity, When they want judgment or resolution: as this is the reason that thousands escape that deserve to be capitally punished, sb it is likewise the cause that there are so many offenders, who boldly venture, in hopes that if they are taken they shall have the same good fortune of getting off.

But if men did imagine, and were fully persuaded, that as surely as they committed a fact that deserved hanging, so surely they would be hanged; executions would be very rare, and the most desperate felon would almost as soon hang himself as he would break open a house. To be stupid and ignorant is seldom the character of a thief. Robberies on the highway, and other bold crimes, are generally perpetrated by rogues of spirit, and a genius; and villains of any fame are commonly subtle cunning fellows, that are well versed in the method of trials, and acquainted with every quirk in the law that can be of use to them; that overlook not the smallest flaw in an indictment, and know how to make an advantage of the least flip of an evidence, and every thing else, that can serve their turn to bring them off.

It is a mighty saying, that it is better that sive hundred guilty people should escape, than that one innocent person should suiter: this maxim is only true as to futurity, and in relation to another world; but it is very false in regard to the temporal welfare of society. It is a terrible thing a man should be put to death for a crime he is not guilty of; yet so oddly circumstances may meet in the insinite variety of accidents, that it is possible it should come to pass, all the wisdom that judges, and consciousness that juries may be possessed of, notwithstanding. But where men endeavour to avoid this, with all the care and precaution human prudence is able to take, should such a misfortune happen perhaps once or twice in half a score years, on condition that all that time justice sliould be administred with all the strictness and severity, and not one guilty person suffered to escape with impunity, it would be a vast advantage to a nation, not only as to the securing of every ones property, and the peace of the society in general, but would likewise save the lives of hundreds, it not thousands, of necessitous wretches, that are daily hanged for trifles, and who would never have attempted any thing against the law, or at least have ventured on capital crimes, if the hopes of getting off, should they be taken, had not been one of the motives that animated their resolution. Therefore where the laws are plain and severe, all the remissnel) in the execution of them, lenity of juries, and frequency of pardons, are in the main a much greater cruelty to a populous state or kingdom, than the use of racks and the most exquisite torments.

Another great cause of those evils, is to be looked for in the want of precaution in those that are robbed, and the many temptations that are given. Abundance of families are very remiss in looking after the safety of their houses; some are robbed by the carelessness of servants, others for having grudged the price of bars and shutters. Brass and pewter are ready money, they are every where about the house; plate perhaps and money are better secured; but an ordinary lock is soon opened, when once a rogue is got in.

It is manifest, then, that many different causes concur, and several scarce avoidable evils contribute to the misfortune of being pestered with pilferers,

thieves, and robbers, which all countries ever were, and ever will be, more or less, in and near considerable towns, more especially vast and overgrown cities. It is opportunity makes the thief; carelessness and neglect in fastening doors and windows, the excessive tenderness of juries and prosecutors, the small dissiculty of getting a reprieve and frequency of pardons; but above all, the many examples of those who are known to be guilty, are destitute both of friends and money, and yet by imposing on the jury, baffling the witnesses, or other tricks and stratagems, sind out means to escape the gallows. These are all strong temptations that conspire to draw in the necessitous, who want principle and education.

To these you may add as auxiliaries to mischief, an habit of floth and idleness, and strong aversion to labour and assiduity, which all young people, will contract that are not brought up to downright working, or at least kept employed most days in the week, and the greatest part of the day. All children that are idle, even the best of either sex, are bad company to one another whenever they meet.

It is not, then, the want of reading and writing, but the concurrence and complication of more substantial evils, that are the perpetual nursery of abandoned profligates in great and opulent nations; and whoever would accuse ignorance, stupidity, and dastardness, as the sirst, and what the physicians call the procataric cause, let him examine into the lives, and narrowly inspect the conversations and actions of ordinary rogues and our common felons, and he will sind the reverse to be true, and that the blame ought rather to be laid on the excessive cunning and subtlety, and too much knowledge in general, which the worst of miscreants and the scum of the nation are possessed of.

Human nature is every where the fame: genius, wit, and natural parts, are always sharpened by application, and may be as much improved in the practice of the meanest villany, as they can in the exercise of industry, or the most heroic virtue. There is no station of life,

where pride, emulation, and the love of glory may not be displayed. A young pickpocket, that makes a jest of his angry prosecutor, and dextrousty wheedles the old justice into an opinion of his innocence, is envied by his equals, and admired by all the fraternity. Rogues have the fame passions to gratify as other men, and value themselves on their honour and faithfulness to one another, their courage, intrepidity, and other manly virtues, as well as people of better professions; and in daring enterprises, the resolution of a robber may be as much supported by his pride, as that of an honest soldier, who sights for his country.

The evils then we complain of, are owing to quite other causes than what we assign for them. Men must be very wavering in their sentiments, if not inconsistent with themselves, that at one time will uphold knowledge and learning to be the most proper means to promote religion, and defend at another, that ignorance is the mother of devotion.

But if the reasons alleged for this general education are not the true ones, whence comes it, that the whole kingdom, both great and small, are so unanimously fond of it? There is no miraculous conversion to be perceived among us, no iniverial bent to goodness and morality that has on a sudden overspread the island; there is as much wickedness as ever, charity is as cold, and real virtue as scarce: the year seventeen hundred and twenty, has been as prolisic in deep villany, and remarkable for selsisli crimes and premeditated mischief, as can be picked out of any century whatever; not committed by poor ignorant rogues, that could neither read nor write, but the better fort of people as to wealth and education, that most of them were great masters in arithmetic, and lived in reputation and splendor. To say, that when a thing is once in vogue, the multitude follows the common cry, that charity schools are in fashion in the same manner as hooped petticoats, by caprice, and that no more reason can be given for the one than the other, I am afraid will not be satisfactory to the curious, and at the fame time 1 doubt much, whether it will be thought of great weight by many of my readers, what I can advance besides.

The real source of this present folly, is certainly very abstruse and remote from sight; but he that asfords the least: light in matters of great obscurity, does a kind ossice to the inquirers. I am willing to allow, that in the beginning, the sirst design of those schools, was good and charitable; but to know what increases them so extravagantly, and who are the chief promoters of them now, we must make our search another way, and address ourselves to the rigid partymen, that are zealous for their cause, either episcopacy or presbytery; but as the latter are but the poor mimicks of the sirst, though equally pernicious, we shall consine ourselves to the national church, and take a turn through a parish that is not blessed yet with a charity school But here I think myself obliged in conscience to ask pardon of my reader, for the tiresome dance I am going to lead him, if he intends to follow me, and therefore I desire, that he would either throw away the book and leave me, or else arm himself with the patience of Job, to endure all the impertinences of low life; the cant and tittle-tattle he is like to meet with before he can go half a street's length.

First we must look out among the young shop-keepers, that have not half the business they could wish for, and consequently time to spare. If such a new-beginner has but a little pride more than ordinary, and loves to be meddling, he is soon mortisied in the vestry, where men of substance and long standing, or else your pert litigious oropinionated-bawlers, that have obtained the title of notable men, commonly bear the sway. His stock and perhaps credit are but inconsiderable, and yet he sinds within himself a strong inclination to govern. A man thus qualised, thinks it a thousand pities there is no charity-school in the parish: he communicates his thoughts to two or three of his acquaintance sirst; they do the fame to others, and in a month's time there is nothing else talked of in the parish. Every body

invents discourses and arguments to the purpose, according to his abilities.—It is an arrant shame, says one, to see so many poor that are not able to educate their children, and no provision made for them, where we have so many rich people. What do you talk of rich, answers another, they are the worst: they must have so many servants, coaches and horses: they can lay out hundreds, and some of them thousands of pounds for jewels and furniture, but not spare a shilling to a poor creature that wants it: when modes and fashions are discoursed of, they can hearken with great attention, but are wilfully deaf to the cries of the poor. Indeed, neighbour, replies the sirst, you are very right, I do not believe there is a worse parish in England for charity than ours: It is such as you and I that would do good if it was in our power, but of those that are able there is very few that are willing.

Others more violent, soil upon particular persons, and fasten slander on every man of substance they dislike, and a thousand idle stories in behalf of charity, are raised and handed about to defame their betters. While this is doing throughout the neighbourhood, he that sirst broached the pious thought, rejoices to hear so many come into it, and places no small merit in being the sirst cause of so much talk and bustle: but neither himself nor his intimates, being considerable enough to set such a thing on foot, some body must be found out who has greater interest: he is to be addressed to, and showed the necessity, the goodness, the usefulness, and Christianity of such a design: next he is to be flattered.—Indeed, Sir, if you would espouse it, nobody has a greater influence over the best of the parish than yourself: one word of you I am sure would engage such a one: if you once would take it to heart, Sir, I would look upon the thing as done, Sir.—If by this kind of rhetoric they can draw in some old fool, or conceited busy-body that is rich, or at least reputed to be such, the thing begins to be feasible, and is discoursed of among the better sort. The parson or his curate, and the lecturer, are every where extolling the pious pro-

ject. The sirst promoters meanwhile are indefatigable: if they were guilty of any open vice, they either sacrisice it to the love ot reputation, or at least grow more cautious and learn to play the hypocrite, well knowing that to be flagitious or noted for enormities, is inconsistent with the zeal which they pretend to, for works of supererogation and excessive piety.

The number of these diminutive patriots increasing, they form themselves into a society, and appoint stated meetings, where every one concealing his vices, has liberty to display his talents. Religion is the theme, or else the misery of the times occasioned by atheism and profaneness. Men of worth, who live in splendour, and thriving people that have a great deal of business of their own, are seldom seen among them. Men of sense and education likewise, if they have nothing to do, generally look out for better diversion. All those who have a higher aim, shall have their attendance easily excused, but contribute they must, or else lead a weary life in the parish Two sorts of people come in voluntarily, stanch churchmen, who have good reasons for it in petto, and your sly sinners that look upon it as meritorious, and hope that it will expiate their guilt, and Satan be nonsuited by it at a small expence Some come into it to save their credit, others to retrieve i according as they have either lost or are afraid of losing it: others again do it prudentially, to increase their trade and get acquaintance, and many would own to you, if they dared to be sincere and speak the truth, that they would never have been concerned in it, but to be better known in the parish. Men offense that see the folly of it, and have nobody to fear, are persuaded into it not to be thought singular, or to run counter to all the world; even those who are resolute at sirst in denying it, it is ten to one but at last they are teazed and imported into a compliance.. The charge being calculated for most of the inhabitants, the insignisicancy of it is another argument that prevails much, and many are drawn in to be contributors, who, without that, would have stood out and strenuously opposed the whole scheme.

The governors are made of the middling people, and many inferior to that class are made use of, if the forwardness of their zeal can but over-balance the meanness of their condition. If you mould alk these worthy rulers, why they take upon them so much trouble, to the detriment of their own affairs and loss of time, either singly or the whole body of them, they would all unanimously answer, that it is the regard they have for religion and the church, and the pleasure they take in contributing to the good, and eternal welfare of so many poor innocents, that in all probability would run into perdition, in these wicked times of scoffers and freethinkers. They have no thought of interest; even those who deal in and provide these children with what they want, have not the least design of getting by what they sell for their use; and though in every thing else, their avarice and greediness after lucre be glaringly conspicuous, in this affair they are wholly divested from selsishness, and have no worldly ends. One motive above all, which is none of the least with the most of them, is to be carefully concealed, I mean the satissaction there is in ordering and directing: there is a melodious found in the word governor, that is charming to mean people: every body admires sway and superiority; even *imperium in belluas* has its delights: there is a pleasure in ruling over any thing; and it is this chiefly that supports human nature in the tedious slavery of schoolmasters. But if there be the least satisfaction in governing the children, it must be ravishing to govern the schoolmaster himself. What sine things are said and perhaps wrote to a governor, when a school-master is to be chosen! How the praises tickle, and how pleasant it is not to sind out the fulsomeness of the flattery, the stisfness of the expreflions, or the pedantry of the stile!

Those who can examine nature, will always sind, that what these people most pretend to is the least, and what they utterly deny their greatest motive. No habit or quality is more easily acquired than hypocrisy, nor any thing

sooner learned than to deny the sentiments of our hearts, and the principle ve act from: but the feeds of every passion are innate to us, and nobody comes into the world without them. If we will mind the pastimes and recreations of young children, we shall observe nothing more general in them, than that all who are susfered to do it, take delight in playing with kittens and little puppy dogs. What makes them always lugging and pulling the poor creatures about the house, proceeds from nothing else but that they can do with them what they please, and put them into what posture and shape they list; and the pleasure they receive from this, is originally owing to the love of dominion, and that usurping temper all mankind are bom with.

When this great work is brought to bear, and actually accomplished, joy and serenity seem to overspread the face ot every inhabitant, which likewise to account for, I must make a short digression. There are every where slovenly sorry fellows, that are used to be seen always ragged and dirty: these people we look upon as miserable creatures in general, and unlets they are very remarkable, we take little notice or them, and yet among these there are handsome and wellshaped men, as well as among their betters. But if one 01 these turns soldier, what a vast alteration is there observed in him for the better, as soon as he is put in his red coat, and we fee him look smart with his grenadier's cap and a great ammunition sword! All who knew him before are struck with other ideas of his qualities, and the judgment which both men and women form of him in their minds, is very different from what it was. There is something analogous to this in the sight of charity children; there is a natural beauty in uniformity, which most people delight in. It is diverting to the eye to fee children well matched, either boys or girls, march two and two in good order; and to have them all whole and tight in the lame clothes and trimming, must add to the comeliness of the sight; and what makes it still more generally entertaining, is the imaginary share which even servants, and the meanest in the parish,

have in it, to whom it costs nothing: our parish church, our charity children. In all this there is a shadow of property that tickles every body, that has a right to make use of the words, but more especially those who actually contribute, and had a great hand in advancing the pious work.

It is hardly conceivable, that men should so little know their own hearts, and be so ignorant of their inward condition, as to mistake frailty, paflion, and enthusiasm, for goodness, virtue and charity; yet nothing is more true than that the satisfaction, the joy and transports they feel on the accounts I named, pass with these miserable judges for principles of piety and religion. Whoever will consider of what 1 have said for two or three pages, and suffer his imagination to rove a little further on what he has heard and seen concerning this subject, will be furnished with sufficient reason, abstract srom the love of God and true Christianity, why charity-schools are in such uncommon vogue, and so unanimously approved of and admired among all sorts and conditions of people. It is a theme which every body can talk of, and understands thoroughly; there is not a more inexhaustible fund for tittle-tattle, and a variety of low conversation in hoy-boats and stage-coaches. If a governor that in behalf of the school or the sermon, exerted himself more than ordinary, happens to be in company, how he is commended by the women, and his zeal and charitable disposition extolled to the skies! Upon my word, sir, fays an old lady, we are all very much obliged to you; I do not think any of the other governors could have made interest enough to procure us a bisliop; it was on your account, I am told, that his lordship came, though he was not very well: to which the other replies very gravely, that it is his duty, but that he values no trouble nor fatigue, so he can be but serviceable to the children, poor lambs: indeed, fays he, I was resolved to get a pair of lawn sleeves, though 1 rid all night for it, and I am very glad I was not disappointed.

Sometimes the school itself is discoursed of, and of whom. in all the parish it is most expedted he should build one: The old room where it is now kept is ready to drop down; such a one had a vast estate left him by his uncle, and a great deal of money besides; a thousand pounds would be nothing in his pocket.

At others, the great crowds are talked of that are seen at some churches, and the considerable sums that are gathered; from whence, by an easy transition, they go over to the abilities, the disferent talents and orthodoxy of clergymen. Dr. is a man of great parts and learning, and I believe he is very hearty for the church, but 1 do not like him for a charity sermon. There is no better man in the world than; he forces the money out of their pockets. When he preached last for our children, I am sure there was abundance of people that gave more than they intended when they came to church. I could fee it in their faces, and rejoiced at it heartily.

Another charm that renders charity-schools so bewitching to the multitude, is the general opinion established among them, that they are not only actually benesicial to society as to temporal happiness, but likewise that Christianity enjoys and requires of us, we should erect them for our future welfare. They are earnestly and fervently recommended by the whole body of the clergy, and have more labour and eloquence laid out upon them than any other Christian duty; not by young persons, or poor scholars of little credit, but the most learned of our prelates, and the most eminent for orthodoxy, even those who do not often fatigue themselves on any other occasion. As to religion, there is no doubt but they know what is. chiefly required of us, and consequently the most necessary to salvation: and as to the world, who should understand the interest of the kingdom better than the wisdom of the nation, of which the lords spiritual are so considerable a branch? The consequence of this sanction is, sirst, that those, who, with their purses or power, are instrumental to £he increase or maintenance of these schools, are tempted to place a greater merit in

what they do, than otherwise they could suppose it deserved. Secondly, that all the rest, who either cannot, or will not anywise contribute towards them, have still a very good reason why they should speak well or them; for though it be dissicult, in things that interfere with our passions, to act well, it is always in our power to wisli well, because it is performed with little cost. There is hardly a person so wicked among the superstitious vulgar, but in the liking he has for charity schools, he imagines to fee a glimmering hope that it will make an atonement for his sins, from the fame principle as the most vicious comfort themselves with the love and veneration they bear to the church; and the greatest profligates sind an opportunity in it to show the rectitude of their inclinations at no expence.

But if all these were not inducements sussicient to make men stand up in defence of the idol I speak of, there is another that will infallibly bribe most people to be advocates for it. We all naturally love triumph, and whoever engages in this course is sure of conquest, at least in nine companies out often. Let him dispute with whom he will, considering the speciousnefs of the pretence, and the majority he has on his side, it is a castle, an impregnable fortress he can never be beat out of; and was the most sober, virtuous man alive to produce all the arguments to prove the detriment charityschools, at least the multiplicity of them, do to society, which 1 shall give hereafter, and such as are yet stronger, against the greatest scoundrel in the world, who should only make use of the common cant of charity and religion, the vogue would be against the sirst, and himself lose his cause in the opinion of the vulgar.

The rise, then, and original of all the bustle and clamour that is made throughout the kingdom in behalf of charity schools, is chiefly built on frailty and human passion, at least it is more than poliible that a nation should have the fame fondness, and feel the fame zeal for them as are shown in ours, and yet not be prompted to it by any principle of virtue or religion. Encour-

aged by this conlideration, I shall, with the greater liberty, attack this vulgar error, and endeavour to make it evident, that far from being benesicial, this forced education is pernicious to the public, the welfare whereof, as it demands of us a regard superior to all other laws and considerations, so it shall be the only apology 1 intend to make for ditlenng from the present sentiments of the

N learned and reverend body of our divines, and venturing plainly to deny, what I have just now owned to be openly asserted by most of our bishops, as well as inferior clergy. As our church pretends to no insatiability even in spirituals, her proper province, so it cannot be an affront to her to imagine that me may err in temporals, which are not so much under her immediate care. But to my task.

The whole earth being cursed, and no bread to be had but what we eat in the sweat of our brows, vast toil must be undergone before man can provide himself with necessaries for his sustenance,.and the bare support of his corrupt and defective nature, as he is a single creature; but insinitely more to make life comfortable in a civil society, where men are become taught animals, and great numbers of them have, by mutual compact, framed themselves into a body politic; and the more man's knowledge increases in this state, the greater will be the variety of labour required to make him easy. It is impossible that a society can long subsist, and suffer many of its members to live in idleness, and enjoy all the ease and pleasure they can invent, without having, at the same time, great multitudes of people that to make good this defect will condescend to be quite the reverse, and by use and patience inure their bodies to work for others and themselves besides.

The plenty and cheapness of provisions depends, in a great measure, on the price and value that is set upon thi labour, and consequently the welfare of all societies, even before they are tainted with foreign luxury, requires,that it should be performed by such of their members as, in the sirst place, are sturdy and robust, and never used to ease or idleness; and, in the second, soon contented as to the necessaries of life; such as are glad to take up with the coarsest manufacture in every thing they wear,' and in their diet have no other aim than to feed their bodies when their stomachs prompt them to eat, and, with little regard to taste or relish, refuse no wholesome nourishment that can be swallowed when men are hungry, or ask any thing for their thirst but to quench it.

As the greatest part of the drudgery is to be done by daylight, so it is by this only that they actually measure the time of their labour without any thought of the hours they are employed, or the weariness they feel; and the hireling in the country mult get up in the morning, not because he has rested enough, but because the sun is going to rife. This last article alone would be an intolerable hardship to grown people under thirty, who, during nonage, had been used to Le a-bed as long as they could sleep: but all three together make up such a condition of life, as a man more mildly educated would hardly choose, though it should deliver him from a goal or a shrew.

If such people there must be, as no great nation can be happy without vast numbers of them, would not a wife legislature cultivate the breed of them with all imaginable care, and provide against their scarcity as he would prevent the scarcity of provision itself? No man would be poor, and fatigue himself for a livelihood, if he could help it: The absolute necessity all stand in for victuals and drink, and in cold climates for clothes and lodging, makes them submit to any thing that can be bore with. If nobody did want, nobody would work; but the greatest hardships are looked upon as solid pleasures, when they keep a man from starving.

From what has been said, it is manifest, that in a free nation, where slaves are not allowed of, the surest wealth consists in a multitude of laborious poor; for besides that they are the never-failing nursery of fleets and armies, without them there could be no enjoyment, and no product of any country

could be valuable. To make the society happy, and people easy under the meanest circumstances, it is requisite that great numbers of them should be ignorant, as well as poor. Knowledge both enlarges and multiplies our desires, and the fewer things a man wishes for, the more easily his necessities may be supplied.

The welfare and felicity, therefore, of every state and kingdom, require that the knowledge of the working poor should be consined within the verge of their occupations, and never extended (as to things visible), beyond what relates to their calling. The more a shepherd, a ploughman, or any other peasant, knows of the world, and the things that are foreign to his labour or employment, the less sit he will be to go through the fatigues and hardships of it with cheerfulness and content.

Reading, writing, and arithmetic, are very necessary to those whose business require such qualisications; but where people's livelihood has no dependence on these arts, they are very pernicious to the poor, who are forced to get their daily bread by their daily labour. Few children make any progress at school, but, at the fame time, they are capable of being employed in some business or other, so that every hour thole of poor people spend at their book is so much time lost to the society. Going to school, in comparison to working, is idleness, and the longer boys continue in this easy sort of life, the more unsit they will be when grown up for downright labour, both as to strength and inclination. Men who are to remain and end their days in a laborious, tiresome, and painful station of life, the sooner they are put upon it at sirst, the more patiently they will submit to it for ever after. Hard labour, and the coarsest diet, are a proper punishment to several kinds of malefactors, but to impose either on those that have not been used and brought up to both, is the greatest cruelty, when there is no crime you can charge them with.

Reading and writing are not attained to without some labour of the brain and assiduity, and before people are tolerably versed in either, they esteem them-

selves insinitely above those who are wholly ignorant of them, often with so little justice and moderation, as if they were of another species. As all mortals have naturally an aversion to trouble and pains-taking, so we are all fond of, and apt to overvalue those qualisications we have purchased at the expence of our ease and quiet for years together. Those who spent a great part of their youth in learning to read, write, and cypher, expect, and not unjustly, to be employed where those qualisications may be of use to them; the generality of them will look upon downright labour with the utmost contempt, I mean labour performed in the service of others in the lowest station of life, and for the meanest consideration. A man, who has had some education, may follow husoandry by choice, and be diligent at the dirtiest and most laborious work; but then the concern must be his own, and avarice, the care of a family, or some other pressing motive, must put him upon it; but he will not make a good hireling, and serve a farmer for a pitiful reward; at least he is not so sit for it as a day labourer that has always been employed about the plough and dung cart, and remembers not that ever he has lived otherwise.

When obsequiousness and mean services are required, we shall always observe that they are never so cheerfully nor so heartily performed, as from inferiors to superiors; I mean inferiors not only in riches and quality, but likewise in knowledge and understanding. A servant can have no unseigned respect for his master, as soon as he has sense enough to sind out that he serves a fool. When we are to learn or to obey, we shall experience in ourselves, that the greater opinion we have of the wisdom and capacity of rhose that are either to teach or command us, the greater deference we pay to their laws and instrucions. No creatures submit contentedly to their equals; and should a horse know as much as a man, I should not desire to be his rider.

Here I am obliged again to make a digression, though I declare I never had a less mind to it than I have at this minute;

but I see a thousand rods in pise, and the whole posse of diminutive pedants against me, for assaulting the Christ-cross-row, and opposing the very elements of literature.

This is no panic fear, and the reader will not imagine my apprehensions ill grounded, if he considers what an army of petty tyrants I have to cope with, that all either actually persecute with birch, or else are soliciting for such a preferment. For if I had no other adversaries than the starving wretches of both sexes, throughout the kingdom of Great Britain, that from a natural antipathy to work'iig, have a great dislike to their present employment, and perceiving within a much stronger inclination to command than ever they felt to obey others, think themselves qualisied, and wish from their hearts to be masters and mistresses of charity schools, the number of my enemies would, by the most modest computation, amount to one hundred thousand at least.

Methinks I hear them cry out, that a more dangerous doctrine never was broached, and Popery is' a fool to it, and alk what brute of a Saracen it is that draws his ugly weapon for the destruction of learning. It is ten to one but they will indict me for endeavouring, by instigation of the prince of darkness, to introduce into these realms greater ignorance and barbarity, than ever nation was plunged into by Goths and Vandals since the sight of the gospel sirst appeared in the world. Whoever labours under the public odium, has always crimes laid to his charge he never was guilty of, and it will be suspected that I have had a hand in obliterating the Holy Scriptures, and perhaps assirmed, that it was at my request that the small Bibles, published by patent in the year 1721, and chiefly made use of in charity schools, were, through badnels of print and paper, rendered illegible; which yet 1 protest I m as innocent of as the child unborn. But 1 am in a thousand fears; the more I consider my cafe, the worse I like it, and the greatest comfort I have is in my sincere belief, that hardly any body will mind a word of what 1 fay; or else, if ever the people suspected that

what I write would be of any weight to any considerable part of the society, I should not have the courage barely to think on all the trades I should disoblige; and I cannot but smile, when I reflect on the variety of uncouth sufferings that would be prepared for me, if the punishment they would disferently inflict upon me was emblematically to point at my crime. For if I was not suddenly stuck full of useless pen knives up to the hilts, the company of stationers would certainly take me in hand, and either have me buried alive in their hall, under a great heap of primers and spelling-books, they would not be able to fell; or else send me up against tide to be bruised to death in a paper mill, that would be obliged to stand still a week upon my account. The ink-makers, at the fame time, would, for the public good, offer to choke me with astringents, or drown me in the black liquor that would be left upon their hands; which, if they joined stock, might easily be performed in less than a month; and if I should escape the cruelty of these united bodies, the resentment of a private monopolist would be aS fatal to me, and 1 should soon sind myself pelted and knocked on the head with little squat Bibles clasped in brass, and ready armed for mischief, that, charitable learning ceasing, would be sit for nothing but unopened to sight with, and exercises truly polemic.

The digression 1 spoke of just now, is not the foolish trifle that ended with the last paragraph, and which the grave critic, to whom all mirth is unseasonable, will think very impertinent; but a serious apologetical one 1 am going to make out of hand, to clear myself from having any design against arts and sciences, as some heads of colleges and other careful preservers of human learning might have apprehended, upon seeing ignorance recommended as a necessary ingredient in the mixture of civil society.

In the sirst place, I-would have near double the number *of* professors in every university of what there is now. Theology with us is generally well provided, but the two other faculties have

very little to boast of, especially physic. Every branch of that art ought to have two or three protestors, that woi.ld take pains to communicate their skill and knowledge lo others. In public lectures, a vain man has great op portunities to set off his parts, but private instructions are more useful to.students. Pharmacy, and the knowledge of the simples, are as necessary as anatomy or the history of diseases: it is a shame, that when men have taken their degree, and arc by authority intrusted with the lives of the subject, they should be forced to come to London to be acquainted with the Materia Medica, and the composition of medicines, and receive instructions from others that never had university education themselves; it is certain, that in the city I named, there is ten times more opportunity for a man to improve himself in anatomy, botany, pharmacy, and the practice of physic, than at both universities together. What has an oil shop to do with silks; or who would look for hams and pickles at a mercers? Where things are well managed, hospitals are made as subservient to the advancement of students in the art of physic, as they are to the recovery of health in the poor.

Good fense ought to govern men in learning as well as in trade: no man ever bound his son apprentice to a goldsmith to make him a linen draper; then why should he have a divine for his tutor to become a lawyer or a physician? It is true, that the languages, logic and philosophy, should be the sirst studies in all the learned professions; but there is so little help for physic in our universities that are so rich, and where so many idle people are well paid for eating and drinking, and being magnisicently, as well as commodiously lodged, that bar books, and what is common to all the three faculties, a man may as well qualify himself at Oxford or Cambridge to be a Turkey merchant, as he can to be a physician; which is, in my humble opinion, a great sign that some part of the great wealth they are possessed of is not so well applied as it might be.

Professors should, besides their stipends allowed them by the public, have gratisications from every student they teach, that self-interest, as well as emulation and the love of glory, might spur them on to labour and assiduity. When a man excels in any one study or part of learning, and is qualisied to teach others, he ought to be procured, if money will purchase him, without regarding what party, or indeed what country or nation he is of, whether black or white. Universities should be public marts for all manner of literature, as your annual fairs, that are kept at Leipsic, Frankfort, and other places in Germany, ai for different wares and merchandises, where no difference is made between natives and foreigners, and which men resort to from all parts of the world with equal freedom and equal privilege.

From paying the gratisicationsl spoke of, I would excuse all students designed for the ministry of the gospel. There is no faculty so immediately necessary to the goverment of a nation as that of theolgy, and as we ought to have great numbers of divines for the service of this island, I would not have the meaner people discouraged from bringing up their children to that function. For though wealthy men, if they have many sons, sometimes mke one of them a clergyman, as we fee even persons of quahcy take up holy orders, and there are like vise people of good sense, especially divines, that from a principle of prudence bring up their children to that prosession, when they are morally assured that they have friends or interest enough, and shall be able, either by a good fellowship at the university, advowsons, or other means to procure them a livelihood: but these produce not the large number of divines that are yearly ordained, and for the bulk of the clergy, we are indebted to another original.

Among the middling people of all trades there are bigots who have a superstitious awe for a gown and cassoc: of these there are multitudes that feel an ardent desire of having a son promoted to the ministry of the gospel, without considering what is to become of them afterwards; and many a kind mother in

this kingdom, without consulting her own circumstances or her child's capacity, transported with this laudable wish, is daily feasting on this pleasing thought, and often before her son is twelve years old, mixing maternal love with devotion, throws herself into ecstasies and tears of satisfaction, by reflecting on the future enjoyment ihe is to receive from seeing him stand in a pulpit, and, with her own ears, hearing him preach the word of God. It is to this religious zeal, or at least the human frailties that pass for and represent it, that we owe the great plenty of poor scholars the nation enjoys. For, considering the inequality of livings, and the smallness of benesices up and down the kingdom, without this happy disposition in parents of small fortune, we cpuld not possibly be furnished from any other quarter with proper persons for the ministry, to attend all the cures of souls, so pitifully provided for, that no mortal could live upon them that had been educated in any tolerable plenty, unless he was possessed of real virtue, which it is foolish and indeed injurious, we should more expect from the clergy than we generally sind it in the laity.

The great care I would take to promote that part of learning which is more immediately useful to society, should n it make me neglect the more curious and polite, but all the liberal arts, and every branch of literature should be encouraged throughout the kingdom, more than they are, if my wishing could do it. In every county, there should be one or more large schools, erected at the public charge, for Latin and Greek, that should be divided into six or more classe"!, with particular masters in each of them. The whole should be under the care and inspection of some men cf letters in authority, whg would not only be titular governors, but actually take pains at least twice a-year, in hearing every class thoroughly examined by the master of it, and not content themselves with judging of the progress the scholars had made for the themes and other exercises that had been made out of their sight.

At the fame time, I would discharge and hinder the multiplicity of those pet-

ty schools, that never would have had any existence had the masters of them not been extremely indigent. It is a vulgar error, that nobody can spell or write Englim well without a little smatch of Latin. This is upheld by pedants for their own interest, and by none more strenuously maintained than such of them as are poor scholars in more than one fense; in the mean time it is an abominable falsehood. 1 have known, and 1 am still acquainted with several, and some of the fair sex, that never learned any Latin, and yet kept to strict orthogragphy, and write admirable good sense; where, on the other hand, every body may meet with the scriblings of pretended scholars, at least such as went to a grammer school for several years, that have grammar faults and are ill spelled. The understanding of Latin thoroughly, is highly necessary to all that are designed for any of the learned profeslions, and I would have no gentleman without literature; even those who are to be brought up attorneys, surgeons, and apothecaries, should be much better versed in that language than generally they are; but to youth, who afterwards are to get a livelihood in trades and callings in which Latin is not dady wanted, it is of no use, and the learning of it an evident loss of just so much time and money as are bestowed upon it. When men come into business, what was taught them of it, in those petty schools is either soon forgot, or only sit to make them impertinent, and often very troublesome in company. Few men can forbear valuing themselves on any knowledge they had once acquired, even after they have lost it; and, unless they are very modest and discreet, the undigested scraps which such people commonly remember of Latin, seklora fail of rendering them, at one time or other, ridiculous to those who understand it.

Reading and writing I would treat as we do music and dancing, I would not hinder them nor force them upon the society: as long as there was any thing to be got by them, there would be masters enough to teach them; but nothing should be taught for nothing but at church: and here I would exclude even those who might be designed for the ministry of the gospel; for, if parents are so miserably poor that they cannot aftbrd their children these sirst elements of learning, it is impudence in them to aspire any further.

It would encourage, likewise, the lower sort of people to give their children this part of education, if they could see them preferred to those of idle sots or lorry rake-hells, that never knew what it was to provide a rag for their brats but by begging. Bet now, when a boy or a girl are wanted for any small service, we reckon it a duty to employ our charity children before any other. The education of them looks like a reward for being vicious and unactive, a benesit commonly bestowed on parents, who deserve to be punilhed for shamefully neglecting their families. In one place you may hear a rascal half drunk, damning himself, call for the other pot, and as a good reason for it, add, that his boy is provided for in clothes, and has his schooling for nothing: In another you shall see a poor woman in great necessity, whose child is to be taken care Qf, because herself Is a lazy flut, and never did any thing to remedy her wants in good earnest, but bewailing them at a gin-mop.

If every body's children are well taught, who, by their own industry, can educate them at our universities, there will be men of learning enough to supply this nation and such another; and reading, writing, or arithmetic, would never be wanting in the business that requires them, though none were to learn them but such whose parents could be at the charge of it. It is not with letters as it is with the gists of the Holy Ghost, that they may nor be purchased with money; and bought wit, if we believe the proverb, is none of the worst. 5 1 thought it necessary to say thus much of learning, to obviate the clamours of the enemies to truth and fair dealing who, had I not so amply explained myself on this head, would have represented me as a mortal foe to all literature and useful knowledge, and a wicked advocate for universal ignorance and stupid-

ity. I shall now make good my promise, of answering what 1 know the Wellwishers to charity schools would object against me, by saying that they brought up the children under their care, to warrantable and laborious trades, and not to idleness as I did insinuate.

1 have sussiciently showed already, why going to school was idleness if compared to working, and exploded this fort of education in the children of the poor, because it incapacitates them ever after for downright labour, which is their proper province, and, in every civil society, a portion they ought not to repine or grumble at, if exacted from them with discretion and humanity. What remains, is, that, i should speak as to their putting them out to trades, which I shall endeavour to demonstrate to be destructive to the harmony of a nation, and an impertinent intermeddling with what sew of these governors know any thing of.

In order to this, let us examine into the nature of societies, and what the compound ought to consist of, if we would raise it to as high a degree of strength, beauty, and perfection, as the ground we are to do it upon will let us. The variety of services that are required to supply the luxurious and wanton desires, as well as real necessities of man, with all their subordinate callings, is in such a nation as ours prodigious; yet it is certain that though the number of those several occupations be excessively great, it is far from being insinite; if you add one more than is required, it must be superfluous. If a man had a good stock, and the best shop in Cheapside to sell turbants in, he would be ruined; and if Demetrius, or any other silversmith, made nothing but Diana's shrines, he would not get his bread, now the worship of that goddess is out of fashion. As it is folly to set up trades that are not wanted, so what is next to it is to increase in any one trade, the numbers beyond what are required., As things are managed with us, it would be preposterous to have as many brewers as there are bakers, or as many woollendrapers as there are shoemakers. This proportion as to numbers, in every

trade, sinds itself, and is never better kept than when nobody meddles or interferes with it.

People that have children to educate that must get their livelihood, are always consulting and deliberating what trade or calling they are to bring them up to, until they are sixed; and thousands think on this, that hardly think at all on any thing else. First, they consine themselves to their circumstances, and he that can give but ten pounds with his son must not look out for a trade, where they ask an hundred with an apprentice; but the next they think on, is always which will be the most advantageous; it there be a calling where at that time people are more generally employed than they are in any other in the fame reach, there are presently half a score fathers ready to supply it with their sons. Therefore the greatest care most companies have, is about the regulation of the number ofapprentices. Now, when all trades complain, and perhaps justly, that they are overstocked, you manifestly injure that trade, to which you add one member more than would flow from the nature of society. Besides that, the governors of charity schools do not deliberate so much what trade is the best, but what tradesmen they can get that will take the boys, with such a sum; and few men os substance and experience will have any thing to do with these children; they are afraid of a hundred inconveniencies from the necelsito us parents of them: so that they are bound, at least most commonly, cither to sots and neglectful masters, or else such as are very needy and do not care what becomes of their apprentices, after they have received the money; by which it seems as if we studied nothing more than to have a perpetual nursery for charity schools.

When all trades and handicrafts are. overstocked, it is a certain sign there isa fault in the management of the whole; for it is impossible there should be too many people if the country is able to feed them. Are provisions dear? Whosefault is that, as long as you have ground untilled and hands unemployed? But 1 shall be answered, that to increase plenty, must at long-run undo the farmer, or lessen the rents all over England. To which I reply, that what the husband man complains of most, is what I would redress: the greatest grievance of farmers, gardners, and others, where hard labour is required, and dirty work to be done, is, that they cannot get servants for the fame wages they used to have them at. The day-labourer grumbles at sixteen pence to do no other drudgery, than what thirty years ago his grandfather did cheerfully for half the money. As to the rents, it is *impof* sible they should fall while you increase youinumbers; but the price of provilions, and all labour in general, must fall with them, if not before; and a man of a hundred and fifty pounds a-year, has no reason to complain that his income is reduced to one hundred, if he can buy as much for that one hundred as before he could have done for two.

There is no intrinsic worth in money, but what is alterable with the times; and whether a guinea goes for twenty pounds or for a milling, it is (as 1 have already hinted before) the labour of the poor, and not the high and low value that is set on gold or silver, which all the comforts of life must arise from. It is in our power to have a much greater plenty than we enjoy, if agriculture and sishery were taken care os, as they might be; but we are so little capable of increasing our labour, that we have hardly poor enough to do what is neceslary to make us subsist. The proportion of the society is spoiled, and the bulk of the nation, which should every where consist of labouring poor, that are unacquainted with every thing but their work, is too little for the other parts. In all business where downright labour is shunned or over-paid, there is plenty of people. To one merchant you have ten book keepers, or at least pretenders; and every where in the country the farmer wants hands. Ask for a footman that for some time has been in gentlemen's families, and you will get a dozen that are all butlers. You may have chamber-maids by the score, but you cannot get a cook under extravagant wages.

Nobody will do the dirty slavish work, that can help it. I do not discommend them; but all these things show, that the people of the meanest rank, know too much to be serviceable to us. Servants require more than masters and mistrefles can afford; and what madness is it to encourage them in this, by industriously increasing at our cost, that knowledge, which they will be sure to nuke us pay for over again! And it i9 not only that those who are educated at our own expence, encroach upon us, but the raw ignorant country wenches and boobily fellows that can do, and are good for nothing, impose upon us likewise. The scarcity os servants occasioned by the education of the sirst, gives a handle to the latter of advancing their price, and demanding what ought only to be given to servants that understand their business, and have most of the good qualities that can be required in them. There is no place in the world where there are more clever fellows to look at, or to do an errand, than some of our footmen; but what are they good for in the main? The greatest part of them are rogues, and not to be trusted; and if they are honest, half of them are sots, and will get drunk three or four times a week. The surly ones are generally quarrelsome, and valuing their manhood beyond all other considerations, care not what clothes they spoil, or what disappointments they may occasion, when their prowess is in question. Those who are good-natured, are generally sad whore-masters, that are ever running after the wenches, and spoil all the maid-servants they come near. Many of them are guilty of all these vices, whoring, drinking, quarreling, and yet shall have all their faults overlooked and bore with, because they are men of good mien and humble address, that know how to wait on gentlemen; which is an unpardonable folly in masters, and generally ends in the ruin of servants.

Some few there are, that are not addicted to any of these failings, and understand their duty besides; but as these are rarities, so there is not one in sifty but what over-rates himself; his wages must be extravagant, and you can never

have done giving him; every thing in the house is his perquisite, and he will not stay with you unless his vails are i iicient to maintain a middling family; and though you had taKen him from the dunghill, out of an hospital, or a prison, you shall never keep him longer than he can make of his place, what in his high estimation of himself he shall think he deserves;. nay, the best and most civilized, that never were saucy and impertinent, will leave the most indulgent master, and, to get handsomely away, frame sifty excuses, and tell downright lies, as soon as they can mend themselves. A man, who keeps an half-crown or twelve-penny ordinary, looks not more for money from his customers, than a footman does from every guest that dines or sups with his master; and I question whether the one does not often think a shilling or half-a-crown, according to the quality of the person, his due as much as the other.

A hoi sekeepei, who cannot afford to make many entertainments, and does not often invite people to his table, can have no creditable man-servant, and is forced to take up with some country booby, or other awkward fellow, who will likewise give him the flip, as soon as he imagines himself tit for any other service, and is made wiser by his rascally companions. All noted eating-houses, and places that many gentlemen resort to for diversion or business, more especially the precincts of Westminster-hall, are the great schools for servants, where the dullest fellows may have their understandings improved; and get rid at once of their stupidity and their innocence. They are the academies for footmen, where public lectures are daily read, on all sciences of low debauchery, by the experienced protestors of them; and students are instrusted in above seven hundred illiberal arts, how to cheat, impose upon, and sind out the blind side of their masters, with so much application, that in few years they become graduates in iniquity. Young gentlemen and others, that are not thoroughly versed in the world, when they get such knowing sharpers in their service, are commonly indulging above measure;

and for fear of discovering their want of experience, hardly dare to contradict or deny them any thing, which is often the reason, that by allowing them unreasonable privileges, they expose their ignorance when they are most endeavouring to conceal it.

Some perhaps will lay the things I complain of to the charge of luxury, of which I said that it could do no hurt to a rich nation, if the imports never did exceed the exports; but I do not think this imputation just, and nothing ought to be scored on the account of luxury, that is downright the effect of folly. A man may be very extravagant in indulging his ease and his pleasure, and render the enjoyment of the world as operose and expensive as they can be made, if he can asford it, and, at the fame time, show his good fense in every thing about him: This he cannot be said to do, if he industriously renders his people incapable of doing him that service he expects from them. It is too much money, excessive wages, and unreasonable vails, that spoil servants in England. A man may have sive and twenty horses in his stables, without being guilty of folly, if it suits with the rest of his circumstances; but if he keeps but one, and overfeeds 't to show his wealth, he is a fool for his pains. Is it not madness to susfer, that servants should take three, and others sive per cent, of what they pay to tradesmen for their masters, as is so well known to watchmakers, and others that fell toys, superfluous nicknacks, and other curiosities, if they deal with people of quality and fashionable gentlemen, that are above telling their own money? If they should accept of a present when offered, it might be connived at, but it is an unpardonable impudence that they should claim it as their due, and contend for it if refused. Those who have all the necessaries of life provided for, can have no occasion for money, but what does them hurt as servants, unless they were to hoard it up for age or sickness, which, among our ikip-kennels, is not very common, and even then it makes them saucy and insupportable.

I am credibly informed, that a parcel of footmen are arrived to that height of insolence, as to have entered into a society together, and made laws, by which they oblige themselves not to serve for less than such a sum, nor carry burdens, or any bundle or parcel above a certain weight, not exceeding two or three pounds, with other regulations directly opposite to the interest of those they serve, and altogether destructive to the use they were designed for. If any of them be turned away for strictly adhering to the orders of this honourable corporation, he is taken care of till another service is provided for him; and there is no money wanting at any time to commence and maintain a law-suit against any master that shall pretend to strike, or offer any other injury to his gentleman footman, contrary to the statutes of their society. If this be true, as I have reason to believe it is, and they are suffered to go on in consulting and providing for their own ease and ccnveniency any further, we may expect quickly to see the French comedy, *Le Maitre le Valet* acted in good earnest in most families, which, if not redressed in a little time, and those footmen increase their company to the number it is posible they may, as well as assemble when they please with impunity, it will be in their power to make a tragedy of it whenever they have a naind to it.

But suppose those apprehensions frivolous and groundless, it is undeniable that servants, in general, are daily encroaching upon masters and mistresses, and endeavouring to be more upon the level with them. They not only seem solicitous to abolish the low dignity of their condition, but have already considerably raised it in the common estimation from the original meanness which the public welfare requires it should always remain in. I do not fay that these things are altogether owing to charity schools, there are other evils they may be partly ascribed to. London is too big for the country, and, in several respects, we-are wanting to ourselves. But if a thousand faults were to concur before the inconveniences could be produced we labour under, can any man doubt, who will consider what I have said, that charity schools are accessary, or, at least, that they are more likely to create and increase than to lessen or redress those complaints?

The only thing of weight, then, that can be said in their behalf is, that so many thousand children are educated by them in the Christian faith, and the principles of the church of England. To demonstrate that this is not a sussicient plea for them, I must desire the reader, as I hate repetitions, to look back on what I have said before, to which I shall add, that Whatever is necessary to salvation, and requisite sor poor labouring people to know concerning religion, that children learn at school, may fully as well either by preaching or catechizing be taught at church, from which, or some other place of worship, I would not have the meanest of a parim that is able to walk to it be absent on Sundays. It is the Sabbath, the most useful day in seven, that is set apart for divine service and religious exercise, as well as resting from bodily labour s and it is a duty incumbent on all magistrates to take particular care of that day. The poor more especially and their children, should be made to go to church on it both in the fore and afternoon, because they have no time on any other. By precept and example they ought to be encouraged and used to it from their very infancy; the wilful neglect of it ought to be counted scandalous, and if downright compulsion to what I urge might seem too harsh, and perhaps impracticable, all diversions at least ought strictly to be prohibited, and the poor hindered from every amusement abroad that might allure or draw them from it.

Where this care is taken by the magistrates, as far as it lies in their power, ministers of the gospel may instil into the smallest capacities, more piety and devotion, and better principles of virtue and religion, than charity schools ever did or ever will produce; and those who complain, when they have such opportunities, that they cannot imbue their parishioners with sussicient knowledge, of what they stand in need of as Christians, without the assistance of reading and writing, are either very lazy or very ignorant and undeserving themselves.

That the most knowing are not the most religious, will be evident if we make a trial between people of different abilities, even in this juncture, where going to church is not made such an obligation on the poor and illiterate, as it might be. Let us pitch upon a hundred poor men, the sirst we can light . that are above forty, and were brought up to hard la

O bour from their infancy, such as never went to school at all, and always lived remote from knowledge and great towns: Let us compare to these an equal number of very good scholars, that shall all have had university education, and be, if you will, half of them divines, well versed in philology and polemic learning; then let us impartially examine into the lives and conversations of both, and I dare engage that anmng the sirst, who can neither read nor write, we shall meet with more union and neighbourly love, less wickedness and attachment to the world, more content of mind, more innocence, sincerity, and other good qualities that conduce to the public peace and real felicity, than we shall sind among the latter, where, on the contrary, we may be assured of the height of pride and insolence, eternal quarrels and dissensions, irreconcileable hatreds, strife, envy, calumny, and other vices, destructive to mutual concord, which the illiterate labouring poor are hardly ever tainted with, to any considerable degree.

I am very well persuaded, that what I have said in the last paragraph, will be no news to most of my readers; but if it be truth, why should it be stifled, and why must our concern for religion be eternally made a cloak to hide our real drifts and worldly intentions? Would both parties agree to pull off the mask, we mould soon discover that whatever they pretend to, they aim at nothing so much in charity schools, as to strengthen their party; and that the great sticklers for the church, by educating children in the principles of religion, mean inspiring them with a superlative veneration for the clergy of the church of England, and a strong aversion and immortal animosity against all that dissent

from it. To be assured of this, we are but to mind on the one hand, what divines are most admired for their charity sermons, and most fond to preach them; and on the other, whether of late years we havs had any riots or party scusfles among the mob, in which the youth of a famous hospital in this city, were not always the most forward ringleaders.

The grand asserters of liberty, who are ever guarding themselves, and skirmishing against arbitrary power, often when they are in no danger of it, are generally speaking, not very superstitious, nor seem to lay great stress on any modern apostleship: 'yet some of these likewise speak up loudly for charity schools; but what they expect from them has no relation to religion or morality: they only look upon them as the proper means to destroy, and disappoint the power of the priests over the laity. Reading and writing increase knowledge; and the more men know, the better they can judge for themselves, and they imagine that, if knowledge could be rendered universal, people could not be priest-rid, which is the thing they fear the most.

The sirst, I confess, it is very possible will get their aim. But sure wise men that are not red-hot for a party, or bigots to the priests, will not think it worth while to fuller so many inconveniencies, as charity schools may be the occasion of, only to promote the ambition and power of the clergy. To the other I would answer, that if all those who are educated at the charge of their parents or relations, will but think for themselves, and refuse to have their reason imposed upon by the priests, we need not be concerned for what the clergy will work upon the ignorant that have no education at all. Let them make the most of them: considering the schools we have for those who can and do pay for learning, it is ridiculous to imagine that the abolisoing of charity schools would be a step towards any ignorance that could be prejudicial to the nation.

I would not be thought cruel, and am well assured if I know any thing of myself, that I abhor inhumanity; but to be compassionate to excess, where reason

forbids it, and the general interest of the society requires steadiness of thought and resolution, is an unpardonable weakness. I know it will be ever urged against me, that it is barbarous the children of the poor should have no opportunity of exerting themselves, as long as God has not debarred them from natural parts and genius, more than the rich. But I cannot think this is harder, than it is that they mould not have money, as long as they have the fame inclinations to spend as others. That great and useful men have sprung from hospitals, I do not deny; but it is likewise very probable, that when they were sirst employed, many as capable as themselves not brought up in hospitals were neglected, that with the fame good fortune would have done as well as they, if they had been made use of instead of them.

There are many examples of women that have excelled in learning, and even in war, but this is no reason we should bring them all up to Latin and Greek, or else military discipline, instead of needle-work and housewifery. But there is no scarcity of sprightliness or natural parts among us, and no soil and climate has human creatures to boast of better formed, either inside or outside, than this ifland generally produces. But it is not wit, genius, or docility we want, but diligence, application, and assiduity.

Abundance of hard and dirty labour is to be done, and Coarse living is to be complied with: where shall we sind a better nursery for these necessities than the children of the poor? none, certainly, are nearer to it or sitter fork: Besides that the things I called hardships, neither seem nor are such to those who have been brought up to them, and know no better. There is not a more contented people among us, than those who work the hardest, and are the least acquainted with the pomp and delicacies of the world.

These are truths that are undeniable; yet I know few people will be pleased to have them divulged; what makes them odious, is an unreasonable vein of petty reverence for the poor, that runs through most multitudes, and more particularly in this nation, and arises from a mixture of pity, folly, and superstition. It is from a lively fense of this compound, that men cannot endure to hear or fee any thing said or acted against the poor; without considering how just the one, or insolent the other. So a beggar must not be beat, though he strikes you sirst. Journeymen tailors go to law with their masters, and are obstinate in a wrong cause, yet they must be pitied; and murmuring weavers must be relieved, and have sifty silly things done to humour them, though in the midst of their poverty they insult their betters, and, on all occasions, appear to be more prone to make holidays and riots than they are to working or sobriety.

This puts me in mind of our wool, which, considering the posture of our affairs, and the behaviour of the poor, 1 sincerely believe, ought not, upon any account, to be carried abroad: but if we look into the reason, why suffering it to be fetched away is so pernicious, our heavy complaint and lamentations that it is exported can be no great credit to us. Considering the mighty and manifold hazards that must be run before it can be got ost'the coast, and safely landed beyond sea, it is manifest that the foreigners, before they can work our wool, must pay more for it very considerably, than what we can have it for at home. Yet, notwithstanding this great difference in the prime cost, they can afford to fell the manufactures made of it cheaper at foreign markets than ourselves. This is the disaster we groan under, the intolerable mischiefs without which the exportation of that commodify could be no greater prejudice to us than that of tin or lead, as long as our hands were fully employed, and we had still wool to" spare.

There is no people yet come to higher perfection in the woollen manufacture, either as to dispatch or goodness of work, at least in the most considerable branches, than ourselves; and therefore what we complain of can only depend on the difference in the management of the poor, between other nations and ours. If the labouring people in one country will work twelve hours in a day, and six days in a week, and in another

they are employed but eight hours in a day, and not above four days in a week the one is obliged to have nine hands for what the other does with four. But if, moreover, the living, the food, and raiment, and what is consumed by the workmen of the industrious, costs but half the money of what is expended among an equal number of the other, the consequence must be, that the sirst will have the work of eighteen men for the same price as the other gives for the work of sour. I would not insinuate, neither do I think, that the difference, either in diligence or necessaries of life between' us and any neighbouring nation, is near so great as what I speak of, yet 1 would have it considered, that half of that difference, and much less, is sussicient to over-balance the disadvantage they labour under as to the price of wool.

Nothing to me is more evident, than that no nation in any manufacture whatever can undersell their neighbours with whom they are at best but equals as to lkill and dispatch, and the conveniency for working, more especially when the prime cost of the thing to be manufactured is not in their savour, unless they have provisions, and whatever is relating to their sustenance, cheaper, or else workmen that are either more assiduous, and will remain longer at their work, or be content with a meaner and coarser way of living than those of their neighbours. This is certain, that where numbers are equal, the more laborious people are, and the fewer hands the fame quantity of work is performed by, the greater plenty there is in a country of the necessaries for life, the more considerable and the cheaper that country may render its exports.

It being granted, then, that abundance of work is to be done, the next thing which 1 think to be likewise undeniable, is, that the more cheerfully it is done the better, as well for those that perform it, as for the rest of the society. To be happy is to be pleased, and the less notion a man has of a better way of living, the more content he will be with his own; and, on the other hand, the greater a man's knowledge and experience is in

the world, the more exquisite the delicacy of his taste, and the more consummate judge he is of things in general, certainly the more difficult it will be to please him. 1 would not advance any thing that is barbarous or inhuman: but when a man enjoys himself, laughs and sings, and in his gesture and behaviour mows me all the tokens of content and satisfaction, 1 pronounce him happy, and have nothing to do with his wit or capacity. I never enter into the reasonableness of his mirth, at least 1 ought not to judge of it by my own standard, and argue from the effect which the thing that makes him merry would have upon me. At that rate, a man that hates cheese must call me fool for loving blue mold. *De gujlibus non eji disputandum* is as true in a metaphorical, as it is in the literal fense ; and the greater the distance is between people as to their condition, their circumstances and manner of living, the less capable they are of judging of one anothers troubles or pleasures.

Had the meanest and most uncivilized peasant leave *incognito* to observe the greatest king for a fortnight; though he might pick out several things he would like for himself, yet he would stnd a great many more, which, if the monarch and he were to change conditions, he would wish for his part to have immediately altered or redressed, and which with amazement he fees the king submit to. And again, if the sovereign was to examine the peasant in the same manner, his labour would be unsufferable; the dirt and squalor, his diet and amours, his pastimes and recreations would be all abominable; but then what charms would he sind in the other's peace of mind, the calmness and tranquillity of his foul? No necessity tor dissimulation with any of his family, or feigned affection to his mortal enemies; no wife in a foreign interest, no danger to apprehend from his children; no plots to unravel, no poison to fear; no pbpular statesman at home, or cunning courts abroad to manage; no seeming patriots to bribe; no unsociable favourite to gratify; no sclnsh ministry to obey; no divided nation to please, or sickle mob to humour, that would direct and interfere with his pleasures.

Was impartial reaibn to be judge between real good and real evil, and a catalogue made accordingly, of the several delights and vexations differently to be met with in both stations; I question whether the condition of kings would be at all preferable to that of peasants, even as ignorant and laborious as I seem to require the latter to be. The reason why the generality of people would rather be kings than peasants, is sirst owing to pride and ambition, that is deeply riveted in human nature, and which to gratify, we daily fee men undergo and despise the greatest hazards and dissiculties. Secondly, to the difference there is in the force with which our affection is wrought upon, as the objects are either material or spiritual. Things that immediately strike our outward fenses, act more violently upon our passions than what is the result of thought, and the dictates of the most demonstrative reason; and there is a much stronger bias to gain our liking or aversion in the sirst, than there is in the latter.

Having thus demonstrated that what I urge could be no injury, or the least diminution of happiness to the poor, I leave it to the judicious reader, whether it is not more probable we should increase our exports by the methods I hint at, than by sitting still and damning and sinking our neighbours, for beating us at our own weapons; some of them outselling us in manufactures made of our own product, which they dearly purchased, others growing rich in spite of distance and trouble, by the same sish which we neglect, though it is ready to jump into our mouths.

As by discouraging idleness with art and steadiness, you may compel the poor to labour without force; so, by bringing them up in ignorance, you may inure them to real hardships, without being ever sensible themselves that they are such. By bringing them up in ignorance, I mean no more, as I have hinted long ago, than that, as to worldly affairs, their knowledge should be consined within the verge of their own occupations, at least that we mould not

take pains to extend it beyond those limits. When by these two engines we shall have made provisions, and consequently labour cheap, we must infallibly outsell our neighbours; and at the fame time increase our numbers. This is the noble and manly way of encountering the rivals of our trade, and by dint of merit outdoing them at foreign markets.

To allure the poor, we make use of policy in some cases with success. Why mould we be neglectful of it in the most important point, when they make their boast that they will not live as the poor of other nations? If we cannot alter their resolution, why should we applaud the justness of their fentiments against the common interest? I have often wondered formerly how an Englimman that pretended to have the honour and glory, as well as the welfare of his country at heart, could take delight in the evening to hear an idle tenant that owed him above a year's rent, ridicule the French for wearing wooden shoes, when in the morning he had had the mortisication of hearing the great King William, that ambitious monarch, as well as able statesman, openly own to the world, and with grief and anger in his looks, complain of-he exorbitant power of France. Yet I do not recommend wooden shoes, nor do the maxims I would introduce require arbitrary power in one person. Liberty and property i hope may remain secured, and yet the poor be better employed than they are, though their children should wear out their clothes by useful labour, and blacken them with country dirt tor something, instead of tearing them off their backs at play, and daubing them with ink for nothing.

There is above three or four hundred years work, for a hundred thousand poor more than we have in this istand. To make every part of it useful, and the whole thoroughly inhabited, many rivers are to be made navigable; canals to be cut in hundreds of places. Some lands are to be drained and secured from inundations for the future: abundance of barren foil is to be made fertile, and thousands of acres rendered more benessicial, by being made more accessible. D« *laboribus omnia vendunt.* There

is no dissiculty of this nature, that labour and patience cannot surmount. The highest mountains may be thrown into their valleys that stand ready to receive them; and bridges might be laid where now we would not dare to think of it. Let us look back on the stupendous works of the Romans, more especially their highways and aqueducts. Let us consider in one view the vast extent of several of their roads, how substantial they made them, and what duration they have been of; and in another a poor traveller that at every ten miles end is stopped by a turnpike, and dunned for a penny for mending the roads in the summer, with wiiat every body knows will be dirt before the winter that succeeds is expired.

The conveniency of the public ought ever to be the public pare, and no private interest of a town, or a whole country, should ever hinder the execution of a project or contrivance that would manifestly tend to the improvement of the whole; and every member of the legiflature, who knows his duty, and would choose rather to act like a wise man, than curry favour with his neighbours, will prefer the least benesit accruing to the whole kingdom, to the most visible advantage of the place he serves for.

We have materials of our own, and want neither stone nor timber to do any thing; and was the money that, people give uncompelled to beggars, who do not deserve it, and what every housekeeper is obliged to pay to the poor of his parish, that is otherwise employed or ill-applied, to be put together every year, it would make a sussicient fund to keep a great many thousands at work. I do not fay this because I think it practicable, but only to mow that we have money enough to spare, to employ vast multitudes of labourers; neither ihould we want so much for it as we perhaps might imagine. When it is taken for granted, that a soldier, whose strength and vigour is to be kept up at least as much as any body's,, can live upon sixpence a-day, I cannot conceive the necessity of giving the greatest part of the year, sixteen and eighteen pence to a day-labourer.

The fearful and cautious people, that are ever jealous of their liberty, I know will cry out, that where the multitudes I speak of should be kept in constant pay, property and privileges' would be precarious. But they might be answered, that sure means might be found out, and such regulations made, as to the hands in which to trust the management and direction of these labourers, that it would be imp visible tor the prince, or any body else, to make an ill use ot their numbers.

What I have said in the four or sive last paragraphs, I foresee, will, with abundance of scorn, be laughed at by many of my readers, and at best be called building castles in the air; but whether that is my fault or theirs is a question. When the public spirit has left a nation, they not only lose their patience with it, and all thoughts of perseverance, but become likewise so narrow-fouled, that it is a pain for them even to think of things that are of uncommon extent, or require great length of time; and whatever is noble or sublime in luch conjectures, is counted chimerical. Where deep ignorance is entirely routed and expelled, and low learning promiscuously scattered on all the people, self-love turns knowledge into cunning; and the more this last qualisication prevails in any country, the more the people will six all their cares, concern, and application, on the time present, without regard of what is to come after them, or hardly ever thinking beyond the next generation.

.But as cunning, according to my Lord Verulam, is but left-handed wisdom; so a prudent legislator ought to provide against this disorder of the society, as soon as the symptoms of it appear, among which the following are the most obvious. Imaginary rewards are generally despised; every body is for turning the penny, and short bargains; he that is dissident of every thing and believes nothing but what he fees with his own eyes, is counted the most prudent; and in all their dealings, men seem to act from no other principle than that of the devil take the hindmost. Instead of

planting oaks, that will require a hundred and sifty years before they are sit to be cut down, they build houses with a design that they shall not stand above twelve or fourteen years. All heads run upon the uncertainty of things, and the vicissitudes of human affairs. The mathematics become the only valuable study, and are made use of in every thing, even where it is ridiculous, and men seem to repose no greater trust in Providence than they would in a broken merchant.

It is the business of the public to supply the defects of the society, and take that in hand sirst which is most neglected by private persons. Contraries are best cured by contraries, and therefore, as example is of greater essicacy than precept, in the amendment of national tailings, the legislature ought to resolve upon some great undertakings, that must be the work of ages as well as vast labour, and convince the world that they did nothing without an anxious regard to their latest posterity. This will six, or at least help to settle, the volatile genius and sickle spirit of the kingdom; put us in mind that we are not born for ourselves only, and be a means of rendering men less distrustful, and inspiring them with a true love for their country, and a tender affection for the ground itself, than which nothing is more necessary to aggrandize a nation. Forms of government may alter; religions and even languages may change, but Great Britain, or at least (if that likewise might lose its name) the island itself will remain, and in all human probability, last as long as any part of the globe. All ages have ever paid their kind acknowledgments to their ancestors, for the benesits derived from them; and a Christian who enjoys the multitude of fountains, and vast plenty of water to be met with in the city *of* St. Peter, is an ungrateful wretch if he never casts a thank ful remembrance on old Pagan Rome, that took such prodigious pains to procure it.

When this island shall be cultivated, and every inch of it made habitable and useful, and the whole the most convenient and agreeable spot upon earth, all

the cost and labour laid out upon it, will be gloriously repaid by the incense of them that shall come after us; and those who burn with the noble zeal and desire after immortality, and took such care to improve their country, may rest satissied, that a thousand and two thousand years hence, they shall live in the memory and everlasting praises of the future ages that shall then enjoy it.

Here I should have concluded this rhapsody of thoughts; but something comes in my head concerning the main scope and design of this essay, which is to prove the necessity there is for a certain portion of ignorance, in a well-ordered society, that I must not omit, because, by mentioning it, I shall make an argument on my side, of what, if I had not spoke of it, might easily have appeared as a strong objection against me. It is the opinion of most people, and mine among the rest, that the most commendable quality of the present Czar of Muscovy, is his unwearied application, in raising his subjects from their native stupidity, and civilizing his nation: but then we must consider it is what they stood in need of, and that not long ago the greatest part of them were next to brute beasts. In proportion to the extent of his dominions, and the multitudes he commands, he had not that number or variety of tradesmen and artisicers, which the true improvement of the country required, and therefore was in the right, in leaving no stone unturned to procure them. But what is that to us who labour under a contrary disease? Sound politics are to the social body, what the art of medicine is to the natural, and no physician would treat a man in a lethargy as if he was sick for want of rest, or prescribe in a dropsy what should be administred in a diabetes. In short, Russia has too few knowing men, and Great Britain too many.

V SEARCH INTO TBK NATURE OF SOCIETY.

1 He generality of moralists and philosophers have hitherto agreed that there could be no virtue without self-denial; but a late author, who is now much read by men of fense, is of a contrary

opinion, and imagines that men, without any trouble, or violence upon themselves, may be naturally virtuous. He seems to require and expect goodness in his species, as we do a sweet taste in grapes and China oranges, of which, if any of them are four, we boldly pronounce that they are not come to that perfecton their nature is capable of. This noble writer (for it is the Lord Shaftesbury 1 mean in his Characteristics) fancies, that as a man is made for society, so he ought to be born with a kind affection to the whole, of which he is a part, and a propensity to seek the welfare of it. In pursuance of this supposition, he calls every action performed with regard to the public good, Virtuous; and all selsishness, wholly excluding such a regard, Vice. In respect to our species, he looks upon virtue and vice as permanent realities, that must ever be the fame in all countries and all ages, and imagines that a man of found understanding, by following the rules of good fense, may not only sind out that *pulchrum et bonejium* both in morality and the works of art and nature, but likewise govern himself, by his reason, with as much ease and readiness as a good rider manages a well-taught horse by the bridle.

The attentive reader, who perused the foregoing part of this book, will soon perceive that two systems cannot be more opposite than his Lordship's and mine. His notions I confess, are generous and resined: they are a high compliment to human-kind, and capable, by a little enthusiasm, of inspiring us with the most noble sentiments concerning the dignity of our exalted nature. What pity it is that they are not true. 1 would not advance thus much if 1 had not already demonstrated, in almost ever page of this treatise, that the solidity of them is inconsistent with our daily experience. But, to leave not the least shadow of an objection that might be made unanswered, 1 design to expatiate on some things which hitherto I have but slightly touched upon, in order to convince the reader, not only that the good and amiable qualities of men are not those that make him beyond other ani-

mals a sociable creature; but, moreover, that it would be utterly impossible, either to raise any multitudes into a populous, rich, and flourishing nation, or, when so raised, to keep and maintain them in that condition, without the assistance of what we call Evil, both natural and moral.

The better to perform what I have undertaken, I shall previously examine into the reality of the *pulchrum et honejlum,* the To K'ao» that the ancients have talked of so much: the meaning of this is to discuss, whether there be a real worth and excellency in things, a pre-eminence of one above another; which every body will always agree to that well understands' them; or, that there are few things, if any, that have the fame esteem paid them, and which the fame judgment is pasted upon in all countries and all ages. When we sirst set out in quest of this intrinsic worth, and sind one thing better than another, and a third better than that, and so on, we begin to entertain great hopes of success; but when we meet with several things that are all very good or all very bad, we are puzzled, and agree not always with ourselves, much less with others. There are disferent faults as well as beauties, that as modes and fashions alter and men vary in their tastes and humours, will be differently admired or disapproved of.

Judges of painting will never disagree in opinion, when a sine picture is compared to the daubing of a novice; but how strangely have they differed as to the works of eminent masters I There are parties among connoisseurs *;* and few of them agree in their esteem as to ages and countries; and the best pictures bear not always the best prices: a noted original will be ever worth more than any copy that can be made of it by an unknown hand, though it mould be better. The value that is set on paintings depends not only on the name of the master, and the time of his age he drew them in, but likewise in a great measure on the scarcity of his works; but, what is still more unreasonable, the quality of the persons in whose possession they are, as well as the length of time they

have been in great families; and if the Cartons, now at Hampton-Court, were done by a less famous hand than that of Raphael, and had a private person for their owner, who would be forced to sell them, they would never yield the tenth part of the money which, with all their gross faults, they are now esteemed to be worth.

Notwithstanding all this, I will readily own, that the judgment to be made of painting might become of universal certainty, or at least less alterable and precarious than almost any thing else. The reason is plain; there is a standard to go by that always remains the fame. Painting is an imitation of nature, a copying of things which men have every where before them. My good humoured reader I hope will forgive me, if, thinking on this glorious invention, I make a reflection a little out of season, though very much conducive to my main design; which is, that valuable as the art is I speak of, we are beholden to an imperfection in the chief of our senses for all the pleasures and ravishing delight we receive from this happy deceit. 1 mall explain myself. Air and space are no objects of sight, but as soon as we can fee with the least attention, we observe that the bulk of the things we fee is lessened by degrees, as they are further remote from us, and nothing but experience, gained from these observations, can teach us to make any tolerable guesses at the distance of things. If one born blind should remain so till twenty, and then be suddenly blessed with sight, he would be strangely puzzled as to the difference of distances, and hardly able, immediately, by his eyes alone, to determine which was nearest to him, a post almost within the reach of his stick, or a steeple that mould be half a mile osf. Let us look as narrowly as we can upon a hole in a wall that has nothing but the open air behind it, and we shall not be able to fee otherwise, but that the sky sills up the vacuity, and is as near us as the back part of the stones that circumscribe the space where they are wanting. This circumstance, not to call it a defect, in our fense of seeing, makes us liable to be imposed upon, and every thing, but motion, may, by art, be represented to us on a siat, in the fame manner as we fee them in life and nature. If a man had never seen this art put into practice, a looking-glass might soon convince him that such a thing was poflible, and I cannot help thinking, but that the reflections from very smooth and well-pohshed bodies made upon our eyes, must have given the sirst handle to the inventions of drawings and painting.

In the works of nature, worth, and excellency, are as uncertain: and even in human creatures, what is beautiful in one country, is not so in another. How whimsical is the florist in his choice! Sometimes the tulip, sometimes the auricula, and at other times the carnatiof/fhall engross his esteem, and every year a new flower, in his judgment, beats all the old ones, though it is much inferior to them both in colour and shape. Three hundred years ago men were lhaved as closely as they are now: Since that they have wore beards, and cut them in vast variety of forms, that were all as becoming, when fashionable, as now they would be ridiculous. How mean and comically a man looks, that is otherwise well dressed, in a narrow brimed hat, when every body wears broad ones; and again, how monstrous is a very great hat, when the other extreme has been in fashion sor a considerable time? experience has taught us, that these modes seldom last above ten or twelve years, and a man of threescore must have observed sive or six revolutions of them at least! yet the beginnings of these changes, though we have seen several, seem always uncouth, and are offensive afresh whenever they return. What mortal can decide which is the handsomest, abstract from the mode in being, to wear great buttons or small ones? the many ways of laying out a garden judiciously are almost innumerable; and what is called beautiful in them, varies, according to the different tastes of nations and ages. In grafs plats, knots and parterres, a great diversity of forms is generally agreeable; but a round may be as pleasing to the eye as a square: an oval cannot be more suitable to one place, than it is possible for a triangle to be to an-

other; and the pre-eminence an octogon has over an hexagon is no greater in sigures, than at hazard eight has above six among the chances.

Churches, ever since Christians have been able to build them, resemble the form of a cross, with the upper end pointing toward the east; and an architect, where there is room, and it can be conveniently done, who should neglect it, would be thought to have committed an unpardonable fault; but it would be foolish to expect this of a Turkish mosque or a Pagan temple. Among the many benesicial laws that have been made these hundred years, it is not easy to name one of greater utility, and, at the same time, more exempt from all inconveniences, than that which has regulated the dre&s of the dead. Those who were old enough to take notice of things when that act was made, and are yet alive, must remember the general clamour that was made against it. At sirst, nothing could be more mocking to thousands of people than that they were to be buried in woollen, and the only thing that made that law supportable was, that there was room left for people of some fashion to indulge their weakness without extravagancy; considering the other expences of funerals where mourning is given to several, and rings to a great many. The benesit that accrues to the nation from it is so visible, that nothing ever could be said in reason to condemn it, which, in few years, made the horror conceived against it lessen every day. I observed then that young people, who had seen but few in their cossins, did the soonest strike in with the innovation; but that those who, when the act was made, had buried many friends and relations, remained averse to it the longest, and I remember many that never could be reconciled to it to their dying day. By this time, burying in linen being almost forgot, it is the general opinion that nothing could be more decent than woollen, and the present manner of dressing a corps; which shows that our liking or disliking of things chiefly depends on mode and custom, and the precept and example of our betters, and such whom one way or other we think

to be superior to us.

In morals there is no greater certainty. Plurality of wives is odious among Christians, and all the wit and learning of a great genius in defence of it, has been rejected with contempt: rlut polvgamy is not mocking to a Mahometan. What men have learned from their infancy enslaves them, and the force of custom warps nature, and, at the fame time, imitates her in such a manner, that it is often dissicult to know which of the two we are influenced by. In the east, formerly sisters married brothers, and it was meritorious for a man to marry his mother. Such alliances are abominable; but it is certain that, whatever horror we conceive at the thoughts of them, there is nothing in nature repugnant against them, but what is built upon mode and custom. A religious Mahometan that has never tasted any spirituous liquor, and has often seen people drunk, may receive as great an aversion against wine, as another with us of the least morality and education may have against lying with his sister, and both imagine that their antipathy proceeds from nature. Which is the best religion? is a question that has caused more mischief

P than all other questions together. Ask it at Pekin, at Constantinople, and at Rome, and you will receive three distinct answers extremely disferent from one another, ye all of them equally positive and peremptory. Christians are well assured of the falsity of the Pagan and Mahometan superstitions: as to this point, there is a perfect union and concord among them; but inquire of the several sects they are divided into, Which is the true church of Christ? and all of them will tell you it is theirs, and to convince you, go together by the ears.

It is manifest, then, that the hunting after this *pulcbrm 1$ bone/lum,* is not much better than a wild-goose-chafe that is but little to be depended on: But this is not the greatest fault I sind with it. The imaginary notions that men may be virtuous without self denial, are a vast inlet to hypocrisy; which being once made habitual, we must not only deceive others, but likewise become altogether unknown to ourselves; and in an instance I am going to give, it will appear, how, for want of duly examining himself, this might happen to a person of quality, of parts, and erudition, one everyway resembling the author of the Characteristics himself.

A man that has been brought up in ease and affluence, if he is of a quiet indolent nature, learns to shun every thing that is troublesome, and chooses to curb his passions, more because of the inconveniences that arise from the eager pursuit after pleasure, and the yielding to all the demands of our inclinations, than any dislike he has to sensual enjoyments; and it is possible, that a person educated under a great philosopher, who was a mild and good-natured, as well as able tutor, may, in such happy circumstances, have a better opinion of his inward state than it really deserves, and believe himself virtuous, because his passions he dormant. He may form sine notions of the social virtues, and the contempt of death, write well of them in his closet, and talk eloquently of them in company, but you shall never catch him lighting for his country, or labouring to retrieve any national losses. A man that deals in metaphysics may easily throw himself into an enthusiasm, and really believe that he does not fear death while it remains out of sight. But should he be asked, why, having this intrepidity either from nature, or acquired by philosophy, he did not follow arms when his country was involved in war; or when he saw the nation daily robbed by those at the helm, and the affairs of the exchequer perplexed, why he did not go to cdurt; and make use of all his friends and interest to be a lord treasurer, that by his integrity and wife management, he might restore the public credit: It is probable he would answer that he loved retirement, had no other ambition than to be a good man, and never aspired to have any share in the government; or that he hated all flattery and slavish attendance, the insincerity of courts and bustle of the world. I am willing to believe him: but may not a man of an indolent temper and unactive spirit, say, and be sincere

in all this, and, at the fame time, indulge his appetites without being able to subdue them, though his duty summons him to it. Virtue consists in action, and whoever is possessed of this social love and kind asfection to his species, and by his birth or quality can claim any post in the public inanagement, ought not to sit still when he can be serviceable, but exert himself to the utmost for the good of his fellow subjects. Had this noble person been of a warlike genius, or a boisterous temper, he would have chose another part in the drama of life, and preached a quite contrary doctrine: For we are ever pushing our reason which way soever we feel passion to draw it, and self-love pleads to all human creatures for their disferent views, still furnishing every individual with arguments to justify their inclinations.

That boasted middle way, and the calm virtues recommended in the Characteristics, are good for nothing but to breed drones, and might qualify a m«n for the stupid enjoyments of a monastic life, or at beil a country justice of peace, but they would never sit him for labour and assiduity, or stir him up to great achievements and perilous under takings. Man's natural love of ease and idleness, and proneness to indulge his sensual pleasures, are not to be cured by precept: His ltrong habits and inclinations can only be subdued by paflions of greater violence. Preach and demonstrate to a coward the unreafonablenels of his fears, and you will not make him valiant, more than you can make him taller, by bidding him to be ten foot high, whereas the secret to raise courage, as I have made it public in Remaik on l. 321," is almost infallibe.

The fear of death is the strongest when we are in our greatest vigour, and our appetite is keen; when we are sharp%hted, quick of hearing, and every part performs its office. The reason is plain, because then life is molt delicious, and ourselves most capable of enjoying it. How comes it, then, that a man or" honour should so easily accept of a challenge, though at thirty and in perfect health? It is his pride that conquers his fear: For, when his pride is not

concerned, this fear will appear most glaringly. If he is not used to the sea, let him but be in a storm, or, if he never was ill before, have but a fore throat, or a flight fever, and he will show a thousand anxieties, and in them the inestimable value he sets on life. Had man been naturally humble and proof against flattery, the politician could never have had his ends, or known what to have made of him. Without vices, the excellency of the species would have ever remained undiscovered, and every worthy that has made himself famous in the world, is a strong evidence against this amiable system.

If the courage of the great Macedonian came up to distraction, when he fought alone against a whole garrison, his madness was not less when he fancied himself to be a god, or at least doubted whether he was or not; and as soon as we make this reflection, we discover both the passion and the extravagancy of it, that buoyed up his spirits in the most imminent dangers, and carried him through all the dissiculties and fatigues he underwent.

There never was in the world a brighter example of an able and complete magistrate than Cicero: When I think on his care and vigilance, the real hazards he slighted, and the pains he took for the safety of Rome; his wisdom and sagacity in detecting and' disappointing the stratagems of the boldest and most subtle conspirators, and, at the fame time, on his love to literature, arts, and sciences, his capacity in metaphysics, the justness of his reasonings, the force of his eloquence, the politeness of his style, and the genteel spirit that runs through his writings; when I think, I *fay,* on all these things together, I am struck with amazement, and the least I can fay of him is, that he was a prodigious man. But when I have set the many good qualities he had in the best sight, it is as evident to me on the other side, that had his vanity been inferior to his greatest excellency, the good fense and knowledge of the world he was so eminently possessed of, could never have let him be such a fulsome as well as noisy trumpeter as he was of his own praises, or sossered him rather tlmn not proclaim his own merit, to make a verse that a school boy would have been laughed at for. *O! Fortunatam*, &c.

How strict and severe was the morality of rigid Cato, how steady and unaffected the virtue of that grand asserter of Roman liberty! but though the equivalent this stoick enjoyed, for all the self-denial and austerity he practised, remained long concealed, and his peculiar modesty hid from the world, and perhaps himself a vast while, the frailty of his heart, that sorced him into heroism, yet it was brought to light in the last scene of his life, and by his suicide it plainly appeared that he was governed by a tyrannical power, superior to the love of his country, and that the implacable hatred and superlative envy he bore to the glory, the real greatness and personal merit of Cæsar, had for a long time swayed all his actions under the most noble pretences. Had not this violent motive over-ruled his consummate prudence, he might not only have saved himself, but likewise most of his friends that were ruined by the loss of him, and would in all probability, if he could have stooped to it, been the second man in Rome. But he knew the boundless mind and unlimited generosity of the victor: it was his clemency he feared, and therefore chose death because it was less terrible to his pride, than the thoughts of giving his mortal foe so tempting an opportunity of mowing the magnanimity of his soul, as Cæsar would have found in forgiving such an inveterate enemy as Cato, and offering him his friendship; and which, it is thought by the judicious, that penetrating as well as ambitious conqueror would not have Hipped, if the other had dared to live.

Another argument to prove the kind disposition, and real affection we naturally have for our species, is our love of company, and the aversion men that are in their senses generally have to solitude, beyond other creatures. This bears a sine gloss in the Characteristics, and is set off in very good language to the best advantage: the next day after 1 read it sirst, 1 heard abundance of people cry

fresh herrings, which, with the reflexion on the vast shoals of that and other sish that are caught together, made me very merry, though 1 was alone; but as I was entertaining myself with this contemplation, came an impertinent idle fellow, whom I had the misfortune to be known by, and asked me how I did, though 1 was, and dare fay, looked as healthy and as well as ever I yas or did in my life. What I answered him I forgot, but remember that I could not get rid of him in a good while, and felt all the uneasiness my friend Horace complains of, from a persecution of the like'nature.

I would have no sagacious critic pronounce me a manhater from this short story; whoever does is very much mistaken. 1 am a great lover of company, and if the reader is not quite tired with mine, before I show the weakness and ridicule of that piece of flattery made to our species, and which I was just now speaking of, I will give him a description of the man 1 would choose for conversation, with a promise that before he has sinished, what at sirst he might only take for a digression foreign to my purpose, he shall sind the ps; of it.

By early and artful instruction, he should be thoroughly imbued with the notions of honour and shame, and have contracted an habitual aversion to every thing that has the least tendency to impudence, rudeness, or inhumanity. He Ihould be well versed in the Latin tongue, and not ignorant of the Greek, and. moreover understand one or two of the modern languages besides his own. He should be acquainted with the fashions and customs of the ancients, but thoroughly skilled in the history of his own country, and the manners of the age he lives in. He should besides literature, have studied some useful science or other, seen some foreign courts and universities, and made the true use of travelling. He should at times take delight in dancing, fencing, riding the great horse, and knowing something of hunting and other country sports, without being attached to any, and he should treat them all as either exercises for health, or diversions thai ihould never

interfere with business, or the attaining to more valuable qualisications. He should have a lmatch of geometry and astronomy, as well as anatomy, and the economy of human bodies; to understand music so as to perform, is an accomplishment: but there is abundance to be said against it; and instead of it, I would have him know so much of drawing as is required to take a landskip, or explain ones meaning of any form or model we would describe, but never to touch a pencil. He should be very early used to the company *ol* modest women, and never be a fortnight without conversing with the ladies.

Gross vices, as irreligion, whoring, gaming, drinking and quarrelling, 1 will not mention: even the meanest education guards us against them; I would always recommend to him the practice of virtue, but I am for no voluntary ignorance, in a gentleman, of any thing that is done in court or city. It is impossible a man should be perfect, and therefore there are faults I would connive at,,f 1 could not prevent them; and if between the years of nineteen and thiee-and twenty, youthful heat should sometimes get the better os h s chastity, so it was done with caution; should he on some extraordinary occasion, overcome by the pressing solicitations of jovial friends, drink more than was consistent with strict sobriety, so he did it very seldom, and found it not to interfere with his health or temper; or if by the height of his mettle, and great provocation in a just cause, he had been drawn into a quarrel, which true wisdom and a less strict adherence to the rules of honour, might have declined or prevented, so it never befel him above once: if I fay he should have happened to be guilty of these things, and he would never speak, much less brag of them himself, they might be pardoned, or at least overlooked at the age 1 named, if he left off then and continued discreet for ever aster. The very disasters of youth, have sometimes frightened gentlemen into a more steady prudence, than in all probability they would ever have been masters of without them. To keep him from turpitude and things that are openly scandalous, there is nothing better than to procure him free access in one or two noble families, where his frequent attendance is counted a duty: and while by that means you preserve his pride, he is kept in a continual dread of shame.

A man of a tolerable fortune, pretty near accomplished as 1 have required him to be, that still improves himself and sees the world till he is thirty, cannot be disagreeable to oonverse with, at least while he continues in health and prosperity, and has nothing to spoil his temper. When such a ne, either by chance or appointment, meets with three or four of our equals, and all agree to pass away a few hours together, the whole is what 1 call good company. There is nothing said in it that is not either instructive or divertg to a man of fense. It is possible they may not always be os the fame opinion, but there can be no contest between y, but who shall yield sirst to the other he differs from. One only speaks at a time, and no louder than to be plainly understood by him who sits the farthest off. The greatest pleasure aimed at by every one of them, is to have the satisAction of pleasing others, which they all practically know may as effectually be done, by hearkening with attention and an approving countenance, as we said very good things ourselves.

Most people of any taste would like such a conversation, and justly prefer it to being alone, when they knew not how to spend their time; but if they could employ themselves in something from which they expected, either a more solid or a more lasting satisfaction, they would deny themfelves this pleasure, and follow what was of greater consequence to them. But would not a man, though he had seen ho mortal in a fortnight, remain alone as much longer, rather than get into company of noisy fellows, that take delight in contradiction, and place a glory in picking a quarrel? Would not one that has books read for ever, or set himself to write upon some subject or other, rather than be every night with partymen who count the island to be good for nothing, whde their adversaries are suffered to live up-

on it? Would not a man be by himself a month, and go to bed before seven a clock, rather than mix with fox-hunters, who having all day long tried in vain to break their necks, join at night in a second attempt upon their lives by drinking, and to express their mirth, are louder in senseless sounds within doors, than their barking and less troublesome companions are only without? I have no great value for a man who would not rather tire himself with walking; or if he was strut up scatter pins about the room in order to pick them up again, than keep company for six hours with half a score common sailors the day their ship was paid off.

I will grant, nevertheless, that the greatest part of mankind, rather than be alone any considerable time, would submit to the things I named: but 1 cannot fee, why this love of company, this strong desire after society, should be construed so much in our favour, and alleged as a mark of some intrinsic worth in man, not to be found in other animals. For to prove from it the goodness of our nature, and a generous love in man, extended beyond himself on the rest of his species, by virtue of which he was a sociable creature, this eagerness after company and aversion of being alone, ought to have been most conspicuous, and most violent in the best of their kind; the men of the greatest genius, parts and accomplishments, and those who are the least subject to vice; the contrary of which is true. The weakest minds, who can the least govern their passions, guilty consciences that abhor, reflexion, and the worthless, who are incapable of producing any thing of their own that is useful, are the greatest enemies to solitude, and will take up with any company rather than be without; whereas, the men of ienle and of knowledge, that can think and contemplate on things, and such as are but little disturbed by their passions, can bear to be by themselves the longest without reluclancy; and, to avoid noise, folly, and impertinence, will run away from twenty companies; and, rather than meet with any thing disagreeable to their good taste, will prefer their closet or a

garden, nay, a common or a desert to the society of some men.

But let us suppose the love of company so inseparable from our species, that no man could endure to be alone one moment, what conclusions could be drawn from this? Does not man love company, as he does every thing else, for his own fake? No friendships or civilities are lasting that are not reciprocal. In all your weekly and daily meetings for diversion, as well as annual feasts, and the most solemn carous.ls, every member that assists at them has his own ends, and some trequent a club which they would never go to unless they were the top of it. 1 have known a man who was the oracle of the company, be very constant, and as uneasy at any thing that hindered him from coming at the hour, leave his society altogether, as soon as another was added that could match, and disputed superiority with him. There are people who are incapable of holding an argument, and yet malicious enough to take delight in hearing others wrangle; and though they never concern themselves in the controversy, would think a company insipid where they could not have that diversion. A good house, rich furniture, a sine garden, horses, dogs, ancestors, relations, beauty, strength, excellency in any thing whatever; vices as well as virtue, may all be accessary to make men long for society, in hopes that what they value themselves upon will at one time or other become the theme of the discourse, and give an inward sa tisfaction to them. Even the most polite people in the world, and such as I spoke of at sirst, give no pleasure to others that is not repaid to their self-love, and does not at tast centre in themselves, let them wind it and turn it as they will. But the plainest demonstration that in all clubs and societies of conversable" people, every body has the greatest consideration for himself, is, that the disinterested, who rather over-pays than wrangles; the good humoured, that is never. waspish nor soon offended; the easy and indolent, that hatej disputes and never talks for triumph, is every where the darling of the company:

whereas, the man of fense and knowledge, that will not be imposed upon or talked out of his reason; the man of genius and spirit, that can fay sharp and witty things, though he never ladies but what deserves it; the man of honour, who neither gives nor takes an affront, maybe esteemed, but is seldom so well beloved as a weaker man less accomplilhed.

As in these instances, the friendly qualities arise from our contriving perpetually our own satisfaction, so, on other occasions, they proceed from the natural timidity of man, and the solicitous care he takes of himself. Two Londoners, whose business oblige them not to have any commerce together, may know, see, and pass by one another every day upon the Exchange, with not much greater civility than bulls would: let them meet at Bristol they will pull off their hats, and on the least opportunity enter into conversation, and be glad of one another's company. When French, English, and Dutch, meet in China, or any other Pagan country, being all Europeans, they look upon one another as countrymen, and if no passion interferes, will feel a natural propensity to love one another. Nay, two men that are at enmity, if they are forced to travel together, will often lay by their animosities, be affable, and converse in a friendly manner, especially if the road be unsafe, and they are both strangers jn the place they are to go to. These things by supersicial judges, are attributed to mans sociableness, his natural propensity to friendship and love of company; but whoever will duly examine things, and look into man more narrowly, will sind, that on all these occasions we only endeavour to strengthen our interest, and are moved by the causes already alleged.

What I have endeavoured hitherto, has been to prove, that the *pulchrum et honejlum,* excellency and real worth of things are most commonly precarious and alterable as modes and customs vary; that consequently the inferences drawn from their certainty are inlignisicant, and that the generous notions concerning the natural goodness of man are

hurtful, as they tend to misiead, and are merely chimerical: the truth of this latter I have illustrated by the most obvious examples in history. I have spoke of our love of company and avenion to solitude, examined thoroughly the various motives 01 them, and made it appear that they all centre in self-love. I inrend now to investigate into the nature of society, and diving into the very rife of it, make it evident, that not the good and amiable, but the bad and hateful qualities of man, his imperfections and the want of excellencies, which other creatures are endued with, are the sirst causes that made man iociable beyond other animals, the moment after he lost Paradise; and that if he had remained in his primitive innocence, and continued to enjoy the blessings that attended it, there is no shadow of probability that he ever would have become that sociable creature he is now.

How necessary our appetites and passions are for the welsare of all trades and handicrafts, has been sussiciently proved throughout the book, and that they are our bad qualities, or at least produce them, nobody denies. It remains then, that I should set forth the variety of obstacles that hinder and perplex man in the labour he is constantly employed in, the procuring of what he wants; and which in other words is called the business of self-preservation: while, at the lame time, I demonstrate that the sociablenels of man arises orcly from these two things, viz. the multiplicity of his desires, and the continual opposition he meets with in his endeavours to gratify them.

The obstacles I speak of, relate either to our own frame, or the globe we inhabit, I mean the condition of it, since it has been cursed. 1 have often endeavoured to contemplate separately on the two things 1 named last, but could never keep them asunder; they always interfere and mix with one another; and at last make up together a frightful chaos of evil. All the elements are our enemies, water dt owns and fire consumes thole who unskilfully approach them. The earth in a thousand places produces plants, and other vegetables that are

hurtful to man, while shc feeds and chenliies a variety of creatures that are noxious to him; and iutiers a legion of poisons to dwell within her: but the most unkind of all the elements is that which we cannot live one moment without: it is impossible to repeat all the injuries we receive from the wind and weather; and though the greatest part of mankind, have ever been employed in desending their species from the inclemency of the air, yet no art or labour have hitherto been able to find a secuiity against the wild rage of some meteors.

Hurricanes, i' is true, happen but seldom, and few men are swallowed up by earthquakes, or devoured by lions; but while we escape thole gigantic mischiefs, we are persecuted by trifles. What a vast variety of insects are tormenting to us; what multitudes of them insult and make game of us with impunity! The most despicable scruple not to trample and graze upon us ascattledo upon a sield: whichyet is often born with, if moderately they use their fortune; but here again our clemency becomes a vice, and so encroaching are their cruelty and contempt of us on our pity, that they make laystalls of our hands, and devour our young ones if we are not daily vigilant in pursuing and destroying them.

There is nothing good in all the universe to the best-designing man, if either through mistake or ignorance he commits the least failing in the use of it; there is no innocence or integrity, that can protect a man from a thousand mischiefs that surround him: on the contrary, every thing is evil, which art and experience have not taught us to turn into a blessing. Therefore how diligent in harvest time is the husbandman, in getting in his crop and shckering it from rain, without which he could never have enjoyed it! As seasons differ with the climates, experience has taught us differently to make use of them, and in one part of the globe we may see the farmer sow while he is reaping in the other; from all which we may learn how vastly this earth must have been altered since the fall of our sirst parents. For should we trace man from his beautiful, his divine original, not proud of wisdom acquired by haughty precept or tedious experience, but endued with consummate knowledge the moment he was formed; I mean the state of innocence, in which no animal nor vegetable upon earth, nor mineral under ground was noxious to him, and himself secured from the injuries of the air as well as all other harms, was contented with the necessaries of life, which the globe he inhabited furnished him with, without his assistance. When yet not conscious ot guilt, he found himself in every place to be the well obeyed unrivalled lord of all, and unaffected with his greatness, was wholly wrapped up in sublime meditations on the insinity of his Creator, who daily did vouchsafe intelligibly to speak to him, and vilit without mischief.

In such a golden age, no reason or probability can be alleged, why mankind ever should have raised themselves into such large societies as there have been in the world, as *long* as we cast give any tolerable account of it. Where a man has every thing he desires, and nothing to vex or disturb him, there is nothing can be added to his happiness; and it is impossible to name a trade, art, science, dignity, or employment, that would not be superfluous in such a blessed state. If we pursue this thought, we shall easily perceive that no societies could have sprung from the amiable virtues and loving qualities ol man; but, on the contrary, that all of them must have had the origin from his wants, his imperfections, and the variety of his appetites: we shall sind likewise, that the more their pride and vanity are displayed, and all their desires enlarged, the more capable they must be of being raised into large and vastly numerous societies.

Was the air always as inoffensive to our naked bodies, and as pleasent as to our thinking it is to the generality of birds in fair weather, and man had not been affected with pride, luxury and hypocrisy, as well as lust, I cannot fee what could have put us upon the invention of clothes and houses. I stiall fay nothing of jewels, of plate, painting, sculpture, sine furniture, and all that rigid moralists have called unnecessary and fuperfluons: but if we were not soon tired with walking a-foot, and were as nimble as some other animals; if men were naturally laborious, and none unreasonable in seeking and indulging their ease, and likewise free from other vices, and the ground was every where even, solid and clean, who would have thought of coaches or ventured on a horse's back? What occasion has the dolphin for a ship, or what carriage would an eagle ask to travel in?

I hope the reader knows, that by society I understand a body politic, in which man either subdued by superior force, or by persuasion drawn from his savage state, is become a disciplined creature, that can sind his own ends in labouring for others, and where under one head or other form of government, each member is rendered subservient to the whole, and all of them by cunning management are made to act as one. For if by society we only mean a number of people, that without rule or government, should keep together, out of a natural affection to their species, or love of company, as a herd of cows or a flock of sheep, then there is not in the world a more unsit creature for society than man; an hundred of them that stiould be all equals, under no subjection, or fear of any superior upon earth, could never live together awake two hours without quarrelling, and the more knowledge, strength, wit, courage and resolution there was among them, the worse it would be.

It is probable, that in the wild state of nature, parents would keep a superiority over their children, at least while they were in strength, and that even afterwards, the remembrance of what the others had experienced, might produce in them something between love and fear, which we call reverence: it is probable, likewise, that the second generation following the example of the sirst; a man with a little cunning would always be able, as long as he lived and had his fenses, to maintain a superior sway over all his own offspring and descendants, how numerous soever they might grow. But the old stock once dead, the sons would quarrel, and there could be no peace long, before there had been war. Eldership in brothers is of no great force, and the pre-eminence that is given to it, only invented as a slhft to live in peace. Man, as he is a fearful animal, naturally not rapacious, loves peace and quiet, and he would never sight, if nobody offended him, and he could.have what he sights for without it. To this fearful disposition, and the aversion he has to his being disturbed, are owing all the various projects and forms of government. Monarchy, without doubt, was the sirst. Aristocracy and democracy were two different methods of mending the inconveniencies of the sirst, and a mixture of these three an improvement on all the rest.

But be we savages or politicians, it is impossible that man, mere fallen man, should act with any other view but to please himself while he has the use of his organs, and the greatest extravagancy either of love or despair can have no other centre. There is no difference between will and pleasure in one sense, and every motion made in spite of them must be unnatural and convulsive. Since, then, action is so consined, and we are always forced to do what we please, and at the saine time our thoughts are free and uncontroulcd, it is impossible we could be sociable creatures without hypocrisy. The proof of this is plain, since we cannot prevent the ideas that are continually arising within us, all civil commerce would be lost, if, by art and prudent dissimulation we had not learned to hide and stifle them; and if all we think was to be laid open to others, in the fame manner as u is to ourselves, it is impossible that, endued with speech, we could be susserable to one another. l am persuaded that every reader feels the truth of what I fay; and I tell my an tagonist that his conscience flies in his face, while his tongue is preparing to refute me. In all civil societies men are taught insensibly to be hypocrites from their cradle; nobody dares to own that he gets by public calamities, or even by the loss of private persons. The sexton would be Honed should he wish openly for the death of the parishoners, though every body knew that he had nothing else to live up-on.

To me it is a great pleasure, when I look on the affairs of human life, to behold into what various, and often strangely opposite forms, the hope of gain and thoughts of lucre shape men, according to the different employments they are of, and stations they are in. How gay and merry does every face appear at a well ordered ball, and what a solemn sadness is observed at the masquerade of a funeral! but the undertaker is as much pleased with his gains as the dancingmaster: both are equally tired in their occupations, and the mirth of the one is as much forced as the gravity of the other is affected. Those who have never minded the conversation of a spruce mercer, and a young lady his customer that comes to his shop, have neglected a scene of life that is very entertaining. I beg of my serious reader, that he would, for a while, abate a little of his gravity, and suffer me to examine these people separately, as to their inside, and thi different motives they act from.

His business is to sell as much silk as he can at a price by which he shall get what he proposes to be reasonable, according to the customary prosits of the trade. As to the lady, what she would be at is to please her fancy, and buy cheaper by a groat or sixpence per yard than the things she wants are commonly fold at. From the impression the gallantry of our sex has made upon her. she imagines (if she be not very deformed) that she has a sine mien and easy behaviour, and a peculiar sweetness of voice; that she is handsome, and if not beautiful, at least more agreeable than most young women she knows. As lhe has no pretensions to purchase the same things with less money than other people, but what are built on her good qualities, so she sets herlelf off to the best advantage her wit and discretion will let her. The thoughts of love are here out of the case; so on the one hand, she has no room foj playing the tyrant, and giving herielf angry and peevish airs, and, on the other, more liberty f speaking kindly, aud being affable than slie can have almost

on any other occasion. She knows that abundance of well-bred people come to his shop, and endeavours to render herself as amiable as virtue and the rules of decency allow of. Coming with such a resolution of behaviour, she cannot meet with any thing to ruffle her temper.

Before her coach is yet quite stopped, she is approached by a gentleman-like man, that has every thing clean and fashionable about him, who in low obeisance pays her homage, and as soon as her pleasure is known that she has a mind to come in, hands her into the shop, where immediately he flips from her, and through a by-way that remains visible only for half a moment, with great address entrenches himself behind the counter: here facing her, with a profound reverence and modish phrase, he begs the favour of knowing her commands. Let her fay and dislike what she pleases, she can never be directly contradicted: she deals with a man in whom consummate patience is one of the mysteries of his trade, and whatever trouble she creates she is sure to hear nothing but the most obliging language, and has always before her a cheerful countenance, where joy and respect seem to be blended with good humour, and altogether make up an artisicial serenity more engaging than untaught nature is able to produce.

When two persons are so well met, the conversation must be very agreeable, as well as extremely mannerly, though they talk about trifles. While she remains irresolute what to take, he seems to be the fame in advising her; and is very cautious how to direct her choice; but when once she has made it and is sixed, he immediately becomes positive, that it is the best of the sort, extols her fancy, and the more he looks upon it, the more he wonders he mould not besore have discovered the pre-eminence of it over any thing be has in his shop. By precept, example, and great application, he has learned unobserved to slide into the inmost recesses of the soul, sound the capacity of his customers, and sind out their blind side unknown to them: by all which he is in-

structed in sifty other stratagems to make her over-value her own judgment as well as the commodity she would purchase. The greatest advantage he has over her, lies in the most material part of the commerce between them, the debate about the price, which he knows to a farthing, and she is wholly ignorant of: therefore he no where more egregiously imposes on her understanding; and though here he ha» the liberty of telling what lies he pleases, as to the prime cost, and the money he has refused, yet he trusts not to them only; but, attacking her vanity, makes her believe the most incredible things in the world, concerning his own weakness and her superior abilities; he had taken a resolution, he fays, never to part with that piece under such a price, but she has the power of talking him out of his goods beyond any body he ever fold to: he protests that he loses by his silk, but seeing that she has a fancy for it, and is resolved to give no more, rather than disoblige a lady he has such an uncommon value for, he will let her have it, and only begs that another time she will not stand so hard with him. In the mean time, the buyer, who knows that she is no fool, and has a voluble tongue, is easily persuaded that she has a very winning way of talking, and thinking it sussicient, for the sake of good-breeding, to disown her merit, and iri some witty repartee retort the compliment, he makes her swallow very contentedly, the substance of every thing he tells her. The upshot is, that, with the satisfaction of having saved ninepence per yard, she has bought her silk exactly at the fame price as any body else might have done, and often gives sixpence more than, rather than not have sold it, he would have taken.

It is possible that this lady, for want of being susssiciently flattered, for a fault she is pleased to sind in his behaviour, or perhaps the tying of his neckcloth, or some other dislike as substantial, may be lost, and her custom bestowed on some other of the fraternity. But where many of them live m a cluster, it is not always easily determined which shop to go to, and the reasons some of the fair sex have for their choice, are often very whimsical, and kept as great a secret. We never follow our inclinations with more freedom, than where they cannot be traced, and it is unreasonable for others to suspect them. A virtuous woman has preferred one house to all the rest, because she had seen a handsome fellow in it, and another of no bad character for having received greater civility before it, than had been paid her any where else, when she had no thoughts of buying, and was going to Paul's church: for among the fashionable mercers, the fair dealer must keep before his own door, and to draw in random customers, make use of no other freedom or importunities than an obsequious air, with a submissive posture, and perhaps a bow to every well dressed female that offers to look towards his shop.

What I have said last, makes me think on another way of inviting customers, the most distant in the world from what I have been speaking of, I mean that which is practised by the watermen, especially on those whom, by their mien and garb, they know to be peasants. It is not unpleasant to see half a dozen people surround a man they never saw in their lives before, and two of them that can get the nearest, clapping each an arm over his neck, hug him in as loving and familiar a manner, as if he was their brother newly come home from an East India voyage; a third lays hold of his hand, another of his sleeve, his coat, the buttons of it, or any thing he can come at, while a sifth or a sixth, who has scampered twice round him already, without being able to get at him, plants himself directly before the man in hold, and within three inches of his nose, contradicting his rivals with an open mouthed cry, shows him a dreadful set of large teeth, and a small remainder of chewed bread and cheese, which the countryman's arrival had hindered from being swallowed.

At all this no offence is taken, and the peasant justly thinks they are making much of him; therefore, far from opposing them, he patiently suffers himself to be pushed or pulled which way the strength that surrounds him shall di-

rect. He has not the delicacy to sind fault with a man's breath, who has just blown out his pipe, or a greasy head of hair that is rubbing against his chops: Dirt and sweat he has been used to from his cradle, and it is no disturbance to him to hear half a score people, some of them at his ear, and the furthest not sive foot from him, bawl out as if he was a hundred yards off: He is conscious that he makes no lels noise when he is merry himself, and is secretly pleased with their boisterous usages. The bawling and pulling him about he construes the way it is intended; it is a courtship he can feel and understand: He cannot help wishing them well tor the esteem they scem to have for him: He loves to be taken notice of, and admires the Londoners for being so pressing in the offers of their service to him, for the value of threepence or less; whereas, in the country at the shop he uses, he can have nothing but he must sirst tell them what he wants, and, though he lays out three or four shillings at a time, has hardly a word spoke to him unless it be in answer to a queltion himself is forced to ask sirst. This alacrity in his behalf moves his gratitude, and, unwilling to disoblige any, from his heart he knows not whom to choose. I have seen a man think all this, or something like it, as plainly as 1 could fee the nose in his face; and, at the fame time, move along very contentedly under a load of watermen, and with a smiling countenance carry seven or eight stone more than his own weight to the water side.

If the little mirth I have shown, in the drawing of these two images from low life, misbecomes me, I am sorry for it, but I promise not to be guilty of that fault any more, and will now, without loss of time, proceed with my argument in artless dull simplicity, and demonstrate the gross eaor of those, who imagine that the social virtues, and the amiable qualities that are praise-worthy in us, are equally benesicial to the public as they are to the individual persons that are possessed of them, and that the means of thriving, and whatever conduces to the welfare and real happiness of private families, must have the fame

effect upon the whole society. This, I confess, 1 have laboured for all along, and I flatter myself not unsuccessfully: But 1 hope nobody will like a problem the worse for seeing the truth of it proved more ways than one.

It is certain, that the fewer desires a man has, and the less he covets, the more easy he is to himself; the more active he Is to supply his own wants, and the less he requires to be waited upon, the more he will be beloved, and the less trouble he is in a family; the more he loves peace and concord, the more charity he has for his neighbour, and the more he shines in real virtue, there is no doubt but that in proportion he is acceptable to God and man. But let us be just, what benesit can these things be of, or what earthly good can they do, to promote the wealth, the glory, and worldly greatness of nations? It is the sensual courtier that sets nu limits to his luxury; the sickle strumpet that invents new fashions every week; the haughty duchess that in equipage, entertainments, and all her behaviour, would imitate a piincess; the profuse rake and lavish heir, that scatter about their money without wit or judgment, buy every thing they see, and either destroy or give it away the next day; the covetous and perjured villain that squeezed an immense trealure from the tears of widows and orphans, and lest the prodigals the money to spend: It is thele that are the prey and proper food of a full grown Leviathan; or, in other words, such is the calamitous condition of human affairs, that we stand in need of the plagues and monsters I named, to have all the variety of labour performed, which the skill of men is capable of inventing in order to procure an honest livelihood to the vast multitudes of working poor, that are required to make a large society: And it is folly to imagine, that great and wealthy nations can subsist, and be at once powerful and polite without.

I protest against Popery as much as ever Luther and Calvin did, or Queen Elizabeth herself; but I believe from my heart, that the Reformation has scarce been more instrumental in rendering the kingdoms and states that have embraced it, flourishing beyond other nations, than the silly and capricious invention of hooped and quilted petticoats. But is this should be denied me by the enemies of priestly power, at least 1 am sure that, bar the great men who have fought for and against that layman's blelling, it has, from its beginning to this day, not employed so many hands, honest, industrious labouring hands, as the abominable improvement on female luxury, I named, has done in few years. Religion is one thing, and trade is another. He that gives most trouble to thousands of his neighbours, and invents the most operofe manufactures, is, right or wrong, the greatest friend to the society.

What a bustle is there to be made in several parts of the world, before a sine scarlet or crimson cloth can be produced; what multiplicity of trades and artisicers must be employed! Not only such as are obvious, as woolcombers, spinners, the weaver, the cloth worker, the scourer, the dyer, the setter, the drawer, and the packer; but others that are more remote, and might seem foreign to it; as the mill-wright, the pewterer, and the chemist, which yet are all necessary, as well as a great number of other handicrafts, to have the tools, utensils, and other implements belonging to the trades already named: But all these things are done at home, and may be persormed without extraordinary fatigue or danger; the most frightful prospect is left behind, when we reflect on the toil and hazard that are to be undergone abroad, the vast seas we are to go over, the disferent climates we are to endure, and the several nations we must be obliged to for their assistance. Spain alone, it is true, might furnish us with wool to make the sinest cloth; but what skill and pains, what experience and ingenuity, are required to dye it of those beautiful colours! How widely are the drugs, and other ingredients, dispersed through the universe that are to meet in one kettle! Allum, indeed, we have of our own ; argol we might have from the Rhine, and vitriol from Hun-. gary; all this is in Europe; but then for saltpetre in quantity, we are forced to go as far

as the East Indies. Cocheneal, unknown to the ancients, is not much nearer to us, though in a quite different part of the earth: we buy it, it is true, from the Spaniards; but not being their product, they are forced to fetch it for us from the remotest corner of the new world in the East Indies. While so many sailors are broiling in the fun, and sweltered with heat in the east and west of us, another set of them are freezing in the north, to fetch potashes from Russia.

When we are thoroughly acquainted with all the variety of toil and labour, the hardships and calamities that must be undergone to compass the end I speak of, and we consider the vast risks and perils that are run in those voyages, and that few of them are ever made but at the expence, not only of the health and welfare, but even the lives of many: When we are acquainted with, I fay, and duly consider the things I named, it is scarce possible to conceive a tyrant so inhuman, and void of shame, that, beholding things in the fame view, he should exact such terrible services from his innocent slaves; and, at the fame time, dare to own, that he did it for no other reason, than the satisfaction a man receives from having a garment made of scarlet or crimson cloth. But to what height of luxury must a nation be arrived, where not only the king's ossicers, but likewise the guards, even the private soldiers, should have such impudent desires!

But if we turn the prospect, and look on all those labours io many voluntary actions, belonging to different callings and occupations, that men are brought up to for a livelihood, and in which every one works for himself, how much soever he may seem to labour for others: If we consider, that even he sailors who undergo the greatest hardships, as soon as one voyage is ended, even after shipwreck, are looking out, and soliciting for employment in another: It we consider, I say, and look on these things in another view; we mall sind, that the labour of the poor is so far from being a burden and an imposition upon them, that to have employment is a blessing, Which, in their addresses to Heaven,

they pray for, and to to procure it for the generality of them', is the greatest care of every legislature.

As children, and even infants, are the apes of others, so all youth have an ardent desire of being men and women, and become often ridiculous by their impatient endeavours to appear what every body fees they are not; all large societies are not a little indebted to this folly for the perpetuity, or at least long continuance, of trades once established. What pains will young people take, and what violence will they not commit upon themselves, to attain to insignisicant, and often blameable qualisications, which, for want of judgment and experience, they admire in others, that are superior to them in age! This fondness of imitation makes them accustom themselves, by degrees, to the use os things that were irksome, if not intolerable to them at sirst, till they know not how to leave them, and are often very sorry for having inconsiderately increased the necessaries of life without any necessity. What estates have been got by tea and coffee! What a vast trassic is drove, what a variety of labour is performed in the world, to the maintenance of thousands of families that altogether depend on two silly, if not odious customs; the taking of snuff, and smoking of tobacco; both.which, it is certain, do insinitely more hurt than good to those that are addicted to them! 1 sliall go further, and demonstrate the usefulness of private losles and misfortunes to the public, and the folly of our wishes, when we pretend to be most wife and serious. The sire of London was a great calamity; but if the carpenters, bricklayers, smiths, and all, not only that are employed in building, but likewise those that made and dealt in the same manufactures, and other merchandises that were burnt, and other trades again that got by them when they were in full employ, were to vote against those who lost by the sire, the rejoicings would equal, if not exceed the complaints. In recruiting what is lost and destroyed by sire, storms, sea-sights, sieges, battles, a considerable part of trade consists; the truth of which, and whatever I have iuid-#f the nature of society, will plainly appear from what follows.

It would be a dissicult task to enumerate all the advantages and disferent benesits, that accrue to a nation, on account of shipping and navigation; but if we only take into consideration the ships themselves, and every vessel great and small that Is made use of for water-carriage, from the least wherry to a sirst rate man of war; t timber and hands that are employed in the building of them; and consider the pitch, tar, rosin, grease; the masts, yards, fails and riggings; the variety of smiths work; the cables, oars, and every thing else belonging to them; we shall sind, that to furnish only such a nation as ours with all the necessaries, make up a considerable part of the trassic of Europe, without speaking of the stores and ammunition of all forts, that are consumed in them, or the mariners, waterman and others, with their families, that are maintained by them.

But should we, on the other hand, take a view of the manifold mischiefs and variety of evils, moral as well as natural, that befal nations on the score of seafaring, and their commerce with strangers, the prospect would be very frightful; and could we suppose a large populous island, that should be wholly unacquainted with ships and sea affairs, hut otherwise a wise and well-governed people; and that some angel, or their genius, should lay before them a scheme or draught, where they might sec on the one side, all the riches and real advantages that would be acquired by navigation in a thousand years; and on the other, the wealth and lives that would be lost, and all the other calamities, that would be unavoidably sustained on account of it during the same time, I am consident, they would look upon ships with horror and detestation, and that their prudent rulers would ieverely forbid the making and inventing all buildings or machines to go to sea with, of what shape or denomination soever, and prohibit all such abominable contrivances on great penalties, if not the pain of death.

But to let alone the necessary consequence of foreign trade, the corruption of manners, as well as plagues, poxes, and other diseases, that are brought to us by shipping, should we only cast our eyes on what is either to be imputed to the wind and weather, the treachery of the seas, the ice of the north, the vermin of the south, the darkness of nights, and unwholesomeness of climates, or else occasioned by the want fgood provisions, and the faults of manners, and unskilfulnsis of some, and the neglect and drunkenness of others; 'id should we consider the losses of men and treasure swallowed up in the deep, the tears and necessities of widows and orphans made by the sea, the ruin of merchants and the consequences, the continual anxieties that parents and wives are in tor the sufetv of their children and husbands, and not forget the many pangs and heart-aches that are felt throughout a trading nation, by owners and insurers, at every blast of wind; should we cast our eyes, I fay, on these things, consider with due attention and give them the weight they deserve, would it not be amazing, how a nation of thinking people mould talk of their ships and navigation as a peculiar blessing to them, and placing an uncommon felicity in having an insinity of vessels dispersed through the wide world, and always some going to and others coming from every part of the universe?

But let us once, in our consideration on these things, consine ourselves to what the ships suffer only, the vessels themselves, with their rigging and appurtenances, without thinking on the freight they carry, or the hands that work them, and we shall sind that the damage sustained that way only, is very considerable, and must one year with another amount to vast sums; the ships that are foundered at sea, split against rocks and swallowed up by sands, some by the sierceness of tempests altogether, others by that and the want of pilots, experience, and knowledge of the coasts: the masts that are blown down, or forced to be cut and thrown overboard, the yards, fails, and cordage of different sizes that are destroyed by storms, and the anchors that are lost: add to these the necessary repairs of leaks sprung,

and other hurts received from the rage of winds, and the violence of the waves: many ships are set on sire by carelessness, and the effects of strong liquors, which none are more addicted to than sailors: sometimes unhealthy climates, at others the badness of provision breed fatal distempers, that sweep away the greatest part os the crew, and not a few ships are lost for want of hands.

These are all calamities inseparable from navigation, and seem to be great impediments that clog the wheels of foreign commerce. How happy would a merchant think himself, if his ships should always have sine weather, and the wind he wished for, and every mariner he employed, from the highest to the lowest, be a knowing experienced sailor, and a careful, sober, good man! Was such a felicity to be had for prayers, vhat owner of ships is there, or dealer in Europe, nay, the whole world, who would not be all day long teazing Heaven to obtain such a blessing for himself, without regard to what detriment it would do to others? Such a petition would certainly be a very unconscionable one; yet where is the man who imagines not that he has a right to make it? And there fore, as every one pretends to an equal claim to those favours, let us, without reflecting on the impossibility of its being true, suppose all their prayers esfectual and their wishes answered, and afterwards examine into the result of such a happiness.

Ships would last as long as timber houses to the full, because they are as strongly built, and the latter are liable to suffer by high winds and other storms, which the sirst, by our supposition, are not to be: so that, before there would be any real occasion for new ships, the master builders now in being, and every body under them, that is set to work about them, would all die a natural death, if they were not starved or come to some untimely end: for, in the sirst place, all sliips having prosperous gales, and never waiting for the wind, they would make very quick voyages both out and home: secondly, no merchandises would be damaged by the sea, or by stress of weather thrown overboard, but the entire lading would always come safe ashore; and hence it would follow, that three parts in four of the merchant-men already made, would be superfluous for the present, and the stock of ships that are now in the world, serve a vast many years. Masts and yards would last as long as the vessels themselves, and we should not need to trouble Norway on that score a great while yet. The sails and rigging, indeed, of the few ships made use of would wear out, but not a quarter part so fast as now they do, for they often suffer more in one hour's storm, than in ten days fair weather.

Anchors and cables there would be seldom any occasion for, and one of each would last a ship time out of mind: this article alone, would yield many a tedious holiday to the anchor-smiths and the rope-yards. This general want of consumption would have such an influence on the timbermerchants, and all that import iron, sail-cloth, hemp, pitch, tar, &-c. that four parts in sive of what, in the beginning of this rellection on sca-assairs, I said, made a considerable branch of the tralfic of Europe, would be entirely lost.

I have only touched hitherto on the consequences of this blessing in relation to shipping, but it would be detrimental to all other branches of trade besides, and destructive to the poor of every country, that exports any thing of their own growth or manufacture. The goods and merchandises that every year go to the deep, that are spoiled at sea by falt water, by heat, by vermine, destroyed by sire, or lost to the merchant by other accidents, all owing to storms or tediou9 vbyages, or else the neglect or rapacity of sailors; such goods, I fay, and merchandises are a considerable part of what every year is sent abroad throughout the world, and must have employed great multitudes of poor, before they could come on board. A hundred bales of cloth that are burnt or funk in the Mediterranean, are as benesicial to the poor in England, as if they had safely arrived at Smyrna or Aleppo, and every yard of them had been retailed on the grand Signior's dominions.

The merchant may break, and by him

the clothier, the dyer, the packer, and other tradesmen, the middling people, may suffer; but the poor that were set to work about them can never lose. Day-labourers commonly receive their earnings once a-week, and all the working people that were employed, either in any of the various branches of the manufacture itself, or the several land and water carriages it requires to be brought to perfection, from the sheep's back, to the vessel it was entered in, were paid, at least much the greatest part of them, before the parcel came on board. Should any of my readers draw conclusions *in infinitum,* from my assertions, that goods funk or burnt are as benesicial to the poor, as if they had been well fold and put to their proper uses, I would count him a caviller and not worth answering: mould it always rain and the fun never shine, the fruits of the earth would soon be rotten and destroyed; and yet it is no paradox trt assirm, that, to have grafs or corn, rain is as necessary as the sunshine.

Irtswhat manner this blessing of fair winds and sine weather, would affect the mariners themselves, and the breed of iailors, may be easily conjectured from what has been said already. As there would hardly one ship in four be made use of, so the vessels themselves being always exempt from storms, fewer hands would be required to work them, and consequently sive in six of the seamen we have might be spared, which in this nation, most employments of the poor being overstocked, would be but an untoward article. As soon as those superfluous seamen should be extinct, it would be impossible to man such large sleets as we could at present: but I do not look upon this as a detriment, or the least inconveniency: for the reduction of mariners, as to numbers being general throughout the world, all the consequence would be, that in case of war, the maritime powers would be obliged to fight with fewer ships, which would be an happiness instead of an evil: and would you carry this felicity to the highest pitch of perfection, it is but to add one desirable Westing more, and no nation shall ever sight at all:

the blessing I hint at is, what all good Christians are bound to pray for, viz. that all princes and states would be true to their oaths and promises, and just to one another, as well as their own subjects; that they might have a greater regard for the dictates of conscience and religion, than those of state politics and worldly wisdom, and prefer the spiritual welfare of others to their own carnal desires, and the honesty, the safety, the peace and tranquillity of the nations they govern, to their own love of glory, spirit of revenge, avarice, and ambition.

The last paragraph will to many seem a digression, that makes little for my purpose; but what I mean by it, is to demonstrate that goodness, integrity, and a peaceful disposition in rulers and governors of nations, are not the proper qualisications to aggrandize them, and increase their numbers; any more than the uninterrupted series of success that every private person would be blest with, if he could, and which I have shown would be injurious and destructive to a large society, that should place a felicity in worldly greatness, and being envied by their neighbours, and value themselves upon their honour and their strength.

No man needs to guard himself against blessings, but calamities require hands to avert them. The amiable qualities of man put none of the species upon stirring: his honesty, his love of company, his goodness, content and frugality, are so many comforts to an indolent society, and the more real and unaffected they are, the more they keep every thing at rest and peace, and the more they will every where prevent trouble and motion itself. The same almost may be said of the gists and munisicence of Heaven, and all the bounties and benesits of nature: this is certain, that the more extensive they are, and the greater plenty we have of them, the more we save our labour. But the necessities, the vices, and imperfections of man, together with the various inclemencies ot the air and other elements, contain in them the feeds of all arts, industry and labour: it is the extremities of heat and old, the inconstancy and badness of seasons, the violence and uncertainty of winds, the vast power and treachery of water, the rage and untractablenets of sire, and the stubbornness and sterility of the earth, that rack our invention, how we shall either avoid the mischiefs they may produce, or correct the malignity of them, and turn their several forces to ovir own advantage a thousand different ways; while we are employed in supplying the insinite variety of our wants, which will ever be multiplied as our knowledge is enlarged, and our desires increase. Hunger, thirst, and nakedness, are the sirst tyrants that force us to stir: afterwards, our pride, sloth, sensuality, and sickleness, are the great patrons that promote all arts and sciences, trades, handicrafts and callings; while the great task-masters, necessity, avarice, envy, and ambition, each in the class that belongs to him, keep the members of the society to their labour, and make them all submit, most of them cheerfully, to the drudgery of their station; kings and princes not excepted.

The greater the variety of trades and manufactures the more operofe they are, and the more they are divided in many branches, the greater numbers may be contained in a society without being in one another's way, and the more easily they may be rendered a rich, potent, and siourishing people. Few virtues employ any hands, and therefore they may render a small nation good, but they can never make a great one. To be strong and laborious, patient in dissiculties, and asiiduous in all business, are commendable qualities; but as they do their own work, so they are their own reward, and neither art nor industry have ever paid their compliments to them; whereas the excellency of human thought and contrivance, has been, and is yet no where more conspicuous than in the variety of tools and instruments of workmen and artisicers, and the multiplicity of engines, that were all invented either to assist the weakness of man, to correct his many imperfections, to gratify his laziness, or obviate his impatience.

It is in morality as it is in nature, there is nothing so perfectly good in creatures, that it cannot be hurtful to any

one of the society, nor any thing so entirely evil, but it may prove benesicial to some part or other of the creation: so that things are only good and evil in reference to so something else, and according to the light and position they are placed in. What pleases us is good in that regard, and by this rule every man wishes well for himself to the best of his capacity, with little respect to his neighbour. There never was any rain yet, though in a very dry season when public prayers had been made for it, but somebody or other who wanted to go abroad, wished it might be fair weather only for that day. When the corn stands thick in the spring, and the generality of the country rejoice at the pleasing object, the rich farmer who kept his last year's crop for a better market, pines at the sight, and inwardly grieves at the prospect of a plentiful harvest. Nay, we shall often hear your idle people openly wish for the possessions of others, and not to be injurious forsooth add this wife proviso, that it should be without detriment to the owners: but I am afraid they often do it without any such restriction in their hearts.

It is a happiness that the prayers as well as wishes of most people, are insignisicant and good for nothing; or else the only thing that could keep mankind sit for society, and the world from falling into confusion, would be the impossibility that all the petitions made to Heaven mould be granted. A dutiful pretty young gentleman newly come from his travels, lies at the Briel waiting with impatience for an easterly wind, to waft him over to England, where a dying father, who wants to embrace and give him his blessing before he yields his breath, lies hoaning after him, melted with grief and tenderness: in the mean while a British minister, who is to take care of the Protestant interest in Germany, is riding post to Harwich, and in violent haste to be at Ratisbone before the diet breaks up. At the fame time a rich fleet lies ready for the Mediterranean, and a sine squadron is bound for the Baltic. All these things may probably happen at once, at least there is no dissiculty in supposing they should.

If these people are not atheists, or very great reprobates, they will all have some good thoughts before they go to sleep, and consequently about bed-time, they must all differently pray for a foir wind and a prosperous voyage. 1 do not fay but it 's their duty, and it is possible they may be all heard,'but I am sure they cannot be all served at the same time.

After this, I flatter myself to have demonstrated that, neither the friendly qualities and kind affections that are natural to an, nor the real virtues he is capable of acqiring by reason and self-denial, are the foundation of society ; but that what We call evil in this world, moral as well as natural, is the grand principle that makes us sociable creatures, the solid basis, the life and support of all trades and employments without exception: that there we must look for the true origin of all arts and sciences, and that the moment evil ceases, the society must be spoiled, if not totally dissolved.

I could add a thousand things to enforce, and further illustrate this truth, with abundance of pleasure; but for fear of being troublesome, I shall make an end, though I confess that 1 have not been half so solicitous to gain the approbation of others, as 1 have studied to please myself in this amusement: yet if ever I hear, that by following this diversion I have given any to the intelligent reader, it will always add to the satisfaction I have received in the performance. In the hope my vanity forms of this, I leave him with regret, and conclude with repeating the seeming paradox, the substance of which is advanced in the title page; that private vices, by the dexterous management of a skilful politician. may be turned into public benesits.

VINDICATION

Book., from the Aspersions contained in a Presentment of the Grand Jury of Middlesex,

And an Abusive Letter to Lord C 1 Hat the reader may be fully instructed in the merits of the cause between my adversaries and myself, it is requisite that, before he fees my defence, he should know the whole charge, and have before him all the accusations against me at large.

the Presentment of the Grand Jury is worded thus:

W E the Grand Jury for the county of Middlesex, have, with the greatest sorrow and concern, observed the many books and pamphlets that are almost every week published against the sacred articles of our holy religion, and all discipline and order in the church, and the manner in which this is carried on, seems to us to have a direct tendency to propagate insidelity, and consequently corruption of all morals.

We are justly sensible of the goodness of the Almighty, that has preserved us from the phgue, which has visited our neighbouring nation, and for which great mercy, his Majesty was graciously pleased to command, by his proclamation, that thanks mould be returned to Heaven; but how provoking must it be to the Almighty, that his mercies and deliverances extended to this nation, and our thanksgiving that was publicly commanded for it, should be attended with such flagrant impieties.

We know of nothing that can be of greater service to bis Majesty, and the Protestant succession (which is happily established among us for the defence of the Christian Religion), than the suppression of blasphemy and profaneness, which has a direct tendency to subvert the very foundation on which his Majesty's government is sixed.

So restless have these zealots for insidelity been in their diabolical attempts against religion, that they have, *First,* Openly blasphemed and denied the doctrine of the ever Blessed Trinity, endeavouring, by species pretences, to revive the Arian heresy, which was never introduced into any nation, but the vengeance of Heaven pursued it. *Secondly,* They assirm an absolute fate, and deny the Providence and government of the Almighty in the world. *Thirdly,* They have endeavoured to subvert all order and discipline of the church, and by vile and unjust reflections on the clergy, they strive to bring contempt on all religion; that by the libertinism of their opinions they may en-

courage and draw others into the immoralities of their practice. *Fourthly,* That a general libertinism may the more effectually be established, the universities are decried, and all instructions of youth in the principles of the Christian religion are exploded with the greatest malice and falsity. *Fifthly,* The more effectually to carry on these works of darkness, studied artisices, and invented colours, have been made use of to run down religion and virtue as prejudicial to society, and detrimental to the state; and to recommend luxury, avarice, pride, and all kind of vices, as being necessary to public welfare, and not tending to the destruction of the constitution: nay, the very stews themselves have had strained apologies and forced encomiums made in their favour, and produced in print, with design, we conceive, to debauch the nation.

These principles having a direct tendency to the subversion of all religion and civil government, our duty to the Almighty, our love to our country, and regard to our oaths, oblige us to present as the publiffer of a book, intituled the Fable of the Bees; or Private Vices Public Benesits. 2d. Edit. 1723.

And abb as the publisher of a weekly paper, called the British Journal, Numb. 26, 35. 3» 39

A VINDICATION OF THE BOOK,' " «4»

The Letter I complain of is this:

My Lord,

It is welcome news to all the king's loyal subjects and true friends to the established government and succession in'the illustrious house of Hanover, that your Lordship is said to be contriving some esfectual means of securing us from the dangers, wherewith his Majesty's happy government seems to be threatened by Catiline, under the name of Cato; by the writer of a book, intituled, The Fable of the Bees, &c. and by others of their fraternity, who are undoubtedly useful friends to the Pretender, and diligent, for his fake, in labouring to subvert and ruin our consti ution, under a specious pretence of defending it. Your Lordship's wife resolution, totally to suppress such impious writings, and the direction already given

for having them presented, immediately, by some of the grand juries, will esfectually convince the nation, that no attempts against Christianity will be suffered or endured here. And this conviction will at once rid mens minds of the uneasiness which this flagitious race of writers has endeavoured to raise in them; will therefore be a sirm bulwark to the Protestant religion; will effectually defeat the projects and hopes of the Pretender; and best secure us against any change in the ministry. And no faithful Briton could be unconcerned, if the people should imagine any the least neglect in any single person bearing a part in the ministry, or begin to grow jealous, that any thing could be done, which is not done, in defending their religion from every the least appearance of danger approaching towards it. And, my Lord, this jealousy might have been apt to rise, if no measures had been taken to discourage and crush the open advocates of irreligion. It is no easy matter to get jealousy out of one's brains, when it is once got into them, jealousy, my Lord! it is as furious a siend as any of them all. I have seen a little thin weak woman so invigorated by a sit of jealousy, that sive grenadiers could not hold her. My Lord, go on with your just methods of keeping the people clear of this curled jealousy: for amongst the various kinds and occasions of it, that which concerns their religion, is the most: violent, flagrant, frantic fort of all; and accordingly has, in former reigns, produced those various mischiefs, which your Lordship has faithfully determined to prevent, dutifully re garding the royal authority, and conforming to the example of his Majesty, who has graciously given directions (which are well known to your Lordship) for the preserving of unity jn the church; and the purity of the Christian faith. It is in vain to think that the people of England will ever give up their religion, or be very fond of any ministry that will not support it, as the wisdom of this ministry has done, against such audacious attacks as are made upon it by the scriblers; for scrjbler, your Lordship knows, is the just appellation of every author, who, under whatever plausibly appearance of good sense, attempts to undermine the religion, and therefore the content and quiet, the peace and happiness of his fellow-subjects, by subtle and artful, and fallacious arguments and insinuations. May Heaven avert those insufferable miseries, which the Church of Rome would bring upon us! tyranny is the bane of human society, and there is no tyranny heavier than that of the triple crown. And, therefore, this free and happy people has justly conceived an utter abhorrence and dread of Popery, and of every thing that looks like encouragement or tendency to it; but they do also abhor and dread the violence offered to Christianity itself, by our British Catilines, who shelter their treacherous designs against it, under the false colours of regard and good will to our blessed Protestant religion, while they demonstrate, too plainly demonstrate, that the title of Protestants does not belong to them, unless it can belong to those who are in effect protestors against all religion.

And really the people cannot be much blamed for being a little unwilling to part with their religion: for they tell ye that there is a God; and that God governs the world; and that he is wont to bless or blast a kingdom, in proportion to the degrees of religion or irreligion prevailing in it. Your Lordship has a sine collection of books; and, which is a siner thing still, you do certainly understand them, and can turn to an account of any important affair in a trice. I would therefore fain know, whether your Lordship can show, frorri any writer, let him be as profane as the scribblers would have him, that any one empire, kingdom, country, or province, great or small, did not dwindle and sink, and was confounded, when it once failed of providing studiously for the support of religion.

The scribblers talk much of the Roman government, and liberty, and the spirit of the old Romans. But it is undenkble, that their most plausible talk of these things is all pretence, and grimace, and an artisice to serve the purposes of irreligion; and by consequence to render

the people uneasy, and ruin the kingdom. For if they did in reality esteem, and would faithfully recommend to their countrymen, the sentiments and principles, the main purposes and practices of the wife and prosperous Romans, they would, in the sirst place, put us in mind, that old Rome was as remarkable for observing and promoting natural religion, as new Rome has been for corrupting that which is revealed. And as the old Romans did signally recommend themselves to the favour of heaven, by their faithful care of religion; so were they abundantly convinced, and did accordingly acknowledge, with universal consent, that their care of religion was the great means of God's preserving the empire, and crowning it with conquest and success, prosperity and glory. Hence it was, that when their orators were bent upon exerting their utmost in moving and persuading the people, upon any occasion, they ever put them in mind of their religion, if that could be any way asfected by the point in debate; not doubting that the people would determine in their favour, if they could but demonstrate, that the safety of religion depended upon the success of their cause. And, indeed, neither the Romans, nor any other nation upon earth, did ever suffer their established religion to be openly ridiculed, exploded, or opposed: and I am sure, your Lordship would not, for all the world, that this thing would be done with impunity amongst us, which was never endured in the world before. Did ever any man, since the blessed revelation of the gospel, run riot upon Christianity, as some men, nay, and some few women too, have lately done? must the devil grow rampant at this rate, and not to be called *coram nobis?* Why should not he content himself to carry off people in the common way, the way of curling and swearing, Sabbath breaking and cheating, bribery, and hypocrisy, drunkenness and whoring, and such kind of things as he used to do? never let him domineer in mens mouths and writings, as he does now, with loud, tremendous insidelity, blasphemy and prophaneness, enough to

frighten the King's subjects out of their wits. We are now come to a short question: God or the devil? that is the word; and time will sh nv, who and who goes together. Thus much inav be said at present, that those have abundantly shown their spirit of opposition to sacred things, who have not only mveighed against the national profession and exercise of religion; and endeavoured, with bitterness and dexterity, to render it odious and contemptible, but are solicitous to hinder mnlrudp? of the natives of this island from having the very seeds of religion sown among them with advantage.

Qnis est tam vecors qui non inteHigat, numine hoc tantum imperiiim, eJTe natum, actum, et retentum? *Cic. Oral, de Harvjh. Re/p.*

Arguments are urged, with the utmost vehemence, against the education of poor children in the charity schools, though there hath not one just reason been offered against the provision made for that education. The things that hava been objected against it are not, in fact, true; and nothing ought to be regarded, by serious and wife men, as a weighty or just argument, if it is not a true one. How hath Catiline the considence left to look any man in the face, after he hath spent more considence than most mens whole stock amounts to, in saying, that this pretended charity has, in effect, destroyed all other charities, which were before given to the aged, sick, and impotent.

It seems pretty clear, that if those, who do not contribute to any chanty school, are become more uncharitable to any other object than formerly they were, their want of charity to the one, is not owing to their contribution to the other. And as to those who do contribute to these schools; they are so far from being more sparing in their relief of other objects, than they were before, that the poor widows, the aged and the impotent do plainly receive more relief from them, in proportion to their numbers apd abilities, than from any the fame numbers of men under the fame circumstancies of fortune, who do not concern themselves with charity schools, in any respect, but in condemning and decrying them. I will meet Catiline at the Grecian coffee-house any day in the week, and by an enumeration of particular persons, in as great a number as he pleaieth, demonstrate the truth of what I fay. But 1 do not much depend upon his giving me the meeting, because it is his business, not to encourage demonstrations of the truth, but to throw disguises upon it; otherwise, he never could have allowed himself, after representing the charity schools as intended to breed up children to reading and writing, and a sober behaviour, that they may be qualisied to be servants, immediately to *(iqa* these words, a fort of idle and rioting vermin, by which the kingdom is already almost devoured, and are become every where a public nuisance, &c. What? Is it owing to the charity schools, that servants are become so idle, such rioting vermin, such a public nuisance; that women-servants turn whores, and the men-servants robbers, house-breakers, and sharpers? (as he fays they commonly do). Is this owing to the charity schools? or, if it is not, how comes he to allow himself the liberty of representing these schools as a means of increasing this load of mischief, which is indeed too plainly fallen upon the public? The imbibing principles of virtue hath not, usually, been thought the chief occasion of running into vice. If the early knowledge of truth, and of our obligations to it, were the surest mears of departing from it, nobody would, doubt, that the knowledge of truth was instilled into Catiline very early, and with the utmost care. It is a good pretty thing in him to spread a report, arid to lay so much stress upon it as he does, that there is more collected at the church doors in a day, to make these poor boys and girls appear in caps and livery coats, than for allthe poor in a year. O rare Catiline! This point you will carry most swimmingly; for you have no witnesses against you, nor any living foul to contradict you, except the collectors and overseers of the poor, and all other principal inhabitants of most of the parishes, where any charity schools are in England.

The jest of it is, my Lord, that these scribblers would still be thought good moral men. But, when men make it their business to mislead and deceive their neighbours, and that in matters of moment, by distorting and disguising the truth, by misrepresentations and false insinuations; if such men are not guilty of usurpation, while they take upon them the character of good moral men, then it is not immoral, in any man, to be false and deceitful, in cafes where the law cannot touch him for being so, and morality bears no relation to truth and fair dealing. However, 1 shall not be very willing to meet one of these moral men upon Hounslow-heath, if I should happen to ride that way without pistols. For I have a notion, that they who have no conscience in one point, do not much abound with it in another. Your Lordship, who judges accurately of men, as well as books, will easily imagine, if you had no other knowledge of the charity schools, that there must be something very excellent in them because such kind of men as these are so warm in opposing them.

They tell you, that these schools are hindrances to husbandry and to manufacture. As to husbandry; the children are not kept in the schools longer than till they are of age and strength to perform the principal parts of it, or to bear constant labour in it; and even while they are under this course of education, your Lordship may depend upon it, that they shall never be hindered from working in the sields, or being employed in such labour as they are capable of, in any parts of the year, when they can get such employment for the support of their parents and themselves, In this cafe, the parents, in the several counties, are proper judges of their several situations and circumstances, and at the fame time, not so very fond of their childrens getting a little knowledge, rather than a little money, but that they will sind other employment for them than going to school, whenever they can get a penny by so doing. And the case is the fame as to the manufactures; the trustees of the charity schools, and the parents of the children bred in them, would be thank-

ful to those gentlemen who make the objection, if they would assist in removing it, by subscribing to a fund for joining the employment of manusacture, to the business of learning to read and write in the charity schools. This would be a noble work: it is already affected by the supporters of some charity schools, and is aimed at, and earnestly desired by all the rest: but Rome was not built in a day. Till this great thing can be brought about, let the masters and managers of the manufactures in the several places of the kingdom, be so charitable as to employ the poor children for a certain number of hours in every day, in the respective manufactures, while the trustees are taking care to sill up their other hours of the day, in the usual duties of the charity schools. It is an easy matter for party-men, for designing and perverted minds,-to invent colourable, fallacious arguments, and to offer railing, under the appearance of reasoning, against the best things in the world. But undoubtedly, no impartial man, who is affected with a serious fense of goodness, and a real love of his country, can think this proper and just view of the charity schools, liable to any just weighty objection, or refuse to contribute his endeavours to improve and raise them to that perfection which is proposed in them. In the mean time, let no man be so weak or so Wicked as to deny, that when poor children cannot meet with employment in any other honest way, rather than suffer their tender age to be spent in idleness, or in learning the arts of lying, and swearing, and stealing, it is true charity to them, and good service done to our country, to employ them in learning the principles of religion and virtue, till their age and strength will enable them to become servants in families, or to be engaged in husbandry, or manufacture, or any kind of mechanic trade or laborious employment; for to these laborious employments are the charity children generally, if not always turned, as soon as they become capable of them: and therefore Catiline may be pleased to retract his objection concerning shopkeepers, or retailers of commodities, wherein he has asssirmed, that their employments, which he fays ought to fall to the share of children of their own degree, are mostly anticipated and engrossed by the managers of the charity schools. He must excuse my acquainting your Lordship, that this assirmation is in fact directly false, which is an inconvenience very apt to fall upon his assirmations, as it has particularly done upon one of them more, which I would mention. For he is not ashamed roundly to assert, That the principles of our common people aTe debauched in our charity schools, who are taught, as soon as they can speak, to blabber out Highchurch and Ormond, and so are bred up to be traitors before they know what treason signisies. Your Lordship, and other persons of integrity, whose words are the faithful representatives of their meaning, would now think, if I had not given you a key to Catiline's talk, that he has been fully convinced, that the children in the charity" fchoos are bred up to be traitors.

My Lord, if any one master be suffered by the trustees to continue in any charity school, against whom proof can be brought, that he is disaffected to the government, or that hedoes not as faithfully teach the children obedience and loyalty to the King, as any other duty in the catachisin, then I will gratify Catiline with a licence to pull down the schools, and hang up the masters, according to his heart's delire.

These, and such things as these, are urged with the like bitterness, and as little truth, in the book mentioned above, viz. The Fable of the Bees; or, Private Vices, Public Benesits, &c. Cataline explodes the fundamental article:, of faith, impiously comparing the doctrine of the blessed Tri.iit) to fee-fa-fum: this profligate author of the Fable is not i,nly an auxiliary to Catiline in opposition to faith, but has taken up on him to tear up the very foundations of moral virtue, and establish vice in its room. The best physician in the world did never labour more, to purge the natural body of bad qualities, than this bumble-bee has done to purge the bodypol'tic of good ones. He himself bears testimony to the truth

of this charge against him: for when he comes to the conclusion of his book, he makes this observation upon himself and his performance: " After this, 1 flatter myself to " have demonstrated, thnt neither the friendly qualities and " kind affections that are natural to man, nor the real virtues " he is capable of acquiring by reason and self-denial, are " the foundation of society; but that what we call evil in " this world, moral as well as natural, is the grand principle " that makes us sociable creatures, the solid basis, the lite " and support of all trades and employments without excep" tion: that there we must look for the true origin of all " arts and sciences, and that the moment evil ceases, the so" ciety must be spoiled, if not totally dissolved. "

Now, my Lord, you see the grand design, the main drift of Catiline and his confederates; now the scene opens, and the secret springs appear; now the fraternity adventure to speak out, and surely no band of men ever dared to speak at this rate before; now you see the true cause of all their enmity to the poor charity schools; it is levelled against religion: religion, my Lord, which the schools are instituted to promote, and which this confederacy is resolved to destroy; for the schools are certainly one of the greatest instruments of religion and virtue, one of the sirmest bulwarks against Popery, one of the best recommendations of this people to the Divine favour, and therefore one of the greatest blessings to our country of any thing that has been set on foot since our happy Reformation and deliverance from the idolatry and tyranny of Rome. If any trivial inconvenience did arise from so excellent a work, as some little inconvenience attends all human institutions and affairs, the excellency of the work would still be matter of joy, and sind encouragement with all the wise and the good, who despise such inlignisicant"nbjections.against it, as other men are not ashamed to raise and defend.

Now your Lordship also sees the true cause of the satire, which is continually formed against the clergy, by Catiline

and his confederates. Why should Mr. Hall's conviction and execution be any more an objection against the clergy, than Mr. Layer's against the gentlemen of the long robe? Why, because the profession of the law does not immediately relate to religion: and therefore Catiline will allow, that if any persons of that profession should be traitors, or otherwise vicious, all the rest may, notwithstanding the iniquity of a brother, be as loyal and virtuous as any other subjects in the King's dominions: but because matters of religion are the professed concern, and the employment of the clergy; therefore Catiline's logic makes it out, as clear as the day, that if any of them be disaffected to the government, all the rest are so too; or if any of them be chargeable with vice, this consequence from it is plain, that all or most of the rest are as vicious as the devil can make them. I shall not trouble your Lordship with a particular vindication of the clergy, nor is there any reason that I mould, for they are already secure of your Lordship's good affection to them, and they are able to vindicate themselves wheresover such a vindication is wanted, being as faithful, and virtuous, and learned, a body of men as any in Europe; and yet they suspend the publication of arguments in a solemn defence of themselves, because they neither expect nor delire approbation and esteem from impious and abandoned men; and, at the fame time, they cannot doubt that all persons, not only of great penetration, but ot common fense, do now clearly see, that the arrows shot against the clergy are intended to wound and destroy the divine institution of the ministerial ossices, and to extirpate the religion which the sacred ossices were appointed to preserve and promote. This was always supposed and suspected by every honest and impartial man;but it is now demonstrated by those who besore had given occasion to such suspicions, tor they have now openly declared, that faith, in the principal articles of it, is not only needless, but ridiculous, that the welfare of human society must sink and perish under the encouragement of virtue, and that immorality is the only sirm foundation whereon the hiippinelV of mankind can be built and subsist. The publication of such tenets as these, an open avowed propoal to extirpate the Christian faith and all virtue, and to six moral evil for tire basis of the government, is so stunning, so shocking, so frightful, so flagrant an enormity, that it it should be imputed to us as a national guilt, the Divine vengeance must inevitably fall upon us. And how far this enormity would become a national guilt, if it should pass disregarded and unpunished, a casuist less skilful and discerning than your Lordship may easily guess. And, no doubt, your Lordship's good judgment, in so plain and important a cafe, has made you, like a wife and faithful patriot, resolve to use your utmost endeavours in your high station, to defend religion from the hold attacks made upon it.

As soon as I have seen a copy of the bill, for the better security of his Majesty and his happy government, by the better security of religion in Great Britain, your Lordship's just scheme of politics, your love of your country, and your great services done to it, shall again be acknowledged by,

My Lord, *Tour most faithful bumble Servant,*

Theophilus Philo-britannus.

These violent accusations, and the great clamour every where raised against the book, by governors, masters, and other champions of charity schools, together with the advice of friends, and the reflection on what I owed to myself, drew from me the following answer. The candid reader, in the perusal of it, will not be offended at the repetition of some passages, one of which he may have met with twice already, when he shall consider that, to make my defence by itself to the public, I was obliged to repeat what had been quoted in the Letter, since the paper would unavoidably fall into the hands of many who had never seen either the Fable of the Bees, or the Defamatory Letter wrote against it. The Answer was published in the London Journal of August 10. 1723, in these words:

W Hereas, in the Evening Post of Thursday July ii, a presentment was inserted of the Grand Jury of Middlesex, against the publisher of a book, intituled, The Fable of the Bees; or, Private Vices, Public Benesits; and since that, a passionate and abusive Letter has been published against the fame book, and the author of it, in the London Journal ol Saturday, July 27; I think myself indispensibly obliged to vindicate the above said book against the black aspersions that undeservedly have been cast upon it, being conscious that I have not had the least ill design in composing it. The ac cusations against it having been made openly in the public papers, it is not equitable the defence of it should appear in a more private manner. What I have to say in my behalf, I shall address to all men offense and sincerity, asking no other favour of them, than their patience and attention. Setting aside what in that Letter relates to others, and every thing that is foreign and immaterial, I shall begin with th« passage that is quoted from the book, viz. " After this, I flatter my" self to have demonstrated, that neither the friendly quali" ties and kind affections that are natural to man, nor the " real virtues he is capable of acquiring by reason and self" denial, are the foundation of society; but that what we " call evil in this world, moral as well as natural, is the " grand principle that makes us sociable creatures; the " solid basis, the life and support of all trades and employ" ments without exception: That there we must look for " the true origin of all arts and sciences; and that the mo" ment evil ceases, the society must be spoiled, if not totally " dissolved." These words, I own, are in the book, and, being both innocent and true, like to remain there in all future impressions. But I will likewise own very freely, that, if I had wrote with a design to be understood by the meanest capacities, I would not have chose the subject there treated of; or if I had, I would have amplisied and explained every period, talked and distinguished magisterially, and never appeared without the fescue in my hand. As for example; to make the passage pointed at in-

telligible, I would have bestowed a page or two on the meaning of the word Evil; after that I would have taught them, that every defect, every want, was an evil; that on the multiplicity of those wants depended all thole mutual services which the individual members of a society pay to each other; and that consequently, the greater variety there was of wants, the larger number of individuals might sind their private interest in labouring for the good of others, and, united together, compose one body. Is there a trade or handicraft but what supplies us with something we wanted? This want certainly, before it was supplied, was an evil, which that trade or handicraft was to remedy, and without which it could never have been thought of. Is there an art or science that was not invented to mend some detect! Had this latter not existed, there could have been no occasion for the former to move it. I fay, p. 236. " The excellency of human thought " and contivance has been, and is yet nowhere more confpi" cuous, than in the variety of tools and instruments of work" men and artisicers, and the multiplicity of engines, that " were all invented, either to assist the weakness of man, to " correct his many imperfections, to gratify his laziness, or " obviate his impatience." Several foregoing pages run in the fame strain. But what relation has all this to religion or insidelity, more than it has to navigation or the peace in the north?

The many hands that are employed to supply our natural wants, that are really such, as hunger, thirst, and nakedness, are inconsiderable to the vast numbers that are all innocently gratifying the depravity of our corrupt nature, I mean the industrious, who get a livelihood by their honest labour, to which the vain and voluptuous must be beholden for all their tools and implements of ease and luxury. " The mort-sight" ed vulgar, in the chain of causes, seldom can see farther " than one link; but those who can enlarge their view, and " will give themselves leisure of gazing on the prospect of " concatenated events, may" in a hundred places, fee good " spring up, and pullulate from evil, a$ naturally as chickens " do from eggs."

The words are to be found p. 46. in the Remark made op. the seeming paradox; that in the grumbling hive,

The worst of all the multitude

Did something lot the common good.

Where, in many instances, may be amply discovered, how unsearchable Providence daily orders the comforts of the laborious, and even the deliverances of the oppressed, secretly to come forth, not only from the vices of the luxurious, but likewise the crimes of the flagitious and most abandoned.

Men of candour and capacity perceive, at sirst sight, that in the passage censured, there is no meaning hid or expressed that is not altogether contained in the following words:" Man is a necessitous creature on innumerable accounts, " and yet from those very necessities, and nothing else, arise " all trades and employments." But it is ridiculous for men to meddle with books above their sphere.

The Fable of the Bees was designed for the entertainment of people of knowledge and education, when they have an idle hour which they know not how to spend better: it is a book of severe and exalted morality, that contains a strict 3 test of virtue, an infallible touchstone to distinguish the real from the counterfeited, and shows many actions to be faulty that are palmed upon the world for good ones: it describes the nature and symptoms of human passions, detects their force and disguises; and traces self love in its darkest recesses; I might safely add, beyond any other system of ethics: the whole is a rhapsody void of order or method, but no part of it has any thing in it that is sour or pedantic; the style, I confess, is very unequal, sometimes very high and rhetorical, and sometimes very low, and even very trivial; such as it is, I am satissied that it has diverted persons of great probity and virtue, and unquestionable good fense; and I am in no fear that it will ever cease to do so while it is read by such. Whoever has seen the violent charge against this book, will pardon me for saying more in commendation of it, than a man, not labouring un-

der the fame necessity, would do of his own work on any other occasion.

The encomiums upon stews complained of in the presentment are no where in the book. What might give a handle to this charge, must be a political disscrtation concerning the best method to guard and preserve women of honour and virtue from the insults of diflblute men, whose passions are often ungovernable: As in this there is a dilemma between two evils, which it is impracticable to shun both, lo I have treated it with the utmost caution, and begin thus: " I am far from encouraging vice, and should think it an uhfpeak" able felicity for a state, if the sin of uncleanness could be " utterly banished from it; but 1 am afraid it is impossible." I give my reasons why I think it so; and, speaking occasionally of the music-houses at Amsterdam, 1 give a short account of them, than which nothing can be more harmless; and I appeal to all impartial judges, whether, what I have said of them is not ten times more proper to give men (even the voluptuous of any taste) a dilguli and aversion against them, than it is to raise any criminal desire. 1 am lorry the Grand Jury mould conceive that 1 published this with a design to debauch the nation, without conlideiing, that, in the jirstplace, there is not a sentence nor a syllable that can either offend the chastest ear, or sully the imagination of the most vicious; or, in the second, that the matter complained of is manifestly addressed to magistrates and politicians, or, at least, the more serious and thinking part of mankind; whereas a general corruption of manners as to lewdness, to be produced by reading, can only be apprehended from obscenities easily purchased, and every way adapted to the tastes and capacities of the heedless multitude and unexperienced youth of both sexes: but that the performance, so outrageously exclaimed against, was never calculated for either of these classes of people, is self-evident from every circumstance. The beginning of the prose is altogether philosophical, and hardly intelligible to any that have not been used to matters of speculation;

and the running title of it is so far from being specious or inviting,that without having read the book itself, nobody knows what to make of it, while, at the fame time, the price is sive shillings. Fnmi all which it is plain, that if the book contains any dangerous tenets, I have not been very solicitous to scatter them among the people. 1 have not said a word to please or engage them, and the greatest compliment I have made them has been, *Apage vulgus.* But as nothing (I fay, p. 138) would more clearly demonstrate the falsity of my notions than that, the generality of the people should fall in with them, so I do not expect the approbation of the multitude. 1 write not to many, nor seek for any well-wishers, but among the few that can think abstractly, and have their minds elevated above the vulgar." Of this 1 have made no ill use, and ever preserved such a tender regard to the public, that when I have advanced any uncommon sentiments, I have used all the precautions imaginable, that they might not be hurtful to weak minds that might casually dip into the book. When (p. 137.) I owned," That it was my sentiment that no socie" ty could be raised into a rich and mighty kingdom, or so " railed subsist in their wealth and power for any considerable " time, without the vices of man," I had premised, what was true, " That I had never said or imagined, that man could not " be virtuous as well in a rich and mighty kingdom, as in the " most pitiful commonwealth:" which caution, a man less scrupulous than myself might have thought superfluous, when he had already explained himself on that head in the very same paragraph which begins thus: " 1 lay down, as a lirst ' principle, that in all societies, great or small, it is the du" ty of every member of it to be good; that virtue ought " to be encouraged, vice discountenanced, the laws obeyed, " and the transgressors punished" There is not a line in the book that contradicts this doctrine, and I defy my enemies to disprove what I have advanced, p. 139, " That if 1 have *f* shown the way to wordly greatness, I have always, without " hesitation, preferred the road that leads to virtue." No man ever took more pains not to be misconstrued than my-self: mind p. 138, when I say, " That societies cannot be " raised to wealth and power, and the top of earthly glory,. " without vices; I do not think, that by so saying, 1 bid men " be vicious, any more than I bid them be quarrelsome or co" vetous, when I assirm, that the profession of the law could. not be mintained in such numbers and splen-dour, if there was not abundance of too selsish and litigious people." A caution of the fame nature I had already given towards the end of the Preface, on ac-count of a palpable evil inseparable from the felicity of London. To search into the real causes of things, imports no ill design, nor has any tendency to do harm. A man may write on poisons, and be an excellent physician. Page 235, I fay, " No man needs to guard him" self against blessings, but calamities require hands to avert " them." And lower, " It is the extremities of heat and cold,." the inconstancy and badness of seasons, the violence and " uncertainty of winds, the vast power and treachery of water, the rage and untractableness of sire, and the stubbornness " and sterility of the earth, that rack our invention, how we shall ei-ther avoid the mischiefs they produce, or correct the ,, malignity of them, and turn their several forces to our own ad-vantage a thousand disferent ways." While a man is inquiring into the occu-pation of vast multitudes, I cannot fee why he may not fay all this and much more, without being accused of depreci-ating and speaking slightly of the gists and munisicence of heaven; when, at the lame time, he demonstrates, that without rain and sunshine this globe would not be habitable to creatures like ourselves. It is an out-ofthe-way sub-ject, and I would never quarrel with the man who mould tell me that it might as well have been Jet alone: yet I always thought it would please men of any tol-erable taste, and not be easily lost.

My vanity 1 could never conquer, so well as I could wish; andl am too proud to commit crimes.and as to the main scope, the intent of the book, 1 mean the view it was wrote with, I protest that it has been with the utmost sincerity, what I have declared of it in the Preface, where you will sind these words: ` If you ask me.why I have done all this, *cuibono* ? And what " good these no-tions will produce? Truly, besides the reader's f diversion, I believe none at all; but if I was asked, what na 5 turally ought to be expected from them? I would answer, " That, in the sirst place, the people who continuity sind fault with others, by reading them would be taught to look at " home, and examining their own consciences, be made ` ashamed of always railing at what they are more or less guilty of themselves; and that, in the next, those who are so fond of the ease and comforts of a great and flourishing " nation, would learn more patiently to submit to those in con-veniences, which no government upon earth can reme" dy, when they should fee the impossility of enjoying any great share of the sirst, without partak-ing likewise of the " latter."

The sirst impression of the Fable of the Bees, which came out in 1714, was never carped at, or publicly taken notice of; and all the reason I can think on, why this second edition should be so unmercifully treated, though it has many precautions which the former wanted, is an Essay on Charity and Charity Schools, which is added to what was printed before. I confess, that it is my sentiment, that all hard and dirty work, ought, in a well-governed nation, to be the Jot and portion of the poor, and that to divert their children from useful labour till they are fourteen or fifteen years old, is a wrong method to qualify them for it when are they grown up. 1 have given several reasons for my opin-ion in that Essay, to which I refer all impartial men of understanding, assur-ing them that they will not meet with such monstrous impiety in it as report-ed. What an advocate I have been for libertinism and immorality, and what an enemy to all instructions of youth in the Christian faith, may be collected from the pains I have taken on education for above seven pages together: and after-wards again, page 193, where speaking of the instructions the children of the poor might receive at church; from which, I fay, " Or some other place " of worship, I would not have the mean-est of a parish that " is able to walk to it, be absent on Sundays," I have these words: " It is the Sabbath, the most use-ful day in seven, " that is set apart for divine service and religious exercise, as well as resting from bodily labour; and it is a duty incum bent on all magis-trates, to take a particular care of that " day. The poor more especially, and their children, " mould be made to go to church on it, both in the fore and " the afternoon, because they have no time on any other.." By precept and example, they ought to be encouraged tt

" it from their very infancy: the wilful neglect of it ought " to be counted scan-dalous; and if downright compulsion to " what I urge might seem too harsh, and perhaps impractica" ble, all diver-sions at least ought strictly to be prohib-ited, " and the poor hindered from every amusement abroad, that " might allure or draw them from it." If the arguments I have made use of are not convincing, I desire they may berefuted, and I will ac-knowledge it as a favour in any one that shall convince me of my error, with-out ill language, by showing me where-in I have been mistaken: but calumny, it seems, is the shortest way of confut-ing an adversary, when men are touched in a sensible part. Vast sums are gath-ered for these charity schools, and I un-derstand human nature too well to imag-ine, that the sharers of the money should hear them spoke against with any pa-tience. 1 foresaw, therefore, the usage I was to receive, and having repeated the common cant that is made for chari-ty schools, I told my readers, page 165. " This is the general cry, and he that speaks the " least word against it, is an uncharitable, hard-hearted, and " inhu-man, if not a wicked, profane and athe-istical wretch." For this reason, it cannot be thought, that it was a great surprise to me, when in that extraordinary letter to Lord C. I saw myself called " pros-ligate author; the publication of " my tenets, an open and avowed proposal to extirpate the " Christian faith and all virtue, and what 1 had done so stun" ning, so shocking, so frightful, ib fla-grant an enormity, that " it cried for the vengeance of Heaven." This is no more than what I have already expected from the enemies to truth and fair dealing, and I shall retort nothing on the angry author of that letter, who endeavours to expose me to the public fury. I pity him, and have charity enough to believe that he has been imposed upon himself, by trusting to fame and the hearsay of oth-ers; for no man in his wits can imagine that he should have read one quarter part of my hook, and write as he does.

1 am sorry if the words Private Vices, Public Benesits, have ever given any os-fence to a well-meaning man. The mys-tery of them is soon unfolded, when once they are rightly understood; but no man of sincerity will question the in-nocence of them, that has read the last paragraph, where I take my leave of the reader, " and conclude with repeating the seeming paradox, the substance of which is advanced ' in the title page; that private vices, by the dexterous ma

S

" nagement of a skilful politician, may be turned into public " benesits." These are the last words of the book, printed in the fame large character with the rest. But I set aside all what I have said in my vindication; and if, in the whole book called the Fable of the Bees, and presented by the grand jury of Middlesex to the judges of the King's Bench, there is to be found the least title of blasphemy or profaneness, or any thing tending to immorality or the cor-ruption of manners, 1 desire it may be published; and if this be done without invective, personal reflections, or set-ting the mob upon me, things I never de-sign to answer, 1 will not only recant, but likewise beg pardon of the offended public in the most solemn manner: and (if the hangman might be thought too good for the osssice) burn the book my-self, at any reasonable time and place my adversaries shall be pleaied to ap-point.

The Author of the Fable of the Bees. THE FABLE OF THE BEES. PART II. *Opinionum enim Ctmmenta delit dies; Naturet judi-cla cotifirmat.*

Cicero de Nat. Deor. Lib. 2.

PREFACE; (considering the manifold clamours, that have been raised from several quarters, against the Fable of the Bees, even after I had published the vin-dication of it, many of my readers will wonder to fee me come out with a sec-ond part, before I have taken any further notice of what has been said against the sirst. Whatever is published, I take it for granted, is submitted to the judgment of all the world that see it; but it is very unreasonable, that authors should not be upon the same footing with their crit-ics. The treatment I have received, and the liberties some gentlemen have taken with me, being well known, the public must be convinced before now, that, in point of civility, I owe my adversaries nothing: and if those, who have taken upon them to school and reprimand me, had an undoubted right to censure what they thought sit, without asking my leave, and to say of me what they pleased, I ought to have an equal priv-ilege to examine their censures, and, without consulting them, to judge in my turn, whether they are worth answering or not. The public must be the umpire between us. From the Appendix that has been added to the sirst part, ever since the third edition, it is manifest, that I have been far from endeavouring to sti-fle, either the arguments or the invec-tives that were made against me; and, not to have left the reader uninformed of any thing extant of either sort, I once thought to have taken this opportunity of presenting him with a list of the ad-versaries that have appeared in print against me: but as they are in nothing so considerable as they are in their num-bers, I was afraid it would have looked like ostentation, unless I would have an-swered them all, which I shall never at-tempt. The reason, therefore, of my ob-stinate silence has been all along, that hitherto I have not been accused of any thing that is criminal or immoral, for which every middling capacity could not have framed a very good answer, from some part or other, either of the vindication or the book itself.

However, I have wrote, and had by me near two years, a defence of the Fable of the Bees, in which I have stated and endeavoured to solve all the objections that might reasonably be made against it, as to the doctrine contained in it, and the detriment it might be ot' to others: for this is the only thing about which I ever had any concern. Being conscious, that I have wrote with no ill design, I should be sorry to lie under the impu-tation of it: but as to the goodness or badness of the performance itself, the thought was never worth my care; and therefore those critics, that found fault with my bad reasoning, and said of the book, that it is ill wrote, that there is nothing new in it, that it is incoherent stuff, that the language is barbarous, the humour low, and the style mean and pitiful; those critics, 1 fay, are all very welcome to say what they please: In the main, I believe they are in the right; but if they are not, I shall never give myself the trouble to contradict them; for I never think an author more fool-ishly employed, than when he is vindi-cating his own abilities. As I wrote it for my diverlion, so 1 had my ends; if those who read it have not had theirs, 1 am sorry for it, though 1 think myself not at all answerable for the disappoint-ment. It was not wrote by subscription, nor have 1 ever warranted, any where, what use or goodness it would be of: on the contrary, in the very preface, I have called it an inconsiderable trifle; and since that, I have publicly owned that it was a rhapsody. If people will buy books without looking into them, or knowing what they are, I cannot see whom they have to blame but them-selves, when they do not answer expec-tations. Besides, it is no new thing for people to dislike books after they have bought them: this will happen some-times, even when men of considerable sigure had given them the strongest as-surances, before hand, that they would be pleased with them.

A considerable part os the defence *i* mentioned, has been seen by several of my friends, who have been in expecta-tion of it for some time. I have stayed neither for types nor paper, and yet 1 have several reasons, why 1 do not yet publish it; which, having touched nobody's money, nor made any piomise concerning it, 1 beg leave to keep to myself. Most of my adversaries, whenever it comes out, will think it soon enough; and nobody suffers by the delay but myself.

Since 1 was sirst attacked, it has long been a matter of wonder and perplexity to me to sind out, why and how men ibould conceive, that I had wrote with an intent to debauch the nation, and promote all manner of vice: and it was a great while before 1 could derive the charge from any thing, but wilful mistake and premeditated malice. But since I have seen, that men could be serious in apprehending the increase of rogues and robberies, from the frequent representations of the Beggar's Opera, I am persuaded, that there really are such wrongheads in the world, as will fancy vices to be encouraged, when they fee them exposed. To the same perversenese of judgment it must have been owing, that some of my adversaries were highly incensed with me, for having owned, in the Vindication, that hitherto I had not been able to conquer my vanity, as well as I could have wished. From their censure it is manifest, that they must have imagined, that to complain of a frailty, was the fame as to brag of it. But if these angry gentlemen had been less blinded with passion, or seen with better eyes, they would easily have perceived, unless they were too well pleased with their pride, that to have made the same confession themselves, they wanted nothing but sincerity. Whoever boasts of his vanity, and at the fame time shows his arrogance, is unpardonable. But when we hear a man complain of an insirmity, and his want of power entirely to cure it, whilst he suffers no symptoms of it to appear, that we could justly upbraid him with, we are so far from being offended, that we are pleased with the ingenuity, and applaud his candour: and when such an author takes no greater liberties with his readers, than what is usual in the fame manner of writing, and owns that to be the result of vanity, which others tell a thousand lies about, his confession is a compliment, and the frankness of it

ought not to be looked upon otherwise, than as a civility to the public, a condescension he was not obliged to make. It is not in feeling the passions, or in being affected with the frailties of nature, that vice consists; but in indulging and obeying the call of them, contrary to the dictates of reason. Whoever pays great deference to his readers, respectfully submitting himself to their judgment, and tells them at the fame time, that he is entirely destitute of pride; whoever, 1 fay, does this, spoils his compliment whilst he is making of it: for it is no better than bragging, that it costs him nothing. Persons of taste, and the least delicacy, can be but little affected with a man's modesty, of whom they are sure, that he is wholly void of pride within: the absence of the one makes the virtue of the other cease; at least the merit of it is not greater than that of chastity in an eunuch, or humility in a beggar. What glory would it be to the memory of Cato, that he refused to touch the water that was brought him, if it was not supposed that he was very thirsty when he did it?

The reader will sind, that in this second part I have endeavoured to illustrate and explain several things, that were obscure and only hinted at in the sirst.

Whilst I was forming this design, I found, on the one hand, that, as to myself, the easiest way of executing it, would be by dialogue; but I knew, on the other, that to discuss opinions, and manage controversies, it is counted the most unfair manner of writing. When partial men have a mind to demolish an adversary, and triumph over him with little expence, it has long been a frequent practice to attack him with dialogues, in which the champion, who is to lose the battle, appears at the very beginning of the engagement, to be the victim that is to be sacrisiced, and seldom makes a better sigure than cocks on Shrove-Tuelday, that receive blows, but return none, and are visibly set up on purpose to be knocked down. That this is to be said against dialogues, is certainly true; but it is as true, that there is no other manner of writing, by which greater reputation has been obtained. Those, who have most excelled all oth-

ers in it, '.vere the two most famous authors of all antiquity, Plato and Cicero: the one wrote almost all his philosophical works in dialogues, and the other has left us nothing else. It is evident, then, that the fault of those, who have not succeeded in dialogues; was in the management, and not in the manner of writing; and that nothing but the ill use that has been made of it, could ever have brought it into disrepute. The reason why Plato preferred dialogues to any other manner ol writing, he said, was, that things thereby might look, as if they were acted, rather than told: the fame was afterwards given by Cicero in the fame words, rendered into his own language. The greatest objection that in reality lies against it, is the dissiculty there is in writing them well. The chief of Plato's interlocutors was always his master Socrates, who every where maintains his character with great dignity; but it would have been impossible to have made such an extraordinary person speak like himself on so many emergencies, '1 Plato had not been as great a man as Socrates.

Cicero, who studied nothing more than to imitate Plato, introduced in his dialogues lome of the greatest men m Rome, his contemporaries, that were known to be of different opinions, and made them maintain and defend every one his own sentiments, as strenuously, and in as lively a manner, as they could possibly have done themselves; and in reading his dialogues a man may easily imagine himself to be in company with several learned men of different tastes and studies. But to do this, a man must have Cicero's capacity. Lucian likewise, and several others among the ancients, chose for their speakers, persons of known characters. That this interests and engages the reader more than strange names, is undeniable; but then, when the personages fall short of those characters, it plainly shows, that the author undertook what he was not able to execute. To avoid this inconveniency, most dialogue-writers among the moderns, have made use of sictitious names, which they either invented themselves or borrowed of others. These are, generally speaking, judicious compounds, taken from the Greek, that serve for short characters of the imaginary persons they are given to, denoting either the party they side with, or what it is they love or hate. But of all these happy compounds, there is not one that has appeared equally charming to so many authors of different views and talents, as Philalethes; a plain demonstration of the great regard mankind generally have to truth. There has not been a paper-war of note, these two hundred years, in which both parties, at one time or other, have not made use of this victorious champion; who, which side soever he has fought on, has hitherto, like Dryden's Almanzor, been conqueror, and constantly carried all before him. But, as by this means the event of the battle must always be known, as soon as the combatants are named, and before a blow is struck; and as all men are not equally peaceable in their dispositions, many readers have complained, that they had not sport enough for their money, and that knowing so much before hand, spoiled all their diversion. This humour having prevailed for some time, authors are grown less solicitous about the names of the personages they introduce. This careless way, seeming to me at least as reasonable as any other, I have followed; and had no other meaning by the names I have given my interlocutors, than to distinguish them, without the least regard to the derivation of words, or any thing relating to the etymology of them: all the care I have taken about them, that I kiidw of, is, that the. pronum.ation of them shouid not be harsh, nor the sounds offensive.

But though the names I have chosen are feigned, and the circumstances of the persons sictitious, the characters themselves are real, and as faithfully copied from nature as I have been able to take them. I have known critics sind fault with play-wrights for annexing short characters to the names they gave the persons of the drama; alleging, that it is forestalling their pleasure, and that whatever the actors are represented to be, they want no monitor, and are wise enough to sind it out themselves. But

I could never approve of this censure: there is a satisfaction, I think, in knowing ones company; and when I am to converse with people for a considerable time, I desire to be well acquainted with them, and the sooner the better. It is for this reason. I thought it proper to give the reader some account of the persons that are to entertain him. As they are supposed to be people of quality, I beg leave, before I come to particulars, to premise some things concerning the *beau monde* in general; which, though most.people perhaps know them every body does not always attend to. Among the fashionable part of mankind throughout Christendom, there are, in all countries,, persons, who, though they seel a just abhorrence to atheism and professed insidelity,yet have very little religion, and are scarce half-believers, when their lives come to be looked into, and their sentiments examined. What is chiesly aimed at in a resined education, is to procure as much ease and pleasure upon earth, as that can asford: therefore men are sirst instructed in all the various arts of rendering their behaviour agreeable to others, with the least disturbance to themselves. Secondly, they are imbued with the knowledge ot all the elegant comforts of life, as well as the lessons of human prudence, to avoid pain and trouble, in order to enjoy as much of the world, and with as little opposition as it is possible. Whilst thus men study their own private interest, in assisting each other to promote and increase the pleasures os life in general, they sind by experience, that to compass thole ends, every thing ought to be banished from conversation, that can have the least tendency of making others uneasy; and to reproach men with their faults or imperfections, neglects or omissions, or to put them in mind of their duty, are ossices that none are allowed to take upon them, but parents or professed masters and tutors; nor even they before company: but to reprove and pretend to teach others, we have no authority over, is ill manners, even in a clergyman out of the I pulpit; nor is he there to talk magisterially, or ever to mention things, that

are melancholy or dismal, if he should pass for a polite preacher: but whatever we may vouchsafe to hear at church, neither the certainty os a future state, nor the necessity of repentance, nor any thing else relating to the essentials of Christianity, are ever to be talked of when we are out of it, among the *beau monde,* upon any account whatever. The subject is not diverting: belides, every body is supposed to know those things, and to take care accordingly; nay, it is unmannerly to think otherwise. The decency in fashion being the chief, if not the only rule, all modisli people walk by, not a few of them go to church, and receive the facrament, from the same principle that obliges them to pay visits to one another, and now and then to make an entertainment. But as the greatest care of the *beau monde* is to be agreeable, and appear well-bred, so most of them take particular care, and many against their consciences, not to seem burdened with more religion than it is fashionable to have, for fear of being thought to be either hypocrites or bigots.'

Virtue, however, is a very fafliionable word, and some of the most luxurious are extremely fond of the amiable sound; though they mean nothing by it, but a great veneration for whatever is courtly or sublime, and an equal aversion to every thing that is vulgar or unbecoming. They seem to imagine, that it chiefly consists in a strict compliance to the rules of politeness, and all the laws of honour, that have any regard to the respect that is due to themselves. It is the existence of this virtue, that is often maintained with so much pomp of words, and for the eternity of which so many champions are ready to take up arms: whilst the votaries of it deny themselves no pleasure, they can enjoy, either fashionably or in secret, and, instead of sacrisicing the heart to the love of real virtue can only condescend to adandon the outward deformity of vice, for the satisfaction they receive from appearing to be well-bred. It is counted ridiculous for men to commit violence upon themselves, or to maintain, that virtue requires self-denial: all court philosophers are agreed, that nothing can be lovely or desirable, that is mortifying or uneasy. A civil behaviour among the fair in public, and a deportment inoffensive both in words and actions, is all the chastity the polite world requires in men. What liberties soever a man gives himself in private, his reputation lhall never susfer, whilst he conceals his amours from all those that are not unmannerly inquilitive, and takes care that nothing criminal can ever be proved upon him. *Si non caste saltern caute,* is a precept that susficiently shows what every body expects; and though incontinence is owned to be a sin, yet never to have been guilty of it is a character which most single men under thirty would not be fond of, even amongst modest women.

As the world everywhere, in compliment itself, desires to be counted really virtuous, so bare-faced vices, and all trespasses committed in sight of it, are heinous and unpardonable. To fee a man drunk in the open street, or any serious assembly at noon-day, is shocking; because it is a violation of the laws of decency, and plainly shows a want of respect, and neglect of duty, which every body is supposed to owe to the public. Men of mean circumstances likewise may be blamed for spending more time or money in drinking, than they can asford; but when these and all worldly considerations are out of the question, drunkenness itself, as it is a sin, an osfence to Heaven, is seldom censured; and no man of fortune scruples to own, that he was at such a time in such a company, where they drank very hard. Where nothing is committed, that is either beastly, or otherwise extravagant, societies, that meet on purpose to drink and be merry, reckon their manner of palling away the time as innocent as any other, though most days in the year they spend sive or six hours of the four and twenty in that diversion. No man had ever the reputation of being a good companion, that would never drink to excess; and isa man's constitution be so strong, or himself so cautious, that the dose he takes overnight, never disorders him the next clay, the worst

that shall be said of him, is, that he loves his bottle with moderation: though every night constantly he makes drinking his pastime, and hardly ever goes to bed entirely sober.

Avarice, it is true, is generally detested; but as men may be as guilty of it by scraping money together, as they can be by hoarding it up, so all the base, the sordid, and unreasonable means of acquiring wealth, ought to be equally condemned and exploded, with the vile, the pitiful, and penurious way of saving it: but the world is more indulgent; no man is taxed with avarice, that will conform with the *beau monde,* and live every way in splendour, though he mould always be raising the rents of his estate, and hardly sutler his tenants to live under him; though he mould enrich himself by usury, and all the barbarous advantages that extortion can make of the necessities of others: and though, moreover, he should be a bad paymaster himself, and an unmerciful creditor to the unfortunate; it is all one, no man is counted covetous, who entertains well, and will allow his family what is fashionable for a person in his condition. How often do we fee men of very large estates unreasonably solicitous after greater riches! What greediness do some men discover in extending the perquisites of their offices! What dishonourable condescensions are made for places of prosit! What slavish attendance is given, and what low submissions and unmanly cringes are made to favourites for pensions, by men that could subsist without them! Yet these things are no reproach to men, and they are never upbraided with them but by their enemies, or those that envy therri, and perhaps the discontented and the poor. On the contrary, most of the well-bred people, that live, in affluence themselves, will commend them for their diligence and activity; and fay of them, that they take care of the main chance; that they are industrious men for their families, and that they know how, and are sit, to live in the world.

But these kind constructions are not more hurtful to the practice of Christianity, than the high opinion which, in

an artful education, men are taught to have of their species, is to the belief of its doctrine, if a right use be not made of it. That the great pre-eminence we have over all other creatures we are acquainted with, consists in our rational faculty, is very true; but it is as true, that the more we are taught to admire ourselves, the more our pride increases, and the greater stress we lay on the sussiciency of our reason: For as experience teaches us, that the greater and the more transcendent the esteem is, which men have for their own worth, the less capable they generally are to bear injuries without resentment; so we see, in like manner, that the more exalted the notions are which men entertain of their better part, their reasoning faculty, the more remote and averse they will be from giving their assent to any thing that seems to insult over or contradict it: And asking a man to admit of any thing he cannot comprehend, the proud reasoner calls an affront to human understanding. But as ease and pleasure are the grand aim of the *beau monde,* and civility is inseparable from their behaviour, whether they are believers or not, so well-bred people never quarrel with the religion they are brought up in: They will readily comply with every ceremony in divine worship they have been used to, and never dispute with you either about the Old or the New Testament, if, in your turn, you will forbear laying great stress upon faith and mysteries, and allow them to give an allegorical, or any other sigurative fense to the History of the Creation, and whatever else they cannot comprehend or account for by the light of nature.

I am far from believing, that, among the fashionable people, there are not, in all Christian countries, many persons of stricter virtue, and greater sincerity in religion, than I have here described; but that a considerable part of mankind have a great resemblance to the picture I have been drawing, I appeal to every knowing and candid reader. Horatio, Cleomenes, and Fulvia, are the names 1 have given to my interlocutors: The sirst represents one of the modish people I have been speaking of, but rather of the better sort of them as to morality, though he seems to have a greater distrust of the sincerity of clergymen than he has of that of any other profession, and to be of the opinion, which is expressed in that trite and specious, as well as false and injurious faying, priests of all religions are the fame. As to his studies, he is supposed to be tolerably well versed in the classics, and to have read more than is usual for people of quality, that are born to great estates. He is a man of strict honour, and of justice as well as humanity; rather profuse than cuvetous, and altogether disinterested in his principles. He has been abroad, seen the world, and is supposed to be possessed of the greatest part of the accomplishments that usually gain a man the reputation of being very much of a gentleman.

Cleomenes had been just such another, but was much reformed. As he had formerly, for his amusement only, been dipping into anatomy, and several parts of natural philosophy; so, since he was come home from his travels, he had studied human nature, and the knowledge of himself, with great application. It is supposed, that, whilst he was thus employing most of his leisure hours, he met with the Fable of the Bees; and, making a great use of what he read, compared what he felt himself within, as well as what he had seen in the world, with the sentiments set forth in that book, and found the insincerity of men fully as universal, as it was there represented. He had no opinion of the pleas and excuses that are commonly made to cover the real desires ef the heart; and he ever suspected the sincerity of men, whom he saw to be fond of the world, and with eagerness grasping at wealth and power, when they pretended that the great end of their labours was to have opportunities of doing good to others upon earth, and becoming themselves more thankful to Heaven; especially, if they conformed with the *beau monde,* and seemed to take delight in a falhionable way of living: He had the same suspicion of all men of sense, who, having read and considered the gospel, would maintain the possibility

that persons might pursue worldly glory with all their strength, and, at the same time, be good Christians. Cleomenes himself believed the Bible to be the word of God, without reserve, and was entirely convinced of the mysterious, as well as historical truths that are contained in it. Bat as he was fully persuaded, not only of the veracity of the Christian religion, but likewise of the severity of its precepts, so he attacked his passions with vigour, but never scrupled to own his want of power to subdue them, or the violent opposition he felt from within; often complaining, that the obstacles he met with from stem and blood, were insurmountable. As he understood perfectly well the dissiculty of the task required in the gospel, so he ever opposed those easy casuists, that endeavoured to lessen and extenuate it for their own ends; and he loudly maintained, that men's gratitude to Heaven was an unacceptable offering, whilst they continued to live in ease and luxury, and were visibly solicitous after their share of the pomp and vanity of this world. In the very politeness of conversation, the complacency with which fashionable people are continually, soothing each other's frailties, and in almost every part of a gentleman's behaviour, he thought there was a disagreement between the outward appearances, and what is felt within, that was clashing with uprightness and sincerity. Cleomenes was of opinion, that of all religious virtues, nothing was more scarce, or more dissicult to acquire, than Christian humility; and that to destroy the possibility of ever attaining to it, nothing was so effectual as what is called a gentleman's education; and that die more dexterous, by this means, men grew in concealing the outward signs, and every symptom of pride, the more entirely they became enslaved by it within. He caresully examined into the felicity that accrues from the applause "of others, and the invisible wages which men f sense and judicious fancy received for their labours; and what it was at the bottom that rendered those airy rewards so ravishing to mortals. He had often observed, and watched nar-

rowly the countenances and behaviour of men, when any thing of theirs was admired or commended, such as the choice of their furniture, the politeness of their entertainments, the elegancy of their equipages, their dress, their diversions, or the sine taste displayed in their buildings.

Cleomenes seemed charitable, and was a man of strict morals, yet he would often complain that he was not possessed of one Christian virtue, and found fault with his own actions, that had all the appearances of goodness; because he was conscious, he said, that they were performed from a wrong principle. The effects ot his education, and his aversion to infamy, had always been strong enough to keep him from turpitude; but this he ascribed to his vanity, which he complained was in such full possession of his heart, that he knew no gratisication of any appetite from which he was able to exclude it. Having always been a man of unblameable behaviour, the sincerity of his belief had made no visible alteration in his conduct to outward appearances; but in private he never ceased from examining himself. As no man was less prone to enthusiasm than himself, so his lise was very uniform; and as he never pretended to high flights of devotion, ib he never was guilty of enormous offences. He had a (Irong aversion to rigorists of all sorts; and when he saw men quarrelling about forms and creeds, and the interpretation of obscure places, and requiring of others the strictest compliance to their own opinions in disputable matters, it raised his indignation to see the generality of them want charity, and many of them scandalously remiss in the plainest and most necessary duties. He took uncommon pains to search into human nature, and lest no stone unturned, to detect the pride and hypocrisy of it, and, among his intimate friends, to expose the stratagems of the one, and the exorbitant power of the other. He was sure, that the satisfaction which arose from worldly enjoyments, was something distinct from gratitude, and foreign to religion; and he felt plainly, that as it proceeded from within, so it centered in himself:

The very reliso of life, he said, was accompanied with an elevation of mind, that seemed to be inseparable from his being. Whatever principle was the cause ot this, he was convinced within himself, that the sacrisice" os the lieart, which the gospel requires, consisted in the utter extirpation of that principle; confessing, at the fame time, that this satisfaction he found in himself, this elevation of mind, caused his chief pleasure; and that, in all the comforts of life, it made the greatest part of the enjoyment.

Cleomenes, with grief, often owned his fears, that his attachment to the world would never cease whilst he lived; the reasons he gave, were the great regard he continued to have for the opinion of worldly men; the stubborness of his indocile heart, that could not be brought to change the ob»jects of its pride; and refused to be ashamed of what, from his infancy, it had been taught to glory in; and, lastly, the impossibility, he found in himself, of being ever reconciled to contempt, and enduring, with patience, to be laughed at and despised for any cause, or on any consideration whatever. These were the obstacles, he said, that hindered him from breaking off all commerce with the *beau monde,* and entirely changing his manner of living; without which, he thought it mockery to talk of renouncing the world, and bidding adieu to all the pomp and vanity of it.

The part of Fulvia, which is the third person, is so inconsiderable, me just appearing only in the sirst dialogue, that it would be impertinent to trouble the reader with a character of her. I had a mind to fay some things on painting and operas, which I thought might, by introducing her, be brought in more naturally, and with less trouble, than they could have been without her. The ladies, I hope, will sind no reason, from the little she does fay, to suspect that she Vrants either virtue or understanding.

Aj to the fable, or what is supposed to have occasioned the sirst dialogue between Horatio and Cleomenes, it is this. Horatio, who had found great delight in my Lord Shaftsoury's polite manner of writing, his sine raillery, and blending virtue with good manners, was a great stickler for the social system; and wondered how Cleomenes could be an advocate for uch a book as the Fable of the Bees, of which he had heard a very vile character from several quarters. Cleomenes, who loved and had a great friendstrip for Horatio, wanted to undeceive him; but the other, who hated satire, Was prepossessed, and having been told likewise, that martial courage, and honour itself, were ridiculed in that book, he was very much exasperated against the author and his whole scheme: he had two or three times heard Cleomenes. dis

T course on this subject with others; but would never enter into the argument himself; and sinding his friend often pressing to come to it, he began to look cooly upon him, and at lall to avoid all opportunities of being alone with him: till Cleomenes drew him in, by the stratagem which the reader will fee he made use of, as Horatio was one day taking his leave after ashort complimentary visit.

I mould not wonder to fee men of candour, as well as good fense, sind fault with the manner, in which I have chose to publish these thoughts of mine to the world: There certainly is something in it, which I confess I do not know how to 'justify to my own satisfaction. That such a man as Cleomenes, having met with a book agreeable to his own sentiments, should desire to be acquainted with the author of it, has nothing in it that is improbable or unseemly; but then it will be objected, that, whoever the interlocutors are, it was I myself who wrote the dialogues; and that it is contrary to all decency, that a man mould proclaim concerning his own work, all that a friend of his, perhaps, might be allowed to fay: this is true; and the best answer which I think can be made to it, is, that such an impartial man, and such a lover of truth, as Cleomenes is represented to be, would be as cautious in speaking of his friend's merit, as he would be of his own. It might be urged likewise, that when a man professes himself to be an author's friend, and exactly to entertain the fame sentiments with another, it must naturally put every reader upon his guard, and render him as suspicious and distrustful of such a man, as he would be of the author himself. But how good soever the excuses are, that might be made for this manner of writing, I would never have ventured upon it, if I had not liked it in the famous Gassendus, who, by the help of several dialogues and a friend, who is the chief personage in them, has not only explained and illustrated his system, but likewise refuted his adversaries: him I have followed, and I hope the reader will sind, that whatever opportunity l have had by this means, of speaking well of myself indirectly, l had no design to make that, or any other ill use of it.

As it is supposed, that Cleomenes is my friend, and speaks my sentiments, so it is but justice, that every thing which he advances should be looked upon and considered as my own; but no man in his senses would think, that I ought to be equally responsible for every thing that Horatio says, who is his antagonist. If ever he offers any thing that savours of libertinism, or is otherwise exceptionable, which Cleomenes does not reprove him for in the best and most serious manner, or to which he gives not the most satisfactory and convincing answer that can be made, I am to blame, otherwise not. Yet from the fate the sirst part has met with, I expect to fee in a little time several things transcribed and cited from this, in that manner, by themselves, without the replies that are made to them, and so shown to the world, as my words and my opinion. The opportunity of doing this will be greater in this part than it was in the former, and should I always have fair play, and never be attacked, but by such adversaries, as would make their quotations from me without artisice, and use me with common honesty, it would go a great way to the refuting of me; and l should myself begin to suspect the truth of several'things I have advanced, and which hitherto I cannot help believing.

A stroke made in this manner, which

the reader will sometimes meet with in the following dialogues, is a sign, either of interruption, when the person speaking is not suffered to go on with what he was going to fay, or else of a pause, during which something is supposed to be said or done, not relating to the discourse.

As in this part I have not altered the subject, on which a former, known by the name of the Fable of the Bees, was wrote; and the fame unbiassed method of searching after truth, and inquiring into the nature of man and society, made use os in that, is continued in this, I thought it unnecessary. to look out for another title; and being myself a great lover of simplicity, and my invention none of the most fruitful, the reader, 1 hope, will pardon the bald, inelegant aspect, and unusual emptiness of the title page.

Here 1 would have made an end of my Preface, which I know very well is too long already: but the world having been very grossly imposed upon by a false report, that some monthsago was very solemnly made, and as" industriously spread in tnest os the newspapers, for a considerable time, 1 think it would be an unpardonable neglect in me, of the public, should 1 suffer them; to remain in the error they were led into, when 1 am actually addressing them; and there is no other person, from whom they can so justly expect to be undeceived. In the London Evening Post of Saturday March 9,

Tj 1727-8. the following paragraph was printed in small Italic, at the end of the home news.

On Friday evening the sirst instant, a gentleman, welldresled, appeared at the bonsire before St. James's Gate, who declared himself the author of a book, intituled, the Fable of the Bees; and that he was sorry for writing the fame: and recollecting his former promise, pronounced these words: I commit my book to-the flames; and threw it in accordingly.

The Monday following, the fame piece of news was repeated, in the Daily Journal, and after that for a considerable time, as I have said, in most of the papers: but since the Saturday mentioned, which was the only time it was printed by itself, ir appeared always with a small addition to it, and annexed (with a N. B. before it) to the following advertisement.

Apeth-aoha:

Or an Inquiry into the Original of Moral Virtue, wherein the false notions of Machiavcl, Hobbs, Spinosa, and Mr. Bayle, as they are collected and digested by the Author of the Fable of the Bees, are examined and confuted; and the eternal and unalterable nature and obligation of moral virtue is stated and vindicated; to which is presixed, a Prefatory Introduction, in a Letter to that Author, By Alexander Innes, D. D. Preacher Assistant at St. Margaret's, Westminster.

The small addition which I said was made to that notable piece of news, after it came to be annexed to this advertisement, consisted of these sive words (upon reading the above book), which were put in after," sorry for writing the fame. " This story having been often repeated in the papers, and never publicly contradicted, many people, it seems, were credulous enough to believe, notwithstanding the improbability of it. But the least attentive would have suspected the whole, as. soon as they had seen the addition that was made to it, the second time it was published; for supposing it to be intelligible, as it follows the advertisement, it cannot be pretended, that the repenting gentleman pronounced those very words. He must have named the book; and if he had said, that his sorrow was occasioned by reading the ApethAoriA, or the new book of the reverend Dr. Innes, how camesuch a remarkable part of his confession to be omitted in the sirst publication, where the well-dressed gentleman's words and actions seemed to be set down with so much care and exactness? Besides, every body knows the great industry, and general intelligence of our newswriters: if such a farce *had.* really been acted, and a man had been hired to pronounce the words mentioned, and throw a book into the sire, which I have often wondered was not done, is it credible at all, that a thing so remarkable, done so openly, and before so many witnesses, the sirst day of March, should not be taken notice of in any of the papers before the ninth, and never be repeated afterwards, or ever mentioned but as an appendix of the advertisement to recommend Dr. Innes's book?

However, this story has been much talked of, and occ.-fioned a great deal of mirth among my acquaintance, several of whom have earnestly pressed me more than once to advertise the falsity of it, which I would never comply with for fear of being laughed at, as some years ago poor Dr. Patridge was, for seriously maintaining that he was not dead. But all this while we vere in the dark, and nobody could tell how this report came into the world, or what it could be that had given a handle to it, when one evening a friend of mine, who had borrowed Dr. Innes's book, which till then I had never seen, showed me in it the following fines.

But *a propos,* Sir, if I rightly remember, the ingenuous Mr. Law, in his Remarks upon your Fable of the Bees, puts you in mind of a promise you had made, by which you obliged yourself to burn that book at any time or place your adversary should appoint, if any thing should be found in it tending to immorality or the corruption of manners. I have a great respect for that gentleman, though I am not personally acquainted with him, but I cannot but condemn his excessive credulity and good nature, in believing that a man of your principles could be a slave to his word; for my own, part, I think, I know you too well to be so easily imposed upon; or if, after all, you should really persist in your resolution, and commit it to the flames, I appoint the sirst of March before St. James's Gate, for that purpose, it being the birthday of the best and most glorious queen upon earth; and the. burning of your book the smallest atonement you can make, for endeavouring to corrupt and debauch his majesty's subjects in their principles. Now, Sir, if you agree to this, I hope you are not so destitute of friends, but that jou mar sind some charitable neighbour or other, who will lend you a helping hand, and throw in the author at the same time by way of appendix; the doing of which will, in my opinion, complete the solemnity of the day. I am not your patient, but, your most humble servant.

Thus ends what, in the Apeth-aotia, Doctor Innes is pleased to call a Prefatory Introduction, in a Letter to the Author of the Fable of the Bees. It is signed A. 1. and dated Tot-hill-sields, Westminster, Jan. 20. 1727-8.

Now all our wonder ceased. The judicious reader will easily allow me, that, having read thus much, I had an ample dispensation from going on any further; therefore I can say nothing of the book: and as to the reverend author of it, who seems to think himself so well acquainted with my principles, I have not the honour to know either him or his morals, otherwise than from what I have' quoted here. *Ex ptde Herculem.* 1 *London, Odober* 20. 1728.

CLEOMENES.

Always in haste, Horatio?

Hor. 1 must beg of you to excuse me, I am obliged to go. *Cleo.* Whether you have other enagements than you used to have, or whether your temper is changed, I cannot tell, but something. has made an alteration in you, of which I cannot comprehend the cause. There is no man in the world whose friendship I value more than 1 do yours, or whose company 1 like better, yet I can never have it. I profess I have thought sometimes that you have avoided me on purpose. *Hor.* I am sorry, Cleomenes, I should have been wanting incivility to you; I come every week constantly to pay my respects to you, and if ever I fail, I always send to inquire after your health. *Cku.* No man outdoes Horatio in civility-; but I thought something more was due to our affections and long acquaintance, besides compliments and ceremony: Of late I have never been to wait upon you, but you are gone abroad, or I sind you engaged; and when I have the honour to see you here, your stay is only momentary. Pray pardon my rudeness for once: What is it that hinders you now from keeping me company for an hour or two? My coulin talks of go-

ing out, and 1 shall be all alone. *Hor.* I know better than to rob you of such an opportunity for speculation? *Cleo.* Speculation! on what, pray? *Hor.* That vileness of our species in the resined way of thinking you have of late been so fond of, I call it the scheme of deformity, the partisans of which study chiefly to make every thing in our nature appear as ugly and contemptible as it is possible, and take uncommon pains, to persuade men that they are devils. *Cleo.* If that be all, I shall soon convince you. *Hor.* No conviction to me, I beseech you: I am determined, and fully persuaded, that there is good in the world as well as evil;' and that the words, honesty, benevolence, and humanity, and even charity, are not empty sounds only, but that there are such things in spite of the Fable of the Bees; and I am resolved to believe, that, notwithstanding the degeneracy of mankind, and the wickedness of the age, there are men now living, who arc actually possessed of those virtues. *Cleo.* But you do not know what I am going to fay: I am *Hor.* That may be, but I will not hear one word; all you can fay is lost upon me, and if you will not give me leave to speak out, I am gone this moment. That cursed book has bewitched you, and made you deny the existence of those very virtues that had gained you the esteem of your friends. You know this is not my usual language; I hate to say harsh things: But what regard can, or ought one to have for an author that treats every body *de baut en bas,* makes a jest of virtue and honour, calls Alexander the Great a madman, and spares kings and princes no more than any one, would the most abject of the people? The business of his philosophy is just the reverse to that of the herald's ossice; for, as there they are always contriving and rinding out high and illustrious pedigrees for low and obscure people, so your author is ever searching after, and inventing mean contemptible origins for worthy and honourable actions. I am your very humble servant *Cleo.* Stay. I am of your opinion; what I offered to convince you of, was, how entirely 1 am recovered of the folly which you have so justly ex-

posed: I have left that error. *Hor.* Are you in earnest? *Cleo.* No man more: There is no greater stickler for the social virtues than myself; and I much question, whether there is any of Lord Shaftsbury's admirers that will go my. lengths! *Hor.* I shall be glad to see you go my lengths sirst, and as many more as you please. You cannot conceive, Cleomenes, how it has grieved me, when I have seen how many enemies you made yourself by that extravagant way of arguing. If you are but serious, whence comes this change? *Cleo.* In the sirst place, I grew weary of having every body against me: and, in the second, there is more room for invention in the other system. Poets and orators in the social system have sine opportunities of exerting themselves. *Hor.* I very much suspect the recovery you boast of: Are you convinced, that the other system was false, which you might have easily learned from seeing every'body against you? *Giro.* False to be sure; but what you allege is no proof of it: for if the greatest part of mankind were not against that scheme of deformity, as you justly call it, insincerity could not be so general, as the scheme itself supposes it to be: But since my eyes have been opened, I have found out that truth and probability are the silliest things in the world; they are of no manner of use, especially among the people *cie bongout. Hor.* I thought what a convert you was: but what new madness has seized you now? *Cleo.* No madness at all: 1 fay, and will maintain it to the world, that truth, in the sublime, is very impertinent; and that in the arts and sciences, sit for men of taste to look into, a master cannot commit a more unpardonable fault, than sticking to, or being influenced by truth, where it interferes with what is agreeable. *Hor.* Homely truths indeed *Cleo.* Look upon that Dutch piece of the nativity: what charming colouring there is! What a sine pencil, and how just are the outlines for a piece so curiously sinished! But what a fool the fellow was to draw hay, and straw, and water, and a rack as well as a manger: it is a wonder he did not put the bambino into the manger. *Ful.* The *bambino?* That is the child, I suppose: why it should be in the manger; mould it not? Does not the history tell us, that the child was laid in the manger? I have no skill in painting; but I can fee whether things are drawn to the life or not: sure nothing can be more like the head of an ox than that there. A picture then pleases me best when the art in such a manner deceives my eye, that, with. out making any allowance, I can imagine I fee the things in reality which the painter has endeavoured to represent. I have always thought it an admirable piece ; sure nothing in the world can be more like nature. *Cleo.* Like nature! So much the worse: Indeed, cousin, it is easily seen, that you have no skill in painting. It is not nature, but agreeable nature, *la belle nature,* that is to be represented: all things that are abject, low, pitiful, and mean, are carefully to be avoided, and kept out of sight; becaule, to men of the true taste, they are as offensive as things that are shocking, and really nasty. *Ful.* At that rate, the Virgin Mary's condition, and our Saviour's birth, are never to be painted. *Cleo.* That is your mistake; the subject itself is noble: Let us go but in the next room, and I will show you the difference Look upon that picture, which is the fame history. There is sine architecture, there is a colonnade; can any thing be thought of more magnisicent? How skilfully is that ass removed, and how little you fee of the ox: pray, mind the obscurity they are both placed in. It hangs in a strong light, or else one might look ten times upon the picture without observing them: Behold these pillars of the Corinthian order, how lofty they are, and what an effect they have, what a noble space, what an area here is! How nobly every thing concurs to express the majestic grandeur of the subject, and strikes the foul with awe and admiration at the fame time! *Ful.* Pray cousin, has good fense ever any share in the judgment which your men of true taste form about pictures? *Hor.* Madam! *Ful.* I beg pardon, Sir, if I have offended: but to me it seems strange to hear such commendations given to a painter, for turning the stable of a country inn into a palace

of extraordinary magnisicence: This is a great deal worse than Swift's Metamorphosis of Philemon and Baucis; for there some show of resemblance is kept in the changes. *Hor.* In a country stable, Madam, there is nothing but silth aud nastineso, or vile abject things not sit to be seen, at least not capable of entertaining persons of quality. *Ful.* The Dutch picture in the next room has nothing that is offensive: but an Augean stable, even before Hercules had cleaned it, would be less mocking to me than those fluted pillars; for nobody can please my eye that asfronts my understanding: When I desire a man to-paint a considerable history, which every body knows to have been transacted at a country inn, does he not strangely impose upon me, because he understands architecture, to draw me a room that might have served for a great ball, or banqueting-house, to any Roman emperor? Besides, that the poor and abject state in which our Saviour chose to appear at his coming into the world, is the most material circumstance of the history: it contains an excellent moral against vain pomp, and is the strongest persuasive to humility, which, in the Italian, are more than lost. *Hor.* Indeed, Madam, experience is against you; and it is certain, that, even among the vulgar,-the representations *ot'* mean and abject things, and such as they are familiar with,: have not that effect, and either breed contempt, or are insignisicant: whereas vast piles, stately buildings, roofs of uncommon height, surprising ornaments, and all the architecture of the grand taste, are the sittest to raise devotion, and inspire men with veneration, and" a religious awe for the places that have these excellencies to boast of. Is there ever a meeting-house or barn to be compared to a sine cathedral, for this purpose? *Ful.* I believe there is a mechanical way of raising devotion in silly superstitious creatures; but an attentive contemplation on the works of God, I am sure -*Cleo.* Pray, cousin, say no more in defence of your low taste: The painter has nothing to do with the truth of the history; his business is to express the dignity of the subject, and, in com-

pliment to his judges, never to forget the excellency of our "species: All his art and good fense must be employed in raising that to the highest pitch: Great masters do not paint for the common people, but for persons of resined understanding: What you complain of, is the effect of the good, manners and complaisance of the painter. When he had drawn the Infant and the Madona, he thought the least glimpse of the ox and the ass would be susiieient to acquaint you with the history: They who want more fescuing, and a broader explanation, he does not desire his picture should ever be shown to; for the jest, he entertains you with nothing but what is noble and worthy your attention: You fee he is an architect, and completely skilled in, perspective, and he shows you how sinely he can round a pillar, and that both the depth, and the height of a space, may be drawn on a flat, with all the other wonders he performs by his skill in that inconceivable mystery of light and shadows. *Ful.* Why. then is it pretended that painting is an imitation of nature? *Cleo.* At sirst setting out a scholar is to copy things exactly as he fees them; but from a great master, when he is left to his own invention, it is expected he should take the perfections of nature, and not paint it as it is, but as we would wish it to be. Zeuxis, to draw a goddess, took sive beautiful women, from which he culled what was most graceful in each. *Ful.* Still every grace he painted was taken from nature. *Cleo.* That's true; but he. left nature her rubbish, and imitated nothing but what was excellent, which made the assemblage superior to any thing in nature. Demetrius was taxed for being too natural; Dionysus was also blamed for drawing men like us. Nearer our times, Michael Angelo was esteemed too natural, and Lysippus of old upbraided the common fort of sculptors for making men such as they were found in nature. *Ful.* Are these things real? *Cleo.* You may read it yourself in Graham's Preface to The Art of Painting: the book is above in the library. *Hor.* These things may seem strange to you, Madam, but they arc of immense use to the public: the higher we can carry the excellency of our species, the more those beautiful images will sill noble minds with worthy and suitable ideas of their own dignity, that will seldom fail of spurring them on to virtue and heroic actions. There is a grandeur to be expressed in things that far surpafles the beauties of simple nature. You take delight in operas, Madam, I do not question; you must have minded the noble manner and stateliness beyond nature, which every thing there is executed with. What gentle touches, what slight and yet majestic motions are made use of to express the most boisterous passions! As the subject is always lofty, so no posture is to be chosen but what is serious and signisicant, as well as comely and agreeable; should the actions there be represented as they are in common life, they would ruin the sublime, and at once rob you of all your pleasure. *Ful.* I never expected any thing natural at an opera; but as persons of distinction resort thither, and every body comes dressed, it is a sort of employment, and I seldom miss a night, because it is the fashion to go: besides, the royal family, and the monarch himself, generally honouring them with their presence, it is almost become a duty to attend them, as much as it is to go to court. What diverts me there is the ompany, the lights, the music, the scenes, and other decora,tions: but as I understand but very few words of Italian, so what is most admired in the *recitativo* is lost upon me, which makes the acting part to me rather ridiculous than *Hor.* Ridiculous, Madam! For Heaven's fake *Ful.* I beg pardon, Sir, for the expression, I never laughed at an opera in my life; but I confess, as to the entertainment itself, that a good play is insinitely more diverting to me; and I prefer any thing that informs my understanding beyond all the recreations which either my eyes or my ears can be regaled with. *Hor.* I am sorry to hear a lady of your good fense make such a choice. Have you no taste for music, Madam? *Ful.* I named that as part of my diversion. *Cleo.* My cousin plays very well upon the harpsichord herself. *Ful.* I love to hear good

music; but it does not throw me into those raptures, I hear others speak of. *Hor.* Nothing certainly can elevate the mind beyond a fine concert: it seems to disengage the soul from the body, and lift it up to heaven. It is in this situation, that we are most capable of receiving extraordinary impressions: when the instruments cease, our temper is subdued, and beautiful action joins with the sldlful voice, in setting before us in a transcendent light, the heroic labours we are come to admire, and which the word Opera imports. The powerful harmony between the engaging sounds and speaking gestures invades he heart, and forcibly inspires us with those noble sentiments, which to entertain, the most expressive words can only attempt to persuade us. Few comedies are tolerable, and in the best of them, if the levity of the expressions does not corrupt, the meanness of the subject must debase the manners; at least, to persons of quality. In tragedies the style is more sublime and the subjects generally great; but all violent passions, and even the representations of them, rustle and discompose the mind: besides, when men endeavour to express things strongly, and they are acted to the life, it often happens that the images do mischief, because they are too moving, and that the action is faulty for being too natural; and experience teaches us, that in unguarded minds, by those pathetic performances, flames are often raised that are prejudicial to virtue.. The playhouses themselves are far from being inviting, much less the companies, at least the greatest part of them lhat frequent them,, some, of which are almost of the lowest rank of all. The disgust that persons of the least elegance receive from these people are many; besides, the ill scents, and unseemly sights one meets with, of careless rakes and impudent wenches, that, having paid their money, reckon themselves to bfe all upon the level with every body there; the oaths, scurrilities, and vile jells one is often obliged to hear, without resenting them; and the odd mixture of high, and low that are all partaking of the same diversion, without regard to dress or quality, are all

very offensive; and it cannot but be very disagreeable to polite people to be in the same crowd with a variety of persons, some of them below mediocrity, that pay no deference to one another. At the opera, every thing charms and concurs to make happiness complete. The sweetness of voice, in the sirst place, and the solemn composure of the action, serve to mitigate and allay every passion; it is the gentleness of them, and the calm serenity of the mind, that make us amiable, and bring us the nearest to the perfection of angels; whereas, the violence of the passions, in which the corruption of the heart chiefly consists, dethrones our reason, and renders us more like unto savages. It is incredible, how prone we are to imitation, and how strangely, unknown to ourselves, we are shaped and fashioned after the models and examples that are often let before us. No anger nor jealousy are ever to be seen at an opera, that distort the features; no flames that are noxious, nor is any love represented in them, that is not pure and next to seraphic; and it is impossible for the remembrance to carry any thing away from them, that can fully the imagination. Secondly, the company is of another fort: the place itself is a security to peace, as well as every one's honour; and it is impossible to name another, where blooming innocence and irresistible beauty stand in so little need of guardians. Here we are sure never to meet with petulancy or ill manners, and to be free from immodest ribaldry, libertine wit, and detestable satire. If you will mind, on the one hand, the richness and splendour of dress, and the quality of the persons that appear in them; the variety of colours, and the lustre of the fair in a spacious theatre, well illuminated and adorned; and on the other, the grave deportment of the assembly, and the consciousness that appears in every countenance, of the respect they owe to each other, you will be forced to confess, that upon earth there cannot be a pastirae more agreeable: believe me, Madam, there is no place, where both sexes have such opportunities of imbibing exalted sentiments, and raising themselves above the vulgar, as they have at the opera; and there is no other fort of diversion or assembly, from the frequenting of which, young persons of quality can have equal hopes of forming their manners, and contracting a strong and lasting habit of virtue. *Ful.* You have said more in commendation of operas, Horatio, than I ever heard or thought of before; and I think every body who loves that diverlion is highly obliged to you. The grand gout, I believe, is a great help in panegyric, especially, where it is an incivility strictly to examine and overcuriousty to look into matters. *Cleo.* What fay you now, Fulvia, of nature and good fense, are they not quite beat out of doors? *Ful.* 1 have heard nothing yet, to make me out of conceit with good fense; though what you insinuated of nature, as if it was not to be imitated in painting, is an opinion, I must confess, which hitherto I more admire at, than 1 can approve of it. *Hor.* I would never recommend any thing, Madam, that is repugnant to good fense; but Cleomenes must have some design in over-acting the part he pretends to have chosen. What he said about painting is very true, whether he spoke it in jest or in earnest; but he talks so diametrically opposite to the opinion which he is known every where to defend of late, that I do not know what to make of him. *Ful.* I am convinced of the narrowness of my own understanding, and am going to visit some persons, with whom I shall be more upon the level. *Hor.* You will give me leave to wait upon you to your coach, Madam Pray, Cleomenes, what is it you have got in your head? *Cleo.* Nothing at all: I told you before, that I was so entirely recovered from my folly, that"few people went my lengths. What jealousy you entertain of me I do not know; but 1 sind myself much improved in the social system. Formerly I thought, that chief ministers, and all those at the helm of affairs, acted from principles of avarice and ambition; that in all the pains they took, and even in the slaveries they underwent for the public good, they had their private ends, and that they were supported in the fatigue by secret enjoyments they were unwilling to own. It is

not a month ago, that I imagined that the inward care and real solicitude of all great men centered within themselves; and that to enrich themselves, acquire titles of honour, and raise' their families on the one hand, and to have opportunities on the other of displaying a judicious fancy to all the elegant comforts of life, and establishing, without the least trouble of self-denial, the reputation of being wise, humane, and munisicent, were the things, which, besides the satisfaction there is in superiority and the pleasure of governing, all candidates to high ofsices and great posts proposed to themselves, from the places they sued for: I was so narrow minded, that I could not conceive how a man would ever voluntarily submit to be a flave but to serve himself. But 1 have abandoned that ill-natured way of judging: I plainly perceive the public good, in all the designs of politicians, the social virtues shine in every action, and I sind that the national interest is the compass that all statesmen steer bv. *Hor.* That is more than I can prove; but certainly there have been such men, there have been patriots, that without sclsini views' have taken incredible pains for their country's welfare: nay, there are men now that would do the fame, if they were employed; and we have had princes that have neglected their ease and pleasure, and sacrisiced their quiet, to promote the prosperity and increase the wealth and honour of the kingdom and had nothing so much at heart as the happiness of their subjects, *Cleo.* No disaffection, 1 beg of you. The difference between past aud present times, and persons in and out of places, is perhaps clearer to you than it is to me; but it is many years ago, you know, that It has been agreed between us never to enter into party disputes: what I desire your attention to, is my reformation, which you seem to doubt of, and the great change that is wrought in me. The religion of most kings and other high potentates, 1 formerly had but a slender opinion of, but now I measure their piety by what they say of it themselves to their subjects. *Hor.* That is very kindly done. *Cleo.* By thinking meanly of

things, I once had strange blundering notions concerning foreign wars: I thought that many of them arose from trisling causes, magnisied by politicians for their own ends; that the most ruinous misunderstandings between states and kingdoms might spring from the hidden malice, folly, or caprice of one man; that many f them had bean owing to the private quarrels, piques, resentments, and the haughtiness of the chief ministers of the respective nations, that were the sufferers; and that what is called personal hatred between princes seldom was more at sirst, than either an open or secret animosity which the two great favourites of those courts had against one another: but now I have learned to derive those things from higher causes. I am reconciled likewise to the luxury of the voluptuous, which I used to be offended at, because now I am convinced that the money of most rich men, is laid out with the social design of promoting arts and sciences, and that in the most expensive undertakings their principal aim is the employment of the poor. *Hor.* These are lengths indeed. *Cleo.* I have a strong aversion to satire, and detest it every whit as much as you do: the most instructive writings to understand the world, and penetrate into the heart of man, I take to be addresses, epithets, dedications, and above all, the preambles to patents, of which I am making a large colleclection. *Hor.* A very useful undertaking! *Cleo.* But to remove all your doubts of my conversion, I will show you some easy rules I have laid down for young beginners. *Hor.* What to do? *Cleo.* To judge of mens actions by the lovely system of Lord Shaftsbury, in a manner diametrically opposite to that of the Fable of the Bees. *Hor.* I do not understand you. *Cleo.* You will presently. I have called them rules, but they are rather examples from which the rules are to be gathered: as for instance, if we fee an industrious poor woman, who has pinched her belly, and gone in rags for a considerable time to save forty millings, part with her money to put out her son at six years of age to a chimney-sweeper; to judge of her charitably, according to the system of the social virtues, we must imagine, that though me never paid for the sweeping of a chimney in her life, me knows by experience, that for want of this necessary cleanliness the broth has been often spoiled, and many a chimney has been set on sire, and therefore to do good in her generation, as far as me is able, she gives up her all, both offspring and estate, to assist in preventing the several mischiefs that are often occasioned by great quantities of foot disregarded; and, free from selsish U ness, sacrisices her only son to the most wretched employment for the public welfare.

Hor. You do not vie I fee with Lord Shaftfbury, for loftiness of subjects. *Cleo.* When in a starry night with amazement we behold the glory of the sirmament, nothing is more obvious than that the whole, the beautiful all, must be the workmanship of one great Architect of power and wisdom stupendous; and it is as evident, that every thing in the universe is a constituent part of one entire fabric. *Hor.* Would you make a jest of this too. *Cleo.* Far from it: they are awful truths, of which I am as much convinced as I am of my own existence; but I was going to name the consequences, which Lord Shaftsbury draws from them, in order to demonstrate to you, that I am a convert, and a very punctual observer of his Lordship's instructions, and that, in my judgment on the poor woman's conduct, there is nothing that is not entirely agreeable to the generous way of thinking set forth and recommended in the Characteristics. *Hor.* Is it possible a man mould read such a book, and make no better use of it! I desire you would name the consequences you speak of. *Cleo.* As that insinity of luminous bodies, however different in magnitude, velocity, and the sigures they describe in their courses, concur all of them to make up the universe, so this little spot we inhabit is likewise a compound of air, water, sire, minerals, vegetables, and living creatures, which, though vastly disfering from one another in their nature, do altogether make up the body of this terraqueous globe. *Hor.* This is very right, andinthe fame mannerasour

whole species is composed of many nations of disferent religions, forms of government, interests and manners that divide and share the earth between them; so the civil society in every nation consists in great multitudes of both sexes, that widely differing from each other in age, constitution, strength, temper, wisdom and possessions, all help to make up one body politic. *Cho.* The fame exactly which I would have said: now, pray Sir, is not the great end of men's forming themselves into such societies, mutual happiness; I mean, do not all individual persons, from being thus combined, propose to themselves a more comfortable condition of life, than human creaturts, if they were to live like other wild animals, without tie or dependance, could enjoy in a free and savage state? *Hor.* This certainly is not only the end, but the end which is every where attained to by government and society, in some degree or other. *Cleo.* Hence it must follow, that it is always wrong for men to pursue gain or pleasure, by means that are visibly detrimental to the civil society, and that creatures who can do this must be narrow-fouled, short-sighted, selsish people; whereas, wife men never look upon themselves as individual persons, without considering the whole, of which they are but trifling parts in respect to bulk, and are incapable of receiving any satisfaction from things that interfere with the public welfare. This being undeniably true, ought not a!l private advantage to give way to this general interest; and ought it not to be every one's endeavour, to increase this common stock of happiness; and, in order to it, do what he can to render himself a serviceable and useful member of that whole body which he belongs to? *Hor.* What of all this? *Cleo.* Has not my poor woman, in what I have related of her, acted in conformity to this social system? *Hor.* Can any one in his fenses imagine, that an indigent thoughtless wretch, without fense or education, mould ever act from such generous principles? *Cleo.* Poor 1 told you the woman was, and I will not insist upon her education; but as for her being

thoughtless and void of fense, you will give me leave to say, that it is an aspersion for which you have no manner of foundation; and from the account I have given of her, nothing can be gathered but that she was a considerate, virtuous, wife woman, in poverty. *Hor.* I suppose you would persuade me that you are in earnest. *Cleo.* I am much more so than you imagine; and say once more, that, in the example I have given, 1 have trod exactly in my Lord Shaftsbury's steps, and closely followed the social system. If I have committed any error, show it me. *Hor.* Did that author ever meddle with any thing so low and pitiful. *Cleo:* There can be nothing mean in noble actions, whoever the persons are that perform them. But if the vulgar are to be all excluded from the social virtues, what rule or instruction shall the labouring poor, which are by far the greatest part of the nation, have left them to walk by, when the Characteristics have made a jest of all revealed religion, especially the Christian? but if you despise the poor and illiterate, I can, in the same method, judge of men in higher stations. Let the enemies to the social system behold the venerable counsellor, now grown eminent for his wealth, that at his great age continues sweltering at the bar to plead the doubtful cause, and, regardless of his dinner, shorten his own life in endeavouring to secure the possessions of others. How conspicuous is the benevolence of the physician to his kind, who, from morning till night, visiting the sick, keeps several sets of horses to be more serviceable to many, and still grudges himself the time for the necessary functions of life! In the fame manner the indefatigable clergyman, who, with his ministry, supplies a very large parish already, solicits with zeal to be as useful and benesicent to another, though sifty of his order, yet unemployed, offer their service for the same purpose. *Hor.* I perceive your drift: from the strained panegyrics you labour at, you would form arguments *ad absurdum:* the banter is ingenious enough, and, at proper times, might serve to raise a laugh; but then you must own likewise, that those studied encomiums will not bear to be seriously examined into. When we consider that the great business as well as perpetual solicitude of the poor, are to supply their immediate wants, and keep themselves from starving, and that their children are a burden to them, which they groan under, and desire to be delivered from by all possible means, that are not clashing with the low involuntary affection which nature forces them to have for their offspring: when, I fay, we consider this, the virtues of your industrious make no great sigure. The public spirit likewisa, and the generous principles, your sagacity has found out in the three faculties, to which men are brought up for a livelihood, seem to be very for fetched. Fame, wealth, and greatness, every age can witness: but whatever labour or fatigue they submit to, the motives of their actions are as conspicuous as their calling themselves. *Cleo.* Are they not benesicial to mankind, and of use to the public? *Hor.* I do not deny that; we often receive inestimable benesits from them, and the good ones in either profession are not only useful, but very necessary to the society: but though there are several that sacrisice their whole lives, and all the comforts of them, to their business, there is not one of them that would take a quarter of the pains he now is at, if, without taking any, he could acquire the fame money, reputation, and other advantages that may accrue to him from the esteem or gratitude of those whom he has been serviceable to; and I do not believe, there is an eminent man among them that would not own this if the question was put to him. Therefore, when ambition and the love of money are avowed principles men act from, it is very silly to ascribe virtues to them, which they themselves pretend to lay no manner of claim to, But your encomium upon the parson is the merriest jest of all: I have heard many excuses made, and some of them very frivolous, for the covetousness of priests; but what you have picked out in their praise is more extraordinary than any thing I ever met with; and the most partial advocate and admirer of the clergy never yet discovered before yourself a great virtue in their hunting after pluralities, when they were well provided for themselves, and many others for want of employ were ready to starve. *Cleo.* But if there be any reality in the social system, it would be better for the public, if men, in all professions, were to act from those generous principles; and you will allow, that the society would be the gainers, if the generality in the three faculties would mind others more, and themselves less than they do now. *Hor.* I do not know that; and considering what slavery some lawyers, as well as physicians, undergo, I much question whether it would be possible for them to exert themselves in the fame manner though they would, if the constant baits and refreshments of large fees did not help to support human nature, by continually stimulating this darling passion. *Cleo.* Indeed, Horatio, this is a stronger argument against the social system, and more injurious to it than any thing that has been said by the author whom you have exclaimed against with so much bitterness. *Hor.* I deny that: I do not conclude from the selsishness in some, that there is no virtue in others. *Cleo.* Nor he neither, and you very much wrong him if you assert that he ever did. *Hor.* I refuse to commend what is not praise-worthy; hut as bad as mankind are, virtue has an existence as well as vice, though it is more scarce. *Cleo.* What you said last, nobody ever contradicted; but t do not know what you would be at: does not the Lord Shaftsbury endeavour to do good, and promote the social virtues, and am I not doing the very fame? suppose me to be in the wrong in the favourable constructions I have made of things, still it is to be wished for at least, that men had a greater regard to the public welfare, less fondness for their private interest, and more charity for their neighbours, than the generality of them have. *Hor.* To be wished for, perhaps, it may be, but what probability is there that this ever will come to pass? *Cleo.* And unless that can come to pass, it is the idled thing in the world to discourse upon, and demonstrate the excellency of virtue; what signisies it to set forth the beauty of it, unless it was possible that men should fall in love with it? *Hor.* If virtue was never recommended, men might grow worse than they are. *Cleo.* Then, by the same reason, if it was recommended more, men might grow better than they are. But I fee persectly well the reason of these shifts and evasions you make use of against your opinion: You sind yourself under a necessity of allowing my panegyrics, as you call them, to be just; or sinding the lame fault with most of my Lord Shaftsbury's; and you would do neither if you could help it: From mens preferring company to solitude, his Lordship pretends to prove the love and natural affection we have for our own species: If this was examined into with the fame strictness as you have done every thing I have said in behaltor the three faculties, 1 believe that the solidity of the consequences would be pretty equal in both. But I stick to my text, and stand up for the social virtues: The noble author of that system had a most charitable opinion of his species, and extolled the dignity of it in an extraordinary manner, and why my imitation us him should be called a banter, 1 fee no reason. He certainly wrote with a good design, and endeavoured to inspire his readers with resined notions, and a public spirit abstract from religion: The world enjoys the fruits of his labours; but the advantage that is justly expected from his writings, can never be so universally felt, before that pubhe spirit, which he recommended, comes down to the meanest tradesmen, whom you would endeavour to exclude from the generous sentiments and noble pleasures that are already so visible in many. I am now thinking on two sorts of people that stand very much in need of, and yet hardly ever meet with one another: This misfortune must have caused such a chasm in the band of society, that no depth of thought, or happiness of contrivance, could have silled up the vacuity, if a most tender regard for the commonwealth, and the height of benevolence did not influence and oblige others, mere strangers to those people, and commonly men of small education, to assist them with their good ossices, and stop up the gap. Many ingenious workmen, in obscure dwellings, would be starved in spite of industry, only for want of knowing where to sell the product of their labour, if there were not others to dispose of it for them: And again, the rich and extravagant are daily furnished with an insinite variety of superfluous knicknacks and elaborate trifles, every one of them invented to gratify either a needless curiosity, or else wantonness and folly; and which they could never have thought of, much less wanted, had they never seen or known where to buy them. What a blessing, then, to the public, is the social toyman, who lays out a considerable estate to gratify the desires of these two disserent classes of people? He procures food and raiment for the deserving poor, and searches with great diligence after the most skilful artisicers, that no man shall be able to produce better workmanship than himself: with studied civilities, and a serene countenance, he entertains the greatest strangers; and, often speaking to them sirst, kindly osfers to guess at their wants: He consines not his attendance to a few stated hours, but waits their leisure all day long in an open shop, where he bears the summer's heat, and winter's cold, with equal cheerfulness. What a beautiful prospect is here of natural asfection to our kind! For, if he acts from that principle, who only furnishes us with necessaries of life, certainly he shows a more superlative love and indulgence to his species, who will not surfer the most whimsical of it to be an hour destitute of what he shall fancy, even things the most unnecessary. *Hor.* You have made the most of it indeed, but are you not tired yet with these fooleries yourself? *Cleo.* What fault do you sind with these kind constructions; do they detract from the dignity of our species? *Hor.* I admire your invention, and thus much I will own, that, by overacting the part in that extravagant manner, you have set the social system in a more disadvantageous light than ever I had considered it before: But the best things, you know, may be ridiculed. *Cleo.* Whether I know

that or not, Lord Shaftstrary has flatly denied it; and takes joke and banter to be the best and surest touchstone to prove the worth of things: It is his opinion, that no ridicule can be fastened upon what is really great and good. His Lordship has made use of that test to try the Scriptures and the Christian religion by, and exposed then because it seems they could not stand it. *Hor.* He has exposed superstition, and the miserable notions the vulgar were taught to have of Got!; but no man ever had more sublime ideas of the Supreme Being, and the universe, than himself. *Cieo.* You are convinced, that what I charge him with is true *Hor.* I do not pretend to defend every syllable that noble Lord has wrote. His style is engaging, his language is polite, his reasoning strong; many of his thoughts are beautifully expressed, and his images, for the greatest part, inimitably line. I may be pleased with an author, without obliging myself to answer every cavil that mall be made against him. As to what you call your imitation of him, I have no taste in burlesque: but the laugh you would raise might be turned upon you with less trouble than you seem to have taken. Pray, when you conlider the hard and dirty labours that are performed to supply the mob with the vast quantities of strong beer they swill, do not you discover social virtue in a drayman? *Cleo.* Yes, and in a dray-horse too; at least as well as I can in some great men, who yet would be very angry should we refuse to believe, that the most selsish actions of theirs, if the society received but the least benefit from them, were chielly owing to principles of virtue, and a generous regard to the public. Do you believe that, in the choice of a P"P» the greatest dependence of the Cardinals, and what they prin cipally rely upon, is the influence of the Holy Ghost? *Hor.* S«o more than I do transubttantiation. *Cleo.* But if you had been brought up a Roman Catholic, you would believe both. *Hor.* I do not know that. *Cleo.* You would, if you was sincere in your religion, as thousands of them are, that are no more destitute of reason and good fense than you or I. *Hor.* I have nothing

to say as to that: there are many things incomprehensible, that yet are certainly true: These are properly the objects of faith; and, therefore, when matters are above my capacity, and really surpass my understanding, I am silent, and submit with great humility: but I will swallow not.iing which I plainly apprehend to be contrary to my reason, and is directly clashing with my senses. *Cleo.* If you believe a Providence, what demonstration can you have, that God does not direct men in an asfair of higher importance to all Christendom, than any otheryou can name? *Hor.* This is an ensnaring, and a very unfair question. Providence superintends and governs every thing without exception. To defend my negative, and give a reason for my unbelief, it is susssicient, if I prove, that all the instruments, and the means they make use of in those elections, are visibly human and mundane, and many of them unwarrantable and wicked. *Cleo.* Not all the means; because every day they have prayers, and solemnly invoke the Divine assistance. *Hor.* But what stress they lay upon it may be easily gathered from the rest of their behaviour. The court of Rome is, without dispute, the greatest academy of resined politics, and the best school to learn the art of caballing: there ordinary cunning, and known stratagems, are counted rusticity, and designs are pursued through all the mazes of human subtlety. Genius there must give way to sinesse, as strength does to art in wrestling; and a certain skill some men have in concealing their capacities from others, is of far greater use with them, than real knowledge, or the soundest understanding. In the sacred college, where every thing is *auro venale,* truth and justice bear the lowest price: Cardinal Palavicini, and other Jesuits, that have been the stanch advocates of the Papal authority, have owned with ostentation the *Poliiia religiosa della chusa,* and not hid from us the virtues and accomplishments, that were only valuable among the Purpurati, in whose judgment over-reaching,- at any rate, is the highest honour, and to be outwitted, though by the basest artisice, the greatest shame. In conclaves, more especially, nothing is curried on without tricks and intrigue; and in them the heart of man is so deep, and so dark an abyss, that the sinest air of dissimulation is sometimes found to haveTjeen insincere, and men often deceive one another, by counterfeiting hypocrisy. And is it credible, that holiness, religion, or the least concern for spirituals, should have any share in the plots, machinations, brigues, and contrivances of a society, of which each member, besides the gratisication of his own passions, has nothing at heart but the interest of his party, right or wrong, and to distress every faction that opposes it? *Cleo.* These sentiments consirm to me what I have often heard, that renegadoes are the most cruel enemies. *Hor.* Was ever I a Roman Catholic? *Cleo.* I mean from the social system, of which you have been the most strenuous assertor; and now no man can judge of actions more severely, and indeed less charitably, than yourself, especially of the poor cardinals. I little thought, if once I quitted the scheme of deformity, to have found an adversary in you; but we have both changed sides it seems. *Hor.* Much alike, I believe. *Cleo.* Nay, what could any body think to hear me making the kindest interpretations of things that can be imagined, and yourself doing quite the reverse? *Hor.* What ignorant people, that knew neither of us, might have done, I do not know: but it has been very manifest from our discourse, that you have maintained your cause, by endeavouring to movv the absurdity of the contrary side, and that I have defended mine by letting you see, that we were not such fools as you would represent us to be. I had taken a resolution never to engage with you on this topic, but you fee I have broke it: I hate to be thought uncivil; it was mere complaisance drew me in; though I am not sorry that we talked of it so much as we did, because I found your opinion less dangerous than I imagined: you have owned the existence of virtue, and that there are men who act from it as a principle, both which I thought you denied: but I would not have you flatter yourself that you deceived me, by hanging out false

colours. *Cleo.* I did not lay on the disguise so thick, as not to have you fee through it, nor would 1 ever have discoursed upon this subject with any body, who could have been so eaiily 5 imposed upon. I know you to be a man of very good sense and sound judgment; and it is for that very reason I so heartily wish you would suffer me to explain myself, and demonstrate to you, how small the difference is between us, which you imagine to be so considerable: There is not a man in the world, in whose opinion I would less pass for an ill man than in yours; but I am so scrupulously fearful of offending you, that I never dared to touch upon some points, unless you had given me leave. Yield something to our friendship, and condescend for once to read the Fable of the Bees for my fake: It is a handsome volume: you love books: I have one extremely well bound ; do; let me, suffer me to make you a present of it. *Hor.* I am no bigot, Cleomenes; but I am a man of honour, and, you know, of strict honour: 1 cannot endure to hear that ridiculed, and the least attempt of it chafes my blood: Hoiour is the strongest and noblest tie of society by far, and therefore, believe me, can never be innocently sported with. It is a thing so solid and awful, as well as serious, that it can at no time become the object of mirth or diversion; and it is impossible for any pleasantry to be so ingenious, or any jest so witty, that I could bear with it on that head. Perhaps I am singular in this, and, if you will, in the wrong; be that as it will, all I can fay is, *"Je ne'entens pas Raillerie la dejfus* ; and therefore, no Fable of the Bees for me, if we are to remain friends: 1 have heard enough of that. *Cleo.* Pray, Horatio, can there be honour without justice?

Hor. No: Who assirms there can?

Cleo. Have you not owned, that you have thought worse of me, than now you sind me to deserve? No men, nor their works, ought to be condemned upon hearsays and bare surmises, much less upon the accusations of their enemies, without being examined into. *Hor.* There you are in the right: I heartily beg your pardon, and to atone for the wrong

I have done you, fay what you please, I will hear it with patience, be it never so slacking; but 1 beg of you be serious. *Cleo.* I have nothing to fay to you that is distasteful, much less mocking: all 1 delire is, to convince you, that I am neither so ill-natured nor uncharitable, in my opinion of mankind, as you take me to be: and that the notions I entertain of the worth of things, will not differ much from yours, when both come to be looked into. Do but consider what we have been doing: I have endeavoured to set every thing in the handsomest light I could think of; you say, to ridicule the social system; I own it; now reflect on your own conduct, which has been to show the folly of my strained panegyrics, and replace things in that natural view, which all just, knowing men would certainly behold them in. This is very well done: but it is contrary to the scheme you pretended to maintain; and if you judge of all actions in the fame manner, there is an end of the social system; or, at least, it will be evident, that it is a theory never to be put into practice. You argue for the generality of men, that they are possessed of these virtues, but when we come to particulars, you can sind none. I have tried you every where: you are as little satissied with persons of the highest rank, as you are with them of the lowest, and you count it ridiculous to think better of the middling people. Is this otherwise than standing up for the goodness of a design, at the fame time you confess, that it never was, or ever can be executed? What sort of people are they, and where must we look for them, whom you will own to act from those principles of virtue? *Hor.* Are there not in all countries men of birth and ample fortune, that would not accept of places, though they were offered, that are generous and benesicent, and mind nothing but what is great and noble? *Cleo.* Yes: But examine their conduct, look into their lives, and scan their actions with as little indulgence as you did those of the cardinals, or the lawyers and physicians, and then see what sigure their virtues will make beyond those of the poor industrious woman. There is, generally speaking, less truth in panegyrics, than there is in satires. Whea all pur senses are soothed, when we have no distemper of body or mind to disturb us, and meet with nothing that is disagreeable, we are pleased with our being: it is in this situation that we are most apt to mistake outward appearances for realities, and judge of things more favourably than they deserve. Remember, Horatio, how feelingly you spoke half an hour ago in commendation of operas: Your soul seemed to be listed up whilst you was thinking on the many charms you sind in them. I have nothing to fay against the elegancy of the diversion, or the politeness of thole that frequent them: but I am afraid you lost yourself in the contempla tion of the lovely idea, when you asserted that they were the most proper means to contract a strong and lasting habit of virtue; do you think, that among the fame number of people, there is more real virtue at an opera, than there is at a bear-garden? *Hor.* What a comparison! *Cleo.* I am very serious., *Hor.* The noise of dogs, and bulls, and bears, make a sine harmony! *Cleo.* It is impossible you should mistake me, and you know very well, that it is not the different pleasures of those two places 1 would compare together. The things you mentioned are the least to be complained of: the continual sounds of oaths and imprecations, the frequent repetitions of the word *lie,* and other more silthy expressions, the loudness and dissonance of many strained and untuneful voices, are a perfect torment to a delicate ear. The frowsiness of the place, and the ill scents of different kinds, are a perpetual nuisance; but in all mob meetings *Hor. L'odorat souffre beaucoup.* *Cleo.* The entertainment in general is abominable, and all the fenses suffer. 1 allow all this. The greasy heads, some of them bloody, the jarring looks, and threatning, wild, and horrid aspects, that one meets with in those ever-restless asscmblies, must be very shocking to the sight, and so indeed is every thing else that can be seen among a rude and ragged multitude, that are covered with dirt, and have in none of their pastimes one action that is inoffensive: but, after

all, vice and what is criminal, are not to be confounded with roughness and want of manners, no more than politeness and an artful behaviour ought to be with virtue or religion. To tell a premeditated falsehood in order to do mischief, is a greater sin, than to give a man the lie, who speaks an untruth; and it is possible, that a person may suffer greater damage, and more injury to his ruin, from slander in the low whisper of a secret enemy, than he could have received from all the dreadful swearing and cursing, the most noisy antagonist could pelt him with. Incontinence, and adultery itself, persons of quality are not more free from all over Christendom, than the meaner people: but if there are some vices, which the vulgar are more guilty of than the better fort, there are others the reverse. Envy, detraction, and the spirit of revenge, are more raging and mischievous in courts than they are in cottages. Excess of vanity and hurtful ambition are unknown among the poor; they are seldom tainted with avarice, with irrcligion never; and they have much less opportunity of robbing the public than their betters. There are few persons of distinction, whom you are not acquainted with: I desire, you would seriously reflect on the lives of as many as you can think of, and next opera night on the virtues of the assembly. *Hor.* You make me laugh. There is a good deal in what you fay; and I am persuaded, all is not gold that glisten. Would you add any more? *Cleo.* Since you have given me leave to talk, and you are such a patient hearer, I would not slip the opportunity of laying before you some things of high concern, that perhaps you never considered in the light, which you shall'own yourself they ought to be seen in. *Hor.* I am sorry to leave you; but I have really business that must be done to-night: it is about my law-suit, and I have stayed beyond my time already: but if you will come and eat a bit of mutton with me to-morrow, I will see nobody but yourself, and we will converse as long as you please. *Cleo.* With all my heart. I will not fail to wait on you. THE SECOND DIALOGUE HORATIO AND CLEOMENE? HORATIO.

I He discourse we had yesterday, has made a great impression upon me; you said several things that were very entertaining, and some which I mall not easily forget: I do not remember I ever looked into myself so much as 1 have done since last night after I left you. *Cleo.* To do that faithfully, is a more dissicult and a severer talk than is commonly imagined. When, yesterday, I asked you where and among what sort of people we were to look for those whom you would allow to act from principles of virtue, you named a class, among whom I have found very agreeable characters of men, that yet all have their failings. if these could be left out, and the best were picked and culled from the different good qualities that are to be seen in several, the compound would make a very handsome picture. *Hor.* To sinish it well every way would be a great masterpiece. *Cleo.* That I shall not attempt: but I do not think it would be very dissicult to make a little sketch of it, that yet should exceed nature, and be a better pattern for imitation than any can be shown alive. I have a mind to try; the very thought enlivens me. How charming is the portrait of a complete gentleman, and how ravishing is the sigure which a person of great birth and fortune, to whom nature has been no niggard, makes, when he understands the world, and is thoroughly well-bred! *Hor.* I think them so, I can assure you, whether you are in jest or in earnest. *Cleo.* How entirely well hid are his greatest imperfections! though money is his idol, and he is covetous in his heart, yet his inward avarice is forced to give way to his outward liberality, and an open generosity shines through all his actions. *Hor.* There lies your fault: it is this I cannot endure in you. *Cleo.* What is the matter? *Hor.* I know what you are about, you are going to give me the caricatura of a gentleman, under pretence of drawing his portrait. *Cleo.* You wrong me, I have no such thought. *Hor.* But why is it impossible for human nature ever to be good? instead #of leaving out, you. put in failings without the least grounds or colour. When things have a handsome appearance every way, what reason have you to suspect them still to be bad? How came you to know, and which way have you discovered imperfections that are entirely well hid; and why should you suppose a person to be covetous in his heart, and that money is his idol, when you own yourself that he never shews it, and that an open generosity shines through all his actions? This is monstrous. *Cleo.* 1 have made no such supposition of any man, and I protest to you, that, in what I said, I had no other meaning than to observe, that whatever frailties and natural insirmities persons might be conscious of within, good fense and good manners were capable, and, without any other assistance, sussicient to keep them out of sight: but your questions are very seasonable, and since you have started this, I will be very open to you. and acquaint you before hand with my design of the description I am going to make; and the use I intend it for; which in Ihort is, to demonstrate to you, that a most beautiful superstructure may be raised upon a rotten and despicable foundation. You will understand me better presentlv. *Hor.* But how do you know a foundation to be rotten that supports the building, and is wholly concealed from you? *Cleo.* Have patience, and 1 promise you, that 1 shall take nothing for grunted, which you shall not allow of yourself. *Hor.* Stick close to that, and I desire no more: now say what you will. *Cleo.* The true object of pride or vain glory is the opinion of others; and the most superlative wish, which a man posscfled, and entirely silled with it can make, is. that he may be well thought of, applauded, and admired by the whole world, not only in the present but all future ages. This passion is generally exploded; but it is incredible, how many strange and widely different miracles are, and may be performed by the force of it; as persons differ in circumstances and inclinations. In the sirst place, there is no danger so great, but by the help of his pride a man may flight and confront it; nor any manner of death so terrible, but with the same assistance he may court, and if he has a sirm constitution, undergo it

with alacrity. In the second, there are no good ossices or duties, either to others or ourselves, that Cicero has spoke of, nor any instance of benevolence, humanity, or other social virtue, that Lord Shaftsbury has hinted at, but a man of good fense and knowledge may learn to practise them from no better principle than vain glory, is it be strong enough to subdue and keep under all other passions that may thwart and interfere with his design. *Hor.* Shall 1 allow all this? *Cleo.* Yes. *Hor.* When? *Cleo.* Before we part. *Hor.* Very well. *Cleo.* Men of tolerable parts in plentiful circumstances?, that were artfully-educated, and are not lingular in their temper, can hardly fail of a genteel behaviour: the more pride they have, and the greater value they set on the esteem of others, the more they will make it their study to render themselves acceptable to all they converse with; and they will take uncommon pains to conceal and stifle in their bosoms, every thing which their good fense tells them ought not to be seen or understood. *Hor.* 1 must interrupt you, and cannot suffer you to go on thus. What is all-this but the old story over again, that every thing is pride, and all we fee hypocrisy, without proof or argument? Nothing in the world is more false than what you have advanced now; for, according to that, the most noble, the most gallant, and the best bred man would be the proudest; which is so clashing with daily experience, that the very reverse is true. Pride and insolence are no, where more common than among upstarts; men of no family, that raise estates out of nothing, and the most ordinary people, that having had no education, are pulsed up with their fortune whenever they are lifted up above mediocrity, and from mean stations advanced to posts of honour: whereas, no men upon earth, generally speaking, are more courteous, humane, or polite, than persons of high birth, that enjoy the large possessions and known feats of their ancestors; men illustrious by descent, that have been used to grandeur and titles of honour from their infancy, and received an education suitable to their quality. 1 do not believe

there ever was a nation, that were not savages, in which the youth of both sexes were not expressly taught never to be proud or haughty: did you ever know a school, a tutor, or a parent, that did not continually inculcate to those under their care to be civil and obliging; nay, does not the word mannerly itself import as much? *Cleo.* I beg of you, let us be calm, and speak with exactness. The doctrine of good manners furnishes us with a thousand lessons, against the various appearances and outward symptoms of pride, but it has not one precept against the passion itself, *Hor.* How is that? *Cleo.* No, not one against the passion itself; the conquest of it is never attempted, nor talked of in a gentleman's education, where'men are to be continually inspired and kept warm with the fense of their honour, and the inward value they must put upon themselves on all emergencies. *Hor.* This is woith conlideration, and requires time to be examined into; but where is your sine gentleman, the picture you promised? *Cleo.* 1 am ready, and shall begin with his dwelling: Though he has several noble seats indifferent countries, yet I sh.dl only take notice of his chief mansion-house that bears the name, and does the honours of the family: this is amply magnisicent, and yet commodious to admiration. His gardens are very extenlive, and contain an insinite variety of pleasing objects: they are divided into many branches for divers purposes, and every where silled with improvements of art upon nature; yet a beautiful order and happy contrivance are conspicuous through every part; and though nothing is omitted to render them stately and delightful; the whole is laid out to the best advantage Within doors, every thing bespeaks the grandeur and judgment of the master; and as no cost is spared any where to procure beauty or conveniency, so you see none impertinently lavished. All his plate and furniture are completely tine, and you fee nothing but what is fathionable. He has no pictures but of the most eminent hands: the rarities he shows are really such; he hoards up no trifles, nor osters any thing to your light that is shocking: but the several collections he has of this fort, are agreeable as well as extraordinary, and rather valuable than large: but curiosities and wealth are not consined to his cabinet; the matble and sculpture that are displayed up and down are a treasure themselves; and there is abundance ot admirable gilding and excellent carving to be seen in many places. What has been laid out on the great hall, and one gallery, would be a considerable estate; and there is a ialloon and a stair-case not inferior to either: thele are all very spacious and lofty; the architecture of them is of the best taste, and the decorations surprising. Throughout the whole there appears a delicate mixture and allonishing variety of lively embellishments, the splendour of which, joined to a persect cleanliness, no where neglected, are higly entertaining to the most careless and least observing eye; whilst the exactness of the workmanship bestowed on every part of the meanest

Utensil, gives a more'solid satisfaction, and is ravishing to the curious. But the greatest excellency in this model of perfection is this; that as in the most ordinary rooms there is nothing wanting for their purpose, and the least passage is handsomely sinished; so in those of the greatest eclat there is nothing overcharged, nor any part of them encumbered with ornaments.

Hor. This is a studied piece; but I do not like it the worse for it, pray go own. *Cleo.* I have thought of it before, I own. His equipage is rich and well chosen, and there is nothing to be seen about him that art or expence, within the compass of reason, could make better. At his own table his looks are ever jovial; and his heart seems to be as open as his countenance. His chief business there is to take care of others, without being troublesome; and all his happiness seems to consist in being able to please his friends: in his greatest mirth, he is wanting in respect to no man; and never makes use of abbreviations in names, or unhandsome familiarities with the meanest of his guests. To every one that speaks to' him, he gives an obliging attention, and seems never to disregard any thing but what is said in commendation of his fare: he never interrupts any discourse but what is made in his praise, and seldom assents to any encomiums, though the most equitable that are made on any thing that is his. When he is abroad he never spies faults; and whatever is amiss, he either fays nothing, or, in answer to the complaints and uneasiness of others, gives every thing the best-natured turn it can bear; but he seldom leaves a house before he sinds out something to extol in it, without wronging his judgment. His conversation is always facetious and good-humoured, but as solid as it is diverting. He never utters a syllable that has the least tincture of obscenity or profaneness; nor ever made a jest that was offensive. *Hor.* Very sine! *Cleo:* He seems to be entirely free from bigotry and superstition, avoids all disputes about religion; but goes constantly to church, and is seldom absent from his family devotions *Hor.* A very godly gentleman! *Cleo.* I expected we should differ there. *Hor.* I do not sind fault. Proceed, pray. *Cleo.* As he is a man of ertfdition himself, so he is a promoter of arts and sciences; he is a friend to merit a re warder of industry, ami a professed enemy to nothing but. immorality and oppression. Though no man's table is better furnished, nor cellars better stored; he is temperate in his eating, and never commits excess in drinking: though he has an exquisite palate he always prefers wholesome meats to those that are delicious only, and never indulges his appetite in any thing that might probably be prejudicial to his health. *Hor.* Admirably good! *Cleo.* As he is in all other things, so he is elegant in his clothes, and has often new ones: neatness lie prefers to sinery in his own dress; but his retinue is rich. He seldom wears gold or silver himself, but on very solemn occasions, in compliment to others; and to demonstrate that these pompous habits are made for no other purpose, he is never seen twice in the same; but having appeared in them one day, he gives them away the next. Though of every thing he has the best of the sort, and might be culled curious in apparel; yet he leaves the care of it to others; and no man has his clothes put on better that seem so little to regard them. *Hor.* Perfectly right; to be well dressed is a necessary article, and yet to be solicitous about it is below a person of quality. *Cleo.* Therefore he has a domestic of good taste, a judicious man, who saves him that trouble; and the management likewise of his lace and linen, is the province of a skilful woman. His language is courtly, but natural and intelligible; it is neither low nor bombastic, and ever free from pedantic and vulgar expressions. All his motions are genteel without affectation; his mien is rather sedate than airy, and his manner noble: for though he is ever civil and condescending, and no man less arrogant, yet in all his carriage there is something, gracefully majestic; and as there is nothing mean in his humility, so his loftiness has nothing disobliging. *Hor.* Prodigiously'good! *Cleo.* He is charitable to the poor; his house is never shut to strangers; and all his neighbours he counts to be his friends. He is a father to his tenants; and looks upon their welfare as inseparable from his interest. No man is less uneasy at little-offences, or more ready to forgive all trelpafles without design. The injuries that are suffered from other landlords, he turns into benesits; and whatever damages, great or small, are sustained on his account, either from his diversions or otherwise, he doubly makes good. He takes care to be early informed of such losses, and commonly repairs them before they are complained of. *Hor.* Oh rare humanity; hearken ye soxhunters! *Cleo.* He never chides any of his people; yet no man is better served'; and though nothing is wanting in his housekeeping, and his family is very numerous, yet the regularity of it is no less remarkable than the plenty they live in. His orders he will have strictly obeyed; but his commands are always reasonable, and he never speaks to the meanest footman without regard to humanity. Extraordinary diligence in servants, and all laudable actions he takes notice of himself, and often commends them to their faces; but leaves it to his steward to reprove or dismiss those he distikes. *Hor.* Well judged. *Cleo.* Whoever lives with him is taken care of in sickness as well as in health. The wages he gives are above double those of other masters; and he often makes presents to those that are more than ordinary observing and industrious to please: but he sutlers nobody to take a penny of his friends or others, that come" to his house, on any account whatever. Many faults are connived at, or pardoned for the sirst time, but a breach of this order is ever attended with the loss of their places as soon as it is found out; and there is a premium for the discovery. *Hor.* 'fhis is the only exceptionable thing, in my opinion, that I have heard yet. *Cleo.* 1 wonder at that: why so, pray? *Hor.* In the sirst place, it is very ditiicultto enforce obedience to such a command; secondly, it it could be executed, it would be of little use; unless it could be made general, which is imposiible: and therefore 1 look upon the attempt of introducing this maxim to be singular and fantastical. It would phase misers and others, that would never follow the example at home; but it would take' away from generous men a handiome opportunity of showing their liberal and benesicent disposition: besides, it wcnld manifestly make ones house too open to ail sorts of people. *Cleo.* Ways might be found to prevent that; but then it would be a bksting, and do great kindness to men of parts and education, that have little to spare, to many of whom this money to servants is a very grievous burden. *Hor.* What you mention is the only thing that can be said for it, and I own, of great weight: but I beg your pardon for interrupting you,, *Cleo.* fn all his dealings he is punctual and just. As he has an immense estate, so he has good managers to take care of it: but though all his accounts are very neatly kept, yet he makes it part of his business to look them over himself. He suffers ho tradesman's bill to lie by unexamined; and though he meddles not with his ready cash himself, yet he is a quick and cheerful, as well as an exact paymaster; and the only singularity he is guilty of, is, that he never will owe any thing on a new-year's day *Hor.* I like that very well. *Cleo.* He is affable with discre-

tion, of easy access, and never ruffled with passion. To sum up all, no man seems to be less elevated with his condition than himself; and in the full enjoyment of so many personal accomplishments, as well as other possessions, his modesty is equal io the rest of his happiness; and in the midst of the pomp and distinction he lives in, he never appears to be entertained with his greatness, but rather unacquainted with the things he excels in. *Hor.* It is an admirable character, and pleases me exceedingly; but I wdl freely own to you, that I should have been more highly delighted with the description, if I had not known your design, and the use you intend to make of it;. which, I think, is barbarous: to raise so sine, so elegant, and so complete an edisice, in order to throw it down, Is taking great pains to mow one's skill in doing mischief. I have observed the several places where you left room for evasions, and sapping the foundation you have built upon. His heart *seems* to be as open; and he never *appears* to be entertained with his greatness. I am persuaded, that wherever you have put in this *seeming* and *appearing,* you have done it designedly, and with an intent to make use of them as so many back doors to creep out at. I could never have taken notice of these things, if you had not acquainted me with your intention before hand. *Cleo.* I have made use of the caution you speak of: but with no other view than to avoid just censure, and prevent your accusing me of incorrectness, or judging with too much precipitation; if it should be proved afterwards, that this gentleman had acted from an ill principle, which is the thing own I purposed to convince you of; but seeing, that it .would be unpleasant to you, I will be satissied with having given you some small entertainment of the description, and for the rest, I give you leave to think me in the wrong. *Hor.* Why so? 1 thought the character was made and contrived on purpose for my instruction. ' *Cleo.* 1 do not pretend to instruct you: I would have osfered something, and appealed to your judgment; but 1 have been mistaken, and plainly see my error. Both

last night and now, when we began our discourse, I took you to be in another disposition of thinking than 1 perceive you are. You spoke of an impression that had been made upon you, and of looking into yourself, and gave some other hints, which too rashly 1 misconstrued in my favour; but I have found since, that you are as warm as ever against the sentiments 1 profess myself to be of; and therefore I will desist. 1 expect no pleasure from any triumph, and I know nothing that would vex me more, than the thoughts of disobliging you. Pray let us do in this as we do in another matter ot importance, never touch upon it: friends in prudence should avoid all subjects in which they are known essentially to differ. Believe me, Horatio, if it was in my power to divert or give you any pleasure, 1 would grudge no pains to compass that end: but to, make you uneasy, is a thing that I shall never be knowingly guilty of, and 1 beg a thousand pardons for having said so much both yesterday and to-day. Have you heard any thing from Gibraltar? *Hor.* 1 am ashamed of my weakness and your civility: you have not been mistaken in the hints you speak of; what you have said has certainly made a great impression upon me, and I have endeavoured to examine myself: but, as you fay, it is a severe task to do it faithfully. I desired you to dine with me on purpose, that we might talk of these things. It is I that have offended, and it is 1 that ought to ask pardon for the ill manners 1 have been guilty of; but you know the principles I have always adhened to; it is impossible to recede from them at once. I lee great dissiculties, and now and then a glimpse of truth, that makes me start: 1 sometimes feel great struggles within; but I have been so used to derive all actions that are really good from laudable motives, that as soon as 1 return to my accustomed way of thinking, it carries all before it, Pray bear with my insirmities. I am in love with your sine gentleman, and I confess, 1 cannot lee how a person so universally good, so far remote from all selsishness, can act in such an extraordinary manner every, way, but from principles of virtue and religion. Where is there such a land-lord in the world? If I am in an error, I shall be, glad to be undeceived. Pray inform me, and say what you will, I promise you to keep my temper, and I beg of you speak your mind with free-doni. *Cled.* You have bid me before say what I would, and when I did, you seemed displeased; but since you command me

I will try once more Whether there is or ever was such a man as I have described, in the world, is not very material: but I will easily allow, that most people would think it less difficult to conceive one, than to imagine that such a clear and beautiful stream could flow from so mean and muddy a spring, as an excessive thirst after praise, and an immoderate desire of general applause from the most knowing judges: yet it is certain, that great parts and extraordinary riches may compass all this in a man, who is not deformed, and has had a resined education; and that there are many persons naturally no better than a thousand others, who by the helps mentioned, might attain to those good qualities and accomplishments, if they had but resolution and perseverance enough, to render every appetite and every faculty subservient to that one predominant passion, which, if continually gratisied, will always enable them to govern, and, if required, to subdue all the rest without exception, even in the most dissicult cases.

Hor. To enter into an argument concerning the possibility of what you fay, might occasion a long dispute; but the probability, I think, is very clear againil you, and if there was such a man, it would be much more credible, that he acted from the excellency of his nature, in which so many virtues and rare endowments were assembled, than that all his good qualities sprung from "vicious motives. If pride could be the cause of all this, the effect of it would sometimes appear in others. According to your system, there is no scarcity of it, and there are men os great parts and prodigious estates all over Europe: why are there not several such patterns to be seen up and down, as you have drawn us one;

and why is it so very seldom, that many virtues and good qualities are seen to meet in one individual?. *Cleo.* Why so few persons, though there are so many men pf immense fortune, ever arrive at any thing like this high pitch of accomplishments, there are several reasons that an? very obvious. In the sirst; place, men differ in temperament: some are naturally of an active, stirring; others of an indolent, quiet disposition; some of a bold, others of a meek spirit. In the second, it is to be considered, that this temperament in men come to maturity is more or less conspicuous, according as it has been either checked or encouraged by education. Thirdly, that on these two depend the different perception men have of happiness, according to which the love of glory determines them different ways. Some think it the greatest felicity to govern and rule over others; some take the praise ot" bravery and undauntedness in dangers to be the most valuable: others, erudition, and to be a celebrated author: so that, though they all love glory, they set out differently to acquire it. But a man who hates a bustle, and is naturally of a quiet easy temper, and whicli has been encouraged in him by education, it is very likely might think nothing more desirable than the character of a sine gentleman; and if he did, I dare fay that he would endeavour to behave himself pretty near the pattern I have given ybu; I say pretty near, because 1 may have been mistaken in some things, and as I have riot touched upon every thing, some will fay, that 1 have left out several neceflkry ones: but in the main I believe, that in the country and age we five in, the qualisications I have named would get a man the reputation I have supposed him to desire. `, *Hor.* Without doubt, I make no manner of scruple about what you said last; and I told you before that it was an admirable character, and pleased me exceedingly. That I took notice of your making your gentleman so very godly as you did, was because it Is not common; but 1 intended it not as a reflection. One thing, indeed, there was in which 1 differed from you; but that was merely speculative; and,

since I have reflected on what you have answered me, 1 do not know but I may be in the wrong, as 1 should certainly believe myself to be, if there really was such a man, and he was of the contrary opinion: to such a sine genius I would pay an uncommon deference, and with great readiness submit my understanding to his superior capacity. But the reasons you give why those effects which you ascribe to pride, are not more common, the cause being so universal, I think arc insussicient. That men are prompted to follow different ehds, as their inclinations differ, I can easily allow; but there are great numbers of rich men that are likewise of a quiet and indolent disposition, and moreover very desirous of being thought sine gentlemen. How comes it, that among so many persons of high birth, princely estates, and the most resined education, as there are in Christendom, that study, travel, and take great pains to be well accomplished, there is not one, to whom all the good qualities, and every thing you named, could be applied without flattery? *Cleo.* It is very pollible that thousands may aim at this, and not one of them succeed to that degree: in some, perhaps the predominant paflion is not strong enough entirely to subdue the rest: love or covetousness may divert others: drinking, gaming, may draw away many, and break in upon their resolution; they may not have strength to persevere in a design, and steadily to pursue the same ends; or they may want a true taste or knowledge of what is estemed by men of judgment; or, lastly, they may not be so thoroughly wellbred, as is required to conceal themselves oa alt emergencies: for the practical part of diflimulation is insinitely more difficult than the theory: and any one of thse obstacles is sufficient to spoil all, and hinder the sinishing of such a piece. *Hor.* I lhall not dispute that with you: but all this while you have proved nothing, nor given the least reason why yoH should imagme, that a man of a character, to all outivard appearance so bright and beautiful, acted from vicious motives. You would not condemn him without so much as naming the cause why you lulpect him. *Cleo.* By no means; nor have I advanced any thing that is ill natuied or undiamable: for 1 have not laid, that ill found a gentleman in poliellion of all the things J mentioned, 1 would give his raie endowments this turn, and think all his perfections derived from no better stock, than an extraordinary love ot glory. What 1 argue for, and insist upon, is, the poliibility that all these things might be performed by a man from no other views, and with no other helps, than those 1 have named: nay, 1 believe moreover, that 3gentleman so accomplished. all his knowledge and great parts notwithstanding, may himsels be ignorant, or at least not well assured of the motive he acts horn. *Hor.* This is more unintelligible than any thing you have said yet; why will you heap difiicul.ies upun one another, without solving any? 1 detue you would clear up this lat paradox, heroic you do any thing eile. *Cleo.* In order to obey you, I must put you in mind us what happens in early education, by the sirst rudiments of which, infants are taught in the choice of actions to pieter the precepts of others to the dictates of their o.vn inclinations; which, in mort, is no more than doing as they are bid. To gain this point, punishments and rewards are not neglected, and many different methods are made use of; but it is certain, that nothing proves more often esfectual roi tins purpose, or has a greater influence upon children, than ttie handle that is made of shame; which, though a natural patlion, they would not be sensible of so soon, if we did not artrully rouse and stir it up in them, before they can speak or go: by which means, their judgment being then weak, we may teach them to be ashamed of what we please, as scon a? we can perceive them to be any ways atfected with the passion itself f but as the fear of shame is very insignisicant, where there is but little pride, so it is impossible to augment the sirst, without increasing the latter in the same proportion. *Hur.* 1 should have thought that this increase of pride would render children more stubborn and less doc.ile. *Cleo.* You judge right; it would so, and must have been a great hinderance to good manners, till experience taught men, that though.pride was not to be destroyed by force, it might be governed by stratagem, and that the best way to manage it, is by playing the passion against itself. Hence it is, that in an artful education, we are allowed to place as much pride as we please in our dexterity of concealing it. I do not suppose, that this covering ourselves, notwithstanding the pride we take in it, is performed without a dissiculty that is plainly felt, and perhaps very unpleasant at sirst; but this wears osf as we grow up; and when a man has behaved himself with so much prudence as I have described, lived up to the strictest rules of good-breeding for many years, and has gained the esteemof all that know him, when this noble and polite manner is become habitual to him, it is possible he may in time forget the principle he set out with, and become ignorant, or at least insensible of the hidden spring that gives life and motion to all his actions. *Hor.* 1 am convinced of the great use that may be made of pride, if you will call it so; but 1 am not satissied yet, how a man of so much sense, knowledge, and penetration, one that understands himself so entirely well, should be ignorant of his own heart, and the motives he acts from What is it that induces you to believe this, besides the possibility of his forgetfulness? *Cleo.* I have two reasons for it, which I desire may be seriously considered. The sirst is, that in what relates to ourselves, especiallv our own worth and excellency, pride blinds the understanding in men offense and great parts as well as in others, and the greater value we may reasonably set upon ourselves, the sitter we are to swallow the grossest flatteries, in spite ot" all our knowledge and abilities in other matters: witness Alexander the Great, whole vast genius could not hinder him from doubting seriously, whether he was a god or not. My second reason will prove to us, that if the person in question was capable of examining himself, it is yet highly improbable, that he would ever set about it: for, it must be granted, that, in order to search into ourselves, it is required we should be willing as well as able'; and we have all the reason in the world to think, that there is nothing wliich a very proud man of such high qualisications would avoid more carefully than such an inquiry: because, for all other acts of self-denial, he is repaid in his darling passion; but this alone is really mortifying, and the only sacrisice ot his quiet for which he can have no equivalent. If the hearts of the best and sincerest men are corrupt and deceitful, what condition must theirs be in, whose whole life is one continued scene of hypocrisy! therefore inquiring within, and boldly searching into ones own bosom, must be the most shocking employment, that a man can give his mind to, whose greatest pleasure consists in secretly admiring himself. It would be ill manners, after this, to appeal to yourself; but the severity of the task *Hor.* Say no more, I yield this point, though I own I cannot conceive what advantage you can expect from it: for, instead of removing, it will rather help to increase the grand dissiculty, which Is to prove, that this complete perJon you have described, acts from a vicious motive: and if that be not your design, I cannot fee what you drive at. *Cleo.* I told you it was. *Hor.* You must have a prodigious sagacity in detecting abstruse matters before other men. *Cleo.* You wonder, I know, which way I arrogate *to* myself such a superlative degree of.penetration, as to know an artful cunning man better than he does himself, and howl dare pretend to enter and look into a heart, which I have owned to be completely well concealed from all the world; which in strictness is an impossibility, and consequently not to be bragged of but by a coxcomb. *Hor.* You may treat yourself as you please, I have said no such thing; but 1 own that I long to see it proved, that you have this capacity. I remember the character very well: Notwithstanding the precautions you have taken, it is very full: 1 told you before, that where things have a handsome appearance every way, there can be no just cause to suspect them. I will stick close to that; your gentleman is all of a piece: You shall alter nothing, either by retracting any of the good qualities you have given him, or making additions that are either clashing with, or unsuitable to what you have allowed already. *Clco.* I mall attempt neither: And without that decisive trials may be made, by which it will plainly appear whether a person acts from inward goodness,and a principle of religion, or only from a motive of vain glory; and, in the latter cafe, there is an infallible way of dragging the lurking siend from his darkest recelfes into a glaring light, where all the world shall know him. *Hor.* I do not think myself a match for you in argument; but I have a great mind to be your gentleman's advocate against all your infallibility: I never liked a cause better in my life. Come, I undertake to defend him in all the suppositions you can make that are seasonable and consistent with what you have said before. *Cleo.* Very well: let us suppose what may happen to the most inoffensive, the most prudent, and best-bred man; that our sine gentleman differs in opinion before company, with another, who is" his equal in birth and quality, but not so much master over his outward behaviour, and less guarded in his conduct; let this adversary *mal a propos,* grow warm, and seem to be wanting in the respect that is due to the other, and reflect on his honour in ambiguous terms. What is your client to do? *Hor* Immediately to ask for an explanation. *Cleo.* Which, if the hot man disregards with scorn, or flatly refuses to give, satisfaction must be demanded, and tilt they must. *Hor.* You are too hasty: it happened before company; in such cases, friends, or any gentlemen present, should interpose and take care, that if threatening words eniue, they are, by the civil authority, both put under arrest; and before they came to uncourteous language, they ought to have been parted by friendly force, if it were, postible. After that, overtures may be made of reconciliation with the nicest; regard to the point of honour. *Cleo.* I do not ask for directions to prevent a quarrel; what you fay may be done, or it may not be done: The good offices of friends may succeed, and they may not succeed.

I am to make what suppositions I think sit within the verge of possibility, so they are reasonable and consistent with the character I have drawn: can we not suppose these two persons in such a situation that you yourself would advise your friend to send his adversary a challenge? *Hor.* Without doubt such a thing may happen. *Cleo.* That is enough. After that a duel must ensue, in which, without determining any thing, the sine gentleman, we will say, behaves himself with the utmost gallantry.' *Hor.* To have suspected or supposed otherwise would have been unreasonable. *Cleo.* You see, therefore, how fair I am. But what is it, pray, that so suddenly disposes a courteous sweet-tempered man, for so small an evil, to seek a remedy of that extreme violence? But above all, what is it rhat buoys up and supports him against the fear of death? for there lies the greatest difficulty. *Hor.* His natural courage and intrepidity, built on the innocence of his life, and the rectitude of his manners. *Cleo.* But what makes so just and prudent a man, that has the good of society so much at heart, act knowingly against the laws of his country? *Hor.* The strict obedience he pays to the laws of honour, which are superior to all others. *Cleo.* If men of honour would act consistently, they ought all to be Roman Catholics. *Hor.* Why, pray? *Cleo.* Because they prefer oral tradition to all written laws: for nobody can tell when, in what king's or emperor's reign, in what country, or by what authority these laws of honour were sirst enacted: it is very strange they should be of such force. *Hor.* They are wrote and engraved in every ones breast that is a man of honour: there is no dem ing of It; you.are conscious of it yourself; every body feels it Vuhin. *Cleo.* Let them be wrote or engraved wherever you please, they are directly opposite to and clashing with the laws of God; and if the gentle nm I described W.is as sincere in his religion as he appeared to be, he must have been of an opinion contrary to yours; for Christians of all persuasions are unanimous in allowing the divine laws to be far above all other; and that all other considerations ought

to give way to them. How, and under what pretence can a Cbristian, who is a man offense, submit or agree to laws that prescribe revenge, and counrenance murder; both which are so expressly forbid by the precepts of his religion? *Hor.* I am no casuist: but you know, that what I say is true; and that, among persons of honour, a man would be laughed at, that mould make such a scruple. Not but that I think killing a man to be a great sin, where it can be helped; and that all prudent men ought to avoid the occasion, as much as it is in.their power. He is highly blameable who is the tirst aggressor, and gives the assront; and whoever enters upon it out of levity, or seeks a quarrel out of wantonness, ought to be hanged. Nobody would choose it, who is not a fool; and yet, when it is forced upon one, all the wisdom in the world cannot teach him how to avoid it. It has been my cafe you know: I shall never forget the reluctancy I had against it; but necessity has no law. *Cleo.* I saw you that very morning, and you seemed to be sedate and void of passion: you could have no concern. *Hor.* It is silly to show any at such times; but l know best what I felt; the struggle I had within was unspeakable: it is a terrible thing. 1 would then have given a considerable part of my estate, that the thing which forced me into it had not happened; and yet, upon less provocation, 1 would act the fame part again tomorrow. *Cleo.* Do you remember what your concern was chiefly about? *Hor.* How can you ask? It is an affair of the highest importance that can occur in life; I was no boy; it was after we came from Italy; l was in my nine and twentieth year, had very good acquaintance, and was not ill received: a man of that age, in health and vigour, who has seven thousand ayear, and the prospect of being a peer of England, has no reason to quarrel with the world, or wish himself out of it. It is a very gicat hazard a man runs in a duel; besides the remorse and uneasiness one mult feel as long as he lives, if ho has the misfortune of killing his adversary. It is impossible to reflect on all these things, and at the fame time resolve to run those hazards (though there are other considerations os still greater moment), without being under a prodigious concern. *Cleo.* You fay nothing about the sin. *Hor.* The thoughts of that, without doubt, are a great addition;.but the other things are so weighty of themselves, that a man's condition at such a time, is very perplexed without further reflection. *Cleo.* You have now a very sine opportunity, Horatio, of looking into your heart, and with a little of my assistance, examining yourself. If you can condescend to this, I promise you that you shall make great discoveries, and be convinced of truths you are now unwilling to believe. A lover of justice and probity, as you are, ought not to be fond os a road of thinking, where he is always forced to skulk, and never dares to meet with light or reason. Will you sutler me to ask you some questions, and will you answer them directly and in good humour? *Hor.* 1 will, without reserve. *Cleo.* Do you remember the storm upon the coast ef Genoa? *Hor.* Going to Naples? Very well; it makes me cold to think of it. *Cleo.* Was you afraid? *Hor.* Never more in my life: I hate that sickle element; I cannot endure the sea.. *Cleo.* What was you afraid of? *Hor.* That is a pretty question: do you think a young fellow of six-and-twenty, as I was then, and in my circumstances, had a great mind to be drowned? The captain himself laid we were in danger. *Cleo.* But neither he nor any body else discovered half lo much fear and anxiety as you did. *Hor.* There was nobody there, yourself excepted, that had half a quarter so much to lose as I had: besides, they are used to the sea; storms are familiar to them. 1 had never been at sea before, but that line afternoon we crossed srom Dover to Calais. *Cleo.* Want of knowledge or experience may make men apprehend danger where there is none; bus real dangers, when they are known to be such, try the natural courage oi all men; whether they have been used to them or not: sailors are as unwilling to lose their lives as other people. *Hor.* I am not ashamed to own, that I am a great coward at sea: give me *terra Jirma,* and then— *Cleo.* Six or seven months after

you fought that duel, I remember you had the small-pox; you was then very much afraid of dying. *Hor.* Not without a cause. *Cleo.* I heard your physicians fay, that the violent apprehension you was under, hindered your sleep, increased your fever, and-was as mischievous to you as the distemper itself. *Hor.* That was a terrible time; I am glad it is over: I had a sister died of it. Before I had it, I was in perpetual dread of it, and many times to hear it named only has made me uneasy. *Cleo.*-Natural courage is a general armour against the fear of death, whatever shape that appears in, *Si fraSlus illabatur erbis.* It supports a man in tempestuous seas, and in a burning fever, whilst he is in his fenses, as well as in a siege before a town, or in a duel with seconds. *Hor.* What! you are going to mow me, that I have uo courage. *Cleo.* Fatfromit; it would be ridiculous to doubt a man's bravery, that has shown it in such an extraordinary manner as you have done more than once: what I question, is the epithet you joined to it at sirst, the word *natural;* for there is a great difference between that and *artificial* courage. *Hor.* That is a chicane I will not enter into: but I am not of your opinion, as to what you laid before. A gentleman is not required to show his bravery, but where his honour is concerned ; and if he dares to sight for his king, his friend, his mistress, and every thing where his reputation is engaged, you shall think of him what you please for the rest. Besides, that in sickness and other dangers, as weU'as afflictions, where the hand of God is plainly to be seen, courage and intrepidity are impious as well as impertinent. Undauntedness in chastisements is a kind of rebellion: it is waging war with Heaven, which none but atheists and freethinkers would be guilty of; it is only they that can glory in impenitence, and talk of dying hard. All others that have any fense of religion, desire to repent before they go out of the world: the best of us do not always live, as we could wish to die.

Y *Cko.* I am very glad to hear you are so religious: but do not you perceive yet, how inconsistent you are with yourself:

how can a man sincerely wish to repent, that wilfully plunges himself into a mortal sin, and an action where he runs a greater and more immediate hazard of his life, than he could have done in almost any other, without force or necessity?

Hor. I have over and over owned to you that duelling is a sin; and, unless a man is forced to it by necessity, I believe, a mortal one: but this was not my cafe, and therefore I hope God will forgive me: let them look to it that make a sport of it. But when a man comes to an action with the utmost reluctancy, and what he does it not possibly to be avoided, I think he then may justly be said to be forced to it, and to act from necessity. You may blame the rigorous laws of honour, and the tyranny of custom, but a man that will live in the world must, and is bound to obey them. Would nat you do it yourself? *Cleo.* Do not ask me what I would do: the question is, what every body ought to do. Can a man believe the Bible, and at the fame time apprehend a tyrant more crafty or malicious, more unrelenting or inhuman than the devil, or a mischief worse than hell, and pains either more exquisite or more durable than torments unspeakable and yet everlasting? You do not answer. What evil is it? Think of it, and tell me what dismal thing it is you apprehend, shouki you neglect those laws, and despise that tyrant.: what calamity could befall you? Let me know the worst that can be feared. *Hor.* Would you be posted for a coward? *Cleo.* For what? For not daring to violate all human and divine laws? *Hor.* Strictly speaking you aTe in the right, it is unanswerable; but who will consider things in that sight? *Cleo.* All good Christians. *Hor.* Where are they then? For all mankind in general would despise and laugh at a man, who mould move those scruples. I have heard and seen clergymen themselves in company (how their contempt of pbltrons, whatever they might talk or recommend in the pulpit. Entirely to quit the world, and at once to renounce the conversation of all persons that are valvable in it, is a terrible thing to resolve upon. Would you become a town and table-talk? Could you submit to be the jest and scorn of public-houses, stagecoaches, and market-places? Is not this the certain fate of a man, who should refuse to sight, or bear an asfront without resentment? be just, Cleomenes; is it to be avoided? Must he not be made a common laughing-stock, be pointed at in the streets, and serve for diversion to the very children; to link-boys and hackney-coachmen? Is it a thought to be born with patience? *Cleo.* How come you now to have such an anxious regard for what may be the opinion of the vulgar, whom at other times you so heartily despise? *Hor.* All this is-reasoning, and you know the thing will not bear it: how can you be so cruel? *Cleo.* How can you be so backward in discovering and owning the passion, that is so conspicuously the occasion of all this, the palpable and only cause of the uneasiness we feel at the thoughts of being despised? *Hor.* I am not sensible os any; and I declare to you, that I feel nothing that moves me to speak as I do, but the fense and principle of honour within me. *Cleo.* Do you think that the lowest of the mob, and the scum of the people, are possessed of any part of this principle? *Hor.* No, indeed. *Cleo.* Or that among the highest quality, infants can be affected with it before they are two years old? *Hor.* Ridiculous. *Cleo.* If neither of these are asfected with it, then honour should be either adventitious, and acquired by culture; or, if contained in the blood of those that are nobly bom, imperceptible until the years of discretion; and neither of them can be said of the principle, the palpable cause I speak of. For we plainly fee on the one hand, that scorn and ridicule are intolerable to the poorest wretches, and that there is no beggar so mean or miserable, that contempt will never osfend him: on the other, that human creatures are so early influenced by the sense of shame; that children, by being laughed at and made a jest of, may be set a crying before, they can well speak or go. Whatever, therefore, this mighty principle is, it is born with us, and belongs to our nature; are you unacquainted with the proper, genuine,

homely name of it? *Hor.* I know you call it pride. I will not dispute with you about principles and origins of things; but that high value which men of honour set upon themselves as such, and Y a which is no more than what is due to the dignity of our nature, when well cultivated, is the foundation of their character, and a support to them in all difsiculties, that is of great use to the society. The desire, likewise, of being thought well of, and the love of praise and even of glory are commendable qualities, that are benesicial to the public. The truth of this is manifest in the reverse; all shameless people that are below infamy, and matter not what is said or thought of them, these, we see nobody can trust; they stick at nothing, and if they can but avoid death, pain, and penal laws, are always ready to execute all manner of mischief, their selsishness or any brutal appetite shall prompt them to, without regard to the opinion of others: such are justly called men of no principles, because they have nothing of any strength within, that can either spur them on to brave and virtuous actions, or restrain them from villany and baseness.

Cleo. The sirst part of your assertion is very true, when that high value, that desire, and that love are kept within the bounds of reason: But, in the second, there is a mistake; those whom we call shameless, are not more destitute of pride rhan their betters. Remember what I have said of educa'ion, and the power of it; you may add inclinations, knowledge, and circumstances; for, as men differ in all these, so they are differently influenced and wrought upon by all the passions. There is nothing that some men may not be taught to be ashamed of. The fame passion that makes the well bred man, and prudent ossicer, value and secretly admire themselves for the honour and sidelity they display, may make the rake and scoundrel brag of their vices, and boast of their impudence. *Hor.* I cannot comprehend, how a man of honour, and one that has none, should both act from the fame principle. *Cleo.* This is not more strange, than that self-love may make a man destroy him-

self, yet nothing is more true; and it is as certain, that some men indulge their pride in being shameless. To understand human nature, requires study and application, as well as penetration and sagacity. All passions and instincts in general, were given to all animals for some wife end, tending to the preservation and happiness of themselves, or their species: It is our duty to hinder them from being detrimental or offensive to any part of the society; but why should we be ashamed of having them? The instinct of high value, which every individual has for himself, is a very useful passion: but a passion it is, and though I could demonstrate, that we should be miserable creatures without it, yet, when it is excessive, it often is the cause of endless mischiefs. *Hor.* But in well-bred people it never is excessive. *Cleo.* You mean the excess of it never appears outwardly: But we ought never to judge of its height or strength from what we can discover of the passion itself, but from the effects it produces: It often is jnost superlative, where it is most concealed; and nothing increases and influences it more, than what is called a resined education, and a continual commerce with the *beau monde:* The only thing that can subdue, or any ways curb it, is a strict adherence to the Christian religion. *Hor.* Why do you so much insist upon it, that this principle, this value men set upon themselves, is a passion? And why will you choose to call it pride rather than honour? *Cleo.* For very good reasons. Fixing this principle in human nature, in the sirst place, takes away all ambiguity: Who is a man of honour, and who is not, is often a disputable point; and, among those that are allowed to be such, the several degrees of strictness, in complying with the rules of it, make great disference in the principle itself. But a passion that is born with us is unalterable, and part of our frame, whether it exerts itself or not: The essence of it is the fame, which way soever it is taught to turn. Honour is the undoubted offspring of pride, but the fame cause produces not always the fame effect. All the vulgar, children, savages, and many others that are not affected with any fense of honour, have all of them pride, as is evident from the symptoms. Secondly, it helps us to explain the phenomena that occur in quarrels and affronts, and the behaviour of men of honour on these occasions, which cannot be accounted for any other way. But what moves me to it most of all, is the prodigious force and exorbitant power of this principle of self esteem, where it has been long gratified and encouraged. You remember the concern you was under, when you had that duel upon your hands, and the great reluctancy you felt in doing what you did; you knew it to be a crime, and, at the fame time, had a strong aversion to it; what secret power was it that subdued your will, and gained the victory over that great reluctancy yOu felt against it? You call it honour, and the too strict, though unavoidable adherence to the rules of it: But men never commit violence upon themselves but in struggling with the passions that are innate and natural to them. Honour is acquired, and the rules of it are taught: Nothing adventitious, that some afe possessed, and others destitute of, could raise such intestine wars and dire commotions within us; and therefore, whatever is the cause that can thus divide us against ourselves, and, as it were, rend human nature in twain, must be part of us; and, to speak without disguise, the struggle in your breast was between the fear of shame and the fear of death: had this latter not been so considerable, your struggle would have been less: Still the sirst conquered, because it was strongest; but if your fear of shame had been inferior to that of death, you would have reasoned otherwise, and found out some means or other to have avoided sighting. *Hor.* This is a strange anatomy of human nature. *Cleo.* Yet, for want of making use of it, the subject we are upon is not rightly understood by many; and men have discoursed very inconsistently on duelling. A divine who wrote a dialogue to explode that practice, said, that those who were guilty of it, had mistaken notions of, and went by false rules of honour; for which my friend justly ridiculed him, saying, You may as well deny, that

it is the fashion what you see every body wear, as to fay, that demanding and giving satisfaction, is against the laws of true honour. Had that man understood human nature, he could not have committed such a blunder: But when once he took it for granted, that honour is a just and good principle, without inquiring into the cause of it among the passions, it is impossible he should have accounted for duelling, in a Christian pretending to act from such a principle; and therefore, in another place, with the same justice, he said, that a man who had accepted a challenge was not qualisied to make his will, because he was not *compos mentis:* He might, with greater show of reason, have said, that he was bewitched. *Hor.* Why so? *Cieo.* Because people out of their wits, as they think at random, so commonly they act and talk incoherently; but when a man of known sobriety, and who shows no manner of dilcomposure, discourses and behaves himself in every thmg, as he is used to do; and, moreover, realons on points of great nicety with the utmost accuracy, it is impoJlible we should take him to be either a fool or a madman; and when such a person, in an asfair of the highest importance, acts so diametrically against his interest, that a child can fee it, and with deliberation pursues his own destruction, those who believe that there are malignant spirits of that power, would rather imagine that he was led away by some enchantment, and overruled by the enemy of mankind, than they would fancy a palpable absurdity: But even the supposition of that is not sufficient to solve the dissiculty, without the help of that strange anatomy. For what spell or witchcraft is there, by the delusion of which a man of understanding shall, keeping his fenses, mistake an imaginary duty for an unavoidable necessity to break all real obligations? But let us wave all ties of religion, as well as human laws, and the person we speak of to be a professed Epicure, that has no thoughts of futurity ; what violent power of darkness is it, that can force and compel a peaceable quiet man, neither inured to hardship,

nor valiant by nature, to quit his beloved ease and security; and seemingly by choice go sight in cold blood for his life, with this comfortable reflection, that nothing forfeits it so certainly as the entire defeat of his «nemy? *Hor.* As to the law and the punishment, persons of quality have little to fear of that. *Cleo.* You cannot fay that in France, nor the Seven Provinces. But men of honour, that are of much lower ranks, decline duelling no more than those of the highest quality. How many examples have we, even here, of gallant men, that have suffered for it either by exile or the hangman! A man of honour must fear nothing: Do but consider every obstacle which this principle of self-esteem has conquered at one time or other; and then tell me whether it mutt not be something more than magic, by the fascination of which a man of taste and judgment, in health and vigour, as well as the flower of his age, can be tempted, and actually drawn from the embraces of a wise he loves, and the endearments of hopeful children, from polite conversation and the charms of friendship, from the fairest possessions and the happy enjoyment of all worldly pleasures, to an unwarrantable combat, of which the victor must be exposed either to an ignominious death, or perpetual banishment. *Hor.* When tilings are set in this light, I confess it is very

Y unaccountable: but will your system explain this; can you make it clear yourself?

CJeo. Immediately, as the fun: If you will but observe two things, that must necessarily follow, and are manifest from what I have demonstrated already. The first is, that the fear of shame, in general, is a matter of caprice, that varies with modes and customs, and may be sixed on different objects, according to the different lessons we have received, and the precepts we are imbued with; and that this is the reason, why this fear of shame, as it is either well or ill placed, sometimes produces very good effects, and at others is the cause of the most enormous crimes. Secondly, that, though shame is a real passion, the evil to be feared from it is altogether imaginary, and has no existence but in our own reflection on the opinion of others. *Hor.* But there are real and substantial mischiefs which a man may draw upon himself, by misbehaving in point of honour; it may ruin his fortune, and all hopes of preferment: An officer may be broken for putting up an affront: No body will serve with a coward, and who will employ him? *Cleo.* What you urge is altogether out of the question; at least it was in your own cafe; you had noming to dread or apprehend but the bare opinion of men. Besides, when the fear of shame is superior to that of death, it is likewise superior to, and outweighs all other considerations; as has been sussiciently proved: But when the fear of ffiame is not violent enough to curb the fear of death, nothing else can; and whenever the fear of death is stronger than that of shame, there is no consideration that will make a man sight in cold blood, or comply with any of the laws of honour, where life is at stake. Therefore, whoever acts from the fear of shame as a motive, in sending and accepting of challenges, must be sensible, on the one hand, that the mischiefs he apprehends, should he disobey the tyrant, can only be the otfspring of his own thoughts; and, on the other, that if he could be persuaded anywise to lessen the great esteem and high value he sets upon himself, his dread of shame would likewise palpably diminisli. From all which, it *is* most evident, that the grand cause of this distraction, the powerful enchanter we are seeking after, is pride, excess of pride, that highest pitch of self-esteem, to which some men may be wound up by an artful education, and the perpetual flatteries bestowed upon our species, and the excellencies of our nature. This is the sorcerer, that is able to divert all other passions from their natural objects, and make a rational creature ashamed of what is most agreeable to his inclination, as well as his duty; both which the duellist owns, that he has knowingly acted against. *Hor.* What a wonderful machine, what an heterogenous compound is man! You have almost conquered me. *Cleo.* I aim at no victory,

all I wish tor is to do you service, in undeceiving you. *Hor.* What is the reason that, in the same person, the fear of death should be so glaringly conspicuous in sickness, or a storm, and so entirely well hid in a duel, and all military engagements? Pray, solve that too. , " *Cleo.* I will as well as I can: On all emergencies, where reputation is thought to be concerned, the fear of shame is effectually roused in men of honour, and immediately their pride rushes in to their assistance, and summons all their strength to fortify and support them in concealing the fear of death; by which extraordinary efforts, the latter, that is the fear of death, is altogether stifled, or, at least, kept out of sight, and remains undiscovered. But in all other perils, in which they do not think their honour engaged, their pride lies dormant. And thus the fear of death, being checked by nothing, appears without disguise. That this is the true reason, is manifest from the different behaviour that is observed in men of honour, according as they are either pretenders to Christianity, or tainted with irreligion; for there are of both sorts; and you shall see, most commonly at least, that your *esprits forts,* and those who would be thought to disbelieve a future state (I speak of men of honour), show the greatest calmness and intrepidity in the fame dangers, where the pretended believers among them, appear to be the most ruffled and pusillanimous. *Hor.* But why pretended believers? at that rate there are no Christians among the men of honour. *Cleo.* I do not see how they can be real believers. *Hor.* Why so? *Cleo.* For the fame reason that a Roman Catholic cannot be a good subject, always to be depended upon, in a Protestant, or indeed any other country, but the dominions of his Holiness. No sovereign can conside with safety in a man's allegiance, who owns and pays homage to another superior power upon earth. 1 am sure you understand me. *Hor.* Too well. *Cleo.* You may yoke a knight with a prebendary, and put them together into the same stall; but honour, and the Christian religion, make no couple, *nee in undsede morantur,* any more

than majesty and love. Look back on your own conduct, and you shall sind, that what you said of the hand of God was only a shift, an evasion you made to serve your then present purpose. On another occasion, you had said yesterday yourself, that Providence superintends and governs every thing without exception; you must," therefore, have known, that the hand of God is as much to be seen in one common accident in life, and in one misfortune, as it is in another, that is not more extraordinary. A severe sit of sickness may be less fatal, than a slight skirmish between two hostile parties; and, among men of honour, there is often as much danger in a quarrel about nothing, as there can be in the most violent storm. It is impossible, therefore, that a man offense, who has a solid principle to go by, should, in one sort of danger, think it impiety not to show fear, and in another be ashamed to be thought to have any. Do but consider your own inconsistency with yourself. At one time, to justify your fear of death, when pride is absent, you become Teligious on a sudden, and your conscience then is so tenderly scrupulous, that, to be undaunted under chastisements ' from the Almighty, seems no less to you than waging war with Heaven; and, at another, when honour calls, you dare not knowingly and willingly break the most positive command of God, but likewise to own, that the greatest calamity which, in your opinion, can befal you, is, that the world should believe, or but suspect of you, that you had any scruple about it. I defy the wit of man to carry the affront to the Divine Majesty higher. Barely to deny his being, is not half so daring, as it is to do this after you have owned him to exist. No Atheism *Hor.* Hold, Cleomenes; I can no longer resist the force of truth, and 1 am resolved to be better acquainted with myself for the future. Let me become your pupil. *Cleo.* Do not banter me, Horatio; I do not pretend to instruct a man of your knowledge; but if you will take my advice, search into yourself with care and boldness, and, at your leisure, peruse the book I recommended. *Hor.* I promise you I will, and shall be glad to accept of the handsome present I refused: Pray, send a servant with it to-morrow morning. *Cleo.* It is a trifle. You had better let one of yours go with me now; I shall drive home directly. *Hor.* I understand your scruple. It shall be as you please. THE THIRD DIALOGUE HORATIO AND CLEOMENES. HORATIO. 1 Thank, you for your book. *Cleo.* Your acceptance of it I acknowledge as a great favour. *Hor.* I confess, that once I thought nobody could have persuaded me to read it; but you managed me very skilfully, and nothing could have convinced me so well as the instance of duelling: The argument, *a majori ad minus,* struck me, without your mentioning it. A passion that can subdue the fear of death, may blind a man's understanding, and do almost every thing else. *Cleo.* It is incredible what strange, various, unaccountable, and contradictory forms we may be shaped into by a passion, that is not to be gratised without being concealed, and never enjoyed with greater ecstacy than when we are most fully persuaded, that it is well hid: and therefore, there is no benevolence or good nature, no amiable quality or social virtue, that may not be counterfeited by it; and, in short, no achievement, good or bad, that the human body or mind are capable of, which it may not seem to perform. As to its blinding and infatuating the persons pollened with it to a high dei-ree, there is no doubt of it: for what strength of realon, i pray, what judgment or penetration, has the greatest gen: r-. if lie pretends to any religion, to boast os, after he hab owned himself to have been more terrisied by groundless apprehensions, and an imaginary evil from vain impotent men, whom he has never injured, than he was alarmed with the just fears of a real punishment from an all-wise and omnipotent God, whom he has highly offended? *Hor.* But your friend makes no such religious reflections: he actually speaks in favour of duelling. *Cleo.* W hat, because he would have the laws against it as severe as possible, and nobody pardoned, without exception, that offends that way? *Hor.* That indeed seems to discourage it; but he shows the necessi-

ty of keeping up that custom, to polish and brighten society in general. *Cleo.* Do not you see the irony there? *Hor.* No, indeed: he plainly demonstrates the usefulness of it, gives as good reasons as it is possible to invent, and shows how much conversation would suffer, if that practice was abolished. *Cleo.* Can you think a man serious on a subject, when he leaves it in the manner he does? *Hor.* I do not remember that. *Cleo.* Here is the book: I will look for the passage Pray, read this.

Hor. It is strange, that a nation should grudge to see, perhaps, half a dozen men sacrisiced in a twelvemonth, to obtain so valuable a blessing, as the politeness of manners, the pleasure of conversation, and the happiness of company in general, that is often so willing to expose, and sometimes loses as many thousands in a *tew* hours, without knowing whether it will do any good or not. This, indeed, seems to be said with a sneer: but in what goes before he is very serious. *Cleo.* He is so, when he fays that the practice of duelling, that is the keeping up of the fashion of it, contributes to the politeness of manners and pleasure of conversation, and this is very true; but that politeness itself, and that pleasure, are the things he laughs at and exposes throughout his book. , *Hor.* But who knows, what to shake of a man, who recommends a thing very seriously in one page, and ridicules it in the next? *Cleo.* It is his opinion, that there is no solid principle to go by but the Christian religion, and that few embrace it with sincerity: always look upon him in this view, and you will never sind him inconsistent with himself. Whenever at sirst fight he seems to be so, look again, and upon nearer inquiry you will sind, that he is only, pointing at, or labouring to detect the inconsistency of others with the principles they pretend to. *Hor.* He seems to have nothing less at heart than religion. *Cleo.* That is true, and if he had appeared otherwise, he would never have been read by the people whom he designed his book for, the modern deists and all the *beau monde:* It is those he wants to come at. To the sirst he sets forth the origin and insuf-

siciency of virtue, and their own insincerity in the practice of it: to the rest he shows the folly of vice and pleasure, the vanity of worldly greatness, and the hypocrisy of all those divines, who, pretending to preach the gospel, give and take allowances that are inconsistent with, and quite contrary to the precepts of it. *Hor.* But this is not the opinion the world has of the book; it is commonly imagined, that it is wrote for the encouragement of vice, and to debauch the nation. *Cleo.* Have you found any such thing in it? *Hor.* To speak my conscience, 1 must confess, I have not: vice is exposed in it, and laughed at; but it ridicules war and martial courage, as well as honour and every thing else. *Cleo.* Pardon me, religion is ridiculed in no part of it. *Hor.* Bvit if it is a good book, why then are so many of the clergy so much against it as they are? *Cleo.* For the reason I have given you: my friend has exposed their lives, but he has done it in such a manner, that nobody can say he has wronged them, or treated them harshly. People are never more vexed, than when the thing that offends them, is what they must not complain of: they give the book an ill name because they are angry; but it Is not their interest, to tell you the the true reason why they are so. Tcould draw you a parallel case that would clear up this matter, if you would have patience to hear me, which, as you are a great admirer of operas, I can hardly expect. *Hor.* Any thing to be informed. *Cleo.* I always had such an aversion to eunuchs, as no sine singing or acting of any of them has yet been able to conquer; when I hear a feminine voice, I look for a petticoat; and I perfectly loath the sight of those, sexless animals. Suppose that a man with the same dislike to them had wit at will, and a mind to laih that abominable piece of luxury, by which men are taught in cold blood to spoil males for diverlion, and out of wantonness to make waste of their own species. In order to this, we will fay, he takes a handle from the operation itself; he describes and treats it in the most inoffensive manner; then shows the narrow bounds of human knowledge, and the small assistance we can have, either from dissection or philosophy, or any part of the mathematics, to trace and penetrate into the cause *a priori,* why this destroying of manhood mould have that surprising effect upon the voice; and afterwards demonstrates, how sure we are *a posteriori,* that it has a considerable influence, not only on the pharinx, the glands and muscles of the throat, but likewise the windpipe, and the lungs themselves, and in short on the whole mass of blood, consequently all the juices of the body, and every sibre in it. He might fay likewise, that no honey, no preparations of sugar, raisins, or spermaceti; no emulsions, lozenges or other medicines, cooling or balsamic; no bleeding, no temperance or choice in eatables; no abstinence from women, from wine, and every thing that is hot, sharp or spirituous, were of that essicacy to preserve, sweeten, and strengthen the voice; he might insist upon it, that nothing could do this so effectually as castration. For a blind to his main scope, and to amuse his readers, he might speak of this practice, as made use of for other purposes; that it had been inflicted as a solemn punishment for analogous crimes; that others had voluntarily submitted to it, to preserve health and prolong life; whilst the Romans, by Cæsar's testimony, thought it more cruel than death, *morte gravius.* How it had been used sometimes by way of revenge; and then fay something in pity of poor Abelard; at other times for precaution; and then relate the story of Combabus and Stratonice: with scraps from Martial, Juvenal, and other poets, he might interlard it, and from a thousand pleasant things that have been said on the subject, he might pick out the most diverting to embellish the whole. His design being satire, he would blame our fondness for these castrati, and ridicule the age in which a brave English nobleman and a general ossicer, serves his country at the hazard of his life, a whole twelvemonth, for less pay than an Italian no-man of scoundrel extraction receives, for now and then singing a song in great safety, during only the winterseason. He would

laugh at the caresses and the court that are made to them by persons of the sirst quality, who prostitute their familiarity with these most abject wretches, and misplace the honour and civilities only due to their equals, on things that are no part of the creation, and owe their being to the surgeon; animals so contemptible, that they can curie their maker without ingratitude. If he should call this book, the Eunuch is the Man; as soon as I heard the title, before I saw the book, I should understand by it, that eunuchs were now esteemed, that they were in fashion and in the public favour, and considering that a eunuch is in reality not a man, I should think it was a banter upon eunuchs, or a satire against those, who had a greater value for them than they deserved. But if the gentlemen of the academy of music, displeased at the freedom they were treated with, should take it ill, that a paultry scribbler should interfere and pretend to censure their diversion, as well as they might; if they should be very angry, and study to do him a mischief, and accordingly, not having much to say in behalf of eunuchs, not touch upon any thing the author had said against their pleasure, but represent him to the world as an advocate for castration, and endeavour to draw the public odium upon him by quotations taken from him proper for that purpose, it would not be dissicult to raise a clamour against the author, or sind a grand jury to present his book. *Hor.* The simile holds very well as to the injustice of the accusation, and the insincerity of the complaint; but is it as true, that luxury will render a nation flourishing, and that private vices are public benesits, as that castration preserves and strengthens the voice? *Cleo.* With the restrictions my friend requires, I believe it is, and the cafes are exactly alike. Nothing is more effectual to preserve, mend, and strengthen a sine voice in youth than castration: the question is not, whether this is true, but whether it is eligible; whether a sine voice is an equivalent for the loss, and whether a man would prefer the satisfaction of singing, and the advantages that may accrue from it, to the comforts of mar-

riage, and the pleasure of posterity, of which enjoyments it destroys the possibility. In like manner, my friend demonstrates, in the sirst place, that the national happiness which the generality wish and pray for, is wealth and power, glory and worldly greatness; to live in ease, in asfluence and splendour at home, and to be feared, courted, and esteemed abroad: in the second, that such a felicity is not to be attained to without avarice, profuseness, pride, envy, ambition, and other vices. The latter being made evident beyond contradiction, the question is not, whether it is true, but whether this happiness is worth having at the rate it is only to be had at, and whether any thing ought to be wished for, which a nation cannot enjoy, unless the generality of them are vicious. This he offers to the consideration of Christians, and men who pretend to have renounced the world, with all the pomp and vanity of it. *Hor.* How does it appear that the author addresses himself to such? *Cleo.* From his writing it in English, and publishing it in London. But have you read it through yet? *Hor.* Twice: there are many things I like very well, but I am not pleased with the whole. *Cleo.* What objection have you against it? *Hor.* It has diminished the pleasure I had in reading a much better book. Lord Shaftibury is my favourite author: I can take delight in enthusiasm; but the charms of it cease as soon as I am told what it is I enjoy. Since we are such odd creatures, why should we not make the most of it? *Cleo.* I thought you was resolved to be better acquainted with yourself," and to search into your heart with care and boldness. *Hor.* That is a cruel thing; I tried it three times since I saw you last, till it put me into a sweat, and then I was forced to leave off. *Cleo.* You should try again, and use yourself by degrees to think abstractly, and then the book will be a great help to you. *Hor.* To confound me it will: it makes a jest of all politeness and good manners. *Cleo.* Excuse me, Sir, it only tells us, what they are. *Hor.* It tells us, that all good manners consist in flattering the pride of others, and concealing our own. Is not that a horrid thing? *Cleo.* But is it not true? *Hor.* As soon as I had read that paflage, it struck me: down I laid the book, and tried in above sifty instances, sometimes of civility, and sometimes of ill manners, whether it would answer or not, and I profess that it held good in every one. *Cleo.* And so it would if you tried till doomsday, *Hor.* But is not that provoking? I would give a hundred guineas with all my heart, that I did not know it. I cannot endure to fee so much of my own nakedness. *Cleo.* I never met with such an open enmity to truth in a man of honour before. *Hor.* You stiall be as severe upon me as you please; what I say is fact. But since I am got in so far, I must go through with it now: there are sifty things that I want to be informed about. *Cleo.* Name them, pray; if I can be of any service to you, I shall reckon it as a great honour; I am perfectly well acquainted with the author's sentiments. *Hor.* I have twenty questions to ask about pride, and I do not know where to begin. There is another thing I do not understand; which is, that there can be no virtue without self-denial. *Cleo.* This was the opinion of all the ancients. Lord Shaftsbury was the sirst that maintained the contrary. *Hor.* But are there no persons in the world that are good by choice? *Cleo.* Yes; but then they are directed in that choice by reason and experience, and not by nature, I mean, not by untaught nature: but there is an ambiguity in the word good which I would avoid; let us stick to that of virtuous, and then I assirm, that no action is such, which does not suppose and point at some conquest or other, some victory great or small over untaught nature; otherwise the epithet is improper. *Hor.* But if by the help of a careful education, this victory is obtained, when we are young, may we not be virtuous afterwards voluntarily and with pleasure? *Cleo.* Yes, if it really was obtained: but how shall we be sure of this, and what reason have we to believe that it ever was? when it is evident, that from our infancy, instead of endeavouring to conquer our appetites, we have always been taught, and have taken pains ourselves to conceal them; and we

are conscious within, that whatever alterations have been made in our manners and our circumstances, the passions themselves always remained? The system that virtue requires to self-denial, is, as my friend has justly observed, a vast inlet to hypocrisy: it will, on all accounts, iurnish men with a more obvious handle, and a greater opportunity of counterfeiting the love of society, and regard to the public, than ever they could have received from the contrary doctrine,

Z viz. that there is is no merit but in the conquest of the pafsions, nor any virtue without apparent self-denial. Let us ask those that have had long experience, and are well skilled inhuman asfairs, whether they have found the generality of men such impartial judges of themselves, as never to think better of their own worth than it deserved, or so candid in the acknowledgment of their hidden faults and slips, they could never be convinced of, that there is no fear they should ever stifle or deny them. Where is the man that has at no time covered his failings, and screened himself with false appearances, or never pretended to act from principles oi social virtue, and his regard to others, when he knew in his heart that his greatest care had been to oblige himself? The best of us. sometimes receive applause without undeceiving those who give it; though, at the same time, we are conscious that the actions, for which we suffer ourselves to be thought well of, are the result of a powerful frailty in our nature, that has often beca prejudicial to us, and which we have wished a thousand times in vain, that we could have conquered. The fame motives may produce very different actions, as men differ in temper and circumstances. Persons of an easy fortune may appear virtuous, from the lame turn of mind that would show their frailty if they were poor. If we would know the world, we mult look into it. You take no delight in the occurrences of low life; but if we always remain among persons of quality, and extend our inquiries no farther, the transactions there will not furnish us with a sussicient knowledge of every

thing that belongs to our nature. There are, among the middling people, men of low circumstances, tolerably well educated, that set out with the same slock of virtues and vices, and though equally qualisied, meet with very different success; visibly owing to the difference in their temper. Let us take a view of two persons bred to the fame business, that have nothing but their parts and the world before them, launching out with the fame helps and disadvantages: let there be no difference between them, but in their temper; the one active, and the other indolent. The latter will never get an estate by his own industry, though his profession be gainful, and himself master of it. Chance, or some uncommon accident, may be the occasion of great alterations in him, but without that he will hardly ever raise himself to mediocrity. Unless his pride affects him in an extraordinary manner, he must always be poor, and nothing but some share of vanity can hinder him from being despicably so. If he be a man os sense, he will be strictly honest, and a middling stock of covetousness will never divert him from it. In the active stirring man, that is easily reconciled to the buslle of the world, we shall discover quite different symptoms, under the fame circumstances; and a very little avarice will egg him on to pursue his aim with eagerness and assiduity: small scruples are no opposition to him; where sincerity will not serve, he uses artisice; and in compassing his ends, the greatest use he will make of his good sense will be, to preserve as much as is possible, the appearance of honesty; when his interest obliges him to deviate from it. To get wealth, or even a livelihood by arts and sciences, it,is not sussicient to understand them: it is a duty incumbent on all men, who have their maintainance to seek, to make known and forward themselves in the world, as far as decency allows of, without bragging of themselves, or doing prejudice to others: here the indolent man is very desicient and wanting to himself; but seldom will own his fault, and often blames the public for not making use of him, and encouraging that merit, which they never were acquainted with, and himself perhaps took pleasure to conceal; and though you convince him of his error, and that he has neglected even the most warrantable methods of soliciting employment, he will endeavour to colour over his frailty with the appearance of virtue; and what is altogether owing to his too easy temper, and an excessive fondness for the calmness of his mind, he will ascribe to his modesty and the great aversion he has to impudence and boasting. The man of a contrary temper trusts not to his merit only, or the setting it off to the best advantage; he takes pains to heighten it in the opinion of others, and make his abilities seem greater than he knows them to be. As it is counted folly for a man to proclaim his own excellencies, and speak magnisicently of himself, so his chief business is to seek acquaintance, and make friends on purpose to do it for him: all other passions he sacrisices to his ambition; he laughs at disappointments, is inured to refusals, and no repulse dismays him: this renders the whole man always flexible to his interest; he can defraud his body of necessaries, and allow no tranquillity to his mind; and counterfeit, if it will serve his turn, temperance, chastity, compassion, and piety itself, without one grain of virtue or religion: his endeavours to advance his fortune *per fas ct nefas* are always restless, and have no bounds, but where he is obliged to act openly, and has reason to sear the censure of the world. It is very diverting to fee how, in the different persons I speak of, natural temper will warp and model the very passions to its own bias: pride, for example, has not the fame, but almost a quite contrary effect on the one to what it has on the other: the stirring active man it makes in love with sinery, clothes, furniture, equipages, building, and every thing his superiors enjoy: the other it renders sullen, and perhaps morose; and if he has wit, prone to satire, though he be otherwise a goood-natured man. Self-love, in every individual, ever bestirs itself in soothing and flattering the darling inclination; always turning from us the dismal side of the prospect;

and the indolent man in such ciicumstances,sinding nothing pleasing without, turns his view inward upon himself; and there, looking on every thing with great indulgence, admires and takes delight in his own parts, whether natural or acquired: hence he is eailly induced to despise all others who have not the same good qualisications, especially the powerful, and wealthy, whom yet he never hates or envies with any violence; because that would ruffle his temper. All things that are dissicult he looks upon as impossible, which makes him despair of meliorating his condition; and as he has no possessions, and his gettings will but just maintain him in a low itation of life, sb his good fense, if he would enjoy so much as the appearance of happiness, must necessarily put him iipon two things; to be frugal, and pretend to have no value for riches; for, by neglecting either, he must be blown up, and his frailty unavoidably discovered. *Hor.* I am pleased with your observations, and the knowledge you display of mankind; but pray, is not the frugality you now speak of a virtue r *Cleo.* I think not. *Hor.* Where there is but a small income, frugality is built Upon reason; and in this cafe there is an apparent self-denial, without which an indolent man that has no value for money cannot be frugal and we fee indolent men, that have no regard for wealth, reduced to beggary, as it often happens, it is most commonly for want of this virtue. *Cho.* 1 told you before, that the indolent man, setting out as he did, would be poor; and that nothing but some share of vanity could hinder him from being despicably so. A strong fear of shame may gain so much upon the indolence of a man of sense, that he will bestir himself sussiciently to escape contempt; but it will hardly make him do any more; therefore he embraces frugality, as being instrumental and assisting to him in procuring his *summum bonum,* the darling quiet of his easy mind; whereas, the active man, with the fame mare of vanity, would do any thing rather than submit to the same frugality, unless his avarice forced him to it. Frugality is no virtue, when it is im-

posed upon us by any ot the paflions, and the contempt of riches is seldom sincere. I have known men of plentiful estates, that, on account of posterity, or other warrantable views of employing their money, were saving, and more penurious, than they would have been, if their wealth had been greater: but I never yet found a frugal man, without avarice or neceflity. And again, there are innumerable spendthrifts, lavifli and extravagant to a high degree, who seem not to have the least regard to money, whilst they have any to fling away: but these wretches are the least capable of bearing poverty of any, and the money once gone, hourly discover how uneasy, impatient, and miserable they are without it. But what several in all ages have made pretence to, the contempt of riches, is more scarce than is commonly imagined. To fee a man of a very good estate, in health and strength of body and mind, one that has no reason to complain of the world or fortune, actually despise both, and embrace a voluntary poverty, for a laudable purpose, is a great Tariry. I know but one in all antiquity, to whom all this may be applied with strictness of truth. *Hor.* Who is that, pray? *C/eo.* Anaxagoras of Clav. omene in Ionia: He was very rich, of noble extraction, and admired for his great capacity r he divided and gave away his estate among his relations, and refused to meddle with the administration of public asfairs that was ottered him, for no other reason, than that he might have leisure for contemplation of the works of nature, and the study of philosophy. *Hor.* To me it seems to be more dissicult to be virtuous without money, than with: it is senseless for a man to be poor, when he can help it, and if I saw any body choose it, when he might as lawfully be rich, I would think him to be distracted. *Cleo.* But you would not think him so, if you saw hin sell his estate, and give the money to the poor: you know where that was required. *Hor.* It is not required of us. *Cleo.* Perhaps not: but what fay you to renouncing the world, and the solemn promise we have made of it? *Hor.* In a literal sense that is impossible, unless we go out of it;

and therefore 1 do not think, that to renounce the world signisies any more, than not to comply with the vicious, wicked part of it. *Cleo.* I did not expect a more rigid construction from you, though it is certain, that wealth and power are great snares, and strong impediments to all Christian virtue: but the gerality of mankind, that have any thing to lose, are of your opinion; and let us bar faints and madmen, we shall sind every where, that those who pretend to undervalue, and are always haranguing against wealth, are generally poor and indolent. But who can blame them? They act in their own defence; nobody that could help it would ever be laughed at; for it must be owned, that of all the hardships of poverty, it is that which is the most intolerable.

Nil habet inselix paupertas durius in fe, Qmuu ijund ridiculos homines faciat.

In the very satisfaction that is enjoyed by thostj who excel Sn, or are possessed of things valuable, there is interwoven a spice of contempt for others, that are destitute of them, which nothing keeps from public view, but a mixture of pity and good manners. Whoever denies this, let them consult within, and examine whether it is not the fame with happiness, as what Seneca fays of the reverse., *nemo ejl miser niji comparatus.* The contempt and ridicule I speak of, is,, without doubt, what all men of fense and education endeavour to avoid or disappoint. Now, look upon the behaviour os the two contrary tempers before us, and mind how differently they set about this talk, every one suitably to his own inclination. The man of action, you fee, leaves no stone unturned to acquire *quod oportet babere:* but this is impossible for the indolent; he cannot stir; his idol ties him down hand and foot; and, therefore, the easiest, and, indeed the only thing he has left, is to quarrel with the world, and sind out arguments to depreciate what others value themselves upon.

Hor. I now plainly see, how pride and good sense must put an indolent man. that is poor, upon frugality; and likewise the reason, why they will make him asiect to be content, and seem

pleased with his low condition: for, if he will not be frugal, want and misery are at the door: and if he shows any fondness for riches, or a more ample way of living, he loses the only plea he has for his darling frailty, and immediately he will be atked, why he does not exert himself in a better manners and he will be continually told of the opportunities he neglects. *Cleo.* It is evident, then, that the true reasons, why men speak against things, are not always writ upon their foreheads. *Hor.* But after all this quiet easy temper, this indolence you talk of, is it not what, in plain English, we call laziness? *Cleo.* Not at all; it implies no sloth, or aversion to labour: an indolent man may be very diligent, though he cannot be industrious: be will take up with things below him, if they come in his vay; he will work in a garret, or any where else, remote from public view, with putience and assiduity, but he knows not how to solicit and teaz.e others to employ him, or demand his due of a shuffling, designing master, that is either dissicult of access, or tenacious of his money: if he be a man of letters, he will study hard for a livelihood, but generally parts with his labours at a disadvantage, and will knowingly sell them at an under-rateto an obscure man, who osters to purchase, rather than bear the insults of haughty booksellers, and be plagued with the sordid language of the trade. An indolent man may, by chance, meet with a person of quality, that takes a fancy to him; but he will never get a patron by his own address; neither will he ever be the better for it, when he has one, further than the unasked-for bounty, and downright generosity of his benefactor make him. As he speaks for himself with reluctancy, and is always afraid of asking savours, io, for benessits received, he shows no other gratitude, than what the natural emotions of his heart suggest to him. The striving, active man studies all the winning ways to ingratiate himself, and hunts after patrons with design and sagacity: whilst they are benesicial to him, he affects a perpetual fense os thankfulness; but all his acknowledgments of past obliga-

tions, he turns into solicitations for fresh favours: his complaisance may be engaging, and his flattery ingenious, but the beart is untouched: lie has neither leisure, nor the power to love his benefa!o:3; the eldest he has, he will always sacrisice to a new one; and lie has no other esteem for the fortune, the greatness, or the credit of a patron, than as he can make them subservient either to raise or maintain his own. From all this, and a little attention on human asfairs, we may easily perceive, in the liril place, that the man of action, and an enterprising temper, in following the dictates of his nature, must meet with more rubs and obstacles insinitely, than the indolent, and a multitude of strong temptations, to deviate from the rules of strict virtue, which hardly ever come in the other's way; that, in many" circumstances, he will be forced to commit such actions, for which, all his skill and prudence notwithstanding, he will, by some body or other, deservedly be thought to be an:ll man; and that to end with a tolerable reputation, after a long course of life, he must have had a great deal of good fortune, as well as cunning. Secondly, that the indolent man may indulge his inclinations, and be as sensual as his circumstances may let him, with little offence or disturbance to his neighbour; that the excessive value he sets upon the tranquillity of his mind, and the grand aversion he has to part with it, must prove a strong curb to every passion that conies uppermost; none of which, by this means, can ever affect him in any high degree, and consequently, that the corruption of his heart remaining, he may, with little art and no great trouble, acquire many valuable qualities, that shall have all the appearances of social virtues, whilst nothing extraordinary befals him. As to his contempt of the world, the indolent man perhaps will scorn to make his court, and cringe to a haughty favourite, that will browbeat him at sirst; but he will run with joy to a rich nobleman, that he is sure will receive him with kindness and humanity: With him he will partake, without reluctancy, of all the elegant comforts of life that are offered, the most expensive not excepted. Would you try him further, confer upon him honour and wealth in abundance. If this change in his fortune stirs up no vice that lay dormant before, as it may by rendering him either covetous or extravagant, he will loon conform himself to the fashionable world: Perhaps he will be a kind master, an indulgent father, a benevolent neighbour, munisicent to merit that pleases him, a patron to virtue, and a wellwisher to his country; but for the rest, he will take all the pleasure he is capable of enjoying; stifle no pastion he can calmly gratisy, and, in the midst of a luxuri ant plenty, laugh heartily at frugality, and the contempt of riches and greatness he profesied in his poverty; and cheerfull)' own the futility of those pretences. *Hor.* I am convinced, that, in the opinion of virtue's requiring self-denial, there is greater certainty, and hypocrites have less latitude than in the contrary system. *Clco.* Whoever follows his own inclinations, be they never so kind, benesicent, or human, never quarrels with any vice, but what is clashing with his temperament and nature; whereas those who act from a principle of virtue, take always reason for their guide, and combat, without exception, every passion that hinders them from their duty! The indolent man will never deny a just debt; but, if it be large, he will not give himself the trouble which, poor as he is, he might, and ought to take to discharge it, or, at least, satisfy his creditors, unless he is often dunned, or threatened to be sued for it. He will not be a litigious neighbour, nor make mischief among his acquaintance; but he will never serve his friend or his country, at the expence of his quiet. He will not be rapacious, oppress the poor, or commit vile actions for lucre; but then he will never exert himself, and be at the pains another would take on all opportunities, to maintain a large family, make provision for children, and promote his kindred and relations; and his darling frailty will incapacitate him from doing a thousand things for the benesit of the society, which, with the same parts and opportunities, he might, and would have done, had he been of another temper. *Hor.* Your observations are very curious, and, as far as I can judge from what I have seen myself, very just and natural. *Cleo.* Every body knows that there is no virtue so often counterfeited as charity, and yet so little regard have the generality of men to truth, that how gross and bare-faced soever the deceit is in pretences of this nature, the world never fails of being angry, with, and hating those who detect or take notice of the fraud. It is possible, that, with blind fortune on his fide, a mean shopkeeper, by driving a trade prejudicial to his country on the one hand, and grinding, on all occasions, the face of the poor on the other, may accumulate great wealth; which, in process of time, by continual scraping, and sordid saving, may be raised into an exorbitant, an unheard-of estate for a tradesman. Should such a one, when old and decrepit, lay out the greatest part of his immense riches in the building, or largely endowing an hospital, and I was thoroughly acquainted with his temper and manners, I could have no opinion of his virtue, though he parted with the money, whilst he was yet alive; more especially, if 1 was allured, that, in his last will, he had been highly unjust, and had not only left unrewarded several, whom he had great obligations to, but likewise defrauded others, to whom, in his conscience, he knew that he was, and would die actually indebted. I desire you to tell me what name, knowing all 1 have said to be true, you would give to this extraordinary gift, this mighty donation! *Hor.* 1 am of opinion, than when an action of our neighbour may admit of different constructions, it is our duty to iide wth, and embrace the most favourable. *Clso.* The most favourable constructions with all my heart: But what is that to the purpose, when all the straining in the world cannot make it a good one? I do not mean the thing itself, but the principle it came from, the inward motive of the mind that put him upon performing it; for it is that which, in a free agent, I call the action: And, therefore, call it what you please, and judge as charitably of it as you can, what can you fay of it? *Hor.* He might have had several motives, which I do not pretend to determine; but it is an admirable contrivance of being extremely benesicial to all posterity in this land, a noble provision that will perpetually relieve, and be an unspeakable comfort to a multitude of miserable people; and it is not only a prodigious, but likewise a well-concerted bounty that was wanting, and for which, in after ages, thousands of poor wretches will have reason to bless his memorv, when every body else lhall have neglected them. *Cleo.* All that I have nothing against; and if you would add more, I shall not dispute it with you, as long as you confine your praises to the endowment itself,.and the benesit the public is l;ke to receive from it. But to ascribe it to, or suggest that it was derived from a public spirit in the man, a generous fense of humanity and benevolence to his kind, a liberal heart, or any other virtue or good quality, which it is manifest the donor was an utter stranger to, is the utmost absurdity in an intelligent creature, and can proceed from no other caulc than either a wilful wronging of his own understanding, or else ignorance and f jlly. *Hor.* I am persuaded, that many actions are put off for virtuous, that are not so; and that according as men differ in natural temper, and turn of mind, lb they are differently influenced by the fame pastions: I believe likewise, that these la st are born with us, and belong to our nature; that some of them are in us, or at least the feeds of them, before we perceive them: but lince they are in every individual, how comes it that pride is more predominant in some than it is in, others? For from what you have demonstrated already, it must follow, that one person is more affected with the passion within than another; 1 mean, that one man has actually a greater snare of pride than another, as well among the artful that are dexterous in concealing it, as among the ill-bred that openly mow it. *C'/eo.* What belongs to our nature, all men may justly be said to have actually or virtually in them at their birth; and whatever is not bom with us, either the thing itself, or that which afterwards produces it, cannot be said to belong to our nature: but as we differ in our faces and stature, so we do in other things, that are more remote from light: but all these depend only upon the different frame, the inward formation qf either the solids or the fluids; and there are vices of complexion, that are peculiar, some to the pale and phlegmatic, others to the sanguine and choleric: some are more lustful, others more fearful in their nature, than the generality are: but I believe of man, generally speaking, what my friend has observed of other creatures, that the best of the kind, I mean the best formed within, such as have the sinest natural parts, are born with the greatest aptitude to be proud; but I am convinced, that the difference there is in men, as to the degrees of their pride, is more owing to circumstances and education, than any thing in their formation. Where pastions are most gratisied and least controuled, the indulgence makes them stronger; whereas those persons, that have been kept under, and whole thoughts have never been at liberty to rove beyond the sirst neecstaries of life; such as have not been luffered, or had no opportunity to gratify this pastion, have commonly the least share of it. But whatever portion of pride a man may feel in his heart, the quicker his parts are, the better his understanding is; and the more experience he has, the more plainly he will perceive the averlion which all men have to those that discover their pride: and the looner persons are imbued with good manners, the sooner they grow perfect in concealing that passion. Men of mean birth and education, that have been kept in great subjection, and consequently had no great opportunities to exert their pride, if ever they come to command others, have a sort of revenge mixed with that passion, which makes it often very mischievous, especially in places where they have no superiors or equals, before whom they are obliged to conceal the odious passion. *Hor.* Do you think women have more pride from nature than men? *Cleo.* I believe not: but they have a great deal more from education. *Hor.* I do not fee the reason: for among the better sort,

the sons, especially the eldest, have as many ornaments and sine things given them from their infancy, to stir up their pride, as the daughters. *Cteo.* But among people equally well-educated, the ladies have more flattery bestowed upon them, than the gentlemen, and it begins sooner. *Hor.* But why should pride be more encouraged in women than in men? *Cleo.* For the same reason, that it is encouraged in soldiers, more than it is in other people; to increase their fear of shame, which makes them always mindful of their honour. *Hor.* But to keep both to their respective duties, why must a lady have more pride than a gentleman? *Cleo.* Because the lady is in the greatest danger of straying from it: she has a passion within, that may begin to affect her at twelve or thirteen, and perhaps sooner, and she has all the temptations of the men to withstand besides: she has all the artillery of our sex to fear; a seducer of uncommon address and resistless charms, may court her to what nature prompts and solicits her to do; he may add great promises, actual bribes; this may be done in the dark, and when nobody is by to dissuade her. Gentlemen very seldom have occasion to show their courage before they are sixteen or seventeen years of age, and rarely so soon: they are not put to the trial, till, by conversing with men of honour, they are consirmed in their pride: in the affair of a quarrel they have their friends to consult, and these are so many witnesses of their behaviour, that awe them to their duty, and in a manner oblige them to obey the laws of honour: all these things conspire to increase their fear ofishame 3 and if they can but render that superior to the fear of death, their business is done; they have no pleasure to expect from breaking the rules of honour, nor any crafty tempter that solicits them to be cowards. That pride which is the cause of honour in men, only regards their courage; and if they can but appear to be brave, and will but follow the fashionable rules of manly honour, they may indulge all other appetites, and brag of incontinence without reproach: the pride likewise that produces honour in women, has no

other object than their chastity; and whilst they keep that jewel entire, they can apprehend no shame: tenderness and delicacy are a compliment to them; and there is no fear of danger so ridiculous, but they may own it with ostentation. But notwithstanding the weakness of their frame, and the softness in "which women are generally educated, if overcome by chance they have sinned in private, what real hazards will they not run, what torments will they not stiste, and what crimes will they not commit, to hide from the world that frailty, which they were taught to be most ashamed of! *Hor.* It is certain, that we seldom hear of public prostitutes, and such as have lost their shame, that they murder their infants, though they are otherwise the most abandoned wretches: 1 took notice of this in the Fable of the Bees, and it is very remarkable. *Cleo.* It contains a plain demonstration, that the fame passion may produce either a palpable good or a palpable evil in the same person, according as self-love and his present circumstances mall direct; and that the fame fear of shame, that makes men sometimes appear so highly virtuous, may at others oblige them to commit the most heinous crimes: that, therefore, honour is not founded upon any principle, either of real virtue or true religion, must be obvious to all that will but mind what sort of people they are, that are the greatest votaries of that idol, and the different duties it requires in the two sexes: in the sirst place, the worihippers of honour are the vain and voluptuous, the strict observers of modes and fashions, that take delight in pomp and luxury, and enjoy as much of the world as they are able: in the second, the word itself, I mean the sense of it, is so whimsical, and there is such a prodigious difference in the signisication of it, according as the attribute is differently applied, either to a man or to a woman, that neither of them mall forfeit their honour, though each should be guilty, and openly boast of what would be the others greatest shame. *Hor.* I am sorry that I cannot charge you with injustice: but it is very strange; that to encourage and industriously increase pride in a resined education, should be the most proper means to make men solicitous in concealing the outward appearances of it. *Cleo.* Yet nothing is more true; but where pride is so much indulged, and yet to be so carefully kept from all human view, as it is in persons of honour of both sexes, it would be impoflible for mortal strength to endure the restraint, if men could not be taught to play the passion against itself, and were not allowed to change the natural home-bred symptoms of it, for artisicial foreign ones. *Hor.* By playing the passion against itself, I know you mean placing a secret pride in concealing the barefaced signs of it: but I do not rightly understand what you mean by changing the symptoms of it. *Cleo.* When a man exults in his pride, and gives a loose to that passion, the. marks of it are as visible in his countenance, his mien, his gait and behaviour, as they are in a prancing horse, or a strutting turkey-cock. These are all very odious; every one feeling the fame principle within, which is the cause of those symptoms; and man being endued with speech, all the open expressions the fame passion can suggest to him, must for the same reason be equally displeasing: these, therefore, have in all societies been strictly prohibited by common consent, in the very infancy of good manners; and men have been taught, in the room of them, to substitute other symptoms, equally evident with the sirst, but less offensive, and more benesicial to others. *Hor.* Which are they? *Cleo.* Pine clothes, and other ornaments about them, the cleanliness observed about their persons, the submission that is required of servants, costly equipages, furniture, buildings, titles of honour, and every thing that men can acquire to make themselves esteemed by others, without discovering any of the symptoms that are forbid: upon a satiety of enjoying these, they are allowed likewise to have the vapours, and be whimsical, though otherwise they are known to be in health and of good sense. *Hor.* But since the pride of others is displeasing to us in every shape, and these latter symptoms, you

fay, are equally evident with the sirst, what is got by the change? *Cleo.* A great deal: when pride is designedly expressed in looks and gestures, either in a wild or tame man, it is known by all human creatures that fee it; it is the fame, when vented in words, by every body that understands the language they are spoken in. These are marks and tokens that are all the world over the fame: nobody mows them, but to have them seen and understood, and few persons ever display them without designing that osfence to others, which they never fail to give: whereas, the other symptoms may be denied to be what they are; and many pretences, that they are derived from other motives, may be made for them, which the fame good manners teach us never to refute, nor easily to disbelieve: in the very excuses that are made, there is a condescension that satissies and pleases us. In thole that are altogether destitute of the opportunities to display the symptoms of pride that are allowed of, the least portion of that paflion is a troublesome, though often an unknown guest; for in them it is easily turned into envy and malice, and on the least provocation, it sallies out in those disguises, and is often the cause of cruelty; and there never was a mischief committed by mobs or multitudes, which this paflion had not a-hand in: whereas, the more room men have to vent and gratify the passion in the warrantable ways, the more easy it is for them to stifle the odious part of pride, and seem to be wholly free from it. *Hor.* 1 fee very well, that real virtues requires a conquest over untaught nature, and that the Christian religion demands a still stricter self-denial: it likewise is evident, that to make ourselves acceptable to an omniscient Power, nothing is more necessary than sincerity, and that the heart should be pure. But setting aside sacred matters, and a future state, do not you think that this complaisance and easy construction of one another's actions, do a great deal of good upon earth; and do not you believe that good manners and politeness make men more happy, and their lives more comfortable in this world, than any

thing else could make them without those arts? *Cleo.* If you will set aside what ought to employ our sirst care, and be our greatest concern; and men will have no value for that felicity and peace of mind, which can only arise from a consciousness of being good, it is certain, that in a great nation, and among a flourishing people, whose highest wishes seem to be ease and luxury, the upper part could not, without those arts, enjoy so much of the world as that can afford; and that none Hand more in need of them than the voluptuous men of parts, that will join worldly prudence to sensuality, and make it their chief study to resine upon pleasure. *Hor.* When I had the honour of your company at my house, you said that nobody knew when or where, nor in what king's or emperor's reign the laws of honour were enacted; pray, can you inform me when or which way, what we call good manners or politeness came into the world? what moralist or politician was it, that could teach men to be proud of hiding their pride? *Cleo.* The resistless industry of man to supply his wants, and his constant endeavours to meliorate his condition upon earth, have produced and brought to perfection many useful arts and sciences, of which the beginnings are of uncertain eras, and to which we can assign no other causes, than human sagacity in general, and the joint labour of many ages, in which men have always employed themselves in studying and contriving ways and means to sooth their various appetites, and make the best of their insirmities. Whence had we the sirst rudiments of architecture; how came sculpture and painting to be what they have been these many hundred years; and who taught every nation the respective languages they speak now. When I have a mind to dive into the origin of any maxim or political invention, for the use of society in general, I do not trouble my head with inquiring after the time or country in which it was sirst heard of, nor what others have wrote or said about it; but I go directly to the fountain head, human nature itself, and look for the frailty or defect in man, that is remedied or supplied by that invention: when things are very obscure, 1 sometimes make use of conjectures to sind my way. *Hor.* Do you argue, or pretend to prove any thing from those conjectures? *Cleo.* No; I never reason but from the plain observations which every body may make on man, the phenomena that appear in the lesser world. *Hor.* You have, without doubt, thought on this subject before now; would you communicate to me some of your guesfles? *Cleo.* With abundance of pleasure. *Hor.* You will give me leave, now and then, when things are not clear to me, to put in a word for information's fake. *Cleo.* I desire you would: you will oblige me with it. That self-love was given to all animals, at least, the most perfect, for self-preservation, is not disputed; but as no creature can. love what it dislikes, it is necessary, moreover, that every one mould have a real liking to its own being, superior to what they have to any other. I am of opinion, begging pardon for the novelty, that if this liking was not always permanent, the love which all creatures have for themselves, could not be so unalterable as we fee it is. *Hor.* What reason have you to suppose this liking, which creatures have for themselves, to be distinct from self-love; since the one plainly comprehends the other? *Cleo.* I will endeavour to explain myself better. I fancy, tbat to increase the care in creatures to preserve themselves, nature has given them an instinct, by which every individual values itself above its real worth; this in us, 1 mean in man, seems to be accompanied with a dissidence, arising from a consciousness, or at least an apprehension, that ve do overvalue ourselves: it is that makes us so fond of the approbation, liking, and afl'ent of others; because they strengthen and consirm us in the good opinion we have of ourselves. The reasons why this self-liking, give me leave to call it so, is not plainly to be seen in all animals that are of the fame degree of perfection, are many. Some want ornaments, and consequently the means to express it; others are too stupid and listless: it is to be considered likewise, that creatures, which are always in the fame circumstances,

and meet with little variation in their way of living, have neither opportunity nor temptation to shcw it; that the more mettle and liveliness creatures have, the more visible this liking is; and that in those of the same kind, the greater spirit they are of, and the more they excel in the perfections of their species, the fonder they are of mowing it: in most birds it is evident, especially in those that have extraordinary sinery to display: in a horse it is more conspicuous than in any other irrational creature: it is most apparent in the swiftest, the strongest, the most healthy and vigorous; and may be increased in that animal by additional ornaments, and the presence of

A a man, whom ha knows, to clean, take care of, and delight in him. It is not improbable, that this great liking which creatures have for their own individuals, is the principle on which the love to their species is built: cows and sheep, too dull and lifeless to make any demonstration of this liking, yet herd and feed together, each with his own species; because no others are so like themselves: by this they seem to know likewise, that they have the same interest, and the same enemies; cows have often been seen to join in a common defence against wolves: birds of a feather flock together; and I dare fay, that the screechowl likes her own note better than that of the nightingale.

Hor. Montain seems to have been somewhat of your opinion, when he fancied, that if brutes were to paint the Deity, they would all draw him of tbeir own species. But what you call self-liking is evidently pride. *Cleo.* I believe it is, or at least the cause of it. I believe, moreover, that many creatures show this liking, when, for want of understanding them, we do not perceive it: When a cat washes her face, and a dog licks himself clean, they adorn themselves as much as it is in their power. Man himself, in a a savage state, feeding on nuts and acorns, and destitute of all outward ornaments, would have insinitely less temptation, as well as opportunity, of showing this liking of himself, than he has when civilized; yet if a hundred

males of the sirst, all equally free, were together, within less than half an hour, this liking in question, though their bellies were full, would appear in the desire of superiority, that would be shown among them; and the most vigorous, either in strength or understanding, or both, would be the sirst that would display it: If, as supposed, they were all untaught, this would breed contention, and there would certainly be war before there could be any agreement among them; unless one of them had some one or more visible excellencies above the rest. I said males, and their bellies full; because, if they had women among them, or wanted food, their quarrel might begin on another account. *Hor.* This is thinking abstractly indeed: but do you think that two or three hundred lingle savages, men and women, that never had been under any subjection, and were above twenty years of age, could ever establish a society, and be united into one body, if, without being acquainted with one another, they should meet by chance L *Cleo.* No more, I believe, than so many horses: but societies never were made that way. It is possible that several families of savages might unite, and the heads of them agree upon some sort of government or other, for their common good: I but among them it is certain likewise, that, though superiority was tollerably well settled, and every male had females enough, strength and prowess in this uncivilized state would be insinitely more valued than understanding: I mean in the men; for the women will always prize themselves for what they fee the men admire in them: Hence it would follow, that the women would value themselves, and envy one another for being handsome; and that the ugly and deformed, and all those that were least favoured by nature, would be the sirst, that would fly to art and additional ornaments: seertg that this made them more agreeable to the men, it would soon be followed by the rest, and in a little time they would strive to outdo one another, as much as their circumstances would allow of; and it is possible, that a woman, with a very handsome nose, might envy her neighbour with a much worse, for having a ring through it. *Hor.* You take great delight in dwelling on the behaviour of savages; what relation has this to politeness? *Cleo.* The feeds of it are lodged in this self-love and self-liking, which I have spoke of, as will soon appear, if we would consider what would be the consequence of them in the affair of self-preservation, and a creature endued with understanding, speech, and risibility. Self-love would sirst make it scrape together every thing it wanted for sustenance, provide against the injuries of the air, and do every thing to make itself and young ones secure. Self-liking would make it seek for opportunities, by gestures, looks, and sounds, to display the value it has for itself, superior to what it has for others; an untaught man would desire every body that came ear him, to agree with him in the opinion of his superior worth, and be angry, as far as his fear would let him, with U that should refuse it: he would be highly delighted with, and love every body whom he thought to have a good opinion of him, especially those, that, by words or gestures, mould own it to his face: whenever he met with any visible marks in others of inferiority to himself, he would laugh, and do the same at their misfortunes, as far as his own pity

A a a would give him leave, and he would insult every body that would let him.

Hor. This self-liking, you fay, was given to creatures for felt-preservation: 1 should think rather that it is hurtful to men, because it must make them odious to one another; und I cannot fee what benesit they can recive from it, either in a savage or a civilized state: is there any instance of its doing any good? *Cleo.* I wonder to hear you ask that question. Have you forgot the many virtues which I have demonstrated, may be counterfeited to gain applause, and the good qualities a man offense in great fortune may acquire, by the sole help and instigation of his pride? *Hor.* I beg your pardon: yet what you fay only regards man in the society, and after he has been perfectly well educated: what advantage

is it to him as a single creature? Self-love I can plainly fee, induces him to labour for his maintenance and safety, and makes him fond of every thing which he imagines to tend to his preservation; but what good does the self-liking to him? *Cleo.* If I should tell you, that the inward pleasure and satisfaction a man receives from the gratisication of that passion, is a cordial that contributes to his health, you would laugh at me, and think it far fetched. *Hor.* Perhaps not; but I would set against it the many siiarp vexations and heart-breaking sorrows, that men suffer on the score of this passion, from disgraces, disappointments, and other misfortunes, which, I believe, have sent millions to their graves much sooner than they would have gone, if their pride had less affected them. *Cleo.* I have nothing against what you fay: but this is no proof that the passion itself was not given to man for seltpreservation; and it only lays open to us the precarioufnels of sublunary happiness, and the wretched condition ofmor tals. There is nothing created that is always a blessing; the rain and sunshine themselves, to which all earthly comforts are owing, have been the causes of innumerable calamities. All animals of prey, and thousand others, hunt aster foods with the hazard of their lives, and the greater part of them perish in their pursuits after sustenance. Plenty itself is not: less fatal to some, than want is'to others; and of our own species, every opulent nation has had great numbers, that in full safety from all otner dangers, have destroyed themselves J by excesses of eating and drinking: yet nothing is more certain, than that hunger and thirst were given to creatures, to make them solicitous after, and crave hole necesiaries, wi tout which it would be impossible for them to subsist. *Hor.* Still I can see no advantage accruing from their selfliking to man, considered as a single creature, which can induce me to believe, that nature should have given it us for self-preservation. What you have alleged is obscure; can you name a benesit every individual person receives from that principle within him, that is manifest, and clearly

to be understood? *Cleo.* Since it has been in disgrace, and every body disowns the passion, it seldom is seen in its proper colours, and disguises itself in a thousand disterent shapes: we are often affected with it, when we have not the least suspicion of it; but it seems to be that which continually furnishes us with that relish we have for life, even when it is not worth having. Whilst men are pleased, self-liking has every moment a considerable mare, though unknown, in procuring the satisfaction they enjoy. It is so necessary to the well-being of those that have been used to indulge it, that they can taste no pleasure without it; and such is the deference, and the submissive veneration they pay to it, that they are deaf to the loudest calls of nature, and will rebuke the strongest appetites that fliould pretend-to be gratisied at the expence of that passion. It doubles our happiness in prosperity, and buoys us up against the frowns of adverse fortune. It is the mother of hopes, and the end as well as the foundation of our best wishes: it is the strongest armour against despair; and as long as we can like any ways our situation, either in regard to present circumstances, or the prospect before us, we take care of ourselves; and no man can resolve upon suicide, whilst selfliking lasts: but as soon as that is over, ail our hopes are extinct, and we can form no wishes but for the dissolution of our frame; till at last our being becomes so intolerable to us, that self-love prompts us to make an end of it, and seek refuge in death. *Hor.* You mean self-hatred; for you have said yourself, that a creature cannot love what it dislikes. *Cleo.* If you turn the prospect, you are in the right: but this only proves to us what I have often hinted at, that man is made up of contrarieties; otherwise nothing seems to be more certain, than that whoever kills himself by choice, must do it to avoid something, which he dreads more than that death which he chooses. Therefore, how absurd soever a person's reasoning, may be, there is in all suicide a palpable intention of kindness to one's self. *Hor.* I mull own that your observations are entertaining. I am very well pleased with your discourse, and I see an agreeable glimmering of probability that runs through it; but you have said nothing that comes up to a half proof on the side of your conjecture, if it be seriously considered. *Cleo.* I told you before that I would lay no stress upon, nor draw any conclusions from it: but whatever nature's design was in bestowing this self-liking on creatures, and whether it has been given to other animals besides ourselves or not, it is certain, that in our own species every individual person likes himself better than he does any other. *Hor.* It may be so, generally speaking: but that it is not univerfally true, I can assure you, from my own experience; for I have often wished myself to be Count Thcodati, whom you knew at Rome. *Cleo.* He was a very sine person indeed, and extremely well accomplished; and therefore you wished to be such another, which is all you could mean. Celia has a very handsome face, sine eyes, sine teeth; but she has red hair, and is ill made: theresore she wishes for Chine's hair and Belinda's shape; but she would still remain Celia. *Hor.* But I wished that I might have been that person, that very Theodati. *Cleo.* That is impossible. *Hor.* What, is it impossible to wish it? *Cleo.* Yes, to wish it; unless you wisiied for annihilation at the fame time. It is that self we wish well to; and therefore we cannot wish for any change in ourselves, but with a proviso, that « self, that part of us that wishes, sliould still remain: for take away that consciousness you had of yourself whilst you was washing, and tell me, pray, what part of you it is that could be the better for the alteration you wished for? *Hor.* I believe you are in the right. No man can wish but to enjoy something, which no part of that same man could do, if he was entirely another. *Cleo.* That *be* itself, the person wishing, must be destroyed before the change could be entire, *Hor.* But when shall we come to the origin of politeness? *Cleo.* We are at it now, and we need not look for it any further than in the self-liking, which I have demonstrated every individual man to be possessed of. Do but consider these two

things: First, that from the nature of that passion, it must follow, that all untaught men will ever be hateful to one another in conversation, where neither interest nor superiority are considered: for, if of two equals, one only values himself more by half, than he does the other, though that other should value the sirst equally with himself, they would both be dissatisfied, if their thoughts were known to each other; but if both valued themselves more by half, than they did each other, the difference between them would still be greater, and a declaration of their sentiments would render them both insufferable to each other; which, among uncivilized men, would happen every moment, because, without a mixture of art and trouble, the outward symptoms of that passion are not to be stifled. The second thing 1 would have you consider, is, the effect which, in all human probability, this inconveniency, arising from self-liking, would upon creatures endued with a great share of understanding, that are fond of their ease to the last degree, and as industrious to procure it. These two things, I fay, do but duly weigh, and you shall sind that the disturbance and uneasiness that must be caused by self-liking, whatever strugglings and unsuccessful trials to remedy them might precede, must necessarily produce, at long run, what we call good manners and politeness. *Hor.* I understand you, I believe. Every body in this undisciplined state, being affected with the high value he has for himself, and displaying the most natural symptoms which you have described, they would all be offended at the barefaced pride of their neighbours: and it is impossible that this mould continue long among rational creatures, but the repeated experience of the uneasiness they received from such behaviour, would make some of them reflect on the cause of it; which, in tract of time, would make them sind out, that their own barefaced pride, must be as offensive to others, as that of others is to themselves. *Cleo.* What you fay is certainly the philosophical reason of the alterations that are made in the behaviour of men, by their being civilized:

but all this is done without reflection; and men by degrees, and great length of time, fall as it Were into these things spontaneously. *Hor.* How is that possible, when it must cost them trouble, and there is a palpable self-denial to be seen in the restraint they put upon themselves? *Cleo.* In the pursuit of self-preservation, men discover a restless endeavour to make themselves easy, which insensibly teaches them to avoid mischief on all emergencies: and when human creatures once submit to government, and are used to live under the restraint of laws, it is incredible how many useful cautions, shists, and stratagems they will learn to practise by experience and imitation, from converling together, without being aware of the natural causes that oblige them to act as they do, viz. the passions within, that, unknown to themselves, govern their will and direct their behaviour. *Hor.* You will make men as mere machines as Cartes does brutes. *Cleo.* 1 have no such design: but I am of opinion, that men sind out the use of their limbs by instinct, as much as brutes do the use of theirs; and that, without knowing any thing of geometry or arithmetic, even children may learn to peform actions that seem to bespeak great skill in mechanics, and a considerable depth of thought and ingenuity in the contrivance besides. *Hor.* What actions are they which you judge this from? *Cleo.* The advantageous postures which they will choose in resisting force, in pulling, pushing, or otherwise removing weight; from their sleight and dexterity in throwing stones, and other projectiles; and the stupenduous cunning made use of in leaping. *Hor.* What stupenduous cunning, I pray? *Cleo.* When men would leap or jump a great way, you know, they take a run before they throw themselves off the ground. It is certain, that, by this means, they jump farther, and with greater force than they.could do otherwise: the reason likewise is very plain. The body partakes of, and is moved by two motions; and the velocity, impressed upon it by leaping, must be added to so much, as it retained of the velocity it was put into by running:

Whereas, the body of a person who takes this leap, as he is Handing still, has no other motion, than what is received from the muscular strength exerted in the act of leaping. See a thousand boys, as well as men, jump, and they will make use of this stratagem; but you will not sind one of them that does it knowingly for that reason. What I have said of that stratagem made use of in leaping, I desire you would apply to the doctrine of good manners, which is taught and practised by millions, who never thought on the origin of politeness, or so much as knew the real benesit it is of to society. The most crafty and designing will every where be the sirst, that, for interest-fake, will learn to conceal this passion of pride, and, in a little time, nobody will show the least symptom of it, whilst he is asking favours, or stands in need of help. *Hor.* That rational creatures should do all this, without thinking or knowing what they are about, is inconceivable. Bodily motion is one thing, and the exercise of the understanding is another; and therefore agreeable postures, a graceful mien, an easy carriage, and a genteel outward behaviour, in general, may be learned and contracted perhaps without much thought; but good manners are to be observed every where, in speaking, writing, and ordering actions to be performed by others. *Cleo.* To men who never turned their thoughts that way, it certainly is almost inconceivable to what prodigious height, from next to nothing, some arts may be, and have been raised by human industry and application, by the uninterrupted labour and joint experience of many ages, though none but men of ordinary capacity mould ever be employed in them. ' What a noble, as well as beautiful, what a glorious machine is a sirst rate man of war when stie is under fail, well rigged, and well manned! As in bulk and weight it is vastly superior to any other moveable body of human invention, so there is no other that has an equal variety of differently surprising contrivances to boast of. There are many sets of hands in the nation, that, not wanting proper materials, would be

able in less than half a-year, to produce, sit out, and navigate a sirst rate: yet it is certain, that this task would be impracticable, if it was not divided and subdivided into a great variety of different labours; and it is as certain, that none of these labours require any other, than working men of ordinary capacities. *Hor.* What would you infer from this? *Cleo.* That we often ascribe to the excellency of man's genius, and the depth of his penetration, what is in reality owing to length of lime, and the experience of many generations, all of them very little differing from one another in natural parts and sagacity. And to know what it must have cost to bring that art of making ships for different purposes, to the perfection in which it is nowj it we are only to consider, in the sirst place, that many, considerable improvements have been made in it within these fifty years and less; and. in the second, that the inhabitants of this island did build, and make use of ships eighteen hundred years ago, and that, from that time to this, they have never been without. *Hor.* Which altogether make a strong proof of the flow progress that an has made to be what it is. *Cleo.* The Chevalier Reneau has wrote a book, in whxh he shows the mechanism of sailing, and accounts mathematically for every thing that belongs to the working and steering of a ship. I am persuaded, that neither the sirst inventors of ships and sailing, or those who have made improvements since in any part of them, ever dreamed of those reasons, any more than how the rudest and most illiterate of the vulgar do, when they are made sailors, which time and practice will do in spite of their teeth. We have thousands of them that were sirst hauled on board, and detained against their wills, and yet, in less than three years time, knew every rope and every pully in the ship, and without the least scrap of mathematics, had learned the management as well as use of them, much better than the greatest mathematician could have done in all his lifetime, if he had never been at sea. The book I mentioned, among other curious things, demonstrates what angle the rudder must make with the keel, to ren-

der its influence upon the ship the most powerful. This has its merit; but a lad of sifteen, who has served a year of his time on board of a hoy, knows every thing that is useful in this demonstration, practically. Seeing the poop always answering the motion of the helm, he only minds the latter, without making the least reflection on the rudder, until in a year or two more his knowledge in sailing, and capacity of steering his veslel, become ib habitual to him, that he guides her, as he does his own body, by instinct, though he is half asleep, or thinking on quite another thing. *Hor.* If, as you said, and which 1 now believe to be true, the people who sirst invented, and afterwards improved upon ships and sailing, never dreamed of those reasons of Monsieur Reneau, it is impoflible that they mould have acted from them, as motives that induced them *a priori,* to put their inventions and improvements in practice, with knowledge and design, which, I suppose, is what you intended to prove. *Cleo.* It is; and I verily believe, not only that the raw beginners, who made the sirst essays in either art, good manners as well as sailing, were ignorant of the true cause; the real foundation those arts are built upon in nature; but likewise that, even now both arts are brought to great perfection, the greatest part of those that are most expert, and daily making improvements in them, know as little of the *rationale* of them, as their predecessors did at sirst: though I believe, at the fame time, Monsieur Reneau's reasons to be very just, and yours as good as his; that is, I believe, that there is as much truth and solidity in your accounting for the origin of good manners, as there is in his for the management of ships. They are very seldom the same sort of people, those that invent arts and improvements in them, and those that inquire into the reason of things: this latter is most commonly practised by such as are idle and indolent, that are fond of retirement, hate business, and take delight in speculation; whereas, none succeed oftener in the sirst, than active, stirring, and laborious men, such as will put their hand to the plough, try experiments, and give all their attention to what they are about. *Hor.* It is commonly imagined, that speculative men are best at invention of all sorts. *Cleo.* Yet it is a mistake. Soap-boiling, grain-drying, and other trades and mysteries, are, from mean beginnings, brought to great perfection; but the many improvements that can be remembered to have been made in them, have, for the generality, been owing to persons, who either were brought up to, or had long practised, and been conversant in those trades, and not to great prosicients in chemistry, or other parts of philosophy, whom one would naturally expect those things from. In some of these arts, especially grain or scarlet-dying, there are processes really astonishing; and, by the mixture of various ingredients, by sire and fermentation, several operations are performed, which the most sagacious naturalist cannot account for by any system yet known; a certain sign that they were not invented by reasoning *a priori.* When once the generality begin to conceal the high value they have for themselves, men must become more tolerable to one another. Now, new improvements must be made every day, until some of them grow impudent enough, not only to deny the high value they have for themselves, but likewise to pretend that they have greater value for others, than they have for themselves. This will bring in complaisance; and now flattery will rush in upon them like a torrent. As soon as they are arrived at this pitch of insincerity, they will sind the benesit of it, and teach it their children. The passion of shame is so general, and so early discovered in all human creatures, that no nation can be so stupid, as to be long without observing and making use of it accordingly. The same may be said of the credulity os infants, which is very inviting to many good purposes. The knowledge of parents is communicated to their offspring, and every one's experience in life being added to what he learned in his youth, every generation after this must be better taught than the preceding; by which means, in two or three centuries, good manners must be brought to great perfection. *Hor.* When they are thus far advanced, it is easy to conceive the rest: For improvements, I suppose, are made in good manners, as they are in all other arts and sciences. But to commence from savages, men, I believe, would make but a small progress in good manners the sirst three hundred years. The Romans, who had a much better beginning, had tteen.a nation above six centuries, and were almost matters of the world, before they could be said to be a polite people. What I am most astonished at, and which I am now convinced of, is, that the basis of all this machinery is pride. Another thing I wonder at, is, that you chose to speak of a nation that entered upon good manners before they had any notions of virtue or religion, which, I believe, there never was in the world. *Cleo.* Pardon me, Horatio; I have nowhere insinuated that they had none, but I had no reason to mention them. In the sirst place, you asked my opinion concerning the use of politeness in this world,, abstract from the contiderations of a future state: Secondly, the art of good manners has nothing to do with virtue or religion, tliough it seldom clashes with either. It is a icience that is ever built on the lame steady principle in our nature, whatever the age or the climate may be in which it is practised. *Hor.* How can any thing be said not to clash with virtue or religion, that has nothing to do with either, and consequently disclaims both? *Cleo.* This, I confess, seems to be a paradox; yet it is true. The doctrine of good manners teaches men to speak well os all virtues, but requires no more of them in any age or country, than the outward appearance of those in fashion. And as to facred matters, it is every where satissied with seeming conformity in outward worship; for all the religions in the universe are equally' agreeable to good manners, where they are national; and pray what opinion must we fay a teacher to be of, to whom all opinions are probably alike? All the precepts of good manners throughout the world have the fame tendency, and are no more than the various methods of making ourselves acceptable to others, with as little prejudice to ourselves as is possible: by which artisice we assist one another in the enjoyments of life, and resining upon pleasure; and every individual person is rendered more happy by it in the fruition of all the good things he can purchase, than he could have been without such behaviour. I mean happy, in the sense of the voluptuous. Let us look back on old Greece, the Roman empire, or the great eastern nations that flourished before them, and we shall sind, that luxury and politeness ever grew up together, and were never enjoyed asunder; that comfort and delight upon earth have always employed the wishes of the *beau monde;* and that, as their chief study and greatest solicitude, to outward appearance, have ever been directed to obtain happiness in this world, so what would become of them in the next, seems, to the naked eye, always to have been the least of their concern. *Hor.* I thank you for your lecture: you have satissied me in several things, which I had intended to ask: But you have said some others, that I must have time to consider; after which I am resolved to wait upon you again ; for I begin to believe, that, concerning the knowledge of ourselves, most books are either very defective or very deceitful. *Cleo.* There is not a more copious, nor a more faithful volume than human nature, to those who will diligently peruse it; and I sincerely believe, that I have discovered nothing to you, which, if you had thought of it with attention, you would not have found out yourself. But I shall never be better pleased with myself, than when I can contribute to any entertainment you shall think diverting. THE FOURTH DIALOGUE BETWEEN HORATIO AND CLEOMENES. CLEOMENES. JL Our servant. *Hor.* What say you now, Cleomenes; is it not this without ceremony? *Cleo.* You are very obliging. *Hor.* When they told me where you was, I would suffer nobody to tell you who it was that wanted you, or to come up with me. *Cleo.* This is friendly, indeed! *Hor.* You fee what a prosicient I am: In a little time you will teach me to lay aside all good manners. *Cleo.* You make a sine tutor of me. *Hor.* You will pardon me, I know: this study of yours is a very pretty place. *Cleo.* I like it, because the sun never enters it. *Hor.* A very pretty room! *Cleo.* Shall we sit down in it? It is the coolest room in the house. *Hor.* With all my heart. *Cleo.* I was in hopes to have seen you before now: you have taken a long time to consider. *Hor.* Just eight days? *Cleo.* Have you thought on the novelty I started? *Hor.* I have, and think it not void of probability; for that there are no innate ideas, and men come into the world without any knowledge at all, I am convinced of, and therefore it is evident to me, that all arts and sciences must once have had a beginning in somebody's brain, whatever obhvion that may now be lost in. I have thought twenty times iince I saw you last, on the origin of good manners, and what a pleasant scene it would be to a man who is tolerably well versed in the world, to see among a rude nation those sirst essays they made of concealing their pride from one another. *Cleo.* You fee by this, that it is chiefly the novelty of things that strikes, as well in begetting our aversion, as in gaining our approbation; and that we may look upon many indifferently, when they come to be familiar to us, though they were shocking when they were new. You are now diverting yourself with a truth, which eight days ago you would have given an hundred guineas not to have known. *Hor.* I begin to believe there is nothing so absurd, that it would appear to us to be such, if we hud been accustomed to it very young. *Cleo.* In a tolerable education, we are so industriously and so assiduously instructed, from our most early infancy, in the ceremonies of bowing, and pulling off hats, and other rules of behaviour, fhat even before we are men we hardly look upon a mannerly deportment as a thing acquired, or think conversation to be a science. Thousand things are called easy and natural in postures and motions, as well as speaking and writing, that have caused insinite pains to others as well as ourselves, and which we know to be the product of art. What awkward lumps have I known, which the dancingmaster has put limbs to! *Hor.* Yesterday morn-

ing as I fat musing by myself, an expression of yours which I did not so much reflect upon at sirst, when I heard it, came into my head, and made me smile. Speaking of the rudiments of good manners in an infant nation, when they once entered upon concealing their pride, you said, that improvements would bcmade every day, " till some of them grew impudent enough, not only to " deny the high value they had for themselves, but like" wife to pretend that they had greater value for others than " they had for themselves." *Q'eo.* it is certain, that this every where must have been the forerunner of flattery. *Hor.* When you talk of flattery and impudence, what do you think of the sirst man that had the face to tell hib equal, that he was his humble servant? *Cleo.* If that had been a new compliment, I should have wondered much more at the simplicity of the proud man that swallowed, than I would have done at the impudence of the knave that made it. *Hor.* It certainly once was new: which pray do you believe more ancient, pulling off the hat, or saying, your humble servant? *Cleo.* They are both of them Gothic and modern. *Hor.* I believe pulsing off the hat was sirst, it being the emblem of liberty. *Cleo.* I do not think so: for he who pulled of his hat the sirst time, could not have been understood, if saying your servant had not been practised: and to show respect, a man as well might have pulled off one of his shoes, as his hat; if saying, your servant, had not been an estabsished and well' known compliment. *Hor.* So he might, as you fay, and had a better authority for the sirst, than he could have for the latter. *Cleo.* And to this day, taking of the hat is a dumb show of a known civility in words: Mind now the power of custom, and imbibed notions. We both laugh at this Gothic absurdity, and are well assured, that it must have had its origin from the basest flattery; yet neither of us, walking with our hats on, could meet an acquaintance with whom we are not very familiar, without mowing this piece of civility; nay, it it would be a pain to us not to do it. But we have no reason to think, that the compliment of saying,

your servant, began among equals; but rather that, flatterers having given it to princes, it grew afterwards more common: for all those postures and flexions of body and limbs, had in all probability their rife from the adulation that was paid to conquerors and tyrants; who, having every body to fear, were always alarmed at the least shadow of opposition, and never better pleased than-with submissive and defenceless postures: and you fee, that they have all a tendency that way; they promise security, and are silent endeavours to ease and rid them, not only of their fears, but likewise every suspicion ol harm approaching them: such as lying prostrate on our faces, touching the ground with our heads, kneeling, bowing low, laying our hands upon our breasts, or holding them behind us, folding our arms together, and all the cringes that can be made to demonstrate that we neither indulge our eale, nor stand upon our guard. These are evident signs and con vincing proofs to a superior, that we have a mean opinion of ourselves in respect to him, that we are at his mercy, arid have no thought to resist, much less to attack him; and therefore it is highly probable, that saying, your servant, and pulling osf the hat, were at sirst demonstrations of obedience to those that claimed it. *Hor.* Which in tract of time became more familiar, and were made use of reciprocally in the way of civility. *Cleo.* I believe so; for as good manners increase, we see, that the highest compliments are made common, and new ones to superiors invented instead of them. *Hor.* So the word *grace* which hot long ago was a title, that none but our kings and queens were honoured with, is devolved upon archbishops and dukes. *Cleo.* It was the fame with *highness,* which is now given to the children, and even the grandchildren of kings. *Hor.* The dignity that is annexed to the signisication of the word *lord,* has been better preserved with us, than in most countries: in Spanish, Italian, high and low Dutch, it is prostituted to almost every body. *Cleo.* It has had better fate in France; where likewise the *vtox&Jire* has lost nothing of its majesty, and is

only used to the monarch: whereas, with us, it is a compliment of address, that may be made to a cobler, as well as to a king. *Hor.* Whatever alterations may be made in the sense of words, by time; yet, as the world grows more polished, flattery becomes less barefaced, and the design of it upon man's pride is better disguised than it was formerly. To praise a man to his face, was very common among the ancients: considering humility to be a virtue particularly required of Christians, I have often wondered how the fathers of the church could suffer those acclamations and applauses, that were made to them whilst they were preaching; and which, though some of them spoke against them, many of them appear to have been extremely fond of. *Cleo.* Human nature is always the fame; where men exert themselves to the utmost, and take uncommon pains that spend and waste the spirits, those applauses are very reviving: the fathers who spoke against them, spoke chiefly against the abuse of them. *Hor.* It must have been very odd to hear people bawling out, as often the greatest part of an audience did, *Scphas, divinitus, nun poteji melius, mirabiliter, acriter, ingeniofe:* thev
B b told the preachers likewise that they were orthodox, and sometimes called them, *apqllolus decimus tertius. Cleo.* These words at the end of a period might have passed, but the repetitions of them were often so loud and so ge-' neral, and the noise they made with their hands and feet, so disturbing in and out of season, that they could not hear a quarter of the the sermon; yet several fathers owned that it was highly delightful, and soothing human frailty.
Hor. The behaviour at churches is more decent, as it is now, *Cleo.* Since paganism has been quite extinct in the old western world, the zeal of Christians is much diminished from what it was, when they had many opposers: the want of fervency had a great hand in abolishing that fashion. *Hor.* But whether it was the fastrion or not, it must always have been shocking. *Cleo.* Do you think, that the repeated acclamations, the clapping, stamping, and the most extravagant tokens of applause, that are now used at our several theatres, were ever shocking to a favourite actor; or that the huzzas of the mob, or the hideous mouts of soldiers, were ever shocking to persons of the highest distinction, to whose honour they were made? *Hor.* I have known princes that were very much tired with them. *Cleo.* When they had too much of them; but never at sirst. In working a machine, we ought to have regard to the strength of its frame: limited creatures are not susceptible of insinite delight; therefore we see, that a pleasure protracted beyond its due bounds becomes a pain: but where the custom of the country is not broken in upon, no noise, that is palpably made in our praise, and which we may hear.with decency, can ever be ungrateful, if it do not outlast a reasonable time; but there is no cordial so sovereign, that it may not become osfensive, by being taken to excess. *Hor.* And the sweeter and more delicious liquors are, the sooner they become fulsome, and the less sit they are to sit by. *Cleo.* Your simile is not amiss; and the fame acclamations that are ravishing to a man at sirst, and perhaps continue to give him an unspeakable delight for eight or nine minutes, may become more moderately pleasing, indisferent, cloying, troublesome, and even so oflensive as to create pain, all i» less than three hours, if they were to continue so long without intermission *Hor.* There must be great witchcraft in sounds, that they sliould have such different effects upon us, as we often fee they have. *Cleo.* The pleasure we receive from acclamations, is not in the hearing; but proceeds from the opinion we form of the cause that produces those sounds, the approbation of others. At the theatres all over Italy you have heard, that, when the whole audience demands silence and attention, which there is an established mark of benevolence and applause, the noise they make comes very near, and is hardly to be distinguimed from our hissing, which with us is the plainest token of dislike and contempt: and without doubt the catcalls to affront Faustina were far more agreeable to Cozzcni, than the most artful sounds she ever heard from her triumphant rival. *Hor.* That was abominable! *Cleo.* The Turks show their respects to their sovereigns by a profound silence, which is strictly kept throughout the seraglio, and still more religiously observed the nearer you come to the Sultan's apartment. *Hor.* This latter is certainly the politer way of gratifying one's pride. *Cleo.* All that depends upon mode and custom. *Hor.* But the offerings that are made to a man's pride in silence, may be enjoyed without the loss of his hearing, which the other cannot. *Cleo.* That is a trifle, in the gratisication of that passion: we never enjoy higher pleasure, from the appetite we would indulge, than when we feel nothing from any other. *Hor.* But silence expresses greater homage, and deeper veneration, than noise. *Cleo.* It is good to sooth the pride of a drone; but an active man loves to have that passion roused, and as it were kept awake, whilst it is gratisied; and approbation from noise is more unquestionable than the other: however, I will not determine between them; nmch may be laid on both sides. The Greeks and Romans used sounds, to llir up men to noble actions, with great success; and the silerice observed among the Ottomans has kept them very well in the slavish submission which their sovereigns require of them: perhaps the one does better where absolute power is lodged in one person, and the other where there is some show of liberty. Both are proper tools to flatter the pride of man, when they are understood and made use of as such. I have known a very brave man used to the shouts of war, and highly delighted with loud applause, be very angry with his butler, for making a little rattling with his plates. *Hor.* An old aunt of mine the other day turned away a very clever fellow, for not walking upon his toes; and I must own myself, that the stamping of footmen, and all unmannerly loudnefs of servants, are very offensive to me; though I never entered into the reason of it before now. In our last conversation, when you described the symptoms of self-liking, and what the behaviour would be of an uncivilized

man, you named laughing: I know it is one *of* the characteristics of our species; pray do you take that to be likewise the result of pride? *Cleo.* Hobbes is of that opinion, and in most instances it might be derived from thence; but there are some phenomena not to be explained by that hypothesis; therefore I would choose to say, that laughter is a mechanical motion, which we are naturally thrown into when we are unaccountably pleased. When our pride is feelingly gratised; when we hear or (ee any thing which we admire or approve of; or when we are indulging any other passion or appetite, and the reason why we are pleased seems, to be just and worthy, we are then far from laughing: but when things or actions are odd and out of the way, and happen to please us when we can give no just reason why they mould do so, it is then, generally speaking, that they make us laugh. *Hor.* I would rather side wth what you said was Hobbes's opinion: for the things we commonly laugh at are such as are some way or other mortifying, unbecoming, or prejudicial to others. *Ceo.* But what will you fay to tickling, which will make an infant laugh that is deaf and blind? *Hor.* Can you account for that by your system? *CLo.* iSiot to my satisfaction; but I will tell you what might be. said for it. We know by experience, that the s.noother, the loiter, and the more sensible the skin is, the more tickliih prisons are, generally speaking: we know likewise, that things rough, sharp, and haid, when they touch the skin, are dilpleasing to us, even before they give pain; and that, on the contrary, every thing applied to the ikin that is soft and smooth, and not otherwiie ostensive, is de. lightful. It is possible that gentle touches being impressed on several nervous silaments at once, every one of them producing a pleasing sensation, may create that confused pleasure which is the occasion of laughter. *Hor.* But how came you to think of mechanic motion, in the pleasure of a free agent? *Cleo.* Whatever free agency we may pretend to in the forming of ideas, the effect of them upon the body is independent of the will. Nothing is more direct-

ly opposite to laughing than frowning: the one draws wrinkles on the forehead, knits the brows, and keeps the mouth shut: the other docs quite the reverse; *exporrigere frontem,* you know, is a Latin phrase for being merry. In sighing, the muscles of the belly and breast are pulled inward, and the diaphragm is pulled upward more than ordinary; and we seem to endeavour, though in vain, to squeeze and compress the heart, whilst we draw in our breath in a forcible manner; and when, in that squeezing posture, we have taken in as much air as we can contain, we throw it out with the fame violence we sucked it in with, and at the same time give a sudden relaxation to all the muscles we employed before. Nature certainly designed this for something in the labour sot self-preservation which she forces upon us. How mechanically do all creatures that can aiake any sound, cry out, and complain in great afflictions, as well as pain and imminent danger! In great torments, the efforts of nature are so violent that way, that, to disappoint her, and prevent the discovery of what we feel by sounds, and which she bids us make, we are forced to draw our mouth into a purse, or else suck in our breath, bite our lips, or squeeze them close together, and use the most effectual means to hinder the air from coming out. In grief we sigh, in mirth we laugh: in the latter little stress is laid upon the respiration, and this is performed with less regularity than it is at any other time; all the muscles without, and every thing within feel loose, and seem to have no other motion than what is communicated to them by the convulsive shakes os-laughter. *Hor.* I have seen people laugh till they lost all their strength. *Cleo* How much is all this the reverse of what we observe in sighing! When pain or depth of woe make us cry out, the mouth is drawn round, or at least into an oval; the lips are thrusted forward without touching each other, and the tongue is pulled in, which is the reason that all nations, when they exclaim, cry, Oh! *Hor.* Why pray! *Ck'o.* Because whilst the mouth, lips, and tongue, remain in those postures, they

can found no other vowel, and no consonant at all. In laughing, the lips are pulled back, and strained to draw the mouth in its fullest length. *Hor.* I would not have you lay a great stress upon that, for it is the fame in weeping, which is an undoubted sign of sorrow. *Cko.* In great afflictions, where the heart is oppressed, and anxieties which we endeavour to resist, few people can weep; bnt when they do, it removes the oppression, and sensibly relieves them: for then their resistance is gone; and weeping in distress is not so much a sign of sorrow as it is an indication that we can bear our sorrow no longer; and therefore it is counted uumanly to weep, because it seems to give up our strength, and is a kind of yielding to our grief. But the action of weeping itself is not more peculiar to grief than it is to joy in adult people; and there are men who show great fortitude in assilictions, and bear the greatest misfortunes with dry eyes, that will cry heartily at a moving scene in a play. Some are easily wrought upon by one thing, others are sooner affected with another; but whatever touches us so forcibly, as to overwhelm the mind, prompts us to weep, and is the mechanical cause of tears; and therefore, besides grief, joy, and pity, there are other things no way relating to ourtelves, that may have this effect upon us; such as the relations of surprising events and sudden turns of Providence in behalf of merit; instances of heroism, of generosity;-in love, in friendship in an enemy; or the hearing or reading of noble thoughts and sentiments of humanity; more especially if these things are conveyed to us suddenly, in an agreeable manner, and unlooked for, as well as lively expressions. We shall observe, likewise, that none are more subject to this siaiity of (bedding tears on such foreign accounts, than persons of ingenuity and quick apprehension; and those among them that are most benevolent, generous, and open-hearted; whereas, the dull and stupid, the cruel, selsish.and designing, are very seldom troubled with it. Weeping, therefore, in earnest, is always a sure and involuntary demonstration that something strikes and overcomes the mind, whatever that be wli-icli asects it. We sind likewise, that outward violence, as sharp winds and smoke, the effluvia of onions, and other volatile-salts, &c. have the fame effect upon the external sibres of the lachry-mal ducts and glands that are exposed, which the sudden swelling and pressure of the spirits has upon those within. The Divine Wisdom is in nothing more con-spicuous than in the insinite variety of living creatures of different construc-tion ; every part of them being contrived with stupendous skill, and sitted with the utmost accuracy for the different purposes they were designed for. The human body, above all, is a most aston-ishing master piece of art: the anatomist may have a perfect knowledge of all the bones and their ligaments, the muscles and their tendons, and be able to dis-sect every nerve and every membrane with great exactness; the naturalist, like-wise, may dive a great way into the in-ward economy, and different symptoms of health and sickness: they may all ap-prove of, and admire the curious ma-chine; but no man can have a tolerable idea of the contrivance, the art, and the beauty of the workmanship itself, even in those things he can fee, without being likewise versed in geometry and me-chanics. *Hor.* How long is it;.go that mathematics were brought into physic? that art, I have heard, is brought to great certainty by them. *Cleo.* What you speak of is quite another thing. Math-ematics never had, nor ever can have, any thing to do with physic, if you mean by it the art of curing the sick. The structure and motions of the body, may perhaps be mechanically accounted for, and all fluids are under the laws of hy-drostatics; but we can have no help from any part of the mechanics in the dis-covery of things, insinitely remote from sight, and entirely unknown as to their shapes and bulks. Physicians, with the rest of mankind, are wholly ignorant of the sirst principles and constituent parts of things, in which all the virtues and properties of them consist; and this, as well of the blood and other juices of the body, as the simples, and consequent-ly all the medicines they make use of.

There is no art that has less certainty than theirs, and the most valuable knowledge in it arises from observation, and is such, as a man of parts and ap-plication, who has sitted himself for that study, can only be possessed of aster a long and judicious experience. But the pretence to mathematics, or the useful-ness of it in the cure of diseases, is a cheat, and as arrant a piece of quackery as a stage and a Merry-Andrew. *Hor.* B ut since there is so much kill displayed in the bone9, muscles, and grosser parts, is it not reasonable to think, that there is no less art bellowed on those that are beyond the reach os our senses? *Cleo.* I nowise doubt it: Microscopes have opened a new world to us, and I am far from thinking, that nature should leave off her work where we can trace her no further. I am persuaded that our thoughts, and the affections of the mind, have a more certain and more mechan-ical influence upon several parts of the body than has been hitherto or, in all human probability, ever will be discov-ered. The visible effect they have on the eyes and muscles of the face, must show the least attentive the reason I have for this assertion. When in mcns company we are upon our guard, and would pre-serve our dignity, the lips are shut and the jaws meet; the muscles of the mouth are gently braced, and the rest all over the face are kept sirmly in their places: turn away from theseinto another room, where you meet with a sine young lady that is affable and easy; immediately, before you think on it, your counte-nance will be strangely altered; and without being conscious of having done any thing to your face, you will have quite another look; and every body that has observed you, will discover in it more sweetness and less severity than you had the moment before. When we suffer the lower jaw to sink down, the mouth opens a little: if in this posture we look straight before us, without six-ing our eyes on any thing, we may im-itate the countenance of a natural; by dropping, as it were, our features, and laying no stress on any muscle of the face. Infants, before they have learned to swallow their spittle, generally keep

their mouths open, and are always dri-velling: in them, before they show any underllanding, and whilst it is yet very confused, the muscles of the face are, as it were, relaxed, the lower jaw falls down, and the sibres of the lips are un-braced; at least, these phenomena we observe in them, during that time, moje often than we do afterwards. In extreme old age, when people begin to doat, those symptoms return; and in most id-iots they continue to be observed, as long as they live: Hence it is that we fay, that a man wants a slabbering-bib, when he behaves very sillily, or talks like a natural fool. When we reflect on all this, on the one hand, and consider on the other, that none are less prone to anger than idiots, and no creatures are less af-fected with pride, I would atk, whether there is not some degree of self-liking, that mechanically influences, and seems to assist us in the decent wearing of our faces. *Hor.* I cannot resolve you; what I know very well is, that by these conjec-tures on the mechanism of man, I sind my understanding very little informed: I wonder how we came upon the sub-ject. *Cleo.* You inquired into the origin of risibility, which nobody can give an account of, with any certainty; and in such cases every body is at liberty to make guelsos. so they draw no conclu-sions from them to the prejudice of any thing better established. But the chief design I had in giving you these indi-gested thoughts, was to hint to you, how really mysterious the works of nature are; I mean, how replete they are every where, with a power glaringly conspic-uous, and yet incomprehensible beyond all human reach; in order to demon-strate, that more useful knowledge may be acquired from unwearied observa-tion, judicious experience, and arguing from facts *a posteriori,* than from the haughty attempts of entering into sirst causes, and reasoning *a priori.* I do not believe there is a man in the world of that sagacity, if he was wholly unac-quainted with the nature of a spring-watch, that he would ever sind out by dint of penetration the cause of its mo-tion, if he was never to fee the inside: but every middling capacity may be certain, by feeing only the outside, that its pointing at the hour, and keeping to time, proceed from the exactness of some curious workmanship that is hid; and that the motion of the hands, what number of resorts soever it is communicated by, is originally owing to something else that sirst moves within. In the fame manner we are sure, that as the effects of thought upon the body are palpable, several motions are produced by it, by contact, and consequently mechanically: but the parts, the instruments which that operation is performed with, are so immensely far remote from our senses, and the swiftness of the action is so prodigious, that it insinitely surpasses our capacity to trace them. *Hor.* But is not thinking the business of the soul? What has mechanism to do with that? *Cleo.* The soul, whilst in the body, cannot be said to think, otherwise than an architect is said to build a house, where the carpenters, bricklayers, &-C do the work, which he chalks out and superintends. *Hor.* Which part of the brain do you think the soul to be more immediately lodged in; or do you take it to be diffused through the whole? *Cleo.* I know nothing of it more than what I have told you already. *Hor.* I plainly feel that this operation of thinking is a labour, or at least something that is transacting in my head, and not in my leg nor my arm: what inlight or real knowledge have we from anatomy concerning it? *Cleo.* None at all *a priori:* the most consummate anatomist knows no more of it than a butcher's apprentice. We may admire the curious duplicate of coats, and close embroidery of veins and arteries that environ the brain: but when directing it we have viewed the several pairs of nerves, with their origin, and taken notice of some glands of various fliapes and sizes, which differing from the brain in substance, could not but rush in view; when these, I say, have been taken notice of, and distinguimed by different names, some of them not very pertinent, and less polite, the best naturalist must acknowledge, that even of these large visible parts there are but few, the nerves and blood-vessels excepted, at the use of

which he can give any tolerable guesses: but as to the mysterious structure of the brain itself, and the more abstruse economy of it, that he knows nothing; but that the whole seems to be a medullary substance, compactly treasured up in insinite millions of imperceptible cells, that, disposed in an unconceivable order, are clustered together in a perplexing variety of folds and windings. He will add, perhaps, that it is reasonable to think this to be the capacious exchequer of human knowledge, in which the faithful lenses depoiite the vast treasure of images, constantly, as through their organs they receive them; that it is the ossice in which the spirits are separated from the blood, and afterwards sublimed and volatilized into particles hardly corporeal; and that the most minute of these are always, either searching for, or variously disposing the images retained, and shooting through the insinite meanders of that wonderful substance, employ themselves, without ceasing, in that inexplicable performance, the contemplation of which sills the most exalted genius with amazement. *Hor.* These are very airy conjectures; but nothing of all this can be proved: The smallness of the parts, you will fay, is the reason; but if greater improvements were made in optic glasses, and microscopes could be invented that magnisied objects three or four millions of times more than they do now, then certainly those minute particles, so immensely remote from the senses you speak of, might be observed, if that which does the work is corporeal at all. *Cleo.* That such improvements are impossible, is demonstrable; but if it was not, even then we could have little help from anatomy. The brain of an animal cannot be looked and searched into whilst it is alive. Should you take the main spring out of a watch, and leave the barrel that contained it standing empty, it would be impossible to sind out what it had been that made it exert itself, whilst it showed the time. We might examine all the wheels, and every other part belonging either to the movement or the motion, and, perhaps, sind out the use of them, in relation to the

turning of the hands; but the sirst cause of this labour would remain a mystery for ever. *Hor.* The main spring in us is the soul, which is immaterial and immortal: but what is that to other creatures that have a brain like ours, and no such immortal substance distinct from body? Do not you believe that dogs and horses think? *Cleo.* I believe they do, though in a degree of perfection far inferior to us. , *Hor.* What is it that superintends thought in them? where must we look for it? which is the main spring? *Cko.* I can answer you no otherwise, than life. *Hor.* What is life? *Cleo.* Every body understands the meaning of the word, though, perhaps, nobody knows the principle of life, that part which gives motion to all the rest. *Hor.* Where men are certain that the truth of a thing is not to be known, they will always dilfer, and endeavour to impose upon one another. *Cleo.* Whilst there are fools and knaves, they will; but I have not imposed upon you: what I said of the labour of the brain, I told you, was a conjecture, which I recommend no farther to you than you shall think it probable. You ought to expect no demonstration of a thing, that from its nature can admit of hone. When the breath is gone, and the circulation-ceased, the inside of an animal is vastly different from what it was whilst the lungs played, and the blood and juices were in full motion through every part of it. You have seen those engines that raise water by the help of fire; the steam you know, is that which forces it up; it is as impossible to fee the volatile particles that perform the labour of the brain, when the creature is dead, as in the engine it would be to fee the steam (which yet does all the work), when the sire is out and the water cold. Yet if this engine was shown to a man when it was not at work, and it was explained to him, which way it raised the water, it would be a strange incredulity, or great dullness of apprehension, not to believe it; if he knew perfectly well, that by heat, liquids may be rarisied into vapour. *Hor.* But do not you think there is a difference in fouls; and are they all equally good or equally bad? *Cleo.* We have some tolerable ideas of matter and motion; or, at least, of what we mean by them, and therefore we may form ideas of things corporeal, though they are beyond the reach of our fenses; and we can conceive any portion of matter a thousand trmes less than our eyes, even by the help of tbe best microscopes, are able to fee it: but the foul is altogether incomprehensible, and we can determine but little about it, that is not revealed to us. 1 believe that the, difference of capacities in men, depends upon, and is entirely owing to the difference there is between them, either in the fabric itself, that is, the greater or lesser exactness in the composure of their frame, or else in the use that is made of it. The brain of a child, newly born, is *charte blanche;* and, as you have hinted very justly, we have no ideas, which we are not obliged for to our fenses. 1 make no question, but that in this rummaging of the spirits through the brain, in hunting after, joining, separating, changing, and compounding of ideas with inconceivable swiftness, under the superintendency of the soul, the action of thinking consists. The best thing, therefore, we can do to infants after the sirst month, besides feeding and keeping them from harm, is *to* make them take in ideas, beginning by the two most useful senses, the sight and hearing; and dispose them to set about this labour of the brain, and by our example encourage them to imitate us in thinking; which,on their side, is very poorly performed at sirst. Therefore the more an infant in health is talked to and jumbled about, the better it is for it, at least, for the sirst two years; "and for its attendance in this early education, to the wisest matron in the world, I would prefer an active young wench, whose tongue never stands

Jtill, that should run about, and never cease diverting and playing with it whilst it was awake; and where people can afford it, two or three of them, to relieve one another when they are tired, are better than one.

Hor. Then you think children reap great benessit from the nonsensical chat of nurses? *Cleo.* It is of inestimable use to them, and teaches them to think, as well

as speak, much sooner and better, than with equal aptitude of parts they would do without. The business is to make, them exert those faculties, and keep infants continually employed about them; for the time which is lost then, is never to be retrieved. *Hor.* Yet we seldom remember any thing of what we saw or heard, before we were two years old: then what would be lost, if children should not hear all that impertinence? *Cleo.* As iron is to be hammered whilst it is hot and ductile, so children are to be taught when they are young: as the flesh and every tube and membrane about them, are then tenderer, and will yield sooner to flight imprcssions, than afterwards; so many of their bones are but cartilages, and the brain itself is much softer, and in a manner fluid. This is the reason, that it cannot so well retain the'images it receives, as it does afterwards, when the substance of it comes to be of a better consistence. But as the sirst images are lost, so they are continually succeeded by new ones; and the brain at sirst serves as a flate to cypher, or a sampler to work upon. What infants should chiefly learn, is the performance itself, the exercise of thinking, and to contract a habit of disposing, and with ease and agility managing the images retained, to the purpose intended; which Is never attained better than whilst the matter is yielding, and the organs are most flexible and supple. So they but exercise themselves in thinking and speaking, it is no matter what they think on, or what they fay, that is inoffensive. In sprightly infants, we soon fee by their eyes the efforts they are making to imitate us, before they are able; and that they try at this exercise of the brain, and make essays to think, as well as they do to hammer out words, we may know from the incoherence of their actions, and the strange absurdities they utter: but as there are more degrees of thinking well, than there are of speaking plain, the sirst is of the greatest consequence. *Hor.* 1 wonder you should talk of teaching, and lay so great a stress on a thing that comes so naturally to us, as thinking: no action is performed with greater velocity hy every body: as quick

as thought, is a proverb, and in less than a moment a stupid peasant may remove his ideas from London to Japan, as easily as the greatest wit. *Cleo.* Yet there is nothing, in which men differ so immensely from one another, as they do in the exercise of this faculty: the differences between them in height, bulk, strength, and beauty, are trifling in comparison to that which I speak of; and there is nothing in the world more valuable, or more plainly perceptible in persons, than a happy dexterity of thinking. Two men may have equal knowledge, and yet the one st.all speak as well ofthand, as the other can after two hour; study. *Hor.* I take it for granted, that no man would study two hours for a speech, if he knew how to make it in less; and therefore I cannot fee what reason you have to suppose two such persons to be of equal knowledge. *Cleo.* There is a double meaning in the word *knowing,* which you seem not to attend to. There is a great difference between knowing a violin when you fee it, and knowing how to play upon it. The knowledge I speak ot is of the sirst fort; and if you consider it in that fense, you must be of my opinion; for no study can fetch any thing out of the brain that is not there. Suppose you conceive a short epistle in three minutes, which another, who can make letters and join them together as fast as yourself, is yet an hour about, though both of you write the lame thing, it is plain to me, that the flow person knows as much as you do; at least it dees not appear that he knows less. He has received the fame images, but he cannot come at them, or at least not dispose them in that order, so soon as yourself. When we fee two exercises of equal goodness, either in prole or verse, if the one is made *ex tempore,* and we are sure of it, and the other has cost two days labour, the author of the sirst isa person of siner natural pa.ts than the other, though their knowledge, for ought we know, is the fame. You fee, then, the difference between knowledge, as it signisies the treasure of images received, and knowledge, or rather skill, to sind out those images when, we want them, and work them readily to our purpose, *Hor.* When we know a thing, and cannot readily think of it, or bring it to mind, I thought that was the fault of the memory. *Cleo.* So it may be in part: but there are men of prodigious reading, that have likewise great memories, who judge ill, and seldom say any thing *a propos,* or say it when it is too late. Among the *belluones Ubrorum,* the cormorants of books, there are wretched reasoners, that have canine appetites, and. no digestion. What numbers of learned fools do we not meet with in large libraries; from whose works it is evident, that knowledge must have lain in their heads, as furniture at an upholder's; and the treasure of the brain was a burden to them instead of an ornament! All this proceeds from a defect in the faculty of thinking; an unskilfulness, and want of aptitude in managing, to the best advantage, the ideas we have received. We fee others, on the contrary, thut have very sine fense, and no literature at all. The generality of women are quicker of invention, and more ready at repartee, than the men, with equal helps of education; and it is surprising to see, what a considerable sigure some of them make in conversation, when we consider the small opportunities they have had of acquiring knowledge. *Hor.* But sound judgment is a great rarity among them. *Cleo.* Only for want of practice, application, and assiduity. Thinking on abstruse matters, is not their province in life; and as the stations they are commonly placed in sind them other employment; but there is no labour of the brain which women are not as capable of performing, at least as well as the men, with the fame assistance, if they set about, and persevere in it: sound judgment is no more than the result of that labour: he that uses himself to take things to pieces, to compare them together, to consider them abstractly and impartially; that is, he who of two propositions he is to examine seems not to care which is trise; he that lays the whole stress of his mind on every part alike, and puts the fame thing in all the views it can be seen in: he, I say, that employs himself most often in this exercise, is most likely *cœteris*

paribus to acquire what we call a found judgment. The workmanship in the make of women seems to be more elegant, and better 'sinished: the features are more delicate, the voice is sweeter, the whole outside of them is more curiously wove, than they are in men; and the difference in the skin between theirs and ours is the fame, as there is between sine cloth and coarse. There is no reason to imagine, that nature should have been more neglectful of t-hem out of sight, than slie has where we can trace her; and not have taken the same care of them in the formation, of the bruin, as lo the nicety of the structure, and superior accuracy in the fabric, which is lo visible in the rest of their frame. *Hor.* Beauty is their attribute, as strength is ours. *Cleo.* How minute soever thole particles of the brain are, that contain the several images, and are assisting in the operation of thinking, there must be a difference in the justness, the symmetry, and exactness of them between one person and another, as well as there is in the grosser parts: what the women excel us in, then, is the goodness of the instrument, either in the harmony or pliableness of the organs, which must be very material in the art of thinking, and is the only thing that deserves the name of natural parts, since the aptitude 1 have spoke of, depending upon exercise, is notoriously acquired. *Hor.* As the workmanship in the brain is rather more curious in women than it is in men, so, in sheep and oxen, dogs and horses, I suppose it is insinitely coarser. *Lteo.* We have no reason to think otherwise. *Hjr.* But aiter all, that self, that part' of us that wills and willies, that chooses one thing rather than another, must be incorporeal: For if it is matter, it must either be one single p=.ricle, whch 1 can almost seel it is not, or a combination oi many, which is more tlian inconceivable. *Uto.* 1 do not deny what you fay; and that the principle of thought and action is inexplicable in all creatures I have hinted already: But its being incorporeal does not mend the matter, as to the difsiculty of explaining or conceiving it. That there must be a mutual contact between this principle, whatever

it is, and the body itself, is what we are certain of *a posteriori;* and a reciprocal action upon each other, between an immaterial lubllance and matter, is as incomprehensible to human capacity, as that thought should he the result of matier and motion. *Hor.* Though many other animals seem to be endued with thought, there is no creature we are acquainted with, besides man, that shows or seems to feel a confeiouinefs of his thinking. *Cleo.* It is not easy to determine what-instincts, properties, or capacities other creatures are either poflefled or destitute of, when those qualisications fall not under our fenses: But it is highly probable, that the principal and most necessary parts of the machine are less elaborate in animals, that attain to all the perfection they are capable of in three, four, sive, or six years at furthest, than they are in a creature that hardly comes to maturity, its full growth and strength in sive and twenty. The consciousness of a man of sifty, that he is the fame man that did such a thing at twenty, and was once the boy that had such and such masters, depends wholly upon the memory, 'and can never be traced to the bottom: I mean, that no man remembers any thing of himself, or what was transacted before he was two years old, when he was but a novice in the art of thinking, and the brain was not yet of a due consistence to retain long the images it received: But this remembrance, how far soever it may reach, gives us no greater surety of ourselves, than we mould have of another that had been brought up with us, and never above a week or a month out of sight. A mother, when her son is thirty years old, has more reason to know that he is the fame whom she brought into the world than himself; and such a one, who daily minds her son, and remembers the alterations of his features from time to time, is more certain of him that he was not changed in the cradle, than me can be of herself.. So that all we can know of this consciousness, is, that it consists in, or is the result of the running and rummaging of the spirits through all the mazes of the brain, and their looking there for facts concerning ourselves: He that has lost his memory, though otherwise in perfect health, cannot think better than a fool, and is no more conscious that he is the fame he was a-year ago, than he is of a man whom he has known but a fortnight. There are several degrees of losing our memory; but he who has entirely lost it becomes, *ipjofadlo,* an idiot. *Hor.* I am conscious of having been the occasion of ouf rambling a great way from the subject we were upon, but I do not repent of it: What you have said of the economy of the brain, and the mechanical influence of thought upon the grosser parts, is a noble theme for contemplation on the insinite unutterable wisdom with which the various instincts are so visibly planted in all animals, to sit them for the respective purposes they were designed for; and every appetite is so wonderfully interwove with the very substance of their frame. Nothing could be more seasonable, a/ter you had showed me the origin of politeness, and in the management of ielf-hking, set forth the excellency of our specie?

Cc beyond all other animals so conspicuously in the superlative docility and indefatigable industry, by which all multitudes are capable of drawing innumerable benesits, as well for the ease and comfort, as the welfare and safety of congregate bodies, from a most stubborn and an unconquerable passion, which, in its nature, seems to be destructive to soda bleness artd society, and never fails, in untaught men, to render thens insufferable to one another.

Cleo. By the same method of reasoning from facts *a posteriori,* that has laid open to us the nature and usefulness of self-liking, all the rest of the passions may easily be accounted for, and become intelligible. It is evident, that the necessaries of life stand not every where ready dished up before all creatures; therefore they have instincts that prompt them to look out for those necessaries, and teach them how to come at them. The zeal and alacrity to gratify their appetites, is always proportioned to the strength, and the degree of force with which those instincts work upon every creature: But, considering the dis-

position of things upon earth, and the multiplicity of animals that have all their own wants to supply, it must be obvious, that these attempts of creatures, to obey the different calls of nature, will be often opposed and frustrated, and that, in many animals, they would seldom meet with success, if every individual was not endued with a passion, that, summoning all his strength, inspired him with a transporting eagerness to overcome the obstacles that hinder him in his great work of self-preservation. The paslion I describe is called anger. How a creature postessed of this passion and self-liking, when he sees others enjoy what he wants, should be affected with envy, can likewise be no mystery. After labour, the most savage, and the most industrious creature seeks rest: Hence we learn, that all of them are furnished, more or less, with a love of ease: Exerting their strength tires them; and the loss of spirits, experience teaches us, is best repaired by food and sleep. We fee that creatures, who, in their way of living, must meet with the greatest opposition, have the greatest mare of anger, and are bom with offensive arms. If this anger was to employ a creature always, without consideration of the danger he exposed himseli to, he would soon be destroyed: For this reason, they are all endued with fear; and the lion himself turns tail, it the hunters are armed, and too numerous.-From what we observe in the behaviour of brutes, we have reason to think. that among the more perfect animals, those of the same species have a capacity, on many occasions, to make their wants known to one another; and we are sure of several, not only that they understand one another, but likewise that they may be made to understand us. In comparing our species with that of other animals, when we coniider the make of man, and the qualisications that are obvious in him, his superior capacity in the faculties of thinking and reflecting beyond other creatures, his being capable of learning to speak, and the usefulness of his hands and singers, there is no room to doubt, that he is more sit for society than any other an-

imal we know. *Hor.* Since you wholly reject my Lord Shaftsbury's system, I wish you would give me your opinion at large concerning society, and the sociableness of man; and I will hearken to you with great attention. *Cleo.* The cause of sociableness in man, that is, his sitness for society, is no such abstruse matter: A person of middling capacity, that has some experience, and a tolerable knowledge of human nature, may soon sind it out, if his desire of knowing the truth be sincere, and he will look for it without prepossession; but most people that have treated on this subject, had a turn to serve, and a cause in view, which they were resolved to maintain. It is very unworthy of a philosopher to say, as Hobbes did, that man is born unsit for society, and allege no better reason for it, than the incapacity that infants come into the world with; but some of his adversaries have as far overihot the mark, when they asserted, that every thing which man can attain to, ought to be esteemed as a cause of his sitness for society. *Hor.* But is there in the mind of man a natural affection, that prompts him to love his species beyond what other animals have for theirs; or, are we born with hatred and aversion, that makes us wolves and bears to one another? *Cleo.* I believe neither. From what appears to us in human affairs, and the works of nature, we have more reason to imagine, that the desire, as well as aptness of man to associate, do not proceed from his love to others, than we have to believe that a mutual affection of the planets to one another, superior to what they feel to stars more remote, is not the true cause why they keep always moving together in the fame solar system. *Hor.* You do not believe that the stars have any love for one another, I am sure: Then why more reason? *Cleo.* Because there are no phenomena plainly to contradict this love of the planets; and we meet with thousands every day to convince us, that man centres every thing in himself, and neither loves nor hates, but for his own lake. Every individual is a little world by itself, and all creatures, as far as their understanding and abilities will let them, endeavour to make that self happy: This, in all'of them, is the continual labour, and seems td be the whole delign of life. Ilcr.ce it follows, that in the choice of things, men must be determined by the perception they have of happiness; and no person can commit, or set about an action, which, at that then present time, seems not to be the bell to him. *Hor.* What will you then fay to, *video inelhra proboqur, deteriora sequor? Cleo.* That only shows the turpitude of our inclinations. But men may fay what they please: Every motion in a free agent, which he does not approve of, is either convulsive, or it is not his; I speak of those that are subject to the will. When two things are left to a person's choice, it is a demonstration that he thinks that most eligible which he chooses, how contradictory, impertinent, or pernicious soever his reason for choosing it may be: Without this, ihere could be no voluntary suicide; and it would be injustice to punisti men for their crimes. *Hor.* I believe every body endeavours to be pleased; but it is inconceivable that creatures osthe same species should differ so much from one another, as men do in their notions ct pleasure; and that some of them should take delight in what is the greatest aversion to others:-All aim at happiness; but the question is, Where is it to be found? *Cleo.* It is with complete felicity in this world, as it is with the philosopher's stone: Both have been sought after many different ways, by wife men as well as fools, though neither of them has been obtained hitherto: But in searching aster cither, diligent inquirers have often stumbled by chance on useful discoveries of things they did not look for, and which human sagacity, labouring with design *d priori,* never would have detected. Multitudes of our species may, in any habitable part of the globe, assist one another in a common defence, and be raised into a politic body, in which men mall live comfortably together for many ccuturies, without being acquainted with a thousand things, that if known, would every one of them be instrumental to render the happiness of the public move complete,

according to the common notions men have of happiness. In one part of the world, we have found great and flourishing nations that knew nothing of ships; and in others, trassic by sea had been in use above two thousand years, and navigation had received innumerable improvements, before they knew how to fail by the help of the loadstone: It would be ridiculous to allege this piece of knowledge, either as a reason why man sirst chose to go to sea, or as an argument to prove his natural capacity for maritime asfairs. To raise a garden, it is necessary that we should have a soil and a climate sit for that purpose. When we have these, we want nothing besides patience, but the feeds of vegetables and proper culture. Fine walks and canals, statues, summer-houses, fountains, and cascades, are great improvements on the delights of nature; but they are not essential to the existence of a garden. All nations must have hud mean beginnings; and it is in those, the infancy of them, that the sociableness of man is as conspicuous as it can be ever after. Man is called a sociable creature chiesly for two reasons: First, because it is commonly imagined that lie is naturally more fond and desirous of society, than any other creature. Secondly, because it is manifest, that associating in men turns to better account than it possibly could do in other animals, if they were to attempt it. *Hor.* But why do you fay of the sirst, that it is commonly imagined; is it not true then? *Ck'o.* I have a very good reason for this caution. All men born in society, are certainly more desirous of it than any other animal; but whether man be naturally so, that is a question: But, if he was, it is no excellency, nothing to brag or": The love man has for his ease and security, and his perpetual desire of meliorating his condition, must be sussicient motives to make him fond of society, concerning the necessitous'and helpless condition of his nature. *Hor.* Do not you fail into the fame error, which, you fay, Hobbes has been guilty of, when you talk of man's necestitous and helpless condition? *Cleo.* Not at all; I speak of men and women full grown;

and the more extensive their knowledge is, the higher their quality, and the greater tiuir possessions arc, the nore necesJituus and helpless they are in their nature. A uoblcm.au of twenty-sive or thirty thousand pounds a-year, that has three or four coaches and six, and above sifty people to serve him, is in his person considered singly, abstract from what he possesses, more necessitous than an obscure man that has but sifty pounds a year, and is used to walk a-foot; so a lady, who nevet stuck a pin in herself, and is dresscd and undressed from head to foot like a jointed baby by her woman, and the assistance of another maid or two, is a more helpless creature than doll the diary-maid, who, all the winter long, dresses herself in the dark in less time than the other bestows in placing of her patches. *Hor.* But is the desire of meliorating our condition which you named, so generak that no man is without it? *Cleo.* Not one that can be called a sociable creature; and I believe this to be as much a charasteristic of our species as any can be named: For there is not a man in the wprld, educated in society, who, if he could compass it by wishing, would not have something added to, taken from, or altered in his person, possessions, circumstances, or any part of the society he belongs to. This is what is not to be perceived in any creature but man; whose great industry in supplying what he calls his wants, could never have been known so well as it is, if it had not been for the unreasonableness, as well as multiplicity of his desires. From all which, it is manifest, that the most civilized people stand most in need of society, and consequently, none less than savages. The second reason for which I said man was called sociable, is, that associating together turned to better account in our species than it would do in any other, if they were to try it. ' To sind out the reason of this, we must search into human nature for such qualisications as we excel all other animals in, and which the generality of men are endued with, taught or untaught: But in doing this, we should neglect nothing that is observable in them, from their most early youth to their extreme old age. *Hor.* I cannot see why you use this precaution, of taking in the whole age of man; would it not be susssicient to mind those qualisications which he is possessed of, when he is come to the height of maturity, or his greatest perfection? *Cleo.* A considerable part of what is called docility in creatures, depends upon the pliableness of the parts, and their sit, ness to be moved with facility, which are either entirely lost, or very much impaired, when they are full grown. There is nothing in which our species so far surpasses all others, than in the capacity of acquiring the faculty of thinking and speaking well: that this is a peculiar property belonging to our nature is very certain,, yet it is as manisest, that this capacity vanishes, when we come to maturity, if till then it has been neglected. The term of life likewise, that is commonly enjoyed by our species, being longer than it is in most other animals, we have a prerogative above them in point of time; and man has a greater opportunity of advancing in wisdom, though not to be acquired but by his own experience, than a creature that lives but half his age, though it had the fame capacity. A man of threescore, *cateris paribus,* knows better what is to be embraced or avoided in life, than a man of thirty. What Mitio, in excusing the follies of youth, said to his brother Demea, in the Adelphi, *ad omnia alia Ætate sapimus retlius,* holds among savages, as well as among philosophers. It is the concurrence of these, with other properties, that together compose the sociableness of man. *Hor.* But why may not the love of our species be named, as one of these properties? *Cleo.* First, because, as I have said already, it does not appear, that we have it beyond other animals: secondly, because it is out of the question: for if we examine into the nature of all bodies politic, we shall sind, that no dependance is ever had, Or stress laid on any such affection, either for the raising or maintaining of them. *Hor.* But the epithet itself, the signisication of the word, imports this love to one another; as is manifest from the contrary. One who loves solitude, is

averse to company, or of a singular, reserved, and sullen temper, is the very reverse of a sociable man. *Cleo.* When we compare some men to others, the word, I own, is often used in that sense: but when we speak of a quality peculiar to our species, and fay, that man is a sociable creature, the word implies no more, than that in our nature we have a certain sitness, by which great multitudes of us cooperating, may be united and formed into one body; that endued with, and able to make use of, the strength, lkill and prudence of every individual, shall govern itself, and act on all emergencies, as if it was animated by one foul, and actuated by one will. I am willing to allow, that among the motives that prompt man to enter into society, there is a desire which he has naturally after company; but he has it for his own fake, in hopes of being the better for it; and lie would never wish for either company or any thing else, but for some advantage or other be proposes to himself from it. What I deny is, that man naturally has such a desire, out of a fondness of his species, superior to what other animals have for theirs. It is a compliment which we commonly pay to ourselves, but there is no more reality in it, than in our being one another's humble servants; and I insill upon it, that this pretended love of our species, and natural asfection we are laid to have for one another, beyond other animals, is neither instrumental to the erecting os societies, nor ever trusted to in our prudent commerce with one another when associated, any more than if it had no existence. The undoubted basis of all societies is government: this truth, well examined into, will furnish us with all the reasons of man's excellency, as to sociablenefs. It is evident from it, that creatures, to be raised iuto a community, must, in the sirst plact, be governable: This is a qualisication that requires fear, and some degree of underllanding; for a creature not susceptible of fear, is never to be governed; and the more fense and courage it has, the more refractory and untractable it will be, withou: the influence of that useful passion: and again, fear without understanding puts

creatures only upon avoiding the danger dreaded, without considering what will become ot themselves afterwards: so wild birds will beat out their brains against the cage, before they will save their fives by eating. There is a great difference between being submilfive, and being governable; for he who barely submits to another, only embraces what lie diflikcs, to shun what hediilikes more; and we may be very submissive, and be of no use to the person we submit to: but to be governable, implies an endeavour to please, and a willingness to exert ourselves in behalf of the person that governs: but love beginning every where at home, no creature can labour for others, and be easy long, whilst self is wholly out of the question: therefore a creature is then truly governable, when reconciled to submission, it has learned to construe his servitude to his own advantage; and rests satissied with the account it sinds tor itself, in the labour it performs for others. Several kind ot animals are, or may, with little trouble, be made thus governable; but there is not one creature so tame, that it can be made to serve its own species, but man ; yet without this he could never have been made sociable. *Hor.* But was not man by nature designed for society? *Cleo.* We know from revelation that man was made for society. *Hor.* But if it had not been revealed, or you had been a Chinese, or a Mexican, what would you answer me as a philosopher? *Cleo.* That nature had designed man for society, as she has made grapes for wine. *Hor.* To make wine is an invention of man, as it is to press oil from olives and other vegetables, and to make ropes of hemp. *Ceo.* And so it is to form a society of independent multitudes; and there is nothing that requires greater skill. *Hor.* But is not the fociableness of man the work of nature, or rather of the author of nature, Divine Providence? *Cleo.* Without doubt: But so is the innate virtue and peculiar aptitude of every thing; that grapes are sit to make wine, and barley and water to make other liquors, is the work of Providence; but it is human sagacity that sinds out the uses we make of them: all the other capacities of man likewise, as well as his fociableness, are evidently derived' from God, who made him: every thing therefore that our industry can produce or compass, is originally owing to the Author of our being. But when we speak os the works of nature, to distinguish them from those of art, we mean such as were brought forth without our concurrence. So nature, in due season produces pease; but in England you cannot have them green in January, without art and uncommon industry. What nature designs, she executes herself: there are creatures, of whom it is visible, that nature has designed them for society, as is most obvious in bees, to whom she has given instincts for that purpose, as appears from the effects. We owe our being and every thing else to the great Author of the universe; but as societies cannot subsist without his preserving power, so they cannot exist without the concurrence of human wisdom: all of them must have a dependance either on mutual compact, or the force of the strong exerting itself upon the patience of the weak. The disference between the works of art, and those of nature, is so immense, that it is impossible not to know them asunder. Knowing, *a priori*, belongs to God only, and Divine Wisdom acts with an original certainty, of which, what we call demonstration, is but an imperfect borrowed copy. Amongst the works of nature, therefore, we fee no trials nor essays; they are all complete, and such as she would have them, at the sirst production; and, where she has not been interrupted, highly sinished, beyond the reach of our understanding, as well as fenses. Wretched man, on the contrary is sure of nothing, his own existence not excepted, but from reasoning, *a posteriori*. The consequence of this is, that the works of art and human invention are all very lame and defective, and most of them pitifully mean at sirst: our knowledge is advanced by slow degrees, and some arts and sciences require the experience of many ages, before they can be brought to any tolerable perfection. Have we any reason to imagine that the society of bees, that sent forth the sirst

swarm, made worse wax or honey than any of their posterity have produced since? And again the laws of nature are sixed and unalterable: in all her orders and regulations there is a stibility, no where to be met with in things of human contrivance and approbation;

Quid placet aut odio est, quod non mutabile credas?

Is it probable, that amongst the bees, there has ever been any other form of government than what every swarm submits to now? What an insinite variety of speculations, what ridiculous schemes have not been proposed amongst men, on the subject of government; what dissensions in opinion, and what fatal quarrels has it not been the occasion of! and which is the best form of it, is a question to this day undecided. The projects, good and bad, that have been stated for the benesit, and more happy establishment of society, are innumerable; but how short sighted is our sagacity, how fallible human judgment! What has seemed highly advantageous to mankind in one age, has often been tound to be evidently detrimental by the succeeding; and even among contemporaries, what is revered in one country, is the abomination of another. What changes have ever bees made in their furniture or architecture? have they ever made cells that were not scxangular, or added any tools to those which nature furnished them with'at the beginning? What mighty structures have been raised, what prodigious works have been performed by the great nations of the world! Toward all 4hese nature has only found materials: the quarry yields 7 marble, but it is tbe sculptor that makes a statue of it. To have the insinite variety of iron tools that have been invented, nature has given us nothing but the oar, which she has hid in the bowels of the earth.

Hor. But the capacity of the workmen, the inventors of arts, and those that improved them, has had a great share in bringing those labours to perfection; and their genius they had from nature. *Cleo.* So far as it depended upon the make of their frame, the accuracy of the machine they had, and no further; bus

this I have allowed already; and if you remember what I have said on this head, you will sind, that the part which nature contributed toward the skill and patience of every single person, that had a hand in those works, was very inconsiderable. *Hor.* If I have not misunderstood you, you would insinuate two things: First, that the sitness of man for society, beyond other animals, is something real; but that it is hardly perceptible in individuals, before great numbers of them are joined together, and artfully managed. Secondly, that this real something, this sociableness, is a compound that consists in a concurrence of several things, and not in any one palpable quality, that man is endued with, and brutes are destitute of. *Cleo.* You are perfectly right: every grape contains a small quantity of juice, and when great heaps of them are squeezed together, they yield a liquor, which by skilful management may be made into wine: but if we consider how necessary fermentation is to the vinosity of the liquor, I mean, how essential is it to its being wine, it will be evident to us, that without great impropriety of speech, it cannot be said, that in every grape there is wine. *Hor.* Vinosity, so far as it is the effect of fermentation, is adventitious; and what none of the grapes could ever have received whilst they remained single; and, therefore, if you would compare the sociableness of man to the vinosity of wine, you must show me, that in society there is an equivalent for fermentation; I mean something that individual persons are not actually possessed of, whilst they remain single, and which likewise is palpably adventitious to multitudes when joined together; in the fame manner as fermentation is to the juice of grapes, and as necessary and essential to the completing of society as that is, that fame fermentation, to procure the vinosity of wine. *Cleo.* Such an equivalent is demonstrable in mutual commerce: for if we examine every faculty and qualisication, from and for which we judge and pronounce man to be a sociable creature beyond other animals, we mall sind, that a very considerable, if not the greatest part of the attribute is acquired, and comes upon multitudes, from their conversing with one another. *Fabricundo fabrijimus.* Men become sociable, by living together in society. Natural affection prompts all mothers to take care of the offspring they dare own; so far as to feed and keep them from harm, whilst they are helpleis: but w here people arc poor, and the women have no leisure to indulge themselves in the various expressions of their fondness for their infants, which fondling of them ever increases, they are often very remiss in tending and playing witli them; and the more healthy and quiet such children are, the more they are neglected. This want of prattling to, and stirring up the spirits in babes, is often the principal cause of an invincible stupidity, as well as ignorance, when they are grown up; and we often ascribe to natural incapacity, what is altogether owing to the neglect of this early instruction. We have so few examples of human creatures, that never conversed with their own species, that it is hard to guess, what man would be, entirely untaught; but we have good reaion to believe, that the faculty of thinking would be very imperfect in such a one, if we consider, that the greatest docility can be of no use to a creature, whilst it has nothing to imitate, nor any body to teach it. *Hor.* Philosophers therefore are very wisely employed, when they discourse about the laws of nature; and pretend to determine what a man in the state of naturewou'd think, and which way he would reason concerning himself and the creation, uniustructed. *Cleo.* Thinking, and reasoning justly, as Mr. Loclcc has rightly observed, require time and practice. Those that have not used themselves to thinking, but just on their present necessities, make poor w'ork of it, when they try beyond that. Inxcmote parts, and such as are least inhabited, we lliall iind our species come nearer the state of nature, than it does in and near great cities and considerable towns, even in the moii civilized nations. Among the most ignorant of such people you may learn the truth of my assertion; talk to their, abou: any thing, that requires abstract thinking, and there

is not one in sifty that will understand you, any more than a horse would; and yet many of them are useful labourers, and cunning enough to tell lies and deceive. Man is a rational creature, but he is not endued with reason when he comes into the world; nor can he afterwards put it on when he pleases, at once, as he miy a garment. Speech likewise is a characteristic of our species, but no man is born with it; and a dozen generations proceeding from two savages would not produce any tolerable language; nor have we reason to believe, that a man could be taught to speak after sive-andtwenty, it he had never heard others before that time. *Hor.* The necessity of teaching, Whilst the organs are supple, and easily yield to impression, which you have spoke of before, I believe is of great weight, both in speaking and thinking; but could a dog, or a monkey, ever be taught to speak? *ilh'o.* I believe not; but I do not think, that creatures of another species had ever the pains bestowed upon them, that some children have, before they can pronounce one word. Another thing to be conlidered is, that though some animals perhaps live longer than we do, there is no species that remains young so long as ours; and besides what we owe to the superior aptitude to learn, which we have from the great accuracy of our frame and inward structure, we are not a little indebted for our docility, to the flowness and long gradation of our increase, before we are full grown: the organs in other creatures grow stisf, before ours are come to half their perfection. *Hor.* So that in the compliment we make to our species, of i's being endued with speech and sociableness, there is no other reality, than that by care and industry men may be taught to speak, and be made sociable, if the discipline begins when they are very young. *Cleo.* Not otherwise. A thousand of our species all grown up, that is above sive-and-twenty, could never be made sociable, if they had been brought up wild, and were all strangers to one another. *Hor.* 1 believe they could not be civilized, if their education began so late. *Cko.* But I mean barely sociable, as

it is the epithet peculiar to man; that is, it would be impossible by art to govern them, any more than so many wild horses, unless you had two or three times that number to watch and keep them in awe. Therefore it is highly probable, that most societies, and beginnings of nations, were formed in the manner Sir William Temple supposes it; but nothing near so fast: and I wonder how a man of his unquestionable good fense, could form an idea of justice, prudence, and wildom, in an untaught creature; or think of a civilized man, before there was any civil society, and even before men had commenced to associate. *Hor.* I have read it, I am sure, but I do not remember what it is you mean. *Cleo.* He is just behind you; the third shelf from the bottom; the sirst volume: pray reach it me, it is worth your hearing. It is in his Essay on Government. Here it is. " For if we consider man multiplying his kind by the birth " of many children, and his cares by providing even necessa," ry food for them, until they are able to do it for themselves " (which happens much later to the generations of men, and " makes a much longer dependence of children upon pa" rents, than we can observe among any other creatures); ii " we consider not only the cares, but the industry he is " forced to, for the necessary sustenance of his helpless brood, " either in gathering the natural fruits, or raising those " which are purchased with labour and toil: if he be forced " for supply of this stock, to catch the tamer creatures, and " hunt the wilder, sometimes to exercise his courage in de" fending his little family, and sighting with the strong and " savage beasts (that would prey upon him, as he does upon " the weak and mild): if we suppose him disposing with dis" cretion and order, whatever he gets among his children, " according to each of their hunger or need; sometimes lay" ing up for tomorrow, what was more than enough for to" day; at other times pinching himself, rather than suffering " any of them should want.

Hor. This man is no savage, or untaught creature; he is sit to be a justice of peace. *Cleo.* Pray let me go on, I shall only read this paragraph: " And as each of them grows up, and able to share in the " common support, teaching them, both by lesson and ex" ample, what he is now to do, as the son of his family, and " what hereafter, as the father of another; instructing them " all, what qualities are good, and what are ill, for their " health and life, or common society (which will certainly " comprehend whatever is generally esteemed virtue or vice ' among men), cherishing and encouraging dispositions to " the good, disfavouring and punishing those to the ill: And lastly, among the various accidents of life, lifting up his eyes to Heaven, when the earth affords him no relief; and " having recourse to a higher and a greater nature, whenever " he sinds the frailty of his own: we must needs conclude, " that the children of this man cannot fail of being bred up " with a great opinion of his wisdom, his goodness, his va" lour, and his piety. And if they fee constant plenty in " the family, they believe well of his fortune too. " Hor. Did this man spring out of the earth, I wonder, or did he drop from the sky? Cleo. There is no manner of absurdity in supposing Hor. The discussion of this would too far engage us: I am sure, I have tired you already with my impertinence. Cleo. You have pleased me extremely: the questions you have asked have all been very pertinent, and such as every man of fense would make, that had not made it his business to think on these things. I read that passage on purpose to you, to make some use of it; but if you are weary of the subject, I will not trespass upon your patience any longer. Hor. You mistake me; I begin to be fond of the subject: but before we talk of it any further, I have a mind to run over that Essay again; it is a great while since I read it: and after that I shall be glad to resume the discourse; the sooner the better. I know, you are a lover of sine fruit, if you will dine with me to-morrow, 1 will give you an ananas. Cleo. 1 love your company so well, that I can refuse no opportunity of enjoying it. Hor. A revoir then. Cleo. Your servant. THE FIFTH DIALOGUE BETWEEN HORATIO AND CLEOMENES.

CLEOMENES.

It excels everv thing; it is extremely rich without heing luscious, and I know nothing to which I can compare the taste of it: to me it seems to be u collection of different sine flavours, that puts me in mind of several delicious fruits, which yet are all outdone by it.

Hor. I am glad it pleased you. Cleo. The scent of it likewise is wonderfully reviving. As you was paring it, a fragrancy, I thought, perfumed the room that was perfectly cordial. Hon The inside of the rliind has an oiliness of no disagreeable smell, that upon handling of it sticks to ones singers for a considerable time; for though now I have waihed and wiped my hands, the flavour of it will not be entirely gone from them by to-morrow morning. Cleo. This was the third I ever tasted of our own growth; the production of them in these northern climates, is no small instance of human industry, and our improvements in gardening. It is very elegant to enjoy the wholesome air of temperate regions, and at the fame Lime be able to raise fruit to its highest maturity, that naturally requires the fun of the Torrid Zone. Hor. It is easy enough to procure heat, but the great art consists in sinding out, and regulating the degrees of it at pleasure; without which it would be impossible to ripen an ananas here, and to compass this with that exactness, as it is done by the help of thermometers, was certainly a sine invention. Cleo. I do not care to drink any more. Hor. Just as you please; otherwise I was going to name a. health, which would not have come mal a propos. Cleo. Whose is that, pray? Hor. I was thinking on the man to whom we are in a great measure obliged for the production and culture of the exotic, we were speaking of, in this kingdom; Sir JVTatthew Decker, the sirst ananas or pine-apple, that was brought to perfection in England, grew in his garden at Richmond. Cleo. With all my heart; let us sinish with that; he is 3 benesicent, and, I believe, a very honest man. Hor. It would not be easy to name another, who, with the fame knowledge bf the world, and capacity of getting money, is equally disinterested and inoffensive.

Cleo. Have you considered the things we discoursed of yesterday? Hor. I have thought on nothing else since I saw you: This morning 1 went through the whole Essay, and with more attention than I did formerly: 1 like it very well; only that passage which you read yesterday, and some others to the fame purpose, I cann t reconcile with the account we have of man's origin from the Bible: Since all are descendants from Adam, and consequently of Noah and his posterity, how came savages into the world? . Cleo. The history of the world, as to very ancient times,' is very imperfect: What devastations have been made by war, by pestilence, and by famine; what distress some men have been drove to, and how strangely our race has been dispersed and scattered over the eartn since the flood, we do not know. Hor. But persons that are well instructed themselves, never fail of teaching their children; and we have no reason to think, that knowing, civilized men, as the sons of Noah were, should have neglected their ossspring; but it is altogether incredible, as all are descendants from them, that succeeding generations, instead of increasing in experience and wisdom, should learn backward, and still more and more abandon their broods in such a manner, as to degenerate at last to what you call the state of nature. Cleo. Whether you intend this as a sarcasm or not, I do' not know; but you have raised no dilhculty that can gender the truth of the sacred history suspected. Holy writ has acquainted us with the miraculous origin of Our species, and the small remainder of it aiter the deluge: But it is far from informing us of all the revolutions that have happened among mankind since: The Old Testament hardly touches upon any particulars that hud no relation to the Jews; neither does Moses pretend to give a full account of every thing that happened to, or was transacted by our sirst parents: He names none of Adam's daughters, and takes no notice of several things that mull have happened in the beginning of the world, as is evident from Cain's building a city, and several other circumstances; from which it is plain, that Moses meddled with nothing but what was material, and to his purpose; which, in that part of his history, was to trace the descent of the Patriarchs, from the sirst man. But that there are savages is certain: Most nations of Europe hare met with wild men and women in several parts of the world, that were ignorant of the use of letters, and among whom they could observe no rule or government. *Hor.* That there are savages, I do not question; and from the great number of slaves that are yearly fetched from Africa, it is manifest, that in some parts there must be vail swarms of people, that have not yet made a great hand ot their fociahlenefs: But how to derive them from all the sons of Noah, 1 own, is past my skill. *Cleo.* You sind it as difsicult to account for the loss of the many sine arts, and useful inventions of the ancients, which the world has certainly sustained. But the fault I sind with Sir William Temple, is in the character of his savage. Just reasoning, and such an orderly way of proceeding, as he makes him act in, are unnatural to a wild man: In such a one, the passions must be boisterous, and continually jostling, and succeeding one another; no untaught man could have a regular way of thinking, or pursue any one design with steadiness. *Hor.* You have strange notions of our species: But has not a man, by the time that he comes to maturity, some notions of right and wrong, that are natural? ' *Cleo.* Before 1 answer your question, I would have you consider, that, among savages, there must be always a great disference as to the wildness or tameness of them. All creatures naturally love their ofspring whilst they are helplels, and so does man: But in the savage state, men are more liable to accidents and misfortunes than they are in society, as to the rearing of their young ones; and, therefore, the children of savages mull very often be put to iheir shifts, so as hardly to remember, by the time that they are grown up, that they had any parents. If this happens too early, and they are dropt or lost before they are four or sive years of age, they must perish; either die for want, or be devoured by beasts of

prey, unless some other creature takes care of them. Those orphans that survive, and become their own mailers very young, must, when they are come to maturity, be much wilder than others, that have lived many years under the tuition of parents. *Hor.* But would not the wildest man you can imagine, have from nature some thoughts of justice and injustice? *Cleo.* Such a one, I believe, would naturally, without much thinking in the cafe, take every thing to be his own that he could lay his hands on. *Hor.* Then they would soon be undeceived, if two or three of them met together. *Cleo.* That they would soon disagree and quarrel, is highly probable; but I do not believe they ever would be undeceived. *Hor.* At this'rate, men could never be formed into an aggregate body: How came society into the world?'. *Cleo.* As I told you, from private families; but not without great dissiculty, and the concurrence of many favourable accidents; and many generations may pass before there is any likelihood of their being formed into a society. *Hor.* That men are formed into societies, we fee: But if they are all born with that false notion, and they can never be undeceived, which way do you account for it? *Cleo.* My opinion concerning this matter, is this: Selfpreservation bids all creatures gratify their appetites, and that of propagating his kind never fails to affect a man in health, many years before he comes to his full growth. If a wild man and a wild woman should meet very young, and live together for sifty years undisturbed, in a mild wholesome climate, where there is plenty of provisions, they might see a prodigious number of descendants: For, in the wild state of nature, man multiplies his kind much faster, than can be allowed of in any regular society: No male at fourteen would be long without a female, if he could get one; and no female of twelve would be refractory, if applied to, or remain long uncourted, if there were men. *Hor.* Considering that consanguinity would be no bar among these people, the progeny of two savages might soon amount
Dda to hundreds: All this I can grant

you; but as parents, no better qualisied, could teach their children but little, it would be impossible for them to govern these sons and daughters when they grew up, if none of them had any notions of right or wrong; and society is as far off as ever; the false principle, which you say all men are born with, is an obstacle never to be surmounted.

Cleo. From that false principle, as you call it, the right men naturally claim to every thing they can get, it must follow, that man will look upon his children as his property, and make such use of them as is most conlistent with his interest. *Hor.* What is the interest of a wild man that pursues nothing with steadiness. *Cleo.* The demand of the predominant passion for the time it lasts. *Hur.* That may change every moment, and such children would be miserably managed. *Cleo.* That is true; but still managed they would be; I mean they would be kept under, and forced to do as they were bid, at least till they were strong enough to resist. Natural affection would prompt a wild man to love and cherish his child; it would make him provide food, and other necessaries for his. son, till he was ten or twelve years old, or perhaps longer: But this affection is not the only passion he has to gratify; if his son provokes him by stubbornness, or doing otherwise than he would have him, this love is suspended; and if his displeasure be strong enough to raise his anger, which is as natural to him as any other passion, it is ten to one but he will knock him down: If he hurts him very much, and the condition he has put his son in, moves' his pity, his anger will cease; and, natural affection returning, he will fondle him again, and be sorry for what he has done. Now, if we consider that all creatures hate and endeavour to avoid pain, and that benesits beget love in all that receive them, we shall sind, that the consequence of this management would be, that the savage child would learn to love and tear his father: These two passions, together with the esteem which we naturally have for every thing that far excels us, will seldom fail of producing that compound which we call reverence. *Hor.* 1 have it now; you have opened my eyes, and I see the origin of society, as plain as 1 do that table. *Cleo.* I am afraid the prospect is not so clear yet as you imagine. *Hor.* Why so? The grand obstacles are removed: Untaught men, it is true, when they are grown up, are never to be governed; and our subjection is never sincere where the superiority of the governor is not very apparent: Bit both these are obviated; the reverence we have for a person when we are young, is easily continued as long as we live; and where authority is once acknowledged, and. that acknowledgmentwell established, it cannot be a dissicult matter to govern. If thus a man may keep up his authority over his childern, he will do it still with greater ease over his grand-childern: For a child that has the least reverence for his parents, will seldom refuse homage to the person to whom he sees his father pay it. Besides, a man's pride would be a sussicient motive for him to maintain the authority once gained; and, if some of his progeny proved refractory, he would leave no stone unturned, by the help of the rest to reduce the disobedient. The old man being dead, the authority from him would devolve upon the eldest of his children, and so on. *Qeo.* 1 thought you would go on too last. If the wild man had understood the nature of things, and been endued with general knowledge, and a language ready made, as Adam was by miracle, what you fay might have been easy; but an ignorant creature that knows nothing but what his own experience has taught him, is no more sit to govern than he is sit to teach the mathematics. *Hor.* He would not have above one or two children to govern at sirst; and his experience would increase by degrees, as well as his family. This would require no such consummate knowledge. *Cleo.* I do not say it would: An ordinary capacity of a man tolerably well educated, would be sussicient to begin with; but a man who never had been taught to curb any of his passions, would be very unsit for such a task. He would make his children, as soon as they were able, assist him in getting food, and teach them how and where

to procure it. Savage children, as they got strength, would endeavour to imitate every action they saw their parents do, and every sound they heard them make; but all the instructions they received, would be consined to things immediately necessary. Savage parents would often take osience at their children, as they grew up, without a caule; and as these increased i» years, so natural asfection would decrease in the other. The consequence would be, that the children would often suffer for failings that were not their own. Savages would often discover faults in the conduct of what was past; but they would not be able to establish rules for future behaviour, which they would approve of themselves sor any continuance; and want of foresight would be an inexhaustible fund for changes in their resolutions. The savage's wife, as well as himself, would be highly pleased to see their daughters impregnated and bring forth; and they would both take great delight in their grand-children. *Hor.* I thought, that in all creatures the natural asfection of parents had been consined to their own young ones. *C!eo.* It is so in all but man; there is no species but ours, that are so conceited of themselves, as to imagine every thing to be theirs. The desire of dominion is a never-failing consequence of the pride that is common to all men; and which the brat of a savage is as much born with as the son of an emperor. This good opinion we have of ourselves, makes men not only claim a right to their children, but likewise imagine, that they have a great share of jurisdiction over their grandchildren. The young ones of other animals, as soon as they can help themselves, are free; but the authority which parents pretend to have over their children, never ceases: How general and unreasonable this eternal claim is naturally in the heart of man, we may learn from the laws; which, to prevent the usurpation of parents, and rescue childem from their dominion, every civil society is forced to make; limiting paternal authority to a certain term of years. Our savage pair would have a double title to their grandchildren, from

their undoubted property in each parent of them; and all the progeny being sprung from their own sons and daughters, without intermixture of foreign blood, they would look upon the whole race to be their natural vassals; and I am persuaded, that the more knowledge and capacity of reasoning this sirst couple acquired, the more just and unquestionable their sovereignty over all their descendants would appear to them, though they should live to see the sifth or sixth generation. *Hor.* Is it not strange that nature should send us all into the world with a visible desire after government, and no ca pacity fork at all? *Cleo.* What seems strange to you, is an undeniable instance of Divine Wisdom. For, if all had not been born with this desire, all must have been destitute of it; and multitudes could never have been formed into societies, if some of them had not been possessed of this thirst of dominion. Creatures may commit force upon themselves, they may learn to warp their natural appetites, and divert them from their proper objects: but peculiar instincts, that belong to a whole species, are never to be acquired by art or discipline; and those that are born without them, must remain destitute of them for ever. Ducks run to the water as soon as they are hatched; but you can never make a chicken swim any more than you can teach it to suck. *Hor.* I understand you very well. If pride had not been innate to all men, none of them could ever have been ambitious: And as to the capacity of governing, experience shows us, that it is to be acquired; but how to bring society into the world, I know no more than the wild man himself. What you have suggested to me of his unskilfulness, and want of power to govern himself, has quite destroyed all the hopes I had conceived of society from this family. But would religion have no influence upon them? Pray, how came that into the world? *Cleo.* From God, by miracle. *Hor. Obscurum per obscurius.* I do not understand miracles, that break in upon, and subvert the order of nature; and I have no notion of things that come to pass, *en deplt de hon fens,* and are such; that judging from sound reason and known experience, all wise men would think themselves mathematically sure that they could never happen. *Cleo.* It is certain, that by the word miracle, is meant an interposition of the Divine Power, when it deviates from the common course of nature. *Hor.* As when matters, easily combustible, remain whole and untouched in the midst of a sire siercely burning, or lions in vigour, industriously kept hungry, forbear eating what they are most greedy after. These miracles are strange things. *Cleo.* They are not pretended to be otherwise; the etyrrrtslogy of the word imports it; but it is almost as unaccountable, that men shoulddisoelieve them, and pretend to be of a religion that is altogether built upon miracles. *Hor.* But when I asked you that general question, why did you consine yourself to revealed religion? *Cko.* Because nothing, in my opinion, deserves the name of religion, that has not been revealed: The Jewish was the first that was national, and the Christian the next. *Hvr.* But Ahraham, Noah, and Adam himself, were no Jews, and yet they had religion. *Cleo.* No other than what was revealed to them, God appeared to our sirst parents, and gave them commands immediately after he had created them: The lame intercourse was continued between the Supreme Being and the Patriarchs; but the father of Abraham was an idolater. *Hor.* But the Egyptians, the Greeks, and the Romans had xeligion, as well as the Jews. *Cleo.* Their gross idolatry, and abominable worship, I call superstition. *Hor.* You may be as partial as you please, but they all called their worship religion, as well as we do ours. You fay, man brings nothing with him, but his passions; and when I asked you, how religion came into the world, I meant what is there in man's nature that is not acquired, from, which he has a tendency to religion; what is it that disposes him to it? *Cleo.* Fear. *Hor.* How! *Primus in orbe Deos fecit timor:* Are you of that ppinion. *Cleo.* No man upon earth less: But that noted Epicurean axiom, which irreligious men are so fond of, is a very poor one; and it is silly, as well as impious to fay, that fear made

a God; you may as justly fay, that fear made grafs, or the fun and the moon: but when I am speaking of savages, it is not clashing either with good fense, nor the Christian religion, to assert, that, whilst such men are ignorant of the true Deity, and yet very defective in the art of thinking and reasoning, fear is the passion that sirst gives them an ppportunity of entertaining some glimmering notions of an invisible Power;.which afterwards, as by practice and experience they grow greater prosicients, and become more perfect in the labour of the brain, and the exercise of their highest faculty, will infallibly lead them to the certain knowledge of an Insinite and Eternal Being; whose power and wildom will always appear the greater, and more stupendous to them, the more they themselves advance in knowledge and penetration, though both should be carried on to a much higher piich, than it is possible for our limited nature eyer tq arrive at. *Hor.* T beg your pardon for suspecting you; though I am glad it gave you an opportunity or explaining yourself. The *Vfovdfeur,* without any addition, sounded very harsh; and even now I cannot conceive how an invisible cause should become the object of a man's fear, that should be so entirely untaught, as you have made "he sirli savage: which way can any thing invilible, and that affects none of the fenses, make an impression upon a wild creature? *Cleo.* h.very mischief and every disaster that happens to him, of which thecause is not very plain and obvious; excessive heat and cold ; wet and drought, that are offensive; thunder and ligh ning, even when they do no visible hurt; noiles in the dark, obscurity itself, and every thing that is frightful and unknown, are all administering and contributing to the eslablislment of this fear. The wildest man that can be conceived, by the time that he came to maturity, would be wile enough to know, that fruits and other eatables are not to be had, either always, or every where: this would naturally put him upon hoarding, when he had good store: his prpvilion might be spoiled by the rain: he would lee that trees were blasted, and

yielded not always the fame plenty: he might not always be in health, or his young ones might grow sick, and die, without any wounds or external force to be seen. Some of these accidents might at sirst escape his attention, or only alarm his weak understanding, without occasioning much reflection for some time; but as they come often, he would certainly begin to suspect some invilible cause; and, as his experience increased, be consirmed in his sulpicion. It is likewise highly probable, that a variety of ditlerent sufferings, would make him apprehend several such causes; and at last induce him to believe, that there was a great number of them, which he had to fear. What would very much contribute to this credulous disposition, and naturally lead him into such a belief, is a false notion we imbibe very early, and which we may observe in infants, as soon as by their looks, their guestures, and the signs they make, they begin to be intelligible to us. *Hor.* What is that, pray? *Cleo.* All young children seem to imagine, that every thing thinks and feels in the fame manner as they do themselves; and, that they generally have this wrong opinion of things inanimate, is evident, from a common practice among them; whenever they labour under any m.sfortune, wh.ch their own wildness, and want of care have drawn upon them. In all such cases, you fee them angry at and strike, a table, a chair, the floor, or any thing else, that can seem to have been accessary to their hurting themselves, or the production of any other blunder, they have committed. Nurses we fee, in compliance to their frailty, seem to entertain the same ridiculous sentiments; and adually appease-.vrathful brats, by pretending to take their part: Thus you will often fee them very' serious, in scolding at and beating, either the real object of the baby's indignation, or something else, on which the blame of what has happened, may be thrown, with any show of probability. It is not to be imagined, that this natural folly mould be so easily cured in a child, that is destitute of all instruction and commerce with his own species, as it is in those that are brought up in society, and hourly improved by conversing with others that are wiser than themselves; and 1 am persuaded, that a wild man would never get entirely rid of it whilst he lived. *Hor.* I cannot think so meanly of human understanding. *Cleo.* Whence came the Dryades and Hama-Dryades? How came it ever to be thought impious to cut down, or even to wound large venerable oaks or other stately trees; and what root did the Divinity spring from, which the vulgar, among the ancient heathens, apprehended to be in rivers and fountains? *Hor.* From the roguery of designing priests, and other impostors, that invented those lies, and made fables for their own advantage. *Cleo.* But still it must have been want of understanding; and a tincture, some remainder of that folly which is discovered in young children, that could induce, or would luster men to believe those fables. Unless fools actually had frailties, knaves could not make use of them. *Hor.* There may be something in it; but, be that as it will, you have owned, that man naturally loves those he receives benesits from; therefore, how comes it, that man, sinding all the good things he enjoys to proceed from an invisible cause, his gratitude should not sooner prompt him to be religious, than his fear? *Cleo.* There are several substantial reasons, why it does not. Man takes every thing to be his own, which he has from nature: sowing and reaping, he thinks deserve a crop, and whatever he has the lealt hand in, is always reckoned to be Ills. Every art, arid every invention, as soon as we know them, are our right and property; and whatever we perform by the assistance of them, is, by the courtesy of the species to itself, deemed to be our own. We make use of fermentation, and all the chemistry of nature, without thinking ourselves beholden to any thing but our own knowledge. She that churns the cream, makes the butter; without inquiring into the power by which the thin lymphatic particles are forced to separate themselves, and Hide away from the more unctuous. In brewing, baking, cooking, and almost every thing we have a hand in, nature is the drudge that

makes all the alterations, and does the principal work;'yet all, forsooth, is our own. From all which, it is manifest, that man, who is naturally for making every thing centre in himself, must, in his wild state, have a great tendency, and be very prone to look upon every thing he enjoys as his due; and every thing he meddles with, as his own performance. It requires knowledge and reflection; and a man must be pretty far advanced in the art of thinking justly, and reasoning consequentially, before he can, from his own light, and without being taught, be sensible of his obligations to God. The less a man knows, and the more shallow his understanding is, the less he is capable either of enlargmg his prospect of things, or drawing consequences from the little which he does know. Raw, ignorant, and untaught men, six their eyes on what is immediately before, and seldom look further than, as it is vulgarly expressed, the length of their noses. The wild man,-if gratitude moved him, would much sooner pay his respects to the tree he gathers his nuts from, than he would think of an acknowledgement to him who had planted it; and there is no property so well established, but a civilized man would suspect his title to it sooner, than a wild one woidd question the sovereignty he has over his own breath. Another reason, why fear is an elder motive to religion than gratitude, is, that an untaught man would never inspect that the same cause, which he received good from, would ever do him hurt; and evil, without doubt, would always gain his attention sirst. *Hor.* Men, indeed, seem to remember one ill turn, that is served them, better than ten good ones; one month's sickness better than ten years health. *Cleo.* In all the,labours of self-preservation, man is intent on avoiding what is hurtful to him; but in the enjoyment of what is pleasant, his thoughts are relaxed, and he is void of care: he can swallow a thousand delights, one after another, without asking questions; but the least evil makes him inquisitive whence it came, in order to shun it. It is very material, therefore, to know the cause os evil; but to know that of good, which is always welcome, is

of little use; that is, such a knowledge seems not to promise any addition to his happiness. When a man once apprehends such an invisible enemy, it is reasonable to think, that he would be glad to appease, and make him his friend, if he could sind him out; it his highly probable, likewise, that in order to this, he would search, inve'.ligate, and look every where about him; and that sinding all his inquiries upon earth in vain, he would iift up his eyes to the sky. *Her.* And so a wild man might; and look down and up again long enough before he would be the wiser. I can easily conceive, that a creature must labour under great perplexities, when it actually fears something, of which it knows neither what it is, nor where it is; and that, though a man had all the reason in the world to think it invisible, he would still be more afraid of it in the dark, than when he could see. *Cleo.* Whilst a man is but an imperfect thinker, and wholly employed in furthering self preservation in the most simple manner, and removing the immediate obstacles he meets with in that pursuit, this affair, perhaps, affects him but little; but when he comes to be a tolerable reasoner, and has leisure to reflect, it must produce strange chimeras and surmises; and a wild couple would not converse together long, before they would endeavour to express their minds to one another concerning this matter; and, as in time they would invent and agree upon, certain sounds of distinction for several things, of which the ideas would often occur, so I believe, that this invisible cause would be one of the sirst, which they would coin a name for. A wild man and a wdd woman would not take less care of their helpless brood than other animals; and it is not to imagined, but the children that were brought up by them, though without instruction or discipline, would, before they were ten years old, observe in their parents this fear of an invisible cause. It is incredible likewise, considering, how much men differ from one another in features, complexion, and temper, that all should form the lame idea of this cause; from whence it would follow, that a$ soon as any considerable jramber of men could intelligibly converse together, it.would appear, that there were different opinions among them concerning the invisible cause: the fear and acknowledgment of it being universal, and man always attributing his own passions to every thing, which he conceives to think, every body would be solicitous to avoid the hatred and ill-will, and, if it was possible, to gain the friendlhip of such a power. If we consider these things, and what we know of the nature of man, it is hardly to be conceived, that any considerable number of our species could have any intercourse together long, in peace or otherwise, but wilful lies would be raised concerning this power, and some would pretend to have seen or heard it. How different opinions about invisible power, may, by the malice and deceit of impostors, be made the occasion of mortal enmity among multitudes, ie easily accounted for. If we want rain very much, and I can be persuaded, that it is your fault we have none, there needs greater cause to quarrel; and nothing has happened in the world, of priestcraft or inhumanity, folly or abomination, on, religious accounts, that cannot be solved or explained, with the least trouble, from these data, and the principle of fear. *Hor.* 1 think 1 must yield to you, that the sirst motive of religion, among savages, was fear; but you must allow me in your turn, that from the general thankfulness that nations have always paid to their gods, for signal benesits and success; the many hecatombs that have been offered after victories; and the various institutions of games and festivals; it is evident, that when men came to be wiser, and more civiliied, the greatest part of their resigion was built upon gratitude. *Cleo.* You labour hard, I see, to vindicate the honour of our species; but we have no such cause to boast of it: and I shali demonstrate to you, that a well-weighed consideration, and a thorough understanding of our nature, will give us much less reason to exult in our pride, than it will furnilh us with, for the exercise of our humility. In the sirst place, there is no difference between the original nature of a savage, and that of

a civilized man: they are both born with fear j and neither of them, if they have their senses about them, can live many years, but an invisible Power, will, at one time or other, become the object of that fear; and this will happen to every man, whether he be wild and alone, or in society, and under the best discipline. We know by experience, that empires, slates, and kingdoms, may excel in arts and sciences, politeness, and ail worldly wisdom, and at the same time be slaves to the grossest idolatry, and submit to all the inconsistencies of a false religion. The most civilized people have been as foolish and absurd in sacred worship as it is possible for any savages to be; and the sirst have often been guilty of studied cruelties, which the latter would never have thought of. The Carthaginians were a subtle flourishing people, an opulent and formidable nation, and Hannibal had half conqueredthe Romans, when still to their idols they sacrisiced the children of their chief nobility. And, as to private persons, there are innumerable instances in the most polite ages of men offense and virtue, that have entertained the most miserable, unworthy, and extravagant notions of the Supreme Being. What confused and unaccountable apprehensions must not some men have had of Providence, to act as they did! Alexander Severus, who succeeded Heliogabalus, was a great reformer of abuses, and thought to be as good a prince as his predecessor was a bad one: In his palace he had an oratory, a cabinet set aside for his private devotion, where he had the images of Appollonius Tyanæus, Orpheus, Abraham, Jesus Christ, and such like gods, fays his historian. What makes you smile? *Hor.* To think how industrious priests are in concealing a man's failings, when they would have you think well of him. What you fay of Severus, I had read before; when looking one day for something in Moreri, I happened to cast my eye on the article of that emperor, where no mention is made either of Orpheus or Appollonius! which, remembering the passage in Lampridius, I wondered at; and thinking that I might have been mis-

taken, I again consulted that author, where I found it, as you have related it. I do not question but Moreri left this out on purpose to repay.the civilities of the emperor to the Christians, whom, he tells us, Severus had been very favourable to. *Cleo.* That is not impossible in a Roman Catholic. But what I would speak to, in the second place, is the festivals you mentioned, the hecatombs after victories, and the general thankfulness of nations to their gods. I desire you would consider, that in sacred matters, as well as all human affairs, there are rites and ceremonies, and many demonstrations 01 respect to be seen, that to outward appearance seem to proceed from gratitude, which, upon due examination, will be found to have been originally the result of tear. At what time the floral games were sirst instituted, is not well known: but they never were celebrated every year constantly, before a very unseasonable spring put the senate upon the decree that made them annual. To make up the true compound of reverence or veneration, love and esteem are as necessary ingredients as fear; but the latter alone is capable of making men counterfeit both the former; as is evident from the duties that are outwardly paid to tyrants, at the fame time that inwardly they are execrated and hated. Idolators have always behaved themselves to every invisible cause they adored, as men do to a lawless arbitrary power; when they reckon it as captious, haughty, and unreasonable, as they allow it to be sovereign, unlimited, and irresistible. What motive could the frequent repetitions of the fame solemnities spring from, whenever it was suspected that the least holy trifle had.been omitted? You know, how often the same farce was once acted over again, because after every performance there was still room to apprehend that something had been neglected. Do but consult, I beg of you, and call to mind your own reading; cast your eyes on the insinite variety of ideas men have formed to themselves, and the vast multitude of divisions they have made of the invisible cause, which every one imagines to influence human affairs: run over the history of all ages; look into every considerable nation, their straits and calamities, as well as victories and. successes; the lives of great generals, and other famous men, their adverse fortune and prosperity: mind at which times their devotion was most fervent; when oracles were most consulted, and on what accounts the gods were most frequently addressed. Do but calmly consider every thing you can remember relating to superstition, whether grave,, ridiculous, or execrable, and you will sind, in the sirst place, that the heathens, and all that have been ignorant of the true Deity, though many of them were persons otherwise of great knowledge, sine understanding, and tried probity, have represented their gods, not as wife, benign, equitable, and merciful; but, on the contrary, as passionate, revengesul, capricious, and unrelenting beings; not to mention the abominable vices and grols immoralities, the vulgar were taught to ascribe to them: In the second, that for every one instance that men have addresled themselves to an invisible cause, from a principle of gratitude, there are a thousand in every false religion to convince you, that divine worship, and men's submission to Heaven, have always proceeded from their fear. The word religion itself, and the fear of God, are synonimous; and had man's acknowledgment been originally founded in love, as it is in fear, the craft of impostors could have made no advantage of the passion; and all their boasted acquaintance with gods and goddesses, would have been useless to them, if men had worshipped the immortal powers, as they called their idols, out of gratitude. *Hor.* All lawgivers and leaders of people gained their point, and acquired what they expected from those pretences, which is reverence; and which to produce, you have owned yourself, love and esteem to be as requisite as fear. *Cleo.* But from the laws they imposed on men, and the punishments they annexed to the breach and neglect of them, it is easily seen which of the ingredients they most, relied upon. *Hor.* It would be dissicult to name a king, or other great man, in very an-

cient times, who attempted to govern an infant nation that laid no claim to some commerce or other with an invisible power, either held by himself or his ancestors. Between them and Moses, there is no other difference, than that he alone was a true prophet, and really inspired, and all the rest were impostors. *Cleo.* What would you infer from this? *Hor.* That we can fay no more for ourselves, than what men of all parties and persuasions have done in all ages, every one for their cause, viz. That they alone were in the right, and all that differed from them in the wrong. *Cleo.* Is it not sussicient that we can say this ot ourselves with truth and justice, after the strictest examination; when no other cause can stand any test, or bear the least inquiry? A man may relate miracles that never were wrought, and give an account of things that never happened; but a thousand years hence, all knowing men will agree, that nobody could have wrote Sir Isaac Newton's *Priucipia,* unless he had been a great mathematician. "When Moses acquainted the Israelites with what had been revealed to him, he told them a truth, which nobody then upon earth knew but himself. *Hor.* You mean the unity ot God, and his being the Author of the universe. *Cleo.* 1 do 16.. *Hor.* But is not every man of fense capable of knowing this from his reason? *Cleo.* Yes, when the art of reasoning consequentially is come to that perfection, which it has been arrived at these several hundred years, and himself has been led into the method of thinking justly. Every common sailor could steer a course through the midst of the ocean, as soon as the use of the loadstone, and the mariners compass were invented. But before that, the most expert navigator would have trembled at the thoughts of such an enterprise. When Moses acquainted, and imbued the posterity of Jacob with this sublime and important truth, they were degenerated into slaves, attached to the superstition of the country they dwelled in; and the Egyptians, their masters, though they were great prosicients in many arts and sciences, and more deeply skilled in the mysteries of nature

than any other nation then was, had the most abject and abominable notions of the Deity, which it is possible to conceive; and no savages could have exceeded their ignorance and stupidity, as to the Supreme Being, the invisible cause that governs the world. He taught the Israelites *a priori;* and their children, before they were nine or ten years old, knew what the greatest philosophers did not attain to, by the light of nature, till many ages after. *Hor.* The advocates for the ancients will never allow, that any modern philosophers have either thought or reasoned better, than men did in former ages. *Cleo.* Let them believe their eyes: What you fay every man offense may know, by his own reason, was in the beginning of Christianity contested, and denied with zeal and vehemence by the greatest men in Rome. Celsus, Symmachus, Porphyry, Hierocles, and other famous rhetoricians, and men of unquestionable good sense, wrote in defence of idolatry, and strenuously maintained the plurality and multiplicity of their gods. Moses lived about sisteen hundred years before the reign of Augustus. If in a place where I was very well assured that nobody understood any thing of colouring or drawing, a man should tell me, that he had acquired the art of painting by inspiration, I should be more ready to laugh at him than to believe him; but if I saw him draw several sine portraits before my face, my unbelief would cease, and I should think it ridiculous any longer to suspect his veracity. All the accounts that other lawgivers and founders of nations have given of the deities, which they or
E e their predecessors conversed with, contained ideas that were unworthy of the Divine Being; and by the light of nature only, it is easily proved, that they must have been false: But the image which Moses gave the Jews of the Supreme Being, that He was One, and had made heaven and earth, will stand all tests, and is a truth that will outlast the world. Thus, I think, I have fully proved, on the one hand, that all true religion must be revealed, and could not have come into the world without mira-

cle; and, on the other, that what all men are born with towards religion, before they receive any instruction, is fear.

Hor. You have convinced me many ways, that we are poor creatures by nature; but I cannot help struggling against those mortifying truths, when I hear them started iirst. I long to hear the origin of society, and I continually retard your account of it myself with new questions. *Cleo.* Do you remember where we left off? *Hor.* I do not think we have made any progress yet; for we have nothing towards it but a wild man, and a wild woman, with some children and grandchildren, which they are not able either to teach or govern. *Cleo.* I thought that the introduction of the reverence, which the wildest son must feel, more or less, sor the most savage father, if he stays with him, had been a considerable step. *Hor.* I thought so too, till you destroyed the hopes I had conceived of it yourself, by showing me the incapacity of savage parents to make use of it: And since we are still as far from the origin of society as ever we were, or ever can be, in my opinion, I desire, that before you proceed to that main point, you would answer what you have put off once already, which is my question concerning the notions of right and wrong: 1 cannot be easy before 1 have your sentiments on this head. *Cleo.* Your demand is very reasonable, and I will satisfy you as well as 1 can. A man of sense, learning, and experience, that has been well educated, will always sind out the difference between right and wrong in things diametrically opposite; and there are certain facts, which he will always condemn, and others which he will always approve of: To kill a member of the fame society that has not offended us, or to rob him, will always be bad; and to cure the sick, and be benesicent to the public, he will always pronounce to be good actions: and for a man to do as he will be done by, he will always fay is a good rule in life; and not only rqen of great accomplishments, and such as have learned to think abstractly, but all men of middling capacities, that have been brought up in society, will agree in this, in all

countries and in all ages. Nothing likewise seems more true to all, that have made any tolerable use of their faculty of thinking, than that out of the society, before any division was made, eitherby contract or otherwise, all men would have an equal right to the earth: But do you believe that our wild man, if he had never seen any other human creature but his savage consort and his progeny, would ever have entertained the fame notions of right and wrong, *Hor.* Hardly; his small capacity in the art of reasoning, would hinder him from doing it so justly; and the power he found he had over his children, would render him very arbitrary. *Cleo.* But without that incapacity, suppose that at threescore he was, by a miracle, to receive a sine judgment, and the faculty of thinking and reasoning consequentially, in as great a perfection as the wisest man ever did, do you think he would ever alter his notion of the right he had to every thing he could manage, or have other sentiments in relation to himself and his progeny, than from his behaviour it appeared he entertained, when he seemed to act almost altogether by instinct? *Hor.* Without doubt: For, if judgment and reason were given him, what could hinder him from making use of those faculties, as well as others do? *Cleo.* You seem not to consider, that no man can reason but *a po/leriori,* from something that he knows, or supposes to be true: What I said of the difference between right and wrong, 1 spoke of persons who remembered their education, and lived in society; or, at least, such as plainly saw others of their own species, that were independent of them, and either their equals or superiors. *Hor.* 1 begin to believe you are in the right: But at second thoughts, why might not a man, with great justice, think himself the sovereign of a place, where he knew no human creature but his own wife, and the defeendents of both? *Cleo.* With all my heart: But may there not be an hundred such savages in the world with large families, that might never meet, nor ever hear of one another? *Hor.* A thousand, if you will, and then there would be so many natural sovereigns., *Cleo.*

Very well: what I would have you observe, is, that there are things which are commonly esteemed to be eternal truths, that an hundred or a thousand people of sine sense and judgment, could have no notion of. What if it mould be true, that every man is born with this domineering spirit, and that we cannot be cured of it, but by our commerce with others, and the experience of facts, by which we are convinced that we have no such right? Let us examine a man's whole life, from his infancy to his grave, and fee which of the two seems to be most natural to him; a desire of superiority, and grasping every thing to himself, or a tendency to act according to the reasonable notions of right and wrong; and we shall sind, that, in his early youth, the sirst is very conspicuous; that nothing appears of the second before he has received some instructions, and that this latter will always have less influence upon his actions, the more uncivilized he remains: From whence I infer, that the notions of right and wrong are acquired; for if they were as natural, or if they affected us as early as the opinion, or rather the instinct we are born with, of taking every thing to be our own, no child would ever cry for his eldest brother's play-things. *Hor.* I think there is no right more natural, nor more reasonable, than that which men have over their children; and what we owe our parents can never be repaid. *Cleo.* The obligations we have to good parents for their care and education, is certainly very great. *Hor.* That is the least. We are indebted to them for our being; we might be educated by an hundred others, but without them we could never have existed. *Cleo.* So we could have no malt liquor, without the ground that bears the barley: I know no obligations for benesits that never were intended. Should a man fee a sine parcel of cherries, be tempted to eat, and devour them accordingly with great satisfaction, it is possible he might swallow some of the stones, which we know by experience do not digest: If twelve or fourteen months after, he mould sind a little sprig of a cherry-tree growing in a sield, where nobody would expect it, if he recollected the time, he had been there before, it is not improbable that he might gutfs at the true reason how it came there. It is possible, likewise, that for curiosity's fake, this man might take up this plant, and take care of it; I am well assured, that whatever became of it afterwards, the right he would have to it from the merit of his action, would be the fame which a savage would have to his child. *Hor.* I think there would be a vast difference between the one and the other: the cherry-stone was never part of himself, nor mixed with his blood. *Cleo.* Pardon me; all the difference, as vast as you take it to be, can only consist in this, That the cherry-stone was not part of the man who swallowed it, so long, nor received so great an alteration in its sigure, whilst it was, as some other things which the savage swallowed, were, and received in their sigure, whilst they stayed with him. *Hor.* But he that swallowed the cherry-stone, did nothing to it; it produced a plant as a vegetable, which it might have done as well without his swallowing it. *Cleo.* That is true; and I own, that as to the cause to which the plant owes its existence, you are in the right: but 1 plainly spoke as to the merit of the action, which in either cafe could only proceed from their intentions as free agents; and the savage might, and would in all probability act with as little design to get a child, as the other had eat cherries in order to plant a tree. It is commonly said, that our children are our own flesh and blood: but this way of speaking is strangely sigurative. However, allow it to be just, though rhetoricians have no name for it, what does it prove what benevolence in us, what kindness to others in the intention? *Hor.* You mall fay what you please, but 1 think, that nothing can endear children to their parents more, than the reflection that they are their own flesh and blood. *Cleo.* I am of your opinion; and it is a plain demonstration of the superlative value we have for our own selves, and every thing that comes from us, if it be good, and counted laudable; whereas, other things that are offensive, though equally

our own, are in compliment to ourselves, industriously concealed; and, as soon as it is agreed upon that any thing is unseemly, and rather a disgrace to us than otherwise, presently it becomes ill manners to name, or so much as to hint at it. The contents of the stomach are variously disposed of, but we have no hand in that; and whether they go to the blood, or elsewhere, the last thing we did to them voluntarily, and with our knowledge, was swallowing them; and whatever is afterwards performed by the animal economy, a man contributes no more to, than he does to the going of his watch. This iff another instance of the unjust claim we lay to every performance we are but in the least concerned in, if good comes of it, though nature does all the work; but whoever places a merit in his prolisic faculty, ought likewise to expect the blame, when he has the stone, or a fever. Without this violent principle of innate folly, no rational creature would value himself on his free agency, and at the fame time accept of applause for actions that are vilibly independent of his will. Life in all creatures is a compound action, but the share they have in it themselves, is only passive. We are forced to breathe before we know it; and our continuance palpably depends upon the guardianship and perpetual tutelage of nature; whilst every part of her works, ourselves not excepted, is an impenetrable secret to us, that eludes all inquiries. Nature furnishes us with all the substance of our food herself, nor does she trust to our wisdom for an appetite to crave it; to chew it, me teaches us by instinct, and bribes us to it by pleasure. This seeming to be an action of choice, and ourselves being conscious of the performance, we perhaps may be said to have a part in it; but the moment after, nature resumes her care, and again withdrawn-from our knowledge, preserves us in a mysterious manner, without any help or concurrence of ours, that we are scnsible of. Since, then, the management of what we have eat anddrank remains entirely under the direction of nature, what honour or shame ought,we to receive from any part of the product,

whether it is to lerve as a doubtful means toward generation, or yields to vegetation a less fallible assistance? It is nature that prompts us to propagate as well as to eat; and a favage man multiplies his kind by instinct as other animals do, without more thought or design of preserving his species, than a newborn infant has of keeping itself alive, in the action of sucking. *Hor.* Yet nature gave the different instincts to both, for those reasons. *Cleo.* Without doubt; but what I mean, is, that the reason of the thing is as much the motive of action in the one, as it is in the other; and I verily believe, that a wild woman who had never seen, or not minded the production of any young animals, would have several children before she would guei's at the real cause of them; any more than if Ihe had the cholic, she would luspect. that it proceeded from some de. licious fruit she had eaten; especially if she had feasted upon it for several months, without perceiving any inconveniency from it. Children, all the world over, are brought forth with pain, more or less, which seems to have no assinity with pleasure; and an untaught creature, however docile and attentive, would want several clear experiments, before it would believe that the one could produce or be the cause of the other. *Hor.* Most people marry in hopes, and with a design of having children. *Cleo.* I doubt, not; and believe that there are as many that would rather not have children, or at least not so fast as often they come, as there are that wish for them, even in the state of matrimony ; but out of it, in the amours of thoufands, that revel in enjoyments, children are rekoned to be the greatest calamity that can befal them; and often what criminal love gave birth to, without thought, more criminal pride destroys, with purposed and considerate cruelty. But all this belongs to people in society, that are knowing, and well acquainted with the natural consequences of things; what I urged, I spoke of a savage. *Hor.* Still the end of love, between the different sexes, in all animals, is the preservation of their species. *Cleo.* I have allowed that already. But once more the savage is not prompted to love from that consideration: he propagates before he knows the consequence of it; and I much question, whether the most civilized pair, in the most chaste of their embraces, ever acted from the care of their species, as a real principle. A rich man may, with great impatience, wish for a son to inherit his name and his estate; perhaps he may marry from no other motive, and for no other purpose; but all the fatisfaction he seems to receive, from the flattering prospect of an happy posterity, can only arise from a pleasing reflection on himself, as the cause of those descendants. How much soever this man's posterity might be thought to owe him for their being, it is certain, that the motive he acted from, was to oblige himself: still here is a wishing for posterity, a thought and design of getting children, which no wild couple could have to boast of; yet they would be vain enough to look upon themselves, as the principal cause of all their osfspring and descendants, though they should live to see the sifrh or sixth generation *Hor.* I can sind no vanity in that, and I should think them so myself. *Cleo.* Yet, as free agents, it would be plain, that they had contributed nothing to the existence of their prosperity. *Hor.* Now surely, you have overshot the mark; nothing? *Cleo.* No, nothing, even to that of their own children, knowingly; if you will allow that men have their appetites from nature. There is but one real cause in the universe, to produce that insinite variety of stupendous effects, and all the mighty labours that are performed in nature, either within, or far beyond the reach of our fenses. Parents are the efsicients of their offspring, with no more truth or propriety of speech, than the tools of an artisicer, that were made and contrived by himself, are the cause of the most elaborate of his works. The senseless engine that raises water into the copper, and the passive mash-tub, have between them, as great a share in the art and action of brewing, as the liveliest male and female ever had in the production of an animal. *Hor.* You make stocks and stones of us; is it not in our choice to act, or not to act? *Cleo.* Yes, it

is my choice now, either to run my head against the wall, or to let it alone; but, I hope, it does not puzzle you much to guess which of the two I shall choose. *Hor.* But do not we move our bodies as we list *;* and is not every action determined by the will? *Cleo.* What lignisies that, where there isa passion that manifestly sways, and with a strict hand governs that will? *Hor.* Still we act with consciousness, and are intelligent creatures. *Cleo.* Not in the affair I speak of; where, willing or not willing, we are violently urged from within, and in a manner compelled not only to assist in, but likewise to long for, and, in spite of our teeth, be highly pleased with a performance that insinitely surpasses our understanding. The comparison 1 made is just, in every part of it; for the most loving, and, if you will, the most sagacious couple you can conceive, are as ignorant in the mystery of generation, nay, must remain, after having had twenty children together, as much uninformed, and as little conscious of nature's transactions.,:nd what has been wrought within them, as inanimate utensils are of the most mystic and most ingenious operations they have been employed in. *Hor.* I do not know any man more expert in tracing human pride, or more severe in humbling it than yourself; but when the subject comes in your way, you do not know how to leave it. I wish you would, at once, go over to the origin of society; which, how to derive, or bring about at all, from the savage family, as we left it, is past my skill. It is impossible but those children, when they grew up, would quarrel on innumerable occalions: if men had but three appetites to gratify, that are the most obvious, they could never live together in peace, without government: for though they all paid a deference to the father, yet if he was a man void of all prudence, that could give them no good rules to walk by, I am persuaded that they would live in a perpetual state of war; and the more numerous his offspring grew, the more the old savage would be puzzled between his desire and incapacity of government. As they increased in numbers,

they would be forced to extend their limits, and the spot they were born upon would not hold them long: nobody would be willing to leave his native vale, especially if it was a fruitful one. The more 1 think upon it, and the more 1 look into such multitudes, the less 1 can conceive which way they could ever be formed into a society. *Cleo.* The sirst thing that could make man associate, would be common danger, which unites the greatest enemies: this danger they would certainly be in, from wild beasts, considering that no uninhabited country is without them, and the defenceless condition in which men come into the world. This often must have been a cruel article, to prevent the in crease of our species. *Hor.* The fupposition then, that this wild man, with his progeny, should for sifty years live undisturbed, is not very probable; and I need not trouble myself about our savages being embarrassed with too numerous an offspring. *Cleu.* You fay right; there is no probability, that a man and his progeny, all unarmed, should so long escape the ravenous hunger of beaus of prey, that are to live upon what animals they can get; that leave no place unsearched, nor pains untried, to come at food, though with the hazard of their lives. The reason why I made that supposition, was to ihow you, sirst, the improbability that a wild and altogether untaught man should have the knowledge and discretion which Sir William Temple gives him; secondly, that children who conversed with their own species, though they were brought up by savages, would be governable; and conscquently, that all such, when come to maturity, would be sit for society, how ignorant and unskilsul soever their parents might have been. *Hor.* I thank you for it; for it has shown me, that the very sirst generation of the most brutish savages, was sussicient to produce sociable creatures; but that to produce a man sit to govern others, much more was required. *Cleo.* 1 return to my conjecture concerning the sirst motive that would make savages associate: it is not possible to know any thing with certainty of beginnings, where men were destitute of letters; but

I think, that the nature of the thing makes it highly probable, that it must have been their common danger from beasts of prey; as well such fly ones as lay in wait for their children, and the defenceless animals, men made use of for themselves, as the more bold, that would openly attack grown men and women. What much consirms me in this opinion is, the general agreement of all the relations we have, from the most ancient times, in different countries: for, in the infancy of all nations, profane history is stuffed with the accounts of the conflicts men had with wild beasts. It took up the chief labours of the heroes of remotest antiquity, and their greatest prowess was shown in killing of dragons, and subduing of other monsters. *Hor.* Do you lay any stress upon sphinxes, basilisks, flying dragons, and bulls that spit sire? *Cleo.* As much as I do on modern witches. But I believe that all those sictions had their rise from noxious beasts, the mischiefs they did, and other realities that struck terror into man; and I believe, that if no man had ever been seen on a horse's back, we should never have heard of Centaurs. The prodigious force and rage that are apparent in some savage animals, and the astonishing power, which, from the various poisons of venomous creatures, we are sure must be hid in others; the sudden and unexpected assaults of serpents, the variety of them; the vast bulk of crocodiles; the irregular and uncommon ihapes of some sisties, and the wings of others, are all things that are capable of alarming man's fear; and it is incredible what chimeras that passion alone may produce in a terrisied mind: the dangers of the day often haunt men at night with addition of terror; and from what they remember in their dreams, it is easy to forge realities. If you will consider, likewise, that the natural ignorance of man, and his hankering after knowledge, will augment the credulity which ho ie and f.-ar sirst give birth to; the desire the generality ha /e of applause, and the great esteem that is commonly had for the *metveilleux,* and the witnesses and relaters of it: If, I fay, you will consider all these, you will eas-

ily discover, how many creatures came to be talked of, described, and formally painted, that never had any existence. *Hor.* I do not wonder at the origin of monstrous sigures, or the invention of any fables whatever; but in the reason you gave for the sirst motive, that would make men combine in one interest, I sind something very perplexing, which I own I never thought of before. Wiien I rested on the condition of man, as you have set it before me, naked and defenceless, and the multitude of ravenous animals that thirst after his blood, and are superior to him in strength, and completely armed by nature, it is inconceivable to me, how" our species should have subsisted. *Cleo.* What you observe is well worthy our attention. *Hor.* It is astonishing. What silthy, abominable beasts are lions and tigers! *Cleo.* I think them to be very sine creatures; there is nothing I admire more than a lion. *Hor.* We have strange accounts of his generosity and gratitude; but do you believe them? *Cicj.* I do not trouble my head about them: What I admire is his fabric, his structure, and his rage, so justly proportioned to one another. There are order, symmetry, and superlative wisdom to be observed in all the works of nature; but she has not a machine, of which every part more visibly answers the end for which the whole was formed. *Hor.* The destruction of other animals. *Cleo.* That is true; but how conspicuous is that end, without mystery or uncertainty! that grapes were made for wine, and man for society, are truths not accomplished in every individual: but there is a real majesty stamped on every single lion, at the sight of which the stoutest animals submit and tremble. When we look upon and examine his massy talons, the size of them, and the laboured sirmness with which they are sixed in, and fastened to that prodigious paw; his dreadful teeth, the strength of his jaws, and the width of his mouth equally terrible, the use of them is obvious; but when we consider, moreover, the make of his limbs, the toughness of his flesh and tendons, the solidity of his bones, beyond that of other animals, and the whole frame of him,

together with his never-ceasing anger, speed, and agility; whilst in the desart he ranges king of beasts! When, I fay, we consider all these things, it is stupidity not to fee the design of nature, and with what amazing skill the beautiful creature is contrived for offensive war and conquest. *Hor.* You are a good painter. But after all, why would you judge of a creature's nature from what it was perverted to, rather than from its original, the state it was sirst produced in? The lion in Paradise was a gentle, loving creature. Hear what Milton fays of his behaviour before Adam and Eve, " as they fate recline on the soft downy bank, da" mask'd with flowers:" About them frisking play'd
All hearts of the earth, since wild, and of all chafe
In wood or wilderness, forest or den;
Sporting the lion ramp'd, and in his paw
Dandel'd the kid; bears, tigers, ounces, pards,
GambolM before them.
What was it the lion fed upon ; what sustenance had all these beasts of prey in Paradise?
Cleo. I do not know. Nobody who believes the Bible, doubts, but that the whole state of Paradise, and the intercourse between God and the sirst man, were as much preternatural, as the creation out of nothing; and, therefore, it cannot be supposed, that they should be accounted for by human reason; and if they were, Moses would not be answerable for more than he advanced himself. The history which he has given us of those times is extremely succinct, and ought not to be charged with any thing contained in the glosses and paraphrases that have been made upon it by others. *Hor.* Milton has said nothing of Paradise, but what he could justify from Moses. *Cleo.* It is no where to be proved, from Moses, that the state of innocence lasted so long, that goats, or any viviparous animals could, have bred and brought forth young ones. *Hor.* You mean that there could have been no kid. I should never have made that cavil in so sine a poem. It was not in my thoughts: what I aimed at in repeating those lines, was to show you how su-

perfluous and impertinent a lion must have been in Paradise; and that those who pretend to find fault with the works of nature, might have censured her with justice, for lavishing and throwing away so many excellencies upon a great beast, to no purpose. What a sine variety of destructive weapons, would they fay, what prodigious strength of limbs and sinews are here given to a creature! What to do with? to be quiet and dandle a kid. I own, that to me, this province, the employment assigned to the lion, seems to be as proper and well chosen, as if you would make a nurse of Alexander the Great. *Cleo.* You might make as many flights upon a lion now, if you saw him asleep. Nobody would think that a bull had occasion for horns, who had never seen him otherwise than quietly grazing among a parcel of cows; but, if one should fee him attacked by dogs, by a wolf, or a rival of his *own* species, he would soon sind out that his horns were of great use and service to him. The lion was not made to be always in Paradise. *Hor.* There I would have you. If the lion was contrived for purposes to be served and executed out of Paradise, then it is manifest, from the very creation, that the tail of man was determined and predestinated. *Cleo.* Foreknown it was: nothing could be hid from Omniscience; that is certain: But that it was predestinated so as to have prejudiced, or anywise influenced the free will of Adam, 1 utterly deny. But that word, predestinated, has made ib much noise in the world, and the thing itself has been the cause of so many fatal quarrels, and is so inexplicable, that 1 am resolved never to engage in any dispute concerning it. *Hor.* I cannot make you; but what you have extolled so much, must have cost the lives of thousands of our species; and it is a wonder to me how men, when they were but few, could possibly defend themselves, before they had sire arms, or at least bows and arrows; for what number of naked men and women, would be a match for one couple of lions? *Cleo.* Yet, here we are; and none of those animals are suffered to be wild, in any civilized nation; our superior under-standing has got the start of them. *Hor.* My reason tells me it must be that; but I cannot help observing, that when human understanding serves your purpose to solve any thing, it is always ready and full grown; but at other times, knowledge and reasoning are the work of time, and men are not capable of thinking justly, until after many generations. Pray, before men had arms, what could their understanding do against lions, and what hindered wild beasts from devouring mankind, as soon as they were born? *Cleo.* Providence. *Hor.* Daniel, indeed, was saved by miracle; but what is that to the rest of mankind? great numbers, we know, have, at different times, been torn to pieces by savage beasts: what I want to know, is, the reason that any of them elcaped, and the whole species was not destroyed by them; when men had yet no weapons to defend, nor strong holds to shelter themselves from the fury of those merciless creatures. *Cleo.* I have named it to you already, Providence. *Hor.* But which way can you prove this miraculous affist Cico. You still talk of miracles, and I speak of Providence, or the all-governing Wisdom of God. *Hor.* If you can, demonstrate to me, how that Wisdom interposed between uiir species and that of lions, in the beginning of the world, without miracle, any more than it does at present, *eris mihi magnus Apollo:* for now, I am sure, a wild lion would prey upon a naked man, as soon, at least, as he would upon an ox or an horse. *Cleo.* Will not you allow me, that all properties, instincts, and what we call the nature of things, animate or inanimate, are the produce, the estects of that Wiidom? *Hor.* I never thought otherwise. *Cleo.* Then it will not be dissicult to prove this to you. Lions are never brought forth wild, but in very hot countries, as bears are the product or the cold. But the generality of our species, which loves moderate warmth, are most delighted with the middle regions. Men may, against their wills, be inured to intense cold, or by use and patience, accustom themselves to excessive heat; but a mild air, and weather between both extremes, being more agreeable to human bodies, the greatest part of mankind would naturally settle in temperate climates, and with the lame conveniency, as to every thing else, never choose any other. This would very much lessen the danger men would be in from the siercest and most irrelistible wild beasts. *Hor.* But would lions and tigers in hot countries keep so close within their bounds, and bears in cold ones, as never to straggle or stray beyond them? *Cleo.* I do not suppose they would; and men, as well as cattle, have often been picked up by lions, far from the places where these were whelped No wild beasts are more fatal to our species, than often we are to one another; and men pursued by their enemies have fled into climates and countries, which they would never have chose. Avarice likewise and curiosity, have, without force or necessity, often exposed men to dangers, which they might have avoided, if they had been satissied with what nature required; and laboured for self-preservation in that simple manner, which creatures less vain and fantastical content themselves with. In all these cases, I do not question, but multitudes of our species have suffered from Ravage beasts, and other noxious animals; and on their account only, 1 verily believe, it would have been impossible for any number of men, to have settled or subsisted in either very hot or very cold countries, before the invention of bows and arrows, or better arms. But all this does nothing to overthrow my assertion: what I wanted to prove, is, that all creatures choosing by instinct that degree of heat or cold which is most natural to them, there would be room enough in the world for man to multiply his species, for many ages, without running almost any risk of being devoured either by lions br by bears; and that the most savage man would sind this out, without the help of his reason. This I call the work os Providence; by which I mean the unalterable wisdom of the Supreme Being, in the harmonious disposition of the universe; the fountain of that incomprehensible chain of causes, on which all events have their undoubted dependance. *Hor.*

You have made this out better than I had expected; but I am afraid, that what you alleged as the sirst motive towards society, is come to nothing by it. *Cleo.* Do not fear that; there are other savage beasts, against which men could not guard themselves unarmed, without joining, and mutual assistance: in temperate climates, most uncultivated countries abound with wolves. *Hor.* I have seen them in Germany; they are of the size of a large mastiff; but 1 thought their chief prey had been sheep. *Cleo.* Any thing they can conquer is their prey: they are desperate creatures, and will fall upon men, cows, and horses, as well as upon sheep, when they are very hungry: they have teeth like mastiffs; but besides them they have sharp claws to tear with, which dogs have not. The stoutest man is hardly equal to them in strength; but what is worse, they often come in troops, and whole villages have been attacked by them; they have sive, six, and more whelps at a litter, and would loon over-run a country where they breed, if Ttien did not combine against, and make it their business to destroy them. Wild boars likewise, are terrible creatures, that few large forests, and uninhabited places, in temperate climates, are free from. *Hor.* Those tusks of theirs are dreadful weapons. *Cl-co.* And they are much superior to wolves in bulk and strength. History is full of the mischief they have done in ancient times, and of the renown that valiant men have gained by conquering them. *Hor.* That is true; but those heroes that fought monsters in former days, were well armed; at least, the generality of them; but what could a number of naked men, before they had any arms at all, have to oppose to the teeth and claws of ravenous wolves that came in troops; and what impression could the greatest blow a man can strike, make upon the thick bristly hide of a wild boar? *Cleo.* As on the one hand, I have named every thing that man has to fear from wild beasts; so, on the other, we ought not to forget the things that are in his favour. In the sirst place, a wild man inured to hardship, would far exceed a tame one, in all feats of strength,

nimbleness and activity; in the second, his anger would iooner and more usefully transport and assist him in his savage state, than it can do in society; where, from his insancy he is so many ways taught, and forced in his own defence, to cramp and stifle with his fears the noble gift of nature. In wild creatures we fee, that most of them, when their own life or that of their young ones is at stake, sight with great obstinacy, and continue sighting to the last, and do what mischief they can, whilst they have breath, without regard to their being overmatched, or the disadvantages they labour under. It is observed, likewise, that the more untaught and inconsiderate creatures are, the more entirelv they are swayed by the passion that is uppermost: natural affection would make wild men and women too, sacrisice their lives, and die for their children; but they would die sighting; and one wolf would not sind it an easy matter to carry of a child from his watchful parents, if Jhey were both resolute, though they were naked. As to man's being born defenceless, it is not to be conceived, that he should long know the strength of his arms, without being acquainted with the articulation of his singers, or at least, what is owing to it, his faculty of grasping and holding fast; and the most untaught savage would make use of clubs and staves before he came to maturity. As the danger men are in from wild beasts would be of the highest consequence, so it would employ their utmost care and industry: they would dig holes, and invent other stratagems, to distress their enemies, and destroy their' young ones: as soon as they found out sire, they would make use of that element to guard themselves and annoy their foes: by the help of it they would soon learn to sharpen wood, which presently would put them upon making spears and other weapons that would cut. When men are angry enough with creatures to strike them, and these are running away, or flying from them, they are apt to throw at what they cannot reach: this, as soon as they had spears, would naturally lead them to the invention of darts and javelins. Here,

perhaps, they may stop a while; but the fame chain of thinking would, in time, produce bows and arrows: the elasticity of sticks and boughs of trees is very obvious; and to make strings of the guts of animals, I dare fay, is more ancient than the use of hemp. Experience teaches us, that men may have all these, and many more weapons, and be very expert in the use of them, before any manner of government, except that of parents over their children, is to be seen among them: it is likewise very well known, that savages furnished with no better arms, when they are strong enough in number, will venture to attack, and even hunt after the siercest wild beasts, lions and tigers not excepted. Another thing is to be considered, that likewise favours our species, and relates to the nature of the creatures, of which intemperate climates man has reason to stand in bodily fear of. *Hor.* Wolves and wild boars? *Cleo.* Yes. That great numbers of our species have been devoured by the sirst, is uncontested; but they most naturally go in quest of sheep and poultry; and, as long as they can get carrion, or any thing to sill their bellies with, they seldom hunt after men, or other largo animals; which is the reason, that in the summer our species, as to personal insults, havenot much-to fear from them. It is certain likewise, that savage swine will hunt after men, and many of their maws

F f / have been crammed with human flesh: but they naturally feed on acorns, chesnuts, beach-mast:, and other vegetables: and they are only carnivorous upon occasion, and through necestity, when they can get nothing else; in great frosts, when the country is bare, and every thing covered with snow. It is evident, then, that human creatures are not in any great and immediate danger from either of these species of beasts, but in hard winters, which happen but seldom in temperate climates. But as they are our perpetual enemies, by spoiling and devouring every thing that may serve for the sustenance of man, it is highly necessary, that we should not only be always upon our guard against them, but likewise never cease to asiist one another in routing and destroying them. *Hor.* I plainly see, that mankind might subsist and survive to multiply, and get the mastery over all other creatures that should oppose them; and as this could never have been brought about, unless men had assisted one another against savage beasts, it is possible that the necessity men were in of joining and uniting together, was the sirst step toward society. Thus far 1 am willing to allow you to have proved your main point: but to ascribe all this to Providence, otherwise than that nothing is done without the Divine permission, seems inconsistent with the ideas we have of a perfectly good and merciful Being. It is possible, that all poisonous animals may have something in them that is benesicial to men; and I will not dispute with you, whether the most venomous of all the serpents which Lucan has made mention of, did not contain some antidote, or other sine medicine, still undiscovered: but when I look upon the vast variety of ravenous and blood-thirsty creatures, that are not only superior to us in strength, but likewise visibly armed by nature, as it were on purpose for our destruction; when, I say, I look upon these, I can sind out no use for them, nor what they could be designed for, unless it be to punish us: but 1 can much less conceive, that the Divine Wisdom mould have made them the means without which men could not have been civilized. How many thousands of our species must have been devoured in the conflicts with them! *Cleo.* Ten troops of wolves, with sifty in each, would make a terrible havoc, in a long winter, among a million of ourspe,cies with their hands tied behind them; but among half that number, one pestilence has been known to slaughter more,. than so many wolves could have eaten in the fame time; hot withstanding the great resistance that was made against it, by approved of medicines and able physicians. It is owing to the principle of pride we are born with, and the high value we all, for the fake of one, have for our species, that men imagine the whole universe to be principally made for their use; and this error makes them commit a

thousand extravagancies, and have pitiful and most unworthy notions ot God and his works. It is not greater cruelty, or more unnatural, in a wolf to eat a piece of a man, than it is in a man to eat part of a lamb or a chicken. What, or how many purposes wild beasts were made for, is not for us to determine; but that they were made, we know; and that some of them must have been very calamitious to every infant nation, and settlement of men, is almost as certain: this you was fully persuaded of; and thought, moreover, that they must have been such an obstacle to the very sublistence of our species, as was insurmountable: In answer to this dissiculty, which you started, I showed you, from the different instincts and peculiar tendencies of animals, that in nature a manifest provision was made for our species: by which, notwithstanding the rage and power of the siercest beasts, we mould make a shift, naked and defenceless, to escape their fury, so as to be able to maintain ourselves and multiply our kind, till by our numbers, and arms acquired by our own industry, we could put to flight, or destroy all savage beasts without exception, whatever spot of the globe we might have a mind to cultivate and settle on. The necessary blessings we receive from the fun, are obvious to a child; and it is demonstrable, that without it, none of the living creatures that are now upon the earth, could subsist. But if it were of no other use, being eight hundred thousand times bigger than the earth at least, one thousandth part of it would do our business as well, if it was but nearer to us in proportion. From this consideration alone, I am persuaded, that the sun was made to enlighten and cherish other bodies, besides this planet of ours. Fire and water were designed for innumerable purposes; and among the uses that are made of them, some are immensely different from others. But whilst we receive the benesit of these, and are only intent on ourselves, it his highly probable, that there are thousands of things, and perhaps our own machines among them, that, in the vast system of the universe, Ff?

are now serving some very wise ends, which we shall neves know. According to that plan of this globe, I mean the scheme of government, in relation to the living creatures that inhabit the earth, the destruction of animals is as necessary aa the generation of them.. *Hor.* I have learned that from the Fable of the Bees; and I believe what I have read there to be very true; that, if any one species was to be exempt from death, it would in time crush all the rest to pieces, though the sirst were sheep, and the latter all lions: but that the Supreme Being should have introduced oc ety at the expence of so many lives of our species, I cannot believe, when it might have been done much better in a milder way. *Cleo.* We are speaking of what probably was done, and not of what might have been done. There is no question, but the fame Power that made whales, might have made us seventy feet high, and given us strength in proportion. But since the plan of this globe requires, and you think it necessary yourself, that in every species some should die almost as fast as others are born, why mould you take away any of the means of dying? *Hor.* Are there not diseases enough, physicians and apothecaries, as well as wars by sea and land, that may take off more than the redundancy of our species? *Cleo.* They may, it is true; but in fact they are not always sussicient to do this: and in populous nations we fee, that war, Wild beasts, hanging, drowning, and an hunded casualties together, with sickness and all its attendants, are hardly a match for one invisible faculty of ours, which is the instinct men have to preserve their species. Every thing is easy to the Deity; but to speak after an human manner, it is evident, that in forming this earth, and every thing that is in it, no less wisdom or solicitude was required, in contriving the various ways and means, to get rid and destroy animals, than seems to have been employed in producing them; and it is as demonstrable, that our bodies were made on purpose not to last beyond such a period, as it is, that some houses are built with a design not to stand longer than such a term of years.

But it is death itself to which our aversion by nature is universal; as to the manner of dying, men differ in their opinions; and I never heard of one yet that was generally liked of. *Hor.* But nobody chooses a cruel one. What an unspeakable and insinitely excruciating torment must it be, to be torn to pieces, and eat alive by a savage beast! *Cleo.* Not greater, I can assure you, than are daily occasioned by the gout in the stomach, and the stone in the bladder. *Hor.* Which way can you give me this assurance; how can you prove it? *Cleo.* From our fabric itself, the frame of human bodies, that cannot admit of any torment, insinitely excruciating. The degrees of pain, as well as of pleasure, in this life are limited, and exactly proportioned to every one's strength; whatever exceeds that, takes away the fenses; and whoever has once fainfed away with the extremity of any torture, knows the full extent of what here he can susfer, if he remembers what he felt. The real mischief which wild beasts have done to our species, and the calamities they have brought upon it, are not to be compared to the cruel usage, and the multiplicity of mortal injuries which men have received from one another. Set before your eyes a robust warrior, that having lost a limb in battle, is afterwards trampled upon by twenty horses; and tell me, pray, whether you think, that lying thus helpless with most of his ribs broke, and a fractured skull, in the agony of death, for several hours, he susfers less than if a lion had dispatched him? *Hor.* They are both very bad. *Cleo.* In the choice of things we are more often directed by the caprice of fashions, and the custom of the age, than we are by solid reason, or our own understanding. There is no greater comfort in dying of a dropsy, and in being eaten by worms, than there is in being drowned at sea, and becoming the prey of simes. But in our narrow way of thinking, there is something that subverts and corrupt our judgment; how else could persons of known elegancy in their taste, prefer rotting and stinking in a loathsome sepulchre, to their being burnt in the open air to inoffensive allies? *Hor.* I freely own, that I have an aversion to every thing that is shocking and unnatural. *Cleo.* What you call mocking, I do not know; but no thing is more common to nature, or more agreeable to her ordinary course, than that creatures fliould live upon one another. The whole system of animated beings on the earth seems to be built upon this; and there is not one species that we know of, that has not another that feeds upon it, either alive or dead; and most kind of sish are forced to live upon 'sish. That this in the last-mentioned, was not an omission or neglect, is evident from the large provision nature has made for it, far exceeding any thing she has done for other animals. *Hor.* You mean the prodigious quantity of roe they spawn. *Hor.* Yes; and that the eggs contained in them, receive not their fecundity until after they are excluded; by which means the female may be silled with as many of them as her belly can hold, and the eggs themselves may be more closely crowded together, than would be consistent with the admission of any substance from the male: without this, one silh could not bring forth yearly such a prodigious shoal. *Hor.* But might not the *aura seminalis* of the male be subtile enough to penetrate the whole cluster of eggs, and insluence every one of them, without taking up any room, as it does in fowls and other oviparous animals? *Cleo.* The ostrich excepted in the sirst place: in the second, there are no other oviparous animals in which the eggs are so closely compacted together, as they are in sish. But suppose the prolisic power siiould pervade the whole mass of them; if ail the eggs which some of the females are crammed with, were to be impregnated whilst they are within the sish, it is impossible but the *aura seminalis,* the prolisic spirit of the male, though it took up no room itself, would, as it does in all other creatures, dilate, and more or less distend every egg; and the least expansion of so many individuals would swell the whole roe to a bulk that would require a much greater space, than the cavity that now contains them. Is not here a contrivance beyond imagination sine, to provide for the continuance of a species, though every individual of it should be born with an instinct to destroy it! *Hor.* What you speak of, is only true at sea, in a considerable part of Europe at least: for in fresh water, most kinds of sisti do not feed on their own species, and yet they spawn in the same manner, and are as full of roe as all the rest: among them, the only great destroyer with us, is the pike. *Cleo.* And he is a very ravenous one: We fee in ponds, that where pikes are suffered to be, no other sissi shall ever increase in number. But in rivers, and all waters near any land, there are amphibious fowls, and many sorts of them, that live mostly upon sish: Of these water-fowls in many places are prodigious quantities. Besides these, there are otters, beavers, and many other creatures that live upon sish. In brooks and shallow waters, the hearn and bittern will have their share: What is taken off by them, perhaps is but little; but the young fry, and the spawn that one pair of swans are able to consume in one year, would very well serve to stock a considerable river. So they are but eat, it is no matter what eats them, either their own species or another: What I would prove, is, that nature produces no extraordinary numbers of any species, but she has contrived means answerable to destroy them. The variety of insects in the several parts of the world, would be incredible to any one that has not examined into this matter; and the disferent beauties to be observed in them is insinite: But neither the beauty, nor the variety of them, are more surprising, than the industry ofnature in the multiplicity of her contrivances to kill them; and if the care and vigilance of all other animals in destroying them were to cease at once, in two years time the greatest part of the earth, which is ours now, would be theirs, and in many countries insects would-be the only inhabitants. *Hor.* I have heard that whales live upon nothing else; that must make a sine consumption. *Cleo.* That is the general opinion, I suppose, because they never sind any sish in them; and because there are vast multitudes of insects in those seas, hovering on the surface of the water. This creature likewise helps to corroborate my assertion, that in the numbers produced of every species, the greatest regard is had to the consumption of them: This prodigious animal being too big to be swallowed, nature in it has quite altered the economy observed in all other sish; for they are viviparous, engender like other viviparous animals, and have never above two or three young ones at a time. For the continuance of every species among such an insinite variety of creatures as this globe yields, it was highly necessary, that the provision for their destruction should not be less ample, than that which was made for the generation of them; and therefore the solicitude of nature in procuring death, and the consumption of animals, is visibly superior to the care she takes to feed and preserve them. *flor.* Prove that prav. *Cleo.* Millions of her creatures are starved every year, and doomed to perish for want of sustenance; but whenever any die, there is always plenty of mouths to devour them. But then, again, she gives all she has: nothing is so siue or elaborate, as that she grudges it for food; nor is any thing more extensive or impartial than her bounty: she thinks nothing too good for the meanest of her broods, and all creatures are equally welcome to every thing they can sind to eat. Ho% curious is the workman (hip in the structure of a common fly; how inimitable are the celerity of his wings, and the quickness of all his motions in hot weather! Should a Pythagorean, that was likewise a good master in mechanics, by the help of a microscope, pry into every minute part of this changeable creature, and duly consider the elegancy of its machinery, would he not think it great pity, that thousands of millions of animated beings, so nicely wrought and admirably sinished, should every day be devoured by little birds and spiders, of which we stand in so little need? Nay, do not you think yourself, that things would have been managed full as well, if the quantity,of flies had been less, and there had been no spiders at all? *Hor.* I remember the fable of the Acorn and the Pumkin too well to answer you; I do not trouble

my head about it. *Cleo.* Yet you found fault with the means, which I supposed Providence had made use of to make men associate; I mean the common danger they were in from wild beasts: though you owned the probability of its having been the sirst motive of their uniting. *Hor.* 1 cannot believe that Providence should have no greater regard to our species, than it has to slies, and the spawn of tish: or that nature has ever sported with the fate os human creatures, as she does with the lives of insects, and been as wantonly lavish of the sirst, as she seems to be of the latter. 1 wonder how you can reconcile this to religion; you that are such a stickler for Christianity. *Cleo.* Religion has nothing to do with it. But we are so full of our own species, and the excellency of it, that we have no leisure seriously to.consider the system of this earth; I mean the plan on which the economy of it is built, in relation to the living creatures that are in and upon it. *Hor.* 1 do not speak as to our species, but in respect to the Deity: has religion nothing to do with it, that you make God the author of lo much cruelty and malice? *Cleo.* It is impossible, you should speak otherwise, than in relation to our species, when you make use of those expressions, which can only signify to us the intentions things were done with, or the sentiments human creatures have of them; and nothing can be called cruel or malicious in regard to him who did it, unless his thoughts and designs were such in doing it. All actions in nature, abstractly considered, are equally indifferent; and whatever it may be to individual creatures, to die is not a greater evil to this earth, or the whole universe, than it is to be born. *Hor.* This is making the First Cause of things not an intelligent being. *Cleo.* Why so? Can you not conceive an intelligent, and even a most wife being, that is not only exempt from, but likewise incapable of entertaining any malice or cruelty? *Hor.* Such a being could not commit, or order things that are malicious and cruel. *Cleo.* Neither does God. But this will carry us into a dispute about the origin of evil; and from thence we must in-

evitably fall on free-will and predestination, which, as 1 have told you before, is an inexplicable mystery I will never meddle with. But 1 never said nor thought any thing irreverent to the Deity: on the contrary, the idea I have of the Supreme Being, is as transcendently great, as my capacity is able to form one, of what is incomprehensible; and 1 could as soon believe, that he could cease to exist, as that he should be the author of any real evil. But I should be glad to hear the method, after which you think society might have been much better introduced: Pray, acquaint me with that milder way you spoke of. *Hor.* You have thoroughly convinced me, that the natural love which it is pretended we have for our species, is not greater than what many other animals have for theirs: but if nature had actually given us an affection for one another, as sincere and conspicuous as that which parents are seen to have for their children, whilst they are helpless, men would have joined together by choice; and nothing could have hindred them from associating, whether their numbers had been great or small, and.thersti'elves either ignorant or knowing. M *Cleo. 0 mentes bominum cæcas! 0 Petlora cæca! Hor.* You may exclaim as much as you please; I am persuaded that this would have united men in sirmer bonds of friendship, than any common danger from wild beasts could have tied them with: but what fault can you sind with it, and what mischief could have befallen us from mutual asfection? *Cleo.* It would have been inconsistent with the scheme, thp plan after which, it is evident, Providence has been pleased to order and dispose of things in the universe. If such an asfection had been planted in man by instinct, there never could have be&n any fatal quarrels among them, nor mortal hatreds; men could never have been cruel to one another: in short, there could have been no wars of any duration; and no considerable numbers of our species could ever have been killed by one another's malice. *Hor.* You would make a rare state-physician, in prescribing war, cruelty and malice, for the welfare and maintenance of civil society. *Cleo.* Pray, do not misrepresent me: I have done no such thing: but if you believe the world is governed by Providence at all, you must believe likewise, that the Deity makes use of means to bring about, perform, and execute his will and pleasure: As for example, to have war kindled, there must be sirst misunderstandings and quarrels between the subjects of disferent nations, and disfentions among the respective princes, rulers, or governors of them: it is evident, that the mind of man is the general mint where the means of this fort must be coined; from whence I conclude, that if Providence had ordered matters after that mild way, which you think would have been the best, very little of human blood could have been spilt, if any at all. *Hor.* Where would have been the inconveniency of that: *Cleo.* You could not have had that variety of living creatures, there is now; nay, there would not have been room for man himself, and his sustenance: our species alone would have overstocked the earth, if there had been no wars, and the commmon course of Providence had not been more interrupted than it has been. Might 1 not justly fay then, that this is quite contrary and destructive to the scheme on which it is plain this earth was built? This is a consideration which you will never give its due.jWjeight. I have once already put you in mind of it, that you yourself have allowed the destruction of animals to be as necessary as the generation of them. There is as much wisdom to be seen in the contrivances how numbers of living creatures might always be taken osf and destroyed, to make room for those that continually succeed them, as there is in making all the different forts of them, every one preserve their own species. What do you think is the reason, that there is but one way for us to come into the world? *Hor.* Because that one is sussicient. *Cko.* Then from a parity of reason, we ought to think, that there are several ways to go out of the world, because one would not have been sussicient. Now, if for the support and maintenance of that variety of creatures which are here that they

should die, is a *pojlulatum* as necessary as it is, that they mould be born; and you cut off or obstruct the means of dying, and actually stop up one of the great gates, through which we fee multitudes go to death; do you not oppose the scheme, nay, do you mar it less, than if you hindered generation! If there never had been war, and no other means of dying, besides the ordinary ones, this globe could not have born, or at least not maintained, the tenth part of the people that would have been in it. By war, I do not mean only such as one nation has had against another, but civil as well as foreign quarrels, general massacres, private murders, poison, sword, and all hostile force, by which men, notwithstanding their pretence of love to their species, have endeavoured to take away one another's lives throughout the world, from the time that Cain slew Abel to this day. *Hor.* I do not believe, that a quarter of all these mischiefs are upon record: but what may be known from history, would make a prodigious number of men: much greater, I dare fay, than ever was on earth at one time: But what would you infer from this? They would not have been immortal; and if they had not died in war, they must soon after have been slain by diseases. When a man of threescore is killed by a bullet in the sield, it is odds, that he would not have lived four years longer, though he had stayed at home. *Cleo.* There arc soldiers of threescore perhaps in all armies, but men generally go to the war when they are young; and-when four or sive thousand are lost in battle, you will sind the greatest number to have been under sive-and-thirty: consider now, that many men do not marry till after that age, who get ten or a dozen children. *Hor.* If all that die by the hands of another, were to get a dozen children before they die *Cleo.* There is no occasion for that; I suppose nothing, that is either extravagant or improbable; but that all such, as have been wilfully destroyed by means of their species, should have lived, and taken their chance with the rest; that eveiy thing should have befallen them, that has befallen those that

have not been killed that way; and the same likewise to their posterity; and that all of them should have been subject to all the casualties as well as diseases, doctors, apothecaries, and other accident's, that take away man's life, and shorten his days; war, and violence from one another, only excepted. *Hor.* But if the earth had been too full of inhabitants, might not Providence have sent pestilences and diseases oftener? More children might have died when they were young, or more women might have proved barren. *Cleo.* 1 do not know whether your mild way would hare been more generally pleasing; but you entertain notions os the Deity that are unworthy of him. Men might certainly have been born with the instinct you speak of; but if this had been the Creator's pleasure, there must have been another economy; and things on earth, from the beginning, would have been ordered in a manner quite different from what they are now. But to make a scheme sirst, and afterwards to mend it, when it proves defective, is the business os finite wisdom; it belongs to human prudence alone to mend faults, to correct and redress what was done amiss before, and to alter the measures which experience teaches men, were ill concerted: but the knowledge of God was consummate from eternity. Insinite Wisdom is not liable to errors or mistakes; therefore all his works are universally good, and every thing is made exactly as he would have it: the sirmness and stability of his laws and councils are everlasting, and therefore his resolutions are as unalterable, as his decrees are eternal. It is not a quarter of an hour ago, that you named wars among the necessary means to carry off the redundancy of our species; how come you now to think them uscless? I can demonstrate to you, that nature, in the production of our species, has amply provided against the losses of our sex, occasioned by wars, by repairing them visibly, where they are sustained, in as palpable a manner, as she has provided for the great destruction that is made of sish, by their devouring one another. *Hor.* How is that, pray? *Cleo.* By sending more males into the world than females. "You will easily allow me that our sex bears the brunr of all the toils and hazards that are undergone by sea and land; and that by this means a far greater number of men must be destroyed than there is of women: now if we fee, as certainly we do, that of the infants yearly born, the number of males is always considerably superior to that os the females, is it mot manifest, that nature has made a provision for great multitudes, which, if they were not destroyed, would be not only superfluous, but of pernicious consequence in great nations? *Hor.* That superiority in the number of males born is wonderful indeed; I remember the account that has been published concerning it, as it was taken from the bills of births and burials in the city and suburbs. *Cleo.* For fourscore years; in which the number of females born was constantly much inferior to that of the males, sometimes by many hundreds: and that this provision of nature, to supply the havoc that is made of men by wars and navigation, is still greater than could be imagined from that difference only, will soon appear, if we consider that women, in the sirst place, are liable to all diseases, within a trifle, that are incident to men; and that, in the second, they are subject to many disorders and calamities on account of their sex, which great numbers die of, and which men are wholly exempt from. *Hor.* This could not well be the effect of chance; but it spoils the consequence which you drew from my affectionate scheme, in case there had been no wars: for your fear that our species would have increased beyond all bounds, was entirely built upon the supposition, that those who have died in war should not have wanted women if they had lived; which, from this superiority in the number of males, it is evidfint, they should and must have wanted. *Cleo.* What you observe is true; but my chief aim was to show you how disagreeable the alteration you required would have been every.vay to the rest of the scheme, by which iris manifest things are governed at present. For, if the provision had been made on the oth-

er side; and nature, in the production of our species, had continually taken care to repair the loss of women that die of calamities n jt incident to.men, then certainly there would have been women for all the men that have been destroyed by their own species, if they had lived; and the earth without war, as I have said, would have been over-stocked; or, if nature had ever been the same as she is now, that is, if more males had been born than females, and more females had died of diseases than males, the world would constantly have had a great superfluity of men, if there never had been any wars; and this disproportion between their number and that of the women would have caused innumerable mischiefs, that are now prevented by no other natural causes, than the small value men set upon their species, and their dissensions with one another. *Hor.* I can fee no other mischief this would produce, than than that the number of males which die without having ever tried matrimony, would be greater than it is now; and whether that would be a real evil or not, is a very disputable point. *Cleo.* Do not you think, that this perpetual scarcity of women, and superfluity of men, would make great uneasiness in all societies, how well soever people might love one another; and that the value, the price of women, y6uld be so enhanced by it, that none but men in tolerable good circumstances would be able to purchase them? This alone would make us another world; and mankind could never have known that most necessary and now inexhuastible spring, from which all nations, where staves are not allowed of, are constantly supplied with willing hands for all the drudgery of hard and dirty labour; I mean the children of the poor, the greatest and most extensive of all temporal blessings that accrue from society, on which all the comforts of life, in the civilized state, have their unavoidable dependance. There are many other things, from which it is plain, that such a real love of man for his species would have been altogether inconsistent with the present scheme; the world must have been destitute of all that industry, that

is owing to envy and emulation; no society could have been easy with being a flourishing people at the expence of their neighbours, or enduring to be counted a formidable nation. All men would have been levellers; government would have been unnecessary ; and there could have been no great bustle in the world. Look into the men of greatest renown, and the most celebrated atchievements of antiquity, and every thing that has been cried up and admired in past ages by the fashionable part of mankind: if the fame labours were to be per formed over again, which qualisication, which help of nature do you think would be the most proper means to have them executed; that instinct of real affection you required, without ambition or the love of glory; or a staunch principle of pride and selsishness, acting under pretence to, and assuming the resemblance of that affection? Consider, I beseech you, that no men governed by this instinct would require services of any of their species, which they would not be ready to perform for others; and you will easily fee, that its being universal would quite alter the scene of society from what it is now. Such an instinct might be very suitable to another scheme different from this, in another world; where, instead of sickelness, and a restless desire after changes and novelty, there was observed an universal steadiness, continually preserved by a serene spirit of contentment among other creatures of different appetites from ours, that had frugality without avarice, and generosity without pride; and whose solicitude after happiness in a future state, was as active and apparent in life as our pursuits are aYter the enjoyments of this present. But, as to the world we live in, examine into the various ways of earthly greatness, and all the engines that are made use of to attain to the felicity of carnal men, and you will sind, that the instinct you speak of must have destroyed the principles, and prevented the very existence of that pomp and glory to which human societies have been, and are still raised by worldly wisdom. *Hor.* I give up my affectionate scheme; you have convinced me that there could not have been that stir and variety, nor, upon the whole, that beauty in the world, which there have been, is all men had been naturally humble, good, and virtuous. I believe that wars of all forts, as well as diseases, are natural means to hinder mankind from increasing too fast; but that wild beasts should likewise have been designed to thin our species, I cannot conceive; for they can only serve this end, when men are but few, and their numbers should be increased, instead of lessened; and afterwards, if they were made for that purpose, when men are strong enough, they would not answer it. *Cleo.* I never said that wild beasts was designed to thin our species. I have showed that many things were made to serve a variety of different purposes; that in the scheme of this earth, many things must have been considered that man has nothing to do with; and t£at it is ridiculous to think that 6 the universe was made for our fake. I have said likewise, that as all our knowledge conies, *a posteriori,* it is imprudent to reason otherwise than from facts. That there are vild. beau's, and that there are savage men, is certain; and that where there are but few of the latter, the sirst must always be very Troublesome, and ofren fatal to them, is as certain; and when I reflect on the passions all men are born with, and their incapacity whilst they are untaught, I can sind no cause or motive which is so likely to unite them together, and make them espouse the same interest, as that common danger they must always be in from wild beasts, in uncultivated countries, whilst they live in small families that all shift for themselves, without government or depenjlance upon one another: This sirst step to society, I believe to be au esfect, which that same cause, the common danger so often mentioned, will never fad to produce upon our species in such circumstances: what other, and how many purposes wild beasts might have been.designed for besides, 1 do not pretend to determine, as I have told you before. *Hor.* But whatever other purposes wild beasts were designed for, it still follows from your opinion, that the unit-

ing of savages in common defence, must have been one;-which to me seems clashing with our idea of the Divine Goodness. *Cleo.* So will every thing seem to do, which we call natutal evil; if you ascribe human paflions to the Deity, and measure Insinite Wisdom by the standard of our most shallow capacity; you have been at this twice already; I thought I had answered it. I would not make God the author of evil, any more than yourself; but I am likewise persuaded, that nothing could come by chance, in respect to the Supreme Being; and, therefore, unless you imagine the world not to be governed by Providence, you must believe that wars, and all the calamities we can susfer frym man or beast, as well as plagues and all other diseases, are under a wife direction that is unsathomable. As there can be no esfect without a cause, so nothing can be laid to happen by chance, but in respect to him who is ignorant of the cause of it. I can make this evident to you, in an obvious and familiar example. To a man who knows nothing of the tennis-court, the skips and rebounds of the ball seems to be all fortuitous; as he is not able to guess at the several disferent directions it will receive before it comes to the ground; so, as soon as it has hit the place to which it was plainly directed at sirst, it is chance to him"where it will fall: whereas, the experienced player, knowing perfectly well the journey the ball will make, goes directly to the place, if he is not there already, where it will certainly come within his reach. Nothing seems to be more the effect of chance than a cast of the dice: yet they obey the laws of gravity and motion in general, as much as any thing else; and from the impressions that are given them, it is impossible they should fall otherwise than they do: but the various directions which they shall receive in the whole course of the throw being entirely unknown, and the rapidity with which they change their situation being such, that our flow apprehension cannot trace them, what the cast will be is a mystery to human understanding, at fair play. But if the fame variety of directions was

given to two cubes of ten feet each, which a pair of dice receive, as well from one another as the box, the caster's singers that cover it, and the table they are flung upon, from the time they are taken up until they lie still, the fame effect would follow; and if the quantity of motion, the force that is imparted to the box and dice was exactly known, and the motion itself was so much retarded in the performance, that what is done in three or four seconds, should take up an hour's time, it would be easy to sind out the reason of every throw, and men might learn with certainty to foretell which side of the cube would be uppermost. It is evident, then, that the words fortuitous and casual, have no other meaning than what depends upon our want of knowledge, foresight, and penetration; the reflection on which will show us, by what an insinity of degrees all human capacity falls short of that universal intuitus, with which the Supreme Being beholds at once every thing without exception, whether to us it be visible or invisible, past, present, or to come. *Hor.* I yield: you have solved every dissiculty I have been able to raise; and I must confess, that your supposition concerning the sirst motive that would make savages associate, is neither clashing with good sense, nor any idea we ought to have of the Divine attributes; but, on the contrary, in answering my objections, you have demonstrated the probability of your conjecture, and rendered the wisdom and power of providence, in the scheme of this earth, both as to the contrivance and the execution of it, more conspicuous and palpable to me, than any thing I ever heard or read, had done before.

Gg *Cleo.* I am glad you are satissied; though far from arrogating to myself so much merit as your civility would coniplinent rre wi'h.

Hor. It is very clear to me now; that as it is appointed for all men to die. so 't is neceflary rhere should be means to compass this end; that from the number of thole means, or causes of death, it is impossible to exclude either the malice of men, or the rae of wild beasts, and all noxious animals; and that if they had been actually designed by nature, and contrived for that purpose, we should have no more reason justly to complain os them, than we have to sind fault with death itself, or that frightful train of diseases which are daily and houily the manifest occasion of it. *Cleo.* They are all equally included in the curse, which after the fall was deservedly pronounced against the whole earth; and if they be real evils, they are to be looked upon as the consequence of sin, and a condign punishment, which the transgression os our sirst parents has drawn and entailed upon all their posterity. I am fully persuaded, that all the nations in the world, and every individual of our species, civilized pr savage, had their origin from Seth, Sham, or Japhet: and as experience has taught us, that the greatest empires have their periods, and the best governed states and kingdoms may come to ruin; so it is certain, that the politest people being scattered and distressed, may soon degenerate, and some of them by accidents and misfortunes, from knowing and" well taught ancestors, be reduced at last to savages of the sirst and lowest class. *Hor.* If what you are fully persuaded of, be true, the other Is self-evident, from the savages that are still subsisting. *Cleo.* You once seemed to insinuate, that all the danger men were in from wild beasts, would entirely cease as soon as they were civilized, and lived in large and well-ordered societies; but by this you may see, that our species will never be wholly exempt from tliat danger; because mankind will always be liable to be reduced to savages; for, as this calamity has actually befallen vast multitudes that were the undoubted descendants of Noah; lo the greatest prince upon earth, that has children, cannot be sure, that the same disaster will never happen-to any of his posterity. Wild beasts may be entirely extirpated in some countries that are duly cultivated; but they will multiply in others that are wholly, neglected; and great numbers of them range now, and are masters in many places, where they had been rooted and kept out before. I lhall always believe that every species of living crea-

tures in and upon this globe, without exception, continues to be, as it was at sirst, under the care of that fame Providence that thought sit to produce it. You have had a great deal of patience, but I would not tire it: This sirst step towards society, now we have mastered it, is a good resting place, and so we will leave osf for to day. *Hor.* With all my heart: I have made you talk a great deal; but I long to hear the rest, as soon as you are at leisure. *Cleo.* I am obliged to dine at Windsor to-morrow; if you are not otherwise engaged, I can carry you where the honour of your company will be highly esteemed: my coach shall be ready at nine; you know you are in my way. *Hor.* A sine opportunity, indeed, of three or four hours chat. *Cleo.* I shall be all alone without you. *Hor.* I am your man, and shall expect you. *Cleo.* Adieu.

THE SIXTH DIALOGUE Betwiin
HORATIO AND CLEOMENE3
Horatio. JN ow we are off the stones, pray let us lose no time; I expect a great deal of pleasure from what I am to hear further, *Cleo.* The second step to society is the danger men are in from one another: for which we are beholden to that staunch principle of pride and ambition, that all men are born with. Different families may endeavour to live to

Gg a gether, and be ready to join in common danger; but they are all of little use to one another, when there is no common enemy to oppose. If we consider that strength, agility, and courage would, in such a state, be the most valuable qualisications, and that many families could not live long together, but some, actuated by the principle I named, would strive for superiority: this must breed quarrels, in which the most weak and fearful will, for their own safety, always join with him of whom they have the best opinion.
Hor. This would naturally divide multitudes into bands and companies, that would all have their different leaders, and of which the strongest and most valiant would always swallow up the weakest and most fearful. *Cleo.* What you say agrees exactly with the accounts we have of the uncivilized nations that are still subsisting in the

world; and thus men may live miserably many ages. *Hor.* The very sirst generation that was brought up under the tuition of parents, would be governable: and would not every succeeding generation grow wiser than the foregoing? *Cleo.* Without doubt they would increase in knowledge and cunning: time and experience would have the same effect upon them as it has upon others; and in the particular things to which they applied themselves, they would become as expert and ingenious as the most civilized nations: but their unruly passions, and the discords occasioned by them, would never suffer them to be happy; their mutual contentions would be continually spoiling their improvements, destroying their inventions, and frustrating their designs. *Hor.* But would not their sufferings in time bring them acquainted with the causes of their disagreement; and would not that knowledge put them upon making of contracts, not to injure one another? *Cleo.* Very probably they would; but among such ill-bred and uncultivated people, no man would keep a contract longer than that interest lasted which made him submit to it. *Hor.* But might not religion, the fear of an invisible cause, be made serviceable to them, as to the keeping of their contracts? *Cleo.* It might, without dispute; and would, before many generations pasted away. But religion could do no more among them, than it does among civilized nations; where the Divine vengeance is seldom trusted to only, and oaths themselves are thought to be of little service, where there is no human power to enforce the obligation, and punish perjury. *Hor.* But do not think, that the fame ambition that made a man aspire to be a leader, would make him likewise desirous of being obeyed in civil matters, by the numbers he led? *Cleo.* I do; and moreover that, notwithstanding this unsettled and precarious way communities would live in, after three or four generations, human nature would be looked into, and begin to be understood: leaders would sind out, that the more strife and discord there was amongst the people they headed, the less use they could make of them: this would put them upon various ways of curbing mankind; they would forbid killing and striking one another; the taking away by force the wives or children of others in the fame community; they would invent penalties, and very early find out that nobody ought to be a judge in his own cause; and that old men, generally speaking, knew more than young. *Hor.* When once they have prohibitions and penalties, I should think all the dissiculty surmounted; and I wonder why you said, that thus they might live miserably for many ages. *Cleo.* There is one thing of great moment, which has not been named yet; and until that comes to pass, no considerable numbers can ever be made happy; what signify the strongest contracts when we have nothing to show for them; and what dependence can we have upon oral tradition, in matters that require exactness; especially whilst the lan guage that is spoken is yet very imperfect? Verbal reports are liable to a thousand cavils and disputes that are prevented by Tecords, which every body knows to be unerring witnesses; and from the many attempts that are made to wrest and distort the sense of even written laws, we may judge how impracticable the administration of justice must be among all societies that are destitute of them. Therefore the third and last step to society, is the invention of letters. No multitudes can live peaceably without government; no government can subsist without laws; and no laws can be effectual long, unless they are wrote down: the consideration of this is alone sussicient to give us a great insight into the nature ot" man. *Hor.* I do not think so: the reason why no government can subsist without laws, is, because there are bad men in all multitudes; but to take patterns from them, when we would judge of human nature, rather than from the good ones that follow the dictates of their reason, is an in justice one would not be guilty of to brute beasts; and it would be very wrong in us, for a few vicious horses, to condemn the whole species as such, without taking notice of the many sinespirited creatures that are naturally tame

and gentle. *Cleo.* At this rate I must repeat every thing that I have faid yesterday and the day before: I thought you was convinced, that it was with thought as it is with speech; and that though man was born with a capacity beyond other animals, to attain to both, yet, whilst he remained untaught, and never conversed with any of his species, these characteristics were of little use to him. All men uninstructed, whilst they are let alone, will follow the impulse of their nature, without regard to others; and therefore all of them are bad, that are not taught to be good; so all horses are ungovernable that are not well broken: for what we call vicious in them, is, when they bite r kick, endeavour to break their halter, throw their rider, and exert themselves with all their strength to shake off the yoke, and recover that liberty which nature prompts them to assert and desire. What you call natural, is evidently artisicial, and belongs to education: no sine spirited horse was ever tame or gentle, without management. Some, perhaps, are not backed until they are four years old; but then long before that time, they are handled, spoke to, and dressed; they are fed by their keepers, put under restraint, sometimes caressed, and sometimes made to smart; and nothing is omitted whilst they are young, to inspire them with awe and veneration to our species; and make them not only submit to it, but likewise take a pride in obeying the superior genius of man. But would you judge of the nature of horses in general, as to its sitness to be governed, take the foals of the best bred mares and sinest stallions, and turn an hundred of them loose, sillies and colts together, in a large forest, till they are seven years old, and then see how tractable they will be. *Hor.* But this is never done. *Cleo.* Whose fault is that? It is not at the request of the Jiorses, that they are kept from, the mares; and that any of them are ever gentle or tame, is entirely owing to the management or'man. Vice proceeds from the lame origiu in men, as it does in horses; the delire of uncontrolled liberty, and impatience of restraint, are not more visible in the one

than they are in the other; and a man is then called vicious, when, breaking the curbs of precepts and prohibitions, he wildly follows the unbridled appetites of his untaught or illmanaged nature. The complaints against this nature of ours, are every where the fame: man would have every thing he likes, without considering whether he has any right to it or not; and lie would do every thing he has a mind to do, without regard to the consequence it would be of to others; at the fime time that he diflikes every body, that acting from the fame principle, have in all their behaviour not a lpecial regard to him. *Hor.* That is, in short, man naturally will not do as he would be done by. *Cleo.* That is true; and for this, there is another reason in his nature: all men are partial in their judgments, when they compare themselves to others; no tvo equals think lo well of each other, as both do of themselves; and where all men have an equal right to judge, there needs no greater cause of quarrel, than a present amongst them, with an inscription of *(Ictur digniori.* Man in his anger behaves htmseli in the fame manner as *o* 'her animals; ditlurbing, in the pursuit ol selfpreservation, those they are angry with; and all of them endeavour, according as the degree of their passion is, either to destroy, or cause pain and displeasure to their adversaries. That these obstacles to soeiery are the faults, or rather properties of our nature, we may know by this, that all regulations and prohibitions that have been contrived for ihe temporal happiness of mankind, are made exictiy to tally with them, and to obviate thole complaints, which I laid were every where made against mankind. The principal laws of all countries have the lame tendency; and there is not one that does not point at soroe frailty, deled, or unsitnels tor iociety, that men are naturally subject to; but all ot them are plainly deligned as lo many iemedies, to cure and disappoint that natural instinct ot sovereignty, which teaches man to look upon every thing as centring in himself, and prompts him to put in a claim to every thing he can lay his hands on. This tendency and design to n».nd our nature, for the.temporal good of society, is no where more visible, than in that compendious as well as complete body of laws, that was given by God himself. The Israelites, whilst they were slaves in Egypt, were governed by the laws of their masters; and as they were many degrees removed from the lowest savages, so they were yet far from being a civilized nation. It is reasonable to think, that, before they received the law of God, they had regulations and agreements already established, which the ten commandments did not abolish; and that they must have had notions of right and wrong, and contracts among them against open violence, and the invasion of property, is demonstrable. *Hor.* How is that demonstrable? *Cleo.* From the decalogue itself: all wise laws are adapted to the people that are to obey them. From the ninth commandment, for example, it is evident, that a man's own testimony was not sussicient to be believed in his own affair, and that nobody was allowed to be a judge in his own case. *Hor.* It only forbids us to bear false witness against our neighbour. *Cleo.* That is true; and therefore the whole tenor and design of this commandment presupposes, and must imply what I fay. But the prohibitions of stealing, adultery, and coveting any thing that belonged to their neighbours, are still more plainly intimating the fame; and seem to be additions and amendments, to supply the defects of some known regulations and contracts that had been agreed upon before. If, in this view, we behold the three commandments last hinted at, we shall sind them to be strong evidences, not only of that instinct of sovereignty within us, which at other times I have called a domineering spirit, and a principle of selsishness; but likewise of the dissiculty there is to destroy, eradicate, and pull it out of the heart of man: for, from the eighth commandment it appears, that, though we debar ourselves from taking the things of our neighbour by force, yet there is danger that this instinct will prompt us to get them unknown to him in a clandestine manner, and deceive us with the inlinuations of an *oportet habere.* From

the foregoing precept, it is likewise manifest, that though we agree not to take away, and rob a man of the woman that is his own, it is yet to be scared, that if we like her, this innate principle that bids us gratify every appetite, will advise us to make use of her as *u* she was our ov n; though our neighbour is at the charge of maintaining her and all the chduren she brings forth. The last more especially is very ample in consirming my assertion. It strikes directly at the root of the evil, and lays open the real source of the mischiefs that are apprehended in the seventh and the eighth commandment: for without sirst actually trespassing against this, no man is in danger of breaking either of the former. This tenth commandment, moreover, insinuates very plainly, in the sirst place, that this instinct of ours is of great power, and a frailty hardly to be cured; in the second, that there is nothing which our neighbour can be possessed of, but, neglecting the consideration of justice and property, we may have a desire after it; for which reason it absolutely forbids us to covet any thing that is his: The Divine Wisdom, well knowing the strength of this selsish principle, which obliges us continually to assume every thing to ourselves; and that, when once a man heartily covets a thing, this instinct, this principle will over-rule and persuade him to leave no stone unturned to compass his desires. *Hor.* According to your way of expounding the commandments, and making them tally so exactly with the frailties of our nature, it should follow from the ninth, that all men are born with a strong appetite to forswear themselves, which I never heard before. *Cleo.* Nor I neither; and I confess that the rebuke there is in this smart turn of yours is very plausible; but the censure, how specious soever it may appear, is unjust, and you shall not sind the consequence you hint at, if you will be pleased to distinguish between the natural appetites themselves, and the various crimes which they make us commit, rather than not be obeyed: For, though we are born with no immediate appetite to forswear ourselves, yet we are born with more

than one, that, if never checked, may in time oblige us to forswear ourselves, or do worse, if it be possible, and they cannot be gratisied without it; and the commandment you mention plainly implies, that by nature we are so unreasonably attached to our interest on all emergencies, that it is possible for a man to be swayed by it, not only to the visible detriment of others, as is manifest from the seventh and the eighth, but even though it should be against his own conscience: For nobody did ever knowingly bear false witness against his neighbour, but he did it for some end or other; this end, whatever it is, I call his interest. The law which forbid:, murder, had already demonstrated to us, how immensely we undervalue every thing, when it comes in competition with ourselves; for, though our greatest dread be destruction, and we know no other calamity equal to the dissolution of our being, yet such unequitable judges this instinct of sovereignty is able to make of us, that rather than not have our will, which we count our happiness, we choose to inflict this calamity on others, and bring lot al ruin on such as we think to be obstacles to the gratisication of our appetites; and this men do, not only for hindrances that are present, or apprehended as to come, but likewise for former offences, and things that are past redress. *Hor.* By what you said last, you mean revenge, I suppose. *Cleo.* I do so; and the instinct os sovereignty which I assert to be in human nature, is in nothing so glaringly conspicuous as it is in this passion, which no mere man was ever born without, aud which even the most civilized, as well as the most learned, are seldom able to conqrer: For whoever pretends to revenge himself, must claim a right to a judicature within, and an authority to punish: vv hich, being destructive to the mutual peace of all multitudes, are for that reason the sirst things that in every civil society are snatched away out os every man's hands, as dangerous tools, and vested in the governing part, the supreme power only. *Hor.* This remark on revenge has convinced me more than any thing you have laid yet, that there is some such thing as a principle of sovereignty in our nature; but 1 cannot conceive yet, why the vices of private, 1 mean particular persons, mould be thought to belung to the whole species. *Cleo.* Because every body is liable to fall into the vices that are peculiar to his species; and it is with them, as it is with distempers among creatures of different kinds: There are many ailments that horses are subject to, which are not incident to cows. There is no vice, but whoever commits it had within him before he was guilty of it, a tendency towards it, a latent cause that disposed him to it: Theresore, all lawgivers have two main points to conlider at setting out: First, what things will procure happiness to the society under their care: Secondly, what pallions and properties there are in man's nature, that may either promote or obstruct this happiness. It is prudence to watch your sish ponds againit the iniults ot heains and bitterns; but the fame precaution would be ridiculous against turkeys and peacocks, or any other creatures, that neither love sish, nor are able to catch them. *Hor,* What frailty or defect is it in our nature, that the two sirst commandments have a regard to, or, as you call it, tally with? *Cleo.* Our natural blindness and ignorance of the true Deity: For, though we all come into the world with an instinct toward religion that manifests itself before we come to maturity, yet the fear of an invisible cause, or invisible causes, which all men are born with, is not more universal, than the uncertainty which all untaught men fluctuate in, as to the nature and properties of that cause, or those causes: There can be no greater proof of this *Hor.* I want none; the history of all ages is a sussicient witness.

Cleo. Give me leave: There can, I fay, be no greater proof of this, than the second commandment, which palpably points at all the absurdities and abominations which the ill guided fear of an invisible cause had already made, and would still continue to make men commit; and in doing this, 1 can hardly think, that any thing but Divine Wisdom could, in so few words, have comprehended the vast extent and sum total of human extravagancies, as it is done in that commandment: For there is nothing so high or remote in the sirmament, nor so low or abject upon earth, but some men have worshipped it, or made it one way or other the object of their superstition. *Hor.*——Crocodilon adnrat Pjrs hæc: ilia pavet saturam serpentibus Ibitl.

Effigies sacri nitet aurea Cercopitheci.

A holy monkey! I own it is a reproach to our species, that ever any part of it should have adored such a creature as a god. But that is the tip-top of folly, that can be charged on superstition.

Cleo. 1 do not think so; a monkey is still a living creature, and consequently somewhat superior to things inanimate. *Hor.* I should have thought mens adoration of the fun or m)on insinitely less absurd than to have seen them fall down be ore so vile, so ridiculous an animal. *Cleo.* Those who have adored the sun and moon never questioned, but they were intelligent as well as glori beings. But when I mentioned the word inanimate, I was thinking on what the fame poet you quoted said of the veneration men paid to leeks and onions, deities they raised in their own gardens. they are apt to undervalue, if not despise the best, when they grow common. I am of opinion, that the third commandment points at this frailty, this want of steadiness in our nature; the ill consequences of which, in our duty to the Creator, could not be better prevented than by a strict observance of this law, in never making use of his name, but in the most solemn manner, on necessary occasions, and in matters of high importance. As in the foregoing part of the decalogue, care had been already taken, by the strongest motives, to create and attract reverence, so nothing could be more wisely adapted to strengthen, and make it everlasting, than the contents of this law: For as too much familiarity breeds contempt, so our highest regard due to what is most sacred, cannot be kept up better than by a quite contrary practice.

Porrura & cepe nefas violare, & frangere morsu:

O sanctas genteis, quibus hxc nascuntur in hortis
Nuroina!

But this is nothing to what has been done in America fourteen hundred years after the time of Juvenal. If the portentous worship of the Mexicans had been known in his days, he would not have thought it worth his while to take notice of the Egyptians. 1 have often admired at the uncommon pains those poor people must have taken to express the frightful and mocking, as well as bizarre and unutterable notions they entertained of the superlative malice and hellish implacable nature of their vitzliputzli, to whom they sacrisiced the hearts of men, cut out whilst they were alive. The monstrous sigure and laboured deformity of that abominable idol, are a lively representation of the direful ideas those wretches framed to themselves of an invisible over-ruling power; and plainly show us, how horrid and execrable they thought it to be, at the fame time that they paid it the highest adoration; and at the expence of human blood endeavoured, with fear and trembling, if not to appease the wrath and rage of it, at least to avert, in some measure, the manifold mischiefs they apprehended from it.

Hor. Nothing, I must own, can render declaiming against idolatry more seasonable than a reflection upon the second commandment: But as what you have been saying required no great attention, 1 have been thinking of something else. Thinking on the purport of the third commandment, furnishes me with an objection, and 1 think a strong one, to what you have assirmed about all laws in general, and the decalogue in particular. You know I urged that it was wrong to ascribe the faults of bad men to human nature in general. *Cleo.* I do; and thought I had answered you. *Hor.* Let me try only once more. Which of the two, pray, do you think profane swearing to proceed from, a frailty in our nature, or an ill custom generally contracted by keeping of bad company? *Cleo.* Certainly the latter. *Hor.* Then it is evident to me, that this law is levelled at the bad men only, that are guilty of the vice forbid in it; and not any frailty belonging to human nature in general. *Cleo.* I believe you mistake the design of this law; and am of opinion, that it has a much higher aim than you seem to imagine. You remember my saying, that reverence to authority was necessary, to make human creatures governable. *Hor.* Very well; and that reverence was a compound of fear, love, and esteem. *Cleo.* Now let us take a view of what is done in the decalogue: In the short preamble to it, expressly made that the Israelites should know who it was that spoke to them, God manifests himself to those whom he had chosen for his people, by a most remarkable instance of his own great power, and their strong obligation to him, in a fact, that none of them could be ignorant of. There is a plainness and grandeur withal in this sentence, than which nothing can be more truly sublime or majestic; and I defy the learned world to show me another as comprehensive, and of equal weight and dignity, that so fully executes its purpose, and answers its design with the fame simplicity of words. In that part of the second commandment, which contains the motives and inducements why men should obey the Divine laws, are set forth in the most emphatical manner: First, God's wrath on those that hate him, and the continuance of it on their posterity: Secondly, the wide extent of his mercy to those who love him and keep his commandments. If we duly consider these passages, we shall sind, that fear, as well as love, and the highest esteem, are plainly and distinctly inculcated in them ; and that the best method is made use of there, to inspire men with a deep sense of the three ingredients that make up the compound of reverence. The reason is plain: If people were to be governed by that body of laws, nothing was more necessary to enforce their obedience to them, than their awful regard and utmost veneration to him, at whose command they were to keep them, and to whom they were accountable for the breaking of them. *Hor.* What answer is all this to my objection? *Cleo.* Have a moment's patience; I am coming to it. Mankind are naturally

sickle, and delight in change and variety; they seldom retain long the same impression of things they received at first, when they were new to them; and *Hor.* I am answered. *Cleo.* What weight reverence is thought to be of to procure obedience, we may learn from the fame body of laws in another commandment. Children have no opportunity of learning theirduty but from their parents and those whoact by their authority or in their stead: Therefore, it was requilite, that men should not only stand in great dread of the law of God, but likewise have great reverence for those who sirst inculcated it, and communicated to them that this was the law of God. *Hor.* But you said, that the reverence of children to parents was a natural consequence of what they sirst experienced from the latter. *Cleo.* You think there was no occasion for this law, if man would do what is commanded in it of his own accord: But I delire you would consider, that though the reverence of children to parents is a natural consequence, partly of the benesits and chastisements they receive from them, and partly of the great opinion they form of the superior capacity they observe in them; experience teaches us, that this reverence may be over-ruled by stronger pallions; and therefore it being of the highest moment to all government and fociableneis itself, God thought sit to fortisy and strengthen it in us, by a particular command of his own; and, moreover, to encourage it, by the promise of a reward for the keeping of it It is our parents that sirst cure us of our natural wildness, and break in us the spirit of independency we are all born with: It is to them we owe the sirst rudiments of our submission ; and to the honour and deference which childreQ pay to parents, all societies are obliged for the principle of human obedience. The instinct of sovereignty in our nature, and the waywardness of infants, which is the consequence of it, discover themselves with the least glimmering of our understanding, and before children that have been most neglected, and the least taught, are always the most stubborn and obstinate; and none are more

unruly, and fonder of following their own will, than those that are least capable of governing themselves. *Hor.* Then this commandment you think not obligatory, when we come to years of maturity. *Cleo.* Far from it: for though the benesit politically intended by this law be chiefly received by us, whilst we are under age and the tuition of parents; yet, for that very reason, ought the duty commanded in it, never to cease. We are fond of. imitating our superiors from our cradle, and whilst this honour and reverence to parents continue to be paid by their children, when they are grown men and women, and act for themselves, the example is of singular use to all minors, in teaching them their duty, and not to refuse what they see others, that are older and wiser, comply with by choice: For, by this means, as their understanding increases, this duty, *by* degrees, becomes a fashion, which at last their pride will not fuller them to neglect. *Hor.* What you said last is certainly the reason, that among fashionable people, even the most vicious and wicked do outward homage, and pay respect to parents, at least before t-he world; though they act against, and in their hearts hate them. *Cleo.* Here is another instance to convince us, that good manners are not inconsistent with wickedness; and that men may be strict observers of decorums, and take pains to seem well bred, and at the same time have no regard to the laws of God, and live in contempt of religion: and therefore to procure an outward compliance with this sifth commandment, no lecture can be of such force, nor any instruction so edifying to you'h, among the modest sort of people, as the light of a strong and vigorous, as well as polite and welt drelied man, in a dispute giving way and submitting to a decrepit parent. *Hor.* But doyou imagine that all the divine laws, even those that seem only to relate to God himielf, his power a.id glory, and our obedience to his will, abstract from any connderation of our neighbour, had likewise a regard to the good of society, and the temporal happiness of his people? *Cleo.* There is no doubt of that; witness the keeping of the Sabbath. *Hor.* We have seen that very handsomely proved in one of the Spectators. *Cleo.* But the usefulness of it in human asFairs, is of far greater moment, than that which the author of that paper chiefly takes notice of. Of all the dissiculties that mankind have laboured under in completing society, nothing has been more puzzling or perplexing than the division of time. Our annual course round the sun, not answering exactly any number of complete days or hours, has been the occasion of immense study and labour: and nothing has more racked the brain of man, than the adjusting the year to prevent the confusion of seasons: but even when the year was divided into lunar months, the computation of time must have been impracticable among the common people: To remember twenty-nine, or thirty days, where feasts are irregular, and all other days show alike, must have been a great burden to the memory, and caused a continual confusion among the ignorant; whereas, a shoft period soon returning is easily remembered, and one sixed day in seven, so remarkably distinguished from the rest, must rub up the memory of the most unthinking. *Hor.* I believe that the Sabbath is a considerable help in the computation of time, and of greater use in human affairs, than can be easily imagined by those, who never knew the want of it. *Cleo.* But what is most remarkable in this fourth commandment, is God's revealing himself to his people, and acquainting an infant nation with a truth, which the rest of the world remained ignorant of for many ages. Men were soon made sensible of the fun's power, observed every meteor in the sky, and suspected the influence of the moon and other stars: but it was a long time, and man was far advanced in sublime notions, before the light of nature could raise mortal thought to the contemplation of an Insinite Being that is the author of the whole. *Hor.* You have descanted on this susssiciently when you spoke of Moses: pray let us proceed to the further establishment of society. I am satissied that the third step towards it is the invention of letters; that without

them no laws can be long effectual, and that the principle laws of all countries are remedies against human frailties; I mean, that they are deiigned as antidotes, to prevent the ill conscquences of some properties, inseparable from our nature; which yet in themselves, without management or restraint, are obstructive and pernicious to society: I am persuaded likewise, that these frailties are palpably pointed at in the decalogue; that it was wrote with great wisdom, and that there is not one commandment in it, that has not a regard to the temporal good of society, as well as matters of higher moment. *Cleo.* These are the things, indeed, that I have endeavoured to prove; and now all the great difficulties and clues oInstructions, that can hinder a multitude from being formed into a body politic, are removed: when once men come to be governed by written laws, all the rest comes on a pace. Now property, and safety of life and limb may be sccured: this naturally will forward the love of peace, and make it spread. No number of men, when once they enjoy quie,t, and no man needs to fear his neighbour, will be long without learning to divide and subdivide their labour. *Hor.* I do not understand you. *Cleo.* Man, as I have hinted before, naturally loves to imitate what he lees others do, which is the reason that savage people all do the same thing: this hinders them from meliorating their condition, though they are always wishing for it: but if one will wholly apply himself to the making of bows and arrows, whilst another provides food, a third builds huts, a fourth makes garments, and a sifth utensils: they not only become useful to one another, but the callings and employments themselves will in the fame number of yeais rece.ve much greater improvements, than if all had been promilcuously followed by every one of the sive. *Hor.* I believe you are persectly right there; and the truth of what you fay is in nothing so conspicuous, as it is in watchmaking, which is come to a higher degree of perfection, than it would have been arrived at yet, if the whole had always remained the employment of one perion; and I

am persuaded, that even the plenty we have of clock? and watches, as well as the exactness and beauty they may be made of, are chiefly owing to the divilion that has been made ot that art into many branches.

H h *Cleo.* The use of letters must likewise very much improver speech itself, which before that time cannot but be very barren and precarious.

H'jr. I am glad to hear you mention speech again I would not interrupt you when you named it once before: Piay what language did your wild couple speak, when suit they met? *Cleo.* From what I have said already, it is evident, that they could have had none at all; at lcast, that it is my opinion. *Hor.* Then wild people mast have an instinct to understand one another, which they lose when they are civilized. *Cleo.* 1 am persuaded that nature has made all animals of the fame kind, in their mutual commerce, intelligible to one another, as far as is requisite for the preservation of themselves and their species: and as to my wild couple, as you call them, I believe there would be a very good understanding before many sounds passed between them. It is not without som£ dissiculty, that a man born in society can form an idea of such savages, and their condition; and unless he has used himself to abstract thinking, he can hardly represent to himself such a state of simplicity, in which man can have so few desires, and no appetites roving beyond the immediate call of untaught nature: to me it seems very plam, that such a couple would not only be destitute of language, but likewise never sind out, or imagine that they stood in need of any; or that the want of it was any real inconvenience to them. *Hor.* Why do you think so? *Cleo.* Because it is impossible that any creatures should know the want of what it can have no idea of: I believe, moreover, that if savages, after they are grown men and women, mould hear others speak, be made acquainted with the usefulness of speech, and consequently become sensible of the want of it in themselves, their inclination to learn it would be as inconsiderable as their capacity; and if they should attempt it, they would sind it an immense labour, a thing not to be surmounted; because the suppleness and flexibility in the organs of speech that children are endued with, and which 1 have often hinted at, would be lost in them; and they might learn to play masterly upon the violin, or any other the most dissicult mufical instrument, before they coud make any tolerable proiiaeucy in speaking. *Hor.* Brutes make several distinct sounds to express different passions by: as for example, anguish, and great danger, dogs of all forts express with another noise than they do rage and anger; and the whole species express grief by howling. *Cleo.* This is no argument to make us believe, that nature has endued man with speech; there are innumerable other privileges and instincts which some brutes enjoy, and men are destitute of: chickens run about as soon as they are hatched; and most quadrupeds can walk without help, as soon as they are brought forth. If ever language came by instinct, the people that spoke it must have known every individual word in it; and a man in the wild state of nature "would have no occasion for a thousandth part of the moll barren language that ever had a name. When a man's knowledge isconsined within a narrow compass, and he has nothing to obey, but the simple dictates of nature, the want of speech is easily supplied by dumb signs; and it is more natural to untaught men to express themselves by gestures, than by sounds; but we are all born with a capacity of making ourselves understood, beyond other animals, without speech: to express grief, joy, love, wonder and fear, there are certain tokens that are common to the whole species. Who doubts that the crying of children was given them by nature, to call assistance and raise pity, which latter it does so unaccountably beyond any other sound? » *Hor.* In mothers and nurses, you mean. *Cleo.* I mean in the generality of human creatures. Will you allow me, that warlike music generally rouses and supports the spirits, and keeps them from sinking. *Hor.* I believe I must. *Cleo.* Then I will engage, that the crying (I

mean the *vagitus)* of helpless infants will stir up compassion in the generality of our species, that are within the hearing of it, with much greater certainty than drums and trumpets will dissipate and chafe away fear, in those they are applied to. Weeping, laughing, smiling, frowning, sighing, exclaiming, we spoke of before. How universal, as well as copious, is the language of the eyes, by the help of which the remotest nations understand one another at sirst sight, taught or. uiu taught, in the weightiest temporal concern that belongs to the species? and in that language our wild couple would at their sirst meeting intelligibly fay more to one another without guile, than any civilized pair would dare to name without blushing. *Hor.* A man, without doubt, may be as impudent with his eyes, as he can be with his tongue. *Cleo.* All such looks, therefore, and several motions, that are natural, are carefully avoided among polite people, upon no other account, than that they are too signisicant: it is for the fame reason that stretching ourselves before others, whilst we are yawning, is an absolute breach of good manners, especially in mixed company of both sexes. As it is indecent to display any of these tokens, so it is unfashionable to take notice of, or seem ro understand them: this disuse and neglect of the n is the cause, that whenever they happen to be made, either through ignorance or wilful rudeness, many of the n are lost and really not understood, by ihe *beau monde,* that would be very plain to savages without language, who could have no other means of conversing than by ligns and motions. *Hor.* But if the old stock would never either be able or willing to acquire speech, it is potlible they could teach it their children: then which way could any language ever come into the woild from two savages? *Cleo.* By stow degrees, as all other arts and sciences have done, and length of time; agriculture, physic, astronomy, architecture, painting, &-c. From what we see in children that are backward with iheir tongues, we have reason to think, that a wild p..ir would make themselves intelligible to each

other by lign» and gestures, before they would attempt it by sounds: but when they lived together for many years, it is very probable, that for the things they were most conversant with they would sind out founds, to stir up in each other the ideas of such things, when they were out of light; these founds they would communicate to their young ones; and the longer they lived together the greater variety of founds they would invent, as well for actions as the things themselves: they would sind that the volubility of tongue, and flexibility of voice, were much greater in their young ones, than they could remember it ever to have been in themitives: it is impollible, but. tome of these young ones would either by accident or design, make use of.this superior aptitude of the orgrns at one time or other; which every generation would lit 1 mpn ve upi-n; and this must have been the origin of all languages, ana speech itself, that were not ta"ght by inspiration. I believe moreover, that aster language (I mean such as is of human invention) was come to a great degree of perfection, and even when people had distinct words for every action in life, a., well as every thing they meddled or conversed with, signs and gestures still c ntinued to be made for a great while, to accompany speech.; because both are intended for the same purpose. *Hor.* The design of ipeech is to make our thoughts known to others. *Cleo.* 1 do not think so. *Hot.* What! do not men speak to be understood? *Cleo.* In one sense they do; but there is a double meaning in those words', which 1 believe you did not intend: if by man's (peaking to be understood you mean, that when men speak. thy desire that the purport of the sounds they-ntter should be known and apprehended by others I answer in the arlirmitive: but if you mean by it, that men speak, in order that their thoughts may be known, and their sentiments laid open and seen through by others, which likewise may be meant by speaking to be understood, 1 answer in the negative. The sirst lign or sound that ever man made, bom of a woman, was made in behalf, and intended for the use of him who made it; and I am of opinion, that the sirst design of speech was to persuade others, either to give credit to what the spc. king person would have them believe; or else to act or suffer such things, as he would compel them to act or suffer, if they were entirely in his power. *Hor.* Speech is likewise made use of to teach, advise, and inform others for their benesit, as well as to persuade them in our own behalf. *Cleo.* And so by the help of it men may accuse themselves and own their crimes; but nobody would have invented speech for those purposes; l speak of the design, the sirst motive and intension that put man upon speaking. We see in children that the sirst things they endeavour to express with words, are their wants and their will; and their speech is but a consirmation of what they aiked, denied, or astirmed, by signs before. *Hor.* But why do you imagine that people would continue to make use of signs and gestures, after they could sussiciently express themselves in words? *Cleo.* Because signs consirm words, as much as words do signs; and we lee, even in polite people, that when they are very eager they can hardly forbear making use of both. 'yVhen an infant, in broken imperfect gibberish, calls for a cake or a play-thing, and at the fame time points at and reaches after it, this double endeavour makes a stronger impression upon us, than if the child had spoke its wants in plain words, without making any signs, or else looked at and reached after the thing wanted, without attempting to speak. Speech and action assist and corroborate one another, and experience teaches us that they move us much more, and are more persuasive jointly than separately; *vis unit a fortior;* and when an infant makes use of both, he acts from the fame principle that an orator does when he joins proper gestures to an elaborate declamation. *Hor.* From what you have faid it should seem that action is not only more natural, but likewise more ancient than speech itself, which before I should have thought a paradox. *Cleo.* Yet it is true; and you shall always sind that the most forward, volatile, and siery tem-

pers make more use of gestures when they speak, than others that are more patient and sedate. *Hor.* It is a very diverting scene to see how this is overdone among the French, and stills more among the Portuguese: I have often been amazed to see what distortions of face and body, as well as other strange gesticulations with hands and feet, some of them will make in their ordinary discourses: But nothing was more offensive to me, when I was abroad, than the loudness and violence which most foreigners speak with, even among persons of quality, when a dispute arises, or any thing is to be debated: before I was used to it, it put me always upon my guard; for I did not question but they were angry; and I often recollected what had been said in order to consider whether it was not something I ought to have resented. *Cleo.* The natural ambition and strong desire men have to triumph over, as well as persuade others, are the occasion of all this. Heightening and lowering the voice at proper seasons, is a bewitching engine to captivate mean understandings; and loudness is an assistant to speech, as well as action is: uncorrectness, false grammar, and even want os serise, are often happily drowned in noise and great bustle; and many an argument has been convincing, that had all its force from the vehemence it was made with: the weakness. "*&T* the language itself may be palliatively cured by strength of elocution. *Hor.* I am glad that speaking low is the fashion among-well-bred people in England; for bawling and impetuosity I cannot endure, *Cleo.* Yet this latter is more natural; and no man ever gave in to the contrary practice, the fashion you like, that was not taught it, either by precept or example: and if men do not accustom themselves to it whilst they are young, it is very dissicult to comply with it afterwards: but it is the most lovely, as well as most rational piece of good manners that human invention has to boast of in the art of flattery; for when a man addresses himself to me in a calm manner, without making gestures or other motions with head or body, and continues his discourse in the

same submiflive strain and composure of voice, without exalting or depressing it, he, in the sirst place, displays his own modesty and humility in an agreeable manner; and, in the second, makes me a great compliment in the opinion which he seems to have of me; for by such a behaviour he gives me the pleasure to imagine that he thinks me not influenced by my passions, but altogether swayed by my reason: he seems to lay his stress on my judgment, and therefore to delire, that 1 should weigh and conlider what he says without being ruffled or diiturbed: no man would do this unless he trusted entirely to my good fense, and the rectitude of my understanding. *Hor.* I have always admired this unaffected manner of speaking, though I never examined so deeply into the meaning of it. *Cleo.* I cannot help thinking, but that, next to the laconic and manly spirit that runs through the nation, we are very much beholden for the strength and beauty of our language to this tranquillity in discourse, which for many years has been in England, more than any where else, a custom peculiar to the *beau monde,* who, in all countries, are the undoubted resiners of language. *Hor.* I thought that it was the preachers, play-wrights, orators, and sine writers that resined upon language. *Cleo.* They make the best of what is ready coined to their hands; but the true and only mint of words and phrases is the court; and the polite part of every nation are in postesiion of *the Jus et norma loquendi.* . All technic words indeed, #nd terms of ait, belong to the respective artists and dealers, that primarily and literally make use of them in their business; but whatever is borrowed from them for metaphorical use, or from other languages, living or dead, must sirst have the stamp of the court, and the approbation of *beau monde* before it can pass for current; and whatever is not used among them, or comes abroad without their sanction, is either vulgar, pedantic, or obsolete. Orators therefore, historians, and all wholesale dealers in words, are consined to those that have been already well received, and from that treasure they may pick aud choose what ib most for their purpose; but they are not allowed to make new ones of their own, any more than bankers are fullered to coin. *Hor.* All this while 1 cannot comprehend what advantage or disadvantage speaking loud or low can be of to the language itself; and if what 1 am saying now was set down, it mult be a real conjurer that, half a year hence, should be able to tell by the writing, whether it had been bawled out or whispered. *Cleo.* 1 am of opinion that when people of skill and address accustom themselves to speak in the manner aforesaid, it must in time have an influence upon the language, and render it strong and expressive. *Hor.* But your reason? *Cleo.* When a man has only his words to trust to, and the hearer is not to be asfected by the delivery of them, otherwise than if he was to read them himself, it will infallibly put men upon Undying not only for nervous thoughts and perspicuity, but likewise for words of great energy, for purity of diction, compactness of style, and fullness, as well as elegancy of expressions. *Hor.* This teems to be far fetched, and yet 1 do not know but there may be something in it. *Cleo.* I am sure you will think so, when you consider that men that do speak are equally desirous and endeavouring to persuade and gain the point they labour for, whether they speak loud or low, with gestures or without. *Hor.* Speech, you fay, was invented to persuade; I am afraid you lay too much stress upon that: it certainly is made ule of likewise for many other purposes. *Cleo.* 1 do not deny that. *ILr.* When people scold, call names, and pelt one another with fcuriilnies, what design is that done with? If it, be to persuade others, to have a worse opinion of themselves

J than they are supposed to entertain, 1 believe it is seldom done with success. *Cleo.* Calling names is showing others, and showing them with pleasure and ostentation, the vile and wretched opinion we have of them; and persons that make use of opprobrious language, are often endeavouring to make those whom rhey give it to, believe that they think worse of them than they really do. *Hor.* Worse

than they do! Whence does that ever appear? *Cleo.* From the behaviour and the common practice of thole that scold and call names. They rip up and exaggerate not only the faults and imperfections of their adversary himself, but likewise every thing that is ridiculous or contemptible in his friends or relations: They will fly to,"and reflect upon every thing which he is but in the least concerned in, if any thing can possibly be said of it that is reproachful; the occupation he follows, the party he lides with, or the country he is of. They repeat with joy the calamities and misfortunes that have befallen him or his family: They fee the justice or Providence in-them, and they are sure they are punishments he has deserved. Whatever crime he has been suspected of, they charge him with, as if it had been proved upon him. They call in every thing to their assistance; bare surmises, loose reports, and known calumnies; and often upbraid him with what they themselves, at other times, have owned not to believe. *Hor.* But how conies the practice of scolding and calling names to be so common among the vulgar all the world over? there must be a pleasure in it, though 1 cannot conceive it: 1 ask to be informed; what satisfaction or other benesit is it, that men receive or expect from it? what view is it done with? *Cleo.* The real cause and inward motive men act from, when they use ill language, or call names in earnest, is, in the sirst place, to give vent to their anger, which it is troublesome to stifle and conceal. Secondly, to vex and afflict their enemies with greater hopes of impunity than they could reasonably entertain, if they did them any more substantial mischief, which the law would revenge: but this never comes to be a custom, nor is thought ot, before language is arrived to great perfection, and society is carried to some degree of politenels. *Hor.* '1 hat is merry enough, to assert that scurrility is the effect of politeness, *Cleo.* You shall call it what you please, but in its original it is a plain shift to avoid sighting, and the ill consequences of it; for nobody ever called another rogue and rascal, but he would

have struck him if it had been in his own power, and himself had not been withheld by the fear of something or other: therefore, where people call names without doing further injury, it is a sign not only that they have wholesome laws amongst them against open force and violence, but likewise that they obey and stand in awe of them; and a man begins to be a tolerable subject, and is nigh half civilized, that in his passion will take up and content himself with this paultry equivalent; which never was done without great self-denial at sirst: for otherwise the obvious, ready, and unstudied manner of venting and expressing anger, which nature teaches, is the same in human creatures that it is in other animals, and is done by sighting; as we may observe in infants of two or three months old, that never yet saw any body out of humour; for even at that age they will scratch, flmg, and strike with their heads as vvell as arms and legs, when any thing raises their anger, which is easily, and at most times unaccountably provoked; often by hunger, pain, and other inward ailments. That they do this by instinct, something implanted in the frame, the mechanism of the body before any marks of wit or reason are to be seen in them, I am fully persuaded; as I am likewise, that nature teaches them the manner of sighting peculiar to their species; and children strike with their arms as naturally as horses kick, dogs bite, and bulls push with their horns. 1 beg your pardon for this digrelhon. *Hor.* It was natural enough, but if it had been less so, you. would not have slipt the opportunity of having a fling at human nature, which you never spare. *Cleo.* We have not a more dangerous enemy than our own inborn pride: I mall ever attack, and endeavour to mortify it when it is in my power: For the more we are persuaded that the greatest excellencies the best men have to boast of, are acquired, the greater stress it will teach us to lay upon education; and the more truly solicitous it will render us about it: And the absolute necessity of good and early instructions, can be no way more clearly demonstrated, than by exposing the deformity as well as the weakness of our untaught nature, *Hor.* Let us return to speech: if the chief design of it is to persuade, the French have got the start of us a great way; theirs is really a charming language. *Cleo.* So it is without doubt to a Frenchman. *Hor.* And every body else, 1 should think, that understands it, and has any taste: do not you think it to be very engaging? *Cleo.* Yes, to one that loves his belly; for it is very copious in the art of cookery, and every thing that belongs to eating and drinking. *Hor.* But without banter, do not you think that the French tongue is more proper, more sit to persuade in, than ours? *Cleo.* To coax and wheedle in, I believe it may. *Hor.* 1 cannot conceive what nicety it is you aim at, in that distinction. *Cleo.* The word you named includes no idea of reproach or disparagement; the greatest capacities may, without discredit to them, yield to persuasion, as well as the least; but those who .can be gained by coaxing and wheedling, are commonly supposed to be persons of mean parts and weak understandings. *Hor.* But pray come to the point: which of the two do you take to be the sinest language? *Cleo.* That is hard to determine: Nothing is more dissicult than to compare the beauties of two languages together, because what is very much esteemed in the one, is often not relished at all in the other: In this point, the *Pulcbrutn i$ Honejlum* varies, and is diserent every where, as the genius of the people differs. I do not set up for a judge, but what 1 have commonly observed in the two languages, is this: All favourite expreflions in French, are such as either sooth or tickle; and nothing is more admired in English than what pierces or strikes. *Hor.* Do you take yourself to be entirely impartial now? *Cleo.* I think so; but if I am not, 1 do not know how to be sorry for it: There are some things in which it is the interest of the society that men should be biassed; and I do not think it amiss, that men should be inclined to love their own language, from the fame principle that they love their country. The French call us barbarous, and we fay they are fawning: I will not believe the sirst, let them believe what

they please. Do you remember the six lines in the.

Cid, which Corneille is said to have had a present of six thousand Lvres for? *Hor.* Very well.

Mon Pere est mort, F.lvirc. & la premiere Espee

D"nt s'est arme Ro.irijMi a sa trnit cuunee.

Pkuies pitures mes tux, & fonder v us en eau,

La moitir de m.i vie i mis l'autre au tm eau j

Et m'ohlicje a ven 'er, nprt" ce coupfunestt,

Cell qui *y* n'ay plus fur Ctlie qui me rtlte.

Cleo. The fame thought expressed in our language, to all the advantage it has in the French, would be hissed by an Englilh audience.

Hor. That is no compliment to the taste of your country. *Cieo.* 1 do not know that: Men may have no bad taite," and yet not be so ready at conceiving, which way one half of one's life can put the other into th. grave: To me, I own it is puzzling, and it has too much the air ox a riddle to be seen in heroic poetry. *Hor.* Can you sind no delicacy at all in the thought? *Cleo.* Yes; but it is too sine spun; it is the delicacy of a cobweb; there is no strength in it. *Hor.* I have always admirtd these lines; but new you have made me out of conceit with them: Methinkb I spy another fault that is much greater. *Cleo.* What is that? *Hor.* The author makes his heroine fay a thing which was false in fact: One half, fays Chimene, of my lite has pi:t the other into the grave, and obliges me to revenge, tsc. Which is the nominative of the verb obliges? *Cleo.* One half of my life. *Hor.* Here lies the fault; it is this, which I think is not true; for the one half of her life, here mentioned, is plainly that half which was left; it is Rodngues her lover: Which ivay did he oblige her to seek for revenge? *Cleo.* By what he had done, killing her father. *Hor.* No, Cleomenes, this excuse is insufficient. Ghimene's calamity sprung, from the dilemma she was in between her love and her duty; when the latter was inexorable, and violentlv pressing

her to solicit the punishment, and employ with zeal all her interest and eloquence to obtain the death ot him, whom the sirst had made dearer to her than her own hie; jnd therefore it was the half that vas gone, that was put in the grave, her dead father, and nor Rodrigues wh.ch obliged her to sue for juilice: Had rhe obligation Ihe lav under come from this quarter, it might soon have been cancelled, and herself released without crying out her eyes. *Cleo.* 1 beg pardon for differing from you, but I believe the poet is in the riht. *Hor.* Pray, consider which it was that made Chimenc prosecute Rodrigues, love, or honour. *Cieo.* 1 do; biit still I cannot help thinking, but that her lover, by having killed her father, obliged Chimene to prosecute him, in the fame manner as a man, who will give to fatisfaction to his creditors, obliges them to arrell htm; ot as we would fay to a coxcomb, who is offending us with his discourse. If you go on thus, Sir, you will oblige me to tieat you ill: Though all this while the debtor might be as little delirous of being arrested, and the coxcomb of being ill treated, as Rodrigues was of being prosecuted. *Hor.* I believe you are in the right, and 1 beg Corneille's pardon. But now 1 desire you would tell me what you hae further to fay of society: What other advantages do multitudes receive from the invention of letters, besides the improvements it makes in their laws and language? *Cleo.* It is an encouragement to all other inventions in general, by preserving the knowledge of every useful improvement that is made. When laws begn to be well known, and the execution of them is facilitated by genera! approbation, multitudes may be kept in tolerable concord ann.ng themselves: It is then that it appears and not before, how much the superiority of man's understanding beyond other animals, contributes to his soctablends, which is only retaided by it in his savage state. *Hor.* How so, pray; 1 do not understand you. *Cleo.* The superiority of underiiar.ding, in the sirst place, makes man sooner semible of grief and joy, and capable of entertaining either with greater Gilierence as;o the degrees, than they are felt in otuer creatures: secondly, it renders him more industrious to plcaie himielf; tin; is, ir furnishes self-love with a greater variety of Mitts to exeit itlelf m all emergencies, than is made ule of *by* animals of lels capacity. Superiority of undeutui.dnig like wile gives us a feuhc, and inspires us with hopes, ot wh.ch other cieatures have little, and that only of ihaigs lmuxd.utely before ihe.u. All these things are so many tools, arguments, by which self-lov£ reasons us into content, and renders us patient under many afflictions, for the fake of supplying those wants that are most pressing: this is of insinite use to a man, who sinds himself born in a body politic, and it must make him fond of society; whereas, the fame endowment before that time, the fame superiority of understanding in the state of nature, can only serve to render man incurably averse to society, and more obstinately tenacious of his savage liberty, than any other creature would be, that is equally necessitous. *Hor.* I do not know how to refute you: there is a justness of thought in what you fay, which 1 am forced to assent to; and yet it seems strange: How come you by this inlight into the heart of man, and which way is that skill of unravelling human nature to be obtained? *Cleo.* By diligently observing what excellencies and qualisications are really acquired in a well-accomplished man) and having done this impartially, we may be sure that the remainder of him is nature. It is for want of duly separating and keeping assunder these two things, that men have uttered such absurdities on this subject; alleging as the causes of man's sitness for society, such qualisications as no man ever was endued with, that was not educated in a society, a civil establishment, of several hundred years standing. But the flatterers of our species keep this carefully from our view: instead of separating what is acquired from what is natural, and distinguishing between them, they take pains to unite and confound them together. *Hor.* Why do they? I do not see the compliment; since the acquired, as well as natural parts, belong to the

fame person; and the one is not more inseparable from him than the other. *Cleo.* Nothing is so near to a man, nor so really and entirely his own, as what he has from nature; and when that dear self, for the sake of which he values or despises, loves or hates every thing else, comes to be stript and abstracted from all foreign acquisitions, human nature makes a poor sigure: it shows a nakedness, or at least an undress, which no man cares to be seen in. There is nothing we can be possessed of that is worth having, which we do not endeavour, closely to annex, and make an ornament of to ourselves; even wealth and power, and all the gifts of fortune, that are plainly adventitious, and altogether remote from our persons whilst they are our right and property, we do not love to he considered without them. We fee likewise that men, who are come to be great in the world from despicable beginnings, do not love to hear of their origin. *Hor.* That is no general rule. *Cleo.* I believe it is, though there may be exceptions from it; and these are not without reasons. When a man is proud of his parts, and wants to be esteemed for his diligence, penetration, quickness and assiduity, he will make perhaps an ingenuous confession, even to the exposing of his parents; and in order to set osf the merit that raised him, bespeaking himself of his original meanness. But this is commonly done before inferiors, whose envy will be lessened by it, and who will applaud his candour and humility in owning this blemish: but not a word of this before his betters, who value themselves upon their families; and such men could heartily wish that their parentage was unknown, whenever they are with those that are their equals in quality, though superior to them in birth; by whom they know that they are hated for their advancement, and despised for the lowness of their extraction. But I have a shorter way of proving my assertion. Pray, is it good manners to tell a man that he is meanly born, or to hint at his descent, when it is known to be vulgar? *Hor.* No: I do not fay it is. *Cleo.* That decides it, by showing the general opinion about it. Noble an-

cestors, and every thing else that his 1knourable and esteemed, and can be drawn within our sphere, are an advantage to our persons, and we all desire they ihould be looked upon as our own. *Hor.* Ovid did not think so, when he said, *Nam genus & proavos is! qua non-fecimus ipji, vix ea nojira voco. Cleo.* A pretty piece of modesty in a speech, where a man takes pains to prove that Jupiter was his great grandfather. What signisies a theory, which a man destroys by his practice? Did you ever know a person of quality pleased with being called a bastard, though he owed his oeing, as well as his greatness, chiefly to his mother's impudicity. *Hor.* By things acquired, 1 thought you meant learning and virtue; how come you to talk of birth and descent? *Cleo.* By showingyou, that men are unwilling to have any thing that is honourable separated srom themselves, though it is remote from, and has nothing to do with their persons: *I* would convince you of the little probability there is, that we iiiould be pleased with being considered, abstract from what really belongs to us; and qualisications, that in the opinion of the best and wisest are the only things for which we ought to be valued. When men are well-accomplished, they are aihamed of the lowest steps from which they rose to that perfection; and the more civilized they are, the more they think it injurious to have their nature seen, without the improvements that have been made upon it. The most correct authors would blush to fee every thing published, which in the composing of their works they blotted out and stifled; aud which yet it it is certain they once conceived: for this reason they are justly compared to architects, that remove the scasfolding before they show their buildings. All ornaments bespeak the value we have for the things adorned. Do not you think, that the sirst red or white that ever was laid upon a face, and the sirst false hair that was wore, were put on with great secrecy, and with a design to deceive? *Hor.* In France, painting is now looked upon as part of a woman's dress; they make no mystery of it. *Qeo.* So it is with all the impositions of this nature, when they come to be so gross that they can be hid no longer; as men's perukes all over Europe: but if these things could be conceased, and were not known, the tawny coquette would heartily wish that the ridiculous dawbing she plasters herfelf with might pass for complexion; and the bald-pated beau would be as glad to have his fall-bottomed wig looked upon as a natural head of hair. Nobody puts in artificial teeth, but to hide the loss of his own. *Hor.* But is not a man's knowledge a real part of himself: *Cuo.* Yes, and so is his politeness; but neither of them belong to his nature, any more than his gold watch or his diamond ring; and even from these he endeavours to draw a vaiue and respect to his person. The most admired among t'ue fashionable people that delight in outward vanity, and know how to dress well, would be highly displeased if their clothes, and skill in putting them on, should be looked upon otherwise than as part of themselves; nay, it is this part of them ouly, which, whilst they are unknown, can procure them access to the highest companies, the courts of princes; where it is manifest, that both sexes are either admitted or refused, by no other judgment than what is formed of them from their dress, without the least regard to their goodness, or their understanding. *Hor.* I believe I apprehend you. It is our fondness of that self, which we hardly know what it consists in, that could sirst make us think of embellishing our persons; and when we have taken pains in correcting, polishing, and beautifying nature, the fame self-love makes us unwilling to have the ornaments seen separately from the thing adorned. *Cleo.* The reason is obvious. It is that self we are in love with, before it is adorned, as well as after, and every thing which is confessed to be acquired, seems to point at our original nakedness, and to upbraid us with our natural wants; I would fay, the meanness and desiciency of our nature. That no bravery is so useful in war, as that which is artisicial, is undeniable; yet the soldier, that by art and discipline has manifestly been tricked and whec died into courage, after he

has behaved himself in two or three battles with intrepidity, will never endure to hear that he has not natural valour; though all his acquaintance, as well as himself, remember the time that he was an arrant coward. *Hor.* But since the love, affection, and benevolence we naturally have for our species, is not greater than other creatures have for theirs, how comes it, that man gives more ample demonstrations of this love on thousand occasions, than any other animal? *Clco.* Because no other animal has the fame capacity or opportunity to do it. But you may ask the fame of his hatred: the greater knowledge and the more wealth and power a man has, the more capable he is of rendering others sensible of the paflion he is affected with, as well when he hates as when he loves them. The more a man remains uncivilized, and the leis he is removed from the slate of nature, the less his love is to be depended upon. *Hor.* There is more honesty and less deceit among plain, untaught people, than their is among thole that are more artful; and therefore I mould have looked for true love and unfeigned affection among those that live in a natural simplicity, rather than any where else. *Cleo.* You speak of sincerity; but the love which I said was less to be dependend upon in untaught than in civilized people, I supposed to be real and sincere in both. Artful people may dissemble love, and pretend to friendship, where they have none; but they are influenced by their passions and natural appetites as well as savages, though they gratify them in another manner: well-bred people behave themselves in the choice of diet and the taking of their repasts, very differently from savages; so they do in their amours; but hunger and lust are the fame in both. An artful man, nay, the greatest hypocrite, whatever his behaviour is abroad, may love his wife and children at his heart, and the sincerest man can do no more. My business is to demonstrate to you, that the good qualities men compliment our nature and the whole species with, are the result of art and education. The reason why love is little to be depended upon in those that

are uncivilized, is because the passions in them are more fleeting and inconstant; they oftener jostle out and succeed one another, than they are and do in well-bred people, persons that are well educated, have learned to study their ease and the comforts of life; to tie themselves up to rules and decorums for their own advantage, and often to submit to small inconveniencies to avoid greater. Among the lowest vulgar, and those of the meanest education of all, you seldom see a lasting harmony: you shall have a man and his wife that have a real affection for one another, be full of love one hour, and disagree the next for a trifle; and the lives of many are made miserable from no other faults in themselves, than their want of manners and discretion. Without design they will often talk imprudently, until they raise one another's anger; which neither of them being able to stifle, she scolds at him; he beats her; she bursts out into tears; this moves him, he is sorry; both repent, and are friends again: and with all the sincerity imaginable resolve never to quarrel for the future, as long as they live: all this will pass between them in less than half a day, and will perhaps be repeated once a month, or oftener, as provocations offer, or either of them is more or less prone to anger. Affection never remained long uninterrupted between two persons without art; and the best friends, if they are always together, will fall out, unless great discretion be used on both sides. *Hor.* 1 have always been of your opinion, that the more men were civilized the happier they were; but since nations can never be made polite but by length of time, and mankind must have been always miserable before they had written laws, how come poets and others to launch out so much in praise of the golden age, in which they pretend there was so much peace, love, and sincerity? *Cleo.* For the same reason that heralds compliment obscure men of unknown extraction with illustrious pedigrees: as there is no mortal of high descent, but who values himself upon his family, so extolling the virtue and happiness of their ancestors, can never fail plealing every member of a society: but what stress would you lay upon the sictions of poets? *Hor.* You reason very clearly, and with great freedom, against all heathen superstition, and never surfer yourself to be imposed upon by any fraud from that quarter; but when you meet with any thing belonging to the Jewish or Christian religion, you are as credulous as any of the vulgar. *Cleo.* I am sorry you should think so. *Hor.* What I say is fact. A man that contentedly swallows every thing that is said of Noah and his ark, ought not to laugh at the story of Deucalion and Pyrrha. *Cleo.* Is it as credible, that human creatures should spring from stones, because an old man and his wife threw them over their heads, as that a man and his family, with a great number of birds and beatls, should be preserved in a large ship, made convenient for that purpose? *Hor.* But you are partial: what odds is there between a stone and a lump of earth, for either of them to become a human creature? I can as easily conceive how a stone should be turned into a man or a woman, as how a man or a woman should be turned into a stone; and I think it not more strange, that a woman should be changed into a tree, as was Daphne, or into marble as Niobe, than that she should be transformed into a pillar of salt, as the wife of Lot was. Pray susfer me to catechise you a little. *Cleo.* You will hear me afterwards, I hope. *Hor.* Yes, yes. Do you believe Hesiod? *Cleo.* No. *Hor.* Ovid's Metamorphosis? *Cleo.* No. *Hor.* But you believe the story of Adam and Eve, and Paradise. *Cleo.* Yes. *Hor.* That they were produced at once, I mean at their full growth; he from a lump of earth, and she from one of his ribs? *Cleo.* Yes. *Hor.* And that as soon as they were made, they could speak, reason, and were endued with knowledge? *'Cleo.* Yes. *Hor.* In short, you believe the innocence, the delight, and all the wonders of Paradise, that are related by one man; at the same time that you will not believe what has been told us by many, of the uprightness, the concord, and the happiness of a golden age. *Cleo.* That is very true. *Hor.* Now give me leave to

show you, how unaccountable, as well as partial, you are in this. In the sirst place, the things naturally impossible, which you believe, are contrary to your own doctrine, the opinion you have laid down, and which I believe to be true: tor you have proved, that no man would ever be able to speak, unless he was taught it; that reasoning and thinking come upon us by flow degrees; and that we can know nothing that has not from without been conveyed to the brain, and communicated to us through the organs of the fenses. Secondly, in what you reject as fabulous, there is no manner of improbability. We know from history, and daily experience teaches us, that almost all the wars and private quarrels that have at any time disturbed mankind, have had their rife from the differences about superiority, and the *meum iS tuum:* therefore before cunning, covetousness and deceit, crept into the world; before titles of honour, and the distinction between servant and master were known; why might not moderate numbers of people have lived together in peace and amity, when they enjoyed every thing in common; and have been content with the product of the earth in a fertile foil and a happy climate? Why cannot you believe this? *Cleo.* Because it is inconsistent with the nature of human creatures, that any number of them should ever live together in tolerable concord, without laws or government, let the foil, the climate, and their plenty be whatever the most luxuriant imagination mall be pleased to fancy them. But Adam was altogether the workmanship of God; a preternatural production: his speech and knowledge, his goodness and innocence were as miraculous, as every other part of his frame. *Hor.* Indeed, Cleomenes, this is insufferable; when we are talking philosophy you foist in miracles: why may not I do the fame, and say that the people of the golden age were made happy by miracle? *Cleo.* It is more probable that one miracle should, at a stated time, have produced a male and female, from whom, all the rest of mankind are descended in a natural way; than that by a continued series of miracles several

generations of people should have all been made to live and act: contrary to their nature; for this must follow from the account we have of the golden and silver ages. In Moses, the sirst natural man, the sirst that was born of a woman, by envying and flaying his brother, gives an ample evidence of the domineering spirit, and the principle of sovereignty, which I have asserted to belong to our nature. *Hor.* You will not be counted credulous, and yet you believe all those stories, which even some of our divines have called ridiculous, if literally understood. But I do not insist upon the golden age, if you will give up Paradise: a man of sense, and a philosopher, should believe neither. *Cleo.* Yet you have told me that you believed the Old and New Testament. *Hor.* I never said that I believed every thing that is in them, in a literal fense. But why should you believe miracles at all? *Cleo.* Because I cannot help it: and I promise never to mention the name to you again, if you can show me the bare possibility that man could ever have been produced, brought into the world without miracle. Do you believe there ever was a man who had made himself? *Hor.* No: that is a plain contradiction. *Cleo.* Then it is manifest the sirst man must have been made by something; and what I say of man, I may say of all matter and motion in general. The doctrine of Epicurus, that every thing is derived from the concourse and fortuitous jumble of atoms, is monstrous and extravagant beyond all other follies. *Hor,* Yet there is no mathematical demonstration against it. *Cleo.* Nor is there one to prove, that the fun is not in love with the moon, if one had a mind to advance it; and yet I think it a greater reproach to human understanding to believe either, than it is to believe the most childish stories that are told of fairies and hobgoblins. *Hor.* Bat there is an axiom very little inferior to a mathematical demonstration, *ex nihilo nihilsit,* that is directly clashing with, and contradicts the creation out of nothing. Do you understand how something can come from nothing? *Cleo.* I do not, I confess, any more than I can comprehend eternity, or the Deity itself:

but when I cannot comprehend what my reason assures me must necessarily exist, there is no axiom or demonstration clearer to me, than that the fault lies in my want of capacity, the shallowness of my understanding. From the little we know of the fun and stars, their magnitudes, distances, and motion; and what we are more nearly acquainted with, the gross visible parts in the structure of animals and their economy, it is demonstrable, that they are the effects of an intelligent cause, and the contrivance of a Being insinite in wisdom as well as power. *Hor.* But let wisdom be as superlative, and power as extensive as it is possible for them to be, still it is impossible to conceive how they mould exert themselves, unless they had something to act upon. *Cleo.* This is not the only thing which, though it be true, we are not able to conceive: How came the sirst man to exist? and yet here we are. Heat and moisture are the plain effects from manifest causes, and though they bear a great sway, even in the mineral as well as the animal and vegetable world, yet they cannot produce a sprig of grass without a previous feed. *Hor.* As we ourselves, and every thing we fee, are the undoubted parts of some one whole, some are of opinion, that this all, the « «-», the universe, was from all eternity. *Cleo.* This is not more satisfactory or comprehensible than the system of Epicurus who derives every thing from wild chance, and an undesigned struggle of senseless atoms. When we behold things which our reason tells us could not have been produced without wisdom and power, in a degree far beyond our comprehension, can any thing be more contrary to, or clashing with that same reason, than that the things in which that high wisdom and great power are visibly displayed, should be coeval with the wisdom and power themselves that contrived and wrought them? Yet this doctrine which is spinosisin in epitome, after having been neglected many years, begins to prevail again, and the atoms lose ground: for of atheism, as well as superstition, there are different kinds that have their periods and returns, after they have been

long exploded. *Hor.* What makes you couple together two things so diametrically opposite? *Cleo.* There is greater assinity between them than you imagine: they are of the fame origin. *Hor.* What, atheism and superstition! *Cleo.* Yes, indeed; they both have their rife from the fame cause, the same defect in the mind of man, our want of capacity in discerning truth, and natural ignorance of the Divine efl'ence. Men that from their most early youth hare not been imbued with the principles of the true religion, and have not afterwards continued to be strictly educated in the fame, are all in great danger of falling either into the one or the other, according to the disference there is in the temperament and complexion they are of, the circumstances they are in, and the company they converse with. Weak minds, and those that are brought up in ignorance, and a low condition, such as are much exposed to fortune, men of slavish principles, the covetous and mean-spirited, are all naturally inclined to, and easily susceptible of superstition; and there is no absurdity so gross, nor contradiction so plain, which the dregs of the people, most gamesters, and nineteen women in twenty, may not be taught to believe, concerning invisible causes. Therefore multitudes are never tainted with irreligion; and the less civilized nations are, the more boundless is their credulity. On the contrary, men of parts and spirit, of thought and reflection, the assertors of liberty, such as meddle with mathematics and natural philosophy, most inquisitive men, the disinterested that live in ease and plenty; if their youth has been neglected, and they are not well-grounded in the principles of the true religion, are prone to insidelity; especially such amongst them, whose pride and sussiciency are greater than ordinary; and if persons of this sort fall into Innds of unbelievers, they run great hazard of becoming atheists or sceptics. *Hor.* The method of education you recommend, in pinning men down to an opinion, may be very good to make bigots, and raise a strong party to the priests; but to have good subjects, and moral men,

nothing is better than to inspire youth with the love of virtue, and strongly to imbue them with sentiments of justice and probity, and the true notions of honour and politeness. These are the true specifics to cure man's nature, and destroy in him the savage principles of sovereignty and selsishness, that infest and are i ' mischievous to it. As to religious matters, preposlelTing the mind, and forcing youth into a belief, is more partial and unfair, than it is to leave them unbiassed, and unprejudiced till they come to maturity, and are tit to judge as well as choose for themselves. *Cleo.* It is this fair and impartial management you speak in praise of, that will ever promote and increase unbelief; and nothing has contributed more to the growth of deism in this kingdom, than the remiflhess of education in sacred matters, which for some time has been in fashion among the better sort. *Hor.* The public welfare ought to be our principal care; and 1 am well assured, that it is not bigotry to a sect or persuasion; but common honesty, uprightness in all dealings, and benevolence to one another, which the society stands most in need of. *Cleo.* 1 do not speak up for bigotry; and where the Christian religion is thoroughly taught as it should be, it is impossible, that honesty, uprightness, or benevolence should ever be forgot; and no appearances of those virtues are to be trusted to, unless they proceed from that motive; for without the belief of another world, a man is under no obligation for his sincerity in this: his very oath is no tie upon him. *Hor.* What is it upon an hypocrite that dares to be perjured? *Cleo.* No man's oath is ever taken, if it is known that once he has been forsworn: nor can 1 ever be deceived by an hypocrite, when he tells me that he is one; and 1 shall never believe a man to be an atheist, unless he owns it himself. *Hor.* I do not believe there are real atheists in the world. *Cleo.* I will not quarrel about words; but our modern deism is no greater security than atheism: for a man's acknowledging the being of a God, even an intelligent sirst Cause, is of no use, either to himself or others, if he denies a Providence and a future state. *Hor.* After all, I do not think that virtue has any more relation to credulity, than it has to want of faith. *Cleo.* Yet it would and ought to have, if we were consistent with ourselves; and if men were swayed in their actions by the principles they side with, and the opinion they profess themselves to be of, all atheists would be devils, and superstitious men saints: but this is not true; there are atheists of good morals, and great villains superstitious: nay, I do not believe there is any wickedness that the worst atheist can commit, but superstitious men may be guilty of it; impiety not excepted; for nothing is more common amongst rakes and gamesters, than to hear men blaspheme, that believe in spirits, and are afraid of the devil. I have no greater opinion of superstition than I have of atheism; what I aimed at, was to prevent and guard against both; and I am persuaded that there is no other antidote to be obtained by human means, lo powerful and infallible against the poison of either, as what 1 have mentioned. As to the truth of our descent from Adam, I would not be a believer, and cease to be a rational creature: what I have to say for it, is this. We are convinced that human understanding is limited; and by the help of every little reslection, we may be as certain that the narrowness of its bounds, its being so limited, is the very thing, the sole cause, which palpably hinders us from diving into our origin by dint of penetration: the consequence is, that to come at the truth, of this origin, which is of very great concern to us, something is to be believed: but what or whom to believe is the question. If I cannot demonstrate to you that Moses was divinely inspired, you will be forced to confess, that there never was any thing more extraordinary in the world, than that, in a most superstitious age, one man brought up among the grossest idolaters, that had the' vilest and most abominable notions of the Godhead, should,.without help, as we know of, sind out the most hidden and most important truths by his natural capacity only; for, besides the deep insight he had in human nature, as appears from the decalogue, it is manifest that

he was acquainted with the creation out of nothing, the unity and immense greatness of that Invisible Power that has made the universe; and that he taught this to the Israelites, sifteen centuries before any other nation upon earth was so far enlightened: it is undeniable, moreover, that the history of Moses, concerning the beginning of the world and mankind, is the most ancient and least improbable of any that are extant; that others, who have wrote after him on the fame subject, appear most of them to be imperfect copiers of him; and that the relations which seem not to have been borrowed from Moses, as the accounts we have of *Sommona-codam, Confocius,* and others, are less rational, and sifty times more extravagant and incredible, than any thing contained in the Pentateuch. As to the things revealed, the plan itself, abstract from faith and religion; when we have weighed every system that has been advanced, we ishall sind; that, since we must have had a beginning, nothing is more rational or more agreeable to good fense, than to derive our origin from an incomprehensible creative Power, that was the sirst Mover and Author of all things. *Hor.* I never heard any body entertain higher notions, or more noble sentiments of the Deity, than at different times I have heard from you; pray, when you read Moses, do not you meet with several things in the economy of Paradise, and the conversation between God and Adam, that seem to be low, unworthy, and altogether inconsistent with the sublime ideas you are used to form of the Supreme Being. *Cleo.* I freely own, not only that 1 have thought so, but likewise that I have long stumbled at it: but when I consider, on the one hand, that the more human knowledge increases, the more consummate and unerring the Divine Wisdom appears to be, in every thing we can have any insight into; and on the other, that the things hitherto detected, either by chance or industry, are very inconsiderable both in number and value, if compared to the vast multitude of weightier matters that are left behind and remain still undiscovered: When, I say, I consider these things, I cannot

help thinking, that there may be very wife reasons for what we sind fault with, that are, and perhaps ever will be, unknown to men as long the "world endures. *Hor.* But why should he remain labouring under dissiculties we can easily solve, and not say with Dr. Burnet, and several others, that those things are allegories, and to be understood in a sigurative fense? *Cleo.* I have nothing against it; and shall always applaud the ingenuity and good ossices of men, who endeavour to reconcile religious mysteries to human reason and probability; but I insist upon it, that nobody can disprove any thing that is said in the Pentateuch, in the most literal senie; and I defy the wit of man to frame or contrive a story, the best concerted fable they can invent, how man came into the world, which 1 shall not sind as much fault with, and be able to make as strong objections to, as the enemies of religion have found with, and raised against the account of Moses: If I may be allowed to take the fame liberty with their known forgery, which they take with the Bible, before they have brought one argument against the veracity of it. *Hor.* It may be so. But as sirst I was the occasion of this long digrellion, by mentioning the golden age; so now, desire we may return to our subject. What time, how many ages do you think it would require to have a well-civilized nation from such a savage pair as yours? *Cleo.* That is very uncertain; and I believe it impossible, to determine any thing about it. From what has been said, it is manifest, that the family descending from such a stock, would be crumbled to pieces, reunited, and dispersed again several times, before the whole of any part of it could be advanced to any degree of politeness. The best forms of government are subject to revolutions, and a great many things must concur to keep a society of men together, till they become a civilized nation. *Hor.* Is not a vast deal owing, in the raising of a nation, to the difference there is in the spirit and genius of people? *Cleo.* Nothing, but what depends upon climates, which is soon over-balanced by skilful government. Courage and cowardice, in all bodies of men, depend entirely upon exercise and discipline. Arts and sciences seldom come before riches, and both flow in faster or flower, according to the capacity of the governors, the situation of the people, and the opportunities they have of improvements; but the sirst is the chief: to preserve peace and tranquillity among multitudes of disferent views, and make them all labour for one interest, is a great task; and nothing in human asfairs requires greater knowledge, than the art of governing. *Hor.* According to your system, it should be little more, than guarding against human nature. *Cleo.* But it is a great while before that nature can be rightly understood; and it is the work of ages to sind out the true use of the passions, and to raise a politician that can make every frailty of the members add strength to the whole body, and by dextrous management turn private Vices into public Benesits. *Hor.* It must be a great advantage to an age, when many extraordinary persons are born in it. *Cleo.* It is not genius, so much as experience, that helps men to good laws: Solon, Lycurgus, Socrates and Plato, all travelled for their knowledge, which they communicated to others. The wisest laws of human invention are generally owing to the evasions of bad men, whose cunning had eluded the force of former ordinances that had been made with less caution. *Hor.* I fancy that the invention of iron, and working the oar into a metal, mull contribute very much to the completing of society; because men can have no tools nor agriculture without it. *Clc-o.* Iron is certainly very useful; but shells and flints, and hardening of wood by sire, are substitutes that men make a shift with; if they can but have peace, live in quiet, and enjoy the fruits of their labour. Could you ever have believed, that a man without hands could have shaved himself wrote good characters, and made use of a needle and thread with his feet? Yet this we have seen. It is said by some men of reputation, that the Americans in Mexico and Peru have all the signs of an infant world; because, when the Europeans sirst came among them, they

wanted a great many things, that seem to be of easy invention. But considering that they had nobody to borrow from, and no iron at all, it is amazing which way they could arrive at the perfection we found them in. First, it is impossible to know, how long multitudes may have been troublesome to one another, before the invention of letters came among them, and they had any written laws. Secondly, from the many chasms in history, we know by experience, that the accounts of transactions and times in which letters are known, may be entirely lost. Wars and human discord may destroy the most civilized nations, only by dispersing them; and general devastations spare arts and sciences no more than they do cities and palaces. That all men are born with a strong desire, and no capacity at all to govern, has occasioned an insinity of good and evil. Invasions and persecutions, by mixing and scattering our species, have made strange alterations in the world. Sometimes large empires are divided into several parts, and produce new kingdoms and principalities; at others, great conquerors in few years bring disferent nations under one dominion. From the decay of the Roman empire alone we may learn, that arts and sciences are more perishable, much sooner lost, than buildings or inscriptions; and that a deluge of ignorance may overspread countries, without their ceasing to be inhabited. *Hor.* But what is it at last, that raises opulent cities and powerful nations from the smallest beginnings?-*Cleo.* Providence. *Hor.* But Piovidence makes use of means that are visible; I want to know the engines it is performed with. *Cleo.* All the ground work that is required to aggrandize nations, you have seen Li the Fable of the Bees. All sound politics, and the whole art of governing, are entirely built upon the knowledge of human nature. The great business in general of a politician is to promote, and, if he can, reward all good and useful actions on the one hand; and on the other, to punish, or at least discourage every thing that is destructive or hurtful to society. To name particulars would be an endless task. Anger, lust, and

pride, may be the causes of innumerable mischiefs, that are all carefully to be guarded against: but setting them aside, the regulations only that are required to defeat and prevent all the machinations and contrivances that avarice and envy may put man upon, to the detriment of his neighbour, are almost insinite. Would you be convinced of these truths, do but employ yourself for a month or two, in surveying and minutely examining into every art and science, every trade, handicraft and occupation, that are professed and followed in such a city as London; and all the laws, prohibitions, ordinances and restrictions that have been found absolutely necessary, to hinder both private men and bodies corporate, in so many different stations, sirst from interfering with the public peace and welfare; secondly, from openly wronging and secretly over-reaching, or any other way injuring one another: if you will give yourself this trouble, you will sind the number of clauses and provisos, to govern a large slourishing city.well, to be prodigious beyond imagination; and yet every one of them tending to the fame purpose, the curbing, restraining, and disappointing the inordinate passions, and hurtful frailties of man. You will sind, moreover, which is still more to be admired, the greater part of the articles in this vast multitude of regulations, when well understood, to be the result of consummate wisdom. *Hor.* How could these things exist, if there had not been men of very bright parts and uncommon talents? *Cleo.* Among the things I hint at, there are very few that are the work of one man, or of one generation; the greatest part of them are the product, the joint labour of several ages. Remember what in our third conversation I told vou, concerning the arts of ship-building and politeness. The wisdom 1 speak of, is not the offspring of a sine understanding, or intense thinking, but of sound and deliberate judgment, acquired from a long experience in business, and a multiplierty of observations. By this sort of wisdom, and length of time, it may be brought about, that there shall be no greater dissiculty in governing a large city, than (pardon the lowneis of the simile) there is in weaving of stockings. *Hor.* Very low indeed. *Cleo.* Yet I know nothing to which the laws and established economy of a well ordered city may be more justly compared, than the knitting-frame. The machine, at sirst view, is intricate and unintelligible; yet the effects of it are exact and beautiful; and in what is produced by it, there is a surprising regularity: but the beauty and exactness in the manufacture are principally, if not altogether, owing to the happiness of the invention, the contrivance of the engine. For the greatest artist at it can furnish us with no better work, than may be made by almost any scoundrel after half a year's practice. *Hor.* Though your comparison be low, I must own that it very well illustrates your meaning. *Cleo.* Whilst you spoke, I have thought of another, which is better. It is common now, to have clocks that are made to play several tunes with great exactness: the study and labour, as well as trouble of disappointments, which, in doing and undoing, such a contrivance must necessarily have cost from the beginning to the end, are not to be thought of without astonishment: there is something analogous to this in the government of a flourishing city, that has lasted uninterrupted for several ages: there is no part of the wholesome regulations belonging to it, even the most trifling and minute, about which great pains and consideration have not been employed, as well as length of time; and if you will look into the history and antiquity of any such city, you will sind that the changes, repeals, additions and amendments, that have been made in and to the laws and ordinances by which it is ruled, are in number prodigious: but that when once they are brought to as much perfection as art and human wisdom can curry them, the whole machine may be made to play of itself, with as little skill as it required to wind up a clock; and the government of a large city once put into good order, the magistrates only following their noses, will continue to go right for a while, though there was not a wife man in it; provided that the care of

Providence was to watch over it in tne fame manner as it did before. *Hor.* But supposing the government of a large city, when it is once established, to be very easy, it is not so with whole states and kingdoms: is it not a great blessing to a nation, to have all places of honour and great trust silled with men of parts and application, of probity and virtue? *Cleo.* Yes; and of learning, moderation, frugality, candour and asfability: look out for such as fast as you can; but in the mean time the places cannot stand open, the ossices must be served by such as you can get. *Hor.* You seem to insinuate, that there is a great scarcity-of good men in the nation. *Cleo.* I do not speak of our nation in particular, but of all states and kingdoms in general. What I would fay, is, that it is the interest of every nation to have their home government, and every branch of the civil administration so wisely contrived, that every man of middling capacity and reputation may be sit for any of the highest posts. *Hor.* That is absolutely impossible, at least in such a nation as ours: for what would you do for judges and chancellors? *Cleo.* The study of the law is very crabbed and very tedious; but the profession of it is as gainful, and has great honours annexed to it: the consequence of this is, that few come to be eminent in it, but men of tolerable parts and great application. And whoever is a good lawyer, and not noted for dishonesty, is always sit to be a judge, as soon as he is old and grave enough. To be a lord chancellor, indeed, requires higher talents; and he ought not only to be a good lawyer and an honest man, but likewise a person of general knowledge and great penetration. But this is but one man: and considering what I have said of the law, and the power which ambition and the love of gain have upon mankind, it is morally impossible, that, in the common course of things among the practitioners in chancery, there should not at all times be one or other sit for the seals. *Hor.* Must not every nation have men that are sit for public negotiations, and persons of great capacity to serve for envoys, ambassadors and plenipotentaries? must they not have

others at home, that are likewise able to treat with foreign ministers? *Cleo.* That every nation must have such people, is certain; but I wonder that the company you have kept both at home and abroad, have not convinced you that the things you speak of require no such extraordinary qualisications. Among the people of quality that are bred up in courts of princes, all middling capacities must be persons of address, and a becoming boldness, which are the moll useful talents in all conferences and negotiations. *Hor.* In a nation so involved in debts of diferent kinds, and loaded with such a variety of taxes as ours is, to be thoroughly acquainted with all the funds, and the appropriations of them, must be a science not to be attained to without good natural parts and great application; and therefore the chief management of the treasury must be a post of the highest trust, as well as endless dissiculty. *Cleo.* I do not think so: most branches of the public administration are in reality less dissicult to those that are in them, than they seem tor be to those that are out of them, and are strangers to them. If a jack and the weights of it were out of sight, a sensible man unacquainted with that matter, would be very much puzzled, if he was to account for the regular turning of two or three spits well loaded, for hours together; and it is ten to one, but he would have a greater opinion of the cook or the scullion, than either of them deserved. In all business that belong to the exchequer, the constitution does nine parts in ten; and has taken effectual care, that the happy person whom the king shall be pleased to favour with the l'uperintendency of it, should never be greatly tired or perplexed with his ossice; and likewise that the trust, the considence that must be reposed in him, should be very near as moderate as his trouble. By dividing the employments in a great office, and subdividing them into many parts, every man's business may be made so plain and certain, that, when he is a little used to it, it is hardly possible for him to make mistakes: and again, by careful limitations of every man's power, and judicious checks upon every body's trust, every officer's sidelity may be placed in so clear a light, that the moment he forfeits it, he must be detected. It is by these arts that the weightiest affairs, and a vast multiplicity of them, may be managed with safety as well as dispatch, by ordinary men, whose highest good is wealth and pleasure; and that the utmost regularity may be observed in a great ossice, and every part of it; at the same time, that the whole economy of it seems to be intricate and perplexed to the last degree, not only to strangers, but the greatest part of the very officers that are employed in it. *Hor.* The economy of our exchequer, I own, is an admirable contrivance to prevent frauds and encroachments of all kinds; but in the ossice, which is at the head of it, and gives motion to it, there is greater latitude. *Cleo.* Why so? A lord treasurer, or if his ossice be executed by commissioners, the chancellor of the exchequer, are no more lawless, and have no greater power with impunity to embezzle money, than the meanest clerk that is employed under them. *Hor.* Is not the king's warrant their discharge? *Cleo.* Yes; for sums which the king has a right to dispose of, or the payment of money for uses directed by parliament; not otherwise; and if the king, who can do no wrong, should be imposed upon, and his warrant be obtained for money at random, whether it is appropriated or not, contrary to, or without a direct order of the legislature, the treasurer obeys at his peril. *Hor.* But there are other posts, or at least there is one still of higher moment, and that requires a much greater, and more general capacity than any yet named. *Cleo.* Pardon me: as the lord chancellor's is the highest ossice in dignity, so the execution of it actually demands greater, and more uncommon abilities than any other whatever. *Hor.* What fay you to the prime minister who governs all, and acts immediately under the king? *Cleo.* There is no such ossicer belonging to our constitution; for by this, the whole administration is, for very wife reasons, divided into several branches. *Hor.* But who must give orders and instructions to admirals, generals governors, and all cur ministers in

foreign courts? Who is to take care of the king's interest throughout the kingdom, and of his safety? *Cleo.* The king and his council, without which, royal authority is not supposed to act, superintend, and govern all; and whatever the monarch has not a mind immediately to take care of himself, falls in course to that part of the administration it belongs to, in which every body has plain laws to walk by. As to the king's interest, it is the fame with that cf the nation; his guards arz to take care of his person; and there is no business of what nature soever, that can happen in or to the nation, which is not within the province, and under the inspection of some one or other of the great ossi Kk cers of the crown, that are all known, dignisied, and distinguished by their respective titles; and amongst them, I can assure you, there is no such name as prime minister.

Hor. But why will you prevaricate with me after this manner? You know yourself, and all the world knows and fees, that there is such a minister; and it is easily proved, that there always have been such ministers: and in the situation we are, I do not believe a king could do without. When there are a great many disaffected people in the kingdom, and parliament-men are to be chosen, elections must be looked after with great care, and a thousand things are to be done, that are necessary to disappoint the sinister ends of malecontents, and keep out the Pretender; things of which the management often requires great penetration, and uncommon talents, as well as secrecy and dispatch. *Cleo.* How sincerely soever you may seem to speak in defence of these things, Horatio, I am sure, from your principles, that you are not in earnest. I am not to judge of the exigency of our affairs: But as I would not pry into the conduct, or scan the actions of princes, and their ministers, so I pretend to justify or defend no wisdom but that of the constitution itself. *Hor.* I do not desire you should: Only tell me, whether you do not think, that a man, who has and can carry this vast harden upon his moulders, and all Europe's business in his breast, must be a person

of a prodigious genius, as well as general knowledge, and other great abilities. *Cleo.* That a man, invested with so much real power, and an authority so extensive, as such ministers generally have, must make a great sigure, and be considerable above all other subjects, is most certain: But it is my opinion, that there are always sifty men in the kingdom, that, if employed, would be sit for this post, and, after a little practice, shine in it, to one who is equally qualisied to be a Lord High Chancellor of Great Britain. A prime minister has a vast, an unspeakable advantage barely by being so, and by every body's knowing him to be, and treating him as such: A man who in every ossice, and every branch of it throughout the administration, has the power, as well as the liberty, to ask and fee whom and what he pleases, has more knowledge within his reach, and can speak of every thing with greater exactness than any other man, that is much better versed in affairs, and has ten times greater capacity. It is hardly possible, than an active man, of tolerable education, that is not destitute of a spirit nor of vanity, should fail of appearing to be wise, vigilant, and expert, who has the opportunity whenever he thinks sit, to make use of all the cunning and experience, as well as diligence and labour of every ossicer in the civil administration; and if he has but money enough, and will employ men to keep up a strict correspondence in every part of the kingdom, he can remain ignorant of nothing; and there is hardly any asfair or transaction, civil or military, foreign or domestic, which he will not be able greatly to influence, when he has a mind either to promote or obstruct it. *Hor.* There seems to be a great deal in what you fay, I must confess; but I begin to suspect, that what often inclines me to be of your opinion, is your dexterity in placing things in the light you would have seen them in, and the great skill you have in depreciating what is valuable, and detracting from merit. *Cleo.* I protest that I speak from my heart. *Hor.* When I reflect on what I have beheld with my own eyes, and what I still fee every day of the transactions between statesmen and politicians, I am very well allured you are in the wrong: When I consider all the stratagems, and the force as well as sinesse that are made use of to supplant and undo prime ministers, the wit and cunning, industry and address, that are employed to misrepresent all their actions, the calumnies and false reports that are spread of them, the ballads and lampoons that are published, the set speeches and studied invectives that are made against them; when I consider, I fay, and reflect on these things, and every thing else that is said and done, either to ridicule or to render them odious, I am convinced, that to defeat so much art and strength, and disappoint so much malice and envy as prime ministers are generally attacked with, require extraordinary talents: No man of only common prudence and fortitude could maintain himself in that post for a twelvemonth, much less for many years together, though he understood the world very well, and had all the virtue, faithfulness, and integrity in it; therefore, there must be some fallacy in your aifertion.; *Cleo.* Either I have been desicient in explaining myself, or else 1 have had the misfortune to be misunderstood. When I insinuated that men might be prime ministers without extraordinary endowments, I spoke only in regard to the business itself, that province, which, if there was no such minister, the king and council would have the trouble of managing. *Hor.* To direct and manage the whole machine of government, he must be a consummate statesmen in the sirst place. *Cleo.* You have too sublime a notion of that post. To be a consummate statesmen, is the highest qualisication human nature is capable of possessing: To deserve that name, a man must be well versed in ancient and modern history, and thoroughly acquainted with all the courts of Europe, that he may know not only the public interest in every nation, but likewise the private views, as well as inclinations, virtues, and vices of princes and ministers: Of every country in Christendom, and the borders of it, he ought to know the product and geography, the principal cities and fortress-

es; and of these their trade and mamitactures, their situation, natural advantages, strength, and number of inhabitants; he must have read men as well as books, and perfectly well understand human nature, and the use of the passions: He must, moreover, be a great master in concealing the sentiments of his heart, have an entire command over his features, and be well skilled in all the wiles and stratagems to draw out secrets from others. A man, of whom all this, or the greatest part of it, may not be said with truth, and that he has had great experience in public rifairs, cannot be called a consummate statesman; but lie may be sit to be a prime minister, though he had not a hundredth part of those qualisications. As the kinj's favour creates prime ministers, and makes their station the post of the greatest power as well as prosit, so the fame favour is the only bottom which those that are in it have to stand upon: The consequence is, that the most ambitious men in all monarchies are ever contending for this post as the highest prize, of which the enjoyment is easy, and all the dissiculty in obtaining and preserving it. We see accordingly, that the accomplishments 1 spoke of to make a statesman are neglected, and others aimed at and studied, that are more useful and more easily acquired. The capacities you observe in prime ministers are of another nature, and consist in being sinished courtiers, and thoroughly understanding the art of pleasing and cajoling with address. To procure a prince what he wants, when it is known, and to be diligent in entertaining him with the pleasures he calls for, are ordinary services: Asking is no better than complaining; therefore, being forced to ask, is to have cause of complaint, and to see a prince submit to the slavery of it, argues great rusticity in his courtiers; a polite minister penetrates into his master's wishes, and furnishes him with what he delights in, without giving him the trouble to name it. Every common flatterer can praise and extol promiscuously every thing that is said or done, and sind wisdom and prudence in the most indifferent actions; but it belongs

to the skilful courtier to set sine glosses upon manifest imperfections, and make every failing, every frailty of his prince, have the real appearance of the virtues that are the nearest, or, to speak more justly, the least opposite to them. By the observance of these necessary duties, it is that the favour of princes may be long preserved, as well as obtained. Whoever can make himself agreeable at a court, will seldom fail of being thought necessary; and when a favourite has once established himself in the good opinion of his master, it is easy for him to make his own family engross the king's ear, and keep every body from him but his own creatures: Nor is it more dissicult, in length of time, to turn out of the administration every body that was not of his own bringing in, and constantly be tripping up the heels of those who attempt to raise themselves by any other interest or assistance. A prime minister has by his place great advantages over all that oppose him; one of them is, that nobody, without exception, ever silled that post but who had many enemies, whether he was a plunderer or a patriot: Which being well known, many things that are laid to a prime minister's charge are not credited among the impartial and more discreet part of mankind, even when they are true. As to the defeating and disappointing all the envy and malice they are generally attacked with, if the favourite was to do all thai: himself, it would certainly, as you fay, require extraordinary talents and a great capacity, as well as continual vigilance and application; but this is the province of their creatures, a task divided into a great number of parts; and every body that has the least dependence upon, or has any thing to hope fnm the minister, makes it his business and his study, as it is his interest, on the one hand, to cry up their patron, magnify his virtues and abilities, and justisy his conduct; on the other, to exclaim against his adversaries, blacken their reputation, and play at them every engine, and the same strata-gems that are made use of to supplant the minister. *Hor.* Then every well-polished courtier is sit to be a prime minister, without learning or languages, skill in politics, or any other qualisication besides. *Cldo.* Wo other than what are often and easily met with: It is necessary that he should be a man, at least, of plain common fense, and not remarkable for any gross frailties or imperfections; and.of such, there is no scarcity almost in any nation: He ought to be a man of tolerable health and constitution, and one who delights in vanity, that he may relish, as well as be able to bear the gaudy crowds that honour his levees, the constant addresses, bows, and cringes of solicitors, and the rest of the homage that is perpetually paid him. The accomplishment he stands most in need of, is to be bold and resolute, so as not to be easily shocked or ruffled; if he be thus qualisied, has a good memory, and is, moreover, able to attend a multiplicity of business, if not with a continual presence of mind, at least seemingly without hurry or perplexity, his capacity can never fail of being extolled to the Ikies. *Hor.* You fay nothing of his virtue nor his honesty; there is a vast trust put in a prime minister: If he should be covetous,, and have no probity, nor love for his country, he might make strange havoc with the public treasure. *Cleo.* There is no man that has any pride, but he has some value for his reputation; and common prudence is sussicient to hinder a man of very indifferent principles from stealing, where he would be in great danger of being detected, and has no manner of security that he shall not be punished for it. *Hor.* But great confidence is reposed in him where he cannot be traced; as in the money for secret services, of which, for reasons of slate, it may be often improper even to mention, much more to scrutinize into the particulars; and in negotiations with other courts, mould he be only swayed by selsishness and private views, without regard to virtue or the public, is it not in his power to betray his country, fell the nation, and do all manner of mischief? *Cleo.* Not amongst us, where parliaments are every year sitting. In foreign affairs nothing of moment can be transacted but what all the world must know; and should any thing be done or attempted that would be palpably ruin-

ous to the kingdom, and in the opinion of natives and foreigners grossly and manifestly clashing with our interest, it would raise a general clamour, and throw the minister into dangers, which no man of the least prudence, who intends to stay in his country, would ever run into. As to the money for secret services, and perhaps other sums, which ministers have the disposal of, and where they have great latitudes, I do not question hut they have opportunities of embezzling the nations treasure: but to do this without being discovered, it must be done sparingly, and with great discretion: The malicious overlookers that envy them their places, and watch all their motions, are a great awe upon them: the animosities between those antagonists, and the quarrels between parties, are a considerable part of the nation's security. *Hor.* But would it not be a greater security to have men of honour, of sense and knowledge, of application and frugality, preferred to public employments? *Cleo.* Yes, without doubt. *Hor.* What contidence can we have in the justice or integrity of men; that, on the one hand, mow themselves on all occasions mercenary and greedy after riches; and on the other, make it evident, by their manner of living, that no wealth or estate could ever sussice to support their expences, or satisfy their desires! besides, would it not be a great encouragement to virtue and merit, if from the posts of honour and prosit all were to be debarred and excluded, that either wanted capacity or were enemies to business; all the selsish, ambitious, vain, and voluptuous? *Cleo.* Nobody disputes it with you ; and if virtue, religion, and future happiness were sought after by the generality of mankind, with the same solicitude, as sensual pleasure, politeness, and worldly glory are, it would certainly be best that none but men of good lives, and known ability, mould have any place in the government whatever: but to expect that this ever mould happen, or to live in hopes of it in a large, opulent, and fiounstiing kingdom, is to betray great ignorance in human asfairs? and whoever reckons a general temperance, frugality, and dis-

interestedness among the national blessing, and at the fame time solicits Heaven for ease and plenty, and the increase of trade, seems to me, little to understand what he is about. The best of all, then, not being to be had, let us look out for the next best, and we shall sind, that of all possible means to secure and perpetuate to nations their establishment, and whatever they value, there is no better method than with wife laws to guard and entrench their constitution, and contrive such forms of administration that the commonweal can receive no great detriment from the want of knowledge or probity of ministers, if any of them should prove less able or honest, than they could wish them. The public administration must always go forward; it is a ship that can never lie at anchor: the most knowing, the most virtuous, and the least self-interested ministers are the best; but, in the mean time there must be ministers. Swearing and drunkenness are crying sins among seafaring men, and I should think it a very desirable blessing to the nation, if it was possible to reform them: but all this while we must have sailors; and if none were to be admitted on board of any of his majesty's ships, that had sworn above a thousand oaths, or had been drunk above ten times in their lives. I am persuaded that the service would suffer very much by the well-meaning regulation. *Hor.* Why do not you speak more openly, and say that there is no virtue or probity in the world? for all the drift of your discourse is tending to prove that. *Cleo.* I have amply declared myself upon this subject already in a former conversation; and I wonder you will lay again to my charge what I once absolutely denied: I never thought that there were no virtuous or religious men; what I differ in with the flatterers of our species, is about the numbers which they contend for; and I am persuaded that you yourself, in reality, do not believe that there are so many virtuous men as you imagine you do. *Hor.* How come you to know my thoughts better than I do myself? *C/eo.* You know I have tried you upon this head already, when I ludicrously extolled and set a sine gloss on the merit of several callings and professions in the society, from the lowest stations of life to the highest: it then plainly appeared, that, though you have a very high opinion of mankind in geneial, when we come to particulars, you was as severe, and every whit as censorious as myself. I must observe one thing to you, which is worth consideration. Most, if not all people, are desirous of being thought impartial; yet nothing is more difficult than to preserve our judgment unbiassed, when we are influenced either by our love or out hatred; and how just and equitable soever people are, we see that their friends are seldom so good, or their enemies so bad as they represent them, when they are angry with the one, or highly pleased with the other. For my part, I do not think that, generally speaking, prime ministers are much worse than their adversaries, who for their own interest defame them, and at the fame time, move Heaven and earth to be in their places. Let us look out for two persons of eminence in any court of Europe, that are equal in merit and capacity, and as well matched in virtues and vices, but of contrary parties; and whenever we meet with two such, one in favour and the other neglected, we shall always sind that whoever is uppermost, and in great employ, has the applause of his party; and if things go tolerably well, his friends will attribute every good success to his conduct, and derive all his actions from laudable motives: the opposite side can discover no virtues in him; they will not allow him to act from any principles but his passions; and if any thing be done amiss, are very sure that it would not have happened if their patron had been in the same post. This is the way of the world. How immensely do often people of the lame kingdom disfer in the opinion they have of their chiefs and commanders, even when they are successful to admiration! we have been witnesses ourselves that one pare of the nation has ascribed the victories of a general entirely to his consummate knowledge in martial asfairs, and superlative capacity in action; and maintained that it was im-

possible for a man to bear all the toik and fatigues he underwent with alacrity, or to court the dangers he voluntarily exposed himself to, if he had not been supported, as well as animated, by the true spirit of heroism, and a most generous love for his country: these, you know, were the sentiments of one part of the nation, whilst the other attributed all his successes to the bravery os his troops, and the extraordinary care that was taken at home to supply his army; and insisted upon it, that from the whole course of his life, it was demonstrable, that he had never been buoyed up or actuated by any other principles than excess ot ambition, and an unl'atiable greediness after riches. *Hor.* I do not know but I may have said so myself. But after all, the Duke os Marlborough was a very great man, an extraordinary genius. *Cleo.* Indeed was he, and I am glad to hear you own it at last.
Virtutera incolumem odimus,
Sublatum ex oculis quæiimus inviJi.
Hor. A propvs. I wish you would bid them stop for two or three minutes: some of the horses perhaps may stale the

While.
Cleo. No excuses, pray. You command here. Besides, we have time enough. Do you want to go out? *Hor.* No; but I want to set down something, now I think of it which I have heard you repeat several times. I have often had a mind to ask you for it, and it always went out of my head again. It is the epitaph which your friend made upon the Duke. *Cleo.* Of Marlborough? with all my heart. Have you paper? *Hor.* I will write it upon the back of this letter; and as it happens, I mended my pencil this morning. How does it begin? *Cleo. %ui belli, aid paucis virtutibus qlira petebant. Hor.* Well. *Cleo. Finxerunt homines sœcula prifea Deos. Hor.* I have it. But tell me.a whole distich at a time; the fense is clearer. *Cleo.* Quae martem sine patre tulit, sine matre Mincrvam,
Illustres mendax Giitcia jactet avos.
Hor. That is really a happy thought. Courage and conduct: just the two qualisications he excelled in. What it the next? *Cleo.* Anglia quern genuit jacet

bac, Homo, conditus Urna,
Antiqui, qualeni non habuere Deum.
H. 1 thank you. They may go on now. I have seen several things since sirst I heard this epitaph of you, that are manifestly borrowed from it. Was it never published? *Cleo.* I believe not. The sirst time I saw it was the day the Duke was buried,and ever since it has been handed about in manuscript; but 1 never met with it in print yet. *Hor.* It is worth all his Fable of the Bees, in my opinion. *Cleo.* If you like it so well, I can show you a translation of it, lately done by a gentleman of Oxford, if I have not lost it. It only takes in the sirst and last distich, which indeed contain the main thought: The second does not carry it on, and is rather a digression. *Hor.* But it demonstrates the truth of the sirst in a very convincing manner; and that Mars had no father, and Minerva no mother, is the most fortunate thing a man could wish for, who wanted to prove that the account we have of them is fabulous. *Cleo.* Oh, here it is. I do not know whether you can read k; I copied it in haste. *Hor.* Very well.
The grateful ages past a God dcclar'd,
Who wisely council'd, or who bravely wr'd:
Hence Greece her Mars and Pallas deify'd;
Made him the heroe's, her the patriot's guide.
Ancients,within this urn a mortal lies
Shew me his peer among your deities.
It is very good.
Cleo. Very lively; and what is aimed at in the Latin, is rather more clearly expressed in the English. *Hor.* You know I am fond of no English verse but Milton's. But do not let this hinder our conversation. *Cleo.* I was speaking of the partiality of mankind in general, and putting you in mind how differently men judged of actions, according as they liked or disliked the persons that performed them. *Hor.* But before that you was arguing against the necessity, which I think there is, for men of great accomplishments and extraordinary qualisications in the administration of public affairs. Had you any thing to add? *Cleo.* No; at least 1 do not remem-

ber that I had. *Hor.* I do not believe you have an ill design in advancing these notions; but supposing them to be true, I cannot comprehend that divulging them can have any other effect than the increase of sloth and ignorance; for if men may rill the highest places in the government without learning or capacity, genius or knowledge, there is an end of all the labour of the brain, and the fatigue of hard study. *Cleo.* I have made no such general assertion; but that an artful man may make a considerable sigure in the highest post of the administration, and other great employments, without extraordinary talents, is certain: as to consummate statesmen, 1 do not believe there ever were three persons upon earth at the fame time, that deserved that name. There is not a quarter of the wisdom, solid knowledge, or intrinsic worth in the world that men talk of and compliment one another with; and of virtue or religion there is not an hundredth part in reality of what there is in appearance. *Hor.* 1 atlow that thole who set out from no better motives, than avarice and ambition, aim at no other ends but wealth and honour; which, if they can but get anywise they are satissied; but men who act from principles of virtue and a public spirit, take pains with alacrity to attain the accomplishments that will make them capable of serving their country: and if virtue be so scarce, how come there to be men of skill in their professions? for that there are men of learning and men of capacity, is most certain. *Ck'o.* The foundation of all accomplishments must be laid in our youth, before we are able or allowed to choose for ourselves, or to judge, which is the most prositable way of employing our time. It is to good discipline, and the prudent care of parents and masters, that men are beholden for the greatest part of their improvements; and few parents are so bad as not to wisti their offspring might be well accomplished: the same natural affection that makes men take pains to leave their children rich, renders them solicitcu about their education. Besides, it is unfashionable, and consequently a disgrace to neglect them. The chief design

of parents in bringing up their children to a calling or profession, is to procure tnem a livelihood. What promotes and encourages arts and sciences, is the reward, money and honour; and thousands of perfections are attained to, that would have had no existence, if men had been less proud or less covetous. Ambition, avarice, and often necessity, are great spurs to industry and application; and often rouse men from sloth and indolence, when they are grown up, whom no persuasions or chastisement of fathers or tutors, made any impression upon in their youth, Whilst professions are lucrative, and have great dignities belonging to them, there will always be men that excel in them, in a large polite nation, therefore, all forts of learning will ever abound, whilst the people flourish. Rich parents, and such as can afford it, seldom fail bringing up their children to literature: from this inexhaustible spring it is, that we always draw much larger supplies than we stand in need of, for all the callings and professions where the knowledge of theJearned languages is required. Of those that are brought up to letters, some neglect them, and throw by their books as soon as they are their own masters; others grow fonder of study, as they increase in years; but the greatest part will always retain a value for what has cost them pains to acquire. Among the wealthy, there will be always lovers of knowledge, as well as idle people: every science will have its admirers, as men differ in their tastes and pleasures; and there is no part of learning but somebody or other will look into it, and labour at it, from no better principles than some men are fox-hunters, and others take delight in angling. Look upon the mighty labours of antiquaries, botanists, and the vertuosos in butterflies, cockleshells, and other odd productions of nature; and mind the magnisicent terms they all make use of in their respective provinces, and the pompous names they often give to what others, who have no taste that way, would not think worth any mortal's notice. Curiosity is often as bewitching to the rich, as lucre is to the poor; and

what interest does in some, vanity does in others; and great wonders are often produced from a happy mixture of both. Is it not amazing, that a temperate man mould be at the expence of four or sive thousand a-year, or, which is much the fame thing, be contented to lose the interest of above a hundred thousand pounds, to have the reputation of being the possessor and owner of rarities and knicknacks in a very great abundance, at the fame time that he loves money, and continues slaving for it in his old age! It is the hopes either of gain or reputation, of large revenues and great dignities that promote learning; and when we fay that any calling, art or science, is not encouraged, we mean no more by it, than that the masters or professors of it are not sussiciently rewarded for their pains, either with honour or prosit. The most holy functions are no exception to what I fay; and few ministers of the gospel are so disinterested as to have a lel's regard to the honours and emoluments that are or ought to be annexed to their employment, than they have to the service and benesit they should be of to others; and among those of them that study hard and take uncommon pains, it is not easily proved that many are excited to their extraordinary labour by a public spirit or solicitude for the spiritual welfare of the laity: on the contrary, it is visible, in the greatest part of them, that they are animated by the love of glory and the hopes of preferment; neither is it common to fee the most useful parts of learning neglected for the moll trisling, when, from the latter, men have reason to hope that they shall have greater opportunities of showing their parts, than osfer themselves from the former. Ostentation and envy have made more authors than virtue and benevolence. Men of known capacity and erudition are often labouring hard to eclipse and ruin one another's glory. What principle must we fay two adversaries act from, both men of unquestionable good fense and extensive knowledge, when all the skill and prudence they are masters of are not able to stifle, in their studied performances, and hide from the world, the rancour of their minds, the spleen and animosity they both write with against one another. *Hor.* I do not say that such act from principles of virtue. *Cleo.* Yet you know an instance of this in two grave divines, men of fame and great merit, of whom each would think himself very much injuredj should his virtue be called in question. *Hor.* When men have an opportunity, under pretence of zeal for religion, or the public good, to vent their passion, they take great liberties. What was the quarrel? *Cleo. De lana caprina. Hor.* A trifle. I cannot guess yet. *Clco.* About the metre of the comic poets among the ancients. *Hor.* I know what you mean now; the manner of scanding and chanting those verses. *Cleo.* Can you think of any thing belonging to literature, of less importance, or more useless? *Hor.* Not readily. *Cleo.* Yet the great contest between them, you fee, is which of them understands it best, and has known it the longest. This instance, 1 think, hints to us how highly improbable it is, though men should act from no better principles than envy, avarice, and ambition, that when learning is once established, any part of it, even the most unprositable, should ever be neglected in such a large opulent nation as ours is; where there are so many places of honour, and great revenues to be disposed of among scholars. *Hor.* But since men are sit to serve in most places with so little capacity, as you insinuate, why should they give themselves that unnecessary trouble of studying hard, and acquiring more learning than there is occasion for? *Cleo.* I thought 1 had answered that already; a great many, because they take delight in study and knowledge. *Hor.* But there are men that labour at it with so much application, as to impair their healths, and actually to kill themselves with the fatigue of it. *Cleo.* Not so many as there are that injure their healths, and actually kill themselves with hard drinking, which is the most unreasonable pleasure of the two, and a much greater fatigue. But I do not deny that there are men who take pains to qualify themselves in. order to serve their country; what I insist upon is, that the number of those who do the

fame thing to lerve themselves with little regard to their country, is insinitely greater. Mr. Hutchefon, who wote the Inquiry into the Original of our Ideas of Beauty and Virtue, seems to be very expert at weighing and measuring the. quantities of affection, benevolence, &c. I wish that curious metaphysician would give himself the trouble, at his leisure, to weigh two things separately: First, the real love men have for their country, abstracted from selsishness. Secondly, the ambition they have of being thought to act from that love, though they feel none. I wish, I fay, that this ingenious gentleman would once weigh these two asunder; and afterwards, having taken in impartially all he could sind of/either, in this or any other nation, show us in his demonstrative way, what proportion the quantities bore to each other.—*uijquejibi commiffus eft,* fays Seneca; and certainly, it is not the care of others, but the care of itself, which nature has trusted and charged every individual creature with. When men exert themselves in an extraordinary manner, they generally do it to be the better for it themselves; to excel, to be talked of, and to be preferred to others, that follow the fame business, or court the fame favours. *Hor.* Do you think it more probable, that men of parts and learning should be preferred, than others of less capacity? *Cleo. Cceteris paribus,* I do, *Hor.* Then you must allow that there is virtue at least in those who have the disposal of places. *Cleo.* I do not fay there is not; but there is likewise glory and real honour accruing to patrons for advancing men of merit; and isa person who has a good living in his gift, bestows it upon a very able man, every body applauds him, and every parishioner is counted to be particularly obliged to him, A vain man does not love to have his choice disapproved of, and exclaimed against by all the world, any more than a virtuous man; and the love of applause, which is innate to our species, would alone be sussicient to make the generality of men, and even the greatest part of the most vicious, always choose the most worthy, out of any number ef candidates; if they knew

the truth, and no stronger motive arising from consanguinity, friendship, interest, or something else, was to interfere with the principle I named. *Hor.* But, methinks, according to your system, those should be soonest preferred that can best coax and flatter. *Cleo.* Among the learned there are persons of art and addrsis, that can mind their studies without neglecting the the world: thele are the men that know how to ingratiate themselves with persons of quality; employing to the best advantage all their parts and industry for that purpose. Do but look into the lives and the deportment of such eminent men, as we hae been speaking of, and you will soon discover the end and advantages they seem to propose to themselves from their hard study and severe lucubrations. When you fee men in holy orders, without call or necessity, hovering about the courts of princes; when you fee them continually addrefling and scraping acquaintance with the favourites; when you hear them exclaim against the luxury of the age, and complain of the necessity they are under os complying with it; and at the same time you see, that they are forward, nay eager and take pains with satisfaction, in the way of living, to imitate the *beau monde,* as far as it is in their power: that no sooner they are in posselsion of one preferment, but they are ready, and actually soliciting for another, more gainful and more reputable; and that on all emergencies, wealth, power, honour and superiority are the things they grasp at, and take delight in; when, 1 say, you see these things, this concurrence of evidences, is it any longer dissicult to guess at, or rather is there room to doubt of the principles they act from, or the tendency of their labours? *Nor.* 1 have little to fay to priests, and do not look for virtue from that quarter. *Cleo.* Yet you will sind as much of it among divines, as you will among any other class of men; but every where less in reality, than there is in appearance, Nobody would be thought insincere, or to prevaricate; but there are few men, though they are so honest as to own what they would have, that will acquaint us with the true reason why they would have it: therefore the disagreement between the words and actions of men is at no time more conspicuous, than when we would learn from them their sentiments,' concerning the real worth of things. Virtue, is without doubt, the most valuable treasure which man can be possessed of; it has every body's good word; but where is the country in which it is heartily embraced, *præmiafi tollas?* Money, on the other hand, is deservedly called the root of all evil: there has not been a moralist nor'a satirist of note, that has not had a fling at it; yet what pains are taken, and what hazards are run to acquire it, under various pretences of designing to do good with it! As for my part, I verily believe, that as an accessary cause, it has done more mischief in the world than any one thing besides: yet it is impossible to name another, that is so absolutely necessary to the order, economy, and the very existence of the civil society; for as this is entirely built upon the variety of our wants, so the whole superstructure is made up of the reciprocal services which men do to each other. How to get these services performed by others, when we have occasion for them, is the grand and almost constant solicitude in life of every individual person. To expect that others should serve us for nothing, is unreasonable; therefore all commerce that men ca.n have together, must be a continual bartering of one thing for another. The seller who transfers the property of a thing, has his own interest as much at heart as the buyer who purchases that property: and, if you want or like a thing, the owner of it, whatever stock or provision he may have of the fame, or how gTeatly soever you may stand in need of it, will never part with it, but for a consideration which he likes better than he does the thing you want. Which way shall I persuade a mant to serve me, when the service I can repay him in, is such as he does not want or care for? Nobody who is at peace, and has no contention with any of the society, will do any thing for a lawyer; and a physician can purchase nothing of a man, whose whole family is in perfect health. Money obviates and

takes away all those dissiculties, by being an acceptable reward for all the services men can do to one another. *Hor.* But all men valuing themselves above their worth, every body will over-rate his labour. Would not this follow from your system? *Cleo.* It certainly would, and does. But what is to be admired is, that the larger the numbers are in a society, the more extensive they have rendered the variety of their desires, and the more operose the gratisication of them is become among them by custom j the less mischievous is the consequence of that evil, where they have the use of money: whereas, without it, the smaller the number was of a society, and the more strictly the members of it, in supplying their wants, would consine themselves to those only that were necessity for their subsistence, the more easy it would be for them to agree about the reciprocal services I spoke of. But to procure all the comforts of life, and what is called temporal happiness, in a large polite nation, would be every whit as practicable without speech, as it would be without money, or an equivalent to be used'instead of it. Where this is not wanting, and due care is taken of it by the legislature, it will always be the standard, which the worth of every thing will be weighed by. There are great blessings that arise from necessity; and that every body is obliged to eat and drink, is the cement of civil society. Let men set what high value they please upon themselves, that labour which most people are capable of doing, will ever be the cheapest. Nothing can be dear of which there is great plenty, how benesicial soever it may be to man; and scarcity enhances the price of things much ofrener than the usefulness of them. Hence it is evident why thole arts and sciences will always be the most lucrative, that cannot be attained to, but in great length of time, by tedious study and close application; or elle require a particular genius, not often to be met with. It is likewise evident, to whose lot, in all societies, the hard and dirty labour, which nobody would meddle with, if he could help it, will ever fall: but you have seen enough of this in the

Fable of the Bees. *Hor.* 1 have so, and one remarkable saying I have read there on this subject, which I shall never forget. " The poor," says the author, " have nothing to stir them up to labour, " but their wants, which it is wisdom to relieve, but folly to " cure." *Cleo.* I believe the maxim to be just, and that it is not less calculated for the real advantage of the poor, than it appears to be for the benesit of the rich. For, among the labouring people, those will ever be the least wretched as to themselves, as well as most useful to the public, that being meanly born and bred, submit to the station they are in with cheerfulness; and contented, that their children should succeed them in the same low condition, inure them from their infancy to labour and submission, as well as the cheapest diet and apparel; when, on the contrary, that fort of them will always be the least serviceable to others, and themselves the most unhappy, who, dissatisfied with their labour, are always grumbling and repining at the meanness of their condition; and, under pretence of having a great regard for the welfare of their children, recommend the education of them to the charity of others; and you shall always sind, that of this latter class of poor, the greatest part are idle sottish people, that, leading dissolute lives themselves, are neglectful to their families, aud only want, as far as it is in their power, to shake off that burden of providing for their brats from their own shoulders. *Hor.* I am no advocate for charity schools; yet I think it is barbarous, that the children of the labouring poor, mould be for ever pinned down, they, and all their posterity, to that ilavish condition; and that those who are meanly born, what parts or genius soever they might be of, should be hindered and debarred from raising themselves higher. *Cleo.* So should 1 think it barbarous, if what you speak of was done any where, or proposed to be done. But there is no degree of men in Christendom that are pinned down, they and their posterity, to siavery for ever. Among the very lowest fort, there are fortunate men in every country; and we daily fee persons, that without education, or friends, by their own industry and application, raise themselves from nothing to mediocrity, and sometimes above it, if once they come rightly to love money and take delight in saving it: and this happens more often to people of common and mean capacities, than it does to those of brighter parts. But there is a prodigious difference between debarring the children of the poor from ever rising higher in the. world, and refusing to force education upon thousands of them promiscuously, when they mould be more usefully employed. As some of the rich must come to be poor, so some of the poor will come to be rich in the common course of things. But that universal benevolence, that mould every where industriously lift Lla up the indigent labourer from his meanness, would not be less injurious to the whole kingdom than a tyrannical power, that should, without a cause, cast down the wealthy from their ease and affluence. Let us suppose, that the hard and dirty labour throughout the nation requires three millions of hands, and that every branch of it is performed by the children of the poor. Illiterate, and such as had little or no education themselves; it is evident, that isa tenth part of these children, by force and design, were to be exempt from the lowest drudgery, either there must be so much work left undone, as would demand three hundred thousand people; or the defect, occasioned by the numbers taken off, must be supplied by the children of others, that had been better bred.

Hor. So that what is done at sirst out of charity to some, may, at long run. prove to be cruelty to others. *Cleo.* And will, depend upon it. In the compound of all nations, the different degrees of men ought to bear a certain proportion to each other, as to numbers, in order to render the whole a well proportioned mixture. And as this due proportion is the result and natural consequence of the difference there is in the qualisications of men, and the vicissitudes that happen among them, so it is never better attained to, or preserved, than when nobody meddles with it. Hence we may learn, how the short-sighted wisdom of

perhaps well-meaning people, may rob us of a felicity that would flow spontaneously from the nature of every large society, if none were to divert or interrupt the stream. *Hor.* I do not care to enter into these abstruse matters; what have you further to fay in praise of money? *Cleo.* I have no design to speak either for or against it; but be it good or bad, the power and dominion of it are both of vast exent, and the insluence of it upon mankind has never been stronger or more general in any empire, state, or kingdom, than io the most knowing and politest ages, when they were in their greatest grandeur and prosperity; and when arts and sciences were the most flourishing in them: Therefore, the invention os money seems to me to be a thing more skilfully adapted to the whole bent of our nature, than any other or human contrivance. There is no greater remedy again 1 sloth or stubborness; and with astonishment I have beheld the readiness and alacrity with which it often makes the proudest men pay homage to their inferiors: It, purchases all services, and cancels all debts; nay, it does more, for when a person is employed in his occupation, and he who sets him to work, a good paymaster, how laborious, how dissicult or irksome soever the service be, the obligation is always reckoned to lie upon him who performs it. *Hor.* Do not you think, that many eminent men in ihs learned professions would dissent from you in this? *Cleo.* I know very well, that none ought to do it, if ever they courted business, or hunted after employment. *Hor.* All you have said is true among mercenary people; but upon noble minds that despise lucre, honour has a far greater essicacy than money. *Cleo.* The highest titles, and the most illustrious births, are no security against covetousness; and persons of the sirst quality, that are actually generous and munisicent, are often as greedy after gain, when it is worth their while, as the most sordid mechanics are for trifles: The year twenty has taught us, how dissicult it is to sind out those noble minds that despise lucre, when there is a prospect of getting vastly. Besides, nothing is more universally

charming than money; it suits with every station, the high, the low, the wealthy, and the poor: whereas, honour has little influence on the mean, slaving people, and rarely affects any of the vulgar; but if it does, money will almost every where purchase honour; nay, riches of themselves are an honour to all those who know how to use them fashionably. Honour, on the contrary, wants riches for its support; without them it is a dead weight that oppresses its owner; and titles of honour, joined to a necessitous condition, are a greater burden together than the fame degree of poverty is alone: for the higher a man's quality is, the more coniiderable arc his wants in life; but the more money he has, the better he is able to supply the greatest extravagancy of them. Lucre is the best restorative in the world, in a literal fense, and works upon the spirits mechanically; for it is not only a spur that excites men to labour, and makes them in love with it, but it likewise gives relief in wearinels, and actually supports men in all fatigues and disticulties. A labourer of any fort, who is paid in proportion to his diiignce, can do more work than anorher who is paid by the uay or the week, and has standing wages. *Hor.* Do not you tbink, then, that there are men in laborious offices, who, for a sixed falary, discharge their duties with diligence and assiduity? *Cido.* Yes, many; but there is no place or employment in which there are required or expected, that continual attendance and uncommon severity of application, that some men harass and punish themselves with by choice, when every fresh trouble meets with a new recompence; and you never faw men so entirely devote themselves to their calling, and pursue business with that eagerness, dispatch, and perseverance in any office of preferment, in which the yearly income is certain and unalterable, as tliey often do in those professions, where the reward continually accompanies the labour, and the fee immediately either precedes the service they do to others, as it is with the lawyers, or follows it, as it is with the physicians. I am sure you have hinted at this in our sirst conversation yourself. *Hor.* Here is the castle before us. *Cleo.* Which I suppose you are not sorry for. *Hor.* Indeed I am, and would have been glad to have heard you speak of kings and other sovereigns with the fame candour, as well as freedom, with which you have treated prime ministers, and their envious adversaries. When I fee a man entirely impartial, I shall always do him that justice, as to think, that if he is not in the right in what he fays, at least he aims at truth. The more I examine your sentiments, by what I fee in the world, the more I am obliged to come into them; and all this morning I have said nothing in opposition to you, but to be better informed, and to give you an opportunity to explain yourself more amply. I am your convert, and shall henceforth look upon the Fable of the Bees very disterently from what I did; tor though, in the Characteristics, the language and the diction are better, the iystem of man's, ibciablenefs is more lovely and more plausible, and things are let off with more art and learning; yet in the other there is certainly more truth, and nature is more faithfully copied in it almost every where. *Cieu.* I with you would read them both once more, and, after that, I believe you will fay that you never faw two authors who seem to have wrote with more different views. My friend, the author of the Fable, to engage and keep his readers in good humour, seems to be very merry, and to do something else, whilst he detects the corruption of our nature; and having shown man to himself in various lights, he points indirectly at the necessity, not only of revelation and believing, but likewise of the practice of Christianity manifestly to be seen in mens lives. *Hor.* 1 have not observed that: Which way has he done it indirectly? *Cleo.* By exposing, on the one hand, the vanity of the world, and the most polite enjoyments of it; and, on the other, the insufficiency of human reason and heathen virtue to procure real felicity: for I cannot see what other meaning a man could have by doing this in a Christian country, and among people that all pretend to seek after happiness. *Hor.* And what fay you of Lord

Shaftsbury? *Cleo.* First, I agree with you that he was a man of erudition, and a very polite writer; he has displayed a copious imagination, and a sine turn of thinking, in courtly language and nervous expressions: But, as on the one hand, it must be confessed, that his sentiments on liberty and humanity are noble and sublime, and that there is nothing trite or vulgar in the Characteristics; so, on the other, it cannot be denied, that the ideas he had formed of the goodness and excellency of our nature, were as romantic and chimerical as they are beautiful and amiable; that he laboured hard to unite two contraries that can never be reconciled together, innocence of manners, and worldly greatness; that to compass this end, he favoured,deism, and, under pretence of lashing priestcraft and superstition, attacked the Bible itself; and, lastly, that by ridiculing many passages of Holy Writ, he seems to have endeavoured to sap the foundation of all revealed religion, with design of establishing Heathen virtue on the ruins of Christianity. FINIS. *uisELARD,* page 334. *Absurd,* nothing is thought so that we have been used to, 367. *Absurdities* in sacred matters not incompatible with politeness and worldly wisdom, 413, 414, 415, 412. *Acclamations* made at church, 369. *Accomplishments.* The foundation of them is laid in our youth, 50S. *Acknowledgment &e* to ancestors,.202. *ASive,* stirring man. The difference between such a one, and an easy indolent man in the lame circumstances, *$t,s* to 346. *Ad.uu.* All men are his descendants, 402. Was not predestinated to sall, 429. A miraculous production, 485. *Adminsration,* the civil, how it ought to be contrived, 495. What men it requires, ibid. Most branches of it seem tu be more difficult than they are, 496. Is I'.iscly divided into several branches, ibid. Is a ship that never lies at anchor, 54 *Ajtiiions* of the mind mechanically instuence the body, 376. *Affectionate* scheme, 441. Would have been inconsistent with the present plan, 442. Whin it might take place, 447. *Age,* the golden, sabulous, 483. Inconsistent with human nature, 452. *Air* and *Sace,* no objects of sight, 207. *Alexander* the

Great. The recompence he had in view, »o. Proved from his own mouth, ibid. Another demonstration of his lrailty, 212. *Alexander Hpuerus,* his absurd worship, 4»4 *At:-crica,* what the conquest of it has cost,
"5 *Americans.* The disadvantage they laboured under, 492, May be very ancient, ibid.
A'lanjs, the, or pine-apple, excels all other fruit, 400. To whom we owe the cultivation of it in England, 401. *Anaxcgcras,* the only man in antiquity that really despised riches and honuur, 34'*Anger* defined, 119. Conquered by fear, ibid, and 122. The operation of strong liquors imitates that of anger, 126. Anger described, 386. The origin of it in nature, ibid. What creatures have most. anger, ibid. The natural way of venting anger is by sighting, 474. *Anitnal Economy.* Man contributes nothing to it, 477, *Animals,* all, of the same species intelligible to one another, 466. *Antagonists,* the, of prime ministers, 503, 501. Are seldom better than the ministers themselves, 504. *Apology,* an, for several passages in the book, 137, 138. An apology for recommending ignorance, 182. *Applause,* always gratesul, 369. The charms of it, 271. *Arts and Sciences.* What encourages them, 509. Which will always be the most lucrative, 514. *Atheism* has hid its martyrs, r2S. *Atheism* and *Superstition* of the same origin, 4S7. What people are most in danger of atheism, ibid. Atheism may be abhorred by mtn of little religion, 260". *Atheists* may be men of good morals, 488. *Avarice,* 52. The realon why it is gene rally hated, ibid. Why the society stands in need of it, 53. Is equally necessary with prodigality, ibid. What ought to be deemed as such, 266. *Author of the Fable of the Bees,* the, desires not to conceal any thing that has been said against him, 261. The reaion os his silence, ibid. How sar only he defends his book, 262. Has called it an inconsiderable tnste, and a rhapsody, ibid. Was unjultly censured for confessinq his vanity, 263. How sar he is anfweiabie for what Horatio says, 275. Hii fears of what will happen, ibid. Ttie report of his having

CPSIA information can be obtained at www.ICGtesting.com
Printed in the USA
BVOW01s1517070214

344280BV00007B/301/P